HOW TO USE THIS B(

D1168418

The *Prentice Hall Handbook for Writers* has been ca
use as a reference source. Here are some suggesti
most out of the book when questions arise in you

1. *Look up the topic* in one of four places:

   - Use the list of **Correction Symbols** inside the front cover
   - Use the **Table of Contents** at the beginning of the book
   - Use the **Index** at the end of the book (see sample entry at right)
   - Use the **Organization Chart** inside the back cover

   section number

   Index entry

   subsection number

   page numbers

2. *Turn to the section or subsection covering the topic.* Use the tabs to help you find the information you need. Tabs and section numbers are printed in red.

3. *Study the rules and explanations.* Basic rules are printed in blue. Explanations are in **black**.

4. *Study the examples.* Examples illustrating patterns you can safely use in college writing are labeled in green. Other examples are labeled in **black**.

5. *Work the exercises.* Even if your instructor doesn't assign the exercises, doing them is a good way to check how well you understand the topic. Exercise headings are printed in red.

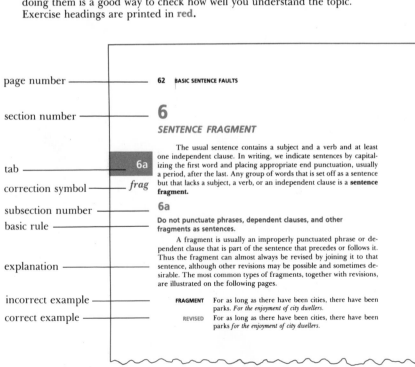

page number — **62** BASIC SENTENCE FAULTS

section number — **6**

SENTENCE FRAGMENT

The usual sentence contains a subject and a verb and at least one independent clause. In writing, we indicate sentences by capitalizing the first word and placing appropriate end punctuation, usually a period, after the last. Any group of words that is set off as a sentence but that lacks a subject, a verb, or an independent clause is a **sentence fragment**.

tab — 6a

correction symbol — *frag*

subsection number — **6a**

basic rule — Do not punctuate phrases, dependent clauses, and other fragments as sentences.

explanation — A fragment is usually an improperly punctuated phrase or dependent clause that is part of the sentence that precedes or follows it. Thus the fragment can almost always be revised by joining it to that sentence, although other revisions may be possible and sometimes desirable. The most common types of fragments, together with revisions, are illustrated on the following pages.

incorrect example — FRAGMENT   For as long as there have been cities, there have been parks. *For the enjoyment of city dwellers.*

correct example — REVISED   For as long as there have been cities, there have been parks *for the enjoyment of city dwellers.*

Prentice Hall

HANDBOOK FOR WRITERS

TENTH EDITION

GLENN LEGGETT
President Emeritus, Grinnell College

C. DAVID MEAD
Michigan State University

MELINDA G. KRAMER
Purdue University

With the editorial supervision of
RICHARD S. BEAL

PRENTICE HALL, Englewood Cliffs, New Jersey 07632

Library of Congress Cataloging in Publication Data

LEGGETT, GLENN H., (date)
   Prentice-Hall handbook for writers / Glenn Leggett, C. David Mead,
Melinda G. Kramer ; with the editorial supervision of Richard S.
Beal. – 10th ed.
   p. cm.

   Includes index.
   ISBN 0-13-695271-2

   1. English language—Rhetoric. 2. English language—
–Grammar—1950– I. Mead, C. David (Carl David), (date)
II. Kramer, Melinda G., (date)   III. Title. IV. Title: Handbook
for writers.
PE 1408.L39 1988
  808'.042—dc19   87–25831
                                        CIP

Cover: Mark Rothko, *Blue, Orange, Red.* 1961.
Hirshhorn Museum and Sculpture Garden, Smithsonian Institution,
Gift of Joseph Hirshhorn Foundation.

Development editor: Ann Torbert
Editorial/production supervision: Virginia Rubens
Interior design: Anne T. Bonanno
Manufacturing buyer: Ray Keating

Acknowledgments for quoted works appear on pages XVI–XVII.

 © 1988 by Prentice Hall, Inc.
A Division of Simon & Schuster
Englewood Cliffs, New Jersey 07632

Printed in the United States of America

10 9 8 7 6 5 4

ISBN 0-13-695271-2 01

Prentice-Hall International (UK) Limited, *London*
Prentice-Hall of Australia Pty. Limited, *Sydney*
Prentice-Hall Canada Inc., *Toronto*
Prentice-Hall Hispanoamericana, S.A., *Mexico*
Prentice-Hall of India Private Limited, *New Delhi*
Prentice-Hall of Japan, Inc., *Tokyo*
Simon & Schuster Asia Pte. Ltd., *Singapore*
Editora Prentice-Hall do Brasil, Ltda., *Rio de Janeiro*

CONTENTS

■ PREFACE

The *Prentice Hall Handbook for Writers* in its tenth edition is designed to meet the needs of today's writers, whether they are in college and university classes or on the job. The point of a handbook is to be "handy"—easy for the individual writer to use as a desk reference tool, easy for instructors and students to use in a classroom setting, and complete enough to support users in both situations. It should be informed by the best of recent composition research while preserving those methods that have been successfully time-tested. A good handbook presents and conserves what is valuable for writers.

The tenth edition of the *Handbook* maintains that kind of balance. Our text presents in efficient and accessible form the rhetorical issues, choices, conventions, and procedures that underlie standard English written for college and the professions.

Among the new material in this edition, Section 41, dealing with the whole essay, has been thoroughly revised. As does the entirety of the *Prentice Hall Handbook,* Section 41 still focuses on meeting the needs of the writer's audience; but its discussion of the recursive activities of the writing process has been augmented and revamped. In addition, we have included information about word processing as a generative writing tool.

Also new, and indicative of our approach to writing tasks, are the "Writers Revising" features that accompany a number of the sections in the tenth edition. Each of these case studies presents an in-process writing sample for users to revise, followed by the original author's revision for comparison. The revisions are accompanied by references to relevant sections of the *Handbook* and, where appropriate, by additional analysis of the author's final draft. The case studies range from a journalism intern writing an article to a library assistant preparing a book display to a student answering an essay question on a biology test.

While the text specifically addresses the needs of students in English composition classes, we are ever mindful of the writing tasks that occur in other courses or on the job. As a result, the writing samples in the sections on the whole essay include not only a personal experience essay written by a freshman composition student but also a memo written by a young businesswoman. The sample research paper was prepared for an undergraduate sociology course. One of the argumentative essays first appeared as an editorial in a campus newspaper; the other is a reprint from a national magazine. Samples throughout the text are from both student and professional authors. We believe it is important to discuss writing by showing a range of writing tasks in which people are routinely engaged—to stress the common features of all writing while acknowledging differences of convention where they become important.

Another new feature of this edition is a four-color format which enhances the easy-to-use reference system that has always character-ized the *Prentice Hall Handbook*. Now references to writing standards and conventions are provided not only through (1) a full index; (2) a detailed table of contents; and (3) organization charts on the endpa-pers of the book; but also through (4) color-coding. Basic rules are printed in blue, as are section subheadings dealing with specific appli-cations or special cases. Examples of acceptable usage are labelled in green, with other examples labelled in black. Exercise headings are printed in red, so that practice sentences will be easy to find.

These and other changes in the tenth edition of the *Handbook*—from new exercises to an expanded discussion of sexist language—reflect our continual recognition of the various audiences a handbook may serve. Believing that all writers are colleagues, sharing many of the same problems and facing many of the same choices, we have again worked to create a text that is at once comprehensive, concise, reliable, thoughtful, and humane.

ACKNOWLEDGMENTS

The *Prentice Hall Handbook for Writers* has benefited from the thoughtful comments of many colleagues who reviewed the tenth edition: Virginia Allen, Iowa State University; Joseph A. Alvarez, Central Piedmont Community College; Lois Avery, Houston Community College; Jim Burns, University of South Carolina; Lennet Daigle, Georgia Southwestern College; Joseph Geckle, Westmoreland County Community College; John W. Johnston, Tyler Junior College; Gary W. Schmidt, Calvin College; Teresita Sellers, Gulf Coast Community College; Louise Z. Smith, University of Massachusetts, Boston; Richard F. Thompson, Northern Virginia Community College; and Clifford Wood, University of Wisconsin, Oshkosh.

Mamie Atkins, Palo Alto College, has once again supplied excellent exercises for Sections 1–40. She merits additional thanks for her preparation of the corresponding sections of the Annotated Instructor's Edition. We are also grateful to Linda Julian for her preparation of the Annotated Instructor's Edition, Sections 41–50.

To Brad Buehler, University of Michigan, we express special thanks for his willingness to supply writing samples and ideas that have been incorporated into this edition. His assistance is greatly appreciated.

This text has also benefited from those students, colleagues, family members, and friends who save memorable examples, circle sentences in letters, tear out magazine articles, and call with material that they think may be usable. Our long list of such thoughtful people includes Linda Buehler, Barbara Doster, John Leland, and Martin Rapisarda—all of Purdue University; John Presley, Augusta College; Lincoln Turner, Hewlett-Packard Company; Joe Buchman, Western Michigan University; and Devona Gamble of Winter Haven, Florida.

Gary Kramer not only kept the word processing equipment running to specifications, but also acted as consultant on scientific and technical topics, and generally helped preserve the author's sanity. A thousand thanks.

Prentice Hall continues to be an outstanding publisher. We are grateful for the guidance we have received from Philip Miller, our acquisitions editor, who is an arranger of supplements *par excellence;* Ann Torbert, our development editor, who has brought freshness and new friendship to the project, as well as keen professionalism; Virginia

Rubens, our production editor, without whom the book would surely never reach the shelves; and Carol Carter, our marketing manager, upon whom so much depends.

To advisors Richard Beal, Boston University, and Joyce Perkins, Prentice Hall, we extend our most heartfelt thanks. At every stage of the project, these two unfailingly offered sound recommendations and words of cheer—in equal and timely measure.

Throughout the *Handbook* we have quoted from copyrighted material, and we are grateful to the copyright holders acknowledged below for their permission.

John M. Allswang, Macintosh: *The Definitive Users Guide*. Bowie: Brady Communications Company, Inc. A Prentice-Hall Publishing Company, 1985.

Maya Angelou, *I Know Why the Caged Bird Sings*. New York: Random House, Inc., 1969. By permission of Random House, Inc.

W. H. Auden, *Tales of Grimm and Andersen*. Copyright © 1952 by Random House, Inc.

Jacques Barzun, *Simple & Direct*. New York: Harper & Row, 1975.

Jacques Barzun, *Teacher in America*. By permission of Little, Brown and Company, in association with the Atlantic Monthly Press.

Isaiah Berlin, *Mr. Churchill in 1940*. By permission of the author and John Murray (Publishers) Ltd.

Newman and Genevieve Birk, *Understanding and Using English*. By permission of the Odyssey Press, Inc.

Alan S. Blinder, "Abolishing the Penny Makes Good Sense," *Business Week*, 12 January 1987. Reprinted by permission of the author.

Lawrence Block, "Fiction: Huffing and Puffing," *Writer's Digest*, August 1982, p. 11.

James V. Catano, "Computer-Based Writing: Navigating the Fluid Text," *College Composition and Communication*, 36 (Oct. 1985), 311.

Winston Churchill, *Blood, Sweat, and Tears*. By permission of G. P. Putnam's Sons and Cassel and Company Ltd.

Peter Davis, "The Game," from *Hometown*. Copyright © 1982 by Peter Davis. Reprinted by permission of Simon & Schuster, Inc.

John Didion, excerpt from "On Keeping a Notebook," from *Slouching Towards Bethlehem*. Copyright © 1966, 1968 by Joan Didion. Reprinted by permission of Farrar, Straus & Giroux, Inc. and Andre Deutsch Ltd.

Maureen Dowd, "Rape: The Sexual Weapon," copyright © 1983 Time Inc. All rights reserved. Reprinted by permission from *Time*.

Peter Drucker, "How to Be an Employee," *Fortune*, May 1952. Copyright © 1952 by Time, Inc.

Kent Durden, *Flight to Freedom*. Reprinted by permission of Simon & Schuster, Inc.

Loren Eiseley, excerpts from "Big Eyes and Small Eyes" and "Instruments of Darkness," in *The Night Country*. Copyright © 1971 Loren Eiseley. Reprinted with permission of Charles Scribner's Sons.

John Erskine, "A Note on the Writer's Craft," in *Twentieth-Century English*. Ed. William Skinkle Knickerbocker. New York: Philosophical Library, 1946.

H. W. Fowler, *Modern English Usage*. Rev. Ernest Gowers, New York: Oxford UP, 1965.

Walker Gibson, *Tough, Sweet, and Stuffy*. Copyright © 1970. Indiana University Press.

S. I. Hayakawa, from *Language in Thought and Action*, Fourth Edition. Copyright © 1978 by Harcourt Brace Jovanovich, Inc. Reprinted by permission of the publisher.

William A. Henry III, "Only 2,500 Miles from Broadway," *Time*, August 4, 1986.

From the book *How Children Fail* by John Holt. Copyright © 1964 by Pitman Publishing Corporation. Reprinted by permission of Fearon-Pitman Publishers, Inc.

Jane Howard, *Families*. Copyright 1978 by Jane Howard. By permission of Simon and Schuster, Inc. Reprinted by permission of A. D. Peters & Co. Ltd.

Elaine Kendall, "An Open Letter to the Corner Grocer," *Harper's* Magazine, December 1960. Reprinted by permission.

Tracy Kidder, *The Soul of a New Machine*. Copyright © 1980 by John Tracy Kidder. By permission of Little, Brown and Company in association with the Atlantic Monthly Press.

Stephen Koepp, excerpt from "Pul-eeze! Will Somebody Help Me?" Copyright 1987 Time Inc. All rights reserved. Reprinted by permission from *Time*.

George Laycock, "Games Otters Play," from *Audubon*, January, 1981. By permission of the National Audubon Society.

Barry Lopez, *Arctic Dreams*. New York: Bantam, 1987.

William H. MacLeish, "The Year of the Coast," from *Smithsonian*, Sept. 1980.

Beryl Markham, *West with the Night*. San Francisco: North Point Press, edition reprinted by arrangement with the author and Houghton Mifflin Co.

Robert K. Massie, *Peter the Great: His Life and World*. New York: Knopf, 1980.

Joan Mills, excerpted with permission from "The One, the Only . . . Joanie!" by Joan Mills, *Reader's Digest*, July 1983. Copyright © 1983 by The Reader's Digest Assn., Inc.

BASIC
GRAMMAR

gr

Writing always presents problems, dilemmas, some of which beset all writers, even great ones; but there is no need to be baffled by *all* the difficulties every time you write. The effort to which you are being invited is to learn the usual pitfalls and how they are avoided, while also learning the devices—tricks of the trade—by which writing can be both improved and made easier than it seems to most people. . . . By the same effort, you may also learn to be clear and to afford pleasure to those who read what you write.

JACQUES BARZUN, *Simple & Direct*

We use grammar whenever we speak or write. When we want to describe the system by which a language works, we talk about its grammar. If you grew up speaking English, as soon as you could distinguish between such pairs as *toy* and *toys*, *home run* and *run home*, and *tiger tails* and *tiger's tail*, you already knew a good deal of English grammar. And by the time you could put together sentences such as *Grandma gave me some new toys*, or *See the monkeys jumping around in the cages*, you had learned some very complicated things about the grammar system that underlies the English language.

In school you studied grammar as a subject, as a way of *describing* what happens to language when you use it. In this sense, grammar is in the same class as physics. Both are concerned with systems that operate according to principles. Physics describes how light, sound, and other kinds of energy and matter work. Grammar describes how language works.

The following pages explain the details of English grammar in terminology that is widely used to describe the way our language functions. Learning the terminology will help you talk about grammar with others; more importantly, it will help you understand the way the English language system works. One basic concept about language may help you to keep the details in perspective: Any language is composed of individual words and grammatical devices for putting them together meaningfully. English has several devices for putting words into meaningful combinations. The three most important are word order, function words, and inflections.

In English, grammatical meaning is largely determined by **word order.** *Blue sky* and *sky blue* mean different things: in the first, *blue* describes *sky;* in the second, *sky* describes *blue.* Here is the principle in action:

> The thief called the lawyer a liar.
> The lawyer called the thief a liar.
> The liar called the lawyer a thief.
>
> Our new neighbors bought an old house.
> Our old neighbors bought a new house.

Word order can be extremely important to meaning, as the following example shows: *The shoes on the steps with the run-down heels are mine.* Word order indicates that *with the run-down heels* describes *steps,* but common sense tells us that steps don't have heels. However, until our common sense overrides the meaning created by word order, as readers we are momentarily confused.

Function words, sometimes called **grammatical words,** are words such as *the, and, but, in, to, because, while, ought,* and *must.* The main use of function words is to express relationships among other words. Compare the following:

I am lonely *at* dark.   The cook prepared *a* rich feast.
I am lonely *in the* dark.   The cook prepared *the* rich *a* feast.

Inflections are changes in the form of words; these changes indicate differences in grammatical relationship. Inflections account for the differences in meaning in the following sentences:

The river*s* flow slowly.   Stop bother*ing* me.
The river flow*s* slowly.   Stop*s* bother me.

Readers depend on your using these grammatical devices—word order, function words, and inflections—to signal what you mean.

A distinction is sometimes made between grammar and *usage.* Grammar is concerned with generally applicable principles about language. **Usage,** in contrast, is concerned with choices, particularly with differences between *formal* (less conversational) and *informal* (more conversational) English and between *standard English* (well established and widely recognized as acceptable) and *nonstandard English* (generally considered unacceptable by educated speakers and writers of English) (see Section **35**).

The differences between *tile floor* and *floor tile, he walks* and *he walked, she was biting the dog* and *the dog was biting her* are grammatical differences of word order and inflection. The differences between *I saw* and *I seen, she doesn't* and *she don't,* and *let me do it* and *leave me do it* are differences in usage. These statements may identify the persons who use them as speakers of standard or nonstandard dialects, but they do not mean different things. Because this book is concerned with writing standard English, it is concerned with both grammar and usage.

1

SENTENCE SENSE

Research regarding how people receive and process language indicates that we are capable of holding between five and nine separate chunks of information in our short-term memories at a time. If this is true, how is it that we can learn complex tasks, express complex ideas, and think even more complex thoughts? Researchers think that by "superchunking" information—by combining individual chunks into condensed, meaningful units—the short-term memory is able to continue receiving new information. If we apply this theory to the words *age, buggy, the, and, horse,* we see that the phrase *the horse-and-buggy age* results in one meaningful superchunk instead of five separate chunks of information. Although we do not yet fully understand how the brain works to create and process language, we are able to describe how language works when we use it.

To describe the way a language works, grammarians assign words to categories according to their function and also classify them by type, assigning terms for each type. These terms, or grammatical function labels, are traditionally referred to as **parts of speech.** The major types of words in English and the functions they usually perform are as follows:

Function	Type	Example
Naming	Nouns and pronouns	*corn, summer, it*
Predicating (stating or asserting)	Verbs	*grows, was*
Modifying	Adjectives and adverbs	*tall, quickly*
Connecting	Prepositions and conjunctions	*in, and*

Nouns and verbs, the naming and stating words, are the basic elements. They are the bones of the sentence. Working together, these chunks of meaning make our simplest sentences: *Corn grows.* Other types of words and word groups expand and refine those simple sentences: *The tall corn grows quickly in the summer.*

1a
Recognizing sentences and their basic parts

A **sentence** is a group of related words that expresses a complete thought. It is an independent construction; that is, it does not depend on any other word group to complete its meaning. *She is studying* and *What is she studying* are sentences. But *although she is studying* is not a sentence because the connecting word *although* makes the whole word group depend upon something else for completion, as in the statement *Although she is still studying, she will be finished soon.* Grammatically, a sentence also must contain a subject and a predicate to be complete.

Subjects and predicates. All complete sentences have two main parts, a subject and a predicate. The **subject** names the person, thing, or concept that the sentence is about. The **predicate** makes a statement or asks a question about the subject:

SUBJECT PREDICATE
My car | won't start.

PREDICATE
SUBJECT
Will | Alexander | take me home?

Nouns. The subject of a sentence is usually a noun or a pronoun. **Nouns** name or classify persons, places, things, activities, conditions, and concepts: *Lynn, Detroit, hat, studio, committee, athletics, courage, wealth.* Nouns have the following characteristics:

1. Nouns naming things that can be counted (sometimes called "count nouns") add *-s* or *-es* to make the plural form which indicates more than one: *chair, chairs; car, cars; church, churches; bush, bushes.* A few nouns have irregular plurals: *woman, women; foot, feet; sheep, sheep.* **Proper nouns** that name particular people, places, or things *(Dorothy, Kansas, Toto)* and **mass nouns,** which name things not usually counted *(gravel, milk, courage, honesty),* do not ordinarily have plural forms.

2. Nouns typically serve as the subjects *(The wind blew; Sally arrived; Honesty pays)* and the objects of verbs and prepositions *(I sent John to the store).*

3. Many nouns have characteristic endings such as *-ance, -ence, -ism, -ity, -ment, -ness, -tion,* and *-ship,* as in *relevance, excellence, realism, activity, argument, darkness, adoption, citizenship.*

Pronouns. Pronouns are words that can substitute for nouns. Thus, pronouns can be subjects or objects of verbs or prepositions. The noun for which a pronoun substitutes is called its **antecedent.** In the sentence *Clara Barton is the woman who founded the American Red Cross,* the pronoun *who* refers to its antecedent, *woman.*

Usually antecedents are expressed, as is *woman* in the previous sentence. Sometimes, however, antecedents are implied and must be deduced from the context. In the sentence *Those who need assistance in boarding the aircraft should come to the gate now,* the meaning of *those* is implied by the context itself; that is, *those* refers to any passengers needing help in boarding. Implied antecedents can cause confusion for readers; in the sentence *Whichever you choose will be acceptable,* it is impossible to know what *whichever* means without the larger context of surrounding sentences that may reveal what *whichever* refers to. **Indefinite pronouns,** words like *anybody, everyone,* and *somebody,* require no antecedent.

The **personal pronouns** *I, we, he, she,* and *they,* and the pronoun *who,* which is used either to relate one group of words to another or to ask a question, change form in the subjective, possessive, and objective cases, for example, *I, my/ mine, me. You* and *it* change form as possessives only: *you/your, it/its.* (See Section **2**).

Verbs. The predicate of a sentence *always* contain a **verb,** a word that makes an assertion about the subject. A sentence cannot exist without a verb. Verbs indicate action, occurrence, being, possession, or the presence of a condition. Examples of verbs are *ask, eat, give, describe, own, am, have, criticize, seem, appear, become, throw.*

In the simplest English sentences, a verb may stand alone as the predicate: *Lions hunt.* Or it may be followed by a word called its **object,** which indicates who or what receives the action of the verb: *Lions hunt prey.*

Verbs have the following characteristics of form:

1. When verbs indicate present time, they usually add *-s* or *-es* to the form listed in the dictionary when their subjects are *he, she,* or *it* or a word for which *he, she,* or *it* can be substituted: *the boys run,* but *the boy* [he] *runs; the logs burn,* but *the log* [it] *burns; the arrows miss,* but *the arrow* [it] *misses.*

2. Almost all verbs have a separate form to indicate past tense. Most add *-d* or *-ed* to the form listed in the dictionary: *save, saved; walk, walked; repeat, repeated.* A few indicate past time in irregular ways: *eat, ate; go, went; run, ran; sleep, slept.* A few verbs do not have a separate form: *cut, put, hit, hurt.*

3. The dictionary form of verbs can always be preceded by any one of the following words: *can could; may, might; will, would; shall, should;* and *must,* as in *can talk, may go, would leave, should pay,* or *must read.* These words are called **auxiliaries** or **helping verbs** and are used to convey special shades of meaning. Other forms of the verb can combine with other auxiliaries to form verb phrases that express various time relationships as well as other shades of meaning such as *have been eating, will be finished, could have been working.* (For a full discussion of auxiliaries, see Section **4.**)

4. Many verbs have typical endings, called **suffixes,** such as *-ate, -en, -fy,* and *-ize,* as in *implicate, operate, widen, hasten, liquefy, simplify, recognize, modernize.*

Basic sentence patterns. All English sentences are built on a limited number of patterns, to which all sentences, no matter how long or complex, can be reduced. The five most basic patterns are illustrated and explained below. In all of them the subject remains a simple noun or pronoun. Differences among the patterns lie in the predicate part of the sentence—the verb and what follows it.

PATTERN 1: S + V

Subject	Verb
Red	fades.
The woman	arrived.
The snow	fell.

The simplest of all English sentence patterns consists of a subject and its verb. Sentences as simple as these are relatively rare in mature writing, yet simple sentences (subject-verb) are the core of all sentences.

PATTERN 2: S + V + DO

Subject	Verb	Direct Object
Dogs	eat	bones.
The carpenter	repaired	the roof.
John	likes	the movies.
Someone	insulted	her.

The verbs in the second pattern are always action words that can pass their action on to another word called an object, or more exactly, a **direct object.** The direct object is always a noun, a pronoun, or a group of words serving as a noun that receives the action of the verb; it answers the question "what?" or "whom?" after the verb. Verbs that can take objects are called **transitive** verbs (See Section **4.**)

PATTERN 3: S + V + DO + OC

Subject	Verb	Direct Object	Object Complement
The press	called	him	a star.
They	appointed	Shirley	chairperson.
We	made	the clerk	angry.
The jury	found	her	innocent.

With a few verbs, such as *appoint, believe, consider, judge, made,* and *name,* the direct object may be followed by another noun or a modifying word that renames or describes the direct object. These are called **object complements,** and they distinguish the third sentence pattern.

PATTERN 4: S + V + IO + DO

Subject	Verb	Indirect Object	Direct Object
My friend	lent	me	his car.
The college	awarded	her	a scholarship.
Wellington	brought	England	victory.
Mark	got	us	tickets.

The fourth pattern includes the indirect object. After such action verbs as *ask, give, send, tell,* and *teach,* the direct object is often preceded by an **indirect object** that names the receiver of the message, gift, or whatever, and always comes before the direct object.

The same meaning can usually be expressed by a phrase that begins with *to* or *for* and is positioned after the direct object: *Wellington brought victory to England; The college awarded a scholarship to her.*

PATTERN 5: S + LV + SC (PN or PA)

Subject	Linking Verb	Subject Complement Predicate Noun	Predicate Adjective
Napoleon	was	a Frenchman.	
My brother	remains	an artist.	
Natalie	may become	president.	
The traffic	seemed		heavy.
Water	was		scarce.
The knife	felt		sharp.

The fifth pattern occurs only with a special kind of verb, called a **linking verb.** (See Section **4.**) The most common linking verb is *be* in its various forms: *is, are, was, were, has been, might be,* etc. Other common linking verbs include *appear, become, seem* and in some contexts such verbs as *feel, grow, act, look, taste, smell,* and *sound.* Linking verbs are followed by a **subject complement,** which may be either a predicate noun or a predicate adjective. A subject complement following a linking verb, in contrast to an object after a transitive verb, identifies or describes the subject of the sentence. **Predicate nouns** rename the subject; **predicate adjectives** modify the subject. It may be helpful to think of a linking verb as an equal sign. The verb "equates" the subject and the complement: *My brother = an artist.*

Other sentence patterns. The preceding five sentence patterns are the basis of all English sentence structure. Other kinds of sentences may be thought of either as additional patterns or as changes, called *transformations* by some grammarians, in these basic patterns. Thus, we create questions by inverting the subject and verb, as in *Will she run,* or by using a function word before the basic pattern, as in *Does she run.* We create commands by omitting the subject, as in *Open the can, Know thyself, Keep calm.*

Two variations on basic patterns are especially important because they involve changes either in the usual actor-action relation of subject and verb or in the usual order of subject and verb.

The first of these is the **passive sentence.** The passive sentence is made from one of the basic patterns that have a direct object. In its most common form, the original object of the verb becomes the subject, and the original subject may be either omitted or expressed in a phrase beginning with *by.* In the passive sentence the subject no longer names the performer of the action described by the verb, as it does in active patterns. Rather, it names the receiver of the action. This characteristic makes the passive sentence especially useful when we do not know who performs an action. Thus we normally say *He was killed in action* rather than *Someone killed him in action.* (See "Voice," in Section **5.**)

The verb in passive sentences consists of some form of the auxiliary, or helping, verb *be* and the past participle.

ACTIVE
The carpenter *repaired* the roof.
Someone *complimented* her.
The doctor *called* my recovery a miracle.
Wellington *brought* England victory.

PASSIVE

Subject	Passive Verb	(Original Subject)
The roof	was repaired	(by the carpenter).
She	was complimented	(by someone).
My recovery	was called a miracle	(by the doctor).
Victory	was brought to England	(by Wellington).

Notice that in all passive sentences the original subject can be expressed in a phrase by starting with the word *by*, but the sentence is grammatically complete without the *by* phrase, e.g., *The roof was repaired.*

The second important variation on basic sentence patterns involves a change in word order that allows us to postpone the subject. By beginning a sentence with the **expletive** *there* or *it*, we can postpone the subject until after the verb.

Expletive	Verb	Complement	Subject
It	is	certain	that they will arrive.
There	was		no reply.
There	are		five letters.
It	will be	hot	early next week.

Expletive constructions, because they postpone the subject, slow the pace of a sentence and can be useful for gaining the reader's attention. They announce "Get ready. Something is coming. Don't miss it." Expletives can provide effective sentence variety, but they can also create unnecessary clutter in a sentence and so should be used thoughtfully. (See "Roundabout Constructions" in Section **39a.**)

EXERCISE 1a
Identify the subjects (S), verbs (V), direct objects (DO), indirect objects (IO), and complements [i.e., object complement (OC), predicate noun (PN), predicate adjective (PA)] in the following sentences. Then use each sentence as a model for writing a sentence of your own, using subjects, verbs, direct objects, indirect objects, and complements as in the model.

1. The detective story is a popular form of modern fiction.
2. Many experts call Edgar Allan Poe the father of the modern detective story.
3. A. Conan Doyle gave readers Sherlock Holmes, the most famous detective of all.

4. In the twentieth century, the late twenties and thirties were called the Golden Age of detective fiction.
5. In the United States, detective stories flourished in the forties.
6. The English detectives were often clever amateurs such as Lord Peter Wimsey.
7. American writers created tough and cynical detectives like Sam Spade and Philip Marlowe.
8. Detective fiction is enjoyable for readers of all ages.
9. Most girls and boys read the adventures of Nancy Drew or the Hardy Boys.
10. Detective fiction can become an addiction for readers.

1b

Recognizing modifiers, connecting words, and verbals

In English, we use modifiers, connecting words, and verbals to embellish the basic sentence patterns. These words and word groups enable us to expand basic sentences with detail and to combine basic sentences in ways that show the relationships among chunks of information. Our writing gains variety, complexity, and—at the same time—clarity and efficiency when we use these words and word groups. Compare the sentences that follow:

> Men wear toupees. Others have hair transplants.

> Some balding men wear toupees, but others have hair transplants because they think transplants look more natural.

When modifying and connecting words are added to the first two sentences, they not only become more precise (telling us exactly which men), but also deliver much more information. Furthermore, the connecting word *but* clearly establishes the contrasting relationship between the ideas in the two sentences.

1. Modifying words: adjectives and adverbs. Modifiers are words or word groups that limit, qualify, or make more exact the other words or word groups to which they are attached. Adjectives and adverbs are the principal single-word modifiers in English.

Adjectives modify nouns or pronouns. Typical adjectives are the underlined words in the following: *brown* dog, *Victorian* dignity, *yellow* hair, *one* football, *reasonable* price, *sleek* boat, *good* work. Adjectives have distinctive forms in the **positive, comparative,** and **superlative:** *happy, happier, happiest; beautiful, more beautiful, most beautiful; good, better, best.*

Adverbs modify verbs, adjectives, or other adverbs, although they may modify whole sentences. Typical adverbs are the underlined words in the following: *stayed outside, walked slowly, horribly angry, worked well, fortunately the accident was not fatal.*

For a discussion of the special forms by which adjectives and adverbs show comparison, and of certain distinctions between the two, see Section **3.**

2. Connecting words: prepositions and conjunctions. Connecting words enable us to link one word or word group with another and to combine them in ways that allow us to express our ideas more concisely and to express the relationships between those ideas more clearly. For example, we don't need to say *We had coffee. We had toast.* Rather, we can say *We had coffee and toast* or *We had coffee with toast.* We don't need to say *We talked. We played cards. We went home.* Rather, we can say *After we talked and played cards, we went home,* or *After talking and playing cards, we went home.* The kinds of words that enable us to make these connections and combinations are prepositions and conjunctions.

A **preposition** links a noun or pronoun (called its **object**) with some other word in the sentence and shows the relationship between the object and the other word. The preposition, together with its object, almost always modifies the other word to which it is linked.

> Skaters glide *over* the ice. [*Over* links *ice* to the verb *glide; over the ice* modifies *glide.*]
>
> The distance *between* us is short. [*Between* links *us* to the noun *distance; between us* modifies *distance.*]

Although a preposition usually comes before its object, in a few constructions it can follow its object.

> *In what town* do you live?   *To whom* do I send the check?
> *What town* do you live *in?*   *Whom* do I send the check *to?*

The most common prepositions are listed below:

about	below	into	through
above	beside	near	to
across	by	next	toward
after	down	of	under
among	during	off	until
around	except	on	up
as	for	out	upon
at	from	over	with
before	in	past	within
behind	inside	since	without

Many simple prepositions combine with other words to form phrasal prepositions, such as *at the point of, by means of, down from, from above, in addition to, without regard to.*

Note that some words, such as *below, down, in, out,* and *up,* occur both as prepositions and as adverbs. Used as adverbs, they never have objects. Compare *He went below* with *He went below the deck.*

Note too that *after, as, before, since,* and *until* also function as subordinating conjunctions. (See below.)

A **conjunction** joins words, phrases, or clauses. Conjunctions show the relationship between the sentence elements that they connect.

Coordinating conjunctions—*and, but, or, nor, for, so, yet*—join words, phrases, or clauses of equal grammatical rank. (See **1d,** "Recognizing Clauses.")

WORDS JOINED	We ate ham *and* eggs.
PHRASES JOINED	Look in the closet *or* under the bed.
CLAUSES JOINED	We wanted to go, *but* we were too busy.

Correlative conjunctions are coordinating words that work in pairs to join words, phrases, clauses, or whole sentences. The most common correlative pairs are *both . . . and, either . . . or, neither . . . nor, not . . . but,* and *not only . . . but also.*

> *both* courageous *and* loyal
> *either* before you go *or* after you get back
> *neither* circuses *nor* sideshows
> *not only* as a child *but also* as an adult

Subordinating conjunctions join clauses that are not equal in rank. A clause introduced by a subordinating conjunction is called a *dependent* or *subordinate* clause (see **1d**) and cannot stand by itself as a sentence; it must be joined to a main, or independent, clause.

> We left the party early *because we were tired.*
> *If the roads are icy,* we will have to drive carefully.
> *Whether we like it or not,* all things must end.

The following are the most common subordinating conjunctions:

after	even if	so that	when
although	even though	than	whenever
as	if	that	where
as if	in order that	though	wherever
as though	rather than	unless	whether
because	since	until	while
before			

3. Verbals. Verbals are special verb forms that have some of the characteristics and abilities of verbs but cannot function as predicates by themselves. Verbs make an assertion. Verbals do not; they function as nouns and modifiers. There are three kinds of verbals: infinitives, participles, and gerunds.

1b

Infinitives are usually marked by a *to* before the actual verb *(to eat, to describe)*. They are used as nouns, adjectives, or adverbs.

ss

> *To see* is *to believe.* [Both used as nouns]
> It was time *to leave.* [Used as adjective]
> I was ready *to go.* [Used as adverb]

Participles may be either present or past. The present form ends in *-ing (eating, running, describing)*. The past form usually ends in *-ed (described)*. But note that some end in *-en (eaten)*, and a few make an internal change *(begun, flown)*. Participles are always used as adjectives.

> *Screaming,* I jumped out of bed. [Present participle]
> *Delighted,* we accepted his invitation. [Past participle]

Gerunds have the same *-ing* form as the present participle. The distinctive name *gerund* is given to *-ing* forms only when they function as nouns.

> *Writing* requires effort. [Subject of *requires*]
> You should try *swimming.* [Object of *try*]

Although verbals can never function by themselves as predicates, they can, like verbs, take objects and complements, and like verbs, they are characteristically modified by adverbs. Note the following:

> I prefer *to believe him. [Him* is the object of *to believe.]*
> It was time *to leave the house. [House* is the object of *to leave.]*
> *Screaming loudly,* I jumped out of bed. [The adverb *loudly* modifies the participle *screaming.]*
> *Swimming in the Atlantic* is refreshing. [The prepositional phrase *in the Atlantic* here functions as an adverb to modify the gerund *swimming.]*

EXERCISE 1b(1)

In the following sentences, identify the adjectives (ADJ), adverbs (ADV), prepositions (P), coordinating conjunctions (CC), and subordinating conjunctions (SC). Then use each sentence as a model for writing a sentence of your own that uses adjectives, adverbs, prepositions, and conjunctions as they are used in the model. Also, go back to Exercise 1a and identify the adjectives, adverbs, prepositions, and conjunctions in those sentences.

1. Filmmakers use special effects to make movies interesting to their audiences.
2. Modern technology allows filmmakers to create fantastic and futuristic worlds.
3. Special effects are not new to filmmaking, for such films as the original *King Kong* and *2001: A Space Odyssey* dazzled audiences with their visual techniques.
4. When George Lucas made *Star Wars*, he began a new era in film technology.
5. Now, filmmakers employ increasingly advanced methods to devise special effects.
6. Artists often build detailed miniature models of scenes and objects to be used in a film.
7. Realistic and elaborate monsters manipulated by cables are commonplace in modern movies.
8. By feeding data on size, shape, and appearance into the computer, technicians can create complicated figures on the screen.
9. Months of effort by artists and technicians may occupy only a few seconds of time on the screen.
10. Although some viewers believe the special effects may eventually become more important than the story, filmmakers constantly search for new effects to thrill their audiences.

EXERCISE 1b(2)
Expand each of the following sentences, using adjectives, adverbs, prepositions, conjunctions, and verbals to add information.

1. People eat snacks at movie theatres.
2. She watched the late movie on television.
3. I took a film history course.
4. Studying movies can be fun.
5. Movie heroes change.

1c

Recognizing phrases

A **phrase** is a group of related words that has no subject or predicate and is used as a single part of speech. As we process language, we recognize phrases as chunks of information that expand a basic sentence, adding to its meaning, but we also recognize that phrases cannot express complete thoughts by themselves. *I fell on the sidewalk* is a complete thought; *on the sidewalk* is not.

Typical phrases are composed of a preposition and its object (*I fell on the sidewalk*) or a verbal and its object (*I wanted to see the parade*). Phrases are usually classified as prepositional, infinitive, participial, or gerund phrases.

Prepositional phrases. Prepositional phrases consist of a preposition, its object, and any modifiers of the object *(under the ground, without thinking, in the blue Ford)*. Prepositional phrases function as adjectives or adverbs and occasionally as nouns.

> He is a man *of action.* [Adjective modifying *man*]
> The plane arrived *on time.* [Adverb modifying *arrived*]
> We were ready *at the airport.* [Adverb modifying *ready*]
> She came early *in the morning.* [Adverb modifying *early*]
> *Before breakfast* is too early. [Noun, subject of *is*]

Infinitive phrases. Infinitive phrases consist of an infinitive, its modifiers, and/or its object *(to see the world, to answer briefly, to earn money quickly)*. Infinitive phrases function as nouns, adjectives, or adverbs.

> I wanted *to buy the house.* [Noun, object of verb]
> It is time *to go to bed.* [Adjective modifying *time*]
> We were impatient *to start the game.* [Adverb modifying *impatient*]

Participial phrases. Participial phrases consist of a present or past participle, its modifiers, and/or its object *(lying on the beach, found in the street, eating a large dinner)*. Note that a prepositional phrase may function as a modifier in a verbal phrase, as in *found in the street.* Participial phrases always function as adjectives describing either nouns or pronouns.

> The dog *running in the yard* belongs to my mother.
> The man *walking his dog* is my father.
> *Covered with ice,* the road was dangerous.
> *Beaten into stiff peaks,* the egg whites were prepared for meringue.

Gerund phrases. Gerund phrases consist of a gerund, its modifiers, and/or its object *(telling the truth, knowing the rules, acting bravely)*. Gerund phrases always function as nouns, as subjects or objects.

> *Collecting stamps* is my hobby. [Subject]
> She earned extra money by *working overtime.* [Object of preposition]
> He hated *living alone.* [Object of verb]
> *Making a profit* is their only purpose. [Subject]

Note that since both the gerund and the present participle end in *-ing,* they can be distinguished only by their separate functions as nouns or adjectives.

Absolute phrases. Absolute phrases are made up of a noun or pronoun and a participle. Unlike participial phrases, absolute phrases do not modify particular words in the sentence to which they are attached. Rather, they modify the whole sentence.

> The whole family sat silent, *their eyes glued to the TV screen.*
> *Mortgage rates having risen drastically,* Isabel gave up searching for a new house.
> The old man lay sprawled on the sofa, *eyes closed, arms folded across his chest, his loud snores almost rousing the dog sleeping near him.*

In absolute phrases with the participle *being* followed by an adjective, *being* is often omitted so that the phrase itself consists simply of a noun followed by an adjective and any other modifiers.

> *Final examinations over,* Linda returned to work.
> The den was thoroughly inviting, *the lights low, the long sofa and over-stuffed chairs luxuriously comfortable, the logs burning brightly in the fireplace,* and *our host open and friendly.*

EXERCISE 1c

In the following sentences, underline the verbal phrases once and put the prepositional phrases in parentheses. Note that a prepositional phrase may sometimes be part of a verbal phrase, as in the verbal phrase *lying on the beach,* in which the verbal *lying* is modified by the prepositional phrase *on the beach.* Then write ten sentences of your own, using these sentences as models for the use of verbal and prepositional phrases.

1. Insomnia or sleeplessness is a common complaint for many people.
2. Insomnia may take the form of lying awake for an hour or more after going to bed.
3. Some people have difficulty going to sleep and then wake up once or more during the night.
4. Some insomnia sufferers wake up very early in the morning and are unable to get back to sleep.
5. Chronic insomnia can be serious, interfering with daily life and leaving the victim exhausted and depressed.
6. For curing occasional insomnia, simple methods may be best.
7. Some doctors recommend getting regular exercise during the day as a cure for sleeplessness.
8. Some people like to take a warm bath before bedtime, while others prefer to read a boring book.
9. Drinking a glass of warm milk may help because tryptophan, an ingredient in milk, helps to induce sleep.
10. Many people choose to use the tried and true method of counting sheep.

1d

Recognizing clauses

A **clause** is a group of words containing a subject and a predicate. The relation of a clause to the rest of the sentence is shown by the position of the clause or by a conjunction. There are two kinds of clauses: (1) main, or independent, clauses and (2) subordinate, or dependent, clauses.

1. Main clauses. A main clause has both subject and verb, but it is not introduced by a subordinating word. A main clause makes an independent statement; it could stand alone. It is not used as a noun or as a modifier.

Eagles are beautiful.

2. Subordinate clauses. Subordinate clauses are usually introduced by a subordinating conjunction (*as, since, because,* etc.) or by a relative pronoun *(who, which, that)*. Subordinate clauses function as adjectives, adverbs, or nouns. They cannot stand alone but must be attached to a main clause. They express ideas that are intended to be subordinate to or dependent on the idea expressed in the main clause. The exact relationship between the two ideas is indicated by the subordinating conjunction or relative pronoun that joins the subordinate and the main clause.

MAIN CLAUSE   SUBORDINATE CLAUSE

Eagles are beautiful when they soar high above the cliffs.

A. An *adjective clause* modifies a noun or pronoun. It usually begins with a relative pronoun that serves as the clauses's subject or object.

This is the jet *that broke the speed record.* [The subordinate clause modifies the noun *jet.*]

Anyone *who is tired* may leave. [The subordinate clause modifies the pronoun *anyone.*]

Canada is the nation *we made the treaty with.* [The subordinate clause modifies the noun *nation,* with the relative pronoun *that* understood.]

B. An *adverb clause* modifies a verb, adjective, another adverb, or a whole main clause. It explains when, where, why, how, or with what result.

The child cried *when the dentist appeared.* [The subordinate clause modifies the verb *cried.*]

1d

ss

My head feels sore *where I bumped it.* [The subordinate clause modifies the predicate adjective *sore.*]

She thinks more quickly *than you do.* [The subordinate clause modifies the adverb *quickly.*]

We can leave for home *unless you are too tired to drive.* [The subordinate clause modifies the entire main clause.]

C. A *noun clause* functions as a noun. It may serve as subject, predicate noun, object of a verb, or object of a preposition.

What you need is a vacation. [The subordinate clause is the subject of the verb *is.*]

This is *where we came in.* [The subordinate clause is a predicate noun.]

Please tell them *I will be late.* [The subordinate clause is the object of the verb *tell,* with the relative pronoun *that* understood.]

I have no interest in *what I am reading.* [The subordinate clause is the object of the preposition *in.*]

EXERCISE 1d(1)
Underline the subordinate clauses twice in the following sentences, and identify each as an adjective, adverb, or noun clause. Then use each sentence as a model for writing a sentence of your own, using adjective, adverb, and noun clauses in similar ways.

1. Birds of prey, which are sometimes called raptors, include eagles, hawks, falcons, and vultures.
2. These birds have sharp, hooked beaks that are used for tearing the flesh from dead prey.
3. Because raptors rely mainly on their excellent eyesight to find food, they are usually active only during the day.
4. What amazes me is the survival of the bald eagle despite threats to its existence.
5. When the eagle sights its prey, it swoops briefly to the ground and strikes with its outstretched talons.
6. Its ten-foot wingspan is what makes the Andean condor the world's largest bird of prey.

EXERCISE 1d(2)
In the following sentences, underline each main clause once and subordinate clauses twice. Indicate the function of each subordinate clause as adjective, adverb, or noun. Then use each sentence as a model for writing a sentence of your own, with a similar structure.

1. The Underground Railroad, which was not literally a railroad but a network of northern whites and free blacks who sheltered fugitive slaves, moved "passengers" from south to north.
2. The paths, river crossings, boats, trains, and wagons of what became

known as the Underground Railroad were an escape route from slavery.

3. Many men and women who opposed slavery kept secret Underground Railroad "stations" in their houses or churches where escaping slaves waited for the next stage in their journey to freedom in the North.
4. Because the Underground Railroad was enveloped in secrecy, no one knows for sure the number of slaves who used it to gain freedom.
5. Although they risked their lives and their jobs, many famous people, both black and white, helped slaves to flee to the North.
6. Before she published *Uncle Tom's Cabin,* Harriet Beecher Stowe operated an Underground Railroad station in Ohio.
7. Levi Coffin, a Quaker who lived in Cincinnati, sheltered hundreds of fugitive slaves in a house which came to be known as the Grand Central Station of the Underground Railroad.
8. Whenever anyone writes of the Underground Railroad, Harriet Tubman is always mentioned.
9. She was born a slave in 1849 and fled to the North, where she joined the Underground Railroad.
10. Harriet Tubman came to be called Moses since she was determined to lead her people to freedom.

---

3. Sentence classification by clausal structure. The number of main or subordinate clauses in a sentence determines its classification: simple, compound, complex, or compound-complex.

A **simple sentence** has a single main clause.

The wind blew.

Note that a sentence remains a simple sentence even though the subject, the verb, or both are compounded.

The cat and the dog fought.
The dog barked and growled.
The cat and the dog snarled and fought.

A **compound sentence** has two or more main clauses.

The wind blew, and the leaves fell.

A **complex sentence** has one main clause and one or more subordinate clauses.

When the wind blew, the leaves fell.

A **compound-complex sentence** contains two or more main clauses and one or more subordinate clauses.

1d

ss

When the sky darkened, the wind blew, and the leaves fell.

See Section **34** for a discussion of how sentence structure and length can be varied to create emphasis and accentuate meaning.

EXERCISE 1d(3)

In the following sentences, underline each main clause once and each subordinate clause twice. Then indicate whether the sentence is simple, compound, complex, or compound-complex. Revise the simple sentences and the compound sentences, adding the necessary clauses to make them compound or compound-complex.

1. Dr. Seuss, who has entertained millions of children with his hilarious drawings and rhyming stories, is actually the pen name of Theodor Seuss Geisel.
2. Over 100 million of Geisel's books have been sold, and children all over the world are familiar with characters such as the Cat in the Hat and the Grinch.
3. Although parents may shudder at the antics in *The Cat in the Hat*, their children beg to hear the book again and again.
4. After reading *Green Eggs and Ham* five times before bedtime, some parents may not be able to face ham and eggs the next morning at breakfast.
5. When children meet the real Dr. Seuss, they often think he looks like a grandfather, yet Geisel has neither grandchildren nor children of his own.
6. Perhaps the rhyming stories of the Dr. Seuss books make them so popular with children; the simple and repetitious rhymes make the stories easy to remember.
7. Children also like the funny characters and their outrageous pranks.
8. Geisel began his career as a political cartoonist, but he eventually turned to writing children's books.
9. After reaching the age of 82, Geisel wrote his first book for adults, *You're Only Old Once!*, which appeared for many months on the *New York Times* best-seller list.
10. The book deals humorously with all the medical problems people face as they grow older.

EXERCISE 1d(4)

Using coordinating and subordinating conjunctions, combine the following sets of simple sentences in two ways. First, combine each set into a single compound sentence. Second, combine each set into a single complex or compound-complex sentence, changing wording and compounding and subordinating sentence parts as necessary.

1. Swimming is enjoyable and relaxing. It can also be a good all-around exercise.
2. Swimming can be an excellent exercise for cardiovascular conditioning. You have to swim continuously for at least twenty minutes. You have to swim at least three times a week.
3. The butterfly stroke is the best stroke for total conditioning. The

butterfly stroke requires the most movement. It's a difficult stroke to continue for long periods. The breast stroke, sidestroke, and Australian crawl also use various muscles and give good conditioning.
4. Swimming is a good exercise for weight control. You burn a considerable number of calories during a vigorous workout. The number of calories depends on the stroke you swim. It also depends on the temperature of the water. The strength of the current also affects how many calories are used.
5. Swimmers get lots of benefits from their exercise. They increase their cardiovascular endurance. They strengthen arm and leg muscles. They relax and feel weightless in the water.

WRITERS REVISING FOR COMPLETE SENTENCES

While brainstorming about a question on his mid-term exam, a student made the notes reproduced below. Turn these phrases and clauses—isolated chunks of information—into complete sentences. Organize the sentences into a paragraph that answers the question "What were the economic effects of the plague—the Black Death—in fourteenth-century Europe?" Then compare the decisions you made to those of the student writer.

Notes on Black Death

```
Killed about 50-75 percent of population

that many dead by end of century

planting and harvesting crops

land returned to wilderness

no laborers--shortages

diminished food supply     villages disappeared

goods scarce    rise in prices
```

As he wrote his answer, the student used two principal techniques to achieve complete sentences. Either he *combined* information from his notes—putting phrases and clauses together into sentences—or he *expanded* the phrases and clauses in his notes—adding subjects or predicates to form complete sentences. The results follow.

Student's Response

IDEAS COMBINED	By the end of the century, the Black Death had killed about 50 to 75 percent of the population. Because
IDEAS COMBINED: CAUSE AND EFFECT	there were not enough laborers for planting and harvesting crops, cleared
CLAUSE EXPANDED WITH MODIFIER: *WHOLE*	land returned to wilderness. Whole villages disappeared. Labor shortages
IDEAS COMBINED: CAUSE AND EFFECT	also meant a diminished food supply and scarce goods, resulting in a rise in prices.

2

CASE

Case shows the function of nouns and pronouns in a sentence. In the sentence *He gave me a week's vacation,* the **subjective case** form *he* indicates that the pronoun is being used as the subject; the **objective case** form *me* shows that the pronoun is an object; the **possessive** form *week's* indicates that the noun is a possessive.

Case endings were important in early English, but Modern English retains only a few remnants of this complicated system. Nouns have only two case forms, the possessive *(student's)* and a common form *(student)* that serves all other functions. The personal pronouns *I, we, he, she, and they* and the relative or interrogative pronoun *who* have three forms: subjective, possessive, and objective. The personal pronouns *you* and *it* have distinctive forms in the possessive.

PERSONAL PRONOUNS

Singular	SUBJECTIVE	POSSESSIVE	OBJECTIVE
FIRST PERSON	I	my, mine	me
SECOND PERSON	you	your, yours	you
THIRD PERSON	he, she, it	his, her, hers, its	him, her, it
Plural			
FIRST PERSON	we	our, ours	us
SECOND PERSON	you	your, yours	you
THIRD PERSON	they	their, theirs	them

RELATIVE OR INTERROGATIVE PRONOUN

Singular	who	whose	whom
Plural	who	whose	whom

2a
Subjective case

We use the subjective form for the pronoun subjects of all verbs and for all pronouns after all forms of the verb *be* (such as *is, are, were,* or *have been*). *They won the game, but in terms of sportsmanship the real victors were we.* Speakers of English are unlikely to say or write "Us are happy" or "Him is going away." But compound subjects and some constructions in which the subject is not easily recognized may cause problems.

1. Use the subjective pronoun form in all parts of a compound subject.

> *He* and *I* went shopping for a doll for my mother.
> My father and *she* collect dolls, so my brother and *I* wanted to buy one for her birthday.

If you are unsure about the pronoun form in a compound subject, you can test for the correct case by separating the compound and saying each pronoun against the verb separately. For example, *My father collect(s) dolls / she collects dolls,* so *my brother wanted to buy one / I wanted to buy one* for her birthday.

2. After the conjunctions *than* and *as,* use the subjective form of the pronoun if it is the subject of an understood verb.

> My brother is better at choosing collectible dolls than *I.* [*I* is the subject of *am at choosing them,* which is understood by the reader.]
> I am not as expert at judging value as *he* [is].

3. Use the subjective form of a pronoun in an appositive describing a subject or a subject complement. An **appositive** is a word or phrase set beside a noun or pronoun that identifies or explains it by renaming it. When an appositive renames a subject or subject complement, it is grammatically equivalent to the subject or complement and thus takes the same case.

> We two, *Sam and I,* went to an antique shop. [*Sam and I* is an appositive renaming the subject *We two.*]
> *We children* had seen a doll there that our mother might like. [Not *Us children. Children* is an appositive defining the pronoun *We.*]

4. Use the subjective case forms of the relative pronouns *who* and *whoever* when they serve as subjects of a clause.

The person *who* thinks dolls are inexpensive should price antique dolls. [*Who* is the subject of the verb *thinks* in the clause *who thinks dolls are inexpensive.*]

Whoever is familiar with antiques knows they can be costly. [*Whoever* is the subject of the verb *is* in the clause *Whoever is familiar with antiques.*]

The form of the pronoun is always determined by its function in its own clause. If it serves as the subject of its own clause, use the subjective form even though the whole clause may be the object of a verb or preposition.

Antique dealers can tell *who* is educated about price and value. [*Who* is the subject of the verb *is educated* in the subordinate clause. The subordinate clause *who is educated about price and value* is the object of the main clause's verb *can tell.*]

They will usually negotiate a fair price for *whoever* knows an object's true worth. [The *whoever . . . worth* clause is the object of the preposition *for. Whoever* is the subject of the clause.]

Note that the form of the pronoun used as subject does not change when such expressions as *I think* and *he says* come between the subject and its verb.

We chose a dealer *who* we knew was reputable. [*Who* is the subject of *was.*]

She was a businesswoman *who* the owner of the antique shop on Grand Street said had a fine collection of dolls for sale. [*Who* is the subject of *had.*]

Who do you think stakes reputation on quality? [*Who* is the subject of *stakes.*]

If you are not sure which form to use in sentences such as these, try testing by temporarily omitting the interrupting words.

She was a businesswoman (who, whom) had a fine collection of dolls for sale.

(Who, Whom) stakes reputation on quality?

The test will help you determine in each case whether the pronoun *who* is the subject of the verb in the subordinate clause.

5. In writing, use the subjective case of the personal pronoun after forms of the verb *be*, except when you are writing dialogue.

In spoken English in all but the most formal situations, *it's me*, using the objective form of the pronoun, is common, and *it's him, her, us, them* is becoming increasingly common. In your writing, however, you should follow the conventions of standard written English, choosing the subjective case for pronouns following forms of *be: It's I*.

> It was *he*, my brother, who first noticed the antique Japanese doll, not *I*.
> It was *we*, however, who had to pay for it.

When you are writing dialogue, choose between the formal subjective case or the conversational objective case depending on the character whose speech you are quoting.

> It was *he* who said, "Since this is a gift for Mom's birthday, it's *her* we should be trying to please, not our bank accounts." I replied, "Since it's *she*, and since this Japanese doll is very unusual, you're right. Let's buy it."

6. In writing, use the subjective case for a pronoun following the infinitive *to be* when the infinitive has no expressed subject.

Spoken English commonly uses the objective case of the pronoun in this construction. [See **2c(5)** for the case of the pronoun after the infinitive when the subject is expressed.]

> WRITTEN   I would like to be *she* when she opens the package. [The infinitive *to be* has no expressed subject.]
>
> SPOKEN   I would like to be *her* when she opens the package.

EXERCISE 2a

In the following sentences, correct any errors of case in accordance with formal written usage. Be ready to explain your reasons.

1. Us American history students went to an exhibition of colonial and early American quilts.
2. Whomever made those quilts must have spent many hours working on the elaborate patchwork designs.
3. We two, Carol and me, were especially interested in the way the quilts served as family records.
4. Her and I noticed that one quilt had patches made from a Revolutionary War uniform.
5. I've made a quilt, but I'll have to admit that the people who made the quilts shown at the exhibition were much better quilters than me.
6. The person whom made the quilt with the log cabin pattern must have been particularly skillful.
7. The organizer of the exhibition told us that her and her associates had gathered the historic quilts from collections and from private owners.
8. The organizers of the exhibit contacted quilt owners whom they thought would be willing to lend their quilts for the display.

2b

ca

9. Anybody whom thinks quilting would be easy to do should look at the intricate patterns and meticulous stitching of these historic quilts.
10. My friends and me really enjoyed seeing an aspect of American history that we had known little about.

2b
Possessive case

1. Generally, use the s-possessive *(boy's, Jane's)* with nouns naming living things. The possessive case of such nouns usually is formed by adding an apostrophe (') and the letter *s*. (See **29a.**) With nouns naming inanimate things, the *of*-phrase *(the point of the pen)* is sometimes preferred, but the *s*-form occurs very often.

ANIMATE	Jane's hair; the cat's meow; a friend's car
INANIMATE	the point of the joke, the wing of the airplane; the words of the title; the city's newsstands; the article's tone

The *s*-possessive is commonly used in expressions that indicate time *(moment's notice, year's labor)* and in many familiar phrases *(life's blood, fool's gold).* Choice of possessive form may also depend on sound or rhythm: the *s*-possessive is more terse than the longer, more sonorous *of*-phrase (the President's signature, the signature of the President). *The title's words,* however, seems more awkward and less pleasing than *the words of the title.*

2. In formal English, use the possessive case for a noun or pronoun preceding a gerund. In informal English, however, the objective case before a gerund is common. A **gerund** is a verb with the suffix *-ing (skiing, reading, driving)* that functions as a noun.

FORMAL	What was the reason for *my* studying Japanese?
INFORMAL	What was the reason for *me* studying Japanese?
FORMAL	You know about *Japan's* dominating the world marketplace.
INFORMAL	You know about *Japan* dominating the world marketplace.

Even in formal English the objective case is frequently used with plural nouns.

I understand *people* wanting to learn about another culture.

Your choice of case may sometimes depend on the meaning you want to convey.

Imagine *my* traveling to Japan. [The act of traveling is emphasized.]
Imagine *me* traveling to Japan. [The emphasis is on *me*. *Traveling* is here used as a participle modifying *me*.]

3. Use *which* to refer to impersonal antecedents. However, substitute *whose* where the phrase *of which* would be awkward.

We bought two tickets for a flight *whose* destination was Tokyo. [Compare *We bought two tickets for a flight the destination of which was Tokyo.*]

Japanese companies *whose* products sell well internationally have captured a large market share. [Compare *Japanese companies the products of which sell well internationally have captured a large market share.*]

2c
Objective case

Objective pronoun forms are used for the objects of all verbs, verbals, and prepositions.

OBJECT OF VERB	Did you see *him* yesterday?
	Our friends visited *us*.
OBJECT OF VERBAL	Visiting *them* was pleasant. [Object of gerund *visiting*]
OBJECT OF VERBAL	I wanted to invite *her* to lunch. [Object of infinitive *to invite*]
OBJECT OF PREPOSITION	Give the check to *me*.
	We will split the total between *us*.

Problems with objective pronoun forms usually occur in the same kinds of constructions that cause problems with subjective pronoun forms (See **2a.**)

1. Use the objective pronoun forms in all parts of a compound object.

We discovered the cat and *him* under the bed. [Not *the cat and he; him* is a part of the compound object of the verb *discovered*.]

They were afraid of you and *me*. [Not *of you and I; me* is a part of the compound object of the preposition *of*.]

If you have trouble deciding whether a singular pronoun form is in the correct case, sometimes it helps to say the sentence aloud, changing the pronoun to the plural as a test for proper case. For example, it may be easier for you to hear the correct form in "They were afraid of *us*." *Us*, the objective form, is equivalent to *me*, the corresponding singular pronoun form.

2. After the conjunctions *than* and *as,* use the objective form for a pronoun that is the object of an understood verb.

> He fears the Great Dane more than [he fears] *me.*
> The cat dislikes the Great Dane as much as [it dislikes] *us.*

In these examples, an error in pronoun case would change the meaning of the sentences. The subjective pronoun, used instead of the objective pronoun, would indicate a different understood verb and, hence, a different meaning.

> He fears the Great Dane more than *I.* [fear the Great Dane.]
> The cat dislikes the Great Dane as much as *we.* [dislike the Great Dane.]

3. Use the objective form of a pronoun in an appositive describing or renaming an object.

> The two of them stared at us—*me* and the dog—and refused to come out from under the bed. [*Me and the dog* is an appositive renaming *us.*]

4. Standard written English requires *whom* for all objects, even though *who* is common in conversation unless it immediately follows a preposition.

> WRITTEN *Whom* do you fear?
> SPOKEN *Who* do you fear?
>
> WRITTEN *Of whom* are you afraid?
> SPOKEN *Who* are you afraid of?

In subordinate clauses, use *whom* and *whomever* for all objects. Remember that the case of the relative pronoun in a subordinate clause depends upon its function in the clause and not upon the function of the whole clause.

> The visitors *whom* we had expected did not come. [*Whom* is the object of the verb *had expected.* The clause *whom we had expected* modifies *visitors.*]
> *Whomever* you like best is the person you should invite. [*Whomever* is the object of the verb *like* in the subordinate clause *whomever you like best.* The entire clause is the subject of the sentence.]

A helpful test is to put the words in the clause in subject-verb-object order *(you like whomever best).* That way you will be able to tell more easily which case form of the pronoun is appropriate.

5. When the infinitive *to be* has an expressed subject, both the subject and the object of the infinitive are in the objective case.

She believed *him* to be *me*. [*Him* is the subject of the infinitive *to be; me* is the direct object.]

The voters selected *them* to be the state senators.

EXERCISE 2b-c

In the following sentences, correct the errors of case in accordance with formal written usage. Be prepared to explain your reasons.

1. Many of we students were so fascinated by the quilt exhibition that we wanted to learn more about quilts.
2. I realized that before the nineteenth century, families had no photographs with which to record their history; instead, them making quilts was a way to make a family record.
3. The librarian gave my friend and I a book about the history of quilt making.
4. I learned that one of the important social events in early American times was the quilting party; the family having the party asked whoever they could find in the neighborhood to come and gather around the quilting frame.
5. In the lonely winters when people were isolated in their houses for days at a time, the people who the host family invited were always eager to come.
6. I can understand them wanting to go to a quilting party, for they could catch up on all the local news.
7. I discovered that my great-aunt had taken part in quilting parties when she was young; she told me, "It was hard work for us—my friends and I—but we also enjoyed ourselves."
8. When I looked at the quilt my great-aunt and her friends had made, I thought they to be very skillful at their craft.
9. Who do you think would put that much work into a quilt today?
10. "I admire you having the skill and patience to make such a beautiful quilt," I said.

EXERCISE 2a-c

In the following paragraph, correct the errors in case forms in accordance with formal written usage. Be prepared to explain your revisions.

After several robberies occurred in our neighborhood, my three roommates and me decided to make our apartment more secure. Stan, whom had gone to a community meeting about preventing crime, told we other three what he had learned there. The people in our community, many of who were very concerned about the robberies, had asked a local police officer to speak at the meeting. The officer said that us citizens can't stop all the break-ins, but we can make our houses or apartments less likely to be a burglar's target. The officer said that tall shrubs or trees around windows make it easy for a burglar to break in without being seen, so John and me decided to trim the shrubs by the bedroom window. Whomever wants to keep burglars away should also light the outside to see whomever is outside the house at night. Burglars prefer to rob unoccupied homes; they want to avoid a confrontation as much as us residents. Thus, people who leave lights or stereos on while they're away discourage burglaries because to whomever passes by the house seems occupied. Having chosen a house or apartment to rob, a burglar usually tries to get in by the easiest way, so Stan asked Mark and I to make sure all windows were locked and that the door frames were solid. When we checked the apartment, Mark was even more surprised than me to discover that only two out of ten windows were locked. After dinner that night, us four sat down and discussed the possibility of him and I buying an alarm system for the apartment. We decided that us having an alarm would help even more in deterring robberies. People who we talked to about such a system had told we four that we could install the alarm ourselves. We decided that in the morning we'd look in the phone book to find a store who sold alarms.

3

ADJECTIVES AND ADVERBS

Adjectives and adverbs are modifying words; that is, they are words that limit or qualify the meaning of other words, thus adding information to a sentence. **Adjectives** modify nouns and pronouns; they are usually placed either immediately before or immediately after the word they modify. Adjectives qualify meaning by indicating *what kind of* about the words they modify.

> Our *local* doctor told me I probably needed *new* glasses; *blurred* vision was giving me headaches too *severe* to treat with aspirin *alone*.

Adverbs normally modify verbs, adjectives, and other adverbs, although they may sometimes modify whole sentences. When they modify adjectives or other adverbs, they are adjacent to the words they modify. When they modify verbs, they are frequently, but not always, adjacent to the verbs.

Adverbs qualify the meaning of the words they modify by indicating such things as *when, where, how, why, in what order,* or *how often.*

> The office closed *yesterday.* [*Yesterday* indicates when.]
> Deliver all mail *here.* [*Here* indicates where.]
> She replied *quickly* and *angrily.* [*Quickly* and *angrily* describe how she replied.]

Consequently, I left. [*Consequently* describes why.]

He *seldom* did any work. [*Seldom* indicates how often.]

Most adverbs are distinguished from their corresponding adjectives by the ending *-ly: strong-strongly, happy-happily, doubtful-doubtfully, hasty-hastily, mad-madly.* But the *-ly* ending is not a dependable indication of the adverb since some adverbs have two forms *(quick, quickly; slow, slowly);* others have the same form as adjectives *(fast, much, late, well);* and some adjectives also end in *-ly.* (See Section **36,** "Vocabulary," for a discussion of the ways adjectives are formed from nouns.)

Most uses of adjectives and adverbs are common to both standard and nonstandard English and to all levels. But formal English uses distinctive adverb forms more frequently than ordinary conversation does. Since certain distinctions in the use of adjectives and adverbs are especially clear markers of differences between standard and nonstandard and between formal and informal English, they should be observed closely.

Where there is a choice between a form with *-ly* and a form without it, formal English prefers the *-ly* form—*runs quickly* rather than *runs quick, eats slowly* rather than *eats slow*—even though the shorter forms are widely used in informal English, particularly in such commands as *Drive slow.*

Four modifying words that can be troublesome are *bad, badly, good,* and *well. Bad* always functions as an adjective: *I had a <u>bad</u> fall and felt too <u>bad</u> to ski afterward* (the first *bad* modifies the noun *fall,* and the second is a predicate adjective). *Badly* always functions as an adverb: *The dress rehearsal went <u>badly</u>. Good* always functions as an adjective: *We had a <u>good</u> time at the concert, and our seats were <u>good</u>* (the first *good* modifies the noun *time,* and the second is a predicate adjective). *Well* may function either as an adjective *(My mother is <u>well</u>, but my father is sick),* or as an adverb *(They live <u>well</u> on their retirement income).* Careful study of Sections **3c** and **3d** will also help you distinguish among these uses.

Note particularly that *good* and *bad* as adverbs are nonstandard. The sentence *He talks <u>good</u> but writes <u>bad</u>* is nonstandard. Standard English requires the use of the adverbs *well* and *badly: He talks <u>well</u> but writes <u>badly</u>.*

3a
Use an adverb, not an adjective, to modify a verb.

INCORRECT   He writes *careless.*

CORRECT   He writes *carelessly.* [The adverb *carelessly* is needed to modify the verb *writes.*]

3b

ad

INCORRECT	We worked *diligent*.
CORRECT	We worked *diligently*. [The adverb is needed to modify the verb.]

3b

Use an adverb, not an adjective, to modify another adverb or an adjective.

INCORRECT	I am *terrible* nearsighted.
CORRECT	I am *terribly* nearsighted. [The adverb *terribly* is needed to modify the adjective *nearsighted*.]
INCORRECT	Contact lenses cost *considerable* more than glasses do.
CORRECT	Contact lenses cost *considerably* more than glasses do. [The adverb *considerably* is needed to modify the other adverb *more*.]

The use of adjectives in place of adverbs is more common in conversation than in writing. The use of the adjective *real* as a substitute for *really* or as an emphatic *very* to modify adjectives and adverbs is heard at all levels of speech. Similarly, the adverb form *surely* should replace *sure* in formal speech and writing.

FORMAL	My flight was *really* late.
COLLOQUIAL*	My flight was *real* late.
FORMAL	You will hear from me *very* soon.
COLLOQUIAL	You will hear from me *real* soon.
FORMAL	I will *surely* be glad to get home.
INFORMAL	I will *sure* be glad to get home.

3c

After a linking verb, use an adjective to modify the subject.

The common **linking verbs** are *be, become, appear, seem*, and the verbs pertaining to the senses: *look, smell, taste, sound, feel*. Predicate adjectives after such verbs refer to the subject and should be in adjective form. In each of the following sentences, for example, the predicate adjective modifies the subject. The verb simply links the two.

> You look *tired* tonight. [*Tired* modifies *you*.]
> The milk smells *sour*. [*Sour* modifies *milk*.]

---

*Colloquial means characteristic of or appropriate to conversation but not formal writing.

One of the most frequent errors in this construction is *I feel badly* in place of the correct subject–linking-verb–predicate-adjective form *I feel bad*. Though *badly* is common even in educated speech, *bad,* an adjective, correctly modifies the subject *I*.

FORMAL	He feels *bad* [ill].
COLLOQUIAL	He feels *badly*.
FORMAL	He felt *bad* about it.
COLLOQUIAL	He felt *badly* about it.

3d

Use an adverb after the verb to describe the manner of the action of the verb.

The cat looked *slyly at the canary*. [The adverb *slyly* modifies the verb *looked*. Contrast *The cat looked sly to the canary*.]

The blind old woman felt *gratefully* for the blanket someone had put at the foot of her bed. [The adverb *gratefully* modifies the verb *felt*, Contrast *The blind old woman felt grateful for the blanket someone had put at the foot of her bed*.]

In these examples the verbs *look* and *feel* express action, and must be modified by adverbs. But in constructions like *She looks tired* or *He feels well*, the verbs serve not as words of action, but as links between the subject and the predicate adjective. The choice of adjective or adverb depends on the function and meaning of the verb— that is, on whether the verb is being used as a linking verb. Ask yourself whether you want to modify the subject or the verb.

EXERCISE 3a-d
In the following sentences, correct in accordance with formal written usage any errors in the use of adjectives and adverbs.

1. Lasers, first developed in 1958, are now used routine in various industries.
2. Some scientists feel surely that lasers will be the primary industrial tool in the future.
3. Lasers work ideal in welding; for instance, aircraft parts manufacturers rely heavy on laser welding, which is faster and more efficient than arc welding.
4. Lasers work good for drilling holes in rubber, metal, glass, and plastic.
5. Lasers also work perfect for measuring straightness and leveling.
6. A laser is light amplified by stimulated emission of radiation; the name laser itself is actual an acronym.
7. Described more simple, a laser is a man-made generation of coherent light.

8. The rapid developing laser industry has created various new jobs.
9. My sister, who is studying physics and math, wants very bad to become a laser scientist.
10. She works real hard, so I feel certainly that she'll achieve her goal.

3e
Distinguish between the comparative and superlative forms of adjectives and adverbs.

Adjectives and adverbs show degrees of quality or quantity by means of their positive, comparative, and superlative forms. The **positive** form *(slow, quickly)* expresses no comparison at all. The **comparative,** formed by adding -er or by prefixing *more* to the positive form *(slower, more quickly)*, expresses a greater degree than the positive form or makes a comparison between two persons or things. The **superlative,** formed by adding -est or by putting *most* before the positive form *(slowest, most quickly)*, indicates the greatest degree of a quality or quantity among three or more persons or things. Some common adjectives and adverbs have irregular forms for the comparative and superlative *(good, better, best; badly, worse, worst)*.

Whether to use *more* or *most* before the adjective or adverb or to add the -er, -est endings depends on the number of syllables in the word. Most adjectives and a few adverbs of one syllable form the comparative and superlative with -er and -est. Adjectives of two syllables often have two possible forms *(fancier, more fancy; laziest, most lazy)*. Adjectives and adverbs of three or more syllables always take *more* and *most (more beautiful, most regretfully)*. Where there is a choice, select the form that sounds better or that is better suited to the rhythm of the sentence. If you are unsure about the appropriate form, consult a dictionary.

Some adjectives and adverbs, such as *unique, empty, dead, favorite, perfect, round,* are considered "absolute" in their meaning and thus cannot be logically compared. Logically, a room is either *empty* or *not empty,* a person is either *dead* or *alive.* Nevertheless, phrases such as "emptier than," "more perfect than," and "more dead than alive" are common in speech and very informal writing.

FORMAL   His diving form is *more nearly perfect* than mine.
INFORMAL   His diving form is *more perfect* than mine.

FORMAL   The new stadium is *more clearly circular* than the old one.
INFORMAL   The new stadium is *more circular* than the old one.

Also, check your writing for "redundant" or "double" comparatives and superlatives. Standard usage does not recognize such expressions as *You are more luckier than I* or *That was the most craziest thing I've ever seen.*

3f

In formal usage, use the comparative to refer only to one of two objects; use the superlative to refer only to one of three or more objects.

COMPARATIVE This car is *cheaper* than that one.
SUPERLATIVE This car is the *cheapest* subcompact on the market.

COMPARATIVE Ruth is the *more* attractive but the *less* good-natured of the twins.

SUPERLATIVE Ruth is the *most* attractive but the *least* good-natured of his three daughters.

EXERCISE 3e-f
In the following sentences, correct in accordance with formal written usage any errors in the use of the comparative and superlative forms of adjectives and adverbs. Then use each corrected form in a sentence of your own.

1. The Tour de France is the most unique bicycle race in the world.
2. The race, which is the longest, richest, and famousest of its kind, lasts for three weeks.
3. The Tour de France begins in Paris and continues through the Pyrenees and the Alps, where the cycling becomes the most hard for the participants.
4. The race is composed of stages which have an average length of not more than 200 kilometers, but no stage can be more long than 260 kilometers.
5. There are twenty stages in the race, and the cyclist who rides better in each of the race's stages is awarded a yellow jersey and a prize.
6. The rider continues to wear the yellow jersey until he is no longer the faster and drops out of first place.
7. Like the Tour de France, the Tour de Spain is another well-known cycling stage race, but because it is in sixteen to eighteen stages over about 1,900 miles, it is the shortest of the two.
8. Italy, Flanders, and Switzerland also host cycling races, but because of its length and the grueling mountain stages, the Tour de France is considered more arduous of all the races.
9. The number of riders who finish the long race is almost always least than the number who started.
10. Although professional cycling is most popular in Europe than in the United States, it is becoming familiarer to Americans as cyclists from the United States compete in major races like the Tour de France.

3g

Avoid the excessive use of nouns to modify other nouns.

The use of nouns to modify other nouns in expressions such as *rock garden, steel mill, silver mine,* and *telephone booth* is very common

3g

ad

in English. (See Section **38**.) When there is no appropriate adjectival form and when the modifying nouns are short, such constructions are usually clear and concise. But when nouns are used to replace appropriate adjectives or when the series of nouns modifying other nouns is long, such expressions are awkward at best, confusing at worst.

1. Choose an adjective instead of a noun modifier whenever possible.

> AWKWARD   *Siberia* railroad line
> IMPROVED   *Siberian* railroad line

2. Avoid long series of nouns modifying other nouns.

> CONFUSING   office management personnel report [A report about the management of office personnel? A report by personnel who are managing an office? Something else?]
> CONFUSING   teacher education program analysis [An analysis of a program for educating teachers? An analysis by teachers of an educational program? Something else?]

EXERCISE 3a-g

In the following sentences, correct in accordance with formal written usage any errors in the use of adjectives and adverbs. Then use the corrected forms in sentences of your own.

1. For those who aren't ready for the Tour de France, cycling for transportation or for exercise has become real popular.
2. People who once drove to work or to class have discovered that cycling is cheapest.
3. Cycling also works good for exercise conditioning.
4. Unfortunate, most people know how to ride a bicycle, but not enough of them know how to ride safe.
5. Every year in the United States, thousands of cyclists are injured in bicycle accidents, and many of these accidents are due to the cyclist riding careless or failing to obey traffic laws.
6. In a collision between a motor vehicle and a bicycle, the cyclist is obvious in the most danger.
7. In large cities pedestrians are frequent in danger from cyclists who ignore traffic regulations.
8. In the past, traffic laws were rare enforced for cyclists, but now a bicycle rider who runs a red light or goes the wrong way on a one-way street is likely to get a ticket.
9. Many elementary schools have established early bicycle safety education classes so that children will learn the basics of bicycle safety.
10. Bicycling can be a safe sport if everyone learns bicycle safety and practices it responsible.

WRITERS REVISING: CASE AND MODIFICATION

While revising a draft of her article about a campus appearance of civil rights leader Jesse Jackson, a reporter for the student newspaper corrected some errors in noun and pronoun case endings as well as in adjective and adverb usage. She also changed some case forms and adjectives and adverbs to make her writing more concise, as newspaper stories need to be. See if you can spot and correct the errors in her first draft. Then compare your revision with hers.

Draft

```
        The highlight of the evening was the

speech by the Reverend Jesse Jackson.

Jackson, whom had been the black contender

for the nomination for President in 1984,

said if a black candidate can succeed in

being nominated it could be him.  In his

speech, Jackson called on minority groups to

get solid behind whomever might better

represent their interests.  Many observers

feel real strong that of the two blacks

who have tried for the Presidency, Jackson

has been the most viable challenger.
```

Notice in the revision how the student reporter revised for conciseness. Once ideas have been fully developed, revising the language for conciseness is an important step for any kind of writing, not just newspaper articles. (The code numbers in the right margin refer to section numbers in this textbook.)

Revision

```
        evening's
    The‸highlight of the evening was the

speech by the Reverend Jesse Jackson.'s speech

        who
Jackson, whom had been the black contender   2a(4)
        Presidential
for the‸nomination for President in 1984,
```

> said if a black candidate can succeed in
>
> being nominated it could be ~~him~~ *he*. In his   2a(5)
>
> speech, Jackson called on minority groups
>
> to get solid~~,~~ *ly* behind ~~whomever~~ *whoever* might ~~better~~ *best*   3a, 2a(4), 3f
>
> represent their interests. Many observers
>
> feel ~~real strong~~ *really strongly* that^ of the two blacks   3b
>
> who have tried for the Presidency, Jackson
>
> has been the ~~most~~ *more* viable challenger.   3f

4

VERB FORMS

Verbs are the most complex parts of speech in English. They have more forms than any other kind of word, and they can be divided into a number of different kinds according to their forms and uses. This section covers the various forms and kinds of verbs, their function, and some common problems in their use. Section **5** covers the forms, use, and problems of tense, voice, and mood in verbs.

FORMS OF THE VERB

All verbs except *be*, which we will discuss separately, have five forms. The first three of these—the plain form, the past tense, and the past participle—are called the **principal parts** of the verb.

Plain form or infinitive. The plain form, sometimes called the base form, is the verb form we use with all plural nouns and the pronouns *I, we, you,* and *they* to indicate present time or habitual action: *rivers flow to the sea; birds fly south every winter; I <u>owe</u> you money; they <u>work</u> downtown.* Verbs are listed in the dictionary by their plain form (*flow, fly, owe, work*). We also use the plain form after all helping verbs, such as *will, can, must, should* (except the forms of the verbs *be* and *have*): *the river will flow; the birds can fly.* The infinitive forms of most verbs are created by adding *to* to the plain form: *he plans <u>to work</u> at home; I used <u>to owe</u> you money.*

Past tense form. The past tense is the form we use to show that the action or state of being indicated by the verb occurred at some time in the past. ("Tense" means the time of the verb's action.) In most verbs the past tense is formed simply by adding *-d* or *-ed* to the plain form (sometimes doubling the final consonant—see Section **40e[4]** for an explanation of this spelling rule): *smoked, worked, planned.* But in about two hundred verbs it is formed in some irregular way, usually by a vowel change: *grow, grew; swim, swam; drive, drove.* (See **4b.**)

Past participle. The past participle is the form we use with *has, have,* or *had* to form the perfect tense (see Section **5**): *has worked, have grown, had driven.* It is also used with the forms of *be* to form the **passive voice:** *is defeated, was being driven, were discovered.* (See Section **5.**) In most verbs the past tense and the past participle have the same form: *played, have played; found, has found; slept, had slept.* But about forty-five verbs, including many very common ones such as *become, do, grow, speak,* and *write,* have separate forms for the past participle. (See Section **4b.**) (For a discussion of the past participle in phrases that function as adjectives, see Section **1c.**)

-s form. The *-s* form is the form we use with the pronouns *he, she,* and *it,* with all singular nouns, and with certain indefinite pronouns (such as *each* or *someone*) to indicate present time or habitual action: *she asks, the dog bites, someone always wins.* For all verbs except *be* and *have,* this form is made by adding *-s* to the plain form: *asks, bites, wins.* For the verbs *be* and *have* the *-s* forms are *is* and *has.*

Present participle. The present participle is the form we use after *am, is, are, was,* or *were* to indicate the progressive tense—action continuing at the time indicated: *I am working, he is playing, they are eating, the corn was growing.* For all verbs this form is made by adding *-ing* to the plain form (sometimes doubling the final consonant).

The five forms of two verbs are summarized below:

		Regular Verb	Irregular Verb
PRINCIPAL PARTS	Plain form	work	begin
	Past tense	worked	began
	Past participle	worked	begun
	-s form (present tense)	works	begins
	Present participle	working	beginning

(For a discussion of the present participle in phrases that function as adjectives, see Section **1c.**)

The verb *be.* The verb *be* is different in having eight forms, three more than any other English verb. Unlike any other verb, it has three present tense forms *(am, are,* and *is),* all different from the plain form *be;* and it has separate singular and plural forms *(was* and *were)* in the past tense. In addition, it has a past participle *(been)* and a present participle *(being).*

4

vb

Plain form	be
Present tense, singular, first person	am
Present tense, singular, -s form	is
Present tense, plural	are
Past tense, singular	was
Past tense, plural	were
Past participle	been
Present participle	being

KINDS OF VERBS

Verbs can be divided into various kinds according to main forms and uses.

Regular and irregular verbs. A verb is either regular or irregular according to the way its past tense and/or past participle are formed.

A **regular verb** forms the past tense and past participle simply by adding -d or -ed to the plain form: *complete, completed, completed; repeat, repeated, repeated.* Occasionally the final consonant of a regular verb doubles in forming the past tense: *plan, planned, planned; hiccup, hiccupped, hiccupped.* (See Section **40e[4]** for an explanation of the applicable spelling rule.)

An **irregular verb** forms the past tense and/or past participle in some unusual way, usually by changing an internal vowel. In many irregular verbs, although the internal vowel is changed, the past tense and past participle have the same form: *keep, kept, kept; sleep, slept, slept.* About forty-five, however, have three distinct forms: *freeze, froze, frozen; give, gave, given.* About twenty irregular verbs keep the same form for all three principal parts: *cut, cut, cut; hit, hit, hit.* Although there are in all only about two hundred irregular verbs in modern English, they include a great many we use most frequently. (See **4b** for a list of the most common ones.)

Main and auxiliary verbs. In a verb phrase such as *is going, had been winning, must have been found,* or *will be helped,* the last verb form indicates the principal meaning and is called the *main verb.* All other verb forms in the phrase indicate special shades of meaning, such as those of time, obligation, and possibility, and are called **auxiliary verbs** or helping verbs.

Auxiliary verbs make up a small group of function words that may be divided into subgroups according to the kinds of functions they perform. All auxiliary or helping verbs except *be, have,* and *do* are marked by the fact that they have only one *form.*

1. The forms of *be (am, is, are, was, were, been,* and *being)* and of *have (has, have, had, having)* combine with main verbs to indi-

cate tense and voice (see Section **5**) as in *have worked, were studying, is planned, had been defeated.* The auxiliaries *will* and *shall* are used to indicate future time, as in *will go.*

2. The auxiliaries *can, could, may, might, must, ought (to), should,* and *would,* sometimes called **modal auxiliaries,** combine with main verbs to indicate ability, obligation, permission, possibility, etc.: *can go, could have gone, must go.*

3. The auxiliary *do* is used to form questions and negative statements and to give emphasis, as in *Does she work; She did not work yesterday; She does work hard.*

Transitive, intransitive, and linking verbs. Verbs may be grouped as intransitive, transitive, or linking according to whether they do or do not pass their action to another word, called their object, or whether they are followed by a word which refers to the subject, called a subject complement. (See also Section **1.**)

Intransitive verbs are those that are not followed by any object or complement. They do not pass their action to a "receiver."

> The church bells rang.
> The book lay on the table.

Transitive verbs are those that are followed by one or more objects, words that receive the action of the verb. In other words, transitive verbs *trans*fer action from the subject to the object.

> The hurricane *struck* the coast.
> Rescue workers *gave* the storm victims aid. [*Victims* is an indirect object, *aid* a direct object.]
> The storm *made* the roads impassable. [*Roads* is a direct object, *impassable* an object complement modifying *roads.*]

Linking verbs are those that are followed by a subject complement, a word that renames or describes the subject. Linking verbs do not transfer action; rather, they join the subject and the complement. Common linking verbs are forms of *be (is, are, was, were,* etc.), *appear, become, seem,* and, in certain contexts, verbs such as *smell, taste, feel, sound, look, act, grow.* (See also Section **3a.**)

> Mata Hari *was* a German spy. [*Spy* describes *Mata Hari.*]
> Her life *appears* glamorous to us now. [*Glamorous* describes *life.*]
> Undoubtedly it *seemed* very dangerous to her. [*Dangerous* describes *it.*]

Many verbs may be used as either intransitive or transitive according to the sentence in which they are used.

4a

vb

The storm *broke* the power lines. [Transitive]
The storm *broke* violently. [Intransitive]

Finite and nonfinite verbs. A **finite verb** can stand alone as the main verb in a sentence or clause. It can function as a main verb without an auxiliary, and it changes form to show person and number: *the bus stops here; the buses stop here.* **Nonfinite verb** forms (infinitives, participles, gerunds) cannot stand alone as main verbs, do not indicate person or number, and cannot by themselves make an assertion about the subject: *the bus stopping here.* They must be accompanied by auxiliaries to form sentences or clauses: *the bus is stopping here.* Unaccompanied nonfinite verbs usually appear in phrases: *This bus goes to Monroe Street after stopping here.*

Compare the finite and nonfinite verbs in the following lists. Note particularly that all the word groups containing a finite verb are complete sentences but that none of those containing only nonfinite verbs are. Note also that the nonfinite verb forms remain unchanged.

FINITE	NONFINITE
The man plans his meals.	The man planning his meals. . .
The men plan their meals.	The men planning their meals. . .
The dog has slept.	The dog having slept. . .
The dogs have slept.	The dogs having slept. . .
She defeats her opponents.	The opponent to defeat. . .
They defeat their opponents.	The opponents to defeat. . .

PROBLEMS WITH VERB FORMS

4a

Use the *-s* and *-ed* forms of the verb when required.

Whenever the subject is (1) *he, she,* or *it,* (2) a singular noun, or (3) an indefinite pronoun such as *someone* or *anybody,* standard written English requires the *-s* ending on most present-tense verbs: *she likes potato chips; he skips lunch; it rains occasionally; the dog wants to go out; everybody sits down.* Similarly, standard written English requires the *-ed* ending on the past tense and the past participle of all regular verbs used with these types of noun and pronoun subjects: *he skipped lunch; the dog wanted to go out.*

EXERCISE 4a

In the blank spaces in the following sentences, supply the correct present-tense form of the verbs given in parentheses. Then use each of these sentences as a model to construct a similar sentence of your own.

1. My neighbor (know) _____ that I (expect) _____ company for dinner, but she won't (get) _____ up and (go) _____ home.
2. She (come) _____ over to our house every chance she (get) _____ and (talk) _____ all afternoon.
3. Obviously, at her house nobody (care) _____ if she (help) _____ out or not.
4. She (be) _____ (suppose) _____ to be watching her little brother (play) _____ in the yard.
5. If somebody (ask) _____ her, I'm sure she (say) _____ she (think) _____ she (be) _____ watching him just fine from my kitchen.

4b

Distinguish carefully among the principal parts of irregular verbs.

Most English verbs are regular; that is, they form their past tense and past participle with *-d* or *-ed*. However, about two hundred verbs are irregular, forming the past tense and past participle another way—sometimes by means of an internal vowel change as in *fly, flew, flown*. Because these irregular verbs break the pattern, so to speak, we have to devote some time and attention to learning their principal parts.

Although nonstandard spoken forms (*I done, I have did, he has broke, we have took, you seen*) seldom seriously interfere with meaning, situations requiring standard English call for the correct use of irregular verbs. When you are in doubt about a verb form, check your dictionary. Dictionaries list the principal parts of all irregular verbs: the plain form (*begin*), the past tense (*began*), and the past participle (*begun*). If your dictionary lists only the plain form and one other form (*bend, bent,* for example), the second form is both the past tense and past participle. If the dictionary lists only the plain form, the verb is regular and forms both its past tense and past participle by adding *-d* or *-ed*.

The principal parts of many of the most commonly used irregular verbs are listed below. When two forms are listed, both are acceptable, although the first is that listed first in most dictionaries and is therefore preferred. Add to the list any other verbs that you find troublesome.

Present Infinitive (Plain Form)	Past Tense	Past Participle
beat	beat	beaten
become	became	become
begin	began	begun
bet	bet	bet
bite	bit	bitten

blow	blew	blown
break	broke	broken
bring	brought	brought
burst	burst	burst
buy	bought	bought
catch	caught	caught
choose	chose	chosen
come	came	come
cut	cut	cut
dive	dived, dove	dived
do	did	done
draw	drew	drawn
drink	drank	drunk
drive	drove	driven
eat	ate	eaten
fall	fell	fallen
feel	felt	felt
find	found	found
fly	flew	flown
forget	forgot	forgot, forgotten
forgive	forgave	forgiven
freeze	froze	frozen
get	got	got, gotten
give	gave	given
go	went	gone
grow	grew	grown
hang (suspend)	hung	hung
hang (execute)	hanged	hanged
hide	hid	hidden
hit	hit	hit
hurt	hurt	hurt
keep	kept	kept
know	knew	known
lead	led	led
leave	left	left
let	let	let
lose	lost	lost
make	made	made
mean	meant	meant
read	read	read
ride	rode	ridden
ring	rang	rung
rise	rose	risen
run	ran	run
see	saw	seen
shake	shook	shaken
shine (emit light)	shone	shone
shine (polish)	shined	shined
sink	sank, sunk	sunk
speak	spoke	spoken
spin	spun	spun

spring	sprang, sprung	sprung
stand	stood	stood
steal	stole	stolen
stink	stank	stunk
strike	struck	struck
swear	swore	sworn
swim	swam	swum
swing	swung	swung
take	took	taken
teach	taught	taught
tear	tore	torn
tell	told	told
think	thought	thought
throw	threw	thrown
wear	wore	worn
weave	wove, weaved	woven, weaved
weep	wept	wept
win	won	won
wind	wound	wound
write	wrote	written

EXERCISE 4b

In the blanks in the following sentences, supply the correct forms of the verbs given in parentheses.

1. Last night a health expert (speak) _____ about physical fitness at the local gym.
2. She had (write) _____ several books about the benefits of exercise.
3. I should have (know) _____ that her speech would make me (feel) _____ guilty for not exercising.
4. As a result, yesterday I (begin) _____ a physical fitness program of my own.
5. I (swim) _____ twenty laps of the pool yesterday, and after I've (swim) _____ twenty more today, I'll feel that I've accomplished something.
6. I (feel) _____ sore all day, for I had (forget) _____ what it was like to use my muscles.
7. At least I haven't (break) _____ any bones; my friend broke his arm the first day he (ride) _____ his bicycle for exercise.
8. My brother (write) _____ to me to tell me that he had (fall) _____ on the racquetball court and sprained his ankle.
9. Another friend gave up jogging after a dog (spring) _____ out at him, (bite) _____ him, and (tear) _____ his expensive jogging suit.
10. I think that my exercise is safe, though, for I remembered everyone else's accidents and (choose) _____ my activity carefully.

4c

Distinguish between *lie* and *lay*, *sit* and *set*.

These two pairs of irregular verbs are often bothersome. *Lie* and *sit* are always intransitive, which means that they cannot pass action to objects or occur in the passive voice. *Lay* and *set* are always transitive and therefore always must either have objects to receive their action or be in the passive. The distinction between the verbs in the two pairs continues to be carefully observed in written English, though not always in speech.

The principal parts of *lie*, meaning "recline," are *lie, lay, lain*. The principal parts of *lay*, meaning "place," are *lay, laid, laid*.

LIE (INTRANSITIVE)

PRESENT	*Lie* down for a while and you will feel better.
PAST	The cat *lay* in the shade and watched the dog carefully.
PRESENT PARTICIPLE	My keys were *lying* on the table where I dropped them.
PAST PARTICIPLE	After I *had lain* down for a while, I felt better.

LAY (TRANSITIVE)

PRESENT	*Lay* the book on the table and leave.
PAST	He *laid* the book on the table and walked out the door.
PRESENT PARTICIPLE	*Laying* the book on the table, he walked out the door.
PAST PARTICIPLE	*Having laid* the book on the table, he walked out the door.

The principal parts of *sit* (meaning "occupy a seat") are *sit, sat, sat;* the principal parts of *set* (meaning "put in place") are *set, set, set*.

SIT (INTRANSITIVE)

PRESENT	*Sit* down and keep quiet.
PAST	I *sat* in the corner for half an hour.
PRESENT PARTICIPLE	*Sitting* down angrily, I glared at my teacher.
PAST PARTICIPLE	*Having sat* in the corner for half an hour, I was subdued.

SET (TRANSITIVE)

PRESENT	*Set* the basket on the table and close the door.
PAST	Yesterday he *set* the grocery cartons on the kitchen table; today he *set* them on the porch.
PRESENT PARTICIPLE	*Setting* her glasses on the table, she rubbed her tired eyes.

PAST PARTICIPLE   *Having set* his skis in the corner, he stooped to take off his boots.

EXERCISE 4c

In sentences 1, 2, and 3 below, supply the correct form of *sit* or *set* in the blanks provided. In sentences 4, 5, and 6, supply the correct forms of *lie* or *lay*. Then write four sentences of your own, one each using a correct form of *sit, set, lie,* or *lay*.

1. Because he had _____ around studying all winter, my friend decided to start a summer exercise program, so he _____ aside a half hour to make a schedule for exercising.
2. He decided to start the next morning, so he _____ his jogging shoes on the end of the bed; that way, he would see them as soon as he _____ up the next morning.
3. The next day he jogged three miles, but he had to _____ down to rest halfway through the run.
4. When I went to see my friend last night, I found him _____ on his bed; his jogging shoes were on the floor where he had _____ them after he took them off.
5. He _____ there on his bed and told me that jogging required more effort than he had realized.
6. After he had _____ there for half an hour, he told me that he was quitting his exercise program and would _____ his jogging shoes in the closet until he felt more energetic.

4d

The main verb in every sentence should be a finite verb.

Remember that only finite verbs or verb phrases can make assertions and serve as the main verbs of sentences. Nonfinite verb forms—infinitives *(to steal)*, present participles *(stealing)*, and past participles *(stolen)*—cannot serve as the main verbs of sentences unless they are accompanied by a helping verb. A group of words that has only a nonfinite verb will always be a sentence fragment. (See Section **6** for a full discussion of sentence fragments.)

INCORRECT   When the pitcher wasn't looking, the runner stole third base. The crowd cheering wildly.

CORRECT   When the pitcher wasn't looking, the runner stole third base. The crowd cheered wildly.

EXERCISE 4a–c

In the blanks in the following sentences, supply the correct form of the verb or verbs given in parentheses. Then use each of these sentences as a model to construct a similar sentence of your own.

1. In 1912 the S.S. *Titanic,* the supposedly unsinkable luxury liner, (sink) _____ after a collision with an iceberg in the North Atlantic; 1,522 people (lose) _____ their lives.
2. The wreckage of the ship now (lie or lay) _____ two-and-a-half miles below the surface of the sea.
3. After hitting the iceberg, which (tear) _____ a 300-foot gash in the starboard side, the ship (remain) _____ afloat for over two hours.
4. Unfortunately, only twenty lifeboats and rafts (be) _____ available for the 2,227 passengers and crew.
5. After the passengers had (enter) _____ the lifeboats, they (begin) _____ to row them away from the tilting ship.
6. Many of those who (sit or set) _____ in the lifeboats (die) _____ because the temperature at sea was below freezing.
7. The nearest ship to respond to the *Titanic's* distress signals (be) _____ two hours away.
8. Another ship, the *Californian,* had (be) _____ nearer the *Titanic* and could have (save) _____ the crew and passengers, but its radio was turned off.
9. Today, a joint French and American expedition has (locate) _____ the *Titanic;* the ship (remain) _____ at the bottom of the sea where it (sink) _____ over seventy years ago.
10. Many of the still-living survivors of the *Titanic* (believe) _____ that the ship should (lie or lay) _____ where it is as a memorial to those who (die) _____.

5

VERBS: TENSE, VOICE, AND MOOD

The form of a verb or verb phrase tells us three things about the action or state it names. It tells what time the action occurs (tense); whether the subject is performing the action or receiving it (voice); and what the attitude of the speaker or writer is (mood).

TENSE

Tense is the time of the action or state expressed by the verb. Almost all verbs show the difference between **present** and **past** time by a change in the verb form. All verbs show **future** time by using *shall* or *will* before the infinitive, or plain form, of the verb.

Tense	Regular Verb	Irregular Verb
PRESENT	She walks today.	The sun rises today.
PAST	She walked yesterday.	The sun rose yesterday.
FUTURE	She will walk tomorrow.	The sun will rise tomorrow.

A few verbs have only one form for both present and past time: *set, burst, cast, hurt, split.* By themselves these verbs cannot show time; to do so, they must depend entirely on modifying words *(I split wood yesterday)* or auxiliary verbs *(I was splitting the wood).*

In addition to the three tenses, which indicate the natural divisions of time into past, present, and future, all verbs have three **perfect tenses.** The perfect tenses indicate that the action named is completed or finished before a given point in time. Thus, for example, the past perfect tense *(had eaten)* indicates that the action named was completed before another past action: *He had eaten before his sister came home.* The three perfect tenses are formed by using the forms of the auxiliary *have* before the past participle of the main verb. The perfect tense forms of the verbs *work* and *see* are shown in the following:

Tense	Regular Verb	Irregular Verb
PRESENT PERFECT	has or have worked	has or have seen
PAST PERFECT	had worked	had seen
FUTURE PERFECT	will have worked	will have seen

The six tenses, together with the way each is formed, are summarized in the following table:

Tense	How Formed	Example
PRESENT	Plain form of verb with *I, we, you, they,* and all plural nouns; *-s* forms of verbs with *he, she, it,* and all singular nouns	I, we, you, they, the men *eat* he, she, it, the man *eats*
PAST	Plain form plus *-ed* in regular verbs; internal change in irregular verbs	she, they *talked* she, they *ate*
FUTURE	*Shall* or *will* before plain form of verb	he, they *will talk/shall eat*
PRESENT PERFECT	*Have* before past participle; *has* with *he, she, it,* and singular nouns	we, you, they, the men *have talked/have eaten* he, she, it, the man *has talked/has eaten*
PAST PERFECT	*Had* before past participle	she, they *had talked/had eaten*
FUTURE PERFECT	*Shall/will have* before past participle	he, they *will have talked/will have eaten*

All six tenses can have **progressive-tense** forms. These progressive forms indicate that the action named is continuing (in progress) at the time indicated. They are made by using the forms of the auxiliary verb *be* with the *-ing* form of the main verb *(is giving, was winning, have been going).*

The most common uses of the tenses of the active verb forms are as follows:

Tense	Use	Example
PRESENT	Expressing a present or habitual action	He *is talking* to the students now. He *talks* to the students at least once every year.
PAST	Expressing an action that was completed in the past	He *talked* to the students yesterday.
FUTURE	Expressing an action yet to come	He *will talk* to the students tomorrow.
PRESENT PERFECT	Usually expressing an action carried out before the present and completed at the present; sometimes expressing an action begun in the past and continuing in the present	He *has talked* to the students before. [Action carried out before the present and now completed] He *has* always *talked* to the students. [Action begun in the past and continuing in the present]
PAST PERFECT	Expressing a past action completed before some other past action	This morning I saw the speaker who *had talked* to the students last month.
FUTURE PERFECT	Expressing an action that will be completed before some future time	He *will have talked* to the students before next Thursday.

For a full synopsis of a regular and an irregular verb, see *conjugation* in the Glossary of Grammatical Terms, p. 545.

PROBLEMS WITH TENSE

In spite of the relatively complicated tense system, writers whose native language is English ordinarily have few problems with its use. The main problems that occur involve either special uses of the present tense or the choice of the appropriate tense in the subordinate clauses of some complex sentences.

5a

Use the present tense to express general truths or accepted facts and to indicate habitual action. Use the present tense in critical writing about literature, arts, and sciences.

GENERAL TRUTHS All that glitters *is* not gold.

Corn *grows* rapidly in warm, humid weather.

HABITUAL ACTION   The old man *exercises* daily.

The bank *closes* at four o'clock.

CRITICAL WRITING   In Dickens' novel, David's harsh stepfather *sends* him to London, where every day David *works* in a warehouse pasting labels on bottles.

Jonas Salk's discovery of a polio vaccine *is* one of the great discoveries of the twentieth century.

Note that the present tense also often expresses future action, as in *Our trip begins tomorrow.*

5b
Place the tenses of verbs in appropriate sequence.

The term **tense sequence** refers to the relation of the times expressed by the verbs in main and subordinate clauses in a complex sentence. When the verb in the main clause of a complex sentence is in any tense except the past or past perfect *(had talked)*, the verb in the subordinate clause will be in whatever tense the meaning requires.

The weather service *predicts* that it *will be* hot again tomorrow. [The prediction occurs in the present but refers to the future.]

Our friends *will* not *know* that we *were* here unless we *leave* them a note. [Future, past, present]

If the verb in a main clause is in the past or past perfect tense, the verb in a subordinate clause following it will usually be in the past or past perfect tense, unless the subordinate clause states a general truth.

You *said* that you *wanted* [not *want*] to live in an apartment.

I *thought* that I *had left* my coat in the car.

The owners *discovered* later that the fire *had destroyed* their house. [The destruction of the house occurred at a time before the owner's discovery of it.]

BUT   The child *discovered* painfully that fire *burns*. [Here *fire burns* states a general truth. Thus the verb is in the present even though the child's discovery occurred in the past.]

EXERCISE 5a–b

In the following sentences, choose the verb form entered in parentheses that is in appropriate tense sequence. Be prepared to explain your choices. Do any of the sentences have more than one possible answer?

1. *Shin splints* is the name given to pain that (occurred, occurs) in the front of the leg between the knee and the ankle.

2. The term *shin splints* may originate from the fact that the front lower-leg muscles (act, acted) as a splint to restrict the jolt and to absorb the impact of running on hard or uneven surfaces.

3. My jogging manual (states, stated) that shin splints (is, was) a stress injury.

4. When I went to see her about pain in my lower front leg, my doctor (tells, told) me that the term *shin splints* (applies, applied) to any pain between the ankle and the knee.

5. In my case, the pain had increased as I (jog, jogged) farther distances for longer periods.

6. My doctor told me that the shin splints will go away if I (use, used) ice on the area and (rest, rested) for a few days.

7. She also told me about some precautions that (help, helped) to avoid shin splints.

8. Because the muscles of the shin do not normally get as much exercise as those of the calf, special exercises, such as toe raises, (develop, developed) these muscles.

9. I also learned that I (have, had) fallen arches; as a result, I (buy, bought) a pair of shoes with built-in arches.

10. If a person who has shin splints (keeps, kept) on running, a more serious injury, such as a stress fracture, could (occur, have occurred).

5c

Use present infinitives and participles to express action occurring at the same time as or later than that of the main verb. Use perfect infinitives and past or perfect participles to express action earlier than that of the main verb.

The infinitive and participle forms are as follows:

	Infinitives	*Participles*
PRESENT	to begin	beginning
PAST	—	begun
PERFECT	to have begun	having begun

Infinitives and participles express only a time that is relative to the time indicated by the main verb of the sentence in which they are used. A present infinitive or participle expresses an action occurring at the same time as or later than that indicated by the main verb. A perfect infinitive or a past or perfect participle expresses a time that is earlier than that indicated by the main verb.

She *wants* [*wanted, had wanted, will want*] *to study* law. [The present infinitive *to study* indicates the same time or time later than that of the main verb *want.*]

She *would have* preferred *to study* [not *to have studied*] law. [The present infinitive *to study* indicates that studying law would occur at the same time or a later time than the expression of her preference.]

She *was* [*is*, *will be*] glad *to have studied* law. She would like *to have studied* law. [The perfect infinitive *to have studied* indicates that the study occurred earlier than the time indicated by the main verbs *was*, *is*, *will be*, or *would like*.]

Wanting to study law, she *works* [*worked*, *had worked*, *will work*] hard. [The present participle *wanting* indicates the same time or a time later than that of the main verb.]

Having passed the entrance exam, she *is celebrating* [*has celebrated*, *will celebrate*]. [The perfect participle *having passed* indicates that passing the exam occurs before the celebrating.]

Defeated in the election, the candidate *retired* [*has retired*, *had retired*, *will retire*] from politics. [The past participle *defeated* indicates that the defeat occurred before the time indicated by the main verb *retire*.]

EXERCISE 5c

In items 1 through 5, choose the infinitive or participle form that is in appropriate sequence. Be prepared to explain your choices. Do any of the sentences have more than one possible answer? In items 6 through 10, create your own sentence in accordance with the instructions.

1. (Warming up, Having warmed up) by doing stretching exercises for ten minutes, I started my five-mile run.
2. I wanted (to relax, to have relaxed) my muscles before starting the run.
3. I want (to avoid, to have avoided) injury, and warming up should also help me (to prevent, to have prevented) soreness after the run.
4. After (completing, having completed) my run, I walk for another quarter of a mile to cool down.
5. My friend, (neglecting, having neglected) to cool down after his run, got dizzy because he stopped too abruptly.

6. Write a sentence in which you use a main verb that expresses present time and a participle that expresses the same time.
7. Write a sentence in which you use a main verb that expresses present time and an infinitive that expresses later time.
8. Write a sentence in which you use a main verb that expresses past time and a participle that expresses earlier time.
9. Write a sentence in which you use a main verb that expresses past time and an infinitive that expresses earlier time.
10. Write a sentence in which you use a main verb that expresses present time and a participle that expresses earlier time.

VOICE

Voice shows whether the subject performs or receives the action named by the verb. When the subject performs the action, the verb is in the **active voice.** When it receives the action, the verb is in the **passive voice.**

5d

t

ACTIVE   The elephant *dragged* its trainer.

The poison *drove* its victim mad.

PASSIVE   The trainer *was dragged* by the elephant.

The victim *was driven* mad by the poison.

The passive voice is formed by using the appropriate form of the verb *be (am, is, are, was, were, been, being)* with the past participle of the main verb: *was driven, will have been driven, is being driven.* Note that although other auxiliaries may be included in the passive verb phrase, some form of the verb *be* must always come immediately before the past participle of the main verb.

Only **transitive verbs,** that is, verbs that can take an object, can show both active and passive voices. We can say *The student wrote the paper* or *The paper was written by the student,* but only *He talked,* not *He was talked.*

Most written sentences use verbs in the active voice, which is almost always more direct, more economical, and more forceful than the passive. But in two situations the passive voice is both useful and natural.

5d
Use the passive voice when the actor is not known.

Consider the following:

> The southside branch of City National Bank was robbed at gunpoint this morning just after ten o'clock.
> The play was first performed in 1591.

The writer of the first of these sentences, presumably not knowing who robbed the bank, was forced to use the passive voice. The only alternative would have been a much less economical construction such as *A person or persons unknown robbed the southside branch. . . .* The second sentence might be written when a record of a play's performance, but not its performers, exists. Otherwise, the sentence might have been written *The Lord Chamberlain's Company first performed the play in 1591.*

5e
Use the passive voice when the receiver of the action is more important than the actor.

Consider the following:

> The new bridge was completed in April.
> The experiment was finished on June 16; on June 17 the conclu-

sions were reviewed by the advisory board and reported immediately to the Pentagon.

In such sentences as these, the focus is not on who completed the bridge or who performed the experiment and reported the results; the important things are the bridge and the experiment.

Problems in the use of voice include awkward and ineffective shifts from one voice to another (see **10a**), and the unnecessary or weak use of the passive (see **39a**).

MOOD

The mood of a verb indicates whether the speaker or writer regards the action named by the verb as a fact, as a command, or as a wish, request, or condition contrary to fact.

English has three moods: the **indicative,** used for ordinary statements and questions *(He is happy, Is he happy);* the **imperative,** used for commands *(Be happy);* and the **subjunctive,** used to express conditions contrary to fact *(If he were happy)* and in clauses following certain verbs. Except for the subjunctive, writers have few problems with mood.

Special forms for the subjunctive have almost disappeared from modern English. The few that do survive are those that appear in *if* clauses expressing unreal conditions; in *that* clauses after verbs expressing requests, recommendations, and demands; and in a few formal idioms.

5f
Use the subjunctive to express conditions contrary to fact.

The subjunctive form uses the plain form of the verb (without the *s*), *have* instead of *has*, and *were* or *be* instead of *is, are, was,* or *am.*

> If the rose bush *were* healthy, it would have more buds. [The bush is not healthy.]
>
> Last year, the bush looked as though it *were* going to die. [But it didn't die.]
>
> Helen could settle the argument if she *were* here. [But she isn't here.]

Note that not all clauses beginning with *if* automatically express a condition contrary to fact.

> If my experiment is successful, I will prove my point. [Here the clause beginning with *if* merely states a condition that, if met, will prove the point.]

5g

Use the subjunctive in *that* clauses after verbs expressing wishes, commands, requests, or recommendations.

> I wish I *were* in Rome. [*that* unexpressed]
> The law requires that there *be* a prompt trial.
> I move that the meeting *be* adjourned.
> Resolved, that the auditor *examine* our books.
> The reporter asked that we *repeat* our last reply.

5h

Use the subjunctive in a few surviving idioms.

> Far be it from me.   Long live the Republic!
> Suffice it to say.   Come what may.
> Heaven help us!   Be that as it may.

Note that except in surviving idioms even the few remaining uses of the subjunctive observed above are often replaced in speech and informal writing by alternative forms. Compare *I wish I was in Rome, The law requires a prompt trial,* or *The reporter asked us to repeat our last reply* with the examples above. In more formal writing, the subjunctive remains quite firm.

EXERCISE 5f–h

In items 1 through 5, choose the appropriate verb form. Be prepared to explain your choices. In items 6 through 10, create your own sentence in accordance with the instructions.

1. The performance of *Hamlet* I saw at the theatre last night was so good that I felt as though I (was, were) in medieval Denmark.
2. If I (was, were) Hamlet, I think I would be terrified to encounter my father's ghost.
3. The audience at the theatre last night demanded that the actor who played Hamlet (is, be) brought back on stage for several bows.
4. I wish I (was, were) an English teacher so that I could assign *Hamlet* for all my students to read.
5. I also would request of the principal that my students (are, be) allowed to go to the theatre to see a performance of the play.

6. Write a sentence that expresses a contrary-to-fact condition.
7. Write a sentence using a verb in a *that* clause after a verb expressing a wish.
8. Write a sentence using a verb in a *that* clause after a verb expressing a command.
9. Write a sentence using a verb in a *that* clause after a verb expressing a request.

10. Write a sentence using a verb in a *that* clause after a verb expressing a recommendation.

EXERCISE 5a–h

In each of the following sentences, choose the correct form of the verbs, infinitives, or participles from each of the pairs given in parentheses. Do any of the sentences have more than one possible answer? Use each of these sentences as a model to construct a similar sentence of your own.

1. I'm glad I (get, got) tired of (sitting, setting) and (lying, laying) around and finally started a regular exercise program.
2. (Having begun, Beginning) to exercise regularly, I'm pleased by how much better I feel.
3. I wish that I (knew, had known) how much better I (would, will) feel.
4. If I (was, were) you, I'd start jogging, swimming, or bicycling right away.
5. Most people say that they (felt, feel) much better both physically and mentally after (starting, having started) a physical fitness program.

Rewrite the following sentences to change the active voice to passive and the passive voice to active. Do not change verb tenses in changing voice.

6. Bicycles were rented by the tourists.
7. They planned a trip through the Lake District.
8. The Lake District features some fairly steep hills.
9. However, the good view of the beautiful scenery was thought by the cyclists to be worth the hard pedaling.
10. Traveling by car had been rejected by them.

WRITERS REVISING: VERBS

A student wrote the following rough draft as he was doing library research for a short paper on the etymology (history) of a common word. He knew the draft had a number of errors in verb usage and more verbs in the passive voice than necessary, but at the time he was primarily interested in recording information. Revise the verb usage, and then compare your version to the student's.

Draft

```
D 1      Although Americans are making blue jeans an

D 2   international fashion, they were not the first on

D 3   the "blue jean scene." Centuries ago, heavy
```

5h

t

D 4   cotton cloth called <u>genes</u> was wove in Genoa,

D 5   Italy. Henry VIII buys a large shipment of the

D 6   cloth for his royal household. <u>Genes</u> is French

D 7   for Genoa, and French immigrants bring the cloth

D 8   to America.

D 9   The word <u>dungarees</u> comes from Dhunga, India,

D10   where during the fifteenth century work pants were

D11   made from cloth that was wove in Nimes, France.

D12   About the same time, the cloth is imported by the

D13   English and the name <u>serge de Nimes</u> (cloth of

D14   Nimes) is shortened to <u>denim</u>.

The rough draft shows a common problem—what verb tense to use when the subject being discussed is historical but has current effects. Is the action past but completed, past but continuing, habitual, or expressing a general truth? These are some of the issues the student tried to resolve in his second draft.

Revision

R 1   Although Americans ~~are making~~ *have made* blue jeans an

R 2   international fashion, they were not the first on

R 3   the "blue jean scene." Centuries ago, heavy

R 4   cotton cloth called genes was ~~wove~~ *woven* in Genoa,   4b

R 5   Italy. Henry VIII ~~buys~~ *bought* a large shipment of the

R 6   cloth for his royal household. <u>Genes</u> is French   5a

R 7   for Genoa, and French immigrants ~~bring~~ *brought* the cloth

R 8   to America.

R 9   The word <u>dungarees</u> ~~comes~~ *came* from Dhunga, India,

R10   where during the fifteenth century work pants were

R11   made from cloth that was ~~wove~~ *woven* in Nimes, France.   4b

R12   About the same time, *the English* ~~the~~ cloth ~~is~~ (imported) ~~by the~~   5d

R13   ~~English~~ and the name serge de Nimes (cloth of

R14   Nimes) ~~is~~ (shortened) to <u>denim</u>.   5d

Analysis

Blue jeans are already an international fashion: the action of the opening clause is completed, so *have made* is required rather than *are making*. The principal parts of wove (lines R4 and R11) are like *freeze, froze, frozen*—not like *get, got, got.* The event described in the third sentence was completed in the past; hence, the use of past tense *bought* is correct, rather than *buys* in the present tense picked up directly from the student's notes.

In the first clause of the fourth sentence (line R6), the present-tense *is* is correct because it states a continuing general truth. *Brought,* the verb in the second clause (line R7), must be in the past tense to show completed past action. Unlike the opening clause in the fourth sentence (line R6), which expresses a continuing general truth, the action expressed in the opening main clause of the fifth sentence (line R9) is completed. The situations described in the two clauses seem similar but are not.

There is no compelling reason for the use of the passive voice (lines D12 and D14). Also, in the revision (lines R12–R14) the "notetaking" present tense has been replaced by past-tense verbs that correctly signal completed past action.

BASIC SENTENCE FAULTS

sen flt

Will [Strunk] felt that the reader was in serious trouble most of the time, a man foundering in a swamp, and that it was the duty of anyone attempting to write English to drain this swamp quickly and get his man up on dry ground, or at least throw him a rope.

E.B. WHITE, ''Introduction to *The Elements of Style*''

Readers have expectations about how sentences should be constructed, expectations based on the system by which our language operates. When you violate this system, you violate your readers' expectations and ask them to work much too hard to understand your meaning—if it can be understood at all. If you want your writing to be understood, you must consider your readers' expectations regarding English grammar.

6

SENTENCE FRAGMENT

The usual sentence contains a subject and a verb and at least one independent clause. In writing, we indicate sentences by capitalizing the first word and placing appropriate end punctuation, usually a period, after the last. Any group of words that is set off as a sentence but that lacks a subject, a verb, or an independent clause is a **sentence fragment.**

Such fragments are common in speech, and they are sometimes used for certain special purposes in writing. But in most writing, the subject-verb sentence is what readers expect, and they will want some special effectiveness if that expectation is not met.

6a

Do not punctuate phrases, dependent clauses, and other fragments as sentences.

A fragment is usually an improperly punctuated phrase or dependent clause that is part of the sentence that precedes or follows it. Thus the fragment can almost always be revised by joining it to that sentence, although other revisions may be possible and sometimes desirable. The most common types of fragments, together with revisions, are illustrated on the following pages.

1. Prepositional phrase. Prepositional phrases consist of a preposition, its object, and any modifiers of the object: *over the mountains, during the long intermission, after eating dinner.* Prepositional phrases usually serve as modifiers. (See **1c.**) The prepositional phrases in the following examples are italicized.

FRAGMENT	For as long as there have been cities, there have been parks. *For the enjoyment of city dwellers.*
REVISED	For as long as there have been cities, there have been parks *for the enjoyment of city dwellers.*
FRAGMENT	Initially parks were for the people in the houses surrounding them. *Not for the city or town as a whole.*
REVISED	Initially parks were for the people in the houses surrounding them, *not for the city or town as a whole.*

6a

frag

Initially parks were for the people in the houses surrounding them—*not for the city or town as a whole.* [Here both revisions join the prepositional phrase introduced by *for* with the main statement, to which it clearly belongs. The dash gives greater emphasis to the phrase. See **23b.**]

2. Verbal phrase. Verbal phrases consist of a verbal (infinitive, participle, or gerund), its object, and any modifiers of the object or verbal. (See **1c.**) The verbal phrases in the following examples are italicized.

FRAGMENT	Architects and developers planned urban parks carefully. *To mix the advantages of city and country living.* [Infinitive phrase]
REVISED	Architects and developers planned urban parks carefully *to mix the advantages of city and country living.*
FRAGMENT	Designers borrowed ideas from fashionable country estates. *Featuring elaborate gardens, artificial lakes, and beautiful vistas.* [Participial phrase]
REVISED	Designers borrowed ideas from fashionable country estates *featuring elaborate gardens, artificial lakes, and beautiful vistas.*
FRAGMENT	American parks frequently were designed on British models. *Being patterned after famous London parks.* [Participial phrase]
REVISED	American parks frequently were designed on British models, *being patterned after famous London parks.*

American parks frequently were designed on British models; in fact, some were patterned after famous London parks. [This second revision changes the participial phrase *(being patterned. . .)* to an independent clause. Consequently, the two sentences could be separated by a period, but the semicolon suggests the close relationship between the ideas expressed by the clauses. See **21b.**]

3. Subordinate clause. Subordinate clauses are usually introduced by such subordinating conjunctions as *after, although, because,* *when, where, while,* or *until* or by a relative pronoun such as *who, which,* or *that.* Subordinate clauses that occur as fragments are almost always modifiers, which properly belong with the preceding or following sentence. (See **1d.**) Subordinate clauses in the following examples are italicized.

FRAGMENT Wealthy English landowners preferred planned parks to nature's own landscaping. *Which was considered too wild and untamed.*

REVISED Wealthy English landowners preferred planned parks to nature's own landscaping, *which was considered too wild and untamed.*

FRAGMENT Regent's Park in London has historical importance. *Because it showed how a large park could be developed within a major city.*

REVISED Regent's Park in London has historical importance, *because it showed how a large park could be developed within a major city.*

Regent's Park in London has historical importance; *it showed how a large park could be developed within a major city.* [Here the fragment has been made into an independent clause by dropping the subordinating conjunction *because,* but the close relationship of the second clause to the first is suggested by separating the two with a semicolon rather than a period.]

FRAGMENT Planners intended New York City's Central Park for everyone's enjoyment. *Although mainly the wealthy used its footpaths and carriageways at first.*

REVISED *Although mainly the wealthy used its footpaths and carriageways at first,* planners intended New York City's Central Park for everyone's enjoyment.

4. Appositives. Appositives are words or phrases that rename or explain a noun or a pronoun standing immediately before them. The appositives in the following examples are italicized.

FRAGMENT Central Park was laid out by F. L. Olmsted. *The same landscape architect who later designed the 1893 World Exposition in Chicago.*

REVISED Central Park was laid out by F. L. Olmsted, *the same landscape architect who later designed the 1893 World Exposition in Chicago.*

REVISED Central Park was laid out by F. L. Olmsted. He was the same landscape architect who later designed the 1893 World Exposition in Chicago. [Here the fragment has been made into an independent clause by adding a subject and a verb. This revision gives greater emphasis to his designing the Chicago exhibition by placing that information in a separate statement.]

FRAGMENT The Exposition grounds formed one of Chicago's large parks. *Jackson Park along the Lake Michigan shore.*

REVISED The Exposition grounds formed one of Chicago's large parks, *Jackson Park along the Lake Michigan shore.*

The Exposition grounds formed one of Chicago's large parks—*Jackson Park along the Lake Michigan shore.* [Here the dash rather than the comma gives greater emphasis to what follows. See **23b.**]

6a

frag

FRAGMENT Both Central Park and Jackson Park were built on seemingly unusable land. *The first being built on garbage-strewn squatters' grounds, the second being dredged from a marshy swamp.*

REVISED Both Central Park and Jackson Park were built on seemingly unusable land, *the first being built on garbage-strewn squatters' grounds, the second being dredged from a marshy swamp.*

Both Central Park and Jackson Park were built on seemingly unusable land. Central Park was built on garbage-strewn squatters' grounds, and Jackson Park was dredged from a marshy swamp.

5. Other fragments.

FRAGMENT New York City's Parks Department has created fifteen "quiet zones" at city parks and beaches. *And declared them off-limits for radio and tape-deck playing.*

REVISED New York City's Parks Department has created fifteen "quiet zones" at city parks and beaches and declared them off-limits for radio and tape-deck playing. [Here the fragment is the second half of a compound predicate: *has created . . . and declared. . . .*]

FRAGMENT The mayor designated some parts of parks for noisy recreation. *But other parts for quiet enjoyment of nature.*

REVISED The mayor designated some parts of parks for noisy recreation *but other parts for quiet enjoyment of nature.* [Here the fragment is the second part of a compound direct object of the verb *designated.*]

FRAGMENT *Earphones only.* Music lovers without them may be fined, and their radios may be impounded.

REVISED *Radios may be played with earphones only.* Music lovers without them may be fined, and their radios may be impounded. [This unusual fragment needs both a subject and a verb. It probably results from a command (You must use earphones) and is similar to such phrases as "Non-smokers only."]

6b

6b

frag

Recognize acceptable incomplete sentences.

Exclamations, commands, and requests have no expressed subject; the subject *you* is always understood. Such sentences as the following are standard sentence patterns rather than incomplete sentences. (See **1a.**)

Look out!	Let the buyer beware!
Close the door.	Please pass the spinach.

Incomplete sentences are common in the questions and answers of speech and in written dialogue, which imitates speech.

"Where do we go tonight?"
"To the movies."
"When?"
"In about an hour."

In most writing, except for the standard sentence patterns of exclamations and commands, incomplete sentences appear only in the following special situations.

1. Transitional phrases and a few familiar expressions. Sometimes experienced writers indicate the conclusion of one topic and the turning to another by using incomplete sentences.

So much for my first point. Now for my second.

In addition, a few familiar expressions such as *The quicker, the better* and *The more, the merrier* occur as incomplete sentences.

2. Answers to rhetorical questions. A rhetorical question is one to which the answer is obvious or one that the asker of the question intends to answer. Experienced writers sometimes follow such questions with incomplete sentences.

How much does welfare do for the poor? Not enough.
Who is to blame for accidents caused by drunk drivers? The drivers, always.

3. Experienced writers sometimes use incomplete sentences for special purposes. Writers sometimes write verbless sentences deliberately. Intentional fragments can convey emphasis or a sense of the writer's "talking" directly to the reader. They can also be used to create special effects such as haste, suspense, anger, and so forth.

I watch the cars go by for a while on the highway. Something lonely about them. Not lonely—worse. Nothing. Like the attendant's expression when he filled the tank. Nothing. A nothing curb by some nothing gravel, at a nothing intersection, going nowhere.

ROBERT M. PIRSIG, *Zen and the Art of Motorcycle Maintenance*

Every day the farmers raised their eyes to the blazing blue sky. Every day, the same message. No rain.

Student Essay

The voice in the ad is a highly fictitious created person, speaking as an individual in a particular situation. In a bathtub, for instance.

WALKER GIBSON, *Tough, Sweet & Stuffy*

6b

frag

EXERCISE 6(1)

In the following sentences, eliminate fragments by combining them with a main clause or by making the fragments into complete sentences.

1. Until the middle of the eighteenth century, the harpsichord was the favorite keyboard instrument. Being used by composers and musicians throughout the world.
2. By the 1750's, however, the harpsichord's popularity was challenged by a new keyboard instrument. The piano, whose full name is pianoforte.
3. The name piano-forte meaning "soft-loud." The new instrument's notes could be played at any volume.
4. Because the harpsichord's strings are plucked by a metal or leather quill. It is not possible to achieve variations in the volume of a single note.
5. The piano allows variations in volume. When a lever-activated hammer hits the string.
6. The first public piano concert was performed in London in 1767. And assured the piano's popularity.
7. Craftsmen began making better pianos for their increasing numbers of customers. Who rushed to own one of these expensive new instruments.
8. In 1771, Thomas Jefferson gave a piano to his fiancée, Martha Wayles Skelton. One of the first pianos to be brought into the United States.
9. By the end of the 1700's. The music of composers such as Mozart and Haydn had made the piano the supreme keyboard instrument. Although the harpsichord was still being played.
10. Having been invented in Italy in 1709. The piano is a relatively young musical instrument.
11. The great age of piano playing began in the middle of the nineteenth century with composers such as Liszt and Chopin. Whose compositions and keyboard techniques brought out the best qualities of the instrument.

12. Since the development of ragtime music in the 1890's. The piano has become an important element in jazz groups.
13. Early pianists like Scott Joplin led the way for later jazz artists. Such as Duke Ellington, Fats Waller, and Errol Garner.
14. The player piano was invented in the latter half of the nineteenth century. For those who couldn't play the piano themselves.
15. Early player pianos required the operator to pump foot pedals, but later models with electric motors were even easier to operate. And needed only the push of a button.

7

cs
fs

EXERCISE 6(2)

In the following paragraph, eliminate fragments by combining them with a main clause or by making the fragments into complete sentences.

Modern technology has enabled scientists to learn a great deal about the human brain. Using the most modern equipment. Researchers have discovered a great deal of information. About how we learn, about how the brain affects the way we feel, about memory, and about the aging of the brain. Contrary to popular opinion. Intelligence is determined not by the size of the brain. But by the number of and the complexity of dendrites in the brain. These dendrites form connections with nerve cells. Thus enabling the brain to receive and use information. Researchers estimate that the human brain functions at only a fraction of its potential. Having lost a portion of the brain through injury or illness. Some people are able to function quite effectively. Acting as a producer of chemicals. The brain produces and secretes substances. Which affect memory, intelligence, and mood. Because brain function deteriorates with age. Some people believe that a person's ability to learn also declines with age. However, older people who engage in intellectual activity or regularly pursue a learning activity. Actually show little or no loss of learning ability. According to recent studies. Therefore, to keep the brain functioning well for a lifetime. A person should continue to learn new things. And be involved in stimulating activities.

7

COMMA SPLICE; RUN-TOGETHER OR FUSED SENTENCE

Readers depend on certain written signals to tell them where one idea stops and another begins. Just as a sentence fragment violates readers' expectations because its capital letter and end punctuation signal a complete thought where none exists, so a comma splice or fused sentence violates expectations because its punctuation signals one complete thought where several exist. Thus readers must un-

tangle ideas, interpret beginnings and endings of thoughts, and deci-
pher relationships among chunks of information that should have
been made plain by the writer. The chances for error and misunderstanding increase accordingly.

7a
**Comma splice: Do not connect two main clauses with only a
comma.**

Placing a comma between two main clauses without a coordinating conjunction *(and, but, for, or, nor, so, yet)* results in the **comma
fault** or **comma splice.** If two main clauses are joined by a coordinating conjunction, a comma must precede the conjunction. If no conjunction is used, the two clauses must be separated by a semicolon or
a period.

Comma splices may be corrected in one of the following ways:

1. Connect the main clauses with a coordinating conjunction
   and a comma.
2. Replace the comma with a semicolon.
3. Make a separate sentence of each main clause.
4. Change one of the main clauses to a subordinate clause.

COMMA SPLICE   I avoided desserts, I was trying to lose weight.

REVISED   I avoided desserts, *for* I was trying to lose weight.

I avoided desserts; I was trying to lose weight.

I avoided desserts. I was trying to lose weight.

Because I was trying to lose weight, I avoided desserts.

The fourth revision would ordinarily be the most effective, for it not
only corrects the comma splice but also indicates a specific relationship
between the clauses. A good revision of a comma-splice error often
entails reworking the sentence rather than merely inserting a punctuation mark. The kind of revision you choose will depend on the larger
context in which the sentences occur and the shades of meaning you
wish to convey.

A comma is sometimes used between main clauses not connected
by a coordinating conjunction if two clauses are in balance or in contrast. Commas are also sometimes used between three or more brief
and closely connected main clauses that have the same pattern.

Good nutrition is not just smart, it's vital. [Balanced main clauses]

Some people eat to live, others live to eat. [Contrasting main clauses]

I'm tired, I'm hungry, I'm bored. [Main clauses with the same pat-
tern]

Although such sentences can be very effective, inexperienced writers would be wiser to use semicolons in them.

7b

7b

cs
fs

Use a semicolon or a period between two main clauses connected by a conjunctive adverb or a transitional phrase.

Conjunctive adverbs are words such as *accordingly, also, consequently, furthermore, however, instead, likewise, moreover, nevertheless, then, therefore,* and *thus.* Transitional phrases are phrases such as *for example, in fact, on the other hand, in conclusion, in the meantime.* When such words or phrases connect main clauses, they must always be preceded by a semicolon or a period.

> First we made coffee. Then we cooked breakfast.
>
> John must be asleep; otherwise he would be here.
>
> I should drink less coffee; however, the caffeine keeps me alert.
>
> Caffeine makes the heart pump faster; in fact, people with heart ailments should avoid caffeine.

7c

Run-together or fused sentence (run-on): Do not omit punctuation between main clauses.

Such omission results in run-together or fused sentences (run-ons)—that is, two grammatically complete thoughts with no separating punctuation. Correct these errors in the same way as the comma splice.

FUSED	Caffeine is a stimulant it gives some people the jitters.
REVISED	Caffeine is a stimulant, *and* it gives some people the jitters.
	Caffeine is a stimulant; it gives some people the jitters.
	Caffeine is a stimulant; *thus* it gives some people the jitters.
	Caffeine is a stimulant. It gives some people the jitters.
	Because caffeine is a stimulant, it gives some people the jitters.

Be especially careful not to fuse main clauses linked by connecting words and phrases. Punctuation is necessary to signal where one clause ends and another begins (see Sections **7b** and **20a**).

FUSED	Coffee contains caffeine furthermore, chocolate, tea, and cola also contain significant amounts of caffeine.
REVISED	Coffee contains caffeine; furthermore, chocolate, tea, and cola also contain significant amounts of caffeine.

FUSED   Many soft drinks have a high caffeine content as a result caffeine-free colas have been developed to respond
to consumers' concerns.

REVISED Many soft drinks have a high caffeine content. As a result, caffeine-free colas have been developed to respond
to consumers' concerns.

7c

cs
fs

EXERCISE 7(1)

Revise the following sentences to eliminate comma splices and fused sentences. Use all four methods of correction.

1. Whales have always been a source of wonder to humans, the earliest seafarers were fascinated by these huge creatures.
2. Whales and dolphins are mammals, they live in the water, they look like fish.
3. Much research has been done on whales during the past ten or fifteen years we now know more about how these mammoth sea creatures live.
4. Blue whales are the largest mammals ever to have lived on the earth, they can grow to a length of nearly 100 feet.
5. Humpback whales can be seen fairly close to the shores of New England, whale-watching trips to sight the humpback are big business.
6. The gray whale migrates annually from its Arctic feeding grounds to the warm waters off Baja California, there the whale-calves are born.
7. The right whale got its name from early whalers they referred to it as the "right" whale to kill because it yielded much blubber and bone.
8. The right whale also swims slowly and floats when killed, therefore it was a convenient and easy target for whalers.
9. Ten years ago the right whale, once the most common whale in the North Atlantic, appeared about to become extinct, although only about 200 right whales exist today, their future as a species looks brighter.
10. Through the centuries, whales have been a subject and a symbol for writers, for instance, Jonah is swallowed by a whale in the Biblical account, and Herman Melville's novel *Moby Dick* uses a white sperm whale as the central symbol and the object of the whale hunt.
11. The sperm whale is the whale species familiar to most people its huge square head appears on T-shirts, tote bags, and posters.
12. Single whales or large groups of whales sometimes become stranded on beaches, the reason for these strandings remains a mystery to scientists, although various theories have been suggested.
13. Some scientists believe strandings are caused by a breakdown in the whale's navigational ability brought on by parasite infestation, others believe the whales may be engaged in some form of mass suicide.
14. "Save the Whales" has become a familiar slogan, the campaign to rescue whales from mass slaughter by commercial fishing seems to be succeeding.

15. The blue, right, humpback, and sperm whales are now protected species others may be hunted in only limited numbers.

EXERCISE 7(2)

Revise the following paragraphs to eliminate comma splices and fused sentences. Use all four methods of correction.

Most people are a bit apprehensive about going to the dentist, some are positively panic-stricken at the thought of a visit to their dentist. The prospect of sitting helplessly in a large mechanical chair while at the mercy of the dentist keeps some people away. These especially fearful people cancel appointments, they delay getting checkups. Some frightened people ignore toothaches they would rather put up with pain than go to the dentist. Some of these people suffer from a dental phobia, they have an irrational fear of the dentist.

No one can promise that a visit to the dentist will be painless, however, modern technology has made dental treatment much more comfortable. Many people fear the pain of the needle that delivers the anesthetic now some anesthetics can be injected into the gums on a jet of air. The old image of a leering dentist with a huge drill in hand is a common one, today's dentists use high-speed, water-cooled drills which are fast and virtually painless.

Such sophisticated equipment and techniques do not help to calm all fears, therefore, dentists have adopted additional techniques for soothing patients. Some dentists give patients headphones for listening to music during treatment, others distract patients with videotapes. Getting patients to do relaxing exercises at the beginning of an appointment sometimes works, other dentists use hypnosis to relax their patients. People who fear dental treatment should tell the dentist of their apprehensions, the dentist can then explain the treatment step by step in order to reduce some of the fear.

WRITERS REVISING: SENTENCE FAULTS

Sentence fragments, comma splices, and fused (run-together) sentences all have one thing in common: a writer's failure to mark accurately for readers the fundamental unit of meaning—a complete thought.

The student intern at the college placement office received the following draft of an article for the placement newsletter. The newsletter was due at the printer's that afternoon, and the author of the article was already on her way home for Christmas vacation. The student intern had a major editing task ahead of her, one that required interpretation of some badly garbled and incomplete sentences.

See if you can revise the draft, fixing the sentence faults

so that the meaning is untangled. Then compare the choices you made with those the intern made as she reworked the article.

Draft

Leave No Stone Unturned

D 1   These next few months will be crucial. For

D 2   many students in their search for that first job.

D 3   And despite feelings of despair when considering

D 4   the task that lies ahead, there is a place to

D 5   start. And a definite path to follow in finding

D 6   the right employer.

D 7   You will find that opportunities do exist.

D 8   If you know where to look when looking you should

D 9   leave no stone unturned. The following are

D10   invaluable sources of help. Your college

D11   placement office. It is not only for the

D12   graduating senior, it also offers opportunities

D13   and services for the student who is seeking a

D14   summer internship. Keep in touch with your

D15   placement counselor. Also your professors and

D16   department heads, they may prove to be the perfect

D17   contacts for job seekers.

Revision

Leave No Stone Unturned

R 1   These next few months will be crucial, for   6a(1)

R 2   many students in their search for that first job.

R 3   And despite feelings of despair when considering   6a(5)

R 4   the task that lies ahead, there is a place to

R 5   start, and a definite path to follow in finding   6a(5)

R 6   the right employer.

R 7   You will find that opportunities do exist,   6a(3)

7c

cs
fs

R 8   If you know where to look. When looking you should   7c

R 9   leave no stone unturned. The following are

R10   invaluable sources of help. Your college

R11   placement office. It is not only for the   6a(4)

R12   graduating senior, *but* it also offers opportunities   7a

R13   and services for the student who is seeking a

R14   summer internship. Keep in touch with your

R15   placement counselor. Also your professors and

R16   department heads, they may prove to be the perfect   7a

R17   contacts for job seekers.

Analysis

To remove the fragment (*For many students* . . . lines (D1–2), it is joined to the first sentence (line R1). A sentence may be started with *And* occasionally, but overuse (lines D3 and D5) suggests the writer is incapable of deciding where one idea stops and another begins. Also, the construction at lines D5–6 is not a sentence at all but the second part of a compound subject begun in the preceding sentence. Making the fragment part of the previous sentence corrects the error (line R5).

The run-on *if you know where to look when looking* . . . (lines D8–9) makes nonsense of the meaning. Combining the first part with the preceding sentence and the second with the following sentence restores meaning (see lines R7–9).

Your college placement office (D10–11) is a fragment, probably the first of the "invaluable sources." Joining the fragment to the sentence that follows not only corrects the error but removes a fairly weak *it* and eliminates some unnecessary words. Also, the constructions *It is not only* . . . *it also* on either side of the comma splice seem to suggest a contrast: inserting a conjunction that indicates contrast *(but)* clarifies the meaning in the revision. These changes are shown in lines R11–12.

The draft's final sentence is a fragment fused to a main clause with a comma. There is no way to tell from the incomplete pieces whether the undergraduate meant *stay in touch with your counselor and professor/department heads* or *stay in touch with your counselor* (one thought) and *your professor/department heads may prove perfect contacts* (a separate thought). In her revision (lines R15–17), the student intern assumed *they* in the last clause referred to the faculty but not also to the counselor.

8

FAULTY AGREEMENT

Agreement is a grammatical relationship that signals the reader about how pieces of information fit together. For example, subject-verb agreement helps the reader to know which actors and which actions go together, even if there are several possibilities in a sentence. Consider the sentence *Poor reading habits that someone acquires when he or she learns to read often prevent reading enjoyment later in life.* The agreement between the plural subject *habits* and plural verb *prevent* helps the reader pick these two key pieces of information from the lengthy intervening subordinate information. Thus the reader is less likely to become confused about the sentence's main idea.

Agreement relationships pertain to subjects and verbs, pronouns and their antecedents, or demonstrative adjectives *(this, that, these, those)* and the words they modify. Modern English nouns and verbs have few inflections or special endings, so their agreement usually presents few problems. However, there are some grammatical patterns, such as the agreement in number of a subject and verb or a pronoun and its antecedent, that you need to watch carefully so that readers will not be confused about your meaning.

8a

Every verb should agree in number with its subject.

Sometimes a lack of agreement between subject and verb results from carelessness in composition or revision. But more often, writers use a singular subject with a plural verb or a plural subject with a singular verb, not because they misunderstand the general rule, but because they are uncertain of the number of the subject or because other words coming between the subject and the verb obscure the real subject.

1. Do not be confused by words or phrases that come between the subject and verb. Find the subject and make the verb agree with it.

The first two *chapters* of the book *were* exciting. [The verb agrees with the subject, *chapters*, not with the nearest noun, *book*.]
The *size* of the bears *startles* the spectators.

> **FAULTY** *Kittle's* has lowered the prices and *are* offering a free TV to anyone who purchases a new set of bedding.
>
> **REVISED** *Kittle's* has lowered the prices and *is* offering a free TV to anyone who purchases a new set of bedding.

Singular subjects followed by such expressions as *with, together with, accompanied by,* and *as well as* take singular verbs. The phrases introduced by such expressions are not part of the subject, even though they do suggest a plural meaning.

8a

agr

FAULTY	The *coach,* as well as the players, *were* happy over the victory.
REVISED	The *coach,* as well as the players, *was* happy over the victory.
FAULTY	*Sally,* together with her friends, *were* here.
REVISED	*Sally,* together with her friends, *was* here.

2. Be alert to agreement problems with indefinite pronouns used as subjects.

Indefinite pronouns ending in *-one, -body,* and *-thing,* such as *anyone, everybody,* and *something,* always take singular verbs. The indefinite pronouns *another, each, either, neither,* and *one* always take a singular verb. (See Section **8a[8]** for use of the phrase *one of the.*)

Everybody in the audience *was* enthusiastic.
Another of the pesticides *has* proved harmful to birds.
Each of the students *needs* individual help.
Neither of the books *was* available in the library.

The indefinite pronouns *all, any, most, more, none,* and *some* may take either a singular or plural verb depending upon the noun they refer to.

Some of the silver *is* missing. [*Some* refers to the singular noun *silver.*]
Some of her ancestors *were* pioneers. [*Some* refers to the plural noun *ancestors.*]

None of the work *is* finished. [*None* refers to the singular *work.*]
None of the birds *have* migrated yet. [*None* refers to the plural *birds.*]

A singular verb is sometimes used with *none* even when it refers to a plural noun. The plural is currently more common, however, in both spoken and written English.

3. Use a plural verb with two or more subjects joined by *and*.

A *dog and a cat* are seldom friends.
The *Ohio River and the Missouri River* empty into the Mississippi.

However, use a singular verb when the two parts of a compound subject refer to the same person or thing.

My *friend and benefactor* was there to help me.

4. Use a singular verb with two or more singular subjects joined by *or* or *nor.* When two or more subjects are joined by *or* or *nor,* make the verb agree with the subject closest to it.

Either the *dean or her assistant <u>was</u>* to have handled the matter.

Either *you or he <u>has</u>* to be here.

Neither the *farmer nor the chickens <u>were</u>* aware of the swooping hawk.

8a

agr

If one of the subjects joined by *or* or *nor* is singular and one plural, as in the last example above, place the plural subject second to avoid awkwardness.

5. When the verb precedes the subject of the sentence, be particularly careful to find the subject and make the verb agree with it.

Do not mistake the expletive *there* for the subject of the verb. (An expletive is a word tht signals that the subject will follow the verb. See **la.**)

There *are* no *trees* in our yard. [*There* is an expletive. The subject is *trees: No trees are in our yard.*]

On this question, there *remains* no *doubt.* [The subject is *doubt: No doubt remains on this question.*]

In some sentences beginning with the adverbs *here* and *there* or with an adverbial word group, the verb comes before the subject.

There *goes* the *man* I was describing. [*There* is an adverb. The subject is the noun *man.*]

Up the trail *race* the *motorcycles.* [The subject is *motorcycles.*]

In the chinks between the bricks *grows moss.* [The subject is *moss.*]

After a big victory *come* the postgame *letdown and fatigue.* [The compound subject, *letdown and fatigue,* requires a plural verb.]

An aid for determining correct subject-verb agreement is to rearrange the sentence into normal order, so that the subject comes first: *<u>Moss grows</u> in the chinks between the bricks.*

6. Use a singular verb with collective nouns when the group is considered as a unit acting together. Use a plural verb when the individual members of the group are acting separately.

Collective nouns have a singular form but name a group of persons or things as a single unit: *audience, band, bunch, class, committee, crowd, family, herd, jury, public, team,* and the like.

Our family *goes* out to dinner weekly. [The family acts together as a single unit.]

The family *have been* arriving all morning. [Members of the family arrived at different times.]

The committee *is* meeting today. [The singular verb *is* emphasizes the committee acting as a unit.]

The committee *are* unable to agree on a plan. [The plural verb *are* emphasizes the members of the committee acting separately.]

8a

agr

7. The verb should agree with its subject, not with a predicate noun.

The best part of the program *is* the vocal duets.

Expensive cars *are* a necessity in his life.

8. When the relative pronouns *who, which,* and *that* are used as subjects, use a singular verb when the antecedent is singular, a plural verb when the antecedent is plural.

They are the employees who *deserve* praise. [*Who* refers to the plural noun *employees;* thus the verb is plural.]

The book that *was* lost belonged to the library. [*That* refers to the singular noun *book;* thus the verb is singular.]

The phrase *one of the* frequently causes problems in such sentences.

Sanderson is one of the council members who *oppose* the plan. [*Who* refers to the plural *members;* several council members oppose the plan.]

Sanderson is the only one of the council members who *opposes* the plan. [*Who* refers to *one;* there is only one council member, Sanderson, opposing the plan. Note that the meaning of the sentence would not be changed if the phrase *of the council members* were omitted.]

9. When the subject is the title of a novel, a play, the name of a business or the like, or a word used as a word, use a singular verb even though the form of the subject is plural.

Romeo and Juliet <u>is</u> a Shakespearean play.

Songs and Satires <u>is</u> a book by Edgar Lee Masters.

Women <u>is</u> the plural of *woman.*

Smith Brothers <u>is</u> a brand of cough drops.

10. Nouns such as *economics, news, physics,* and *mathematics* that refer to an art, science, or body of knowledge usually take singular verbs because they are singular in meaning, although plural in form. Plural-form physical ailments such as *measles* or *hives* are treated similarly.

Linguistics is the study of human speech.

The good *news has* traveled quickly.

Measles carries the threat of severe complications.

11. Some plural-form nouns such as *athletics, hysterics, aerobics, politics, statistics,* and *acoustics* may be either singular or plural, depending on whether they refer to a singular idea or a plural idea. The noun *data,* however, is almost always treated as plural in formal writing.

Aerobics is an extremely strenuous form of exercise. [Singular meaning]

College *athletics are* responsible for generating thousands of dollars from loyal alumni. [Plural meaning: various collegiate sports]

The *data indicate* that consumers are making more credit card purchases.

12. Noun phrases indicating fixed quantities or extents (money, time, distance, or other measurements) may be either singular or plural, depending on whether they are being considered as a unit (singular) or as parts of a unit (plural).

The *majority* in the legislature *is* Republican. [Unit]

The *majority* of the tourists *have* returned to the bus because of the rain. [Individuals]

Three-quarters of the money *is* already spent. [Unit of money]

Sixty percent of the trees *were* damaged by the hurricane. [Individual trees]

Three hundred pounds is a lot for an amateur to bench-press. [Unit]

Five-and-a-half liters were needed to fill the tank. [Parts of unit]

The expression *the number* takes a singular verb, but *a number* takes a plural verb.

The number of candidates for the position *was* large.

A number of candidates *were* applying for the position.

The number of people moving to the Southwest *is* increasing.

A number of business firms *have* moved from New York.

EXERCISE 8a

In the following sentences, correct any errors in agreement.

1. My nephew, along with his eighth-grade classmates, are taking a trip to Washington, D.C., this spring.

2. He and each of his friends has been doing odd jobs to earn money for the trip.
3. Neither the teacher nor the students wants to decide which Washington sights must be omitted for lack of time.
4. None of the famous buildings such as the Lincoln Memorial or the White House has been left off the class's list.
5. But wanting to see everything and having only four days in which to see it is mutually exclusive.
6. There was a number of possible ways to shorten the list; the class have voted for the five things they most want to see.
7. The logistics of herding 130 eighth-graders around Washington make my nephew's teacher rather apprehensive.
8. Fortunately, a group of parents are going along to act as chaperons.
9. Three-quarters of these parents has been to the nation's capital before.
10. Either these parents or the teacher have a good idea of how to get to most of the historical sites in the city.

8b

agr

8b

To achieve pronoun-antecedent agreement, use a singular pronoun in referring to a singular antecedent. Use a plural pronoun in referring to a plural antecedent. Avoid sexist pronoun references.

Most pronoun-antecedent references are straightforward and uncomplicated. Simply make the pronoun agree in number with the word to which it refers.

The *cat* decided *she* wanted to have her kittens in my closet. [*She* refers to the singular antecedent *cat*.]
My closet *floor* is covered with junk; *it* is littered with shoes, old magazines, and a sleeping bag with a broken zipper. [*It* refers to the singular antecedent *floor*.]
The *kittens* were born on the sleeping bag and played *their* first games among my shoes. [*Their* refers to the plural antecedent *kittens*.]

When agreement problems between pronouns and their antecedents do occur, they usually involve (1) indefinite pronouns, (2) collective nouns, and (3) compound antecedents.

1. In writing, use singular pronouns to refer to indefinite antecedents such as *person, one, any, each, either, neither* and compounds ending in *-one, -body,* and *-thing,* such as *someone, anybody,* and *everything.*

Spoken English frequently uses a plural pronoun to refer to indefinite antecedents, but the singular continues to be preferred in writing.

SPOKEN	*Everyone* at the meeting should be allowed to express *their* opinions before the vote is taken.
WRITTEN	*Everyone* at the meeting should be allowed to express *his or her* opinion before the vote is taken.
SPOKEN	*Each* of the Cub Scouts is to bring *their* own tent to the roundup.
WRITTEN	*Each* of the Cub Scouts is to bring *his* own tent to the roundup.
SPOKEN	*None* of us actresses wants you to forget *our* performance.
WRITTEN	*None* of us actresses wants you to forget *her* peformance.

8b

agr

He (him, his) has conventionally been used in English to refer to such antecedents as *one, none, everybody,* and similar indefinite pronouns that designate either male or female. This usage is no longer as common as it once was and is, in fact, offensive to many readers. For a more complete discussion of sexism and pronoun usage, see Section **8c**.

2. With a collective noun as an antecedent, use a singular pronoun if you are considering the group as a unit and a plural pronoun if you are considering the individual members of the group separately.

The *class* finished *their* lab experiments yesterday. [The class members worked as individuals.]

The *sorority* holds *its* rush week in the spring. [The sorority is acting as a unit.]

The *crew* are going about *their* duties preparing the spacecraft for landing. [The members of the crew have separate duties.]

The *crew* is ready for *its* briefing. [The crew is being considered as a unit.]

3. If two or more antecedents are joined by the conjunction *and*, use a plural pronoun to refer to them. If two or more singular antecedents are joined by the conjunctions *or* or *nor*, use a singular pronoun to refer to them. If one of two antecedents joined by *or* or *nor* is singular and one plural, make the pronoun agree with the antecedent that is closer to it.

Dad and Mom have bought *their* tickets.

Either *my sister or my mother* is missing *her* luggage.

Neither *my parents nor my brother* has confirmed *his* reservation.

Either *Jean or my mother and father* are taking *their* vacation in May.

8c

agr

EXERCISE 8b

Revise the following sentences to make every pronoun agree with its antecedent in accordance with written usage. Indicate any sentence that would be acceptable in speech.

1. Everybody has their own way of studying.
2. For instance, neither my brother nor my roommate, John, can study unless their stereo is blasting.
3. Each of these music lovers claims that the sound relaxes them when they study.
4. Usually my roommate or my brother says they can't hear the bass unless the volume is turned to "maximum."
5. I could use earplugs, but it wouldn't allow me to hear the telephone.
6. On the other hand, neither of my sisters can study with music pounding in their ears.
7. I think that every person should consider how their study habits affect the people around them.
8. In my dorm, a committee voted unanimously to enforce quiet hours, but their decision wasn't popular with the music lovers.
9. Anyone who has ever had their study time disrupted by loud music knows how frustrating the experience can be.
10. Friends of mine solved his or her study habits conflict by getting the music lovers earphones.

8c

Avoid sexism in pronoun-antecedent references.

Pronoun-antecedent agreement can become complicated when you are dealing with so-called *common gender* words—words that can refer to either males or females—or when you are dealing with indefinite antecedents. For instance, if you are writing instructions concerning how to apply for a college scholarship, how do you refer to the applicant, who could be either male or female? And how do you refer to "anyone" when discussing those who have taken the Scholastic Aptitude Test or those who have not?

Historically, formal English used masculine pronouns for common gender or indefinite antecedents: *The applicant should have his SAT scores sent to the College Admissions Office. Anyone who has not taken the SAT should indicate when he plans to do so.* The masculine pronouns used in this way were assumed to mean people of either sex.

More recently, however, we have come to recognize that this usage discriminates against women and, in fact, is often illogical because it ignores realities. For example, college applicants are as likely to be women as men, so it makes little sense to write as if all the applicants were male.

Among the substitutes that have been proposed to indicate common gender are (1) the use of *he or she (hers or his)*, (2) alternating pronouns (*she* used in one paragraph, *he* in the next), (3) coined or combined-form pronouns like *s/he* and *his/hers,* and (4) the use of plural pronouns to refer to singular common gender or indefinite words (*Anyone who has not taken the SAT should indicate when they plan to do so*). Each of these alternatives has drawbacks. The first can sometimes result in cumbersome, monotonous pronoun repetition (*Anyone who thinks he or she is eligible for financial aid should send his or her application as early as he or she possibly can*).

The second alternative, although fairly widespread in such places as textbooks, can be confusing to readers. Confusion is particularly likely if a reader is skimming paragraphs and does not notice that the alternation has been deliberate.

General language use tends to reject the third alternative, combining or coining pronouns. The English language is slow to accept such words, particularly when their pronunciation is questionable (as with *s/he*).

Although common in speech, the fourth alternative, using a plural pronoun to refer to a singular antecedent, is regarded by many people as a grammatical error when it appears in writing. Furthermore, such usage can be confusing. Consider the sentences *The fear of growing old is so great that every aged person is seen as an insult and a threat to the society. They remind us of our own death.* Because the pronoun referring to *person* has been made plural, readers might assume that the antecedent is the nearest plural noun construction—*an insult and a threat.*

However, with the following guidelines you can construct clear sentences that are neither awkward nor sexist.

1. To avoid monotonous repetition of pronouns, use the plural rather than the singular if the meaning will not be affected.

An *applicant* who thinks *he or she* is eligible for financial aid should send in *his or her* application forms before December 1.

Applicants who think *they* are eligible for financial aid should send in *their* application forms before December 1.

2. Omit the pronoun altogether to avoid awkward or monotonous pronoun repetition, provided meaning and clarity are preserved.

Applicants who may be eligible for financial aid should send in the application forms before December 1.

3. Indefinite pronoun reference choices often become clear if you consider the probable sex of the people about whom you are writing. Rely on available information rather than stereotypes.

For example, if the person or group is likely to be female, use the feminine pronoun; if the antecedent is likely to be male, use the masculine pronoun.

Each *member* of the college football team had *his* photo taken at the sports banquet.

Everybody on the synchronized swimming team performed *her* best at the Olympic trials.

For groups that could be mixed, choose pronouns that do not presuppose only one sex.

> NOT *Anyone* who wants to be on the athletic training staff ought to choose sports medicine as *his* major.
>
> BUT *Anyone* who wants to be on the athletic training staff ought to choose sports medicine as *his or her* major.
>
> OR *Anyone* who wants to be on the athletic training staff ought to major in sports medicine.

Be careful not to use feminine pronouns for roles stereotyped as female (nurse, teacher, social worker, secretary, telephone operator, flight attendant, etc.) or masculine pronouns for roles stereotyped as male (engineer, auto mechanic, firefighter, government official, airline pilot, etc.) when, in fact, they are mixed.

EXERCISE 8c

Using the range of available options, revise the following sentences so that pronoun references are nonsexist and reflect reality. Be prepared to discuss your choices.

1. A news reporter should be sure of his facts before he writes his story.
2. That open locker probably belongs to somebody who was late for his next class.
3. Whomever they hire to head the Home Economics Department, she will have her work cut out for her.
4. A newly divorced single parent faces a dual role she may be unprepared to handle, that of both breadwinner and primary care-giver.
5. Anyone who wants to attend West Point needs to be nominated by his Congressman.

8d

A demonstrative adjective *(this, that, these, those)* should agree in number with the noun it modifies.

It can be difficult to choose the correct word to use as a demonstrative adjective with *kind of* or *sort of* followed by a plural noun: *This sort of jogging shoes is expensive.* Remember that the demonstrative adjective modifies the singular noun *kind* or *sort* and not the following plural noun. Thus a singular demonstrative is needed. In most cases, standard usage favors agreement among the demonstrative, the noun being modified, and the noun object following the preposition: where appropriate, make them all singular or all plural.

NONSTANDARD	Those kind of strawberries taste sweet.
STANDARD	Those kinds of strawberries taste sweet.
	That kind of strawberry tastes sweet.
NONSTANDARD	This sort of cakes is delicious.
STANDARD	These sorts of cakes are delicious.
	This sort of cake is delicious.
NONSTANDARD	These sort of things happen.
STANDARD	These sorts of things happen.
	This sort of thing happens.

9

ref

EXERCISE 8a-d
In the following sentences, correct every error of agreement in accordance with written usage.

1. There goes Pat and Jean, who have deep tans the year round.
2. Everybody thinks that a suntan makes them look healthy.
3. One of my friends use a tanning booth during the winter, and a number of other friends spend their spring break in Florida.
4. Unfortunately, these sort of activities can do a lot of harm.
5. According to dermatologists, there is several dangers in overexposure to the sun.
6. Anybody who spends long hours unprotected in the hot sun is increasing their chances of developing skin cancer.
7. Another of the sun's adverse effects are more rapid aging of the skin.
8. The American Cancer Society has published their recommendations for safe exposure to the sun's rays.
9. For example, neither a cloudy day nor low air temperature are safeguards against sun damage.
10. Staying out of the sun between 10 A.M. and 2 P.M. and using an effective sunscreen helps in avoiding the damaging effects of the sun.

9

FAULTY REFERENCE OF PRONOUNS

A pronoun depends for its meaning upon its antecedent, the noun or other pronoun to which it refers. If the antecedents of the pronouns in your writing are not clear, your writing will not be clear.

Place pronouns as close to their antecedents as possible, and make all pronoun references exact.

9a

Each pronoun should refer to a single antecedent.

Pronouns can, of course, refer to compound antecedents in such sentences as *Joan and Karen both believed they had performed well,* where the pronoun *they* refers to *Joan and Karen.* However, if a pronoun can refer to either of two possible antecedents, it will be ambiguous, and readers will not know which antecedent is intended.

AMBIGUOUS When Kathy visited her mother, she had a cold. [Who had a cold, Kathy or her mother?]

CLEAR When she visited her mother, Kathy had a cold.

Kathy had a cold when she visited her mother.

Her mother had a cold when Kathy visited her.

AMBIGUOUS Arthur went with John to the airport, where he took a plane to Phoenix. [Who took the plane, John or Arthur?]

CLEAR After going to the airport with John, Arthur took the plane to Phoenix.

After Arthur went to the airport with him, John took the plane to Phoenix.

EXERCISE 9a

Revise the following sentences by eliminating the ambiguous reference of pronouns.

1. Ellen told her sister that she needed a good book to read during her two-week vacation.
2. When Ellen met the manager of the resort hotel, she introduced herself.
3. The hotel manager told Ellen that her job was a demanding one.
4. When Ellen's sister met her at the airport after her vacation, she was exhausted.
5. Ellen had lots of photographs to show her friends, so she decided to get them together right away.

9b

A pronoun should be close enough to its antecedent to ensure clear reference.

In general, the nearer a pronoun is to its antecedent, the more likely it is to be clear. The more remote the antecedent, the more difficulty readers will have in understanding the reference—particularly if other nouns intervene between the antecedent and the pronoun. Readers should never have to search for a pronoun's antecedent.

REMOTE   Credit cards spread throughout the United States and western Europe during the late 1960's. Card issuers make money from the fees paid by card owners and merchants and from interest charged on unpaid balances. Between 1965 and 1970, *they* increased from fewer than 5 million in use to more than 50 million. [*Credit cards* is the only antecedent to which *they* can sensibly refer, but the pronoun is too remote from its antecedent for clear, easy reading.]

CLEAR   . . . Between 1965 and 1970, *credit cards* increased from fewer than 5 million . . . [This revision repeats the subject, *credit cards*.]

Credit cards spread throughout the United States and western Europe during the late 1960's, increasing between 1965 and 1970 from fewer than 5 million in use to more than 50 million . . . [The remote reference is eliminated by combining the first and third sentences.]

9c
Avoid the vague use of *this, that,* and *which* to refer to the general idea of a preceding clause or sentence.

The use of *this, that,* and *which* to refer to an idea stated in a preceding clause or sentence is common in informal English in such sentences as *They keep their promises, which is more than some people do.* Although often used by experienced writers when the meaning is unmistakably clear, such broad reference risks confusing the reader. Less experienced writers should ordinarily eliminate any vague use of *this, that,* and *which,* either by recasting the sentence to eliminate the pronoun or by supplying a specific antecedent for the pronoun.

VAGUE   Their credit cards were stolen after they spent all their cash. That was a real shame.

CLEAR   That their credit cards were stolen after they spent all their cash was a real shame. [The sentence has been recast to eliminate the vague use of *that.*]

VAGUE   The disadvantages of credit cards can offset the advantages, which merits careful consideration. [What merits consideration: the advantages, the disadvantages, the offsetting of one by the other?]

CLEAR   The disadvantages of credit cards can offset the advantages, a fact which merits careful consideration. [*Fact* supplies a clear antecedent for *which.*]

9d

ref

CLEAR	Because the disadvantages can offset the advantages, the consequences of using credit cards should be carefully considered. [The sentence has been revised to eliminate the vague use of *which*.]
VAGUE	I announced that I was going to cut up all my credit cards. This caused a shocked silence.
CLEAR	I announced that I was going to cut up all my credit cards. This announcement caused a shocked silence. [*Announcement* clearly indicates the antecedent for *This*.]

EXERCISE 9b-c
Revise all sentences to eliminate remote or vague pronoun reference.

1. The sandwich had been popular since ancient times, but John Montague, fourth Earl of Sandwich, put a piece of meat between two slices of bread so that he could eat and play cards at the same time. Thus, it got its name in honor of the gambling earl.
2. Today, people all over the world enjoy sandwiches as a fast and convenient food. Sandwich ingredients and shapes differ in each country. As a result, they often eat what might be called a country's national sandwich.
3. Each region of the United States also has its special sandwich. New Yorkers like pastrami on rye, in New Orleans visitors eat a muffuletta or an oyster roll, and in New England tourists enjoy lobster rolls. Therefore, it seems to be a national dish but one with a special flavor in each area of the country.
4. President Franklin D. Roosevelt appointed Frances Perkins, the first woman Cabinet member, to be Secretary of Labor in 1933. This angered some men because unemployment was very high at the time.
5. During her twelve years in the Cabinet, Frances Perkins helped establish Unemployment Insurance and Social Security, which gave American workers benefits they had never had before.
6. At the time Frances Perkins was appointed, some men were demanding that all married women be fired so that men could have their jobs. That was ironic in light of the programs she implemented for workers.

9d

Do not use a pronoun to refer to an implied but unexpressed noun.

To be clear, a pronoun must have a noun or the equivalent of a noun as its specific antecedent. Modifiers, possessives, and other words or phrases that merely suggest an appropriate noun do not provide clear and specific antecedents. Revise faulty sentences so that each pronoun has a specific noun or noun equivalent as antecedent, or otherwise revise the sentence.

FAULTY Because we put a wire fence around the chicken yard, they cannot escape. [*Chicken* here functions as an adjective modifying *yard*. It suggests but does not express the necessary antecedent *chickens*.]

REVISED Because we put a wire fence around the chicken yard, the chickens cannot escape.

FAULTY When the president's committee was established, she appointed several student representatives. [The possessive *president's* implies but does not express the antecedent *president*.]

REVISED When the president established the committee, she appointed several student representatives.

FAULTY The guest speaker for today's class is a banker, and that is a career I want to know more about. [The appropriate antecedent, *banking*, is implied, but it needs to be stated specifically.]

REVISED The guest speaker for today's class is a banker, and I want to know more about careers in banking.

9e

ref

EXERCISE 9d
Revise the following sentences to eliminate all references to unexpressed antecedents.

1. For over a thousand years people believed that the sun and stars revolved around the earth. It remained the belief until Copernicus put forth the heliocentric theory in the 1500's.
2. In the heliocentric theory, the earth and stars revolve around it.
3. In the 1600's Galileo constructed a telescope which enabled him to corroborate the Copernican theory. His theory thus served as the basis for the scientific discoveries of Galileo and others.

9e

In writing avoid the indefinite use of *they* and *it*. Use *you* appropriately.

The indefinite use of *they, it,* and *you* is common at most levels of speech: *In Germany, they drink beer; it says in the dictionary that . . .; you can never find anything where you're looking for it.* In writing, these pronouns all have a much more restricted use.

1. *They* always requires a specific antecedent in all but the most informal writing. Correct its use in your writing by substituting an appropriate noun, or revise the sentence.

9e

ref

SPOKEN   In less industrialized areas, *they* do not understand the problems of the city.

WRITTEN   People living in less industrialized areas do not understand the problems of the city.

SPOKEN   *They* said on the late news that Mount St. Helens had erupted again.

WRITTEN   It was reported on the late news that Mount St. Helens had erupted again.

2. *It* in the phrase *it says* referring to information in newspapers, magazines, books, and the like, though common in speech, is unacceptable in writing, except in dialogue.

SPOKEN   *It* says in the newspaper that Monday will be warmer.

WRITTEN   The newspaper says that Monday will be warmer.

3. *You* in the sense of people in general is common in informal writing: *Differences of opinion among friends can be healthy if you don't take them too seriously,* or *When you're driving you should always be alert.* More formal writing ordinarily prefers a general noun such as *people* or a *person,* or the pronoun *one.*

INFORMAL   Many suburban towns do not permit *you* to drive more than twenty-five or thirty miles an hour.

FORMAL   Many suburban towns do not permit *people* [or *a person* or *one*] to drive more than twenty-five or thirty miles an hour.

You is always correct in writing directions or in other contexts where the meaning is clearly *you, the reader.*

Before turning on your air conditioner, be sure you have closed all your windows.

When using *you* in the sense of *you, the reader,* be sure that the context is appropriate to such use.

INAPPROPRIATE   In early colonial villages, you had to depend on wood for fuel. [The reader is unlikely to be living in an early colonial village.]

REVISED   In early colonial villages, *people* [or *a person* or *one*] had to depend on wood for fuel.

BETTER   Early colonial villagers had to depend on wood for fuel.

EXERCISE 9e
Revise the following sentences to avoid the indefinite use of *they, you,* and *it.*

1. In the newspaper today it says that excessive noise can cause both physical and psychological injuries to those subjected to it.
2. They claim that noise causes damage to hearing, but they also say that noise makes people tired, grouchy, and nervous.
3. In some cities and states, they have passed anti-noise ordinances in order to limit and control excessive noise.
4. Even if the area has anti-noise ordinances, you aren't protected from the everyday noise of air conditioners, vacuum cleaners, and lawn mowers.
5. An inability to hear after a noise has stopped, pain in the ear, or ringing in the ears are warning signs of injury you should be aware of if you're exposed to a loud noise.

9f

Match the relative pronouns *who, which,* and *that* with appropriate antecedents.

In general, use *who* to refer to persons, *which* to refer to things, and *that* to refer to things and sometimes to persons.

Many *students who* major in mathematics today find employment with computer companies.

Arkansas, which became a state in 1836, was earlier a part of Louisiana.

Among the *flowers that* (or *which*) grow most easily are petunias and marigolds.

The possessive *whose* is frequently used to refer to things when the phrase *of which* would be awkward.

Cinderella is a story *whose* ending most of us know. [Compare *the ending of which.*]

The relative pronoun *that* can be used only in restrictive clauses, clauses necessary to meaning and thus not set off by commas. *Which* can be used in both restrictive and nonrestrictive clauses, clauses not necessary to meaning and thus set off by commas. (See **20c.**)

The *Eighteenth Amendment, which* forbade the manufacture, sale, import, or export of intoxicating liquors, instituted nationwide prohibition in 1919.

The *amendment that* (or *which*) repealed prohibition was ratified in 1933.

Some writers prefer to introduce all restrictive clauses with *that* and to limit the use of *which* entirely to nonrestrictive clauses.

9g

9g

ref

Avoid using the pronoun *it* two or more ways in a sentence.

We use *it* as an expletive to postpone a subject (*It is wise to be careful*), in certain idioms *(it is cold)* and colloquial expressions *(He made it to the finish line)*, and of course as a definite pronoun referring to specific antecedents. All of these uses are acceptable when appropriate, but sentences in which two different uses occur are likely to be confusing.

> **CONFUSING** She put her car in the garage because she never leaves *it* out when *it* is bad weather. [The first *it* refers to *car;* the second is idiomatic.]
>
> **IMPROVED** She put her car in the garage because she never leaves it out when the weather is bad [or *in bad weather*].

EXERCISE 9f-g

Revise the following sentences so that pronouns are used appropriately.

1. People that drink coffee, tea, and cola drinks are also ingesting a drug—caffeine.
2. Although coffee has some other ingredients in it, it is caffeine which causes the greatest concern.
3. Caffeine has effects on the human body the consequences of which are not fully known at this time.

EXERCISE 9a-g

Revise the following paragraph to eliminate the faulty reference of pronouns.

Climbers are people which participate in one or all of the three types of climbing—rock, ice, and mountain. Most climbers begin by rock climbing on smaller, less difficult crags and then move to ice and mountain climbing when they feel prepared for it. The best way to learn climbing is to begin by bouldering, a term which means climbing close to the ground. In it, climbers do not use a rope for protection. Starting with bouldering allows you to learn basic techniques without great danger of injury from falling. Many climbers use a spotter when learning bouldering, for this allows someone to be there to break a fall. The climber and the spotter work together so that he won't get hurt by a fall. After climbers master bouldering, they often move on to climbing crags or peaks so high they need ropes. Although some amateur climbers don't realize it, it is vital to have the proper equipment.

10

SHIFTS

Writers keep sentences consistent by using one subject; one tense, voice, and mood in verbs; and one person and number in pronouns, as far as grammar and meaning allow. Unnecessary shifts in any of these elements tend to obscure meaning and make reading more difficult than it has to be. (See Section **42g** for a discussion of consistency within paragraphs.)

10a

Do not shift the subject or the voice of the verb within a sentence unnecessarily.

Particularly in compound and complex sentences, meaning frequently requires the writer to refer to more than one subject, as in the following sentence:

> When the *car* hit their dog, *John* ran home, and *Bill* held the dog until help arrived.

Here the writer is describing an accident involving two boys, their dog, and a car. Meaning clearly requires a shift of subject from one clause to another within the sentence. Such movement of a sentence from one subject to another is perfectly natural.

Less frequently, meaning may justify a shift from active to passive voice within a sentence.

> Three men *escaped* from the state prison yesterday but *were captured* before sundown.

Here the writer could have chosen to write *but the police captured them,* changing the subject but keeping the active voice in both main clauses of a compound sentence. But by choosing to use the compound predicate, *escaped . . . but were captured,* the writer keeps attention focused on the important subject, *three men.*

Unlike the shifts in subject and voice in these sentences, the shifts in the following sentences are unnecessary:

> FAULTY   *As the boys approached* the swamp, *frogs could be heard croaking.* [Here the focus of the sentence is on *the boys.* The shift of subject from *the boys* to *frogs* and of the voice of the verb from the active to the passive are unnecessary and distracting.]
>
> REVISED   *As the boys approached* the swamp, *they could hear* frogs croaking.

10b

FAULTY	*Ellen stayed* at a mountain resort, and most of her *time was spent* skiing. [The sentence is about Ellen. The shift of subject from *Ellen* to *time* and the resulting shift from active to passive voice blurs rather than sharpens the sentence.]
REVISED	*Ellen stayed* at a mountain resort *and spent* most of her time skiing.

EXERCISE 10a

In the following sentences, correct unnecessary shifts in subject or voice.

1. Joggers need to warm up before starting on a strenuous workout; for example, leg muscles can be loosened by stretching exercises.
2. If joggers don't warm up before a run, a tightness in muscles, ligaments, and tendons is felt.
3. Joggers should also have a cool-down period at the end of a run, and the heart needs time to adjust to increased demand when the jogger stops running.
4. As the jogger runs, the heart muscle is helped by the leg muscles to pump blood.
5. When the runner stops too abruptly, the increased demand on the heart may not be able to be met.

10b

Do not shift person or number unnecessarily.

Just as meaning frequently requires us to refer to more than one subject in a single sentence, it may require us to refer to different persons or to combinations of singular and plural subjects, as in the following sentences:

> *I* stayed, but *they* left. [*I* is first person singular; *they* is third person plural.]
> The *snake* held its ground until the *coyotes* finally left. [*Snake* is singular, *coyotes* plural.]

But unless meaning clearly requires such changes, keep person and number within a given sentence consistent.

Unnecessary shifts in person are frequently shifts from the third person (the person being talked about) to the second person (the person being talked to). They occur principally because in English we can make general statements by using either the second person pronoun *you*, the third person pronoun *one*, or one of various third person general nouns such as the singular *a person* or the plural *people*. Thus any one of the following sentences is consistent:

If *you* want to play games, *you* must learn the rules.
If *a person* [or *one*] wants to play games, *he or she* must learn the rules.
If *people* want to play games, *they* must learn the rules.

Failure to follow one of these possible patterns produces faulty shifts, as in the following:

> **FAULTY**   When *a person* has good health, *you* should feel fortunate.
>
> REVISED   When *a person* has good health, *he or she* should feel fortunate.
> When *you* have good health, *you* should feel fortunate.
> When *people* have good health, *they* should feel fortunate.

A second kind of unnecessary shift frequently occurs in sentences in which the writer starts with the first person and inconsistently shifts to the second. Such sentences are ordinarily more effective when the writer maintains the first-person point of view.

> **WEAK**   I refuse to go to a movie theater where you can't buy popcorn.
>
> IMPROVED   I refuse to go to a movie theater where I can't buy popcorn.

These sorts of shifts are sometimes called **shifts in point of view.** Readers find unnecessary shifts disconcerting because expectations about readers' and writers' roles are disrupted. Readers count on point of view to signal their relationship to the writer and to the information being presented. Think, for example, how startling it is to be reading as a third-party "observer" and then suddenly find the language pointing remarks directly at "you."

Faulty shifts in number within a sentence usually involve faulty agreement between pronouns and their antecedents. (See **8b.**)

> **FAULTY**   I like *an occasional cup* of coffee, for *they* give me an added lift. [Shift from singular to plural. The pronoun should agree with the singular antecedent *cup*.]
>
> REVISED   I like *an occasional cup* of coffee, for *it* gives me an added lift.
> I like *occasional cups* of coffee, for *they* give me an added lift.

EXERCISE 10b

In the following sentences, correct unnecessary shifts in person or number.

1. If a person is going to take up jogging or running, you must have properly made and correctly fitted running shoes.
2. Flexible soles and built-up heels are signs of a good running shoe; they should also be well-cushioned.
3. I like to run on soft, even surfaces rather than on concrete because you don't have as much jarring or pounding.
4. Good running shoes may be quite expensive, but it will save pain and perhaps medical expenses later.
5. When a jogger is running, your feet strike the ground with a force two to three times your body weight.

10c

10c

Do not shift tense or mood unnecessarily.

In a sentence such as *Nostalgia is a love of the way things were in our youth,* meaning requires a shift of tense from the present *is* to the past *were.* But except when the meaning or the grammar of a sentence requires such changes in tense, keep the same tense throughout all the verbs in a sentence. (See also Section **5a–c.**)

FAULTY   I *sat* down at the desk and *begin* to write. [The verb shifts unnecessarily from past to present tense.]

REVISED   I *sat* down at the desk and *began* to write.

FAULTY   In chapter one she *accepts* her first job as a kitchen maid, but by chapter three she *was cooking* for an Austrian prince.

REVISED   In chapter one she *accepts* her first job as a kitchen maid, but by chapter three she *is cooking* for an Austrian prince. [In this sentence, the revision uses the present tense in both verbs because it is customary to use the present tense in describing actions in literature. See **5a.**]

Shifts in mood within a single sentence or a series of related sentences are almost never justified. Such shifts often occur in writing directions. Avoid them by casting directions consistently either in the imperative or the indicative mood. (See Section **5** for an explanation of *imperative* and *indicative.*)

FAULTY   *Hold* the rifle firmly against your shoulder, and then you *should take* careful aim. [Shift from imperative to indicative mood.]

REVISED   *Hold* the rifle firmly against your shoulder and then *take* careful aim. [Both verbs are in the imperative mood.]

You *should hold* the rifle firmly against your shoulder and then (you should) take careful aim. [Both verbs are in the indicative. Note that here the second *you should* can be omitted since it will be understood by the reader.]

In general, directions are most economical and effective when they are written in the imperative mood.

EXERCISE 10c
In the following sentences, correct needless shifts in tense or mood.

1. Some people have tried running but have found it too strenuous; try walking for exercise instead.
2. Walking uses fewer calories per minute than jogging did, but it also took more minutes to walk a mile than to jog one.
3. A person decided to walk four miles in an hour; he burns about 300 calories an hour.
4. Experts say that exercise-walking now ranked as the almost perfect exercise: it requires no special equipment, anyone could do it, and it promotes overall physical fitness.
5. Start a walking program gradually, and then you can work up to longer and faster walks as you gain strength and endurance.

10d

Do not shift from indirect to direct quotation unnecessarily.

Direct quotation reports, in quotation marks, the exact words of a speaker or writer. Indirect quotation reports what someone has said or written, but not in the exact words.

DIRECT   She said, "I'm psyched up and ready for the game."

INDIRECT   She said that she was psyched up and ready for the game.

The tense in an indirect quotation should ordinarily be the same as the tense of the main verb. Unnecessary shifts between direct and indirect quotation often cause problems in tense.

FAULTY   Lincoln asked the general *whether his army was well supplied* and *is it ready for battle.* [Shift from indirect to direct quotation. In such mixed constructions, the writer usually omits quotation marks from the direct quotation.]

REVISED   Lincoln asked the general whether his army was well supplied and whether it was ready for battle. [Indirect quotation]

Lincoln asked the general, "Is your army well supplied? Is it ready for battle?" [Direct quotation]

FAULTY   They wondered *if we had missed the train* and *are we trying to telephone them* to let them know.

REVISED   They wondered if we had missed the train and if we were trying to telephone them to let them know. [Indirect quotation]

REVISED   They wondered, "Have they missed the train, and are they trying to telephone us to let us know?" [Direct quotation]

10d

EXERCISE 10a-d

Revise the following sentences, correcting all needless shifts in tense, mood, voice, person, and number and any shifts from indirect to direct quotation. Be prepared to explain your revisions.

1. Any exercise which is aerobic will improve a person's cardiovascular fitness, but you must do the exercise at least three times a week for at least twenty minutes each time.
2. I asked my doctor if walking was an aerobic exercise and how fast and how far should I go.
3. If you want to get aerobic conditioning while you walk, a brisk pace of at least three miles an hour must be achieved.
4. Aerobic exercise helps the heart and lungs to become more efficient at circulating oxygen throughout the body; try some kind of aerobic activity and see how much more fit you'll be.
5. You should choose an aerobic exercise you enjoy, for they must be performed faithfully for their benefits to develop.
6. One hears of people starting ambitious fitness programs, and you know a lot of them will never continue the exercise after a week or two.
7. Jogging, walking, cycling, and swimming are all excellent aerobic exercises, and you should consider each as a possible exercise.
8. Some people live in climates where you can't exercise outdoors all year round, so they choose a stationary bicycle for conditioning.
9. As exercisers continue their fitness programs, benefits can be seen.
10. If you continue with your exercise program, weight control, cardiovascular fitness, increased bone strength, and an improved emotional outlook can be some of the benefits a person achieves.

WRITERS REVISING: SHIFTS AND PRONOUN FAULTS

The Placement Office intern read over another student-written article for the placement newsletter. The writer was supposed to have summarized an article originally appearing in *National Business Employment Weekly*. While attempting to adapt the original for readers of the placement newsletter, the student had created shifts and pronoun faults. See if you can correct the mismatches; then compare your revision with the intern's version.

Student's Article

D 1   There comes a time when we must make a break

D 2   and rely on ourselves as a career expert. To a

D 3   large degree, you are your own expert because only

D 4   you know best about your interests, challenges,

D 5   and what suits you. This means your own judgment

D 6   and intuition must be trusted, if you are going to

D 7   take the initiative in your job search. They say

D 8   we are often our own worst enemies; if you see

D 9   yourself as a bungling idiot during an interview,

D10   you'll probably behave like it.

10d

The intern realized she needed to choose one point of view, and it would be reflected in personal pronouns throughout the article. She could address her audience in either first person plural *(we)* or second person *(you)*. She decided that *we* would encourage readers to identify with the article; the first person plural puts everyone in the same boat—in the scene together. She felt that *you* sounded too much like finger pointing, especially since some negative things were being said *(bungling idiot,* etc.). However, the intern also recognized that she would have to watch agreement carefully so that all the antecedents and verbs were consistent with the plural form.

Intern's Revision

R 1   There comes a time when we must make a break

R 2   and rely on ourselves as ~~a~~ career expert. To a

R 3   large degree, ~~you~~ *we* are ~~your~~ *our* own expert because only **10b**

R 4   ~~you~~ *we* know best about ~~your~~ *our* interests, challenges,

R 5   and what suits ~~you. This means your~~ *us. Being our own experts means we must trust our* own judgment **9c**

R 6   and intuition ~~must be trusted,~~ if ~~you~~ *we* are going to **10a**

R 7   take the initiative in ~~your~~ *our* job search. ~~They say~~

R 8   *We can* ~~are~~ often ~~our~~ own worst enemies; if ~~you~~ *we* see **9e**

R 9   ~~yourself~~ *ourselves* as ~~a~~ bungling idiot, *s* during an interview,

R10   ~~you'll probably~~ *we are likely to* behave like ~~it~~. *idiots*   9d

Analysis

This, the first word of the third sentence (line D5), is an unacceptably vague pronoun, referring to the whole idea in the preceding sentence. Furthermore, the passive voice verb (*must be trusted*, line D6), creates an unnecessary shift in voice **(10a)** and results in a weak sentence as well; the revision to active voice (lines R5-6) is consistent and stronger.

They say. . . (D7) is an indefinite use of the pronoun and serves no real purpose in the sentence, so the intern eliminated the unnecessary opening phrase. Also the final pronoun in the sentence, *it* (D10), has no explicit antecedent that agrees with it in number **(9d)**, so the intern supplied the unexpressed noun (*idiots*) in her revision (R10). Notice that the plural, *idiots*, maintains consistent use of number with the plural pronoun *we*.

11

mis pt

11

MISPLACED PARTS

Modern English relies heavily upon word order to show relationships among words. The Latin sentences *Puella amat agricolam* and *Agricolam amat puella* have the same literal meaning: *The girl loves the farmer*. Even though the subject and object are reversed, the special endings (*-a* and *-am*) make the meaning of the sentence unmistakable. But if the English words are reversed, so is the English meaning: *The girl loves the farmer; The farmer loves the girl*. Word order is crucial to meaning in English.

Just as word order is the principal way to keep subject-verb-object relations clear, so it is the principal way to keep many modifiers attached to the words they modify. Phrases and clauses that modify nouns require special care, since they normally attach to the nearest noun preceding them. Unless writers are alert, sentences such as these can occur:

He bought a horse from a stranger with a lame hind leg.

We returned to Atlanta after a week's vacation on Monday.

Context usually—though not always—allows readers to work out the intended meaning of such sentences. But at best a reader is distracted by the necessary effort; at worst, ludicrous literal meanings can destroy the writer's credibility. Consider, for instance, the following misplaced modifier noted by a national magazine:

> "While a Legion bugler played 'To the Colors,' the first flag was hoisted on DeVane Park's 30-foot flagpole, followed by David Rinald singing the national anthem."   *Lake Placid* (Fla.) *Journal*
>
> Helped him hit the high notes.   *The New Yorker*

11a

In writing, place adverbs of degree or limitation such as *almost, even, hardly, just, only, nearly* immediately before the words they modify.

In speech we commonly put *only* and similar adverbs before the verb, regardless of what we mean them to modify. To avoid any possible ambiguity in writing, place such modifiers immediately before the words they modify.

SPOKEN	I *only* ran a mile.
WRITTEN	I ran *only* a mile.
SPOKEN	He *just* wore a smile.
WRITTEN	He wore *just* a smile.
SPOKEN	She *almost* read the whole book.
WRITTEN	She read *almost* the whole book.

EXERCISE 11a(1)
Revise the following sentences so that limiting adverbs are placed before the words they modify. Then write five sentences of your own, each using a different limiting adverb (*almost, even, hardly, just, only, practically, precisely, nearly, shortly,* and so on) placed appropriately in the sentence.

1. When people in the Northern Hemisphere think of swans, they only consider them as white creatures.
2. However, beautiful black swans are found in Australia and New Zealand, and the blacknecked swan just lives in South America.
3. Swans' habits nearly are the same as those of their close relatives, geese.
4. However, swans breed both north and south of the Equator, while only geese breed in the Northern Hemisphere.
5. In addition, geese mostly feed on land; almost always swans live in water where they feed on water plants.

EXERCISE 11a(2)
Move the italicized adverb to a different place in each of the following

sentences, so that a new meaning is created. Be prepared to explain the differences in meaning between the two sentences. Then write five more sentences of your own that change meaning with a repositioning of the adverb.

11b

mis pt

1. This summer *nearly* all the ducks and geese at the local park died.
2. *Almost* everyone assumed the birds had been poisoned by a vandal.
3. The police put on extra patrols to watch *even* the side streets for the smallest sign of strange activity.
4. *Actually* the university's veterinary laboratory reported that the geese and ducks died from a virus found in the soil and water, not from poison.
5. This news failed to console the neighbors around the park who *only* wanted their old feathered friends back again.

11b

Modifying phrases should refer clearly to the words they modify.

Phrases used to modify nouns must ordinarily be placed immediately after the words they are intended to modify. The following examples show the confusion and misrepresentation created by misplaced modifiers.

> CONFUSING   Joan borrowed a bicycle from a friend *with saddlebags*. [The writer intended the phrase *with saddlebags* to modify *bicycle*, not *friend*.]
>
> CLEAR   Joan borrowed a bicycle *with saddlebags* from a friend.
>
> CONFUSING   "We are committed to eliminating all traces of discrimination in the law *against women*," Ronald Reagan told some 4,000 members of the American Bar Association meeting in Atlanta. [The law is against women?]
>
> CLEAR   President Reagan said that his administration was committed to eliminating from the law all traces of discrimination *against women*.

Phrases used as adverbs may usually be placed either within the sentence close to the words they modify or at the beginning or end of the sentence. In some sentences, however, their placement requires special thought.

> CONFUSING   The author claims the revolt was caused by corruption *in the first chapter*. [*In the first chapter* seems to modify the noun *corruption* although the writer surely intended it to modify the verb *claims*.]
>
> CLEAR   *In the first chapter*, the author claims the revolt was caused by corruption.
>
> CONFUSING   A huge boulder fell as we rounded the corner *with a crash*. [*With a crash* seems to modify the verb *rounded* al-

though the writer intended it to modify the earlier verb, *fell*.]

CLEAR   A huge boulder fell *with a crash* as we rounded the corner.

CONFUSING   Thank you for the beautiful bowl. Right now it's sitting on our buffet *full of fruit*. [That's a lot of fruit!]

CLEAR   Thank you for the beautiful bowl. Right now it's sitting *full of fruit* on our buffet.

11c

mis pt

EXERCISE 11b

Revise the following sentences so the modifying phrases refer clearly to the words they are intended to modify.

1. The shape of the swan is superbly adapted to life in the water with its broad breast like the stern of a ship tapering to the rear.
2. Swans are breathtaking as they extend in flight their long necks and flap their great wings in slow, regular movements.
3. The wing bones of swans in spite of their great strength are hollow.
4. Swans add a regal touch to a pond swimming gracefully.
5. However, the big birds look rather like careening bed pillows getting airborne.

11c

Modifying clauses should refer clearly to the words they modify.

Clauses that modify nouns usually begin with *who, which,* or *that* and follow immediately after the words they modify.

CONFUSING   The dog had a ribbon around his neck *that was tied in a bow.* [The ribbon, not his neck, was tied in a bow.]

CLEAR   Around his neck the dog had a ribbon *that was tied in a bow.*

CONFUSING   The children cautiously approached the deserted house by a winding path, *which was said to be haunted.* [The house, not the path, was said to be haunted.]

CLEAR   By a winding path, the children cautiously approached the house *that was said to be haunted.*

Adverb clauses are introduced by words such as *after, although, because, since,* and *until.* Like adverb phrases, they can usually be placed either within the sentence close to the words they modify or at the beginning or end of the sentence; they can sometimes be confusing unless writers are careful.

CONFUSING   The police towed the stolen station wagon to the city garage *after it was abandoned.* [The clause *after it was abandoned* is intended to modify the verb *towed* but seems to modify the noun *garage*.]

CLEAR *After the stolen station wagon was abandoned,* the police towed it to the city garage.

The police towed the stolen station wagon, *after it was abandoned,* to the city garage.

11d

mis pt

EXERCISE 11c

Revise the following sentences to place the modifying clauses in clear relationships to the words they modify.

1. One of the most graceful of swans is the mute swan with its black forehead and black knob at the base of its bill whose voice is not mute at all.
2. The mute swan has a weaker voice compared to other swans that is caused by its straight windpipe.
3. Mute swans have strong territorial instincts who make up for their weak voices by being aggressive.
4. Europeans have raised mute swans for hundreds of years; in fact, kings often gave mute swans as royal gifts who also had them served for dinner.
5. Swans became a target for thieves because they were prized possessions; as a result, swans were marked with a sign on the upper part of their bills that identified their owners.

11d

Avoid squinting modifiers.

A **squinting modifier** is one that may modify either a preceding word or a following word. It squints at the words on its right and left, and leaves the reader confused.

SQUINTING His physician told him *frequently* to exercise.

CLEAR His physician *frequently* told him to exercise.

His physician told him to exercise *frequently*.

SQUINTING The committee which was studying the matter *yesterday* turned in its report.

CLEAR The committee that was studying the matter turned in its report *yesterday*.

The committee, *which spent yesterday* studying the matter, turned in its report.

SQUINTING He promised *on his way home* to visit us.

CLEAR *On his way home,* he promised to visit us.

He promised to visit us *on his way home*.

EXERCISE 11d
Revise the following sentences to eliminate squinting modifiers.

1. We decided after dinner to go to a movie.
2. We had read often the theater was crowded with people wanting to see the latest horror movie.
3. The movie review in the newspaper reported today when the theater doors open people wanting seats should be in line.
4. We all thought quickly we'd better get to the theater.
5. As I watched the movie, I warned my friend frequently to close his eyes because the scenes were so frightening.

11e
Do not split infinitives awkwardly.

An infinitive is split when an adverbial modifier separates the *to* from the verb. There is nothing ungrammatical about splitting an infinitive, and sometimes a split is useful to avoid awkwardness. But most split infinitives are unnecessary.

AWKWARD	I tried not *to* carelessly *hurt* the kitten.
CLEAR	I tried not *to hurt* the kitten carelessly.
AWKWARD	You should try *to,* if you can, *take* a walk every day.
CLEAR	If you can, you should try *to take* a walk every day.
	You should try *to take* a walk every day if you can.

On the other hand, note the following sentence:

The course is designed *to* better *equip* graduates to go into business.

If *better* is placed before *to equip* it squints awkwardly between *designed* and the infinitive; after *to equip* it modifies *graduates;* at the end of the sentence it is awkward and unnatural, if not entirely unclear. Thus, in this case, the split infinitive is the best choice for conveying the meaning the writer intended.

EXERCISE 11e
Revise the following sentences to eliminate awkward split infinitives.

1. Many airline passengers are upset to at last arrive at their destination to only find that their luggage didn't arrive with them.
2. A good way to at least try to avoid losing luggage is by booking a nonstop flight.
3. It also helps to always check in early at the airport so that luggage has time to correctly be loaded on the right plane.
4. Passengers should also try to, whenever possible, put special mark-

ings on bags so that another passenger won't pick them up by mistake.

5. If a passenger keeps an itemized list of everything in checked baggage, it's easier to accurately document a claim if bags are lost.

11f

mis pt

11f

In general, avoid separating a subject from its predicate, a verb from its object, or the parts of a verb phrase. Intentional separations occasionally make a sentence more effective.

As Section 1 on sentence patterns and sentence parts explained, readers expect certain arrangements of elements in sentences. Remember that readers can hold only a limited number of "chunks" of information in their short-term memories. Thus they rely heavily on related sentence elements and known sentence patterns to help them form the "superchunks" that enable the memory to process more information. Separation of sentence elements puts a strain on readers as they try to derive meaning from pieces of information.

When you go against readers' expectations, you should have a good reason for doing so. Writers intentionally separate related sentence elements to achieve special effects, such as adding suspense or drama to a sentence by delaying the verb. However, what seems like an effective separation to the writer may only try the reader's patience. In other words, effective separation of related sentence elements can be a judgment call, and not everyone will agree on the results. Think carefully about such separations; don't use them unless your subject and purpose warrant the dramatic and artificial impression that separations convey.

EFFECTIVE SEPARATION   The captain, *seeing the ominous storm clouds gathering overhead,* ordered the crew to take in the sail.

And so Pilate, *willing to content the people,* released Barabbas unto them, and delivered Jesus, *when he had scourged him,* to be crucified.

MARK 15:15

Only when a man is safely ensconced under six feet of earth, *with several tons of enlauding granite upon his chest,* is he in a position to give advice with any certainty, and then he is silent.

EDWARD NEWTON

AWKWARD SEPARATION   She *found,* after an hour's search, the *money* hidden under the rug.

CLEAR   After an hour's search, she *found* the *money* hidden under the rug.

AWKWARD SEPARATION	At the convention I saw Mary Ward, whom I *had* many years ago *met* in Chicago.
CLEAR	At the convention I saw Mary Ward, whom I *had met* many years ago in Chicago.

EXERCISE 11f
Revise the following sentences to eliminate the unnecessary separation of related sentence elements.

1. Wilhelm Konrad Röentgen, a German physicist, while doing some experiments with cathode ray tubes, discovered an invisible form of radiation.
2. Röentgen called, X being the common mathematical symbol for the unknown, this invisible radiation X-rays.
3. Röentgen realized, after more work with these rays, that X-rays could pass through many substances which were opaque to regular light.
4. Röentgen's discovery has, for twentieth-century science and medicine, led to many useful applications of X-rays, mainly in medical diagnosis and in treating tumors.
5. Röentgen was, in 1901, the first winner of the Nobel Prize in physics.

EXERCISE 11a-f
Revise the following sentences to eliminate all misplaced parts. Be prepared to explain your revisions.

1. Busy Americans make use of, in order to save time, various labor-saving devices and services.
2. Some people almost eat all their meals in fast-food establishments.
3. Now supermarkets even offer gourmet takeout food.
4. Instead of standing in line in a bank, lots of people use cash machines to quickly get money from their accounts.
5. There are microwave ovens in many kitchens which save time and trouble in food preparation.
6. In today's newspaper the local dry cleaner offered one-hour cleaning service on the back page.
7. Motorists wash their cars often at fast drive-through car washes.
8. Some people listen, while they're driving, to a tape of the latest best-selling novel.
9. Telephone users can punch a one-number code rather than seven digits for numbers they call frequently, which is much faster.
10. Supermarkets, for those who are in a hurry, offer express checkout counters.

12

DANGLING MODIFIERS

A modifier must have something to modify. A **dangling modifier** has nothing to modify because the word it logically should modify is not present in its sentence. For example:

Driving through the mountains, three bears were seen.

Driving through the mountains is a participial phrase that can modify anything capable of driving. The sentence says that the bears are driving, but common sense tells us bears can't drive. Although the writer surely meant that the bears were seen by some person who was driving, the sentence contains no words directly identifying such a person.

Dangling modifiers can occur in mixed constructions when a writer begins a sentence as if he or she intends to use an active verb in the main clause but finishes it by shifting to a passive-voice verb instead (see Section **14b**). The sample sentence above is a good illustration of such a shift. Here is another example of a shift that results in a dangling elliptical clause **(12d).** This one was printed in a financial journal.

When asked to explain why they borrowed money from a particular bank, previous good experience and low interest rates were most frequently mentioned as reasons.

If the sentence is rewritten in the active voice, the dangling modifier will disappear:

When asked to explain why they borrowed money from a particular bank, people most frequently mentioned previous good experience and low interest rates as reasons.

Dangling modifiers may be verbal or prepositional phrases or elliptical clauses **(12d).** They most commonly come at the beginning of a sentence, but they can come at the end as well. To write *There were three bears, driving through the mountains* still leaves the bears apparently doing the driving. Nothing is expressed that *driving* can sensibly modify. Nor is *When a baby, my grandfather gave me a silver cup* improved by moving the clause to the end of the sentence.

Eliminate dangling modifiers (1) by reworking the sentence so that an appropriate word is provided for the modifier to modify or (2) by expanding the dangler into a full subordinate clause. The sentence in the illustration, for example, can be revised as follows:

While driving through the mountains, we saw three bears.
As we were driving through the mountains, we saw three bears.

Through a writer's carelessness, dangling modifiers can slip into writing, especially when an appropriate object for the modifier is present in an adjacent sentence but not in the sentence containing the dangler. Consider this paragraph from a campus newspaper:

12a

dgl

> While wearing a Halloween mask and carrying a handgun, a man entered Marsh Pharmacy and asked for all of the narcotics, said Frank Reinhart, a temporary Marsh employee. According to Reinhart, he was filling in for another pharmacist when a man came up to the desk. *Wearing a green mask and overalls*, Reinhart estimated his height at about six feet and his weight at about 150 pounds.

Presumably the would-be thief, rather than Reinhart, was wearing the green mask and the overalls. The reporter forgot that a modifier and the word it modifies need to be located in the same sentence:

> According to Reinhart, he was filling in for another pharmacist when a man wearing a green mask and overalls came up to the desk.

12a
Avoid dangling participial phrases.

A **participle** is a verb form usually ending in *-ing* or *-ed* and used as an adjective to modify a noun or pronoun. A participial phrase consists of a participle, its object, and any modifiers of the participle or object. (See **1b** and **1c**.)

DANGLING	Coming home late, the house was dark. [There is nothing in the sentence that can sensibly be coming home. A revision must identify some person.]
REVISED	Coming home late, we found the house dark. When we came home late, the house was dark.
DANGLING	Being made of glass, Rick handled the tabletop carefully.
REVISED	Because the tabletop was made of glass, Rick handled it carefully. [The participial phrase is expanded into a subordinate clause.]

EXERCISE 12a
Revise the following sentences to eliminate dangling participial phrases.

1. The Basilica of St. Mark and the huge square in front of it are sights which must not be missed, visiting Venice.

2. Crowded with tourists, you'll see and hear orchestras playing as people sip drinks at outdoor cafés and watch the activity around them.
3. Arriving in Venice, the canals seem at first to be a bewildering maze of waterways.
4. Taking care to establish the cost in advance, a gondola ride can be a good introduction to the beautiful city.
5. Being low on money, a ride on a water bus or a long walk through the streets can be an excellent way to see Venice.

12b
Avoid dangling phrases that contain gerunds.

A **gerund** is an *-ing* form of a verb used as a noun. A gerund phrase consists of a gerund, its object, and any modifiers of the gerund or object. (See **1b** and **1d**.) In typical dangling phrases that contain gerunds, the gerund or gerund phrase serves as the object of a preposition.

DANGLING	Before exploring the desert, our water supply was replenished. [Who replenished it?]
REVISED	Before exploring the desert, we replenished our water supply.
DANGLING	After putting a worm on my hook, the fish began to bite. [A very accommodating fish that will bait the hook for you!]
REVISED	After I put a worm on my hook, the fish began to bite.

Dangling gerunds, like the dangling infinitives discussed in Section 12c, sometimes occur when the subject of the main clause is not the same as the implied subject governing the gerund phrase. In the first example above, the appropriate implied subject to govern the gerund phrase is *we,* and thus the matching subject of the main clause should be *we* as well. But the writer's shift of subject to *water supply* removes the word the gerund phrase should modify. Because a shift of subject is often accompanied by a shift to passive voice, checking the main clause for passive voice verbs is a quick way to test for and correct modifying phrases that may be dangling.

EXERCISE 12b
Revise the following sentences to eliminate dangling gerund phrases.

1. After being in Venice for a day or two, the labyrinthine streets and canals become less confusing.
2. The beauty of Venice can be seen in three or four days by planning an itinerary to include churches, canals, bridges, and artwork.
3. After touring the city itself, the Venetian Lagoon and the islands around it are worth seeing.

4. Before leaving for the islands, decisions need to be made about how much time to spend on each one.
5. On arriving at the island of Murano, glassmaking displays show the beauty of famed Venetian glass.

12c

Avoid dangling infinitive phrases.

An **infinitive** consists of the infinitive marker *to* followed by the plain form of the verb. An infinitive phrase consists of an infinitive, its object, and any modifiers of the infinitive or object.

DANGLING	To take good pictures, a good camera must be used. [Who will use the camera?]
REVISED	To take good pictures, you must use a good camera.
	If you wish to take good pictures, you must use a good camera.
DANGLING	To skate well, practice is necessary
REVISED	To skate well, you [or *one*] must practice.

EXERCISE 12c
Revise the following sentences to eliminate dangling infinitive phrases.

1. To see the Venice where the Venetians actually live, the small streets and canals must be explored.
2. St. Mark's Square should be avoided to get away from the worst crowds.
3. To appreciate the beauty of the light in Venice, the canals should be seen at sunset.
4. A striped shirt and straw hat are necessary to be dressed like a gondolier.
5. To save Venice from the ravages of winter flooding, many plans have been formulated.

12d

Avoid dangling elliptical clauses.

An **elliptical clause** is one in which the subject or verb is implied or understood rather than stated. The clause dangles if its implied subject is not the same as the subject of the main clause. Eliminate a dangling elliptical clause by (1) making the dangling clause agree with the subject of the main clause or (2) supplying the omitted subject or verb.

DANGLING	*When a baby,* my grandfather gave me a silver cup.
REVISED	*When a baby,* I was given a silver cup by my grand-

father. [The subject of the main clause agrees with the implied subject of the elliptical clause.]

REVISED   *When I was a baby,* my grandfather gave me a silver cup. [The omitted subject and verb are supplied in the elliptical clause.]

DANGLING   *While rowing on the lake,* the boat overturned.

REVISED   *While rowing on the lake,* we overturned the boat. [The subject of the main clause agrees with the implied subject of the elliptical clause.]

While we were rowing on the lake, the boat overturned [*or* we overturned the boat]. [The elliptical clause is expanded into a subordinate clause.]

12d

dgl

EXERCISE 12d

Revise the following sentences to eliminate dangling elliptical clauses.

1. When camping and hiking, mosquitoes, bees, ticks, and other insects can be a problem.
2. If left unprotected from insect bites, these pests could ruin a hiker's day.
3. When properly prepared, insect bites can be avoided during a hiking or camping expedition.
4. Ticks can transmit Rocky Mountain Spotted Fever and can be especially dangerous, if not careful.
5. Campers certainly dislike the itching and irritation of mosquito bites, although not dangerous.

EXERCISE 12a-d

Revise the following sentences to eliminate the dangling modifiers.

1. To avoid misery from insect bites, understanding their environment and habits will help.
2. When camping, areas near stagnant water should be avoided, for mosquitoes breed in standing water.
3. Having been bitten by a mosquito, a cold compress, an ice cube, or a first-aid spray will provide some relief from itching.
4. The sting of a bee, wasp, hornet, or ant can be dangerous or even life-threatening, if allergic to the insect's venom.
5. To avoid bee stings, perfumes, hair sprays, shaving lotions, and other heavily scented substances should be avoided.
6. After being stung by a bee, an ice cube can help reduce the swelling.
7. Attaching itself to its host and swelling as it feeds on blood, the hiker will have to be careful to avoid the bites of ticks.
8. If hiking in tick territory, insect repellents and clothing tied tightly at the ankles and wrists will help.
9. To remove a tick, care must be taken not to pull it forcibly off the skin.

10. Before trying to remove the tick, a coating of petroleum jelly, oil, grease, or turpentine should be applied.

WRITERS REVISING: MODIFIERS

Jim, a student in Freshman English, was assigned a personal experience essay. Part of the instructions was to try to achieve variety in sentence construction. When he read over his rough draft, however, Jim noticed that while varying his sentences he had created several dangling and misplaced modifiers. See if you can revise his paragraph, keeping sentence variety but correcting faulty modification. Then compare your version with Jim's retyped revision.

Draft

```
D 1      Last summer I saw a hot-air balloon race. To

D 2   really understand what is going on, a knowledge of

D 3   hares and hounds is helpful. Taking off first,

D 4   one balloon is designated the "hare" balloon, and

D 5   then all the other balloons--the "hounds"--chase

D 6   it.

D 7      The hare balloon after a while lands in a

D 8   field some distance from the starting point.

D 9   Marked with an "x," the hound balloon that is

D10   able to land on or closest to the hare balloon's

D11   spot wins the race. That balloon takes first

D12   prize and gets congratulations from all the other

D13   balloonists having "caught" the hare. Coming

D14   close to the hare balloon's landing spot is not

D15   easy particularly since hot-air balloons float

D16   with the wind and are difficult to maneuver.

D17      Ballooning is the oldest form of aerial

D18   transportation. First flown in France, that

D19   country celebrated its 200th anniversary for

D20   ballooning in 1983.
```

12d

dgl

Revision

R 1   Last summer I saw a hot—air balloon race. To

R 2   really understand what is going on, a knowledge of   11e

R 3   hares and hounds is helpful. Taking off first,

R 4   one balloon is designated the "hare" balloon, and

R 5   then all the other balloons——the "hounds"——chase

R 6   it.

R 7   After a while the hare balloon lands in a   11f

R 8   field some distance from the starting point. The

R 9   hare balloon's landing spot is marked with an   11b

R10   "x," and the hound balloon that is able to land

R11   on or closest to that spot wins the race. Having

R12   "caught" the hare, that balloonist takes first   11b

R13   prize and gets congratulations from all the other

R14   balloonists. Coming close to the hare balloon is

R15   not particularly easy since hot—air balloons float   11d

R16   with the wind and are difficult to maneuver.

R17   Ballooning is the oldest form of aerial

R18   transportation. Hot—air balloons were first flown

R19   in France, where the two—hundredth anniversary of   12a

R20   ballooning was celebrated in 1983.

Analysis

The first sentence of the draft contains no faulty modifiers. Although *To really understand* (lines D1-2) is a split infinitive, the split is not awkward. More importantly, if *really* is to keep modifying *understand,* the only other possibilities are *Really to understand* or *To understand really,* either of which creates a much more awkward sentence. Consequently, Jim wisely made no changes. The third sentence contains no faulty modifiers.

The fourth sentence contains an awkward split of subject and verb (D7-8). As the revision shows (R7-8), moving the modifying phrase to the beginning of the sentence improves the sen-

13

om
comp

tences. The opening phrase of the fifth sentence is misplaced (D9). The landing spot, not the hound balloon, is marked with an "x." Anyone not familiar with ballooning would get an entirely incorrect impression. Jim decided that this important information merited its own independent clause, rather than being subordinated, so he completely restructured the sentence (R9-11).

In sentence 6 (D11-13), the misplaced modifier *having* "caught" the hare suggests that all the balloonists win, rather than just one. Jim solved this problem by moving the phrase to the front of the sentence, placing it closer to the intended noun (R11-14).

In the seventh sentence (D13-16), *particularly* "squints"—it could be interpreted to mean "not particularly easy" or "not easy, particularly since hot air . . . ." Jim transposed the two words (R15).

In the draft's final sentence, France seems to be flying itself, thanks to a dangling phrase. A major revision completely restructures the information; the draft's modifier becomes the main clause—and the major focus—of the last sentence in the revision (R18-20).

Jim located all but one of the misplaced or dangling parts in his draft. He overlooked a subtle error in the second sentence (D1-3)—a dangling infinitive phrase that can be corrected by providing an appropriate subject to perform the action of understanding: *To really understand what is going on, one needs to know something about hares and hounds.*

13

OMISSIONS;
INCOMPLETE AND ILLOGICAL COMPARISONS

A sentence will be confusing if the writer omits words needed for clarity and accuracy. Sometimes, of course, writers omit words through haste or carelessness. This sort of omission can be caught with careful proofreading. Most omissions not caused by carelessness occur in three kinds of constructions: (1) some constructions in which the omission of a preposition or conjunction is common in informal speech, (2) some kinds of compound constructions, and (3) comparisons.

13a

Carefully proofread your writing to avoid careless omissions.

The sample sentences below are confusing because they omit necessary words.

CONFUSING	The opportunities for people television repair are varied.
REVISED	The opportunities for people *in* television repair are varied.
CONFUSING	Many millions people were unemployed last recession.
REVISED	Many millions *of* people were unemployed *during the* last recession.
CONFUSING	The Kentucky Derby is Louisville's best-known attractions, but far from its only one.
REVISED	The Kentucky Derby is *one of* Louisville's best-known attractions, but far from its only one.

Very probably the writer of the third example thought out the sentence with something like the phrase *one of* in mind and was merely careless in getting the idea down on paper.

13b

In writing, express relationships left implied in speech.

Some constructions such as *He left Monday* are idiomatic. In speaking we often extend this pattern to such expressions as *We became friends spring semester,* or *The next few years we'll worry about prices.* In writing, such relationships need to be spelled out.

SPOKEN	Space travel *the last few years* has been exciting.
WRITTEN	Space travel *during the last few years* has been exciting.

Similes or comparisons such as *I feel like a million dollars* are common in both speech and writing. The construction *feel like* also appears in idiomatic expressions such as *I feel like a cookie,* but in this case no comparison is being expressed. Of course the speaker does not actually *feel* like a cookie (he or she merely wants a cookie to eat); the spoken idiom omits the implied participle *having* or *eating.* In most written contexts, the verbal should be expressed.

SPOKEN	Do you feel like some popcorn?
	She feels like a game of tennis.
	I feel like a movie.
WRITTEN	Do you feel like *having* some popcorn?

> She feels like *playing* a game of tennis.
>
> I feel like *going to* a movie.

The omission of *that* can sometimes be confusing.

CONFUSING   He felt completely naked but totally private swimming was indecent.

REVISED   He felt that completely naked but totally private swimming was indecent.

The use of *type, make, brand* and some other similar words immediately before a noun (*this type show, this brand cereal*) is common in speech but is avoided by most writers.

SPOKEN   I have never driven this *make car* before.

WRITTEN   I have never driven this *make of car* before.

EXERCISE 13a-b

Revise the following sentences to correct careless omissions and to supply words that are implied but not stated.

1. Food of the Caribbean is a type cuisine that is new to many Americans.
2. However, there has been a growing interest in the foods of Jamaica, Trinidad, and other Caribbean islands the past few years.
3. As a result, restaurants in large cities are beginning serve such exotic dishes as *asopas de camarone,* which is shrimp with rice in a tomato broth.
4. In large cities shoppers who feel like Caribbean cuisine can find authentic ingredients for Caribbean food in markets specialize in island vegetables and fruits.
5. With the right kinds spices and authentic fruits and vegetables, people can create their own Caribbean dinners at home.

13c

Include all necesssary words in compound constructions.

When we connect two items of the same kind with coordinating conjunctions such as *and* or *but,* we often omit words that unnecessarily duplicate each other: *She could* [go] *and did go; He was faithful* [to] *and devoted to his job.* But such omissions work only if the two items are in fact the same. If they are not, the resulting construction will be incomplete (see also the discussion of parallelism in Section **32**). Such incomplete constructions usually result from omitting necessary prepositions or parts of verb phrases.

INCOMPLETE	Tanya was interested and skillful at photography.
REVISED	Tanya was interested *in* and skillful *at* photography. [*Interested* idiomatically requires the preposition *in;* if it is not present, we tend to read *interested at.*]
INCOMPLETE	My cat never has and never will eat fish.
REVISED	My cat never has *eaten* and never will *eat* fish.
INCOMPLETE	Tom's ideas were sound and adopted without discussion.
REVISED	Tom's ideas were sound and *were* adopted without discussion. [*Were* needs to be repeated here since the two verbs are not parallel; the first *were* is used as the main verb; the second is used as an auxiliary with *adopted.*]

13d

om
comp

EXERCISE 13c
Revise to supply the omitted words in the following sentences.

1. The cuisines of the Caribbean islands have always and continue to be varied because of the islands' French, Spanish, and English colonial backgrounds.
2. The food of the Hispanic Caribbean is plainly prepared and flavorful but not overly spicy.
3. The food of the French-speaking islands of Guadeloupe, Martinique, and Haiti was linked to France and not as familiar in the United States as the food of the Spanish Caribbean.
4. People who say they never have and will taste goat are surprised by the flavor of a Caribbean goat stew.
5. The popularity of Caribbean food has given many Americans the opportunity to indulge and develop a taste for the unusual island flavors.

13d

Make all comparisons complete and logical.

A comparison expresses a relationship between two things: *A is larger than B.* To make a comparison complete and logical, include both items being compared and all words necessary to make the relationship clear, and be sure that the two items are in fact comparable.

1. Avoid incomplete comparisons. Sentences such as *Cleanaid is better* or *Wetherall Paint lasts longer* are popular with advertisers because they let the advertiser avoid telling us what the product is better than or lasts longer than. To be complete, a comparison must state both items being compared.

INCOMPLETE	Our new Ford gets better mileage. [Better than what?]
REVISED	Our new Ford gets better mileage than our old one did.

INCOMPLETE	Louisville features more park land per person than any other in the nation. [Any other what?]
REVISED	Louisville features more park land per person than any other city in the nation.

2. Avoid ambiguous comparisons. In comparisons such as *He enjoys watching football more than* [*he enjoys watching*] *baseball,* we can omit *he enjoys watching* because only one meaning is reasonable. But when more than one meaning is possible, the comparison will be ambiguous.

13d

om
comp

AMBIGUOUS	I admire her more than Jane. [More than Jane admires her? More than you admire Jane?]
CLEAR	I admire her more than I admire Jane.
	I admire her more than Jane does.

3. Avoid illogical comparisons. A comparison will be illogical if it compares or seems to compare two things that cannot be sensibly compared.

ILLOGICAL	A lawyer's income is greater than a doctor. [The sentence compares an income to a doctor. Logic requires the comparison of income to income or of lawyer to doctor.]
REVISED	A lawyer's income is greater than a doctor's.
	A lawyer's income is greater than that of a doctor.
	A lawyer has a greater income than a doctor has.

4. Avoid grammatically incomplete comparisons. Comparisons using the expression *as strong as, as good as,* and the like always require the second *as.*

INCOMPLETE	He is as strong, if not stronger than, Bob.
REVISED	He is as strong as, if not stronger than, Bob.
	He is as strong as Bob, if not stronger.

In comparisons of items in the same class of things, use *other* or *any other.* In comparisons of items in different classes, use *any.*

INCORRECT	Mount Everest is higher than *any* Asian mountain.
CORRECT	Mount Everest is higher than *any other* Asian mountain.
	Mount Everest is higher than *other* Asian mountains. [We are comparing Mount Everest, one Asian mountain, to other Asian mountains.]
	Mount Everest is higher than *any* American mountain. [We are comparing Mount Everest, an Asian mountain, with American mountains, a different class.]

14

awk

EXERCISE 13d

Revise the following sentences to make all comparisons complete and logical.

1. Studies show that nonsmokers are healthier.
2. A smoker's chances of developing lung cancer or of suffering a heart attack are higher than a nonsmoker.
3. Statistics indicate that employees who smoke are absent from work more often than any employees.
4. No reason to quit smoking is more convincing than shortened life expectancy.
5. The desire to live longer is as strong, if not stronger than, any desire in motivating smokers to give up their habit.

EXERCISE 13a-d

The following sentences all contain incomplete constructions. Revise each to supply words that have been omitted. Be prepared to explain your revisions.

1. Ayers Rock, a huge stone mass in the center of Australia, is a type rock geologists call an inselberg.
2. Ayers Rock has been and continues one of the sights travelers to Australia want to see.
3. Ayers Rock is larger than any rock in the Outback, the vast central desert-like area of Australia.
4. The Rock has become more accessible to travelers the last few years as a result improved air transportation as well as four-wheel-drive vehicles.
5. The best time to visit Ayers Rock is Australia's winter (May to September) when days are cooler.
6. The Northern Territory, where the Rock is located, is an area settled by cattle farmers whose cattle stations may cover over 1,000 square miles, making them as large, if not larger than, any others in Australia.
7. People who are fascinated and knowledgeable about folklore will enjoy the fables and myths associated with Ayers Rock.
8. Some people find the mystery of Ayers Rock to be greater.
9. Yet its beauty is considerable, for the Rock changes pink at sunrise to orange at noon to deep red at sunset.
10. Travelers to Australia have found Ayers Rock situated as it is in the middle of nowhere is a perfect symbol of the vast and unusual continent.

14

AWKWARD OR CONFUSED SENTENCES

Sometimes a sentence goes wrong because the predicate says something about the subject that cannot sensibly apply to that subject. Or a sentence goes wrong because it starts with one kind of construction and ends with a different kind of construction. The first of these faults is called **faulty predication;** the second, a **mixed construction.**

14a
Combine only subjects and predicates that make sense together.

Not all subjects and verbs make sense together. For example, many living things can be subjects for the verb *eat*: *women, boys, ants, panthers.* Figuratively, we can speak of water *eating away* rock. But nouns like *bed, fence,* and *idea* are not likely subjects for *eat.* Sometimes however, in haste or carelessness, writers construct sentences in which inappropriate verbs create faulty predications.

In each of the following sentences, the subject and the verb do not fit together.

The *selection* of the committee *was chosen* by the students.

Many *settlers,* moving into a new part of the country, *expanded* into towns.

Any *member* who failed to do his job on the ship *meant* danger for the whole crew.

Illogical combinations of subject and verb are particularly likely to occur when the verb is the linking verb *to be* in its various forms. Linking verbs equate what comes before the verb with what comes after it—the subject with the complement. They say that something equals something else. Thus they cannot be used to connect things that are not equal. *My dog is a beagle* will do, but not *My dog is a reason.*

FAULTY An important step in skiing is stopping. [*Step* does not equal *stopping.*]

REVISED An important step in skiing is learning to stop.

FAULTY His first trick was a pack of cards. [*Trick* does not equal *pack.*]

REVISED His first trick was one with a pack of cards.

FAULTY Schools are a serious quarrel today.

In the third example, *schools* clearly is not equivalent to *quarrel.* But revision is not really possible because the subject, *schools,* is itself so vague. Perhaps the writer meant something like *Increased taxes for schools cause serious quarrels today.*

A common kind of faulty equation occurs with predicates that begin with *is when* and *is where* and with the expression *the reason is because.* Definitions such as *Drunkenness is when you've had too much to drink* or *Subtraction is where you take one thing from another* are common in speech. Written English, however, ordinarily requires a noun or a word group functioning as a noun as both subject and complement in such definitions. Note the following sentences and their revisions.

14a

awk

FAULTY	A documentary is when a movie or a television drama analyzes news events or social conditions.
REVISED	A documentary is a movie or a television drama that analyzes news events or social conditions.
FAULTY	A hasty generalization is when you jump to conclusions.
REVISED	Hasty generalization involves jumping to conclusions.
	To make a hasty generalization is to jump to conclusions.

Another acceptable revision preserves the *when* or *where* but substitutes another verb for the linking verb form *is*.

FAULTY	Frostbite is where skin tissue has been frozen.
REVISED	Frostbite appears where skin tissue has been frozen.
FAULTY	A safety is when a ball carrier gets tackled behind his own goal line.
REVISED	A safety occurs when a ball carrier gets tackled behind his own goal line.

Sentences such as *The reason he didn't come was because he was sick* are also common in speech, but *reason is that* is preferred at all levels of writing. *Because* means *for the reason that;* therefore, the expression *the reason is because* is redundant.

FAULTY	The reason he went to Chicago was because he wanted to visit Kareem.
REVISED	The reason he went to Chicago was that he wanted to visit Kareem.
	He went to Chicago because he wanted to visit Kareem.

EXERCISE 14a

Revise the following sentences to eliminate faulty predications.

1. Printer problems can be frustration for computer users.
2. A printer problem is where nothing happens when the user instructs the machine to send the text to the printer.
3. A page full of lines with only the top half of each character also means a problem for the computer user.
4. The reason printer problems are so annoying is because the computer user has worked hard but has no results.
5. For many students, agony is when the printer fails to work a half hour before a big paper is due.

14b

Do not mix constructions.

A mixed construction is one in which a writer begins a sentence in one construction and then shifts to another. The result is a derailed sentence that must be put back on its track to be clear.

> **MIXED** With every effort the student made to explain his problem got him more confused.

Here the writer began with a prepositional phrase, but was thinking of *every effort* as the subject by the time he or she arrived at the verb *got*. We can untangle the sentence either by giving *got* the subject *he*, or by dropping the preposition *with* and making *every effort* the subject.

> **REVISED** With every effort the student made to explain his problem, he got more confused.
>
> Every effort the student made got him more confused.

Beginnings such as *the fact that, there are,* and *it is* often cause needless complexity and lead to mixed or confusing sentences.

> **MIXED** The fact that Louise was a good student she had many offers for good jobs. [*The fact that* as a beginning requires something like *results* or *leads to* as a main verb in the sentence. But the writer has forgotten that as the sentence develops.]
>
> **REVISED** The fact that Louise was a good student resulted in her having many offers for good jobs.
>
> Because Louise was a good student, she had many offers for good jobs.

Unnecessary shifts from active-voice to passive-voice verbs can also create mixed constructions. When the implied or expressed subject of one clause becomes an implied or expressed object in another clause, readers can have a hard time sorting out meaning (see Section **10a**).

> **MIXED** When they were water-skiing, the tow rope was broken by my friends. [The subject shifts unneccessarily from *they* to *rope*.]
>
> **REVISED** When they were water-skiing, my friends broke the tow rope.

EXERCISE 14b

Revise the following sentences to eliminate mixed constructions.

1. Although a printer has a self-test device does not mean the printer will give warning that it is not working.
2. One of the printer problems a user experiences, it may be in the hardware of the computer.
3. By checking to make sure the on-line switch is set is all a user might have to do to solve the problem.
4. The fact that vibrations may have loosened cables may have caused the user to have printer problems.
5. When you move the printer or load paper, the cables may have been loosened.

14b

awk

EXERCISE 14a-b

Revise the following sentences to eliminate faulty predications and mixed constructions. Be prepared to explain your reasons.

1. The Richter scale, an open-ended measurement of earthquake severity, means how much damage an earthquake can cause.
2. Understanding and predicting earthquake activity is a reason the Richter scale is used.
3. A reading of 6 on the Richter scale is where an earthquake can cause severe damage.
4. The fact that the Richter scale measures 7 widespread and heavy damage can occur.
5. The reason that an earthquake measuring 7 on the Richter scale does much more damage than one measuring 6 is because each unit on the scale represents an increase of thirty times the energy released by the quake.
6. By studying the San Francisco earthquake of 1906 it was estimated to have been above 8 on the Richter scale.
7. To predict exactly where earthquakes might occur is a reason seismologists put sensors along known active faults in the earth's surface.
8. The San Andreas Fault, the best known fault in the United States, is stretching from north of San Francisco to the Mexican border.
9. This 700-mile-long fracture in the earth is an opportunity for geologists to monitor the earth's movement and to test methods of predicting earthquakes.
10. When they design buildings in known earthquake areas, factors for safety during a quake are taken into account by architects.

WRITERS REVISING: OMISSIONS, INCOMPLETE AND MIXED CONSTRUCTIONS

Continuing with the revision of his essay on hot-air ballooning (see pages 113-114 for the first part of the essay), Jim checked for omissions, incomplete comparisons, and confused and mixed constructions. See what you can do with the passage that follows, and then compare your revision with Jim's.

Draft

D 1   I learned ballooning fall semester when

D 2   I attended the Albuquerque International

D 3   Balloon Fiesta with a friend. This event

D 4   attracts over four hundred enthusiasts

D 5   interested and skilled at flying the hot-air

D 6   craft. No other ballooning event attracts

D 7   more people. Several contests that are held

D 8   at the Fiesta have valuable prizes. One is

D 9   where balloonists try to snag keys hanging

D10   from the top of a pole stuck into the

D11   ground. The keys are to the prize, a new car.

Revision

R 1   I learned ˄*about* ballooning ˄*during* fall ˄semester when   13b

R 2   I attended the Albuquerque International

R 3   Balloon Fiesta with a friend. This event

R 4   attracts over four hundred enthusiasts

R 5   interested ˄*in* and skilled at flying the hot-air   13c

R 6   craft. No other ballooning event attracts

R 7   more people ˄*than the Albuquerque fiesta does.* Several contests that are held   13d(1)

R 8   at the Fiesta have valuable prizes. ~~One is~~

R 9   *In one contest* ~~where~~ balloonists try to snag keys hanging   14a

R10   from the top of a pole stuck into the

R11   ground. The keys are to the prize, a new car.

Analysis

Without the preposition *about*, readers would assume from the first draft sentence that Jim knows how to fly a balloon—a major misunderstanding of meaning. *During* is also implied; in writing, the relationship should be expressed. The compound construction in the second sentence requires *in* to be complete (see R5). In the third sentence, *than the Albuquerque Fiesta does* completes the comparison *more people*. The fourth sentence (D7-8) is acceptable as written. In the fifth sentence, *One* can't be "where"—"where" means a place. Also, in this sentence *one* is so far from the word to which it refers *(contests)* that the meaning is likely to be unclear (D8-11). These problems are solved in the revision (R8-11). The final sentence requires no revision.

14b

awk

REVIEW EXERCISE ON BASIC SENTENCE FAULTS (Sections 6-14)
Indicate the principal error in each of the following sentences (faulty agreement, faulty reference, misplaced parts, and so on) and then revise the sentence.

1. A *tsunami* is when a giant ocean wave is set into motion by the force of an earthquake.
2. *Tsunami* are often called tidal waves, they can create much damage to coastal areas.
3. Tidal waves being most commonly caused by earthquakes, particularly those registering above 6.5 on the Richter scale.
4. A volcanic eruption, as well as earthquakes, cause *tsunami*.
5. A giant tidal wave struck Lisbon, Portugal, in 1775, and much of the city is destroyed.
6. In 1883 the volcanic island of Krakatoa exploded, which set off a gigantic *tsunami*.
7. Destroying towns and villages on the neighboring islands of Sumatra and Java, the coasts of India and Australia later felt the effects.
8. Some of the waves set off by the eruption at Krakatoa is estimated to have reached 125 feet.
9. The waves had tremendous speed and force, in fact, accounts of the disaster tell of a steamship which was tossed nearly two miles inland.
10. Fortunately, these sort of disastrous waves do not occur frequently.
11. It says in a recent science magazine article that seismic sea-wave warning systems situated throughout the Pacific allows scientists to detect earthquakes and predict damaging waves which might follow them.
12. After detecting a tidal wave in the Pacific, its travel time to various coastal areas can then be calculated.
13. When in danger of being hit by the wave, authorities issue warnings to people living there.
14. As a result of such warning systems, tidal waves cause less damage.
15. If a person sees the towering wall of water of a *tsunami*, they won't soon forget it.
16. In fact, television now often warns people in coastal areas not to try to see the big waves.
17. To get a glimpse of the phenomenal waves of the *tsunami*, dangerous risks are often taken.
18. The people that go out to the coast to see the wave often don't realize how powerful they are.
19. Anyone that hears of a tidal wave approaching their area should move away from the coast.
20. Although tidal waves can be predicted, they can still cause destruction and death, so don't go to the water to just see the giant waves.

MECHANICS

Of all forms of symbolism, language is the most highly developed, most subtle, and most complicated. It has been pointed out that human beings, by agreement, can make anything stand for anything.

s. i. HAYAKAWA, *Language in Thought and Action*

Many practices of written English are merely conventions. Logic does not justify them; they simply represent standard ways of doing things—codes of meaning that people recognize and accept. The mechanics of writing numbers and abbreviations, of handling acronyms, initialisms, and clipped forms, and of using word division (syllabication) are such conventions. To ignore these conventions is to be a nuisance to readers.

15

NUMBERS

Conventions governing the choice between spelling out numbers *(twenty-two)* and using figures *(22)* vary with the kind of writing. You may have noticed that writing in publications for the humanities uses spelled-out numbers more frequently than does scientific or technical writing, which favors greater use of figures. Consider the following examples:

> There remained to the seventy-five-year-old King only one great-grandson, a pink-cheeked child of two, the last surviving infant in the direct line. . . . This new little Dauphin remained miraculously alive and lived to rule France for fifty-nine years as Louis XV. On his deathbed, Louis XIV called for his great-grandson and heir who then was five. Face to face, these two Bourbons who between them ruled France for 131 years regarded each other.
>
> ROBERT K. MASSIE, *Peter the Great: His Life and World*

> In alphanumeric mode, the video circuit displays characters in 80 or 40 columns by 25 rows. Sixteen foreground and background colors are available, except with character blinking, which reduces available background colors to eight.
> In graphics mode, low resolution provides 16 colors and 160 by 200 pixels, medium resolution provides 4 colors and 320 by 200 pixels, and high resolution offers 2 colors and 640 by 200 pixels.
>
> "The Tandy 1000," *Byte: The Small Systems Journal*

> What is America's biggest regional repertory company, employing as many as 63 actors to mount a dozen productions for a total of 676 performances a year? What company features three spaces ranging from a stripped-down, experimental "black box". . . to a 1,173-seat outdoor Elizabethan playhouse?. . . What company annually attracts more than 300,000 playgoers, 90% of them from

more than 150 miles away?. . . . The answer in each case is the Oregon Shakespearean festival. . . .

"Only 2,500 Miles from Broadway," *Time*

As different as these passages appear to be in their use of numbers versus figures, each follows a coherent set of guidelines used by writers of general nonfiction (the first example), technical description (the second example), and journalism (the third example).

Your own use of numbers and figures in any given piece of writing should be governed by the conventions of the field for which you are writing. Those conventions can be discovered simply by examining publications in the field or by consulting style manuals published by the professional organizations in the field. The following guidelines explain some of the common conventions governing numbers.

15a

nos

15a

In general writing, spell out one- or two-word numbers. In technical writing or journalism, use figures for numbers over ten or numbers in series.

He lived to be one hundred years old. [General]

There are fifty-three people in the room. [General]

I wouldn't give you two cents for that car. [General]

How can anyone govern a country that has 246 different kinds of cheese? [General]

CHARLES DE GAULLE

The larvae of swallow-tail moths feed only on one plant. The leaves, located 15 to 20 meters up into a forest canopy, are difficult to see. [Technical]

Chemistry

Tired volunteers rescued 17 whales beached or stranded Thursday along Cape Cod. . . . Up to 70 scientists and volunteers had worked two days, sometimes in 50-degree water, to aid the giant mammals. [Journalism]

USA Today

15b

Use figures for dates and addresses.

Dates	*Addresses*
May 4, 1914	13 Milford Avenue
July 2, 1947	57 East 121st Street
1862–1924	Route 1 P.O. Box 739 Apt. 2B
17 B.C. to A.D. 21	Grinnell, Iowa 50112

Ordinal numbers (numbers that indicate order: *first*, *third*, *twenty-*

ninth) or the forms 1st, 3rd, 9th, may be used in dates if the year is not given: *March 1, March first, March 1st.*

In formal invitations, dates are usually written out: *Tuesday, September first, nineteen hundred and eighty-seven.* (See **20i** for the punctuation of dates and addresses.)

15c

Ordinarily, use figures for the following:

Decimals	8.72 4.25 13.098
Percentages	72% or 72 percent
Mixed numbers and fractions	27½ 19⅔ (but *one-half pound of coffee*)
Scores and statistics, numbers being compared	score of 35-10 vote of 86-53 it was 5-10 degrees warmer
Identification numbers	Channel 5 Interstate 70
Volume, chapter, and page numbers	Volume V, Chapter 7, page 518
Act, scene, and line numbers	Act II, scene 4, lines 18-47
Numbers followed by symbols or abbreviations	5 cu. ft. 93° F. 31° C. 55 mph 60 Hz 1200 baud
Exact amounts of money	$24.98 $3.49 56¢
Times	4:30 p.m. 11:55 a.m. (but *half past two, quarter of six, seven o'clock*)

Sums of money that can be expressed in two or three words or in round numbers are sometimes written out: *twenty million dollars in losses, fifty cents on the dollar.*

When writing a compound-number adjective, spell out the first of the two numbers or the shorter of the two to avoid confusing the reader: *sixteen 10-foot poles, 500 one-liter bottles.*

15d

Except in legal or commercial writing, do not repeat in parentheses a number that has been spelled out.

COMMERCIAL	The original order was for eight (8) pumps.
STANDARD	Mother dropped six stitches from her knitting.

15e

Spell out numbers that occur at the beginning of a sentence.

Although you may frequently see numbers at the beginning of newspaper headlines, such usage is a journalistic space-saving convention.

17 Whales Saved; 11 Killed

USA Today

If you use a number to begin a sentence, spell it out or revise the sentence to replace the numeral with a word.

    FAULTY   217 bales of hay were lost in the fire.

    REVISED   Two hundred and seventeen bales of hay were lost in the fire.

    FAULTY   1986 was the year the Chicago Bears won the Super Bowl.

    REVISED   In 1986 the Chicago Bears won the Super Bowl.

16

ab

EXERCISE 15 a-e

In the following sentences, make any necessary corrections in the use of numbers. Assume a general audience.

1. 7½ million overseas visitors come to London annually, with twenty percent of these tourists coming from the United States.
2. The average visitor to London must be fairly young, for over eighty percent of visitors are under forty-five.
3. The average stay for a visitor to London is 13 nights.
4. London is divided into thirty-three boroughs, each with a distinctive character of its own.
5. Most tourists feed the pigeons in Trafalgar Square and gaze at the eighteen-foot tall statue of Nelson, a statue which celebrates his victory over the French at the Battle of Trafalgar in eighteen hundred and five.
6. The official residence of the British prime minister at Ten Downing Street is another popular tourist attraction, although visitors cannot actually go into Downing Street itself.
7. During the summer months, thousands of tourists wait outside Buckingham Palace at eleven-thirty A.M. to watch the ceremony of the Changing of the Guard.
8. St. Paul's Cathedral was destroyed by the Great Fire of London in 1666, but 6 days later the famous architect Christopher Wren submitted his 1st proposal for rebuilding the church.
9. London weather isn't really as rainy as people think, and in the summer, temperatures often reach seventy to eighty° F.
10. Visitors to London can also see other interesting areas of England, for Cambridge is only one and one half hours away by train, and Oxford is only 1 hour by train.

16

ABBREVIATIONS

Abbreviations are common in writing for specialized audiences. These readers are usually familiar with the abbreviations common to their field and find them a convenient shorthand. When writing for a general audience, however, you will typically want to avoid abbreviations—with some standard exceptions. The following sections describe standard exceptions, as well as some abbreviated forms that should not be used.

16a
The following abbreviations are appropriate in both formal and informal general writing.

1. Titles before proper names. Use such abbreviations as *Mr., Mrs., Ms., Dr.* only when the surname is given: *Dr. Hart* or *Dr. F. D. Hart.*

> FAULTY He has gone to consult the Dr.
>
> REVISED He has gone to consult Dr. Hart (*or* the doctor).

Use *St.* (Saint) with a Christian name that refers to a person or place: *St. Theresa, St. Louis.* The plural form of the abbreviation is *SS.: SS. Peter and Paul.*

Use abbreviations such as *Hon., Rev., Prof., Sen.* only when both the surname and given name or initials are given: *The Hon. O. P. Jones,* but not *Hon. Jones.* In more formal usage, spell out these titles and use *The* before *Honorable* and *Reverend.*

> INFORMAL Rev. W. C. Case delivered the sermon.
>
> FORMAL The Reverend W. C. Case delivered the sermon.

2. Titles after proper names. Use the following abbreviations only when a name precedes them: *Jr., Sr., Esq.* Abbreviations of academic degrees and professional certifications *(M.S., Ph.D., L.L.D., M.D., J.D., C.P.A.)* can be used after a name, or they can stand by themselves: *Robert Reese, Jr., has an M.A. in philosophy.* Do not, however, use equivalent titles and/or abbreviations both before and after a name.

> NOT Dr. Carolyn Haas, M.D., is a pediatrician.
>
> BUT Carolyn Haas, M.D., is a pediatrician.

3. Abbreviations of terms referring to dates, times, or units of measurement. These terms should be abbreviated only when they appear with numerals specifying exact figures: *34 B.C., A.D. 1066, 6:54 a.m.* (or *A.M.*), *7:15 p.m.* (or *P.M.*), *$87.59, no. 6* (or *No. 6*), *55 mph.*

Note that *B.C.,* which means "before Christ," is always abbreviated and capitalized and always follows the year. *A.D.,* which means "in the year of our Lord" *(anno Domini),* is always abbreviated, capitalized, and always precedes the year. Similarly, *a.m.* (*ante meridiem,* "before noon") and *p.m.* (*post meridiem,* "after noon") are always abbreviated.

The use of abbreviations without numbers should be avoided.

NOT We met in the p.m. to check the no. of ft. the river had risen.

BUT We met in the evening to check the number of feet the river had risen.

See Section **16d** for further discussion of scientific and technical abbreviations.

4. Latin abbreviations. Latin abbreviations such as *i.e.* (that is), *e.g.* (for example), *etc.* (and so forth) are common in most writing. In formal writing the English equivalent is increasingly used. Do not use *etc.* as a catch-all. It is meaningless unless the extension of ideas it implies is unmistakably clear. Do not write *and etc.;* the *and* becomes redundant.

CLEAR The citrus fruits—oranges, lemons, etc.—are rich in Vitamin C. [The reader has no difficulty in mentally listing the other citrus fruits.]

INEFFECTIVE We swam, fished, etc. [The reader has no clues to the implied ideas.]

REVISED We swam, fished, rode horses, and danced.

5. The names of agencies, organizations, corporations, and people ordinarily referred to by their initials.

Agencies	IRS, FBI, SEC
Organizations	AMA, YWCA, NOW, NAACP
Corporations	NBC, IBM, AT&T
People	JFK, FDR

If the name of an organization occurs frequently in a paper or article but is likely to be unfamiliar to readers, it should be spelled out in its first use and the abbreviation given in parentheses. Thereafter the abbreviation may be used: *Zimbabwe African National Union (ZANU).* See Section **17** for further discussion of words formed from initials.

16b

Spell out personal names; the names of countries and states; the names of days, months, and holidays; and the names of courses of instruction.

FAULTY Eliz., a student from Eng. who joined our bio class last Wed., expects to go home for Xmas.

16b

ab

REVISED   Elizabeth, a student from England who joined our biology class last Wednesday, expects to go home for Christmas.

The District of Columbia is spelled out when it is used alone but abbreviated, D.C., when it follows the city name, Washington. The United States and the Soviet Union are commonly abbreviated as the USA (or U.S.A.) or the US, and the USSR (or U.S.S.R.).

16c

16c

ab

Spell out place names and the words *street, avenue, route, company, corporation,* and the like, as well as references to a subject, volume, chapter, line, or page, except in special contexts such as addresses and footnotes.

FAULTY   The Milano Trucking Co. is near the Michigan St. exit of I-70.

REVISED   The Milano Trucking Company is near the Michigan Street exit of Interstate 70.

FAULTY   The vet. med. students are being tested on chs. 4–7 tomorrow in the Life Sciences Bldg.

REVISED   The veterinary medicine students are being tested on Chapters 4–7 tomorrow in the Life Sciences Building.

Use such abbreviations as *Bros., Ltd.* (for *Limited*), *Co., Corp.,* and the ampersand (& for *and*) only if the firms themselves use them in their official names.

Barnes & Noble, Inc.
Sears, Roebuck and Co.

16d

When writing for a general audience, spell out most scientific and technical words unless the abbreviations are well known to readers or unless the words would be excessively long and cumbersome in unabbreviated form.

The number of technical and scientific abbreviations in general use—in everyday speech, newspapers, and magazines—increases constantly. Thus we are more likely to recognize the abbreviation DNA than we are its long form, deoxyribonucleic acid. Almost everyone has heard of AIDS, but fewer people know that it stands for acquired immune deficiency syndrome.

If you are in doubt about whether to use an abbreviation for a technical word, follow your common sense and prevailing general usage. If you think your readers may be unfamiliar with an abbreviation, first use the full name and then follow it with a brief explanation or with the abbreviation in parentheses. Thereafter, the abbreviation may be used alone.

> Thanks to computer-aided-design and computer-aided-manufacturing (CAD-CAM), automobile companies are able to test new models on the drawing board. CAD-CAM saves thousands of dollars and hundreds of hours in engineering time.

Whether to use abbreviations for units of measurement in writing for a nontechnical audience or in a nontechnical context can be a judgment call. For instance, most of us probably accept the use of "45 rpm" in the example that follows:

> Record industry analysts say the 45 rpm single will soon be a thing of the past; revolutions per minute don't mean much when your compact disk player holds just one size.

But many readers resist such usage in general writing as the following:

> The canoe was 8 ft long and 3 ft wide. Empty, it weighed 100 lbs.

16e

Punctuate abbreviations according to the conventions of the field for which you are writing.

In technical writing, the periods are omitted from abbreviations unless they could be confused with words of the same spelling: *The cable is 23 ft 8 in. long.* In general writing, you may omit the periods or not, as you choose, as long as the abbreviations are not confusing and are used consistently throughout the document.

The *MLA Handbook,* the style manual for writing about literature, English, and other modern languages, notes the trend to use neither periods nor spaces between letters of an abbreviation, particularly when the abbreviation is composed of capital letters: *MBA, BC, AD, NY, CPA, USA.* An exception is initials of given names, which require both periods and spacing: *E. F. Hutton, J. Ross Brown.* Periods are recommended for abbreviations composed of or ending in lower-case letters: *a.m., i.e., ft., Dept. of Defense.*

As these examples and others located elsewhere in this text illustrate, conventions regarding abbreviations vary widely between fields and sometimes even within fields. The best advice is to familiarize yourself with the conventions of the group for which you are writing by examining style manuals and periodicals in the field; then apply those conventions with consistency and common sense.

16e

ab

EXERCISE 16a-e

Correct any misuse of abbreviations in the following sentences.

1. One of the most fascinating museums in London is the Victoria and Albert Museum on Cromwell Rd. in the borough of Kensington.
2. The Tower of London is the oldest museum in Gr. Brit. and the biggest tourist attraction of all the Lon. buildings.
3. The central keep of the Tower of London was built by Wm. the Conqueror, who chose its location to give a good view of the River Thames.
4. Bloomsbury, an area which contains a great many publishing houses, is also the site of London Univ.
5. Harley St. is known for the offices of many of the country's top private M.D.'s, and Baker St., which is nearby, was the fictional home of Sherlock Holmes and Dr. Watson.
6. London is the scene of many parades, among them the Easter Sun. Parade in Battersea Park and the London Harness Parade on the Mon. after Easter.
7. Winter can also be exciting in London: Xmas carols are sung in Westminster Abbey, and in the P.M. on Dec. 31 crowds gather to celebrate New Yr.'s Eve in Trafalgar Sq.
8. Because of its large no. of hotels and guest houses, London is an easy place to visit.
9. Amer. students traveling to London sometimes stay at the YMCA hotel on Great Russell St.
10. Many students who have studied Engl. Lit. or Engl. history look forward to a trip to London so that they can see the scene of much that they have read about.

17

ACRONYMS, INITIALISMS, AND CLIPPED FORMS

Acronyms, initialisms, and clipped forms are types of abbreviations, shortened forms of words. In general writing, the following guidelines should be applied.

17a

Spell out acronyms initially if your reader is likely to be unfamiliar with them.

An **acronym** is an abbreviation formed from the initial letters of words. The letters of an acronym are pronounced as a single word, and they are written without periods or spaces between letters.

UNICEF	United Nations International Children's Emergency Fund
MADD	Mothers Against Drunk Driving
OSHA	Occupational Safety and Health Administration
NATO	North Atlantic Treaty Organization

17b

Spell out any initialisms that are likely to be unfamiliar to your reader before using them in their abbreviated form.

17b

An **initialism,** like an acronym, is an abbreviation formed from the first letters of words. However, initialisms are pronounced letter by letter rather than as a single word: *SAT* (Scholastic Aptitude Test), *GRE* (Graduate Record Examination), *CRT* (cathode ray tube), *PCBs* (polychlorinated biphenyls).

> The Securities and Exchange Commission (SEC) began its investigation of insider trading on Wall Street. According to knowledgeable sources, the SEC has a water-tight case against several brokers.

Some abbreviations are a cross between initialisms and acronyms; the first letter may be pronounced as a letter and the remainder pronounced as a word: *GMAT* (pronounced *gee*-mat, Graduate Management Admission Test).

17c

Avoid clipped forms in formal writing. Clipped forms are sometimes appropriate in informal writing, if you are striving for a conversational tone and if your audience will understand them.

Clipped forms are words from which the beginning or end has been cut to create a shorter word: *dorm* (dormitory), *lab* (laboratory), *prof* (professor), *phone* (telephone), *vet* (veteran). Clipped forms are fairly common in the jargon of particular fields such as business *(sales rep)*, medicine *(lab tech)*, and so forth. Strictly speaking, they are not abbreviations and so are not followed by periods.

EXERCISE 17a-c

Write a series of sentences in which you use at least six acronyms, initialisms, and clipped forms. Try to use several from each category, and select several that would not be familiar to some of your audience. Be prepared to discuss whether the clipped forms you have chosen are appropriate for your audience, purpose, and tone.

18

SYLLABICATION

When you find that you can write only part of a word at the end of a line and must complete the word on the next line, divide the word between syllables and use a hyphen to indicate the break. Always place the hyphen at the end of the line after the first part of a divided word, not at the beginning of the next line on which you complete the word.

When you are in doubt about the syllabication of a word, consult a good dictionary. Desk dictionaries normally use dots to divide words between syllables. *bank·rupt, col·lec·tive, ma·lig·nant, punc·ture.* Note that not every syllable marks an appropriate point at which to divide a word at the end of a line. (See **18b** and **18c.**) If a word cannot be correctly divided between syllables, move the entire word to the beginning of the next line.

18

syl

18a
Do not divide words pronounced as one syllable.

WRONG	thr-ee, cl-own, yearn-ed, scream-ed
REVISED	three, clown, yearned, screamed

18b
Do not divide a word so that a single letter stands alone on a line.

WRONG	wear-y, e-rupt, a-way, o-val
REVISED	weary, erupt, away, oval

18c
When dividing a compound word that already contains a hyphen, make the break where the hyphen occurs.

AWKWARD	pre-Dar-winian, well-in-formed, Pan-Amer-ican
REVISED	pre-Darwinian, well-informed, Pan-American

EXERCISE 18a-c

Which of the following words may be divided at the end of a line? Indicate appropriate divisions with a hyphen. Refer to your dictionary if you have doubts.

concentration	visualize	worked
adapt	ready	affair
fortunately	recreational	unique

marched	plague	immunity
create	self-realization	elect

REVIEW EXERCISE ON MECHANICS (Sections 15–18)
Correct any errors in the following sentences. Remember to check for faulty syllabication. Assume a general audience.

1. To see Brit. politics in action, tourists in London can watch Parliament from the Stranger Gallery in the House of Commons, where one hundred and fifty-six seats are available for visitors.

2. 1,000 people line up each summer day to get a ticket to the Galleries, either in the House of Commons or in the House of Lords, where proceedings sometimes go on until nine P.M.

3. London provides easy access to several great castles and palaces; 1 of these is Hampton Court, a palace which was begun in 1515 by Cardinal Wolsey.

4. 15 yrs. after Card. Wolsey started building Hampton Ct., Henry VIII took it over, and it served as a royal residence for the next two hundred years.

5. Hampton Court is surrounded by 50 acres of beautifully landscaped grounds where one of its most popular attractions, a maze, is located.

6. Like many attractions in Engl., Hampton Court has restricted hrs. for visitors from Nov. to Feb. when darkness arrives early on the short winter days.

7. After seeing Hampton Court, visitors can go on along the Thames River to Windsor, a town only 21 miles from London; Windsor can be reached in 50 minutes by train or in ¾'s of an hr. by driving.

8. Windsor's main attraction is its nine hundred yr. old castle, now an official residence of the royal family.

9. The castle, which is the largest castle in the world to be still inhabited, is built around 2 courtyards called the Upper and Lower Wards.

10. In the Lr. Ward, Saint Geo.'s Chapel, a fine ex. of late Perpendicular architecture, was begun in 1477, and many kings and queens are buried there.

18c

syl

WRITERS REVISING: MECHANICS

After an interview with the department chairman, a student wrote up his notes to use in an oral report on government funding of university research. Then the instructor asked for a written version of the oral report, so the student had to make some revisions based on the conventions that a general, nontechnical reader would expect. Turn the interview notes into appropriate written form. Then compare your revision with the student's version.

Interview Notes for Oral Report

Dr. Brown said NSF $ is used to
support a lot of research at colleges
and universities around the U.S. Last
year they distributed grants worth
approx. 1.2 billion $. 14 professors,
forty grad students, and 7 technicians
are currently supported in our school
by the National Science Foundation.
Around the univ. NSF money funds
research in the physical sciences
such as chem., physics, and etc.
Prof. Brown said the analytical chemistry
group has received a 2 hundred thousand
$ grant for a lab robotics project, and
grants worth thousands more support
research on cell repro in the bio.
dept. Profs who wish to apply for an
NSF grant must send a grant proposal to
D.C. Over 29,000 50-page proposals
arrive in the Foundation's mail every
yr.

Revision

the National Science Foundation

Dr. Brown said~ NSF ~~$~~ is used to   **17b, 16a(3)**
money
support a lot of research at colleges
and universities around the U.S. Last

year they distributed grants worth
approximately   *& Fourteen*
~~approx~~ $1.2 billion~~$~~. ~~14~~ professors,   **15c, 15e**
graduate   *seven*
for**ty** ~~grad~~ students, and ~~7~~ technicians   **17c, 15a**

are currently supported in our school

18c

syl

by the ~~National Science Foundation~~. *N S F*   17b,

Around the ~~univ.~~ NSF money funds *university*   16c

research in the physical sciences

such as ~~chem.~~, physics, and ~~etc.~~ *Chemistry* *so forth*   16b, 16a(4)

~~Prof.~~ Brown said the analytical chemistry *Professor*   16a(1)

group has received a ~~2 hundred thousand~~ *$ 200,000*   15c

~~$~~grant for a ~~lab~~ robotics project, and *laboratory*   17c

grants worth thousands more support

research on cell ~~repro~~ in the ~~bio.~~ *reproduction biology*   17c, 16c

~~dept.~~ ~~Profs~~ who wish to apply for an *department. Professors* 17c

NSF grant must send a grant proposal to

D.C. Over 29,000 ~~50~~ page proposals *Washington,* *fifty*   16b, 15c

arrive in the Foundation's mail every

~~yr.~~ *year*   16a(3)

PUNCTUATION

p

Punctuation [is a] code that serves to signal structural, semantic, and rhetorical meanings that would otherwise be missed by the reader . . . and from the reader's point of view, punctuation provides a map for one who must otherwise drive blindly past the by-ways, intersections, and detours of a writer's thought.

MINA SHAUGHNESSY, *Errors and Expectations*

When we speak, we use pauses and gestures to emphasize meaning, and we vary the tempo, stress, and pitch of our voices to mark the beginning and end of units of thought. In other words, we "punctuate" our speech. We punctuate writing for the same purposes, drawing on a whole set of conventional devices developed to give the reader clues to what we are trying to communicate.

The first of these devices is **spacing:** that is, closing up or enlarging the space between letters or words. For example, we do not runwordstogetherthisway. Instead, we identify a word as a word by setting it off from its neighbors. Spacing is the most basic of all punctuating devices. We use spacing also to set off paragraphs, to list items as in an outline, to mark lines of poetry, and the like.

But spacing, of course, is not the only punctuation we need. What, for example, can you understand from this string of words:

> yes madam jones was heard to say to the owl like old dowager without a doubt the taming of the shrew by shakespeare would be a most appropriate new years present for your husband.

To make this passage intelligible, we need to add two other kinds of punctuation: (1) changes in the size and design of letters, namely, **capitals** and **italics;** and (2) marks or points, namely, **periods, commas, quotation marks, apostrophes,** and other special signs.

> "Yes, Madam," Jones was heard to say to the owl-like old dowager, "without a doubt, *The Taming of the Shrew* by Shakespeare would be a most appropriate New Year's present for your husband."

The example shows four functions of punctuation:

1. End punctuation. Capitals, periods, question marks, and exclamation points indicate sentence beginnings and endings.

2. Internal punctuation. Commas, semicolons, colons, dashes, and parentheses within sentences show the relationship of each word or group of words to the rest of the sentence.

3. Direct-quotation punctuation. Quotation marks and brackets indicate speakers and changes of speaker.

4. Word punctuation. Capitals, italics, quotation marks, apostrophes, and hyphens indicate words that have a special character or use.

In questions of punctuation there is often no absolute standard, no authoritative convention to which you can turn for a "correct" answer. But two general rules serve as reliable guides:

19

p

1. Punctuation is a part of meaning, not a substitute for clear and orderly sentence structure. Before you can punctuate a sentence properly, you must construct it properly. No number of commas, semicolons, and dashes can rescue a poorly written sentence.

2. Observe conventional practice in punctuation. Though many of the rules are not hard and fast, still there is a community of agreement about punctuating sentences. Learning and applying the punctuation rules that follow will help you observe these conventions.

19

END PUNCTUATION

Periods, question marks, and exclamation points signal the end of a sentence. Use a *period* after plain statements or commands; use a *question mark* after questions; use an *exclamation point* after strongly emotional expressions.

Ordinarily, the character of the sentence dictates the proper end punctuation; for instance, a clearly interrogative sentence calls for a question mark. Occasionally, however, your readers will not be able to tell from content alone what you intend the meaning of a sentence to be. In such cases, end punctuation is vital to meaning. For example, notice the different intentions of the three sentences below and how the end punctuation contributes to meaning:

> He struck out with the bases loaded.
> He struck out with the bases loaded?
> He struck out with the bases loaded!

THE PERIOD

19a

Use a period to signal the end of a statement, a mild command, or an indirect question.

STATEMENT	She swam the mile with easy strokes.
COMMAND	Swim with easy strokes.
INDIRECT QUESTION	I asked her where she learned to swim with such easy strokes.

19b

Use a period after an abbreviation.

Dr.   Mr.   Mrs.   Ms.   R.N.   C.P.A.   Sen.   B.A.

Omit the period after abbreviations that serve as names of organizations or government agencies (NABISCO, PTA, NFL, UNICEF, CIA, DOD). If you are in doubt about whether to use periods in an abbreviation, consult a good dictionary for the standard practice.

THE QUESTION MARK

19c
Use a question mark after a direct question.

Direct questions often begin with an interrogative pronoun or adverb (*who, when, what,* etc.), and usually have an inverted word order, with the verb before the subject.

> When did you study chemistry?
> Do you ever wonder what your future will be?
> You want to make a good impression, don't you?

19c

end p

19d
Use a question mark inside parentheses (?) to indicate doubt or uncertainty about the correctness of a statement.

The device shows that, even after research, you could not establish the accuracy of a fact. It does not serve as a substitute for checking facts.

> John Pomfret, an English poet, was born in 1667 (?) and died in 1702.

Rather than using (?), you may simply use *about:*

> John Pomfret, an English poet, was born about 1667 and died in 1702.

Do not use a question mark as a form of sarcasm:

> It was an amusing (?) play.

19e
Do not use a question mark after an indirect question.

An **indirect question** is a statement implying a question but not actually asking one. Though the idea expressed is interrogative, the actual phrasing is not.

> They asked me whether I had studied chemistry in high school.
> He asked me whether I wished to make a good impression.
> I wonder what my future will be.

A polite request phrased as a direct question may sometimes be followed by a period rather than a question mark, especially when the intent is more like that of a mild command than an actual question.

> Here is my draft of the committee's report. *When you have finished adding your comments, would you please return it to me.*

However, if you do not use a question mark, you run some risk of your reader's failing to realize that a request has been made. The safest practice is to use the question mark with such requests, particularly if you want a direct response on the reader's part.

> With our presentation only a week away, we don't have much preparation time left. *May I have your graphs by Thursday morning, so that Audio-Visual can make the slides?*

THE EXCLAMATION POINT

19f

Use the exclamation point after an interjection or after a statement that is genuinely emphatic or exclamatory.

> Fire! Help! Oh, no!
> Mom! Dad! Guess what! I've been accepted to law school!
> The rocket's engines have ignited, and we have liftoff!

19g

Do not overuse the exclamation point.

Used sparingly, the exclamation point gives real emphasis to individual statements. Overused, it either deadens the emphasis or introduces an almost hysterical tone in your writing.

> War is hell! Think of what it does to young people to have their futures interrupted and sometimes cut off completely! Think of what it does to their families! Think of what it does to the nation!

EXERCISE 19a–g

Supply the appropriate punctuation marks in the following sentences. If you feel that a choice of marks is possible, state why you chose the one you did. After completing the sentences, go back and revise the indirect questions to make them direct questions and punctuate them accordingly.

1. Do you know how many immigrants entered the United States through the processing station at Ellis Island
2. In the years before World War I, about 33 million European immigrants came to the United States
3. Many of these immigrants came to the United States for economic

reasons, while others were drawn to the democratic society of the United States

4. Many of those immigrants, such as Dr Albert Sabin, the developer of oral polio vaccine, went on to achieve great fame in America

5. Hannah Holborn Gray, the first woman to serve as president of the University of Chicago, came to the United States from Germany when she was three years old and entered college at age fifteen to start work on her BA

6. Wow That's quite an accomplishment for someone who came to America not knowing how to speak English

7. I asked my history teacher where the greatest numbers of immigrants came from

8. Between 1880 and 1919, the largest group came from Italy, but did you know that the second largest group came from Austria-Hungary

9. If you can, you should arrange to visit Ellis Island

10. The National Park Service, which oversees both Ellis Island and the Statue of Liberty, is asking citizens to contribute photographs of and travel documents belonging to their immigrant ancestors for a museum to be built on the island

20-24

int p

20–24
INTERNAL PUNCTUATION

End punctuation indicates whether a whole sentence should be read as a question, a statement, or an expression of emotion. Internal punctuation indicates the relationships and relative importance of elements within the sentence. Five punctuation marks are used for this purpose: commas, semicolons, colons, dashes, and parentheses.

The most important uses of these marks, like those of end punctuation, occur frequently. And like all uses of punctuation, they are a vital way of making the meaning of your sentences clear. In studying the following rules, notice not only how each mark is used but also how it contributes to the total meaning of the sentence.

20
THE COMMA

20a
Use a comma to separate main clauses joined by a coordinating conjunction.

The coordinating conjunctions are *and, but, or, nor, for, so,* and *yet.* When any one of these conjunctions is used to connect main clauses, it is always preceded by a comma. The comma acts as a signal that one independent clause has ended and the next is about to begin.

> Half a million colonists remained loyal to the British Crown during the American Revolution, *and* for their loyalty many of them lost their homes, property, and livelihoods.

> History books used to portray Loyalists as conniving aristocrats with British connections, *but* research has revealed that most were ordinary hard-working farmers and tradespeople.

> Rebel patriots physically abused some Loyalists, *or* more often they verbally abused those who would not shift their allegiance.

> Loyalists were conservatives who did not want change, *nor* did they want separation of the colonies from England.

> About 36,000 Loyalists eventually emigrated to Nova Scotia in Canada, *for* this territory was ruled by the British Crown.

> Approximately 500,000 of the 2.5 million people in colonial America were Loyalists, *so* one in every five Americans could be classified as Loyalist.

> Nearly 100,000 Loyalist Americans fled the colonies in what was the largest exodus in American history, *yet* their suffering has been largely unrecognized.

20a

int p

There are, however, two exceptions.

1. Some writers omit the comma before the coordinating conjunction when one or both of the main clauses are very short: *The spirit is willing but the flesh is weak. Get your coat and let's go.* There is certainly nothing wrong with using a comma in such sentences, and since the comma is sometimes necessary for clarity, it's a good idea simply to establish the habit of using a comma regularly.

2. When one or both of the main clauses joined by a coordinating conjunction are long or internally punctuated, use a semicolon before the coordinating conjunction.

> The Canadian Mounted Police were established in the 1870's to assure peaceful settlement of the northwest wilderness; and they became symbols of political and social order.

> The Mounties, dressed in red tunics and riding well-trained horses, were a familiar sight on the Canadian frontier; but few people in the United States saw Mounties except in the movies.

EXERCISE 20a

Combine the following sentences by using a coordinating conjunction and a comma. If one or both of the main clauses are long or internally punctuated, use a semicolon before the coordinating conjunction. If you have a choice of conjunctions, be prepared to explain your selection.

1. One of the greatest triumphs of medical science was the development of a smallpox vaccine. It was discovered 200 years ago by a rural doctor who knew nothing of the body's immune system.
2. Edward Jenner was an English country physician who had studied in London. In 1773 he settled in Gloucestershire.
3. Jenner's patients often suffered from the mild infection known as cowpox. Some patients contracted the much worse disease, smallpox.
4. The doctor noticed that patients who had contracted cowpox seemed protected from smallpox. He surmised that a person who had had cowpox would be immune to smallpox.
5. Jenner decided to infect people with cowpox. They would then be protected from smallpox.
6. Jenner's method of vaccination was successful. Today the once dreaded smallpox has been virtually eliminated as a disease.

20b

int p

Using coordinating conjunctions preceded by commas, combine at least eight of the sentences in the following paragraph. Use a semicolon before the coordinating conjunction if main clauses are long or internally punctuated.

Doctors in Jenner's time did not know the function of the body's immune system. They did not understand the scientific principles that made vaccination effective. Today, vaccines are available for yellow fever, diphtheria, whooping cough, tetanus, polio, and mumps. Scientists are conducting research on the body's immune system in an effort to develop vaccines against other diseases. Researchers are particularly interested in how the cells of the immune system work. These cells transmit information to and from other cells. There may be a link between the immune system and the mind. Modern immunology is a highly technical field. It had its beginning in a country doctor's simple observation.

20b

Use a comma to separate introductory phrases and clauses from a main clause.

Introductory prepositional or verbal phrases and introductory clauses may be adverbial, modifying the verb in the main clause or the whole main clause; or they may serve as adjectives, modifying the subject of the main clause. Whatever their function, they should always be separated from the main clause by a comma unless they are very short and there is no possibility of misreading.

INTRODUCTORY PREPOSITIONAL PHRASES
According to legend, Hercules had enormous strength. [Adverbial]
After his long exile to France, Charles II returned to England in 1660. [Adverbial]

Like any man of sense and good feeling, I abominate work. [Adjectival]

ALDOUS HUXLEY

INTRODUCTORY VERBAL PHRASES

To succeed as a long-distance runner, a person must have strong legs. [Adverbial]

Announcing a recess, the judge retired to his chambers. [Adjectival]

Exhausted by her effort, the swimmer fell back into the pool. [Adverbial]

To be quite honest about it, that dog has been known to climb trees. [Adverbial]

INTRODUCTORY CLAUSES

As soon as she had finished studying, she left the library. [Adverbial]

If your job is to write every day, you learn to do it like every other job. [Adverbial]

WILLIAM ZINSSER

Whenever I hear anyone arguing for slavery, I feel a strong impulse to see it tried on him personally. [Adverbial]

ABRAHAM LINCOLN

20b

int p

Do not confuse verbal modifiers with verbals used as subjects.

VERBAL MODIFIER	*Having been an arbitrator between labor and management for a decade,* he felt confident in tackling one more labor dispute.
VERBAL AS SUBJECT	*Having been an arbitrator between labor and management for a decade* made him feel confident in tackling one more labor dispute.

The comma is frequently omitted after very short introductory clauses or phrases. However, even when the introductory clause or phrase is very short, a comma is necessary if its omission can cause misreading.

CLEAR	When they arrived she was taking the cat out of the piano.
	After my defeat I retired from public life.
CONFUSING	When he returned home was not what it used to be.
CLEAR	When he returned, home was not what it used to be.
CONFUSING	After dark fireflies came in large numbers.
CLEAR	After dark, fireflies came in large numbers.

20c

int p

EXERCISE 20b

In the following sentences, insert commas wherever they are needed after introductory elements. Then write five sentences of your own containing correctly punctuated introductory elements.

1. Because much land in North America is being converted to pavement and suburbia wild bird populations may be lost unless people make an effort to protect land for birds.
2. By identifying obstacles that limit bird growth people can improve and protect land for birds.
3. To improve wild bird habitats home owners can provide plants which create food, cover, and nesting sites for birds.
4. After being provided with proper plant cover birds may also need additional devices which humans can supply.
5. According to environmental experts these devices might include nest boxes, watering containers, and wooden platforms.
6. In order to determine how to improve your lawn for birds first make a study of which birds come to your property.
7. Having listed the species and numbers of birds you can begin to determine how to attract even more.
8. Even if you provide the proper plants and water birds may also need suitable nesting areas.
9. Although nesting boxes are easy to make it is important to make them from the proper materials and to design the structures to become part of the natural habitat.
10. In winter storms may destroy flimsy cardboard boxes used as nests.

20c

Use commas to set off nonrestrictive elements. Do not set off restrictive elements.

A **restrictive element**—which may be a clause, a phrase, or a word—is an essential modifier. It defines, limits, or identifies the meaning of whatever it modifies. If it is removed from the sentence, the meaning is changed in some basic way. A **nonrestrictive element** may be interesting, but it is incidental to the basic meaning of the sentence. An illustration will help to clarify the difference.

RESTRICTIVE   A person *who is honest* will succeed.
NONRESTRICTIVE   Jacob North, who is honest, will succeed.

In the first sentence the clause *who is honest* identifies the kind of person who will succeed; it restricts the subject of *will succeed* to people *who are honest* as opposed to people *who are not honest*. In other words, the clause is restrictive. It is thus *not* set off with commas. In the second sentence, however, the proper noun *Jacob North* identifies or designates the particular person who *will succeed*; the fact that Jacob North *is honest* is merely amplifying information about a person already sufficiently identified. The clause is nonrestrictive. It *is* set off with commas.

In the illustration just discussed, the meaning is such that there is no question that the clause *who is honest* is restrictive in one sentence and not restrictive in the other. Sometimes, however, a modifying element can be interpreted as either restrictive or nonrestrictive—depending on the particular meaning you intend. In such instances you must decide what you mean. Setting off the modifier or not setting it off is your only way of making your meaning clear to your reader.

> The house, built by my grandfather, faced the mountain. [The phrase *built by my grandfather* is nonrestrictive and is thus set off by commas.]
>
> The house built by my grandfather faced the mountain, and the house built by my father stood only a hundred yards away. [In this compound sentence, the two phrases beginning with *built* limit and define the particular houses, distinguishing them from each other.]
>
> Texans, who have oil wells, can afford high prices. [That is, all Texans have oil wells and can afford high prices.]
>
> Texans who have oil wells can afford high prices. [That is, some Texans have oil wells; only they can afford high prices.]

20c

int p

Always use *two* commas to set off a nonrestrictive element unless it begins or ends the sentence.

> **NOT** The gate, unlocked and wide-open swung on its hinges.
>
> **BUT** The gate, unlocked and wide-open, swung on its hinges.
>
> Unlocked and wide-open, the gate swung on its hinges.

1. Set off nonrestrictive clauses and phrases with commas. Do not set off restrictive clauses and phrases.

NONRESTRICTIVE CLAUSE	Wide porches, *which sometimes run along three sides of the house,* are called verandas.
RESTRICTIVE CLAUSE	Houses *that were built in warm climates* often featured verandas.
NONRESTRICTIVE CLAUSE	Charleston, South Carolina, *where my grandmother lived,* has many old homes with lovely verandas.
RESTRICTIVE CLAUSE	The town *where I grew up* had few porches and no verandas.
NONRESTRICTIVE PHRASE	Grandmother's veranda, *with its enormous length,* was a wonderful place to play. [Prepositional]
RESTRICTIVE PHRASE	The part *with the most appeal* was filled with wicker furniture. [Prepositional]
NONRESTRICTIVE PHRASE	We children, *draping blankets across the furniture,* made tunnels and tents. [Participial]

RESTRICTIVE PHRASE   Anyone *wanting to sit on a chair* had to dismantle childish hide-outs. [Participial]

2. Set off nonrestrictive appositives with commas. Do not set off restrictive appositives. An **appositive** is a noun or a group of words used as a noun that describes or renames another noun, ordinarily the noun that comes immediately before it. Like clauses and phrases, appositives may be either restrictive or nonrestrictive, though appositives of more than one or two words are usually nonrestrictive and therefore set off by commas.

20c

int p

NONRESTRICTIVE APPOSITIVES

Davy Crockett, *the most famous man at the Alamo,* was a former Indian fighter.

No treatment, *not even hypnosis or acupuncture,* helped them stop smoking.

The whale, *a cold-water-dwelling mammal,* is protected by a thick layer of blubber.

"Hello, Mitty. We're having the devil's own time with McMillan, *the millionaire banker and close personal friend of Roosevelt."*

JAMES THURBER

Restrictive appositives limit, define, or designate the noun that they follow in such a way that their absence from the sentence would change its essential meaning. They are often, though by no means always, proper names following a more general noun or identifying phrase.

RESTRICTIVE APPOSITIVES

Robert Frost's poem *"Stopping by Woods on a Snowy Evening"* is one of his best-known poems.

The poet *Bryant* was a leader in New York literary circles.

Do you mean Napoli *the grocer* or Napoli *the doctor*?

The slang term *shrink* is often applied to psychiatrists.

Removing the restrictive appositives from these sentences would create nonsense: *Robert Frost's poem is one of his best-known poems* and *Do you mean Napoli or Napoli?*

EXERCISE 20c

Insert commas in the following sentences to set off nonrestrictive elements. Indicate which sentences are correct as written. Then write five sentences of your own—correctly punctuated—by creating three sentences with nonrestrictive elements and two sentences with restrictive elements.

1. E. B. White who was perhaps most famous as an editor of *The New Yorker* also wrote three well-known children's books.

2. His book *Charlotte's Web* has become a classic in children's literature.
3. Wilbur the runt pig in *Charlotte's Web* is saved from slaughter by Charlotte a spider who lives in a corner of the barn.
4. Charlotte with seemingly miraculous powers keeps Wilbur from becoming the farmer's breakfast bacon.
5. Anyone who likes fantasy will also like White's novel *Stuart Little*.
6. *Stuart Little* is the story of a New York couple whose child is a mouse.
7. The mouse named Stuart by his parents the Littles eventually sets out on a quest for a bird that he has fallen in love with.
8. White's third book is *The Trumpet of the Swan* the story of a trumpeter swan who has no voice.
9. The swan understandably upset at not being able to make noise overcomes his handicap by learning to play the trumpet.
10. E. B. White's children's books beloved for their imagination and humor are favorites with both children and adults.

20d

20d

int p

Use a comma to set off adverbial phrases and clauses following the main clause and explaining, amplifying, or offering a contrast to it. Do not set off such clauses if they are closely related to the main clause.

Adverbial phrases and clauses very often *restrict* the meaning of main clauses that follow and are therefore essential to the meaning of the main clause. Restrictive adverbial clauses should not be set off by a comma when they follow the main clause. When adverbial clauses merely introduce additional *nonrestrictive* information, however, a comma is used to indicate that they are not essential to the meaning.

Consider the logic of your sentence and the meaning you intend when deciding whether to set off adverbial clauses and phrases. Note the following:

> We won't miss the beginning of the movie if we hurry.
>
> We haven't missed the beginning of the movie, even though we're late.

The first of the examples sets up *if we hurry* as the condition for not missing the beginning of the movie. In the second, the main clause makes an unqualified statement of fact; the *even though* clause adds some information but does not change the meaning of the clause.

> Mrs. Jones must have decided not to go outdoors today because the snow hasn't been shoveled from the walk.
>
> Mrs. Jones must have decided not to go outdoors today, because the snow hasn't been shoveled from the walk.

The first of the foregoing examples states that the unshoveled walk is the reason Mrs. Jones has not gone outdoors. The unshoveled walk is an essential condition for keeping her indoors, as indicated by the lack of a comma before the *because* clause. In the second example, the comma before *because* tells us that the writer intends the clause to be nonrestrictive and the information to be understood as nonessential to the basic meaning of the sentence. The *because* clause merely provides evidence for the fact that Mrs. Jones has not gone outside.

Note that in some constructions a comma or the lack of one determines whether the reader will understand a phrase or a clause as a modifier of a final noun in the main clause or as an adverbial modifier.

> He has visited all the small towns in Pennsylvania.
>
> He has visited *all* the small towns, in Pennsylvania, in Ohio, in almost every state of the union.

20e

int p

In the first of these examples, *in Pennsylvania* restricts the location of the small towns and is an adjectival modifier of *towns*. In the second, however, the *in* phrase is additional information amplifying the assertion of the main clause but not essential to it.

EXERCISE 20d
Insert commas in the following sentences wherever they are needed to set off adverbial clauses or phrases. Indicate which sentences are correct as written. Then write five sentences of your own containing adverbial clauses or phrases that require punctuation.

1. Airline pilots practice dealing with emergencies in flight simulators although they hope they will never encounter the real situation.
2. Pilots may not know how to fly through wind shears unless they have encountered that condition in a simulator.
3. Pilots are better equipped to handle emergencies in flight if they have practiced those situations in a simulator.
4. Flight simulators are expensive but save airlines money because flying a real airplane costs up to ten times as much as using a simulator.
5. Pilots return for annual or semiannual checks in flight simulators even though they may have been flying for years.

20e

Use commas to set off all absolute phrases.

Absolute phrases consist of a noun or a pronoun followed by a present or past participle: *the sun shining brightly*. They modify the entire main clause in which they stand rather than any particular word or words in that clause. They are always nonrestrictive, supplying amplifying or explanatory detail rather than essential information. Thus they should always be set off by commas whether they appear at the beginning or end of a sentence or within it.

He was stretched out on his reclining chair in the full sun, *his eyes covered, his head thrown back, his arms spread wide.*

Other things being equal, short familiar words are better than long unfamiliar words.

They were waiting for us, *their figures defined by the light from the half-open door.*

The mastiff, *teeth bared, ears standing erect, body tensed,* refused to give ground.

EXERCISE 20e

Insert commas in the following sentences to set off absolute phrases. Then write five sentences of your own that contain absolute phrases.

1. Their white sandy beaches protected by barrier reefs the Grand Cayman Islands are a paradise for divers.
2. The Grand Caymans group its three small islands spread out in the middle of the Caribbean is still fairly unspoiled by overdevelopment.
3. The seas around the Grand Caymans are clear and silt-free the rainfall not running off but soaking into the limestone base of the islands.
4. The islands are perfect for both experienced and inexperienced divers the diving operators offering short courses, snorkeling trips, and week-long advanced courses.
5. All their attractions being taken into consideration the Grand Cayman Islands offer everything a diver could want.

20f

int p

20f

Use commas to set off elements that slightly interrupt the structure of a sentence.

Words, phrases, and clauses that slightly interrupt the structure of a sentence are often called **parenthetical elements.** Although such elements may add to the meaning of the sentence or relate the sentence to a preceding sentence or idea, they are not essential to grammatical structure. Such elements include words of direct address, mild interjections, the words *yes* and *no,* transitional words and expressions, and phrases expressing contrast.

DIRECT ADDRESS   Can you show me, *Kathy,* how to punctuate this sentence?

Will you speak a little louder, *George?*

MILD INTERJECTIONS   *Well,* no one can do more than his best.

Oh, I hate stewed prunes.

TRANSITIONAL WORDS AND PHRASES   Sales taxes, *moreover,* hurt poor people severely.

Quakers, *on the other hand,* are opposed to military service.

TRANSITIONAL WORDS AND PHRASES	The judge ruled, *nevertheless,* that damages must be paid.
	The result, *in short,* was a complete breakdown of discipline.
CONTRASTED ELEMENTS	He had intended to write 1868, *not 1968.*
	Tractors, *unlike horses,* require gasoline.
	Insecticides and garden sprays now available are effective, *yet safe.*

Note that other elements of a sentence will interrupt its structure and require commas when they are inserted out of their normal grammatical order. Compare the following:

20f

int p

My grandmother always told me that work never killed anyone.
Work, *my grandmother always told me,* never killed anyone.

The exhausted and thirsty construction workers welcomed the cold beer.
The construction workers, *exhausted and thirsty,* welcomed the cold beer.

Always use two commas to set off a parenthetical element unless it begins or ends a sentence.

NOT	She noticed, however that tact worked wonders.
NOT	She noticed however, that tact worked wonders.
BUT	She noticed, however, that tact worked wonders.
	She noticed that tact worked wonders, however.

EXERCISE 20f
Insert commas in the following sentences to set off parenthetical elements. Then write five sentences of your own that contain parenthetical elements requiring commas.

1. Richard have you tried any of the tropical fruits now commonly available in supermarkets?
2. Mangoes and papayas to name two are both exotic and nutritious fruits.
3. The mango according to nutritionists is very high in vitamins A and C.
4. Mangoes a friend from India tells me are eaten there to help offset the effects of the intense tropical heat.
5. Be careful however when you peel a mango, for the skin contains a poison sap which gives some people a rash.

6. The papaya skin like that of the mango can also cause an allergic reaction.
7. Papayas nevertheless are flavorful and nutritious fruits produced mainly in Florida.
8. The yellow or yellow-green fruit of the papaya is rich in vitamins A and C yet low in calories.
9. Many people unfortunately pass up the delicious taste of these nutritious fruits because they're unfamiliar with them.
10. Well they should try a mango or a papaya the next time they see them in the supermarket.

20g
Use commas to separate the items in a series.

A series consists of three or more words, phrases, or clauses of equal grammatical rank. The items of such a series are said to be *coordinate:* they have approximately equal importance. Typical series take the form *a, b,* and *c,* or the form *a, b,* or *c.*

20g

int p

> She talked *fluently, wittily,* and *penetratingly.* [Three adverbs]
>
> The triathlon is an athletic event involving *swimming, running,* and *cycling.* [Three nouns]
>
> Only a generation ago, the Navaho were *horsemen, nomads, keepers of flocks, painters in sand, weavers of wool, artists in silver,* and *singers of the yei-bie-chai.* [Seven nouns, some modified by prepositional phrases]
>
> EDWARD ABBEY
>
> *Her sails ripped, her engines dead,* and *her rudder broken,* the vessel drifted helplessly. [Three absolute phrases]
>
> The city couldn't *issue birth certificates on time, pay overtime when it was due, maintain its automotive fleets, deliver asphalt to men filling potholes, submit claims for federal and state aid payments, supply diaper pins to obstetric wards,* or *hire key staff.* [Seven predicates, each consisting of a verb and its object]
>
> CHARLES R. MORRIS
>
> After the accident, the driver of the car had no idea of *who he was, where he came from,* or *how the accident happened.* [Three dependent clauses]
>
> And that's the news from Lake Wobegon, *where all the women are strong, all the men are good-looking, and all the children are above average.* [Three dependent clauses introduced by a single conjunction]
>
> GARRISON KEILLOR

Some writers treat three or more short, closely related independent clauses not joined by coordinate conjunctions as a series, separating them by commas rather than semicolons.

> Some of the people said the elephant had gone in one direction, some said he had gone in another, some professed not even to have heard of any elephant.
>
> GEORGE ORWELL

Less experienced writers will be safer using semicolons in such a series.

Some writers omit the comma before *and* in simple *a, b,* and *c* series: violins, flutes and cellos; men, women and children. But since the comma is sometimes vital for clarity, it is preferable to establish the habit of always including it. Note how necessary the final comma is in the following:

20h

int p

> Our resort is equipped with comfortable cabins, a large lake with boating facilities, and a nine-hole golf course.
>
> I am interested in a modern, furnished apartment with two bedrooms, kitchenette, living room, bathroom with shower, and garage.

Without the comma after *facilities,* the first sentence seems to suggest that the resort has a lake with a golf course in it. Without the comma after *shower* in the second sentence, the writer seems to be asking for an apartment with a garage in the bathroom.

20h

Use commas to separate coordinate adjectives in a series; do not use commas to separate adjectives that are cumulative rather than coordinate.

Adjectives in a series are *coordinate* if each adjective modifies the noun separately. They are *cumulative,* not coordinate, if any adjective in the series modifies the total concept that follows it.

COORDINATE The British colony of Hong Kong grew up around a *beautiful, sheltered, acccessible* port.

CUMULATIVE Hong Kong is the *third-largest international financial* center in the world.

In the first sentence, each adjective is more or less independent of the other two; the three adjectives could be rearranged without seriously affecting the meaning of the sentence: *accessible, beautiful, sheltered* port; *sheltered, accessible, beautiful* port. Moreover, the conjunction *and* could be inserted in place of the commas and the basic meaning would remain—*beautiful,* and *sheltered* and *accessible* port.

But in the second sentence the adjectives are cumulative and interdependent. Their order may not be changed, nor may *and* be substituted, without making nonsense of the original meaning—*financial third-largest international* center; *third-largest* and *international* and *financial* center. The adjectives in the second sentence constitute, in effect, a *restrictive* phrase, as distinct from the *nonrestrictive* quality of the adjectives in the first sentence, and therefore are not separated from one another by commas.

In actual usage, punctuation of coordinate adjectives varies a great deal. Though few writers would punctuate the sentences above differently from the way we have punctuated them, many writers would be unable to choose between the punctuation of the following sentences:

The *powerful new water-cooled* engine is very fuel-efficient.
The *powerful, new, water-cooled* engine is very fuel-efficient.

It can be argued that the meaning of the two sentences is slightly different: that the first sentence suggests a more unified concept intensified by the cumulative presentation of the adjectives. The point is that the lack of commas, or their inclusion, signals the writer's intentions and tells the reader how a series of adjectives is to be understood.

The same principles governing punctuation for adjectives in a series apply when only two modifiers precede the word being modified. If the two modifiers are coordinate but not joined by a conjunction, use a comma between them. If they are not coordinate, do not use a comma.

20h

int p

Huge, lumbering freighters share Hong Kong's *busy deepwater* port with *ancient Chinese* junks.

EXERCISE 20g–h
In the following sentences, supply commas where they are needed to separate sentence elements in a series. Indicate any sentences which are correct as written. Then write five sentences of your own containing correctly punctuated elements in a series.

1. Franklin Court in Philadelphia is part of a complex of buildings once owned by the multitalented energetic and witty Benjamin Franklin.
2. A replica of an eighteenth-century printing office a museum and various exhibits are available for the modern visitor to Franklin Court.
3. Benjamin Franklin started his own printing business at age twenty-two rose rapidly in Colonial politics and became famous in both America and Europe.
4. Franklin's shrewd inquiring mind led him to invent the lightning rod bifocal glasses and the Franklin stove.
5. Helping to draft the Declaration of Independence persuading the French to aid the Colonists in the War of Revolution and founding the country's first medical center in Philadelphia in 1751 were just a few of Franklin's accomplishments.

6. The witty useful advice Franklin gave to his readers in *Poor Richard's Almanac* helped sell 10,000 copies a year.

In the following paragraph, supply commas where they are needed to separate sentence elements in a series. Indicate any sentences that are correct as written.

Franklin seemed to have unlimited time energy and curiosity. When he had free moments, he studied the weather predicted storms tried to map the Gulf Stream and wrote an essay about the common cold. Although we may picture Benjamin Franklin as a witty old man who stood on a hill with a kite and a key, he was much more than that. Actually, the practical generous Franklin was a problem-solver who improved the everyday lives of people who conducted sensitive diplomatic missions and who played a crucial role in his country's fight for independence.

20i

int p

20i

Follow established conventions for the use of commas in dates, addresses, geographical names, titles, and long numbers.

1. Dates. If a date is written as month-date-year, use a comma between the date and the year. If such a date stands within a sentence, use a comma after the year.

The German surrender ended World War II in Europe on May 7, 1945.
World War II began on September 1, 1939, when Germany invaded Poland.

If only the month and year are given, do not use a comma between them or after the year.

The war in the Pacific ended in August 1945.
The war in the Pacific ended in August 1945 after Japan surrendered.

If a date is written as day-month-year, use no commas.

17 July 1931   6 August 1982

2. Addresses. Standard comma punctuation of addresses is as follows:

205 Hayes Street, San Francisco, California 94102
39 West 12th Street, Olean, NY 71402

If geographical names or addresses appear within a sentence, use a comma after each element—street, city, state (county or province), country—and use a comma after the final item. Note that no comma is used before the zip code.

ADDRESSES	She gave 39 West 12th Street, Olean, New York 71402, as her forwarding address.
GEOGRAPHICAL NAMES	He spent a month at Bremen, Germany, and the rest of his time in Tunbridge Wells, Kent, a small village in England.

3. Titles. Use commas to separate names from titles when the title follows the name. If the name followed by a title occurs within a sentence, use a comma after the title as well as between the name and the title.

Katherine Dugald, M.D.   William Harrington, Sr.

The university recently announced the appointment of Katherine Dugald, M.D., to the faculty of the medical school.

20j

int p

4. Large numbers. Use commas in large numbers to indicate thousands, but do not use commas in social security numbers, telephone numbers, zip codes, and the like. These latter should be written as stated.

1,249	Social security number 391-07-4855
89,129	Telephone number 515-236-7669
1,722,843	Jamaica Plain, MA 02130

20j
Use a comma to prevent misreading.

Sometimes in a sentence two words fall together so that they may be read two ways. In such instances, a comma may be necessary to prevent misreading even though no standard punctuation rule applies.

Long before, she had left everything to her brother.
Pilots who like to see sunbathers, fly low over apartment houses.
Inside the house, cats are sometimes a nuisance.

The omission of a comma after *before* in the first sentence would be momentarily confusing; we get off to a false start by reading *Long before she had left* without interruption. If there were no comma in the second sentence, we might think we were reading about flying sunbathers. A similar difficulty arises in the third sentence if *house* is not separated from *cats*. Often it is best to rewrite such sentences to avoid confusion.

The following sentences present similar problems:

To John, Smith was a puzzle. [Without the comma, the reader will take the introductory phrase to be *To John Smith*.]

People who can, take vacations in the summer. [Without the comma, the reader is likely to assume that the verb is *can take*.]

For the misuse of the comma, see Section **24**. For the use of commas in quoted material, see Section **25d–f**.

20j

int p

EXERCISE 20i–j

In the following sentences, insert commas where conventional usage requires them or where they are needed to prevent misreading.

1. Mont Blanc, the highest and perhaps the most famous mountain in Europe, is located near Chamonix France and soars 15771 feet above the village.
2. The first person to reach the summit of Mont Blanc was Michel Gabriel Pacard M.D. a doctor from Chamonix.
3. Human beings first reached the top of the mountain on August 9 1786 when Pacard and his guide, Jacques Balmat, set foot on the summit.
4. Approximately 2000 people attempt to climb Mont Blanc every year, although only about 300 of them achieve their goal.
5. In winter storms make it extremely treacherous to attempt the climb up Mont Blanc's glaciers and snow fields.
6. In June 1786 when Balmat and Pacard reached the top of Mont Blanc, a German explorer, Baron Adolf Traugott von Gersdorf, watched them through a telescope in order to verify their achievement.
7. Mount Everest, the world's tallest mountain at 29028 feet, was conquered on May 29 1953 by Sir Edmund Hillary and Tenzing Norgay, plus ten other climbers, thirty Sherpa porters, and several hundred team members.
8. Years before Pacard and Balmat had climbed Mont Blanc using only walking sticks and heavy boots.
9. Mount Everest is, of course, over 13000 feet higher than Mont Blanc and is much less accessible, for climbers must first get to Lhasa Tibet in order to start their climb.
10. Because Mont Blanc is more accessible than Mount Everest, many more people attempt to reach its summit; these attempts have resulted in as many as 8000 deaths since the peak was first climbed.

REVIEW EXERCISES ON COMMA USAGE (Section 20)

PART A

Insert commas where they are needed in the following sentences.

1. After over 100 years a great deal of mystery remains concerning General George Armstrong Custer's defeat on June 25 1876 at the Battle of the Little Bighorn in Montana.

2. The Battle of the Little Bighorn which took place during an Army effort to force the Northern Plains Indians back onto their Dakota reservation became one of the most famous military defeats in history.

3. Custer had approximately 225 men but the combined force of the Indians he attacked has been estimated to range from 2500 to 20000.

4. Having graduated from West Point Custer had served with distinction in the Civil War and was considered a brilliant daring cavalry officer.

5. Because no Army personnel survived the attack historians will never know therefore why Custer went into battle against a force that far outnumbered his own.

6. The Battle of the Little Bighorn Custer himself and his decision to attack the Indians remain controversial for some people think of the general as a hero.

7. Others however blame Custer for leading his men into certain death.

8. The Plains Indians won the battle at the Little Bighorn although this victory led to their eventual defeat.

9. Americans having been shocked and outraged by the deaths of Custer and his men the Army mounted a massive campaign against the Indians.

10. The Army continued its pursuit and the Indians were finally defeated at Wounded Knee South Dakota in 1890.

20j

int p

PART B
In the following paragraph, insert any necessary commas.

The twentieth century has produced many fine composers of serious music but perhaps the most distinguished of modern American composers is Aaron Copland. Copland who was born on November 14 1900 in Brooklyn New York has written music which uses American traditions landscapes and folk materials for its basis. Copland's ballets for example draw upon traditional American hymns and folk songs. *Appalachian Spring* which is one of Copland's best-known works is a ballet set in the Pennsylvania frontier of the nineteenth century. The music of *Appalachian Spring* as well that of the ballets *Rodeo* and *Billy the Kid* evokes the wide-open unspoiled land of an earlier America. Copland drew upon other American materials for his *Lincoln Portrait* a composition for narrator and orchestra and his 1942 composition *Fanfare for the Common Man* can be viewed as a symbol of his belief in the democratic principles of America. Although he is best known for his compositions drawn from distinctly American sources Copland who studied music in both New York and Paris also composed more abstract music for piano and orchestra. Throughout his long productive life Aaron Copland has composed a great deal of music written several books about music and has influenced and encouraged a generation of younger American composers.

WRITERS REVISING: COMMAS

As a punctuation exercise for the high school student whom she was tutoring in English, a college junior devised a game she called "Silly Sentences." She wanted to show her tutee that more than merely applying some rules, comma usage determines meaning. Try your hand at removing the nonsense from the following statements by changing the way commas are used.

20j

int p

```
        At the banquet will be many members of
Congress eating roast beef and members of
the press as well. The waiters will serve
the courses of soup, fish, salad, meat, and
vegetables, and dessert with three wines.
For dessert women tend to prefer sherbet, men,
pie and ice cream. Mind your manners
and try not to eat too much pig. Please try
not to drop your spoon, or roll in your
soup. Stay awake during the after-dinner
speech, and if you must yawn do so, quietly.
```

Revision

```
        At the banquet will be many members of
Congress eating roast beef and members of        20c(1)
the press as well. The waiters will serve
the courses of soup, fish, salad, meat and        20g
vegetables, and dessert with three wines.         20j
For dessert women tend to prefer sherbet; men,    20a, 20g
pie and ice cream. Mind your manners
and try not to eat too much pig. Please try       20f
not to drop your spoon or roll in your            20j
soup. Stay awake during the after-dinner
speech, and if you must yawn do so quietly.       20b, 20j
```

21

THE SEMICOLON

21a
Use a semicolon to separate closely related main clauses not joined by a coordinating conjunction.

The main clauses of compound sentences are most commonly joined by a comma and one of the coordinating conjunctions: *and, but, or, nor, for, so,* and *yet: Columbus discovered America in 1492, but the Vikings got here before that.* Conjunctions add meaning to sentences, establishing explicit relationships of equality, addition, simultaneity, choice, contrast, and so forth between independent clauses. There are times, however, when these conjunctions may not be appropriate for the meaning you wish to express—when you wish to suggest only relatedness between thoughts, rather than additional meaning. In those instances, a semicolon can be an effective tool: *Archeologists have uncovered a tenth-century Norse settlement in Newfoundland; these remains place Vikings in America four hundred years before Columbus.* If the ideas in the main clauses are not closely related, or if you don't intend to direct the reader's attention to their relatedness, treat each main clause as a separate sentence and use a period between them: *Norsemen writing to the Vatican reported voyages from Greenland to Canada. Some people believe Columbus was aware of this information.* Whereas a period is a full stop, marking a complete break between sentences, a semicolon separates and stops but does not fully break the flow of thought between grammatically independent statements.

21

int p

> The rabbit is the all-American game; it is everywhere, and everywhere hunted.
>
> JOHN RANDOLPH

> We organize time and myth with music; we mark our lives by it. Music is the way that our memories sing to us across time.
>
> LANCE MORROW

> Initiative in the attack is not much in the nature of the tarantula; most species fight only when cornered so that escape is impossible.
>
> ALEXANDER PETRUNKEVITCH

> Children begin by loving their parents; as they grow older they judge them; sometimes they forgive them.
>
> OSCAR WILDE

> Pay the thunder no mind; listen to the birds.
>
> EUBIE BLAKE

A comma is sometimes used to separate very short main clauses not joined by coordinating conjunctions, particularly if the clauses are parallel, as in *She is not a person, she is a legend* or *Some allow it, some don't.* But the semicolon is always correct in such sentences—and much safer for the inexperienced writer.

21b
Use a semicolon to separate main clauses joined by a conjunctive adverb.

Conjunctive adverbs are words like *however, moreover, therefore, consequently, indeed,* and *then* that carry a thought from one main clause to the next. (See p. 547 for a more extensive list.)

21b

int p

I ordered the concert tickets by mail; *therefore,* I didn't have to stand in line.

Our muscles were tired and sore; *nevertheless,* we kept on jogging.

On February 2 the groundhog saw its shadow; *consequently,* according to folk wisdom, we can expect six more weeks of winter weather.

You can recognize conjunctive adverbs and distinguish them from other kinds of connecting words if you remember that they are the only ones that can be moved from the beginning of a clause to another position in that clause without changing the clause's meaning.

The band struck up a familiar tune; *indeed,* they were playing our song.

The band struck up a familiar tune; they were, *indeed,* playing our song.

When a conjunctive adverb comes within the second main clause instead of at the beginning, the clauses still must be separated by a semicolon and the conjunctive adverb set off by commas. Note that a conjunctive adverb that begins a main clause is followed by a single comma.

Unlike conjunctive adverbs, coordinating conjunctions (*and, but,* etc.) or subordinating conjunctions (*although, because, if, since, when,* and the like) cannot move from their positions without changing or destroying meaning.

Coordinating conjunctions must stand between the clauses they connect.

NOT   Fido barked, we *so* knew he wanted to go out.

BUT   Fido barked, *so* we knew he wanted to go out.

Similarly, subordinating conjunctions must stand at the beginning of the clauses they introduce.

> **NOT**   Fido barked he *because* wanted to go out.
> **BUT**   Fido barked *because* he wanted to go out.

21c

Use a semicolon to separate main clauses joined by a coordinating conjunction if the clauses are long or internally punctuated.

> The meeting last night, the most argumentative and confusing thus far, lasted until midnight; and unless something unexpected happens in the meantime, the next meeting may last even longer.
>
> When New England was first settled, lobsters were plentiful all along the coast; and since the settlers depended heavily on the sea for their food, especially in the early years, they certainly must have eaten lobster frequently.

In some instances, even when relatively short main clauses are joined by a coordinating conjunction, a semicolon instead of a comma may be used for emphasis.

> He could hear the excitement of their talk from the next room; but he could not distinguish what they were saying.

21d

Use a semicolon to separate the items of a series if the items themselves contain commas.

> Compare the following sentences:

> At courtside were Mr. Jones, the owner, and the general manager, a referee, the coach, a former star player, and the current trainer of the team.
>
> At courtside were Mr. Jones, the owner and the general manager; a referee; the coach, a former star player; and the current trainer of the team.

As you can see, the number of people at courtside varies considerably, depending on the punctuation. Without semicolons, readers may have difficulty separating items into subsets.

> Jean Smith, the cardiologist; Angelo Martinez, the dentist; and Alan Wilson, the psychiatrist, meet for lunch every Tuesday.

In other cases, semicolons help to group items with accompanying lengthy modifying phrases or explanations.

21c

int p

The march had been an extraordinary conglomeration of different types of people: students; young middle-class families with children; punks with stiff green Mohawks; a band of bikers with fifties-style pompadours and big Moto Guzzi motorcycles.

The New Yorker

Snobbery has traditionally been founded on birth; knowledge or pseudo knowledge, or merely self-assured ignorance, all of them amounting to the same thing in snob terms; access to power, status, celebrity; circumstances, such as the place one lives or even the things one does not do, such as watch television.

LANCE MORROW

Occasionally, semicolons add an effective emphatic touch as well as provide separation where commas exist.

21d

int p

The bureaucracy consists of functionaries; the aristocracy, of idols; the democracy, of idolators.

G. B. SHAW

You should note that in all the preceding examples semicolons are used to separate items of equal rank—coordinate elements.

EXERCISE 21a–d

PART A

In the following sentence, insert semicolons or substitute them for commas wherever needed.

Today's forecast calls for snow over New England, with scattered snowshowers over the upper Ohio Valley, the lower Great Lakes and eastern upper Michigan, snow across Minnesota, snowshowers scattered over the northern and central Rockies and the Sierra Nevada, rain, with snow in higher elevations, over the southern Rockies, rain and snowshowers scattered over the northern Plateau and from South Dakota to western Kansas, showers and thunderstorms scattered over the southern Plains, Arkansas, eastern Nebraska and northern California and rain over the northern Pacific Coast.

National Weather Service

PART B

In the following sentences, insert semicolons or substitute them for commas wherever needed.

1. Tornadoes are especially dangerous storms, they can strike with little warning and can cause severe damage.
2. Tornadoes, which are created when cool, dry air meets warm, moist

air, usually last only a few minutes and because they strike a very narrow path, surrounding areas are often not affected.

3. Scientists have difficulty studying tornadoes, the violent nature of the tornado makes a field experiment almost impossible.

4. One solution to this problem is the tornado-modeling laboratory, in the lab scientists can create smaller vortices similar to those formed in a tornado.

5. Scientists have discovered that the highest, most dangerous wind-speeds in a tornado occur close to the ground, although hurricanes also contain high windspeeds, the winds may be 200 miles aloft.

PART C

Combine at least eighteen of the twenty sentences in the following paragraphs by using a semicolon and conjunctive adverb that expresses the correct relationship between the clauses. (See p. 547 for a list of conjunctive adverbs.) You may need to delete or rearrange some words to achieve smooth sentences.

21d

int p

Although tornadoes can strike anywhere or any time, conditions must be right for the cool air to meet the warm, moist air. Without these conditions, a tornado cannot form. A thunderstorm must be present in order for a tornado to form. Scientists have generated thunderstorm-like updrafts in the lab in order to study the formation of tornadoes.

While a tornado watch means that conditions are right for a tornado to form, a tornado warning means that a twister has been sighted. It could strike any time within thirty minutes. If a tornado is imminent, the safest place to be is a basement. The next best places are the most interior room of a house or the hall or a closet.

Unlike tornadoes, hurricanes are tropical storms which develop strong winds by feeding off the energy of water. They can last a few hours or a day or two and can cause widespread damage. Hurricanes usually affect the Gulf Coast and the Atlantic states from June to November. Tornadoes can occur anywhere in the United States at any time.

People who live in hurricane areas should keep on hand emergency supplies such as flashlights, batteries, and candles. They should also have a portable radio, a first-aid kit, and nonperishable food. Hurricanes may cause water sources to be cut off. If a hurricane is likely, people in the threatened area should fill their bathtubs with water. Before a hurricane, authorities warn people to evacuate low-lying or otherwise unsafe areas. Some people do not heed these warnings and are injured or killed. During hurricanes and tornadoes, people should stay tuned to the radio for updates or for news that the storm has passed. They will know when it is safe to leave shelter.

22

THE COLON

Whereas the semicolon always indicates a full stop, the colon indicates an addition or expectation. It indicates that what follows will explain, clarify, illustrate, or specify detail.

22a

Use a colon to separate a main clause and another sentence element when the second explains, illustrates, or amplifies the first.

22

int p

It is safe to predict what prices will do in the next decade: they will go up.

If you're considering a hat, remember this cardinal rule: never try to wear a hat that has more character than you do.

Charm, in the abstract, has something of the quality of music: radiance, balance, and harmony.

LAURIE LEE

There are two times in a man's life when he should not speculate: when he can't afford it and when he can.

MARK TWAIN

22b

Use a colon to set off a list or series, including a list or series introduced by *the following* or *as follows.*

For the most part we are an intemperate people: we eat too much when we can, drink too much, indulge our senses too much.

JOHN STEINBECK

Anything is possible on a train: a great meal, a binge, a visit from card players, an intrigue, a good night's sleep, and strangers' monologues framed like Russian short stories.

PAUL THEROUX

If you are interested in reading further about usage, we recommend the following books: Evans, *A Dictionary of Contemporary American Usage;* Follet, *Modern American Usage;* and Bernstein, *The Careful Writer.*

The recommended treatment for a cold is as follows: plenty of fluids, bed rest, and aspirin for fever.

Make sure that a *complete* statement precedes the colon. Do not use a colon after a partial statement, even when that partial statement indicates a list will follow.

NOT	We rented several videocassettes, including: *Ghostbusters, Romancing the Stone,* and *Back to the Future.*
BUT	We rented several videocassettes, including *Ghostbusters, Romancing the Stone,* and *Back to the Future.*
NOT	Tours to Australia feature stops such as: Melbourne, Sydney, and Canberra.
BUT	Tours to Australia feature stops such as Melbourne, Sydney, and Canberra.
OR	Tours to Australia feature such stops as the following: Melbourne, Sydney, and Canberra.

See Section **24k** for more discussion of inappropriate use of colons in lists.

22c

Use a colon to introduce a formal quotation.

The Sixteenth Amendment set up the income tax: "The Congress shall have power to lay and collect taxes on incomes, from whatever source derived, without apportionment among the several states, and without regard to any census or enumeration."

In her book *Stress and the American Woman,* Nora Scott Kinzer writes: "Female alcoholism is on the rise. Psychotropic drugs such as Valium and Equanil are widely used by housewives. Harried male and female executives gulp uppers and downers by the handful. Obesity prevents women from obtaining or keeping good jobs—and can destroy lives as effectively as the bottle of liquor or pills. Stress kills via an intermediary."

22d

Use a colon according to established conventions to separate items in biblical citations, subtitles and titles, and divisions of time.

BIBLICAL CITATION	Isaiah 40:28–31
SUBTITLES	*2001: A Space Odyssey*
	The Panda's Thumb: More Reflections in Natural History
DIVISIONS OF TIME	9:20 a.m. 10:10 p.m.

EXERCISE 22a–d

In the following sentences, insert colons wherever they are needed. Then write five sentences of your own that use colons in various ways.

1. Instead of the first-aid measures traditionally used for treating poisonous snakebite, experts now give this first-aid advice do nothing to the bite, and get the victim to the hospital as quickly as possible.

2. One snakebite expert states "Trying the old remedies may do more harm than good."

3. In the past, recommended first-aid measures for poisonous snakebite included the following using a tourniquet to tie off the bitten area, applying ice to the wound, and sucking out the venom.

4. In the United States, there are only four types of poisonous snakes the coral snake, the water moccasin (cottonmouth), the rattlesnake, and the copperhead.

5. These snakes are found in various areas of the United States the coral snake lives in the southwestern states, the water moccasin inhabits watery areas of the Southeast, the rattlesnake is found mainly in arid and semiarid regions throughout the United States, and the copperhead lives in woody and rocky areas of the central and eastern parts of the country.

6. Snakes do not normally strike unless they're provoked, so any sudden movement is threatening to them; if you encounter a snake, here's what you should do move slowly away from it.

7. The following methods can be effective in protecting oneself against snakebite wearing boots and protective clothing, using a hiking stick in heavy grass or leaves, and being aware of the habitats and habits of poisonous snakes.

8. Swimmers and boaters should be cautious, for snakes also inhabit water they swim well, and they also like to sun themselves on nearby rocks.

9. A bite from a poisonous snake can be distinguished from that of a nonpoisonous snake by one feature fang marks.

10. A nonpoisonous snake bite leaves teeth marks a poisonous snake bite leaves fang marks and may also leave teeth marks.

23

int p

23

THE DASH AND PARENTHESES

Both dashes and parentheses are used to set off interrupting comments, explanations, examples, and other similar parenthetical elements from the main thought of the sentence. Commas are ordinarily used when parenthetical or other nonrestrictive elements are closely related in the main thought of the sentence. Dashes and parentheses are used when the interruption is abrupt and the element set off is only loosely related to the main thought of the sentence.

Though the choice between dashes and parentheses is sometimes a matter of taste, dashes emphasize more strongly the element being set off and give it greater importance than parentheses do. Parentheses are more commonly used when the element enclosed is an incidental explanatory comment, an aside, or a nonessential bit of information.

A single dash is used following an introductory element or preceding a final sentence element. A pair of dashes is used to enclose an element within a sentence. Parentheses are always used in pairs around the enclosed element. In handwriting, distinguish the dash from the hyphen by making the dash longer. In typewritten copy, use two hyphens, with no spacing between them or on either side, to indicate the dash.

THE DASH

23a
Use the dash or a pair of dashes to mark an abrupt shift in sentence structure or thought.

Could she—should she even try to—borrow money from her aunt?

The Queen of England never carries money—too unseemly—but travels with ladies in waiting who pay from the royal purse for whatever Her Majesty fancies.

That puppy is going to grow up to be enormous—check out the size of his paws—and will eat us out of house and home.

23b
Use the dash to set off nonrestrictive appositives and other parenthetical elements for emphasis.

Resorts seeking to expand to other base facilities, such as Winter Park, are also considering the use of funiculars—railroad cars pulled along a track—which can carry up to 5,000 [people] hourly.

Skiing

I think extraterrestrial intelligence—even beings substantially further evolved than we—will be interested in us, in what we know, how we think, what our brains are like, the course of our evolution, the prospects for our future.

CARL SAGAN

Of strong constitution himself, Perron—who had not maintained his health in India without an almost valetudinarian attention to the medicinal needs of his body—had even so not been free of the shortness of temper that was one of the side-effects of an overworked and easily discouraged digestive system.

PAUL SCOTT

Each person is born to one possession which overvalues all his others—his last breath.

MARK TWAIN

The student wandered in at 9:30—half an hour after the class began.

The spoken language does not have the same standards as the written language—the tune you whistle is not the orchestra's score.

WILLIAM SAFIRE

23c
Use the dash for clarity to set off internally punctuated appositives or other parenthetical elements.

To prevent confusion, use dashes rather than commas to set off appositives containing punctuated items in a series. In the following sentence the word *object* appears to be one item in a series.

> Putting a spin on an object, a top, a bullet, a satellite, gives it balance and stability.

But when the commas are replaced by dashes, the meaning is clear.

> Putting a spin on an object—a top, a bullet, a satellite—gives it balance and stability.

Here is another example:

> Because I have so little regard for most of O'Neill's plays, and especially for those hallowed late plays of his—*A Moon for the Misbegotten, The Iceman Cometh,* and *A Touch of the Poet*—I am relieved to have a chance to repeat my opinion that *Long Day's Journey Into Night* is the finest play written in English in my lifetime.

BRENDAN GILL

23d
Use the dash to set off introductory lists or summary statements.

> Gather data, tabulate, annotate, classify—the process seemed endless to the research assistant.
> Black flies, horseflies, little triangular flies, ordinary house flies, unidentified kinds of flies—those are what I mean when I say I'm sick of flies.
> Pound, Eliot, Williams—the course devoted most attention to these poets.

23e
Use the dash to show interruption or hesitation in speech.

> "Why don't you—" He stopped abruptly and looked away.
> "Well, I—uh—we—some of us really want to drop your plan."

23c

int p

PARENTHESES

23f
Use parentheses to set off parenthetical information, explanation, or comment that is incidental or nonessential to the main thought of the sentence.

The lawyer contends (and we can see that the contention has some merit) that this client was convicted on doubtful evidence.

In our society (it's the only one I've experienced, so I can't speak for others) the razor of necessity cuts close.

STUDS TERKEL

More than 1,000 years ago, the Hopis (the word means "the peaceful ones") settled in the mesa-dotted farmland of northern Arizona.

Time

Among the narratives in the text, Maya Angelou's (pp. 58–68) is my favorite.

23f

int p

23g
Use parentheses to enclose numerals or letters labeling items listed within sentences.

To check out a book from our library, proceed as follows: (1) check the catalog number carefully; (2) enter the catalog number in the upper left-hand corner of the call slip; (3) fill out the remainder of the call slip information; and (4) hand in the call slip at the main desk.

EXERCISE 23a–g
In the following sentences, insert dashes or parentheses wherever they are needed.

1. The synthesizer an instrument some people call a machine produces musical sounds by electronic means.
2. Around 1960, such electronic technology as solid-state circuitry gave composers a means of duplicating the sounds of various instruments with only one instrument the synthesizer.
3. Perhaps the best-known synthesizer is that developed by Robert A. Moog b. 1934.
4. The Moog his name rhymes with *vogue* synthesizer is capable of producing extraordinary musical sounds.
5. Since the 1960s, electronic music some people, though, do not consider it music has become more common.

6. Several universities Yale, Brandeis, the University of California at Davis have set up centers for the study of electronic music.
7. Morton Subotnick, Milton Babbitt, and Charles Wuorinen all are successful composers of electronic music.
8. Skeptics ask the following questions about electronic music: 1. Is it true music? 2. Is its sound realistic? 3. Is it practical for the concert hall?
9. My music appreciation text devotes a short chapter pp. 195–206 to the development of electronic music in the second half of the twentieth century.
10. After hearing Bach's *Brandenburg Concerto No. 1* "played" on a synthesizer, I have only one word to describe the performance unusual.

24

int p

24

SUPERFLUOUS INTERNAL PUNCTUATION

Careful punctuation helps readers separate words and ideas, helps group related words together, and enables writers to set off words or word groups for emphasis. Inadequate punctuation can force a reader to go over a passage several times to get its meaning. But too many marks of punctuation confuse a reader as much as too few marks.

The following sentence, for example, is jarring because of unnecessary and confusing punctuation.

> The people of this company, have, always, been aware, of the need, for products of better quality, and lower prices.

None of the commas in that sentence is necessary.

Use all the punctuation marks that will make the reader's work easier or that are required by convention. But do not insert marks that are superfluous. Especially avoid the misuses of the comma, the semicolon, and the colon described below.

24a
Do not separate a single or a final adjective from its noun.

> **NOT** The H.M.S. *Bounty* was a hundred-foot, three-masted, vessel.

BUT   The H.M.S. *Bounty* was a hundred-foot, three-masted vessel.

24b

Do not separate a subject from its verb unless there are intervening words that require punctuation.

NOT   The *Bounty,* had been sent from England by George III in 1787 to Tahiti to trade for breadfruit trees.

BUT   The *Bounty* had been sent from England by George III in 1787 to Tahiti to trade for breadfruit trees.

The *Bounty,* sent from England by George III in 1787 to Tahiti, was to trade for breadfruit trees. [The commas set off a participial phrase.]

24c

Do not separate a verb from its object unless there are intervening words that require punctuation.

NOT   In April 1789 the ship left, Tahiti with its cargo.

BUT   In April 1789 the ship left Tahiti with its cargo.

NOT   The authoritarian captain gave the crew, the brunt of his temper and sharp tongue.

BUT   The authoritarian captain gave the crew the brunt of his temper and sharp tongue.

The authoritarian captain gave the crew, especially Lieutenant Fletcher Christian, the brunt of his temper and sharp tongue. [The commas set off a parenthetical appositive.]

24d

Do not separate two words or phrases that are joined by a coordinating conjunction.

NOT   Captain Bligh called Fletcher Christian a liar, and a scoundrel.

BUT   Captain Bligh called Fletcher Christian a liar and a scoundrel.

NOT   The crew quietly approached Christian, and told him they would follow him if he would lead a mutiny.

BUT   The crew quietly approached Christian and told him they would follow him if he would lead a mutiny.

24b

int p

24e

Do not separate an introductory word, brief phrase, or short clause from the main body of the sentence unless clarity or emphasis requires it.

> **NOT** On April 27, Christian led the crew in the mutiny on the *Bounty.*
>
> BUT On April 27 Christian led the crew in the mutiny on the *Bounty.*

Occasionally, however, a comma must be inserted to prevent misreading. (See **20j.**)

> **NOT** For Christian to mutiny was reprehensible in the abstract but somewhat more ambiguous in reality.
>
> BUT For Christian, to mutiny was reprehensible in the abstract but somewhat more ambiguous in reality.

24e

int p

24f

Do not set off a restrictive modifier. (See 20c.)

> **NOT** They put Bligh and eighteen crewmen, who remained loyal to him, into an open boat.
>
> BUT They put Bligh and eighteen crewmen who remained loyal to him into an open boat.

> **NOT** The boat was fitted, with enough provisions and equipment, to give Bligh and his crew a chance, for survival.
>
> BUT The boat was fitted with enough provisions and equipment to give Bligh and his crew a chance for survival.

Very often, adverbial phrases and clauses that interrupt or follow a main clause *restrict* the meaning of the word or clause to which they are attached. They are therefore essential to the meaning and should *not* be separated by commas from what they modify. (See also **20d.**)

> **NOT** Bligh and his men sailed their small boat, across 3,600 nautical miles, to what is now Indonesia.
>
> BUT Bligh and his men sailed their small boat across 3,600 nautical miles to what is now Indonesia. [The phrases *3,600 nautical miles* and *to what is now Indonesia* restrict the meaning of the verb *sailed,* telling how and where Bligh sailed, and thus are essential to meaning.]

> **NOT** Captain Bligh must be called extraordinary, for the skill and willpower with which he directed the crew to a safe landing with eleven days' rations still remaining.

BUT   Captain Bligh must be called extraordinary for the skill and willpower with which he directed the crew to a safe landing, with eleven days' rations still remaining. [The phrase *for the skill* and the following modifiers restrict the adjective *extraordinary*, explaining the way in which Bligh was extraordinary. On the other hand, *with eleven days' rations still remaining* is a nonrestrictive phrase and so it is set off with a comma.]

24g
Do not separate indirect quotations or direct quotations that are part of a sentence's structure from the rest of the sentence.

NOT   Before the mutiny Bligh had said, he would drive the crew mercilessly.

BUT   Before the mutiny Bligh had said he would drive the crew mercilessly.

NOT   He had called the men, "damned thieving rascals."

BUT   He had called the men "damned thieving rascals."

24g

int p

24h
Do not separate a preposition from its object.

NOT   Now he had driven a skeleton crew safely through, high seas, broiling sun, and impossible odds.

BUT   Now he had driven a skeleton crew safely through high seas, broiling sun, and impossible odds.

24i
Do not use a semicolon to separate a main clause from a subordinate clause, a phrase from a clause, or other parts of unequal grammatical rank.

NOT   Christian and the others sailed the *Bounty* back to Tahiti; where they liked the climate, the lifestyle, and the Polynesian women.

BUT   Christian and the others sailed the *Bounty* back to Tahiti, where they liked the climate, the lifestyle, and the Polynesian women.

NOT   Christian, eight of the men, and several Tahitian women eventually traveled further; sailing to the tiny uninhabited island of Pitcairn.

BUT   Christian, eight of the men, and several Tahitian women eventually traveled further, sailing to the tiny uninhabited island of Pitcairn.

24j

Do not use a semicolon before a direct quotation or before a list.

> **NOT** According to *National Geographic;* "To hide from punishment, the mutineers in 1790 burned their ship in Bounty Bay."
>
> **BUT** According to *National Geographic:* "To hide from punishment, the mutineers in 1790 burned their ship in Bounty Bay."
>
> **NOT** The new residents of Pitcairn faced still more hardship; loneliness, life in a wilderness, even death.
>
> **BUT** The new residents of Pitcairn faced still more hardship: loneliness, life in a wilderness, even death.

24k

Do not use a colon between a verb and its object or complement or between a preposition and its object.

Even though the words that comprise the object or complement may be in series, as in a list, a colon is not needed to precede them. A colon precedes a list only when the words before the colon form a complete statement (see Section **22b**).

> **NOT** Discovering Pitcairn in 1808, an American ship found: a settlement of women, children, and one man.
>
> **BUT** Discovering Pitcairn in 1808, an American ship found a settlement of women, children, and one man.
>
> **NOT** By then every man except one had died by: violence, disease, or mishap.
>
> **BUT** By then every man except one had died by violence, disease, or mishap.
>
> **NOT** Today the descendants of the *Bounty* mutineers number about 1,500; their homes are: Pitcairn Island, New Zealand, Australia, Tahiti, and Norfolk Island near Australia.
>
> **BUT** Today the descendants of the *Bounty* mutineers number about 1,500; their homes are Pitcairn Island, New Zealand, Australia, Tahiti, and Norfolk Island near Australia.

24j

int p

EXERCISE 24a–k

Eliminate any superfluous commas, semicolons, or colons in the following sentences.

1. In the book, *Silent Spring,* Rachel Carson warned that careless use of pesticides was destroying the natural world.

2. *Silent Spring* was published in 1962, and became one of the most significant books of the twentieth century.
3. In the book, Carson predicted that the environment would become so poisoned by pesticides; that the song of birds, in springtime, would be silenced forever.
4. She, also warned readers, of the threat to humans from pesticides.
5. The book helped to make people more aware of the threat to their environment; and particularly the threat of pollutants, and pesticides.
6. At one time, pesticides seemed to be miracle substances, which could destroy pests, and thus boost crop production.
7. *Silent Spring* made people aware, that pesticides could cause damage to both the environment, and the human race.
8. Several chemicals have been banned, or regulated in the twenty-five years, since the publication of *Silent Spring.*
9. Among these chemicals are: DDT, and other chlorinated hydrocarbons.
10. Although, hazardous chemicals continue to be used today, Rachel Carson's book, *Silent Spring,* left its readers with a legacy of awareness, concern, and, activism for their environment.

24k

int p

REVIEW EXERCISE ON INTERNAL PUNCTUATION (Sections 20–24)

The following sentences require various kinds of internal punctuation. Supply the needed punctuation marks and be prepared to explain your choices.

1. Oceanography which is essentially the study of oceans is an ancient science for people have always been curious about these vast expanses of water.
2. In the ancient world sailors from the following places ventured out to explore the sea Egypt Athens Phoenecia and Rome.
3. Although most of this travel took place on the Mediterranean Sea a few bold venturesome crews sailed as far as Scotland.
4. Aided by a better understanding of astronomy and assisted by improved navigational devices ocean explorers made tremendous discoveries during the Renaissance.
5. These discoveries were made by some of the most famous early explorers Ponce de Leon discovered the Gulf Stream Vasco da Gama found the route from Europe to India around the Cape of Good Hope and Ferdinand Magellan circumnavigated the earth.
6. These ocean discoveries increased humankind's knowledge of the scope of the planet moreover they stimulated interest in studying the oceans themselves.
7. By applying his work on gravity to the movement of the tides Sir Isaac Newton precisely explained the behavior of the tides something which had not before been understood completely.
8. Edmund Halley who is most famous for discovering the comet named for him was also an ocean explorer.
9. Benjamin Franklin is known as an inventor writer and statesman but he also had another vocation oceanographer.

10. Franklin had studied the Gulf Stream and his findings which he published described the currents of the Gulf Stream and showed moreover how merchant ships could use these currents to their advantage.

11. Captain James Cook the explorer who sailed around Antarctica took a naturalist with him on his voyages.

12. By the mid-nineteenth century it was common for scientists to go along on exploratory voyages in order to study the sea for example Charles Darwin developed his theories about the origin of species from information he collected while sailing as a scientist on the H.M.S. *Beagle* a survey ship.

13. Its sole purpose being to study the oceans the voyage of the H.M.S. *Challenger* could be called the first oceanographic expedition it sailed over 111000 kilometers 69000 miles in a voyage that lasted four years.

14. Collecting biological specimens obtaining water samples and measuring currents and temperatures those were among the activities carried out by the oceanographers on the *Challenger*.

15. By the end of the nineteenth century oceanography had become an acccepted field of study in universities indeed the Marine Biological Laboratory which was founded at Woods Hole Massachusetts in 1888 is today an important center for the study of marine biology.

25–26

q

25–26

THE PUNCTUATION OF QUOTED MATERIAL

Direct quotations—that is, direct speech and material quoted word for word from other written sources—must always be set off distinctly from a writer's own words. Quotation marks usually indicate the distinction, although when quotations from written sources are long, the distinction may be shown instead by indentation. Section **25** describes the conventional uses of quotation marks and indentation to set off quoted material; the use and punctuation of explanatory words such as *he said;* the conventions controlling the placement of other marks of punctuation with quotation marks; and the special uses of quotation marks in certain titles and with words used as words.

An explanatory comment inserted in a quotation or the omission of some part of the original quotation calls for the use of brackets or the ellipsis mark. These are discussed in Section **26.**

25

QUOTATION MARKS

INDICATING QUOTED MATERIAL

25a

Use double quotation marks to enclose a direct quotation from speech or writing.

> "Don't dive from that rock," she warned me.
> Emerson wrote, "A foolish consistency is the hobgoblin of little minds."

Note that in dialogue, each change of speaker is indicated by a new paragraph.

> "And after dinner, as your personal Mephistopheles, I shall take you up a high hill and show you the second-best place in the world. You agree? A mystery tour?"
> "I want the best," she said, drinking her Scotch.
> "And I never award first prizes," he replied placidly.
>
> JOHN LE CARRÉ

Remember not to set off indirect quotations.

> She warned me not to dive from that rock.
> It was Emerson who wrote that a foolish consistency is the hobgoblin of little minds.

25b

Use single quotation marks to enclose a quotation within a quotation.

> E. B. White wrote, "As an elderly practitioner once remarked, 'Writing is an act of faith, not a trick of grammar.' "

Notice that the end punctuation of the sentence within single quotation marks serves also as the end punctuation for the entire sentence unit of which it is a part.

25c
Set off prose quotations of more than four lines and poetry quotations of more than three lines by indentation.

Long prose quotations. Prose quotations of more than four lines should be displayed—set off from the text of a paper and indented from the left-hand margin. In typewritten papers, indent all lines of the quotation ten character-spaces from the left, and double-space it. Do not enclose a displayed quotation in quotation marks. If quotation marks occur *within* material you are setting off, use them as they are in the original: double for double, single for single.

```
    Professor George Summey's comment on the writer's

responsibility for accuracy in reporting the words of others

is worth quoting:

          Anyone who quotes another person's words has the

          duty of keeping the words unchanged and continuous

          or of giving clear notice to the contrary. It is

          improper to alter wording or punctuation of quoted

          matter, to italicize words without due notice, or

          to make any other change that would misrepresent

          the meaning of the quoted words in their context.

No careful writer would question the need for such accuracy.
```

Quoted poetry. Single lines of poetry are ordinarily run into the text and enclosed in quotation marks unless the writer wishes to give them particular emphasis by setting them off.

```
In the line "A spotted shaft is seen," the hissing s sounds

echo Emily Dickinson's subject: a snake.
```

Two or three lines of poetry may be either enclosed in quotation marks and run into the text or indented ten spaces from the left. If they are enclosed in quotation marks and run into the text, divisions between lines are indicated by a slash mark (/).

```
William Blake combines mystical and military images, as in

the lines "Bring me my Spear: O clouds unfold! / Bring me

my Chariot of fire."
```

```
images, as in the lines
```
> Bring me my spear: O clouds unfold!
>
> Bring me my Chariot of fire.

Poetry quotations of more than three lines should be double-spaced and set off from the text by indenting ten spaces from the left.

EXERCISE 25a–c

In the following sentences, insert double or single quotation marks or slash marks wherever needed.

1. When I was in my advisor's office last week, he said You need to take a literature course next semester, and I think you'd enjoy the poetry course.
2. I wasn't too sure I wanted to read a lot of poetry, but I told him I'd think about the course.
3. After I finally decided to take the course, I got nervous on the first day of class when the instructor announced: In this course you'll probably read more poetry than you've ever read before.
4. One of the first aspects of poetry we studied was figurative language; as a result, I finally understood how to read poetry like Emily Dickinson's two-line description of a hummingbird as A route of evanescence   With a revolving wheel.
5. I worked hard in the course; in fact, one night my roommate said, Everyone in the dorm wonders why they never see you anymore, so I told them you had become a poetry fanatic.

PUNCTUATING EXPLANATORY WORDS WITH QUOTATIONS

25d

In punctuating explanatory words preceding a quotation, be guided by the length and formality of the quotation.

Explanatory words such as *he said* are ordinarily set off from quotations by a comma when they precede the quotation. However, when the quotation that follows is grammatically closely related, explanatory words may be followed by no punctuation, or when they are relatively long and formal they may be followed by a colon.

NO PUNCTUATION	I yelled "Stop!" and grabbed the wheel.
	Auden's poem "In Memory of W.B. Yeats" begins with the line "He disappeared in dead of winter."
	The Preamble begins with the words "We, the people of the United States."
	It was President Franklin Roosevelt who said that "the only thing we have to fear is fear itself."

PUNCTUATION WITH COMMA	The old rancher said very quietly, "Under no circumstances will I tell you where the money is hidden."
	The chairman asked him, "Have I stated your motion correctly?"
PUNCTUATION WITH COLON	The speaker rose and began to rant: "The party in power has betrayed us. It has not only failed to keep its election promises but has sold out to special-interest groups."

25e

Use a comma to separate an opening quotation from the rest of the sentence unless the quotation ends with a question mark or an exclamation point.

"The man is dead," he said with finality.

"Is the man dead?" he asked.

"On, no!" he screamed hysterically. "My brother can't be dead."

25f

When a quotation is interrupted by explanatory words (*I, you, he, she, we, they said*, or their equivalent), use a comma after the first part of the quotation. In choosing the proper punctuation mark to place after the explanatory words, apply the rules for punctuating clauses and phrases.

"I am not aware," she said, "of any dangers from jogging."

"I have always worked hard," he declared. "I was peddling newspapers when I was eight years old."

"Jean has great capacities," the supervisor said; "she has energy, brains, and personality."

EXERCISE 25d–f

In the following sentences, insert appropriate punctuation marks where necessary to separate quotations from the rest of the sentence.

1. "I was worried about my job interview with the accounting firm" said Sherry "but it went very well because I had prepared for the questions I might be asked."
2. "How do you prepare for a job interview" George asked her.
3. "One thing you need to do" replied Sherry "is consider questions the interviewer might ask you and think of how you would respond."
4. "What's the most difficult question you've been asked in an interview" inquired John.
5. His question reminded me of the interviewer who said "Tell me why I should hire you for a position in this accounting firm."

25e

q

USING OTHER MARKS OF PUNCTUATION
WITH QUOTATION MARKS

25g

Follow established conventions in placing other punctuation with quotation marks.

1. Place commas and periods inside quotation marks. Commas are generally used to separate direct quotations from unquoted material.

> "There comes a time," said the politician, "to put principle aside and do what's right."

Note that this rule *always* applies, regardless of the reason for using quotation marks.

> According to Shakespeare, the poet writes in a "fine frenzy."
> The words "lily-livered coward" derive from an earlier expression, "white-livered," which meant "cowardly."

2. Place semicolons and colons outside quotation marks.

> According to Shakespeare, the poet writes in a "fine frenzy"; by "fine frenzy" he meant a combination of energy, enthusiasm, imagination, and a certain madness.

3. Place a dash, question mark, or exclamation point inside the quotation marks when it applies only to the quotation; place it outside the quotation marks when it applies to the whole statement.

> She said, "Will I see you tomorrow?"
> Didn't she say, "I'll see you tomorrow"?
> "You may have the car tonight"—then he caught himself abruptly and said, "No, you can't have it—I need it myself."

When a mark applies to both quotation and sentence, use it only once.

> Have you ever asked, "May I come in?"

EXERCISE 25g

In the following sentences, insert whatever punctuation marks are appropriate for use with quotation marks.

1. How would you reply to an interviewer who asks "What do you expect to be doing in ten years"

2. "I'd like to be retired"   I realized suddenly that probably wouldn't be a good answer and said instead "I'd like to be a senior accountant with your firm."

3. The interviewer then asked "Where can we reach you after we make a decision"

4. In the thank-you note I sent to the interviewer, I wrote, "My background in tax accounting will be useful to your clients" moreover, I reminded her that I would be available for work in two weeks.

5. Unfortunately, I didn't get the job, but I did get a rejection letter that described me as "well-qualified" but "lacking in experience"

OTHER USES OF QUOTATION MARKS

25h

25h

q

Use quotation marks to set off titles of poems, songs, articles, short stories, and other titles that are parts of a longer work.

For the use of italics for the titles of longer works, see **27a** and **27b.**

> Theodore Roethke's poem "My Papa's Waltz" appeared in his book *The Lost Son and Other Poems.*
>
> "The Talk of the Town" has for many years been the opening column of *The New Yorker.*
>
> The song "I Left My Heart in San Francisco" has become an anthem for that city.
>
> "Beowulf to Batman: The Epic Hero in Modern Culture," an article by Roger B. Rollin, originally appeared in the journal *College English.*

25i

Words used in a special sense may be set off by quotation marks.

> When a new book comes into the library, it is first of all "accessioned."
>
> Is this what you call "functional" architecture?

Do not use quotation marks around common nicknames. Do not use them for emphasis. And do not use them apologetically to enclose slang, colloquialisms, trite expressions, or for imprecise words or phrases when you cannot find the right word. If a word is appropriate, it will stand without apology. If it is inappropriate, replace it. If, however, you wish your reader to recognize a slang term or colloquialism as such (to prevent misunderstanding the usage), then you may need to use quotation marks to indicate that the word is being used in a special sense. In your writing, be careful to distinguish between inappropriate use of slang and colloquialisms (to be avoided) and the necessary and legitimate use of such terms in some types of written discourse.

NOT	Katie got a pair of "totally outrageous" socks for her birthday.
BUT	Katie got a pair of brightly colored, wildly patterned socks for her birthday—socks that received full approval from her pre-teen girlfriends: "Totally outrageous!"

EXERCISE 25h–i

In the following sentences, insert quotation marks wherever they are needed.

1. The seventeenth-century writer Ben Jonson was an actor, a poet, a playwright, and a literary critic; in fact, he was the leader of what could be called a literary school.
2. Jonson's poem To the Memory of My Beloved Master William Shakespeare pays tribute to Shakespeare's genius.
3. The song To Celia, from Jonson's play *Cynthia's Revels* is a tender love lyric.
4. Jonson had such an influence on young poets that his followers came to be called his tribe.
5. Ralph S. Walker discusses Jonson's poetry in an article entitled Ben Jonson's Lyric Poetry; the article is included in the book *Seventeenth Century English Poetry.*

26

BRACKETS AND THE ELLIPSIS MARK

Brackets and ellipsis marks signal that a writer has made changes in material being quoted directly. Brackets are used to indicate that a writer has inserted into the quotation some information, comment, or explanation not in the original. The ellipsis mark is used to indicate that something has been deliberately omitted from the material being quoted.

26a

Use brackets to set off editorial remarks in quoted material.

You will sometimes want to insert a clarifying word or explanatory comment in a statement you are quoting. By enclosing such information in brackets, you let the reader know at once that *you* are speaking rather than the original author.

> John Dryden, a famous English poet, said, "Those who accuse him [Shakespeare] to have wanted knowledge give him the greater commendation; he was naturally learned."

> The favorite phrase of their [English] law is "a custom whereof the memory of man runneth not back to the contrary."
>
> RALPH WALDO EMERSON

In bibliographical notations, use brackets to enclose the name of a writer reputed to be the author of the work in question.

[Ned Ward], *A Trip to New England* (1699)

26b

Use the word *sic* ("thus it is") in brackets to indicate that a mistake or peculiarity in the spelling or the grammar of a foregoing word appears in the original work.

> The high school paper reported, "The students spoke most respectively [sic] of Mrs. Hogginbottom."

26c

Use an ellipsis mark (three spaced periods . . .) to indicate an intentional omission from quoted material.

When you wish to quote from an author but want to omit some word or words within a sentence or to omit one or more sentences, in fairness to the original author and to your readers you must indicate that you have omitted material from the original. Such omissions are indicated by inserting an ellipsis mark at the point of omission. For an omission within a sentence, use three spaced periods, leaving a space before and after each period. When the omission comes at the end of a sentence, use four periods; the first is the usual sentence period, and the last three are the ellipsis mark.

For example, the first selection below is taken without any omission from Russel Nye's *The Unembarrassed Muse* (New York, 1971). It describes the comic-strip world of Walt Disney's Mickey Mouse. The second selection shows how a writer quoting from the original passage might use the ellipsis.

> Mickey's is a child's world, safe (though occasionally scary), nonviolent, nonideological, where all the stories have happy endings. Characterization is strong and simple—Mickey is bright and friendly, Minnie eternally feminine, Goofy happily stupid, Donald of the terrible temper a raffish, likeable rascal. No Disney strip ever gave a child bad dreams or an adult anything to ponder.

> Mickey's is a child's world, safe . . . nonviolent, nonideological, where all the stories have happy endings. Characterization is strong and simple—Mickey is bright and friendly, Minnie eternally feminine, Goofy happily stupid, Donald of the terrible temper a raffish, likeable rascal. No Disney strip ever gave a child bad dreams. . . .

If you must omit an entire line or more of poetry or an entire paragraph or more of prose, use a full line of ellipsis marks to indicate the omission. The example below is from Edgar Allan Poe's poem "The Raven."

> Once upon a midnight dreary, while I pondered, weak and weary,
> Over many a quaint and curious volume of forgotten lore—
> While I nodded, nearly napping, suddenly there came a tapping,
>
> . . . .
>
> " 'Tis some visitor," I muttered, "tapping at my chamber door—
> Only this and nothing more."

REVIEW EXERCISES ON THE PUNCTUATION OF QUOTED MATERIAL (Sections 25–26)
Supply the appropriate punctuation in the following sentences.

1. I hadn't realized my friend said to me that there have been so many American women poets; I'm taking an American poetry class this term he continued and we're reading some interesting work.
2. Did you read the Puritan Anne Bradstreet's poetry another friend asked.
3. My friend replied that he had read Bradstreet and that he especially liked her poem The Author to Her Book.
4. My favorite American poet is Emily Dickinson my roommate said and I've read all her poetry.
5. He continued Her description of a snake as A narrow fellow in the grass is one of my favorite images.
6. My other friend asked Have you read the poem that begins with the line I'm nobody! Who are you?
7. I enjoy the poetry of more modern American writers I said because I find their language easier to understand.
8. My friend said When my American literature teacher asked What American poet do you admire most I said that I liked Sylvia Plath's poetry because her images are so vivid.
9. When my friend mentioned Sylvia Plath, I remembered that I had read her poem Lady Lazarus, which was in *Ariel,* her second book of poems.
10. Can you recall some of Plath's other poems my friend asked I'd like to read them.

27–30

WORD PUNCTUATION

Italics, capitals, apostrophes, and hyphens identify words that have a special use or a particular grammatical function in a sentence.

Our two-week reading program, assigned in Wednesday's class, is Shakespeare's *King Lear.*

Here the italics set off the words *King Lear* as a single title. The capitals identify *Wednesday, Shakespeare, King,* and *Lear* as proper names. The apostrophes indicate that *Shakespeare* and *Wednesday* are singular possessives and not plurals. The hyphen between *two* and *week* makes the two words function as a single adjective.

27

ITALICS

In printing, italics are typefaces that slope toward the right. In typed or handwritten manuscript, italics are indicated by underlining.

On the printed page: *italics*

In typewritten copy: <u>italics</u>

In handwritten copy: <u>*italics*</u>

27a
Italicize the titles of books, newspapers, magazines, and all publications issued separately.

"Issued separately" means published as a single work and not as an article or story in a magazine, nor as a chapter or section of a book. (For the proper punctuation of such titles, see **25h**.)

The New York Times	*Death of a Salesman*
Commentary	*Moby Dick*
People	*Webster's New Collegiate Dictionary*
The Lord of the Rings	*USA Today*

Be careful not to add the word *The* to titles unless it belongs there and not to omit it if it does belong.

NOT	*The Reader's Digest*
BUT	the *Reader's Digest*
NOT	the *Red Badge of Courage*
BUT	*The Red Badge of Courage*

Note that the titles of some very well-known works and documents are not italicized nor placed in quotation marks.

the Bible	Psalms
the Koran	the Constitution of the
the Magna Carta	United States
the Declaration of	Matthew
Independence	the Bill of Rights

27b

Italicize the names of ships, spacecraft, and aircraft, and the titles of works of art, movies, television and radio programs, record albums, and the like.

Titanic	*Spirit of St. Louis*	U.S.S. *Saratoga*
The Thinker	*Casablanca*	the *Concorde*
Dallas	*Born in the USA*	*Challenger*

Note that for ships and the like, the prefix U.S.S. (or H.M.S.) is not italicized: U.S.S. *Nimitz;* H.M.S. *Pinafore.*

27c

Italicize letters, words, and numbers used as words.

> Your *r*'s look very much like your *n*'s, and I can't tell your *7*'s from your *1*'s.
>
> The early settlers borrowed Indian words like *moccasin, powwow,* and *wigwam.*

Quotation marks are also sometimes used to set off words as words (see **25i**). However, if a subject you are discussing in a typewritten or handwritten paper requires you to set off many words as words, underlining (italics) will make your manuscript look less cluttered.

27d

Italicize foreign words and phrases that have not yet been accepted into the English language. Also italicize the Latin scientific names for plants, animals, and so forth.

> She graduated *magna cum laude.*
>
> Many of the works of the *fin de siècle* judged so sensational when they were written now seem utterly innocent.
>
> In the fall, the ginkgo tree *(Ginkgo biloba)* produces a yellow fruit that smells indescribably foul.

You may sometimes feel that a foreign word or phrase expresses your meaning more aptly or concisely than an English one. If you are sure that your readers will understand the expression, use it. But overuse of such words is pedantry. Many foreign words have been accepted into the English language and need no longer be italicized. The following words, for example, do not require italics:

bourgeois   milieu   denouement   liqueur

To determine whether a foreign word should be italicized, consult a good dictionary.

27e

Use italics to give a word or phrase special emphasis.

> *Always* turn off the electricity before attempting to work on the wiring.
>
> We have government *of* the people, *by* the people, and *for* the people; dictatorships have government *over* the people.

27f

Avoid the overuse of italics.

Distinguish carefully between a real need for italicizing and the use of italics as a mechanical device to achieve emphasis. The best way to achieve emphasis is to write effective, well-constructed sentences. The overuse of italics will make your writing seem immature and amateurish, as in the following:

> Any good education must be *liberal*.
>
> America is a *true* democracy, in every sense of the word.
>
> This book has what I call *real* depth of meaning.

EXERCISE 27a–f

Italicize words as necessary in the following sentences.

1. Even before the time Homer sang of "the wine dark sea" in the Odyssey, the beauty and mystery of the sea has been a powerful subject and symbol in literature, art, and music.
2. Novelists have often made use of the sea as a setting; for instance, in Herman Melville's novel Moby Dick, much of the action takes place at sea.
3. In Moby Dick, Ishmael, the narrator, tells of the captain and crew of the whaling ship Pequod.
4. Melville was familiar with the sea, for as the author of a recent article in The New York Times points out, Melville spent four years on trading vessels, whaling ships, and U.S. Navy ships in the Atlantic and Pacific.
5. The novelist Joseph Conrad drew upon his own career as a sailor for such sea novels as Lord Jim and Victory, as well as short stories such as "The Secret Sharer."

6. Sea novels have been popular subjects for transformations into movies; for example, Mutiny on the Bounty, a movie based on the novel of the same name, has been remade several times.
7. Artists have also turned to the sea for background and symbol: the Renaissance painter Botticelli shows Venus emerging from the sea in his famous painting Birth of Venus.
8. The English Romantic landscape painter William Turner painted many storms at sea, one of the most striking being the typhoon in his painting The Slave Ship.
9. Composers also looked to the sea for inspiration, and Claude Debussy, who liked to call himself musicien francais (French musician), was influenced by Turner's paintings.
10. Debussy's greatest orchestral composition is La Mer, a work that evokes the changing appearance of the sea as well as its sounds and moods.

28
CAPITALS

Modern writers capitalize less frequently than did earlier writers, and informal writing permits less capitalization than formal writing. Two hundred years ago, a famous author wrote:

> Being ruined by the Inconstancy and Unkindness of a Lover, I hope a true and plain Relation of my Misfortune may be of Use and Warning to Credulous Maids, never to put much Trust in deceitful Men.
>
> JONATHAN SWIFT, "The Story of the Injured Lady"

A modern writer would capitalize no letters but the initial *B* and the pronoun *I*.

28a

Capitalize the first word of a sentence, a line of poetry, a direct quotation that is not structurally part of another sentence, a complete sentence enclosed in parentheses or brackets, or—in some cases—a complete sentence following a colon.

1. A sentence or a line of poetry.

Education is concerned not with knowledge but with the meaning of knowledge.

True ease in writing comes from art, not chance,
As those move easiest who have learned to dance.

ALEXANDER POPE, *Essay on Criticism*

Some modern poets ignore the convention of capitalizing each line of poetry, perhaps because they feel that an initial capital letter gives a word unwanted emphasis.

> a man who had fallen among thieves
> lay by the roadside on his back
> dressed in fifteenthrate ideas
> wearing a round jeer for a hat
>
> e.e. cummings, "a man who had fallen among thieves"

2. A direct quotation.

She thought, "Where shall we spend our vacation—at the shore or in the mountains?"

28a

word p

Notice that the preceding example shows a quotation that is grammatically independent. Before the quotation are words that introduce and attribute it to a speaker, but the quotation itself could stand alone and is, in fact, an independent thought. The capital letter signals this independence.

When a quotation is grammatically incorporated into the sentence in which it appears, the first word of the quotation is not capitalized unless it is a proper noun.

She knew that "the woods are lovely, dark, and deep," but sun, sand, and sea appealed to her, too.

The newspaper's motto was "all the news that's fit to print," which made me wonder how bad the news had to be before it became unfit.

3. A complete sentence enclosed in parentheses or brackets.

The survey shows that cigarette smoking has declined nationally in the last ten years but that smoking among women has increased. (See Table 3 for numerical data.)

"The Black Death killed anywhere between one-third to one-half of the entire population of Europe. [Exact numbers are impossible to derive, given the state of record-keeping in medieval Europe.] Those who survived were often too few to bury the dead."

When a parenthetical or bracketed statement appears within another sentence, the first word is ordinarily not capitalized and the ending period is omitted.

The survey shows that cigarette smoking has declined nationally in the last ten years but that smoking among women has increased (see Table 3 for numerical data).

4. A complete sentence following a colon.

Typically, an independent statement following a colon is not capitalized, particularly when it is closely related to the preceding sentence. However, if the independent statement is not closely related or if the writer wishes to emphasize it, a capital letter may be used.

> There were fifteen or twenty women in the room: None of them was his mother.

28b
Capitalize the pronoun *I* and the interjection *O*.

> How long must I wait, O Lord?

Do not capitalize the interjection *oh* unless it is the first word of a sentence.

> Oh how we enjoyed the party, but oh how we paid for our fun later.

28b

word p

28c
Capitalize proper nouns, their derivatives and abbreviations, and common nouns used as proper nouns.

1. Specific persons, races, nationalities, languages.

Willa	Bob	Rita Mae Browne	Semitic
Asiatic	American	Mongolian	Cuban
Canadian	English	Swahili	Zulu

Usage varies for the term *black (blacks)* as an ethnic designation. Although it is often not capitalized, and is never capitalized in the phrase "blacks and whites," many authors regularly capitalize other uses in current writing.

2. Specific places.

Atlanta	Buenos Aires	California	Lake Erie
Newfoundland	India	Jerusalem	Snake River

3. Specific organizations, historical events, and documents.

Daughters of the American Revolution	the French Revolution
the Locarno Pact	NAACP
Declaration of Independence	

4. Days of the week, months, holidays, and holy days.

Thursday	November	Christmas	Sunday	Labor Day
Easter	Good Friday	Hanukkah	Ramadan	Yom Kippur

5. Religious terms, deities, and sacred texts.

the Virgin   Allah   Holy Ghost   Jehovah   the Torah

6. Titles of books, plays, magazines, newspapers, journals, articles, poems. Capitalize the first word and all others except articles (*a/an, the*), and conjunctions and prepositions of fewer than five letters. (See also **25h** and **27a.**)

Gone with the Wind	*The Country Wife*	*Pippa Passes*
Paradise Lost	*Atlantic Monthly*	*War and Peace*
Ebony	*Much Ado About Nothing*	*Business Week*

28c

word p

7. Titles, and their abbreviations, when they precede a proper noun. Such titles are an essential part of the name and are regularly capitalized. Abbreviations for academic degrees and professional certificates are also capitalized when they follow a proper name.

Professor Berger	Mr. Rothstein	Vice Chairman
Dr. Carolyn Woo	Justice Sandra	Diaz
President Reagan	Day O'Connor	John Leland,
Thomas Hass,	Valarie Petroski,	Ph.D.
M.D.	C.P.A.	Editor-in-Chief
Secretary Dole	Associate Dean	Weil
	G.P. Bass	

When a title follows a name, capitalize it only if it indicates high distinction:

Abraham Lincoln, President of the United States
John Marshall, Chief Justice of the Supreme Court

BUT   Sally S. Fleming, director of corporate communications
J. R. Derby, professor of English

Often the "in-house" conventions of a particular organization include capitalizing titles after names. For example, in an annual report or employee newsletter you would probably see the following:

Sally S. Fleming, Director of Corporate Communications

This use of capitals suggests that the concept of high distinction is strongly related to audience and context. Although a title following a name may not warrant the distinctive treatment of capitalization for a general audience (the readers of your paper about corporate research and development), that same title may well be capitalized for a specialized audience (Fleming's coworkers).

8. **Common nouns used as an essential part of a proper noun.** These are generic names such as *street, river, avenue, lake, county, ocean, college, church, award.*

Vine Street	Lake Huron	Hamilton College
Fifth Avenue	General Motors Corporation	Pulitzer Prize
Pacific Ocean	Penn Central Railroad	Mississippi River

When the generic term is used in the plural, it is not usually capitalized.

Vine and Mulberry streets	the Atlantic and Pacific oceans
Hamilton and Lake counties	the Catholic and Protestant churches in town

28d

Avoid unnecessary capitalization.

A good general rule is not to capitalize unless a specific convention warrants it.

1. **Capitalize *north, east, south, west* only when they come at the beginning of a sentence or refer to specific geographical locations.**

Birds fly south in the winter.

BUT She lives in the western part of the Old South.

2. **The names of seasons need not be capitalized.**

fall   autumn   winter   midwinter   spring   summer

3. **Capitalize nouns indicating family relationships only when they are used as names or titles or in combination with proper names. Do not capitalize *mother* and *father* when they are preceded by possessive adjectives**

I telephoned my mother.

BUT I telephoned Mother.

My uncle has four children.

BUT My Uncle Ben has four children.

4. **Ordinarily, do not capitalize common nouns and adjectives used in place of proper nouns and adjectives.**

I went to high school in Cleveland.

BUT I went to John Adams High School in Cleveland.

I am a university graduate.

BUT   I am a Columbia University graduate.

I took a psychology course in my senior year.

BUT   I took Psychology 653 in my senior year.

She received a master's degree in computer science.

BUT   She received a Master of Science degree from the Computer Science Department.

EXERCISE 28a–d

Capitalize words as necessary in the following sentences. Remove unnecessary capitals.

1. martin luther king, jr., who won the nobel peace prize in 1964 when he was thirty-five years old, was the youngest person ever to receive that award.
2. King was born in 1929 and graduated from morehouse college at age nineteen; later, he received a ph.d. from boston university.
3. When the black boycott of segregated buses began in montgomery, alabama, king was the Pastor of the largest black baptist church in the City.
4. The techniques of mahatma gandhi, the indian Leader, influenced king in his belief in Non-violent protest.
5. through his work in the civil rights movement, king became an important National and International leader.
6. Martin Luther King, jr., wrote several books, among them *where do we go from here?* and *why we can't wait.*
7. king became so well-known that he appeared on the cover of *time* magazine.
8. in 1963, king went South to birmingham, alabama, where he led a huge Demonstration against Segregation and Discrimination.
9. Eventually, king and 2,400 civil rights workers were arrested and jailed in birmingham; one of king's most famous writings, "letter from birmingham jail," came from the experience.
10. In april 1968 martin luther King, jr., was in memphis, tennessee, where he had gone to give support to Striking Garbage Workers; There, on april 4, he was killed by an Assassin's bullet.

29

THE APOSTROPHE

29a

Use an apostrophe to show the possessive case of nouns and indefinite pronouns.

1. If a word (either singular or plural) does not end in s, add an apostrophe and s to form the possessive.

the woman's book   the women's books
the child's book   the children's books
the man's book   the men's books
someone's book   people's books

2. If the singular of a word ends in s add an apostrophe and s unless the second s makes pronunciation difficult; in such cases, add only the apostrophe.

        Lois's car   James's sandwich
BUT Moses' leadership Sophocles' dramas

(The addition of a second s would change the pronunciation of *Moses* to *Moseses* and *Sophocles* to *Sophocleses*.)

29a

word p

3. If the plural of a word ends in s, add only the apostrophe.

the girls' locker room
the boys' blue jeans
the Smiths' house [Referring to at least two persons named Smith]

4. In compounds, make only the last word possessive.

father-in-law's pipe [Singular possessive]
mothers-in-law's birthdays [Plural possessive]
someone else's fault

5. In nouns of joint possession, make only the last noun possessive; in nouns of individual possession, make both nouns possessive.

John and Paul's office [Joint possession]
John's and Paul's offices [Individual possession]

Here is a list showing standard singular and plural possessive forms:

Singular	Possessive Singular	Plural	Possessive Plural
child	child's	children	children's
man	man's	men	men's
lady	lady's	ladies	ladies'
father-in-law	father-in-law's	fathers-in-law	fathers-in-law's
passer-by	passer-by's	passers-by	passers-by's

29b

Use an apostrophe to indicate the omission of a letter or number.

can't	cannot	o'clock	of the clock
doesn't	does not	blizzard of '89	blizzard of 1889
it's	it is	will-o'-the-wisp	will of the wisp

In reproducing speech, writers frequently use an apostrophe to show that a word is given a colloquial or dialectical pronunciation.

"An' one o' the boys is goin' t' be sick," he said.

29c

Use an apostrophe and *s* to form the plurals of letters, numbers, and words used as words.

If the letters, numbers, and words are italicized (see Section **27c**), the *s* is not.

Cross your *t*'s and dot your *i*'s.
Tighten your sentence structure by eliminating unnecessary *and*'s.
The 1970's were known as the "me decade."

These are the only kinds of situations in which the apostrophe is used in forming plurals. It is never used in forming the plurals of proper names or other nouns.

29d

Do not use the apostrophe with the possessive form of personal pronouns.

The personal pronouns *his, hers, its, ours, yours, theirs* and the pronoun *whose* are possessives as they stand and do not require the apostrophe.

his father   an idea of *hers*   a friend of *theirs*

Be particularly careful not to confuse the possessive pronoun *its* with the contraction *it's* (it is).

We couldn't find *its* nest.
We know *it's* a robin.

EXERCISE 29a–d

Insert apostrophes or apostrophes plus *s* as necessary in the following sentences. Then write five sentences of your own that use apostrophes in various ways.

1. Searching for ones ancestors, which might begin as a casual hobby, can become a time-consuming, but rewarding, adventure.
2. Its not easy to trace a genealogy, for a familys records may be difficult to find, and the information thats available may be inaccurate.
3. Over the years, a persons name may have been changed, or as often is the case, the spelling of family names wont be the same on various records.
4. Draw up a family tree by consulting Bibles, letters, and other documents; the chart should show family members names as well as the names of those who married into the family—for example, brothers-in-laws and sisters-in-laws names.
5. Interviewing living relatives can also provide useful information: your grandmothers attic might be a storehouse of helpful information, and your two elderly aunts memories may prove to be very sharp when recalling the people and events of their youth.
6. Its also vital to check your local librarys section dealing with genealogy or local history; also, the county record office, with its files of birth and marriage certificates and land records, can be a genealogists treasure trove.
7. In the United States, various libraries and historical societies that have genealogical collections will often answer writers requests for information.
8. Searching for your ancestors can be confusing as well as fascinating; while youre poring over records, you may discover that your family changed its name, and what you thought were the Smiths records suddenly became the Schwartzs records.
9. For those who dont want to do their own searches, professional genealogists, who charge about $20.00 for each hours work, are available.
10. Although professionals will do peoples searches for them, many people prefer to spend the time it takes to research their familys history, for discovering the facts of mens and womens lives gives the searcher a great deal of satisfaction.

30

word p

30

THE HYPHEN

The hyphen has two distinct uses: (1) to form compound words, and (2) to indicate that a word is continued from one line to the next.

Convention in the latter use of the hyphen, called *syllabication* or *word division,* is arbitrarily fixed. (See Section **18**.) However, convention in the use of hyphens with compounds not only shifts rapidly but is unpredictable. As a noun, *short circuit* is spelled as two words; but the verb *short-circuit* is hyphenated. *Shorthand* and *shortstop* are spelled as single words, but *short order* is spelled as two words. *Short-term* in *short-term loan* is hyphenated, but in *the loan is short term* it is spelled as two words.

In such a rapidly changing and unpredictable matter, your only safe recourse is to consult a good, up-to-date dictionary. The following uses of the hyphen in forming compound words are widely accepted.

30a

Use a hyphen to form compound words that are not yet accepted as single words.

The spelling of compound words that express a single idea passes through successive stages. Originally spelled as two separate words, then as a hyphenated word, a compound word finally emerges as a single word.

> *base ball* became *base-ball* became *baseball*
> *post mark* became *post-mark* became *postmark*

There is no certain way of determining the proper spelling of a compound at any given moment. Your dictionary is your most authoritative reference.

30b

Use a hyphen to join two or more words serving as a single adjective before a noun.

Do not hyphenate such an adjective if it follows the verb as a predicate adjective.

> a well-known speaker
> BUT   The speaker was well known.
>
> a grayish-green coat
> BUT   The coat was grayish green.
>
> nineteenth-century American fiction
> BUT   American fiction of the nineteenth century

Omit the hyphen when the first word is an adverb ending in *-ly*.

> a slow-curving ball
> BUT   a slowly curving ball

a quick-moving runner
BUT a quickly moving runner

30c
Use a hyphen to avoid an ambiguous or awkward union of letters.

re-create [for "create again"]
NOT recreate

bell-like
NOT belllike

There are many common exceptions, however.

coeducational   coordinate   cooperate   readdress

30d
Use a hyphen to form compound numbers from twenty-one through ninety-nine and to separate the numerator from the denominator in written fractions.

twenty-nine   fifty-five   two-thirds   four-fifths

30e
Use a hyphen with the prefixes *self-, all-, ex-,* and the suffix *-elect.*

self-important   all-conference   ex-mayor   governor-elect

Do not capitalize the prefix *ex-* or the suffix *-elect,* even when used in titles that are essential parts of a name.

ex-Mayor Sanchez   Governor-elect Jones   ex-President Ford

EXERCISE 30
Insert hyphens as needed. Then write five sentences containing compound adjectives, some of which precede nouns and some of which follow verbs as predicate adjectives.

1. Ex athletes often become well known as sports commentators.
2. Perhaps their quick reactions on the playing field help them to make the kinds of fast thinking observations expected of a sports commentator.
3. My friend says that there are so many former athletes on sports broadcasts now that it seems as though three fourths of the well known athletes must go into broadcasting.

4. But not all ex athletes go into broadcasting; the senator elect from my state is a former professional football player.

5. He was an All American when he was in college, so he is widely known in my state.

REVIEW EXERCISES ON WORD PUNCTUATION (Sections 27–30)

Supply the necessary italics, capitals, apostrophes, and hyphens in the following sentences.

1. I read an interesting article about the american west in this months issue of national geographic.

2. The article caused me to think of how important the idea of the west is in americas culture.

3. My friend, an ex texan, says she reads westerns and watches old cowboy movies on television to remind her of the wide open spaces of texas and the other western states.

4. My friends favorite western movie is high noon, starring gary cooper and grace kelly.

5. In my american literature class, we read a lot of fiction set in the west; i especially liked bret hartes story "the outcasts of poker flat."

6. The gambler and the good hearted dancehall girl in hartes story remind me of the same kinds of characters who often showed up in television westerns like gunsmoke.

7. After reading various authors depictions of the west, i decided to see how the area has been portrayed by artists.

8. I was fascinated by georgia o'keeffes art; I discovered that she spent a great deal of her long life in new mexico, where the colors of the desert influenced her work.

9. Some people might think o'keeffes paintings are avant-garde, but i like them, especially her painting Cow's Skull—Red, White and Blue, a painting she did in 1931.

10. Although viewers opinions may differ about o'keeffe, i think that everyone would have to admit that living in the western part of the united states influenced much of the artists work.

REVIEW EXERCISES ON PUNCTUATION (Sections 19–30)

EXERCISE A

Make all necessary corrections in internal punctuation and in the use of quotation marks, capitals, italics, apostrophes, and hyphens in the following sentences.

1. Brooklyn New York was once the nations fourth largest city but in 1898 it became an outer borough of new york city.

2. In the late 1800s and in the first half of the twentieth century brooklyns Navy Yard built huge battleships among them the Maine built in 1899 and the Missouri built in 1944.

3. Over two million people live in brooklyn today a figure that gives the 70 square mile area a higher population than seventeen states in the u.s.

4. The early settlers of the area were dutch irish and german later

great waves of jewish italian and scandinavian immigrants arrived giving the neighborhoods of brooklyn a rich ethnic mix.

5. Many people think of the Dodgers a major league baseball team when they think of brooklyn however the dodgers who had been playing at ebbets field in brooklyn since 1913 moved to los angeles california in 1957.

6. The brooklyn dodgers were famous for hiring jackie robinson the first black ballplayer in the major leagues and for winning their first world series by beating their rivals the new york yankees in 1955.

7. The brooklyn bridge is perhaps the most famous landmark associated with the city for its glittering graceful span links brooklyn with manhattan on the other side of the east river.

8. The bridge which was opened on may 24 1883 was at the time of its opening the longest suspension bridge in the world.

9. In his poem The Bridge Hart Crane 1899–1932 uses the brooklyn bridge as his basic symbol, said professor Postle our Literature instructor.

10. In the opening of cranes poem the poet addresses the bridge as he describes its stately beauty And Thee, across the harbor, silver-paced.

30e

word p

EXERCISE B

In the following paragraphs, insert any needed internal punctuation, as well as capitals, italics, apostrophes, and hyphens.

The english novelist charles dickens captured the imagination of his Victorian readers as no other novelist had done. Dickens was born on february 7 1812 in Portsmouth in southern england and later moved with his family to Chatham in Kent. Dickens childhood was affected by his fathers debts at one point the elder Dickens was imprisoned for not paying his debts. When he was twelve years old Charles Dickens worked in a blacking warehouse an experience that inspired the chapters in his novel David Copperfield in which the young david works in a bottle warehouse. After his grim experience in the warehouse Dickens worked in law offices learned shorthand became a reporter of debates at the House of Commons and contributed his writing to various periodicals. Dickens established his writing career with the popularity of The Pickwick Papers a novel that was first issued in twenty monthly installments from april 1836 to november 1837. The sale of The Pickwick Papers rose as high as 40000 copies per issue. Over the next several years Dickens published the novels Oliver Twist Nicholas Nickelby and The Old Curiosity Shop. In 1842 Dickens and his wife visited the united states and later he satirized americans in the novel Martin Chuzzlewit.

Dickens was a prolific writer for his success had made the reading public eager for more novels from him. He had moreover a large family to support with the profits from his writing. During his career as a novelist Dickens also founded and edited several periodicals. It was in one of these periodicals All the Year Round that Dickens published the installments of many of his later works such as

David Copperfield the autobiographical novel drawn from the authors childhood Bleak House a novel that deals with the english legal system A Tale of Two Cities a novel that deals with the french revolution and Great Expectations the story of a young boy who receives wealth from a mysterious source. When Dickens died suddenly on 9 June 1870 he left unfinished the novel The Mystery of Edwin Drood.

Dickens remains as popular with modern readers as he was with nineteenth century readers in fact the novels of Dickens have been made into movies for television and have been transformed into broadway musicals. Families make a tradition of reading A Christmas Carol each christmas a time when many children listen raptly to the transformation of Scrooge and wait eagerly to hear Tiny Tim say God Bless us, Every one! In addition Dickens house at 48 Doughty street London his home from 1837 to 1839 attracts many visitors each year. These visitors see numerous portraits of the author various Dickens memorabilia from all his houses and Dickens desk the desk at which he wrote on the day before he died.

30e

word p

EXERCISE C

In the following sentences, determine which marks of punctuation are used correctly, correct any marks used incorrectly, and add any needed punctuation.

1. Modern pharmacy which has its beginnings in ancient humans herb and root collecting has evolved through the centuries to its place today, as a vital part of the modern health profession.
2. As the practice of pharmacy evolved the pharmacist used methods first developed by the early alchemists, these practices in turn gave way to modern chemistry and its scientific methods.
3. During the early days of pharmacy, many physicians compounded the drugs they prescribed for their patients but today the roles of the physician, and the pharmacist have become quite different.
4. The profession of pharmacy has developed rapidly and widely in the twentieth century; for instance, todays pharmacist may work in industry in hospitals or in community pharmacies.
5. Those pharmacists, who work in industry, may be creating or testing new, and more effective medicines, or they may be developing new methods of delivering medicine—new kinds of tablets powders or capsules.
6. Nuclear medicine has created a need for nuclear pharmacists this group works with the radioactive drugs used by nuclear physicians in order to diagnose and treat disease.
7. Because modern drugs are often more potent have more side effects and can be more dangerous than earlier drugs, the modern pharmacists role often includes counseling and advising patients about the drugs their doctors have prescribed.
8. In the past pharmacists spent much of their time actually mixing drugs but most drugs today are produced by manufacturers in premeasured doses, therefore, community pharmacists spend a lot of

time answering the questions of patients who ask What are the side effects of this drug?

9. Pharmacists in hospitals spend much of their time producing solutions for intravenous fluids (IV's) a crucial task in which the drug must be soluble in the fluid.

10. Some pharmacists continue their studies in graduate school, and eventually teach or conduct research; current research involves such areas as endocrine pharmacology, the study of hormones and the drugs that affect hormones, behavioral pharmacology, the study of how chemicals affect human behavior, neuropharmacology, the study of how drugs affect the nervous system, and toxicology, the study of toxic drugs and their effects.

WRITERS REVISING: PUNCTUATION

On a biology test, students were asked to cite an example of current genetic research that was having a direct and practical impact on everyday life. Following is a draft of one student's answer before she had revised its punctuation. Supply the internal punctuation, word punctuation, and end punctuation you think is most appropriate and effective. Then compare your version with the student's revision. Be sure you can explain the reasons for the choices you made.

Draft

```
      Using the latest research
technology geneticists have
identified 12 characteristic genetic
differences between European honey—
bees and African honey—bees. Because
both types of bees belong to the same
species Apis mellifera they
are very difficult to tell apart a
severe problem for commercial
bee—keepers. The African bees are wild
quick to anger and vicious they will
sting intruders repeatedly pursuing
them for a quarter of a mile in some
```

30e

word p

cases. These bees have spread North
from Brazil to Honduras, and are
expected to reach the continental
united states within a few years.

Commercial bee—keepers in this
country wonder whether the destructive
African bees will take over hives
driving out the domestic European bees?
The results would be: interruption of
pollination of crops that are worth
almost $20 billion a year, and also
probable ruination of commercial honey
production. Isolating the African bees
has previously been nearly impossible,
however thanks to the new genetic,
identification technique bee colonies
can be quarantined or destroyed if they
are "invaded" by africanized
intruders.

Revision

Using the latest research
technology geneticists have   20b
identified 12 characteristic genetic
differences between European honey—
bees and African honey—bees. Because   30a
both types of bees belong to the same
species Apis mellifera they   20b, 27d, 20c(2)
are very difficult to tell apart a   23b
severe problem for commercial   27f
bee—keepers. The African bees are wild 30a, 20h

quick to anger,and vicious;they will   **20h, 22a**

sting intruders repeatedly,pursuing   **20c(1)**

them for a quarter of a mile in some

cases. These bees have spread North   **28d(1)**

from Brazil to Honduras and are   **24d**

expected to reach the continental

United States within a few years.   **28c(1)**

     Commercial bee keepers in this   **30a**

country wonder whether the destructive

African bees will take over hives   **20c(1)**

driving out the domestic European bees.   **19e**

The results would be interruption of   **24k**

pollination of crops that are worth

almost $20 billion a year and also   **24d**

probable ruination of commercial honey

production. Isolating the African bees

has previously been nearly impossible;   **21b**

however,thanks to the new genetic   **20f, 20h**

identification technique,bee colonies   **20b**

can be quarantined or destroyed if they

are invaded by Africanized   **25i, 28c(1)**

intruders.

30e

word p

EFFECTIVE
SENTENCES

ef

When you write, you make a point, not by subtracting as though you sharpened a pencil, but by adding. When you put one word after another, your statement should be more precise the more you add.

JOHN ERSKINE, *"A Note on the Writer's Craft"*

It's one thing to write sentences that are grammatical; it's another to write sentences that not only convey information but also explicitly establish the relationships among the ideas they are intended to express. Writers sometimes think effective sentences are just a matter of style, a concern important in poetry and novels but not vital to everyday writing.

As the following sample paragraph illustrates, nothing could be further from the truth. The writer, a manager at a large manufacturing company, forgot that one of his roles is to *make meaning,* to show his reader the connections among the chunks of information he presents. As they stand, his sentences are correct, but they give equal emphasis to everything—and, consequently, to nothing. What's more, when he reviewed this paragraph, the writer discovered he had actually subordinated major ideas and stressed minor details. He concluded that, indeed, sentence structure had a lot to do with how a reader perceives meaning. Compare the original version with the revision that follows it.

I usually dislike writing. I particularly dislike writing under pressure. My last four written documents were a plant appropriation request, a business letter, and two personal letters. The plant appropriation request was a thirty-five page report. It was prepared for the department staff's review and approval. I was trying to justify a request for funds to purchase a new computer system. The business letter was addressed to a system designer and confirmed a scheduled project review meeting. This letter also contained a list of issues and questions that I wanted discussed during the review. Both the report and the letter had to be written on short notice, and both involved thousands of dollars in business transactions. Thoroughly disliking the task, I really worried about the effect pressure was having on my writing. The two personal letters were written to friends, and I enjoyed writing them because I could relax.

I usually dislike writing, particularly when under pressure. My last four documents were a plant appropriation request, a business letter, and two personal letters. The plant appropriation request, a thirty-five page report that was prepared for the department staff's review and approval, justified my request for funds to purchase a new computer system. The business letter, addressed to a system designer and confirming a scheduled project review meeting, also contained a list of issues and questions I wanted discussed during the review. Both the report and the letter had to be written on short notice. Because both involved thousands of dollars in business transactions, I really worried about the effect pressure was having on my writing. Consequently, I thoroughly disliked the task. In contrast,

because the two personal letters were written to friends, I could relax and enjoy writing them.

Notice that the writer combined some sentences, inserting details
previously placed in separate sentences. He also moved some combinations from one sentence to another. For example, instead of leaving
the ideas concerning short notice and expensive transactions in a coordinated sentence (the ideas connected by *and*), he decided to develop the cause-and-effect relationship between business responsibility, time pressure, and effective writing. He stressed his dislike of the
situation in a short, simple sentence that now varies from the other
sentence patterns, thus drawing extra attention to the idea; but he
used a connecting word *(consequently)* to show the sentence's relationship to the preceding thought. Because the ideas are now shaped by
sentence structures that clarify meaning, the reader is much more
likely to understand what the writer intended. An added benefit is that
during the revising process the writer was able to edit his sentences so
that the number of words in his new paragraph is fewer than in the
original. The final result is not only clearer but also less time-consuming for the reader. The following sections discuss ways you can use
sentence structure to help make clear to your readers the meaning you
intend.

31

sub

31

COORDINATION AND SUBORDINATION

Many effective sentences bring together two or more ideas, relating them to one another by coordination and subordination. In a
broad sense, **coordination** expresses equality: two things that are coordinate have roughly the same importance, the same rank, the same
value. **Subordination** expresses some sort of inequality: when one
thing is subordinate to or dependent upon another, it is in some way
of lesser importance, rank, or value. Coordination and subordination
allow us to indicate relationships between and among ideas by means
of grammatical form and placement, without having to say directly
"This is equal to that" or "This information is additional, qualifying
detail—important, but not as important as the main idea."

31a
Coordination brings equal, related ideas together.

Coordination allows you to combine equal parts of separate
ideas into a single sentence by creating compound subjects, objects,
modifiers, or whole predicates. Using **coordinating conjunctions**

(such as *and, but, or, nor, so, yet, for*) to connect words, phrases, and clauses—and putting them in the same grammatical form—you can express clear relationships between ideas without needless repetition.

> Dogs belong to the Canidae family. Foxes belong to the Canidae family. Jackals belong to the Canidae family.
> *Dogs, foxes,* and *jackals* belong to the Canidae family. [Coordinate subjects]
>
> Members of the Canidae family possess four legs. They eat meat. They have acute senses of smell.
> Members of the Canidae family possess four legs, eat meat, and have acute senses of smell. [Coordinate verbs *possess, eat,* and *have;* coordinate objects *legs, meat,* and *senses*]
>
> One of the family's general characteristics is a long muzzle. Another is large canine teeth. Another is a long tail.
> The family's general characteristics are a long muzzle, large canine teeth, and a long tail. [Coordinate predicate nouns *muzzle, teeth,* and *tail*]

31a

sub

In addition to the more common coordinators, **correlative conjunctions** that work in pairs—*both–and, either–or, neither–nor, not–but, not only–but also*—and **conjunctive adverbs** such as *however, consequently, therefore,* and *nonetheless* can be used to join ideas. Unlike correlative conjunctions, conjunctive adverbs *never* connect words, phrases, or dependent clauses; they coordinate whole sentences only.

> The domestic species is characterized by its worldwide distribution in close association with humans. It is also characterized by its enormous amount of genetic variability.
> The domestic species is characterized not only by its worldwide distribution in close association with humans but also by its enormous amount of genetic variability. [Coordinate adverbial prepositional phrases joined by correlative conjunctions *not only* and *but also*]
>
> The Canidae family is sometimes loosely referred to as the dog family. The term "dog" usually refers only to the domestic species.
> The Canidae family is sometimes loosely called the dog family; however, the term "dog" usually refers only to the domestic species. [Conjunctive adverb *however* coordinating two sentences]

As these examples illustrate, coordination allows you to combine complex ideas and information from several sentences. When the ideas in such sentences are equal and closely related, you aid your readers if you can bring the ideas together into a single, easy-to-follow sentence that reveals those relationships. Compare the following:

Winter is the season when animals get stripped down to the marrow. Humans also do. Animals can take the winter easy by hibernating. Humans are exposed naked to the currents of elation and depression.

Winter is the season when *both* animals *and* humans get stripped down to the marrow, *but* many animals can hibernate, take the winter easy, as it were; we humans are exposed naked to the currents of elation and depression.

MAY SARTON, *Plant Dreaming Deep*

Although the information in both versions is much the same, the first forces the reader to work much harder to discover that animals and humans share the same exposure to winter, but with different effects. May Sarton's single sentence pulls all the relationships tightly and clearly together for the reader by first linking *animals* and *humans* with the coordinating pair *both . . . and.* She then establishes the idea of contrast between them with *but,* and carries out the contrast by linking her statements about animals on the one hand and humans on the other with the semicolon, itself a kind of coordinating link.

31a

sub

EXERCISE 31a

Combine the following sentences using coordinating conjunctions either to form compound sentences or to link similar elements to form compound subjects, objects, predicates, or modifiers. You may need to make slight changes in wording. If appropriate, use a conjunctive adverb to coordinate two sentences. After you have combined the sentences at each number, rewrite them as a paragraph. Revise and recombine as necessary to create a smooth, coherent paragraph.

1. People view bats as frightening creatures. Most of the ideas people have concerning bats are misconceptions.
2. According to experts, bats do not swoop down on people. Bats do not become entangled in people's hair.
3. Bats are not birds. They are not insects. They are mammals. They are also shy creatures. They are secretive. They are nocturnal.
4. Bats usually produce only one offspring a year. Bats can live up to thirty years.
5. Bats are useful as laboratory subjects. They have helped scientists in developing navigational aids. Bats have been useful in producing vaccines. Bats have also been used in developing birth control techniques.
6. Bats are an important link in the ecosystem. They are the major predators of night-flying insects. People try to destroy bat populations.
7. In order to eradicate bats, misguided people use guns to rout them from caves. Others use dynamite to drive out bats. Some bats are destroyed by pesticides.

8. Some people mistakenly believe that bats are vampires. The only breed of vampire bats lives exclusively in Latin America.
9. Vampire bats constitute only one-third of one percent of all bat species. The possibility of ever encountering a vampire bat is extremely small.
10. Misconceptions about bats have caused people to be afraid of them. Bats' peculiar appearance has also caused them to be feared.

31b
Subordination shows connections between unequal but related information; the central idea appears in the main clause, and less important ideas appear in subordinate constructions.

Writing is essentially a process of addition. Subordination allows you to build details, qualifications, and other lesser information into sentences, while keeping the main statement of the sentence clear and sharply focused. When you put information into subordinate constructions, you indicate to your readers that these constructions are less important than the main statement, even though they may be vital to the full meaning of the sentence. Subordinating conjunctions, particularly, enable you to express exact relationships among ideas.

Among the most important relationships expressed by subordinating conjunctions are cause, condition, concession, purpose, time, and location. These relationships, along with the most common subordinating conjunctions expressing them, are illustrated below. Notice how the conjunctions are used to combine ideas so that one idea is subordinated to another.

31b

sub

CAUSE

because, since

Many animal species are nearing extinction. They are protected by law.

Because many animal species are nearing extinction, they are protected by law.

CONDITION

if, even if, provided, unless

Some species can be saved. We can protect their habitats.

Some species can be saved, *if* we can protect their habitats.

Unless we can protect their habitats, some species cannot be saved.

CONCESSION

although, though, even though

Alligators are protected by law in Florida. Poachers still hunt them for their hide and meat.

Although alligators are protected by law in Florida, poachers still hunt them for their hide and meat.

PURPOSE

in order that, so that, that

Land has been drained and cleared. It can be used for real-estate development.

Land has been drained and cleared *so that* it can be used for real-estate development.

TIME

as long as, after, before, when, whenever, while, until

The Florida swamps are drained. The alligators lose more of their natural habitat to human intruders.

Whenever the Florida swamps are drained, the alligators lose more of their natural habitat to human intruders.

LOCATION

where, wherever

New houses now stand on dry ground. Alligators once raised their young amid the sawgrass.

New houses now stand on dry ground *where* alligators once raised their young amid the sawgrass.

31b

sub

The relative pronouns—*who (whose, whom), which,* and *that*—allow you to use adjective clauses for subordinate information and details about nouns.

Humans have legitimate needs. They have come in conflict with the needs of wildlife.

Humans, *who* have legitimate needs, have come in conflict with the needs of wildlife.

Wildlife has given way. Its needs are equally legitimate.

Wildlife, *whose* needs are equally legitimate, has given way.

Land and wildlife management can help save endangered species. It considers the balance between humans and the rest of nature.

Land and wildlife management, *which* considers the balance between humans and the rest of nature, can help save endangered species.

Deciding which information to subordinate and which to place in the sentence's main clause depends on what you consider to be most important and where you want to focus your reader's attention. For example, the last of the preceding sample sentences could have been written *Land and wildlife management, which can help save endangered species, considers the balance between humans and the rest of nature.* However, the writer chose to emphasize the help provided by such management and to place the other information in a subordinate clause. As another illustration, compare the difference in emphasis—and thus in meaning—when the previous example sentence *New houses now stand on dry ground where alligators once raised their young* . . . is rewritten *Alligators once raised their young* . . . *where new houses now stand on dry ground.* In the first instance, the past is subordinated to the present; in the second instance, the present is subordinated to the past.

Readers rely greatly on your sentence construction to reveal the meaning you intend. Consequently, the main clause of a sentence should carry your central idea; details, qualifications, and other relevant information that is closely related but less important than the central idea should be put into subordinate constructions.

Consider the following sentence as a possible topic sentence for a paragraph:

> Gorillas have often been killed to permit the capture of their young for zoos, and humans have recently been occupying more and more of their habitat, and gorillas are now threatened with extinction.

31b

sub

Although the information in the sentence is perfectly clear, it is unclear whether the central concern is with the gorillas' threatened extinction or with the causes for that threat, because the coordinating conjunction *and* gives equal emphasis to each of the ideas the sentence expresses. Readers will probably assume that the principal concern is the threat to the gorillas' existence, but they cannot be sure from the sentence what direction the paragraph will take.

Either of the following versions, however, makes the central concern of the writer unmistakably clear:

> Because gorillas have often been killed to permit the capture of their young for zoos, and humans have recently been occupying more and more of their habitat, *gorillas are now threatened with extinction.*

> Even though gorillas have often been killed to permit the capture of their young and are now threatened with extinction, *humans have recently been occupying more and more of their habitat.*

The first version of the sentence makes it clear that the writer's focus is on the threatened extinction of the gorillas; the second, that the writer's focus is on the current, increasing encroachment on the gorillas' habitat. Neither of these revisions is intrinsically better than the other. Which of them the writer chooses must be determined by the point the writer sees as most important.

EXERCISE 31b(1)

Combine the following pairs of sentences, using subordinating conjunctions that will express the relationships indicated in parentheses. You may need to make slight changes in the wording.

1. Wild lions now live in limited numbers in India and in Africa south of the Sahara Desert. They once roamed through Europe, the Middle East, and all of Africa. (Concession)

2. Lions live in a group called a pride. Lions are social animals. (Relative pronoun)

3. Usually, older males in a pride drive out the young males. This prevents the young male from mating with its mother or sisters. (Purpose)

4. Lionesses are better hunters than male lions. Lionesses are leaner and faster. (Cause)

5. Lions usually gather around a water hole or a lake bed. They wait in order to leap upon weaker animals coming to drink. (Location)

6. Lions like to get their food without too much work. On seeing vultures circling overhead, they will go to find the carcass. (Cause)

7. Another animal has made a kill. Lions will drive away the animal and take the meat for themselves. (Condition)

8. Game is scarce during a drought. Lions have difficulty finding food, and some members of the pride may starve. (Time)

9. Finding game each day is important. A grown lion can eat sixty pounds of meat at one feeding. (Cause)

10. Lions spend most of their time sleeping and resting. Most people picture lions constantly stalking prey. (Concession)

31c

sub

EXERCISE 31b(2)

Examine the sentences in Exercise 31a. Where it makes sense to do so, use subordinating conjunctions to combine sentences, placing one idea in the main clause and subordinating those ideas you think are less important. Then compare your new sentences with the ones you wrote using coordinating conjunctions. Notice the differences in meaning that result from these changes.

31c

Subordinating constructions such as appositives, participial phrases, and absolute phrases add information to sentences.

Although subordinate clauses, simple prepositional phrases, and single-word modifiers are most commonly used for subordinating ideas and details, writing also uses other subordinate constructions. Three useful ones are appositives, participial phrases, and absolute phrases. With these three constructions, you can imbed information in your sentences, making them economical and tightly knit. Appositives, participial phrases, and absolute phrases are also useful for adding variety to your sentences.

Such constructions are even more important to meaning. Participles, for example, are valuable for conveying action; absolutes are valuable for conveying detail; appositives are useful for reducing whole clauses to one or two tightly packed phrases that deliver meaning quickly. Effective and mature writing typically makes use of such subordinating constructions for their force and precision of expression.

APPOSITIVES

An appositive is a word or word group that renames, clarifies, further identifies, or expands the meaning of another word or phrase:

Sweden, *a Scandinavian country,* is very beautiful.

Unlike clauses or whole sentences, appositives have the same grammatical function as the word or phrase they clarify. That is, a word group that serves as an appositive to the subject of a sentence could also serve as the subject; an appositive to the object of a verb could also serve as the verb's object. Appositives most often function as nouns or noun word groups, but they may also serve as adjectives.

31c

sub

Appositives often offer an economical alternative to subordinate clauses. You can, for example, combine the following two sentences by putting the information of the second sentence either in a relative clause or in an appositive:

Sven Nilssen has told me much about Sweden. He is my close friend and an accomplished pianist.

Sven Nilssen, who is my close friend and an accomplished pianist, has told me much about Sweden.

But the combination with an appositive is briefer and moves more quickly:

Sven Nilssen, my close friend and an accomplished pianist, has told me much about Sweden.

In general, any nonrestrictive clause that consists of *who* or *which* as the subject, some form of the verb *to be,* and a complement can be reduced to an appositive, as in the following:

My mother was born in Lima, Ohio. She was the oldest of seven children.

My mother, the oldest of seven children, was born in Lima, Ohio.

Jim Slade, who is a militant labor organizer, has been repeatedly denied admission to the factory.

Jim Slade, a militant labor organizer, has been repeatedly denied admission to the factory.

Often a series of appositives can be used to bring together several details in a single sentence. In the following passage, each of the last three sentences states a separate observation about the way in which keepers of notebooks are a "different breed altogether."

> Keepers of private notebooks are a different breed altogether. They are lonely and resistant rearrangers of things. They are anxious malcontents. They are children afflicted at birth with some presentiment of loss.

But in the sentence she wrote, Joan Didion used a series of appositives to combine all these observations into a single smooth, clear sentence packed with information:

> Keepers of private notebooks are a different breed altogether, lonely and resistant rearrangers of things, anxious malcontents, children afflicted at birth with some presentiment of loss.
>
> JOAN DIDION, *On Keeping a Notebook*

31c

sub

Although appositives are most commonly noun groups, they can function as adjectives, as in the following:

A lovely hand tentatively rose. The hand was almost too thin to be seen.

A lovely hand, almost too thin to be seen, tentatively rose.

HERBERT KOHL, *36 Children*

She was about thirty-five years old. She was dissipated. She was gentle.

She was about thirty-five years old, dissipated and gentle.

JOHN CHEEVER, "The Sutton Place Story"

PARTICIPLES AND PARTICIPIAL PHRASES

Participles are nonfinite verb forms; that is, they cannot serve as main verbs in sentences, but they can help form verb phrases or function as adjectives. Like finite verbs, they can take objects and modifiers to form participial phrases. Present participles end in *-ing (living, studying, flowing, driving, eating).* Past participles of regular verbs end in *-ed (lived, studied, wasted);* past participles of irregular verbs often end in *-n* or *-en (blown, driven, eaten)* but sometimes have other irregular forms *(slept, clung, swum)*. Together with objects or modifiers, participles may form phrases, as in the following:

> *Eating through the sills of the house,* the termites caused great damage.
> *Dressed in the warmest clothes they could find,* Kathie and Mark stepped out into the driving wind.

Because they are comprised of verb forms, participial phrases are particularly useful for conveying action, as the preceding examples indicate.

Participial phrases often provide an alternative way of expressing information or ideas that can be expressed in sentences or dependent clauses. Compare the following:

> Writing is a slow process. It requires considerable thought and time.
> Writing is a slow process *which requires considerable thought and time.*
> Writing is a slow process, *requiring considerable thought and time.*

31c

sub

In contrast to relative clauses, which ordinarily must follow immediately after the nouns they modify, participial phrases can precede the nouns they modify. A participial phrase can usually be placed at more than one point in a sentence.

> The old house, *which was deserted twenty years ago and said to be haunted by the ghost of its former owner,* stood halfway up the hill.
> *Deserted twenty years ago and said to be haunted by the ghost of its former owner,* the old house stood halfway up the hill.
> The old house, *deserted twenty years ago and said to be haunted by the ghost of its former owner,* stood halfway up the hill.

Since participial phrases are somewhat flexible in their position, they often permit you to vary sentence structure to fit a particular purpose in a given paragraph. You must, however, be careful not to create misplaced modifiers with participial phrases (see Section **12a**).

Besides suggesting action, participial constructions are especially useful for describing events that occur at the same time as those in the main clause. Compare the following:

> The hikers struggled on. They were gasping for breath and nearly exhausted.
> The hikers, gasping for breath and nearly exhausted, struggled on.

In the following sentence, notice how John Updike uses a pair of present participial phrases to suggest that his walking through the yard and his clutching the child's hand both occur at the same time as his thinking that "It was all superstition."

[It was all] superstition, I thought, walking back through my yard, and clutching my child's hand tightly as a good luck token.

JOHN UPDIKE, "Eclipse"

ABSOLUTE PHRASES

Absolute phrases consist of a subject, usually a noun or a pronoun, and a participle, together with any objects or modifiers of the participle. They may be formed from any sentence in which the verb is a verb phrase that contains a form of the verb *be* followed by a present or past participle simply by omitting the *be* form. In other sentences they may be formed by changing the main verb of a sentence into its *-ing* form. Note the following:

SENTENCE	Her thoughts were wandering.
ABSOLUTE	Her thoughts wandering . . .
SENTENCE	The wind blew with increased fury, and the drifts rose ever higher.
ABSOLUTE	The wind blowing with increased fury, and the drifts rising ever higher . . .

31c

sub

When the participle of an absolute phrase is a form of the verb *be,* the verb is frequently omitted entirely, so that the absolute consists simply of a noun followed by adjectives.

The pianist played beautifully, her technique flawless, her interpretation sure and sensitive.

Because of its speed and compression, an absolute phrase allows you to add specific, concrete detail to a general statement with greater economy than most alternative constructions. Extremely flexible besides, it can be placed at the beginning or end of a sentence, or often in the middle:

The rain having stopped, we went to the beach.
Their dinner finished, the two industrialists were ready to talk business.
Slouched in our seats, we listened to the soothing music, *eyes closed.*
The little boy stood crying beside the road, *his bicycle broken, his knees bruised,* and *his confidence badly shaken.*
The driver of the wrecked car, *one leg trapped beneath the dashboard, body pinned firmly against the steering wheel,* waited patiently for the rescue squad.

EXERCISE 31c

Combine each of the following sets of sentences, expressing in the main clause what you consider to be the most important idea and using appositives, participial phrases, or absolute phrases to subordinate other ideas. After you have combined the sentences in items 1 through 10, rearrange, revise, and recombine them to create a smooth, coherent paragraph.

1. The Baseball Hall of Fame is a popular attraction for fans of the sport often called "America's pastime." The Hall of Fame is located in the small town of Cooperstown, New York.
2. The upstate New York village of Cooperstown was founded in 1786 by Judge William Cooper. He was the father of author James Fenimore Cooper.
3. The Hall of Fame and its museum attract over 200,000 visitors each year. The museum traces the evolution of baseball from its earliest days to today's multi-million-dollar sport.
4. The museum walls are covered with photographs. Its display cases are filled with memorabilia. The museum stores a wealth of baseball history.
5. Avid baseball fans will see a bat displayed in the exhibit. Roger Maris used the bat to hit his sixty-first home run in 1961.
6. Only two players have been honored with life-size sculptures in the museum. These players are Babe Ruth and Ted Williams.
7. The arm of Ted Williams is posed in his famous swing. The figure looks as though he has just hit a home run.
8. The induction ceremony for the National Baseball Hall of Fame takes place every year in Cooperstown. The Hall of Fame members are elected by baseball writers and a special Hall of Fame committee.
9. Legend claims that Abner Doubleday invented baseball in a Cooperstown pasture in 1839. Today, an exhibition game between two major league teams is played each year at Doubleday Field near the Hall of Fame.
10. Cooperstown is thought of as the home of baseball. It attracts baseball fans, and it continues to lure both young and old fans to its nostalgic displays.

31d

sub

31d

Excessive or faulty coordination and subordination hinder meaning.

If you completed the second half of Exercise 31c, you may have learned that too much of a good thing is no good at all. Too much subordination and coordination, or subordination and coordination used incorrectly, may show the writer's skill at jamming information into dense constructions but is not necessarily easy or pleasant to read. Such sentences force too many chunks of information on the reader at once. Your goal in the use of coordinating and subordinating constructions should be to clarify meaning.

EXCESSIVE COORDINATION

As writers become experienced, they discover that paragraphs composed mainly of short, simple sentences make their writing sound childish. Such sentences are sometimes called "primer" sentences because they resemble those of children's first reading books. Series of sentences such as *He stood on a street corner. The wind was blowing. He peered into the darkness. He had no place to go* are not only monotonous and choppy but indiscriminate, giving equal weight and importance to all the facts and ideas.

•Stringing the sentences together with a series of *and*'s and *but*'s is just as ineffective as a choppy series of simple sentences: *He stood on a street corner and the wind was blowing and he peered into the darkness, but he was a stranger so he had no place to go* sounds equally childish—although more breathless. The ideas still receive equal emphasis with no clue as to which information is more or less important.

Help your readers understand which ideas are important and which are minor by reworking primer sentences into more complex ones that use both coordination and subordination to reflect meaning. The following revisions illustrate two different meanings for the preceding primer sentences.

31d

sub

> Standing on a windy street corner and peering into the darkness, the stranger had no place to go.
> Standing on a windy street corner, the stranger peered into the darkness. He had no place to go.

The first revision emphasizes the stranger's having no place to go by placing this idea in the main clause. The second revision preserves one of the short, simple sentences but combines three others. Thus the writer gains two points of emphasis by means of the two main clauses *the stranger peered into the darkness* and *He had no place to go*. The last main clause, the short, simple sentence, achieves extra impact because its structure differs from the preceding sentence. The revisions show that the writer had in mind a slightly different effect, and hence different meaning, for each.

EXCESSIVE SUBORDINATION

Like excessive coordination, excessive subordination occurs when you include in a sentence details that are inessential or only loosely related to the main line of thought. It also occurs when successive dependent clauses are strung together, each attached to the preceding one without a clear relationship to the main clause. In the following example, the italicized clauses are only remotely related to the main direction of the sentence. They clutter rather than clarify what the writer is saying. The revision shows how the writer decided what he really meant to say and how he restructured the information to convey that meaning.

> EXCESSIVE SUBORDINATION
> My fishing equipment includes a casting rod *which my Uncle Henry gave me many years ago* and which is nearly worn out, and an assortment of lines, hooks, and bass flies, which make good bait *when I can get time off from work to go bass fishing* at Hardwood Lake.

> REVISED
> My fishing equipment includes an old casting rod and an assortment of lines, hooks, and bass flies—which make good bait. When I can get time off from work, I like to go bass fishing at Harwood Lake.

In the following sentence, the successive details are all essential, but the structure of successive dependent clauses makes their relationship hard to grasp.

> EXCESSIVE SUBORDINATION
> We walked down Fifth Avenue, which led us to Washington Square, where we saw the memorial arch, which resembles the *Arc de Triomphe* which is in Paris.

31d

sub

Such sentences can often be improved by changing some of the clauses to modifying phrases.

> REVISED
> We walked down Fifth Avenue to Washington Square, where we saw the memorial arch resembling the *Arc de Triomphe* in Paris.

Sometimes effectiveness requires that a sentence be reworked as two separate sentences. Even when relationships to the main clause are clear, using too many subordinate constructions can overload readers. It may be challenging to see how much information you can pack into a single sentence, but if the meaning becomes too complex many readers will simply stop trying to comprehend it.

FAULTY COORDINATION

Faulty coordination occurs when you coordinate two or more facts or ideas that have no logical connection.

> FAULTY
> The poet John Keats wrote "The Eve of St. Agnes," and he died of tuberculosis.

Two such unrelated facts would make strange bedfellows even if one were subordinated to the other, unless perhaps they were given some such meaningful context as the following:

She could remember only two facts about John Keats: He wrote "The Eve of St. Agnes," and he died of tuberculosis.

Sometimes faulty coordination occurs when writers leave out important information that is evident to them but not to a reader.

> **FAULTY**   My uncle was in the army in World War II, but he didn't have enough money to finish college.
>
> **CLEAR**   Although my uncle's service in World War II entitled him to some education under the G.I. bill for veterans, he didn't have enough money to finish college.

A somewhat different kind of faulty coordination occurs when a writer coordinates items from overlapping classes. In the following sentence, for example, the four-item coordinate series makes it appear that there are four different kinds of animals or birds in the pet show the writer is describing. But clearly there are only three: dogs, parrots, and monkeys. The "mangy cocker spaniel" belongs among the dogs.

> **CONFUSING**   Entered in the pet show were several dogs, two parrots, three monkeys, and a mangy cocker spaniel.
>
> **CLEAR**   Entered in the pet show were two parrots, three monkeys, and several dogs, one of which was a mangy cocker spaniel.

31d

sub

FAULTY SUBORDINATION

Faulty subordination, sometimes called "upside-down" subordination, occurs when the idea the reader would normally expect to be the more important is placed in a subordinate clause. In many sentences, determining which ideas to place in a main clause and which to subordinate depends entirely on context. In one context, you might want to write *While Lincoln was still President, he was shot,* thus emphasizing the assassination itself. In another, you might want to write *When he was shot, Lincoln was still President,* thereby making more prominent the fact that he was still in office. Only your intentions as writer and the demands of a particular context can make one of these versions preferable to the other.

Readers apply the logic of normal expectation to most sentences. A sentence such as *She happened to glance at the sidewalk, noticing a hundred-dollar bill at her feet* contradicts the reader's sense of the relative importance of the two ideas, glancing at the sidewalk and noticing the money. Ordinarily, the finding of one hundred dollars would be the logically emphasized fact; a reader would expect the sentence to say *Happening to glance at the sidewalk, she noticed a hundred-dollar bill at her feet.*

EXERCISE 31d(1)

Revise the first passage to eliminate excessive coordination and excessive subordination. Revise the second passage, using both coordination and subordination where appropriate to eliminate choppy, ineffective sentences. Your revisions should create meaningful relationships between ideas.

1. I was staying at my sister's house for the summer, and I volunteered to take charge of my four-year-old nephew's fifth birthday party, but I didn't know what a mess I was getting myself into. Thinking that my nephew, who is named Johnny, would want a simple cake-and-ice-cream party, and remembering my own birthday parties when I was young, I began to plan the party for Johnny's birthday, which would be a week from Saturday. I planned to make a chocolate cake, and I wanted to get strawberry ice cream, and I thought I'd buy balloons and party hats which would be something the children could take home and keep, but I hadn't asked Johnny what he wanted, so I thought I would just check and make sure he liked my plans.

2. I talked to Johnny that night. I got a big shock. He didn't like my plans. He wanted to go to a fast-food restaurant for his party. He wanted hamburgers. He also wanted cake and ice cream. He said soft drinks had to be served. That wasn't all. He wanted to go to the movies after going to the fast-food restaurant. He wanted to take along all his guests. I couldn't believe it. I said, "That party will last all afternoon." I looked at him. He looked disappointed. I thought about it for a minute. I said, "Well, I guess we can try your ideas." Johnny hugged me. He jumped up and down. He told me it would be the best birthday party anyone ever had.

EXERCISE 31d(2)

Revise the following passage, eliminating faulty coordination and faulty subordination. Add information as necessary to establish logical, meaningful relationships among ideas.

It was the day of Johnny's birthday party, and I took him and nine of his friends, who were all four-year-olds, to the fast-food restaurant. The restaurant was crowded, and other kids were having parties, and I ended up in a hot room filled with screaming kids, and I could hardly stand the noise. Because some of Johnny's friends wanted me to take the pickles off their hamburgers, they were picky eaters. I had to wipe off their faces, clean up their spills, wipe off their hands, and pick up the french fries they dropped on the floor. They all got balloons, although the balloons were part of the party arrangements I had made with the restaurant. While I rushed around, I tried to clean up everyone, but one little girl popped her balloon, and I jumped four feet in the air. We finished with cake and ice cream and then we left the restaurant and went to the movies where we saw an animated movie, and it bored me, but I couldn't go to sleep as fifty four- or five-year-olds were bouncing up and down throughout the theater. The movie ended at last when

I took each child home. Finally, Johnny and I got back to my sister's house, and I was exhausted, since Johnny had energy to spare. The last thing I remember was Johnny saying to me, "That was the best birthday ever," and I collapsed on the couch.

WRITERS REVISING: SUBORDINATION AND COORDINATION

The members of the student council in the business school were asked to nominate a professor for the Outstanding Instructor Award. The nomination was to be presented in writing, with specific discussion of such points as "student evaluations" and "innovations in classroom instruction." Following is a portion of an early draft of their nomination. Revise the draft to eliminate excessive subordination and excessive coordination. Then compare your version with the final draft the business students used to nominate Professor Ashwin Gupta. An analysis of the students' revision follows the final draft.

31d

sub

Draft

D 1   The extraordinary influence that Professor

D 2   Gupta has had in the professional preparation of

D 3   his students can be seen by the strong ratings he

D 4   has received on course evaluations, which

D 5   frequently place him above the 70th percentile on

D 6   such questions as "ability to achieve a

D 7   conceptual understanding of the material" because

D 8   he creates a close relationship between his class

D 9   and the students' educational goals, and he is

D10   rated above the 80th percentile in the "best

D11   course" and "best instructor" categories.

D12   Although the tremendous importance of the

D13   personal computer to the accounting profession is

D14   now well known, Professor Gupta recognized that

D15   importance very early, and four years ago his tax

D16   accounting course was the school's first

D17   undergraduate course to use a personal computer

D18   frequently in homework assignments and classroom

D19   work, thereby giving business students early and

D20   valuable exposure to the computer applications

D21   that have since become commonplace in the

D21   accounting profession.

The major flaw in the first draft is excessive use of coordinating conjunctions, particularly *and*. Each lengthy, strung-together sentence lacks focus and contains too many ideas. Notice that each paragraph, although several lines long, contains only a single sentence. So that readers can focus on points of emphasis and understand the relationships between ideas, the revision breaks the two long sentences into six shorter ones.

31d

sub

Revision

R 1   The extraordinary influence that Professor

R 2   Gupta has had in the professional preparation of

R 3   his students can be seen by the strong ratings he

R 4   has received on course evaluations ~~which~~ *His course evaluations*

R 5   frequently place him above the 70th percentile on

R 6   such questions as "ability to achieve a

R 7   conceptual understanding of the material" *no doubt* because

R 8   he creates a close relationship between his class

R 9   and the students' educational goals ~~and~~ he is *Furthermore,*

R10   rated above the 80th percentile in the "best

R11   course" and "best instructor" categories.

R12   Although the tremendous importance of the

R13   personal computer to the accounting profession is

R14   now well known, Professor Gupta recognized that

R15   importance very early ~~and~~ Four years ago his tax

R16   accounting course was the school's first

R17   undergraduate course to use a personal computer

R18   frequently in homework assignments and classroom

R19 work. ~~thereby giving~~ business students early and
Thus he gave

R20 valuable exposure to the computer applications

R21 that have since become commonplace in the

R22 accounting profession.

Analysis

The first sentence in the revision (R1–4) focuses on Gupta's influence as reflected in course evaluations. The second sentence (R4–9) is constructed from the "which" dependent clause in the first draft (D4–7). Thus, rather than burying the numerical information about Gupta's good ratings in a subordinate clause, the revision focuses on the ratings (in the main clause). The reason for these ratings (close relationship between class and goals) is placed in a dependent clause *(because . . .)* (R7–9), the writer having chosen to subordinate the explanation to the numbers. The third sentence (R9–11) achieves much more emphasis for the 80th percentile ratings by placing the information in a separate sentence (compare lines D9–11 and R9–11). The connection between this idea and the previous sentence is achieved with the transition *furthermore*.

The fourth sentence (R12–15) subordinates the importance of the personal computer (*although* dependent clause, R12–14) to the main clause about Professor Gupta's having *recognized* its importance (R14), thus focusing the reader's attention on the professor rather than the personal computer. However, because the dependent clause occurs first in the sentence, it receives some secondary emphasis. The evidence for the claim stated in the fourth sentence appears in a separate sentence (R15–19) so that both the claim and the evidence will make equally emphatic impressions on the reader's mind. The results—giving students early and valuable exposure to computers—benefit from the focus achieved with a separate sentence (R19–22). The transition word *Thus* provides the cause-and-effect link to the foregoing sentence.

32

PARALLELISM

When you coordinate two or more elements in a sentence, readers expect you to make them *parallel*, that is, to state them in the same grammatical form. Noun should be matched with noun, verb with verb, phrase with phrase, and clause with clause.

A lawyer must be *articulate* and *logical*. [Parallel and coordinate adjectives]

She *closed the door, opened the window,* and *threw herself* into the chair. [Three coordinate and parallel predicates, each consisting of verb plus direct object]

The otter's fur is dark-chocolate brown, and *its eyes are small and black.* [Two coordinate and parallel independent clauses]

Parallelism is a basic principle of effective writing and speaking. Equal form reinforces equal meaning. By putting equally important parts of a sentence or of successive sentences into equal grammatical constructions, you emphasize their relationship to one another. The parallelism confirms the coordinate relationship, the equal importance of the coordinate parts.

32a
Parallelism makes coordinate relationships clear.

32a

||

1. **In single sentences.** Putting equal ideas in a sentence in parallel constructions will help you make their coordinate relationship more immediately clear to your reader. Compare the following sentences:

> If they buy the assigned books, students can usually be successful, but they must read them and careful notes must be taken.
>
> Students can usually be successful if they *buy the assigned books, read them,* and *take careful notes.*

The first sentence really sets three conditions for a student's success: buying the books, reading them, and taking notes. But the sentence muddies this equal relationship by putting the first in an *if* clause separate from the other two; and although the last two conditions—reading the books and taking notes—are coordinated by *and,* the first is active and the second passive, thus further weakening their coordinate relationship. The revised sentence brings the three conditions neatly and clearly together in a single parallel series of predicates.

> The most overworked word in English is the word "set," which has 58 noun uses, 126 verbal uses, and 10 as a participial adjective.
>
> *Environmental Engineering News*

So strong is our desire for parallelism in series that as soon as we see the first two items in the preceding sample sentence, it is very likely that our minds will "fill in" the third phrase—even before we have actually read it. Consequently, when we realize that the sentence does not say . . . *and 10 participial adjective uses,* we may feel annoyed or cheated: the sentence's rhythm has been thwarted, as have our expectations.

2. Among successive sentences. Many times you can increase the coherence of your writing by combining several successive sentences into a single sentence that uses parallelism carefully.

Suppose you are trying to get together your ideas about the things necessary for good writing and that you have written the following in a first draft:

> Logical thinking is one of the things necessary for good writing. Good writers also have to organize their ideas coherently. And finally, anyone who wants to write well must express his or her ideas clearly.

Look at this draft closely; *thinking, organizing,* and *expressing* are the main related processes here. Parallel structure can help you knit these together tightly and emphasize them clearly. Compare the following single sentences with the three original sentences:

Thinking logically, organizing ideas coherently, and expressing ideas clearly	are three requirements of good writing.

32a

‖

or

Logical thought, coherent organization, and clear expression	are the major ingredients of good writing.

or

Anyone who wishes to write well must learn	to think logically, to organize ideas coherently, and to express them clearly.

Each of these versions of the first draft pulls the ideas together into a single economical unit and gives emphasis to the three major items.

Notice how parallelism helps to keep the following sentences clear and to emphasize the relation between the ideas.

Strikes, though sometimes necessary, mean	loss of wages for workers, interference with production for managers, and disruption of services for consumers.

Political language is designed ‖‖ to make ‖ lies sound truthful and murder respectable

and

to give an appearance of solidity to pure wind.

3. In whole paragraphs. Just as you can often make single sentences clearer by coordinating equal ideas and putting them in parallel constructions, so you can often use roughly parallel sentences to increase the coherence of an entire paragraph. (See also Section **42d[2]**.) Study the following paragraph:

> Otters seem to improvise. *When swimming along* in a lake or a stream, *one may push* a leaf or twig ahead of it. Or *it may drop* a pebble, then chase it through the sparkling water, catching it before it touches bottom, only to bring it to the surface and drop it again. *Underwater, it may balance* a rock or mussel on its head as it swims, *or play* cat and mouse games with its prey. *In captivity, it plays* games with every moving object and explores all corners and crevices for string to pull, wires to loosen, latches to open, and new mysteries to solve.
>
> GEORGE LAYCOCK, "Games Otters Play," *Audubon*

32a

‖

The structure of this paragraph is kept unmistakably clear by its careful coordinating and confirming parallelism throughout. The simple topic sentence, *Otters seem to improvise,* is developed by a series of details of their improvisation in three situations: in the water, underwater, or in captivity.

Not only does parallelism provide connecting links between ideas in this paragraph, it also binds information within sentences. A case in point is the final sentence, which uses parallel prepositional objects: *for string to pull, wires to loosen, latches to open, and new mysteries to solve.*

As is true for all the sentence-writing techniques we have been examining, parallelism can be overdone. While two or three parallel sentences in a paragraph may set up a nice rhythm, nine or ten sentences using the same parallel structures can amount to overkill. Monotonous repetition of constructions bores readers, blunting their attention to meaning. To write effective sentences, you also need to pay attention to emphasis and variety (see Sections **33** and **34**).

EXERCISE 32a

Using parallelism and subordination, revise the following passages, combining sentences as necessary.

1. Corn is an ancient crop. It was once a wild grain. The Aztec and Maya Indians grew it as a crop. Columbus and his men found

corn growing in the New World in 1492. Indians had adapted corn to growing conditions all over South America and North America.

2. Columbus took corn back to Spain. Later, Magellan took corn to the Philippines. From the Philippines corn spread to eastern Asia. It also spread to New Zealand. English colonists in North America made good use of corn. The Indians taught them how to grow corn. Most early American settlers dried their corn. They ground the dried corn into meal. They stored it for use during the winter.

3. Today corn is the most widely grown crop in America. Much of the corn grown in the United States is used for livestock production. Other corn is used to make corn syrup. Some corn is used to make cornstarch. It is also used to make alcoholic beverages. It is used to make industrial products. Humans consume corn in various forms. Corn is a nutritious food. We eat corn in cereal. We consume corn-bread. We snack on corn chips. Everybody likes popcorn. Popcorn's kernels have more hard starch than other kinds of corn. This hard starch causes popcorn to burst when it is heated.

32b

32b
Use parallelism for elements joined by coordinating or correlative conjunctions.

Coordinating conjunctions. Parallelism is useful for constructing effective sentences, for combining successive sentences to achieve economy and clarity, and for maintaining coherence throughout an entire paragraph. On the other hand, lack of parallelism can throw a reader off and produce ineffective sentences. To keep your sentences clear, as well as grammatically correct, make sure the structural patterns of the coordinate elements match one another.

FAULTY As an industrial designer, Pam enjoys *her work* with engineers and *creating* the shape of mass-produced products.

PARALLEL As an industrial designer, Pam enjoys *working* with engineers and *creating* the shape of mass-produced products.

FAULTY Industrial designers are *highly trained, with creative ideas,* and *have knowledge* of ergonomics.

PARALLEL Industrial designers are *highly trained, creative,* and *knowledgeable* in ergonomics.

When you are coordinating prepositional phrases or infinitives, clarity will sometimes require you to point up parallel structure by repeating prepositions.

AMBIGUOUS	A poorly designed telephone may be identified by the trouble it gives you with dialing or holding the receiver. [Dialing the receiver?]
CLEAR	A poorly designed telephone may be identified by the trouble it gives you *with* dialing or *with* holding the receiver.
AMBIGUOUS	Industrial designers are trained to study the way people will use a product and then create the most attractive but functional form. [People use and then create?]
CLEAR	Industrial designers are trained *to* study the way people will use a product and then *to* create the most attractive but functional form.

Correlative conjunctions. Correlative conjunctions are coordinating pairs: *either. . .or, neither. . .nor, both. . .and, not. . .but, not only. . .but also.* Parallelism requires that the structure following the second part of the correlative be the same as that following the first part.

FAULTY	A well-designed office chair *both should be* attractive to look at *and comfortable* to sit in.
PARALLEL	A well-designed office chair should be *both attractive* to look at *and comfortable* to sit in.
FAULTY	Industrial designers work *on not only* office furniture and equipment, bathroom fixtures, kitchen appliances, beds, lamps, and cookware *but also on* cars, camping gear, and cameras.
PARALLEL	Industrial designers work *not only on* office furniture and equipment, bathroom fixtures, kitchen appliances, beds, lamps, and cookware *but also on* cars, camping gear, and cameras.

32b

‖

If you are uncertain of the parallelism with correlative conjunctions, try recasting your sentence as two sentences. Take, for example, the sentence *Not only is Pierre Cardin famous for his fashion designs but also the industrial designs that bear his name.* Recast as separate sentences, this becomes

Pierre Cardin is famous for his fashion designs.
Pierre Cardin is famous for the industrial designs that bear his name.

When you combine the common parts of these two sentences to get *Pierre Cardin is famous for,* it is clear that the two distinct parts that belong in parallel form are *his fashion designs* and *the industrial designs that bear his name.* The correct forms of the sentence are as follows:

Pierre Cardin is famous for *not only his fashion designs but also the industrial designs* that bear his name.

OR Pierre Cardin is famous *not only for* his fashion designs *but also for* the industrial designs that bear his name.

32c
Avoid faulty parallelism with *and who, and which, and that.*

Do not use an *and who, and which*, or *and that* clause in a sentence unless you have already used a parallel *who, which,* or *that* clause. (So too with *but* and *who, which,* or *that*.)

FAULTY We met Abner Fulton, a brilliant biologist and who is also an excellent pianist.

PARALLEL We met Abner Fulton, who is a brilliant biologist and who is also an excellent pianist.

PARALLEL We met Abner Fulton, who is both a brilliant biologist and an excellent pianist.

FAULTY I like a detective novel with exciting action and that keeps me guessing.

PARALLEL I like a detective novel that has exciting action and that keeps me guessing.

32c
||

EXERCISE 32b–c(1)
Revise the following sentences, rewording as necessary to express coordinate ideas in parallel form.

1. New parents, and even those who are experienced in child-rearing and having several children, often have trouble coping with their children's fears.
2. Parents shouldn't panic when a child is fearful of a certain situation, for child psychologists believe that experiencing fear is natural and to overcome it is an important step in a child's development.
3. To help a child deal with fear, a parent should understand what kinds of fears to expect at various ages and ways of helping the child with those fears.
4. For example, two-year-olds may not only fear strangers but also may fear new experiences.
5. Parents can help children overcome these fears by introducing new activities gradually and if they talk to them about these new experiences.
6. Older children experience many fears, among them fear of dogs, fear of being alone in the dark, and loud noises.
7. Around the age of five years, children may develop a fear of death; either this fear is of the child's own death or of the death of a parent.
8. If a parent deals with a child's fears calmly and without overreact-

ing, the child learns to accept fears as natural and that there are
ways to make the fears less overwhelming.

9. Older children may be especially fearful of new experiences like
moving to a new school or when they encounter a new group of
children in a club or activity.

10. If parents show that they take their children's fears seriously, supporting them and reassure them, then the children will be more
likely to conquer their fears.

EXERCISE 32b–c(2)
Write at least five sentences, each containing parallel, coordinate elements.

33

EMPHASIS

Effective sentences emphasize main ideas and keep related details in the background. The careful use of coordination, subordination, and parallelism enables you to stress your most important ideas
without losing track of less important, related ideas and information.
Sentence variety enables you to emphasize important ideas by changing the flow and rhythm of a passage. In addition to these useful strategies, you can also emphasize ideas within a single sentence by controlling the arrangement of its elements and by using repetition
carefully.

As you revise sentences to achieve the emphasis you want, keep
in mind that any sentence is part of a paragraph and of a larger
whole. To determine what to emphasize in a given sentence, always
look at the sentence in relation to its context and in relation to your
audience and overall purpose.

33a

Emphatic positions in a sentence highlight important ideas.

The position of a word or idea within a sentence usually determines the emphasis it receives. Generally, the most emphatic place in
the sentence is at its end; the next most emphatic, its beginning; the
least emphatic, its middle. Consider the following sentence:

> Brunhilda, our Great Dane, loves to play with the neighborhood
> children, but she is bigger than most of them.

The end position of *bigger than most of them* gives that information the
heaviest stress in the sentence. As the topic sentence of a paragraph
that contrasts the dog's love of children with their fear of her size, the
sentence is effective.

If, however, the sentence introduces a paragraph that focuses on Brunhilda's love of children, it must be revised.

> Brunhilda, our Great Dane, although bigger than most of the neighborhood children, loves to play with them.

In this version of the sentence, the information about the dog's size is subordinated and placed in the middle of the sentence, and the information about her love of children is held for the most emphatic position, the end.

Compare the emphasis in the following pair of sentences:

> Spanish-speaking people want to be understood, just as much as other minorities in the country.

> Spanish-speaking people, just as much as other minorities in the country, want to be understood.

In the latter sentence, emphasis on the main clause is increased by placing lesser information within the main clause. Such placement of modifying phrases and clauses delays the predicate, the sentence's action, for the final emphatic position in the sentence.

Sometimes you can increase the emphasis on a single-word adverb or a brief adverbial phrase by moving it to the initial position in a sentence.

> Debra reached sleepily for the alarm clock.
> Sleepily, Debra reached for the alarm clock.

33a

emp

On the other hand, don't weaken emphasis by placing minor qualifying phrases before your subject or at the end of the sentence. Any qualifying words or phrases placed at the very beginning or the very end of a sentence will receive emphasis, so be sure the words are worth emphasizing. Otherwise they may seem distracting, illogical, or tacked on. When such words do not merit emphasis, bury them within the sentence or omit them.

WEAK	Such matters as incorrect spelling and unconventional punctuation can distract a reader's attention even in otherwise good writing.
EMPHATIC	Incorrect spelling and unconventional punctuation can distract a reader's attention even in otherwise good writing.
WEAK	The history of English vocabulary is the history of English civilization, in many ways.
EMPHASIS ON HISTORY	The history of English vocabulary is in many ways the history of English civilization.
EMPHASIS ON QUALIFIER	In many ways, the history of English vocabulary is the history of English civilization.

EXERCISE 33a

Write ten pairs of sentences using the phrases listed below. In the first sentence, place the phrase in an emphatic position. In the second, place it so that it is de-emphasized.

1. according to experts
2. as soon as possible
3. opening the door
4. the president of the university
5. moving quickly
6. in the past
7. on the other hand
8. using a knife
9. with concern
10. if you like it

33b

Different sentence structures create different emphases.

33b

emp

The position of subordinate or modifying material can have a definite impact on where the emphasis falls in a sentence (see Section **33a**). There are four basic sentence structures for handling modifying material: the periodic, or left-branching, sentence; the mid-branching sentence; the balanced sentence; and the loose, or right-branching, sentence.

A **periodic** or **left-branching sentence** places a modifying clause at the beginning and holds the main idea until the end. This pattern creates anticipation, first setting up the reader's expectations with background information or qualifying details and then presenting the subject dramatically in the main clause at the end.

PERIODIC, LEFT-BRANCHING   *When her mother was in the hospital for two months and her father was on the edge of a breakdown,* Brenda showed great courage.

Because the structure of a periodic sentence contains built-in suspense, it can be extremely effective. However, it also contains inherent risk. The longer readers must wait to discover the subject, the greater the likelihood that they will become impatient or confused. Consequently, the delivery of the subject in the final clause should have a strong clarifying effect and should be worth the reader's wait.

A **mid-branching sentence** places modifying material between the subject and the verb. Again, you are asking the reader to suspend normal thought patterns and expectations about the way information is delivered. The subordinate information amounts to an interruption, as you imbed detail, before the main idea is carried to completion.

This structure can be used to create drama and suspense, or it can be used to de-emphasize information by sandwiching it between the more powerful parts of the sentence—the subject and the verb.

EMPHASIZED   Death Valley—*without a doubt the hottest spot in the country*—comes by its name honestly.

DE-EMPHASIZED   Death Valley, *the nation's hot spot,* comes by its name honestly.

Notice in the preceding examples that the punctuation and word choice combine with sentence structure to provide additional cues that reinforce the meaning the writer intended.

A **balanced sentence** is a compound sentence in which the independent clauses are exactly, or very nearly, parallel in all elements.

> We always like those who admire us; we do not always like those whom we admire.
>
> LA ROCHEFOUCAULD, *Maxims*

> Grammar maps out the possible; rhetoric narrows the possible down to the desirable and effective.
>
> FRANCIS CHRISTENSEN, *Toward a New Rhetoric*

> It is as natural to die as to be born; and to a little infant, perhaps, the one is as painful as the other.
>
> FRANCIS BACON, "Of Death"

33b

emp

As these three examples illustrate, the balanced sentence is useful for stating contrasts and distinctions. Because it holds two coordinate ideas before the reader, its structure naturally emphasizes meanings involving weighing or choice.

A **loose** or **right-branching sentence,** sometimes called a **cumulative sentence,** completes its main statement and then adds subordinate details. This structure follows the most common pattern of human thought, identifying key informational elements (the subject and verb) first and then providing qualifying material.

LOOSE, RIGHT-BRANCHING   Brenda showed great courage *when her mother was in the hospital for two months and her father was on the edge of a breakdown.*

Because it follows our usual thought patterns, the loose sentence is easy to read and satisfies readers' expectations about normal emphasis in sentences. For the same reason, it does not lend itself to special emphasis and can lead to rambling lists of details that are simply piled on after the subject and verb without regard for effectiveness. Consider the following example, the opening sentence from a newspaper article:

> A bid to set the altitude record for hot-air balloons suffered a setback Saturday when one of the two British crewmen was hurt in a fall and a gust of wind tore the balloon at the Royal Air Force base in Watton, England.

Journalists attempt to include as much pertinent information as possible in the opening sentence of a story: who, what, when, where, why, and how. The foregoing example covers all the bases, its cumulative structure setting forth the main statement (what) followed by the subordinate details (when, who, how, why, where). This loose sentence is easy to read, an important consideration in newspaper writing, but its listlike construction offers little emphasis. Had the writer been striving for dramatic effect, he might have used a periodic sentence like the following:

> Their balloon torn by the wind and one of the two crewmen hurt in a fall at the Royal Air Force base in Watton, England, the British team suffered a setback Saturday in their attempt to set the altitude record for hot-air balloons.

33c

emp

Strictly speaking, any sentence consisting of a main clause followed by an adverbial phrase or clause is loose and can be made periodic simply by moving the adverbial modifier to the beginning. Often, periodic and loose constructions are more or less equally effective. Your choice should be guided by the particular emphasis and effect you want and by the relation of your sentence to those before and after it. In the following passage from a student paper, notice how the writer uses a periodic sentence between two loose, cumulative sentences to emphasize his sense of loss after his mother's death.

> I became aware of myself—who I was and what I was—during the weeks following her funeral. After the relatives had all left and the sympathy cards stopped coming, I was left alone. I had to be independent, find others to shed my tears upon, and look elsewhere for a scolding.

EXERCISE 33b
Write a paragraph describing an accident. Include at least one each of the following sentence structures: periodic, mid-branching, balanced, and loose. Be sure, in each case, that the sentence's structure appropriately reflects the content, meaning, and emphasis you intend.

33c

Expletive constructions can be used to regulate the pace and emphasis of a sentence.

Expletives such as *there are, there was, it is,* and *it was (there* or *it* together with forms of the verb *to be)* are sometimes considered to be wordy time-wasters that weaken the emphasis on a sentence's true subject (Section **39a[3]**). In fact, such is frequently the case. On the other hand, it should also be recognized that expletive constructions can affect the pace, and thus the emphasis, of a sentence.

For example, compare the following two passages, and notice how the expletives in the second add to the suspense by delaying the delivery of information.

> Dead silence prevailed for about a half a minute, during which we might have heard the falling of a leaf, or a feather. A low, but harsh and protracted grating sound which seemed to come at once from every corner of the room interrupted the silence.

> There was a dead silence for about a half a minute, during which the falling of a leaf, or of a feather might have been heard. It was interrupted by a low, but harsh and protracted grating sound which seemed to come at once from every corner of the room.

> EDGAR ALLAN POE, "Hop-Frog"

As the preceding example shows, expletives sometimes occur as part of passive voice constructions—verb forms which de-emphasize the actor in a sentence and focus on the receiver of the action or the result (see Section **33f**). By themselves, expletives can also focus the reader's attention on the outcome of some action rather than on the actor. Compare the following:

33c

emp

> You have no excuse for missing the meeting. You chose to set the time for last night at eight.
> There is no excuse for your missing the meeting. It was your choice to set the time for last night at eight.

When you hear expletives in speech, notice that they are often used in preparation for heavier spoken emphasis on the words that follow them—on the grammatical subject of the sentence. Expletives can have a similar effect in writing. They are relatively content-free themselves, but like the wind-up before a pitch, expletives can help readers anticipate and prepare for the delivery of meaning. Thus in some circumstances they can help to achieve emphasis and variety.

EXERCISE 33c

Write five pairs of sentences in which the difference between the first sentence and the second sentence in each pair is the use of expletives. Try to create sentences that benefit from the use of expletive constructions to delay information.

33d
Items in parallel series create cumulative emphasis.

When items are arranged in a parallel series, emphasis tends to fall on the last item, simply because it is last. Compare the following:

> You are a coward, a thief, a murderer, and a liar.
> You are a liar, a coward, a thief, and a murderer.

Of these two, the first, by placing *a liar* in the end position, tends to suggest that lying is more important than thievery and murder. The second sentence, in contrast, moves in the order that fits our usual sense of values, suggesting that murder is the most serious and therefore most important. Because readers expect order of increasing importance in parallel series, meaning can be especially enhanced in cumulative series. For example:

> Their lives were brief, pitiable, and tragic.
> The life of man [is] solitary, poor, nasty, brutish, and short.
> THOMAS HOBBES, *Leviathan*

33d

emp

The first sentence mentions life's brevity but emphasizes its tragic nature, whereas the second sentence puts the full weight of the cumulative effect on the word *short*. In the first sentence, the words and structure combine to emphasize a more sympathetic view of human beings than that of the second sentence.

The arrangement of a series in descending order of importance can sometimes be used for surprise, humor, or irony.

> If once a man indulges himself in murder, very soon he comes to think little of robbery; and from robbing he next comes to drinking and Sabbath-breaking; and from that to incivility and procrastination.
> THOMAS DE QUINCY

In many series some other principle dictates the arrangement. The controlling principle may be the order of events, increasing or decreasing size, spatial order, or some other order that fits the logic of the writer's purpose. In the following sentence, for example, the writer's intention is to show that even the smallest detail reflected "orderliness."

> The orderliness of their house and their yard mirrored the orderliness of their lives: inside, each chair, each painting, each book had its assigned place; outside, each tree, shrub, and flower seemed planted by design.

Within a paragraph, parallel series can be extremely effective in capturing the sense of a situation, as author Joan Mills does when she reflects on her childhood:

Children are spoiled by overindulgence; but never by love. It was a day's work for me to spend 12 hours inside my own littleness: dragging a stool around to see the top of things; living with my daily failures—shoelaces all adraggle again, the peas rolling off the spoon, my sweater on backward; worrying about goblins long past Halloween. But love let me know all was right with the world, and with me.

JOAN MILLS, "The One, the *Only . . . Joanie!*"

EXERCISE 33d
Revise the following sentences by arranging parallel items in what seems to you to be a more logical order.

1. The Grand Prix driver finished last and ran out of gas halfway through the race.
2. A heart attack can cause severe pain in the chest as well as pain in the left arm and shoulder.
3. My sister should be qualified to practice medicine after a residency, an internship, four years of medical school, and four years of college.
4. Some letters between friends are meant to be read a couple of times, some are meant to be read quickly, and still others are meant to be read and put away to be read again and again.
5. Failing the calculus exam, losing my keys, missing my favorite TV show—it wasn't a good day for me.

Write sentences containing parallel series of items using the following principles of arrangement:

6. Time order
7. Spatial order
8. Order of increasing importance
9. Order of decreasing importance (for humorous effect)
10. Series arranged for contrasting effect

33e
Key words and ideas can be repeated for emphasis.

Careless and awkward repetition of words makes sentences weak and flabby (see Section **39a[6]**), but careful, deliberate repetition of key words, when not overdone, can be an effective way of gaining emphasis, as in the following sentences:

A *moderately* honest man with a *moderately* faithful wife, *moderate* drinkers both, in a *moderately* healthy home: that is the true middle class unit.

G. B. SHAW

33e

emp

> Don't *join* too many gangs. *Join* few if any. *Join* the United States and *join* a family—but not much else in between, unless a college.
>
> ROBERT FROST

> It is the *dull* man who is always *sure,* and the *sure* man who is always *dull.*
>
> H. L. MENCKEN

As you can see from the examples, repetition frequently appears in combination with parallel constructions. This is not surprising, since repeated words are naturally reinforced and emphasized by repeated constructions. (For a discussion of ways in which repetition of words and ideas links sentences within a paragraph, see Section **42**).

EXERCISE 33e

Discuss the effectiveness of repetition of words and phrases in each of the sentences below.

1. No one can be perfectly free till all are free; no one can be perfectly moral until all are moral; no one can be perfectly happy until all are happy.

   HERBERT SPENCER

2. Some books are to be tasted, others to be swallowed, and some few to be chewed and digested; that is, some books are to be read only in parts; others to be read, but not curiously; and some few to be read wholly, and with diligence and attention.

   FRANCIS BACON

3. To know how to say what others only know how to think is what makes men poets or sages; and to dare to say what others only dare to think makes men martyrs or reformers or both.

   ELIZABETH CHARLES

33f

Verbs in the active voice create more emphasis than verbs in the passive voice.

The **active voice** puts the subject (the actor) first, following it with the active verb, and then the object (the receiver of the action): *The cat killed the rat.* The **passive voice** turns things around, putting the receiver in front, then the verb, and finally the actor: *The rat was killed by the cat.* (See Section **5**.)

Of the two, the active is almost always more direct, more forceful and emphatic, and also more economical. Therefore, if your goal is to emphasize the actor and the action itself, the active voice is the better choice. If you want to emphasize the receiver or result of the action, downplaying the action and its initiator, the passive voice is usually preferable.

ACTIVE   The firefighter saved the terrified child.

PASSIVE   The terrified child was saved by the firefighter.

The first example sentence focuses our attention on the rescue; the second focuses on the object of the rescue, the child. Bear in mind that, as its name implies, a sentence in the passive voice will always be less forceful than one in the active voice, and longer as well. If your goal is economy and directness, choose active-voice verbs.

PASSIVE   It was voted by the faculty that all students should be required to take mathematics. [15 words]

ACTIVE   The faculty voted to require that all students take mathematics. [10 words]

EXERCISE 33f

Write five pairs of sentences, using active and passive voices as appropriate to emphasize the actor in the first sentence and to emphasize the recipient of the action in the second sentence.

34

VARIETY

A long series of sentences identical or very similar in length and structure is monotonous. But a series of well-written, varied sentences provides the reader with more than mere absence of monotony. It reflects the writer's careful molding of form to thought and the careful choice of length and structure to supply emphasis that creates meaning.

34a
Varying sentence structure and length creates emphasis and accentuates meaning.

Consider the following paragraph by Jane Howard. Notice the variety in length and structure of the eight sentences that make up the paragraph.

The trouble with the families many of us were born into is not that they consist of meddlesome ogres but that they are too far away. In emergencies we rush across continents and if need be oceans to their sides, as they do to ours. Maybe we even make a habit of seeing them, once or twice a year, for the sheer pleasure of it. But blood ties seldom dictate our addresses. Our blood kin are often too remote to ease us from our Tuesdays to our Wednesdays. For this we must rely on our families of friends. If our relatives are not, do not wish to be, or for whatever reasons cannot be our friends, then by some complex alchemy we must try to transform our friends into our relatives. If blood and roots don't do the job, then we must look to water and branches.

JANE HOWARD, Families

The length of these eight sentences ranges from the seven-word *But blood ties seldom dictate our addresses* to the long thirty-three-word sentence beginning *If our relatives are not.* Structure varies from the simple subject-verb-object pattern of the crisp fourth, fifth, and sixth sentences to the much greater complexity of the opening twenty-six word sentence and the two closing sentences of thirty-three and sixteen words respectively.

Such variety of length and structure is by no means accidental. In the paragraph immediately before this one, Howard has set her thesis: all of us need to belong to a clan, a tribe; if our families don't fit that need, we will find a substitute that does. The quoted paragraph develops that thesis. Its pivotal point falls at the cluster of three comparatively short, subject-verb-object sentences—seven, sixteen, and ten words, respectively—that comes at the approximate center of the paragraph: our blood families often are remote; thus they cannot "ease us from our Tuesdays to our Wednesdays"; for this we need friends. The effect of those pivotal sentences is to focus the reader's attention. By using shorter, simpler sentences, Howard clearly intends to emphasize those ideas that are in an ordinarily unemphatic, mid-paragraph location.

There is no formula for the "right" variety of length and form among the sentences of a paragraph or a paper. The variety of Jane Howard's paragraph above comes not from some predetermined pattern she worked out for the paragraph. It comes, rather, from choosing the length and form best suited to the meaning and emphasis she intended to convey to her readers.

Such fitting of form to meaning is unlikely to come in the first draft of a paragraph or paper. It comes with revision. When you turn to revising the early drafts of your writing, be wary if many or most of your sentences are either short or long or if some single structure seems to recur overfrequently. You will need relatively long and complex sentences to relate ideas clearly to one another and to subordinate minor detail; short sentences to give you emphasis where you want it; variety to avoid monotony. Be aware, too, that the kind of sentences that will be appropriate if you are writing a sports column or a set of simple directions will differ from the kind you will need to explain a complex idea. Remember that short sentences can be vigorous and emphatic, but that they are more likely to be effective when placed in contrast to longer sentences.

34a

var

Most important, always keep in mind that sentence variety is not an end in itself. If you set out to make your sentences alternately short and long, you will end with awkward and artificial writing. If you set out to shift structure with each new sentence without regard to the relationship of one to another, you are more likely to destroy the coherence of the whole than to achieve effective variety. Your choice of length and structure for any one sentence must always depend upon your meaning and upon the relationship of that sentence to those that stand before and after it.

34b

Short, simple sentences and longer, more complex sentences can work together to achieve variety that enhances meaning.

If you are effectively using coordination, subordination, parallelism, and other sentence structures discussed in Sections 31–33, your writing will already contain a good deal of variety. You will have discovered, for instance, that short sentences are good for introducing a topic or summing up a point and that longer sentences lend themselves to elaboration, detailed explanation, or qualification of a main idea. Notice how the following passages use this "push, pull" technique to advantage.

34b

var

> My biology final flopped on my desk. A big, fat *D* stared up at me. Refusing to believe what my eyes had seen, my mind uncomprehending, I scooped up the paper, lunged through the door, and took off across the parking lot. I drove home, cursing the white car that drove so slow I had to pass it and damning the blue truck that drove so fast it had to pass me.
>
> *Student paragraph*

> When I was nine, we moved to Boston. I grew up; got my schooling; larked about a while as a reporter; married, and had a little girl of my own. I adored her. . . . Raising three in the baby boom was louder, funnier, messier; more alarming, marvelous, tearful and tender than any prior experience of mine. My children spent emotions and energies over a range I'd never known in my childhood. So did I.
>
> JOAN MILLS, "The One, the *Only* . . . *Joanie!*"

Both writers take advantage of sentence structure to build details, move their readers forward through the meaning with vigor and energy, and stop them short to make points memorable. The writing is effective not only because the authors have something interesting to say but also because they align the structure of their sentences to the content of those sentences—piling and building, adding and combining, balancing or contrasting, pausing and breaking—in ways that reinforce their thoughts.

34c

Changing the word order, the sentence pattern, or the sentence type can add variety.

WORD ORDER

Certain modifiers, called **free modifiers,** can be moved from one position to another in a sentence. Prepositional phrases, clauses, and single words that modify nouns should be placed next to or very close to the nouns they modify; their position is relatively fixed. But adverbs, adverbial phrases and clauses, many participial phrases, and absolute phrases can often be placed at different positions in a sentence; these are free modifiers. Moving such modifiers into varying positions can help you place emphasis where you want it and increase sentence variety.

ADVERBIAL PHRASES AND CLAUSES

Westerners and Arabs still do not understand each other, *in spite of two thousand years of contact.*

In spite of two thousand years of contact, Westerners and Arabs still do not understand each other.

Westerners and Arabs, *in spite of two thousand years of contact,* still do not understand each other.

The defendant changed his plea to guilty *because the prosecutor had built up such convincing evidence against him.*

Because the prosecutor had built up such convincing evidence against him, the defendant changed his plea to guilty.

The defendant, *because the prosecutor had built up such convincing evidence against him,* changed his plea to guilty.

The bank's vice president kept juggling several customers' large deposits *to cover his own embezzlement.*

To cover his own embezzlement, the bank's vice president kept juggling several customers' large deposits.

The bank's vice president, *to cover his own embezzlement,* kept juggling several customers' large deposits.

PARTICIPIAL PHRASES

The deer, *grazing peacefully in the valley,* were unaware of the approaching hunters.

Grazing peacefully in the valley, the deer were unaware of the approaching hunters.

[Being] unaware of the approaching hunters, the deer were grazing peacefully in the valley.

Gasping for air, the diver came to the surface.

The diver, *gasping for air,* came to the surface.

The diver came to the surface, *gasping for air.*

Note that in placing participial modifiers, you must be alert to the possibility of creating a misplaced modifier (see Section **12a**). Participial phrases can almost always be placed either before or after the nouns they modify. But whether they can be more widely separated will depend upon the sentence. In the example above, *gasping for air* can logically modify only *diver,* not *surface;* and since the sentence is brief, the phrase can comfortably be placed at its end. But in the previous example, if the *grazing* phrase were moved to the end of the sentence, it would modify *hunters* rather than *deer.*

Absolute phrases, since they always modify the entire sentence in which they stand, can usually be placed either at the beginning or end of a sentence or within it.

ABSOLUTE PHRASES

His hair cut close, his arms and legs tanned, his face freckled, Jonathan seemed the typical country boy in summer.

Jonathan, *his hair cut close, his arms and legs tanned, his face freckled,* seemed the typical country boy in summer.

Jonathan seemed the typical country boy in summer—*his hair cut close, his arms and legs tanned, his face freckled.*

Sarah settled back for a quiet evening, *the work day over, the bills paid, some letters written.*

The work day over, the bills paid, some letters written, Sarah settled back for a quiet evening.

Sarah, *the work day over, the bills paid, some letters written,* settled back for a quiet evening.

34c

var

SENTENCE PATTERNS

The subject-verb-object pattern of the basic English sentence is so strongly established that any shift in it causes unusually heavy emphasis. Sentences such as *Over the fence jumped Oscar* or *Siamese cats she adores* are rather infrequent in most modern writing. But such **inversion,** when context justifies it, can be effective. Consider the following example from a student's essay about his mother's death:

> No longer did I have the security of someone being there to greet me when I arrived home from school—all I had was a high-strung Yorkshire terrier with a bladder problem. What I had to do was fend for myself and take on new responsibilities.

The student might have written "I no longer had the security . . .," but because he inverted the word order a bit at the opening of his paragraph, its contrast with the parallel "all I had" and "what I had" of the next two independent clauses highlights the change his mother's death brought to his life.

Notice how the next example uses inversion to emphasize the desire for wealth.

Throughout Dawson's life his great obsession had been to secure wealth, great wealth, wealth that would enable him to indulge his wildest fantasies. Such wealth he constantly dreamed of; and such wealth he was determined to get at all costs.

A more common and much less emphatic inversion occurs when the subject and verb are reversed in a sentence opening with a long adverbial modifier.

Across the boulevard where a milk truck scurries to more lucrative fields lies the sea and miles of empty beach.

JOHN J. ROWLAND, *Spindrift*

SENTENCE TYPES

Except in dialogue, the overwhelming majority of written sentences are statements. But questions, commands, and occasionally even exclamations are useful for achieving emphasis and variety when the context warrants them.

34c

var

Questions at the beginning of a paragraph can point its direction. The following sentence opens a paragraph in which the author argues that television news coverage is superior to that of all but the best newspapers.

Why do I think network TV does a better job of informing than [most] newspapers?

MARYA MANNES, "What's Wrong with the Press?"

Or a question may open a paragraph of definition.

What is civilized man? By derivation, he is one who lives and thinks in a city.

BERNARD IDDINGS BELL

Imperative sentences are the staple sentences of writing that gives directions. But occasionally they are useful in other contexts.

Observations indicate that the different clusters of galaxies are constantly moving apart from one another. To illustrate by a homely analogy, think of a raisin cake baking in an oven.

If not overused, an exclamation is a sure attention-getter that will change the flow of a paragraph momentarily. Notice how the following student paragraph mixes exclamations and questions to create an informal, breezy, comic tone.

Now we all know that college presents many new and exciting experiences to be sampled in the name of education. You want culture and a foreign flavor? There are hundreds of exotic beers and wines to be tasted, especially the foreign ones. Skoal! You want social graces? There are dozens of events to attend where the fine art of genteel behavior can be practiced. Food fight! What about homework? You would ask. Mom, Dad . . . would a well-brought-up son of yours flunk out of school? Get serious!

Avoid the temptation to vary sentences just for the sake of change. Remember that variety should be a function of meaning and emphasis. As the sections on parallelism and effective repetition explained, sameness can be a strength in your writing, just as variety can be. The important thing is to clarify and reinforce your meaning and aid your reader's understanding. Observe how author William Zinsser uses similar sentence structures to suggest the dreamlike quality of a reverie and then introduces sentence variety to shift from the imaginary to the real.

34c

var

Pagination! I have always loved the word and been sorry that it doesn't mean all the things I think it ought to mean. Its sound wafts me to romantic or faraway worlds. I think of the great voyages that paginated the Indies. I watch the moonlight playing across the pagination on the Taj Mahal. I hear glorious music (Lully's pagination for trumpets). I savor gourmet meals (mussels paginated with sage). I see beautiful women—the pagination on their bodice catches my eye—and dream of the nights we will spend in torrid pagination. The wine that we sip will be exquisitely paginated—dry, but not too dry—and as the magical hours slip away we will . . .

But why torture myself? The fact is that it's a dumb word that means just one thing: the process of arranging pages in their proper sequence and getting them properly numbered.

WILLIAM ZINSSER, *Writing with a Word Processor*

EXERCISE 34a–c(1)
Practice the following techniques for achieving sentence variety.

1. Write two sets of sentences in which a short, simple sentence works together with longer ones that elaborate and provide details.
2. Write two sets of sentences in which several of the sentences use inverted word order effectively.
3. Write three pairs of sentences containing free modifiers. Make the second sentence of each pair identical to the first, except move the free modifier to a new position. Use an adverbial phrase or clause in the first pair; a participial phrase in the second; an absolute phrase in the third.
4. Write two sets of sentences in which you vary the second set by recasting some declarative statements as questions, commands, and/or exclamations.
5. Write a paragraph that uses at least four of the techniques for varying sentences that are discussed in Section **34.** Then write a para-

graph explaining why you chose those particular techniques, how you used them, and what effect you wanted to achieve.

EXERCISE 34a–c(2)

Revise the following paragraph by introducing greater variety to enhance meaning.

> Eric realized that the camping trip was a failure. He was to blame. He had convinced his two friends that hiking into the hills and staying two nights would be fun. It hadn't been fun. It had rained for two days. Eric and his friends had had to slosh through mud to get to the campsite. They couldn't get their tent poles to stay in the wet ground. They couldn't find dry wood for a fire. They couldn't warm up the food they had brought. To make matters worse, Eric's two friends grumbled all the time. They didn't try to make the situation any better, so Eric decided to take charge. He decided to be positive. He wanted to make the best of the situation, but it didn't work. His friends ignored his suggestions to make the campsite more comfortable. They resented his taking charge. They blamed him for their being wet and tired and cold, and they just wanted to be left alone.

34c

var

REVIEW EXERCISES ON EFFECTIVE SENTENCES (Sections 31–34)

EXERCISE A

Indicate what you consider to be the principal detraction from the effectiveness of the following sentences (excessive coordination, faulty subordination, lack of emphasis, lack of parallelism, etc.), and then revise the sentences.

1. Silver is a valuable metal. It has been used for thousands of years. The ancient Egyptians called silver "white gold."
2. Silver is like gold and bends and stretches easily, but it also resists acids and corrosions, and it won't rust.
3. Silver reflects light better than any other metal, and that quality gives silver its lustrous shine.
4. Because of its light-collecting qualities, silver is used on solar collectors, and the finest mirrors are backed with silver.
5. Silver conducts heat and electricity better than any other metal, and not even copper is a better conductor.
6. Silver is more abundant than gold. Modern technology continues to create new uses for silver. Silver use exceeds production.
7. Existing deposits of silver neither are easy to mine nor enough to supply the need for the metal.
8. Silver can be melted down and reused because very little metal is lost in each melting, fortunately.
9. Most silver comes from North and South America. It comes from the Rockies and the Andes. It comes from the Sierra Mountains in Mexico. Canada supplies some silver. Australia and the Soviet Union have silver deposits. Mexico produces more silver than any other country.

10. France issues silver coins. West Germany uses silver coins. Mexico has silver coins. The United States used to use silver coins. Now the United States no longer uses silver coins.

11. Because silver became so expensive, the United States, which had issued dimes and quarters that were 90 percent silver, changed the coins to nickel and copper that was coated with silver.

12. Skilled Indian craftsmen in the southwest United States make beautiful jewelry that includes silver and with the turquoise stones found in the region.

13. Silver is used in photographic film, it is used in wires in silicon solar cells, it is used in x-ray film, and doctors use silver creams to disinfect burns.

14. People have died for silver, fought for it, and even searched ships wrecked at sea for it, and have dug into the earth for it.

15. People also eat silver. They eat it in India. They make it into the thinnest sheets possible. They put it on food. They may use it on desserts. The thin silver sheets are called *vark*.

EXERCISE B
Go over a paper you have written recently, revising several paragraphs in which the sentences can be written more effectively.

34c

var

WRITERS REVISING FOR MORE EFFECTIVE SENTENCES

Library users were being asked to share their thoughts on a book that had made a difference in their lives—not just a favorite book, but one that had changed their thinking or their actions. People were being asked to write a page about this book for display in a loose-leaf notebook that would be part of a special exhibit during National Library Week. To start the ball rolling, each library staff member had been asked to write a contribution for the notebook.

Stacy, who worked part-time in the library, drafted several paragraphs, but she wasn't very happy with them. She was challenged by the topic but felt she hadn't effectively conveyed her feeling about it. Her sentences seemed monotonous and uninteresting, without energy and lacking the emotion she felt about the subject.

Although you, of course, cannot bring the same experience to the following draft, experiment with some sentence revisions that help to emphasize the feelings Stacy discusses. Then see what she did in the final version she submitted for the library display. Notice in Stacy's retyped version how her thoughts evolved and how the meaning emerged with the changing sentences.

Draft

D 1   A book that has made a difference in my life

D 2   is Anne Frank's <u>The Diary of a Young Girl</u>.

D 3   Actually, two books have made a difference in my

D 4   life. One is <u>The Diary of a Young Girl</u> by Anne

D 5   Frank and the other is the diary my Aunt Betty

D 6   gave me at Christmas when I was twelve years old.

D 7   That fall I had read the diary of Anne Frank, the

D 8   young Jewish girl only a few years older than I

D 9   who died at Belsen, a Nazi concentration camp, in

D10   1945 during World War II. Then at Christmas, I

D11   received my own diary.

D12   I had never kept a diary before, but Anne

D13   Frank's diary inspired me and served as a model.

D14   Of course my life was very mundane compared to

D15   hers and certainly did not contain the tragedies

D16   she experienced while hiding from the Nazis, but I

D17   understood and appreciated her need to write

D18   things down. Writing was the way she came to

D19   terms with her life, she tempered suffering by

D20   writing about it, and she also kept hope alive

D21   through writing. With my own diary, I had the

D22   opportunity to use writing as a way of

D23   understanding what was happening in my life. I

D24   have kept a diary ever since receiving that first

D25   one when I was twelve. Anne Frank and Aunt Betty

D26   helped me find my voice as a writer, so you can

D27   see why I think the two books made a lot of

D28   difference.

34c

var

Revision

R 1   Two books--Anne Frank's <u>The Diary of a Young</u>

R 2   <u>Girl</u> and a diary given to me by my aunt--have made

R 3   a tremendous difference in my life. When I was

R 4   twelve, I read the diary of Anne Frank, a Jewish

R 5   girl only a few years older than I when she wrote

R 6   her diary. Anne died at Belsen, a Nazi

R 7   concentration camp.

R 8   That Christmas, I received a diary of my own.

R 9   Although I had never kept a diary before, Anne

R10   Frank's diary provided me with both model and

R11   inspiration. Compared to her life, mine was very

R12   mundane, of course, containing none of the

R13   tragedies she experienced while hiding from the

R14   Nazis. Nevertheless, I did understand and

R15   appreciate her need to write things down. Writing

R16   was the way she came to terms with her life, the

R17   way she tempered suffering, the way she kept hope

R18   alive.

R19   Gradually, writing also became my way of

R20   understanding what was happening in my life.

R21   Those two books received when I was twelve--one

R22   filled, one blank--helped me find my voice as a

R23   writer. I have kept a diary ever since. It has

R24   made all the difference.

34c

var

Analysis

Most of the information in the first three draft sentences (D1-6) has been compressed into the first revision sentence (R1-3). Now the paragraph gets off to a faster, smoother start. Stacy decided that, for her readers, her aunt's name was unimportant. She also decided that the information identifying the two books would be more effective in an appositive (**31c**, **33b**) than in separate sentences.

The fourth draft sentence (D7-10) contains a long string of information delivered in prepositional phrases and other modifiers. Some information concerns a comparison between Stacy and Anne Frank, some of it concerns the circumstances of Anne's death. The revision (R3-7) separates the two sets of information, first, so that the reader is not confronted by so many unrelated bits and, second, so that the statement about Anne Frank's death can achieve greater impact (**34a**, **34b**). The contrast between the periodic sentence (R3-6) and the loose sentence (R6-7) in the revision also helps to emphasize the brutal fact of Anne Frank's death. The relatively short, right-branching sentence that concludes the paragraph (R6-7) makes this information easily accessible (**33b**). Also for the sake of emphasis, Stacy chose to move the fifth draft sentence (D10-11) to the beginning of the revision's second paragraph (R8), where it would not detract from the starkness of the first paragraph's ending.

Notice that the sixth draft sentence (D12-13) is a compound sentence, but in the revision (R9-10), Stacy subordinates the information that previously appeared in an independent clause. This change places full emphasis on the idea of Anne Frank's diary as a model and inspiration for Stacy—emphasis achieved both by situating the main idea in an independent clause (**33a**) and by placing it at the end of the sentence (**33a**) (R10-11).

Take over the analysis of Stacy's revision. What are the effects of the changes she has made? Also analyze her revision in relation to yours. Which choices do you prefer?

WORDS

wds

In searching for the precise word, in reaching for the accepted form, and in knowing the rules well enough to break them consciously and for effect, the writer and reader can luxuriate in the language. Fighting the good fight for the good word leads to the good life of the mind.

WILLIAM SAFIRE, *What's the Good Word?*

35

SOURCES AND USES OF WORDS

Like all languages, English changes constantly. Changes in vocabulary are the most rapid and obvious. *Butcher* once meant "a man who slaughters goats"; *neutron* and *proton*, key terms in physics today, were unrecorded sixty years ago; *biofeedback* appeared in dictionaries only in the 1970's; *byte*, a unit for measuring computer memory, became part of the vocabularies of many schoolchildren almost before their parents were aware the word existed.

Language changes in more complex ways too. Today educated speakers avoid the multiple negatives of *She won't never do nothing*, but William Shakespeare's *nor this is not my nose neither* was good Elizabethan English. Even the sounds of the language change. For Shakespeare, four hundred years ago, *deserts* rhymed with our *departs*, and *reason* sounded much like our *raisin;* two hundred years ago, Alexander Pope properly rhymed *joined* with *line* and *seas* with *surveys.* Spelling changes as well. Today *judgment* is more common than *judgement* and *baseball* has replaced *base ball.*

35a

35

wds

The history and development of English

Linguists believe English evolved from a prehistoric parent language called Indo-European. By the time of the Roman Empire, eight or nine language families descended from Indo-European had become established throughout Europe and parts of Asia. These included Indo-Iranian (including Sanskrit and Persian); Slavic (including Russian); Hellenic (Greek); Italic (including Latin and the Romance, or Roman, languages, which became modern-day Italian, French, Spanish, Portugese, and Romanian); Celtic (Gaelic); and Germanic (including the Scandinavian languages, German and English). Sharing its ancestry with these other Indo-European language families, English is **cognate** with them, having many similar words. For example, Latin *rex*, French *roi*, Hindu *raja*, Sanskrit *rajan*, Anglo-Saxon *riht*, and English *regal* are cognates of the Indo-European base form *reg* (straight, lead).

English is directly descended from the language of the Germanic tribes (Angles, Saxons, and Jutes) who invaded the British Isles in the fifth and sixth centuries, driving out or absorbing the Celtic inhabitants after the Romans withdrew. From this Anglo-Saxon invasion we date the three periods of our language: Old English, spoken until about 1100 A.D.; Middle English, spoken from about 1100 to 1500 A.D.; and Modern English.

Old English was composed mainly of Anglo-Saxon words with a

smattering of Old Norse vocabulary that resulted from Viking (Danish) invasions in the eighth through tenth centuries. It was characterized by inflectional endings similar to those in modern German and a much freer word order than exists in Modern English. In other words, Old English depended largely upon changes in the forms, particularly the endings, of words to show their relationship to one another. Pronoun case forms *(I, me, my, mine)* are among the few vestiges of inflection remaining in English today. Old English formed new words by compounding (joining words) and by derivation (developing new words from existing ones); except for some Latin and Greek vocabulary, Old English borrowed few words from other languages.

Middle English is a transitional language heavily influenced by the Norman Conquest in 1066. The Normans (Northmen) were Vikings who had settled in northern France and who had gradually exchanged their native Old Norse of the Germanic language family for Old French, belonging to the Italic family; they brought thousands of Latin, Scandinavian, and, particularly, French words to England. For nearly 400 years French was the major language of the ruling class, and, as a result, standard Old English disappeared, fragmenting into dialects spoken primarily by the common people—the peasants and laborers.

Middle English shows the modification of these Old English dialects as they continued to evolve and to absorb influences from Norman French. As the Normans became culturally and politically more detached from Europe—and as they came to view England as their home—their association with the English-speaking common people gradually led to the resurrection of English as the spoken language of all classes. Even so, associations with social class could be identified in words of French and Anglo-Saxon origin, words that remain in our language today. For example, *beef (boeuf), mutton (mouton),* and *venison (veneison)*—words of French origin—describe meat cooked and served at the table; *cattle (catel), sheep (scēap),* and *deer (dēor)*—words of Anglo-Saxon origin—describe meat on the hoof in the field. Thus, French and Anglo-Saxon vocabulary mingled in one language but still identified the realms of rulers and laborers.

As the Middle English period progressed, the language experienced steady reduction or loss of inflectional endings and a resultant fixing of word order as the principal means of conveying meaningful relationships among words in a sentence. At the same time, function words (articles, prepositions, conjunctions)—words like *the, with, because*—grew in number and importance. French influenced not only vocabulary and meaning but also spelling and pronunciation.

During the Middle English period, the dialect spoken in the London area emerged as the basis for standard English—not surprising since London had become the country's capital and was the hub of activity for the court, the government, and the nearby universities.

35a

wds

The growing dominance of the London dialect as the standard language was strengthened further by the fact that most of the major writers of the late Middle Ages used it. Nevertheless, the flux and uncertainty of the time can be seen in the late-fourteenth-century works of John Gower—one written in Latin, one in English, and one in French. This variety indicates that a single literary language was not yet dominant. A short time later, however, Gower's friend Geoffrey Chaucer was writing his works in the dialect of London, that increasingly powerful political and economic center whose influence would ultimately control the language.

The shift from Middle English to Modern English occurred during a series of pronunciation changes known as the Great Vowel Shift. As a result of these changes that took place between 1350 and 1550, English began to sound more as it does today. Unfortunately for modern spelling, printing was introduced to England in the middle of this shift (1476), thereby preserving a number of Middle English spellings that bore little resemblance to the changed pronunciations. Despite these incongruities, printing had a positive effect on the development of English. Printing, and the subsequent increase in people who could read and write, tended to slow change and foster greater stability and standardization in both the spoken and written language. Printing also helped to foster the acceptance of English as a national language. The stature of English as a national language was signified by the great English translation of the Bible in 1611, named the King James Bible for the monarch reigning at the time.

35a

wds

The following brief passages show some of the developments that occurred as English evolved between the time of King Alfred in the late ninth century and that of Shakespeare in the late sixteenth century.

> Ða   gemette hie   Æpelwulf aldorman on Englafelda, ond
> Then   met   them   Aethelwulf alderman in Englefield,   and
>
> him   þaer wiþ   gefeaht ond sige   nam.
> them there against fought   and victory won.
>
> KING ALFRED, *Anglo-Saxon Chronicle*, c. 880

> But now, if so be that dignytees and poweris be yyven to gode men, the whiche thyng is full selde, what aggreable thynges is there in tho dignytees or power but oonly the goodnesse of folk that usen them?
>
> GEOFFREY CHAUCER, from the translation of *Boethius*, c. 1380

> Hit befel in the dayes of Uther Pendragon, when he was kynge of all Englond, and so regned, that there was a myghty duke in Cornewaill that helde warre ageynst hym long tyme, and the duke was called the duke of Tyntagil.
>
> SIR THOMAS MALORY, *Morte d'Arthur*, c. 1470

A Proude Man contemneth the companye of hys olde friendes, and disdayneth the sight of hys former famyliars, and turneth hys face from his wonted acquayntaunce.

HENRY KERTON, *The Mirror of Man's Lyfe,* 1576

Although their relationship to Modern English is unmistakable, these passages also indicate the changing nature of our language. And change remains continuous in English as the language adapts to the changing needs of those who use it.

As always, change is most easily seen in vocabulary. In its very early history, the Christianization of Britain brought such Latin words as *angel, candle, priest,* and *school* into English. From the Danish invasions came such basic words as *they, their, them, skull, skin, anger, husband, knife, law, root,* and *ill.* Following the Norman Conquest, French borrowings flooded the language, adding thousands of words we have inherited: *dance, tax, mayor, justice, faith, battle, paper, poet, surgeon, gentle, flower, sun,* to name just a few. In the seventeenth century, Latin became greatly respected and avidly studied; hence, Latin words, always a trickle since the first Roman occupation, again poured into English, including not only learned vocabulary but many words we think of as ordinary today: *industry, educate, insane, exist, illustrate, multiply, benefit, paragraph, delicate,* and the like. As English reached other parts of the world through exploration and colonization, it continued its habit of borrowing, drawing on Arabic *(alcohol, assassin),* Hebrew *(cherub, kosher),* East Indian *(jungle, yoga),* Japanese *(jujitsu, tycoon),* Spanish *(adobe, canyon),* and many other languages.

35a

wds

The borrowing process continues today. But in the past hundred years two other developments have had major consequences for English. The first is the rapid development of mass education and the resulting rise in literacy. The second is the advancement of science and technology. Though the effect of the first is difficult to measure, it is clear that a language reaching many of its users in print and an even greater number through electronic mass media will develop differently from a language in which writing is addressed to a special minority or in which speech is limited largely to face-to-face exchange. The effect of the technological revolution and rapid specialization is clearer. It has given us a burgeoning vocabulary of technical terms that, especially when aided by the mass media, frequently become a part of the common language almost overnight.

Changes in grammar since the sixteenth century, though minor compared with the earlier loss of inflections and the accompanying fixing of word order, have continued in Modern English. Reliance upon word order and function words has become even greater. Questions in the form of *Consents she?* and negations in the form of *I say not, I run not* have disappeared, to be replaced by the auxiliary verb *do,* as in *Does she consent?, I do not say, I do not run.* Verb forms with *be* in the pattern of *He was speaking, We are going, It is being built* have multiplied greatly. Other changes include an increase in the number of verbs combined with adverbs or with prepositions, as in *He looked up the word, She looked over their new house, The fireplace was smoking up the room.* Similarly, nouns used as modifiers of other nouns, as in *college student, transistor radio, gasoline station, space flight,* have become more common. Such changes clearly show that the evolution of the language continues.

Why should we be concerned about the history and development of the English language? For one thing, such knowledge gives us an appreciation for our language's richness and variety—for the sources and borrowings that have helped to create the most extensive vocabulary on earth. Experts estimate that English contains over 500,000 words, plus another half million scientific and technical terms. Among the earth's some 2,700 languages, no other language comes close. Says Robert MacNeil, co-author of *The Story of English:* "Today, English is used by at least 750 million people, and barely half of those speak it as a mother tongue. . . . English at the end of the twentieth century is more widely scattered, more widely spoken and written, than any other language has ever been. It has become *the* language of the planet, the first truly global language."

35b

Variety and standards

Language not only changes with time, it also varies widely at any given time—from one geographical area to another and from one occupational and social group to another. Further, the language each of us uses varies from situation to situation—depending on our audience and purpose.

Two recognized categories of variation are standard and nonstandard English. The term **standard English** applies to the written and spoken language of educated people. It is the language of their social discourse and also of the professions: business, journalism, law, education, medicine, politics, engineering, and so forth.

Nonstandard English, language that varies from the standard, differs in verb and pronoun forms and in the use of double negatives: *he give, growed; I seen, have saw; she be going; him and me is; hern, youse; can't never.* Nonstandard is also characterized by a relatively narrow range of vocabulary, deviant pronunciation and spelling, and often by a heavy dependence on a small variety of sentence structures.

Distinctions between standard and nonstandard English are not distinctions between good and bad or right and wrong; any language that communicates clearly and accurately is language functioning as it should. Rather, the reasons for the use of standard English by educated people are social and historical. But the fact remains that standard English is accepted as the norm for public speech and writing: it is the language shared by a wide audience of literate people.

The following passages illustrate standard and one form of non-standard English. Since nonstandard language is primarily spoken, the illustration can only approximate it.

STANDARD

While no country boasts the highest standards in every field, other cultures are more demanding of some services than America is. Most European countries insist on timely and efficient service on their railroads and airlines, which receive state subsidies to assure that performance. Americans who visit London typically come away with fond memories of the city's excellent taxicabs and subway system. The shortage of personal attention comes just when U.S. consumers are enjoying a cornucopia of novel products and services. . . . Shoppers can now find ten kinds of mustard and a dozen varieties of vinegar in a supermarket, but where is a clerk who can give a guiding word about these products?

STEPHEN KOEPP, *Time*

NONSTANDARD

"Well," he said at last, "I got in your springhouse for a fact and drank me some milk." He made a gesture toward the cement sack with his forefinger. "If you look in my poke yonder, you'll find two turnips and a handful of pole beans I grubbed outta your garden." He inclined his head toward the far-off field. "I expect that haystack I bedded down in needs fixin' if it ain't to molder." He took a deep breath and raised his eyebrows quizzically. "I think them's the damages," he said. "I trust they ain't none of em shootin offenses."

JOHN YOUNT, *Hardcastle*

35b

wds

Standard English is divided according to use into **functional varieties,** the most general variations being informal and formal. **Informal English** is everyday speaking and writing, casual conversation between friends and associates, personal letters, and writing close to general speech. **Formal English** is the language of scholarly books and articles; business, scientific, and governmental reports; legal writing; and most literary prose.

Because *informal* and *formal* each encompass wide ranges of degree, what may seem relatively formal to one listener or reader may strike another as fairly informal. Perceived formality or informality is often highly dependent on purpose, subject matter, and audience expectations.

In general, as language moves closer to casual speech, it becomes more informal. Free use of contractions, loose sentence structures, and conversational, everyday words and expressions (such as *shape up* and *get going*) characterize informal language. As formal language moves away from the conversational, its sentence structures become more complex, elaborate, and rigid, its vocabulary often more Latinate, and its tone more serious, less relaxed. The examples that follow illustrate the range possible within formal and informal writing. The first example is quite formal, the second more informal, and the third quite informal.

FORMAL

The enduring social unit is a female [polar bear] and her cubs. They are usually together for two years, during which time the female teaches the cubs to hunt. Their social interaction is constant and intense. Older bears infrequently make sounds—they hiss loudly, growl, and champ their teeth when they are irritated; and when they are agitated they make a soft chuffing sound. Cubs, on the other hand, have an impressive vocal repertoire.

BARRY LOPEZ, *Arctic Dreams*

INFORMAL

The colossal success of the supermarkets is based upon the fact that nobody, but nobody, can sell you something as well as you can by yourself. As a result, supermarkets now stock clothing, appliances, plastic swimming pools, and small trees. The theory is that if you succumb to an avocado today, tomorrow you may fall for an electronic range or a young poplar.

ELAINE KENDALL, "An Open Letter to the Corner Grocer"

Of all the common farm operations none is more ticklish than tending a brooder stove. All brooder stoves are whimsical, and some of them are holy terrors. Mine burns coal, and has only a fair record. With its check draft that opens and closes, this stove occupies my dreams from midnight, when I go to bed, until five o'clock, when I get up, pull a shirt and a pair of pants on over my pajamas, and stagger out into the dawn to read the thermometer under the hover and see that my 254 little innocents are properly disposed in a neat circle around their big iron mama.

E. B. WHITE, *One Man's Meat*

35b

wds

The terms *colloquial* and *edited* are often used in discussing varieties of English. Loosely synonymous with informal, **colloquial** means *spoken*. It describes the everyday speech of educated people and writing that uses easy vocabulary, loose constructions, contractions, and other characteristics of that speech. The informal styles of E. B. White and Elaine Kendall illustrated above are colloquial. **Edited English** is the *written* language of many books, magazines, and newspapers. It may be more or less formal or informal, but it is always marked by its observation of the conventional standards of spelling, punctuation, grammar, and sentence structure accepted by literate people.

That English contains such variety means there can be no rigid standard of correctness. But this does not mean there are no standards. We choose a standard according to its appropriateness for the speaking or writing situation, paying careful attention to the demands of the subject, the purpose in speaking or writing about it, and, particularly, the characteristics and expectations of the audience. Having considered these factors, we select the level of language that will communicate most effectively.

36

THE DICTIONARY

A good dictionary is a biography of words. More than a source for checking spelling, pronunciation, and meaning, it also records word history, part of speech, and, when necessary, principal parts, plurals, or other forms. Frequently it records the level of current usage. Often the dictionary offers other information as well—lists of abbreviations, rules for punctuation and spelling, condensed biographical and geographical information, the pronunciation and source of many given names, and a vocabulary of rhymes. For writers and readers a dictionary is an invaluable resource and an indispensable tool.

Dictionaries are not born; they are made. Modern general dictionaries are researched, compiled, and edited by specialists of all kinds: linguists, meteorologists, artists, theologians, journalists, historians, physicists, architects, psychologists—and many others. The various editorial staffs, contributors, consultants, and panels who work together to produce a first-rate dictionary are interested in where a word has come from, its current meaning and actual usage, and its latest important developments. As William Morris explains in his introduction to the first edition of *The American Heritage Dictionary:* "We have engaged the services of hundreds of authorities in every range of human endeavor and scholarship, from archaeology to space research, from Indo-European to computer programming . . . many thousands of definitions were sent to these specialists for emendation or approval." Good dictionaries record the way our language changes and provide guidance about its use. General dictionaries are of two types: abridged and unabridged.

36

wds

ABRIDGED DICTIONARIES

Also known as desk dictionaries, abridged dictionaries usually list between 150,000 and 200,000 entries and conveniently serve most people's daily reading and writing needs. Of the many dependable ones available, five reputable abridged dictionaries are described below. Although they differ in important ways, all contain more than 150,000 entries, provide careful etymologies and basic grammatical information about each entry, and specify distinctions among synonyms. All but *Webster's New Collegiate* provide helpful style or usage labels.

Webster's New Collegiate Dictionary. 9th ed. Springfield, MA: Merriam, 1983.

Based upon the *Third New International,* this desk dictionary profits from its extensive scholarship. The order of definitions under any one word is historical; a date notes the first instance of use. It has relatively full etymologies, a wide range of synonymies, and full prefatory material (including explanatory notes, history of English, pronunciation guide and symbols, spelling guide, and list of abbreviations). Abbreviations, biographical names, and place names are listed separately at the end of the dictionary. Some users find inconvenient the lack of the label *colloquial* or its equivalent, *informal,* and sparse use of the label *slang.*

Webster's New World Dictionary. 2nd college ed. New York: Simon, 1982.

This dictionary emphasizes simplified definitions even of technical terms and includes a large number of words and phrases that are relatively informal. Usage labels are generously used. Synonymies and etymologies are full and thorough. The sequence of definitions is historical, except that common meanings are placed first before specialized ones. All words are contained in the main alphabetical list. Identification of Americanisms and attention to the origin of American place names are special features. Foreign words that need to be italicized are clearly labeled by double-daggers in the margin. This dictionary is fairly generous in allowing for variant spellings.

The American Heritage Dictionary of the English Language. 2nd college ed. Boston: Houghton, 1982.

The distinguishing features of this dictionary are its generous illustrations and its usage notes based upon a consensus of a panel of some one hundred writers, editors, poets, and public speakers. The initial definition of an entry offers what the editors judge to be the central meaning, and it serves as the base for the arrangement of other senses of the word. Synonymies are generous but lack cross-references. Abbreviations and biological and geographical entries are listed in separate sections. An appendix of Indo-European roots is a special feature.

The Random House Dictionary of the English Language. College ed. New York: Random, 1984.

This dictionary is based on the unabridged *Random House Dictionary of the English Language.* Definitions are ordered by frequency of use; recent technical words receive careful attention. A single alphabetical listing incorporates all biographical and geographical as well as other entries. Among its prefaces, that by Raven I. McDavid, Jr., on usage, dialects, and functional varieties of English, is a particularly valuable summary.

Webster's II: New Riverside University Dictionary. Boston: Houghton, 1984.

This dictionary features some 200,000 definitions and is an updated and slightly condensed version of the same publisher's *American Heritage Dictionary, 2nd College Edition.* Special strengths include clear and adequate usage labels, numerous word histories, and excellent usage notes. Definitions are ordered neither historically nor by frequency of occurrence. Rather, they are ordered according to central meaning clusters from which related meanings and additional meanings may evolve. Reviewers have compared *Webster's II* to the now-out-of-print second edition of *Webster's New International Dictionary* because it is prescriptive, ruling on what is acceptable or unacceptable usage in the notes.

UNABRIDGED DICTIONARIES

Unabridged dictionaries contain the most complete and scholarly description of English words. The three described below are available in most libraries and are the unabridged dictionaries most frequently used.

The Oxford English Dictionary. 13 vols., plus supplements. New York: Oxford UP, 1933, 1972, 1977. Now also available in a photographically reduced edition of two volumes published in 1971.

36

wds

Commonly referred to as the *OED,* this is the greatest dictionary of the English language. Containing over 500,000 entries, it traces the progress of each word through the language, giving dated quotations to illustrate its meaning and spelling at particular times in its history. A single word may occupy several pages. *Set,* for example, occupies twenty-three pages, and a single one of its more than 150 definitions is illustrated by thirteen quotations from writings beginning in 1056 and extending to 1893.

Webster's Third New International Dictionary of the English Language. Springfield, MA: Merriam-Webster, 1981.

This is the unabridged dictionary that people who live in the United States are most likely to be familiar with. Issued originally in 1909, it was revised in 1934. The current edition, thoroughly revised, has 460,000 entries and was first published in 1961. Though not as exhaustive as the *OED,* its definitions are scholarly and exact and frequently supported by illustrative quotations. Since the 1961 edition uses style labels such as *slang* infrequently and does not use the label *colloquial,* some readers continue to prefer the second edition.

Random House Dictionary of the English Language. 2nd ed. New York: Random, 1987.

With only 315,000 entries, the *Random House Dictionary* is considerably briefer than most unabridged dictionaries. But it is a sound and scholarly dictionary with especially up-to-date entries. It is the only entirely new unabridged dictionary to be published in recent years.

Other unabridged dictionaries of English are the *New Standard Dictionary of the English Language, Webster's New Twentieth-Century Dictionary,* and the *Dictionary of American English* (four volumes), which is made on the same plan as the *OED* and follows the history of words as they were used by American writers between 1620 and 1900.

36a
Using a dictionary

Because dictionaries must say a great deal in a very brief space, they use systems of abbreviations, symbols, and type faces to condense information. Although such systems vary from dictionary to dictionary, their format is quite similar. Taking the time to read a dictionary's explanatory pages will save you some puzzlement later; and once you have become familiar with the system in one dictionary, you will find reading any dictionary's entries fairly easy.

The following sample entry, from *Webster's Third New International Dictionary,* shows most of the principal features to be found in a dictionary entry. These are labeled and numbered to correspond with the more detailed descriptions that follow.

36a

wds

1 | spelling and syllabication   2 pronunciation   grammatical function and form 3

¹howl \ˈhau̇l *esp before pause or consonant* -au̇əl\ *vb* -ED/-ING/ -s [ME *houlen;* akin to MD *hūlen* to howl, MHG *hiulen, hiuweln* to howl, OHG *hūwila* owl, Gk *kōkyein* to shriek, wail, lament, Skt *kauti* he cries out] *vi* **1 :** to utter or emit a loud sustained doleful sound or outcry characteristic of dogs and wolves ⟨wolves ∼*ing* in the arctic night⟩ ⟨the only sound is a melancholy wind ∼*ing* —John Buchan⟩ **2 :** to cry out or exclaim with lack of restraint and prolonged loudness through strong impulse, feeling, or emotion ⟨the scalded men ∼*ing* in agony⟩ ⟨the hungry mob ∼*ed* about the Senate house, threatening fire and massacre —J.A.Froude⟩ ⟨proctors ∼*ing* at the blunder⟩ **3 :** to go on a spree or rampage ⟨this is my night to ∼⟩ ∼ *vt* **1 :** to utter or announce noisily with unrestrained demonstrative outcry ⟨newsboys ∼*ing* the news⟩ **2 :** to affect, effect, or drive by adverse outcry — used esp. with *down* ⟨supporters of the Administration . . . ready to ∼ down any suggestion of criticism —*Wall Street Jour.*⟩ **syn** see ROAR

²howl \ˈ\ *n* -s **1 :** a loud protracted mournful rising and falling cry characteristic of a dog or a wolf **2 a :** a prolonged cry of distress **:** WAIL **b :** a yell or outcry of disappointment, rage, or protest **3 :** PROTEST, COMPLAINT ⟨raise a ∼ over high taxes⟩ ⟨set up a ∼ that he was being cheated⟩ **4 :** something that provokes laughter ⟨his act was a ∼⟩ **5 :** a noise produced in an electronic amplifier usu. by undesired regeneration of alternating currents of audio frequency **:** OSCILLATION — called also *squeal*

4 etymology   6 quotation   meanings 5   synonym 7

1. Spelling and syllabication. The main entry of a word in a dictionary shows the spelling and syllabication, using centered dots between syllables to show how to separate the word properly at the ends of the lines (see "Syllabication," Section **18**). The entry also gives the proper spelling of compound words—properness depends on whether the editors found them more often written as two single words (**half broth·er**), as a hyphenated compound (**quar·ter-hour**), or as one word (**drug·store**). Dictionaries also indicate foreign words that require italics (in manuscript, underlining) either by labeling them as foreign (*French, German,* etc.), printing them in boldface italics, or using a symbol such as a double dagger (‡).

Any variant spellings will also be listed in the main entry. Usually, the first listing is, in the opinion of the editors, the more common; some dictionaries indicate that two variants are equally common by joining them with *or* (**cad·die** *or* **cad·dy**) or that one is less common than the other by joining them with *also* (**wool·ly** *also* **wool·y**). In general, choose the first listed variant unless there is a special reason for choosing the second.

The main entry for *howl* shows that it is a one-syllable word, which cannot be divided at the end of a line; that it is not normally capitalized; and that it has no variant spelling.

EXERCISE 36a(1)

Referring to a dictionary, give the preferred spelling of each word.

1. ambiance	4. hiccough	7. partizan
2. cheque	5. labelled	8. sabre
3. favour	6. mediaeval	9. theatre

EXERCISE 36a(2)

Rewrite the following compounds, showing which should be written as they are, which hyphenated, and which written as two or more separate words.

1. bookkeeper	4. goalpost	7. rainfall
2. candlelight	5. heavyduty	8. shortcircuit
3. eyecontact	6. policymaker	9. weightlifter

EXERCISE 36a(3)

Copy the following foreign words, underlining those that require italics and supplying accents where needed.

1. ad nauseam	4. in loco parentis	7. nom de guerre
2. elan	5. manana	8. outre
3. faux pas	6. noblesse oblige	9. Zeitgeist

36a

wds

---

2. Pronunciation. Dictionaries indicate the pronunciation of words by respelling them with special symbols and letters. Explanation of the symbols is given either at the bottom of the page on which the entry appears or in the prefatory pages or both.

In *Webster's Third* the pronunciation appears between slant lines called reverse virgules; some other dictionaries use parentheses. Stressed syllables are indicated by accent marks (´ or '). In most dictionaries, the accent mark follows the stressed syllable. Notice, however, that *Webster's Third* (as well as *Webster's New Collegiate,* based on the *Third*) places the accent mark immediately before the stressed syllable.

Dictionaries show frequently occurring variant pronunciations as they do variant spellings. In the *Webster's Third* sample entry, for instance, you can see that an unabridged dictionary may even show variant pronunciations for such a simple word as *howl.* As with variant spellings, the first pronunciation is sometimes said to be preferred. However, unless there is a limiting label or comment attached to one or more variants, they are all equally correct. Your preference should be determined by the pronunciation you hear in conversation around you.

EXERCISE 36a(4)

Copy the dictionary pronunciations for the following words. If there is variant usage for any, underline the pronunciation that you are accustomed to.

1. again
2. applicable
3. aunt
4. banal
5. hospitable
6. laboratory
7. negate
8. neither
9. trespass

36a

wds

3. Grammatical functions and forms. All dictionaries indicate the part of speech to which a word belongs. If a word can serve as more than one part of speech, most dictionaries include all its functions and meanings under a single entry, grouping the meanings separately for each function. A few dictionaries list a separate entry for each part of speech—as does *Webster's Third,* which groups the intransitive *(vi)* and transitive *(vt)* verb forms in the first entry and the noun form *(n)* in the second.

Dictionaries also show a word's inflected forms, especially if they are irregular or if they might cause spelling problems (as in *travel, traveled, traveling* or *travelled, travelling*). Thus the entry for the verb *drink* lists the irregular past tense *drank* and the past participle *drunk.* The entries for the singular nouns *child* and *alumna* give the plural forms *children* and *alumnae.* Most dictionaries do not show plurals for nouns that are regular, forming their plurals with *-s.* Most dictionaries also show *-er* and *-est* for the comparative and superlative forms of adjectives and adverbs. Where this information is not supplied, you can assume the comparative and superlative forms require the addition of *more* and *most. Webster's Third* is one of several dictionaries that also show the regular as well as irregular forms for various parts of speech.

Other parts of speech formed from the word being defined, and related in meaning, are listed at the end of the entry. They are spelled, divided into syllables, and identified by part of speech, but not defined.

EXERCISE 36a(5)

Write the past tense and the past participle of each of these verbs. Use a dictionary as necessary.

1. bring	4. drive	7. shake
2. broadcast	5. fly	8. sink
3. burst	6. ride	9. wear

EXERCISE 36a(6)

Write the plural (or plurals) of each of the following. Use a dictionary as necessary.

1. alumna	4. elf	7. larva
2. apex	5. focus	8. medium
3. court-martial	6. index	9. synopsis

EXERCISE 36a(7)

Write the comparative and superlative forms of each of the following. Use a dictionary as necessary.

1. boring	4. mad	7. radical
2. good	5. much	8. sweetly
3. lively	6. often	9. terrible

36a

wds

4. **Etymology.** A word's history—its origin and derivation—often helps clarify its present meaning, forms, and spelling. Because the course of history changes, restricts, or extends meanings, many original ones have been lost entirely. *Presently,* for example, formerly meant *at once, immediately;* it now usually means *shortly, in a little while.*

The etymology of a word can be very useful in discriminating between synonyms, so that you can select the one that comes closest to the meaning you intend. Dictionaries place etymologies after the initial grammatical label or at the very end of the entry. When they contain symbols, abbreviations, and different type faces, you should check the key and explanation provided in the dictionary's opening pages.

The material between the brackets in the *Webster's Third* entry for *howl* shows the origin or etymology of the word: *howl* comes from a word in Middle English (ME) spelled *houlen,* and is related to Middle Dutch (MD) *hūlen* and Middle High German (MHG) *hiulen* or *hiuweln,* all meaning "to howl"; to the Old High German (OHG) word *hūwila* meaning "owl"; to the Greek (Gk) *kōkyein* meaning "to wail" or "lament"; and to the Sanskrit (Skt) word *kauti* meaning "he cries out."

EXERCISE 36a(8)

Explain the etymology of each of the following.

1. astonish	4. gossip	7. robust
2. boss	5. investigate	8. sabotage
3. colonel	6. ostracize	9. scapegoat

EXERCISE 36a(9)

From what specific names have the following derived?

1. bikini	4. guppy	7. ritzy
2. dunce	5. leotard	8. saxophone
3. epicure	6. magnolia	9. uranium

EXERCISE 36a(10)

From what language did each of the following words originally come?

1. aloof	6. moose	11. skeptic
2. confetti	7. pariah	12. ski
3. humility	8. poodle	13. tomato
4. jest	9. potato	14. tycoon
5. mammoth	10. robot	15. yacht

36a

wds

5.   Meanings. Strictly speaking, dictionaries do not *define* words; they record meanings that actual usage, past and present, has attached to words. When more than one meaning is recorded for a single word, *Webster's Collegiate* (and *Webster's Third*) lists them in order of historical use, earliest meaning first. Most other dictionaries list the most common or frequently used, most general, or most basic meaning first. Thus it is important to know a dictionary's system of arrangement, explained in the volume's prefatory pages, and to read *all* the meanings in an entry before choosing the one that best suits the context in which you plan to use the word.

Senses of a word within a single part of speech are shown by means of boldface numbers. Where the sense of a word can be subdivided into further shades of meaning (different but related senses), boldface, lower-case letters are used. Words in small capitals (WAIL in meaning 2 of the noun form of *howl*, for example) are both synonyms and also main entries where further related definitions can be found. Special and technical meanings are clearly indicated.

EXERCISE 36a(11)

For each of the following words, (1) indicate the total number of meanings you can find, and (2) write three sentences that illustrate three different meanings.

1. bat	4. figure	7. right
2. clean	5. lock	8. seal
3. digest	6. over	9. try

EXERCISE 36a(12)

Explain the changes in meaning that have taken place in each of the following words, using etymologies where helpful.

1. aisle	6. fossil	11. neighbor
2. charm	7. gamut	12. rigmarole
3. dally	8. lewd	13. slapstick
4. dock	9. libel	14. smirk
5. eerie	10. magazine	15. triumph

6. Quotations. Quotations form a major part of a definition by illustrating actual usage, the context for a word. They are extremely valuable in showing differences in synonyms, distinguishing between closely related meanings, or illustrating unusual uses of a word. Those labeled by authors' names or by sources are actual quotations; those not so labeled are typical phrases created by the dictionary editors. Illlustrative quotations are usually enclosed in angle brackets (< >) or set off by a colon and italicized.

Under meaning 2 of *howl* as a transitive verb, a usage note states that in this meaning *howl* is used especially with *down* in the phrase *howl down*, and an example from *The Wall Street Journal* is provided. *Webster's Third* uses a swung dash (~) in quotations to replace the word itself.

36a

wds

7. Synonyms and antonyms. A **synonym** is a word having approximately the same general meaning as the main-entry word. An **antonym** has approximately the opposite meaning. For practical reasons, not all entries show synonyms and antonyms. Paragraph-length discussions of groups of synonyms are usually located at the end of certain entries and cross-referenced at related entries. For instance, at the end of meaning 2 in the *Webster's Third* transitive verb entry for *howl*, "**syn** see ROAR" means that the entry for *roar* contains a discussion of the synonyms for *howl*. That synonym group is reproduced below.

From *Webster's Third*, for *howl:*

syn HOWL, ULULATE, BELLOW, BAWL, BLUSTER, CLAMOR, VOCIFERATE: ROAR suggests the full loud reverberating sound made by lions or the booming sea or by persons in rage or boisterous merriment ⟨far away guns *roar* —Virginia Woolf⟩ ⟨the harsh north wind . . . *roared* in the piazzas —Osbert Sitwell⟩ ⟨*roared* the blacksmith, his face black with rage —T.B.Costain⟩ HOWL indicates a higher, less reverberant sound often suggesting the doleful or agonized or the sounds of unrestrained laughter ⟨frequent *howling* of jackals and hyenas —James Stevenson-Hamilton⟩ ⟨how the wind does *howl* —J.C.Powys⟩ ⟨*roared* at his subject . . . *howled* at . . . inconsistencies —Martin Gardner⟩ ULULATE is a literary synonym for HOWL but may suggest mournful protraction and rhythmical delivery ⟨an *ululating* baritone mushy with pumped-up pity —E.B.White⟩ BELLOW suggests the loud, abrupt, hollow sound made typically by bulls or any similar

(continued on p. 280)

loud, reverberating sound ⟨most of them were drunk. They went *bellowing* through the town —Kenneth Roberts⟩ BAWL suggests a somewhat lighter, less reverberant, unmodulated sound made typically by calves ⟨a woman *bawling* abuse from the door of an inn —C.E.Montague⟩ ⟨the old judge was in the hall *bawling* hasty orders —Sheridan Le Fanu⟩ BLUSTER suggests the turbulent noisiness of gusts of wind; it often suggests swaggering and noisy threats or protests ⟨expressed her opinion gently but firmly, while he *blustered* for a time and then gave in —Sherwood Anderson⟩ ⟨swagger and *bluster* and take the limelight —Margaret Mead⟩ CLAMOR suggests sustained, mixed and confused noisy outcry as from a number of agitated persons ⟨half-starved men and women *clamoring* for food —Kenneth Roberts⟩ ⟨easy ... for critics ... to *clamor* for action —Sir Winston Churchill⟩ VOCIFERATE suggests loud vehement insistence in speaking ⟨was not willing to break off his talk; so he continued to *vociferate* his remarks —James Boswell⟩

By permission. From *Webster's Third New International Dictionary.* © 1986 by Merriam-Webster, Inc., publisher of the Merriam-Webster® dictionaries.

8. Labels. Dictionaries label words or particular meanings of words to indicate that they are in some way restricted. Words and meanings not so labeled are appropriate for general use. Although the particular labels that dictionaries use vary somewhat, all labels can be divided into four general categories: *geographic* labels, *time* labels, *occupational* or *subject* labels, and *usage* or *style* labels.

Geographic labels indicate that the word or meaning is limited to a particular area. Typical labels of this sort are *British, Australian, New England, Southern U.S.,* and the like. Thus *Webster's Collegiate* labels *lift,* in the meaning of "elevator," *British,* and *outbye,* meaning "a short distance away," *Scottish. Webster's New World* labels *corn pone,* a kind of corn bread, *Southern U.S.* The label *dialectal* or *regional* usually suggests a specialized local or provincial word, often traditional. Thus *larrap,* meaning "a blow" or "to flog," is labeled *dialectal* by *Webster's Collegiate* and *regional* by *American Heritage.*

Time labels indicate that the labeled word has passed out of use entirely or no longer occurs in ordinary contexts. *Obsolete* means that a word has passed out of use entirely, as for example *absume* and *enwheel,* words that have not been used for two hundred years. *Archaic* means that the labeled word or meaning is no longer generally used although it may still be seen occasionally in older writing, as for example *belike,* meaning "probably," and *outland,* meaning "a foreign land."

Subject labels indicate that a word or a particular meaning belongs to a special field such as law, medicine, baseball, finance, mathematics, or psychology. Thus *Webster's New World* identifies *projection* as a psychiatric term *(Psychiatry)* when used to mean the process of assigning one's own undesirable impulses to others and as a photographic term *(Photog.)* when used to mean projecting an image on a screen. *American Heritage* labels as *Law* the meaning of *domain* in the sense of ownership and rights of disposal of property.

Style labels indicate that a word or meaning is restricted to a particular level of usage. Typical style labels are *slang, colloquial, in-*

36a

wds

formal, nonstandard, substandard, illiterate, and *vulgar.* Variations among dictionaries are greatest in their choice of labels and in the words and meanings to which they apply them. Nonetheless, there is broad agreement on the meanings of the labels themselves.

Slang indicates that a word, though widely used, has not yet been accepted in the general vocabulary. Slang terms and meanings often are used humorously; are likely to be short-lived, limited to a particular group of people; and are used almost entirely in speech rather than writing. Typical examples are *gross out* (to fill with disgust), *shaft* (to treat in a harsh, unfair way), *shades* (sunglasses), *snow* (cocaine or heroin), and *megabuck* (a million dollars). Of the dictionaries described, *Webster's Collegiate* is by far the most sparing in its use of the label, allowing many entries labeled *slang* by others to pass without any label.

Colloquial and *informal* are almost synonymous terms. They both indicate that a word is characteristic of speech or of quite informal, rather than more formal, writing. The *American Heritage* and *Webster's II* use the label *informal; Webster's New World* uses *colloquial. Webster's Collegiate* uses neither label and thus may be less useful for those who need to determine how appropriate a word is for a particular writing context.

Illiterate, substandard, and some other similar terms are labels indicating that a word is limited to uneducated speech, as *drownded* for the past tense of *drown.* Though dictionaries vary somewhat in the particular labels they use, their agreement in classifying a word as being limited to uneducated speech is much greater than their agreement in labeling a word *slang, colloquial,* and so on.

To use your dictionary wisely as a guide to usage, you will have to examine carefully the explanatory notes in it to determine exactly what labels are applied and how they are interpreted by the editors.

36a

wds

EXERCISE 36a(13)

Which of the following are standard English and which also have colloquial, informal, or slang usages, according to your dictionary? If possible, check more than one dictionary to determine if they agree.

1. beef	5. fan	9. soft-pedal
2. blowup	6. flop	10. stiff
3. corn	7. gag	11. whitewash
4. drip	8. needle	12. zip

EXERCISE 36a(14)

In what areas of the world would you be likely to hear the following?

1. banyan	5. joey	9. queue
2. chador	6. kibbutz	10. sahib
3. dingo	7. pensione	11. samovar
4. fez	8. piñata	12. sampan

EXERCISE 36a(15)

Any of the desk dictionaries discussed in this section will help you answer the following questions. Look up the meanings of *etymology, homonym,* and *synonym,* if necessary, before answering the questions.

1. What is the etymology of the word *language?*
2. What are three homonyms for the word *right?*
3. What is the syllabication of the word *premonition?*
4. What are some synonyms for the adjective *variable?*
5. Give the meanings of these abbreviations: dial., Q.E.D., sp. gr.

SPECIAL DICTIONARIES

General dictionaries bring together in a single reference all of the information you ordinarily need about a word. Special dictionaries, because they limit their attention to a single kind of information about words or to a single category of words, can give more complete information. Thus a dictionary of slang can devote an entire page to the word *hip,* in contrast to the general dictionary, which can afford no more than four or five lines. Similarly, dictionaries of usage and of synonyms can provide much more complete information of a particular kind than space allows in general dictionaries. Such dictionaries are no substitute for the daily usefulness of a good desk dictionary, but they are extremely useful supplements.

When you need specialized information about words, check the most recent edition of one of the following dictionaries:*

> Bernstein, Theodore M. *The Careful Writer: A Modern Guide to English Usage.*
> Follett, Wilson. *Modern American Usage.*
> Fowler, H.W. *Dictionary of Modern English Usage.* Rev. and ed. Sir Ernest Gowers.
> Partridge, Eric. *A Dictionary of Slang and Unconventional English.* Ed. Paul Beale.
> *Webster's Collegiate Thesaurus.*
> *Webster's New Dictionary of Synonyms.*
> Wentworth, Harold, and Stuart Berg Flexner. *Dictionary of American Slang.* 2nd supp. ed.

36b

wds

36b

Increasing your vocabulary

The English language contains well over a million words. Of these, about two-fifths belong almost exclusively to special fields: e.g., zoology, electronics, psychiatry. Of the remaining three-fifths, una-

---

*See also the lists of reference books in "Research," Section **44**.

bridged dictionaries list 500,000 or more, desk dictionaries between 150,000 and 200,000. Such wealth is both a blessing and a curse. On the one hand, many English words are loosely synonymous, sometimes interchangeable, as in *buy* a book or *purchase* a book. On the other hand, the distinctions between synonyms are fully as important as their similarities. For example, a family may be said to be living in *poverty*, or in *penury*, or in *want*, or in *destitution*. All these words are loosely synonymous; but each in fact indicates a slightly different degree of need, *want* describing the least severe and *destitution* describing the most severe degree. Thus only one of the words will portray the family exactly as you see it and wish your reader to see it. In short, as a writer of English you must use words carefully in order to be precise.

We all have two vocabularies: a **passive**, or **recognition**, **vocabulary**, which is made up of the words we recognize in the context of reading material or conversation but do not actually use ourselves; and an **active vocabulary**, which consists of "working" words—those we use daily in our own writing and speaking. A good vocabulary is the product of years of serious reading, of listening to intelligent talk, and of trying to speak and write forcefully and clearly. This does not mean other methods of vocabulary building are ineffective, but it does mean that acquiring a good vocabulary is inseparable from acquiring an education.

1. **Increasing your recognition vocabulary.** English includes many words derived from other languages. Consequently, it has a number of words based on common root forms to which different prefixes or suffixes have been added. The root form *spec-*, for example, from the Latin *specere (to look)*, appears in *specter, inspection, perspective, aspect, introspection, circumspect, specimen, spectator*. Knowing the common prefixes and suffixes will help you detect the meanings of many words whose roots are familiar.

36b

wds

Prefixes

Prefix	Example	Meaning
ab-	absent	away from
ad-*	adverb	to *or* for
com-*	combine	with
de-	degrade, depart, dehumanize	down, away from *or* undoing
dis-*	disparate, disappoint	separation *or* reversal
ex-*	extend, ex-president	out of *or* former

---

*The spelling of these prefixes varies, usually to make pronunciation easier. *Ad* becomes *ac* in *accuse*, *ag* in *aggregate*, *at* in *attack*. Similarly, the final consonant in the other prefixes is assimilated by the initial letter of the root word: *colleague (com + league); illicit (in + licit); offend (ob + fend); succeed (sub + ceed)*.

Prefix	Example	Meaning
il-*	illogical	not
im-	immobile	not
in-*	input	in *or* on
in-*	inhuman	not
ir-	irrefutable	not
mis-	misprint	wrong
non-	non-Christian, nonsense	not
ob-*	obtuse	against
pre-	prevent, precondition	before
pro-	proceed	for *or* forward
re-	repeat	back *or* again
sub-*	subcommittee	under
trans-	transcribe	across
un-	unclean	not

EXERCISE 36b(1)

Write words denoting *negation* of the following.

> EXAMPLE   movable—able to be moved
> immovable—*not* able to be moved

1. accessible
2. breakable
3. compliant
4. consistent
5. exact
6. hospitable
7. literate
8. measurable
9. responsible

EXERCISE 36b(2)

Write words denoting *reversal* of the following.

> EXAMPLE   accelerate—to move at *in*creasing speed
> decelerate—to move at *de*creasing speed
> increase—to grow *larger*
> decrease—to grow *smaller*

1. associate
2. continue
3. dress
4. engage
5. link
6. load
7. prove
8. satisfy
9. stabilize

Suffixes. These fall into three groups: noun suffixes, verb suffixes, adjectival suffixes.

Noun suffixes denoting *act of, state of, quality of* include the following:

Suffix	Example	Meaning
-dom	freedom	*state of* being free
-hood	manhood	*state of* being a man
-ness	dimness	*state of* being dim
-ice	cowardice	*quality of* being a coward
-ation	flirtation	*act of* flirting
-ion	intercession	*act of* interceding

36b

wds

Suffix	Example	Meaning
⌐-sion	scansion	*act of* scanning
⌊-tion	corruption	*state of* being corrupt
-ment	argument	*act of* arguing
-ship	friendship	*state of* being friends
⌐-ance	continuance	*act of* continuing
|-ence	precedence	*act of* preceding
|-ancy	flippancy	*state of* being flippant
⌊-ency	currency	*state of* being current
-ism	baptism	*act of* baptizing
-ery	bravery	*quality of* being brave

Noun suffixes denoting *doer, one who* include the following:

Suffix	Example	Meaning
-eer (general)	auctioneer	*one who* auctions
-ist	fascist	*one who* believes in fascism
⌐-or	debtor	*one who* is in debt
⌊-er	worker	*one who* works

Verb suffixes denoting *to make* or *to perform the act of* include the following:

Suffix	Example	Meaning
-ate	perpetuate	*to make* perpetual
-en	soften	*to make* soft
-fy	dignify	*to make* dignified
-ize, -ise	sterilize	*to make* sterile

Adjectival suffixes include the following:

Suffix	Example	Meaning
-ful	hateful	full of
-ish	foolish	resembling
-ate	affectionate	having
-ic, -ical	angelic	resembling
-ive	prospective	having
-ous	zealous	full of
-ulent	fraudulent	full of
-less	fatherless	without
-able, -ible	peaceable	capable of
-ed	spirited	having
-ly	womanly	resembling
-like	childlike	resembling

36b

wds

EXERCISE 36b(3)

Make words indicating *act of, state of,* or *quality of* from the following words.

1. assist
2. consult
3. enchant
4. hard
5. kin
6. king
7. process
8. real
9. vex

EXERCISE 36b(4)

Make nouns indicating *doer* from the following.

1. art	4. mediate	7. produce
2. deal	5. mountain	8. research
3. instigate	6. piano	9. sail

EXERCISE 36b(5)

Make verbs indicating *to make or to perform the act of* from the following nouns and adjectives.

1. alien	4. individual	7. pure
2. beauty	5. material	8. red
3. fantasy	6. motive	9. special

EXERCISE 36b(6)

Make adjectives of the following words by adding a suffix.

1. access	4. demon	7. tolerate
2. art	5. illustrate	8. value
3. curve	6. neighbor	9. wish

36b

wds

2. Increasing and strengthening your active vocabulary. Another way to increase word power is to keep transferring words from your recognition vocabulary to your active vocabulary. When you acquire a new word, find opportunities to use it so that it will come to feel natural and comfortable in your speech and writing.

An excellent way to strengthen your vocabulary is to study dictionary discussions of synonyms. As you add words to your vocabulary, look them up in a dictionary to be certain of their meaning and usage, and examine their synonyms at the same time. That way you will be able to increase your vocabulary by not one but several related words at a time. Furthermore, you will have learned the distinctions in meaning that will make your use of these words accurate and effective. Synonym dictionaries and thesauruses, devoted exclusively to the grouping and differentiating of synonyms, are also good sources. Although the various editions of *Roget's Thesaurus* are valuable for long lists of closely related words, they must be used cautiously because they do not discuss distinctions in meaning and offer no guiding examples. A thesaurus should be used in conjunction with a dictionary so that you will be sure of selecting the synonym with the shade of meaning you need.

EXERCISE 36b(7)

Indicate the distinctions in meaning among the words in each of the following groups.

1. abolish, cancel, rescind, quash, revoke
2. careful, economical, thrifty, frugal, provident

3. polite, genteel, cultured, civil, urbane, gracious
4. curious, quaint, odd, singular, fanciful
5. petty, trivial, trifling, insignificant, unimportant

37
APPROPRIATENESS

The Greek philosopher Aristotle wrote that a speech is composed of three things: the speaker, the subject on which he speaks, and the audience he is addressing. These words neatly summarize the factors to consider when you are choosing the words that will best express your ideas. Your language needs to be appropriate not only for your subject matter but also for your readers or listeners. Further, it should reflect the aspects of yourself as writer or speaker that you wish to project.

Author and teacher William Zinsser believes that good writing is a personal transaction between a reader and a writer. His analogy is a helpful one: the language you use reflects not only your attitude about yourself and your subject but also your attitude toward your audience. If the words you choose are inappropriate, you will end up alienating the reader.

There are no words in the English language that cannot be used somewhere, sometime. You may consider yourself a casual, easygoing person and believe that casual, easygoing language is appropriate to your writing. It may be—in a letter to a close friend, for instance. Even in letter writing, however, you must also consider your audience and your subject: a letter to a friend would necessarily be different if you were expressing sympathy for an illness in his or her family than if you were recounting the events of a weekend party.

On the other hand, if you wanted to mention the party in a psychology paper as an example of tension-releasing behavior among college students, your descriptive language would undoubtedly be different from the language you used in the letter to your friend. The writing in the letter would appropriately be informal and colloquial—easy, loose, and full of jargon and slang: *The mixer was a blast, everybody just hanging out, getting ripped, and generally blowing off steam after too many all-nighters and heavy-duty midterms.* In the paper the writing would appropriately be more formal, edited, standard English—the "public" writing of the professions and most college courses: *Many college students release the tension and pressure resulting from concentrated study by attending parties after their exams are over.*

Both examples are right for their situations. But the audience for the first is much more limited than the audience for the second. When you write, bear in mind that the more diverse and general your audience the more you need to rely on standard, formal English, which offers a huge vocabulary of widely understood words. You will usually want to avoid words that only limited groups of readers understand. The vocabularies offered by slang, jargon, colloquialisms, regionalisms, and the like are narrow and specialized, and therefore can be misunderstood. Consequently, their use should generally be limited to special contexts, audiences, and purposes.

37a
Slang is the language of the in-crowd.

Slang consists of the rapidly changing words and phrases in popular speech that people invent to give language novelty and vigor. Slang words, in fact, are fun—unless you don't happen to know what they mean. Then they can seem like the strange tongue of a secret sect.

Slang often is created by the same process we use to create most new words: by combining two words (*ferretface, blockhead*); by shortening words (*pro, prof, vet, max*); by borrowing from other languages (*kaput, spiel*); and by generalizing a proper name (*the real McCoy*). Often slang simply extends the meaning of phrases borrowed from other activities (*lower the boom* from sailing; *tune in, tune out* from radio; *cash in your chips* from poker). A great deal of slang gives a new range of meaning to existing words (*tough, heavy, high, joint, turned on, bombed out*).

Slang is—and has always been—part of the current language, adding spontaneity, directness, color, and liveliness. Over three hundred years ago, Pilgrim youngsters were inventing slang terms, turning the traditional farewell—"God be with you"—into the flippant "good-by." Thus slang often contributes directly to the growth of the language as slang terms move gradually into general use. Words like *rascal* and *sham* were originally slang terms; shortened forms such as *A-bomb, ad, gym,* and *phone* are now appropriate to most informal writing. Reports on education routinely refer to high school *dropouts*. To see soft drinks and potato chips called *junk food* in the pages of a magazine surprises no one. When slang is clear, precise, vivid, and descriptive in ways that more standard words are not, it tends to enter general usage. In informal writing, well-chosen slang terms can be very effective:

> Has Harold Wilson *Lost His Cool?*
>
> Headline, *New York Times*

> Heaven knows there are large areas where a shrewd eye for the *quick buck* is dominant.
>
> FREDERICK LEWIS ALLEN, *The Big Change*

But slang has serious limitations. It is often imprecise, understandable only to a narrow social or age group, and usually changes very rapidly. You may be familiar with the latest slang, but who remembers *lollapalooza, balloon juice,* or *spooning?* The fact that *hep* became *hip* within a few years suggests how short-lived slang can be.

Enjoy slang for the life it can sometimes give to speech. But even in conversation, remember that it may not be understood and that a little goes a long way. If you rely on *nifty, lousy, tough,* and *gross* to describe all objects, events, and ideas, you don't communicate much. In writing, use slang primarily when it serves some legitimate purpose, such as capturing the flavor of conversation.

> The bouncer told the drunk he had better back off or he was likely to get his lights punched out. Then he firmly steered the drunk through the door and out of the bar.

Except in carefully controlled contexts, slang and standard language usually make an inappropriate mixture:

> The very notion of venture capital is so alien in Communist China that no government official was willing to risk giving the two [young Chinese entrepreneurs] permission to set up shop. The decision was bucked up all the way to Premier Zhao Ziyang. He flashed the go-ahead last year, and the company began operation in January.
>
> *Business Week*

37a

appr

While we are not likely to resist such usages as *set up shop* in a magazine aimed at a fairly broad, general business audience, the slang expressions *bucked up* and *flashed the go-ahead* here seem out of place in a news story concerning the head of the Chinese government. The best rule of thumb is to assess your audience and purpose carefully in deciding whether a slang term is appropriate.

EXERCISE 37a(1)

Almost everyone has favorite slang terms. Make a list of your own slang expressions and compare the list with those of your classmates to see how "original" your own slang is. Then ask an individual from an older or younger generation for a list of slang terms to see how expressions for similar things vary from age group to age group.

EXERCISE 37a(2)

For a week or two, keep a list of slang terms you find in the daily newspaper or a weekly news magazine. Which terms strike you as appropriate and effective? Which as poor usage? Why? Here's an example from *Time* to get you started.

> The statistical trends hardly explained Wall Street's loony rise and fall. The main cause of the fierce roller-coaster ride was the

volume of buy and sell orders triggered by computer-driven trading programs at major investment houses. When market prices reach prescribed levels, the so-called program traders can blitz the market in seconds with orders representing many thousands of shares of a broad spectrum of stocks.

37b

Regional or nonstandard language is inappropriate in most writing.

Regional words (sometimes called **provincialisms** or **localisms**) are words whose use is generally restricted to the speech of a particular geographical area. Examples are *tote* for *carry*, *poke* for *bag*, *spider* for *frying pan* or *skillet*. **Nonstandard** words and expressions generally occur only in the language of uneducated speakers. Examples are *ain't, could of, she done,* and double negatives such as *can't never, scarcely none,* and *don't have no*. Dictionaries label such words *nonstandard* or *illiterate*. These have no place in your writing unless you are presenting dialogue or characterizing actual speech that uses such words.

REGIONAL	She *redded up* the house for our *kinfolk*.
GENERAL	She cleaned the house for our relatives.
NONSTANDARD	They *didn't ought to have* spent the money.
STANDARD	They shouldn't have spent the money.
NONSTANDARD	I wish *I'd of drove more careful*.
STANDARD	I wish I had driven more carefully.

37b

appr

EXERCISE 37b

If you are a native of the region in which your college is located, ask a classmate from another region to give you a list of words or expressions that strike him or her as being regionalisms in your own speech. If you come from another area yourself, make up your own list of regionalisms of the college area and compare it with a classmate's.

37c

For a general audience, jargon should be used sparingly.

The term **jargon** has several meanings (see Section **39b**). In a famous essay, "On Jargon," Sir Arthur Quiller-Couch defined the term as vague and "woolly" speech or writing that consists of abstract words, elegant variation, and "circumlocution rather than short straight speech." Linguists often define jargon as hybrid speech or dialect formed by a mixture of languages, for example the English-Chinese jargon known as pidgin English.

To most people, however, jargon is the technical or specialized vocabulary of a particular trade, profession, or field of interest—for example, engineering jargon, computer jargon, or horticultural jargon. Naturally, members of a specialized group use their jargon when communicating with one another. It is their language, so to speak, and its terms are often more precise, more meaningful, and more quickly comprehended than non-jargon expressions would be.

The following example shows how the author of a computer manual carefully defines terms, even though some of his readers may be very familiar with computer jargon. The author knows that the Macintosh computer is relatively new to a significant number of his readers; hence, he is careful to establish meanings for Macintosh jargon.

> The Macintosh makes a useful distinction between *applications* and *documents*, the first being used to create the second. Applications can also be thought of, more generally, as *tools* since the Macintosh manual uses the former term somewhat restrictively. Programs, such as MacWrite and MacPaint, are what are formally referred to as applications. . . . The pointer is a tool, whose use will vary from place to place; the keyboard and mouse are physical tools, as is the video screen on which you see the development of your labors. . . . Documents, on the other hand, are the end result of the process of computing, the reason you bought a computer in the first place.
>
> JOHN M. ALLSWANG, *Macintosh: The Definitive Users Guide*

37c

appr

Technical jargon is inappropriate when you are writing for a general audience unless, of course, the terms have entered everyday language and are widely understood. The mass media have broadened our understanding of many technical terms, especially those relating to newsworthy topics. *Countdown* and *liftoff* from space exploration, *carcinogenic* and *biopsy* from medicine, *printout* and *terminal* from computer technology are but a few of the words that have moved from jargon into fairly general usage. Nevertheless, you should use jargon with care, defining the terms if you think your readers might not know the meanings.

Unfortunately, jargon impresses some people simply because it sounds involved and learned. We are all reluctant to admit that we do not understand what we are reading. What, for example, can you make of the following passage?

THE TURBO-ENCABULATOR IN INDUSTRY

. . . Work has been proceeding in order to bring to perfection the crudely conceived idea of a machine that would not only supply

inverse reactive current for use in unilateral phase detractors, but
would also be capable of automatically synchronizing cardinal grammeters. Such a machine is the Turbo-Encabulator. . . . The original
machine had a base plate of prefabulated amulite surmounted by a
malleable logarithmic casing in such a way that the two spurving
bearings were in a direct line with the pentametric fan. . . . The
main winding was of the normal lotus-o-delta type placed in a pan-
endermic semiboloid slot in the stator, every seventh conductor
being connected by a non-reversible tremie pipe to the differential
girdlespring on the "up" end of the grammeters. . . .

Reprinted by permission of the publishers,
Arthur D. Little, Inc., Cambridge, Mass.

This new mechanical marvel was a joke, the linguistic creation of a
research engineer who was tired of reading jargon. The point is, you
should avoid unnecessary jargon in your writing, words used merely
to impress, words that clutter rather than clarify.

EXERCISE 37c(1)

Make a list of twenty words and/or phrases that constitute jargon in a
field you know. Define these terms in a way that a general reader could
understand. Finally, explain whether you think each term is a justifiable
use of jargon in your field or whether a "plain English" term would work
just as well.

EXERCISE 37c(2)

From an issue of a magazine or newspaper written for a general audience,
list technical or specialized terms that have ceased to be jargon and have
entered the general usage. From what fields did these terms originally
come? How many of them are at least partially defined within the context
of the articles in which they appear?

38

EXACTNESS

Once you have determined the type of language that is appropriate for your subject and audience, you will want to choose from the
available words those that are as precise as possible. That way you
have a much better chance of conveying the exact meaning you intend. To write with precision, you need to know both the denotation
and the connotation of words. **Denotation** is the core of a word's
meaning, sometimes called the "dictionary" or literal meaning: for example, a *tree* is "a woody perennial plant having a single stem or

trunk." **Connotation** refers to the reader's emotional response to a word and to the associations the word carries with it. Thus, *tree* may connote shade or coolness or shelter or stillness or strength.

If you have misunderstood the denotation of a word you are using, you are quite likely to confuse your readers. For example, the student who wrote *In thinking biology would be an easy course, I was thinking wistfully* simply chose the wrong word. She meant *wishfully.* To write *The firefighters who risked their lives to rescue the child were praised for their heroics* will not do. *Heroics* means something quite different from *heroism,* the word the writer surely intended. Worse yet is the case of the following writer who, in seeking to impress his readers with his vocabulary, simply made himself look silly: *The people on this school board are people of their word and are trustworthy. For him to cast* dispersions *on their veracity is just unfair.* The writer should have accused his opponent of casting *aspersions* (slanderous or defamatory remarks). The moral: Be sure you know the meaning before you use the word.

Errors of connotation are more subtle. Connotations cannot be fixed precisely, for individual responses to words differ and meanings can change over time. For example, *gay* commonly means "exuberant," but in recent years its secondary definition, "homosexual," has gained wide usage, no doubt affecting the word's connotative impact. Nonetheless, many words have quite stable connotations. *Home* generally suggests security, a sense of one's own place. Most of us would prefer a *cozy* robe and slippers to *snug* ones.

Make sure, too, that your words fit the association called up by other words in both the individual sentence and the larger context in which they are used. Sentences such as the following go wrong because the words don't fit connotatively:

> *Brandishing* a gun and *angrily demanding* the money, the thief *yelped threateningly* at the frightened teller, "Empty the cash drawer."

The verb *yelped* suggests animal-like anger and abruptness, perfectly appropriate to the situation being described. Yet the connotations seem to conflict with the adverb *threateningly. Yelped* also carries connotations of sharpness caused by alarm and pain. Since the thief appears to have the upper hand in the situation, for most of us *snarled* would suggest connotations more in keeping with the other words in the sentence.

Many words stand for abstractions: *democracy, truth, inadequacy, challenge, beauty.* Because the connotations of such words are both vague and numerous, state specifically what you mean when you use them, or make sure that the context clarifies their meaning (see Section **38f**). Otherwise, readers will misunderstand or, worse, think they understand your terms when they do not.

38

ex

38a

Distinguishing among synonyms increases exactness.

English is rich in **synonyms,** groups of words that have nearly the same meaning: *begin, start, commence; funny, comic, laughable.* But most synonyms differ in connotation. By observing their precise shades of meaning and choosing carefully among them, you can more accurately express your ideas. Occasionally, the difference in meaning between two synonyms is so slight that it makes little difference which you choose: you can *begin a vacation* or *start a vacation*—either will do. But usually the differences will be much greater. To *commence a vacation,* for example, connotes far more formality than ordinarily goes with vacations. And it makes a much more important difference whether you describe a movie as *funny, comic,* or *laughable.*

If you increase the number of synonyms in your vocabulary (see Section **36b**) and distinguish carefully among them when you write, your use of language will be more precise and therefore a greater aid to your readers. Knowing that *fashion* and *vogue* are synonyms for *fad,* or that *renowned* and *notorious* are synonyms for *famous,* gives you the chance to make your writing more exact by selecting the synonym connoting the precise shade of meaning that best expresses your idea. On the other hand, careless use of synonyms not only makes writing inexact, but also often distorts meaning. Notice the importance of connotation in the following sentence:

> Capone was a *renowned* gangster. [*Renowned* has favorable connotations that the writer probably did not intend. *Famous* would do, but it is not very exact. *Notorious,* "known widely and regarded unfavorably," would be exact.]

38a

ex

EXERCISE 38a

Explain the differences in meaning among the italicized words in each of the following groups.

1. a *virtuous,* an *upright,* an *honest,* a *moral* person
2. a *morose,* a *gloomy,* a *sullen,* a *sulky* attitude
3. to *mimic,* to *imitate,* to *mock,* to *ape* someone's actions
4. a *calamity,* a *disaster,* a *misfortune,* a *mishap*
5. an *impressive,* a *stirring,* an *exciting,* an *affecting,* a *moving* sight

For each of the following sentences, choose the italicized synonym that seems to connote the most appropriate and precise shade of meaning for the context.

6. The class didn't understand the equation, so they asked the instructor to *expound, illustrate, explain, interpret, elucidate* her method for solving it.

7. The performer thought that he could *charm, captivate, enchant, enrapture, fascinate* the audience with his wide array of magic tricks.
8. Because the crucial project was already three weeks behind schedule, the supervisor asked the engineers to *accelerate, dispatch, expedite, speed, hasten* their work.
9. The mud pie seemed very plain, so the child who had made it decided to *adorn, embellish, bedeck, beautify* it with her initials, some swirls of grass, and flowers from her parents' garden.
10. The *gleaming, glittering, shining, flashing* jewels in the showcase attracted the attention of the shoppers.

38b

Derogatory references to sex, race, ethnicity, or religion are both inaccurate and offensive.

Language that relies on stereotypes—as do derogatory terms and language with negative connotations referring to women or men or members of racial, ethnic, religious, or other groups—is both inappropriate and inaccurate. Broad-brush stereotypes—for example, that men are insensitive, women prone to hysteria, or Scots tight with their money—will reveal your thinking and your writing to be based on biased, insupportable generalizations. Make sure that the language you choose does not reflect these types of narrow-minded, offensive biases.

The reasons for the nonsexist use of personal pronouns have been discussed elsewhere in this book (see **Section 8c**). But eliminating sexist language from your writing involves more than removing common-gender pronoun references. You need to be sure that you refer to men and women in the same way when the circumstances are similar. For example, two faculty members in the biology department should be referred to as Professor Winston and Professor Levitz, not Professor Winston and Mrs. Levitz. The two poets Richard Wilbur and Sylvia Plath should be referred to as Wilbur and Plath (once their full names have been given), not as Wilbur and Sylvia (or Miss Plath or Mrs. Hughes).

Be aware, also, that professions and occupations once viewed as typically male or typically female now usually employ both sexes. Do not use terms like *nurse* and *doctor* in ways that suggest nurses are always women and doctors always men, for instance. Our language is changing to reflect the awareness that stereotypes are usually inaccurate and frequently discriminatory or demeaning. *Police officer* instead of *policeman, mail carrier* instead of *mailman,* and *flight attendant* instead of *stewardess* are words that have gained widespread use as people come to terms with sexism both as a habit of mind and as a habit of language.

38b

ex

EXERCISE 38b

Put together a list of words that show how standard English is reflecting elimination of sexual stereotyping. Be ready to discuss whether you think the new or preferred term is accurate and/or justified.

38c

Be careful not to confuse words that have similar sound or spelling but different forms or meanings.

Some words are **homonyms;** that is, they have the same pronunciation but different meanings and different spellings *(idol, idle, idyll; aid; aide; aisle, isle).* Other words are sufficiently similar in sound and spelling to be confusing *(marital, martial).* Treat all these words as you would any other unfamiliar term: learn the correct spelling and meaning of each as an individual word.

Many words have two, sometimes three, adjectival forms, each having a distinct meaning: for example, a *changeable* personality, a *changing* personality, a *changed* personality. A roommate whom you *like* is not necessarily a *likeable* roomate, nor is a *matter of agreement* necessarily an *agreeable matter.* Be careful not to substitute one form for the other.

38c

ex

UNACCEPTABLE	The cook served our *favorable* dessert.
ACCEPTABLE	The cook served our *favorite* dessert.
UNACCEPTABLE	He is a good student; he has a *questionable* mind.
ACCEPTABLE	He is a good student; he has a *questioning* mind.

EXERCISE 38c

What are the differences in meaning in each of the following pairs of words?

1. affect, effect
2. ascent, assent
3. capitol, capital
4. compliment, complement
5. compunction, compulsion
6. council, counsel
7. desert, dessert
8. mantel, mantle
9. moral, morale
10. personal, personnel
11. quite, quiet
12. stationary, stationery

13. a *definite* ruling
    a *definitive* ruling
14. a *neglected* child
    a *neglectful* child
15. a *confident* friend
    a *confiding* friend
16. a *sensible* alternative
    a *sensitive* alternative
17. a *judicious* decision
    a *judicial* decision
18. an *economic* plan
    an *economical* plan
19. a *pleased* customer
    a *pleasing* customer
20. a *likely* candidate
    a *likeable* candidate

38d

Invented words tend to confuse meaning.

A **coined word** is a new and outright creation (like *gobbledygook, blurb*). A **neologism** is either a new word or a new use of an old word or words (like travel agents' *package tours* or the traffic department's *gridlock*). A **nonce-word,** literally **once-word,** is a word made up to suit a special situation and generally not used more than once ("My son," he said, "suffers from an acute case of televisionitis"). Though most neologisms and nonce-words are short-lived, they are among the ways by which new words and new functions for old words are constantly working their way into a changing language. *Motel,* for example, an invented word formed from *motor* and *hotel,* is now a permanent fixture in our language.

English is relatively free in shifting words from one part of speech to another. This process, called **functional shift,** is one of the many ways in which our language grows. The noun *iron* is used as an adjective in *iron bar,* and as a verb in *iron the shirts.* The space age has given us *All systems are go,* using the verb *go* as a modifier. *River, paper,* and *tennis* are clearly nouns in form, but we commonly use them as modifiers in *river bank, paper bag,* and *tennis elbow.*

But the fact that such changes are common in English does not mean that there are no constraints on functional shift. In *The jury opinioned that the defendant was guilty, opinion* is used as a verb, a grammatical function to which it is entirely unaccustomed. The meaning may be clear, but the use is not accepted. We *punish* a person. There is perhaps no good reason why we should not speak of *a punish,* but we don't: if we want a noun, we use *punishment.* Advertisers talk about *winterizing* our cars with antifreeze and snow tires, but most of us draw the line at *skiierizing* our automobiles with the addition of a ski rack.

Devote most of your attention to learning and using words whose meanings are already established by usage. Invented words probably confuse readers and obscure meaning more often than they succeed. Still, don't be afraid to try a new coinage if it seems to suit your purpose and audience. Do be careful, however, to avoid unintentional inventions—words that you "invent" because of spelling errors *(disallusion* for *disillusion)* or an inexact knowledge of word forms and functions *(understandment* for *understanding).* If you have any doubt about the accepted grammatical functions of a word, consult your dictionary.

38d

ex

EXERCISE 38d

Correct the italicized words that seem to you needlessly invented. When necessary, check your dictionary to determine whether a particular word is an accepted form as used.

1. The new tax law caused *constornationment* among the workers in the budget department.
2. I ignored their *trivialistic* objections and went on with my proposal for a *fast sell* campaign to clear out old merchandise.
3. The *enthusiastical* response of the audience *prompted* the pianist to perform an encore.
4. After their candidate lost the election, those who had previously supported him tried *to distance* themselves from him.
5. The cab drivers were glad *to garage* their cars for the night, for they had had *unnumerable* troubles with passengers during the long, rainy day.

38e

Follow accepted usage for idioms that include prepositions.

An **idiom** is an expression that does not follow the normal pattern of the language or that has a total meaning not suggested by its separate words: *to catch fire, strike a bargain, ride it out, lose one's head, hold the bag.** Such expressions are a part of the vocabulary of native speakers. In fact, we learn them in the same way we learn new words—by hearing them in the speech around us and by reading them in context. For the most part they give no more, and no less, difficulty than vocabulary itself gives us. Dictionaries usually give the common idiomatic expressions at the end of the definition of a word entry.

For many writers the most troublesome idioms in English are those that require a particular preposition after a given verb or adjective according to the meaning intended. The following list contains a number of such combinations that frequently cause trouble.

ABSOLVED BY, FROM	I was *absolved by* the dean *from* all blame.
ACCEDE TO	He *acceded to* his father's demands.
ACCOMPANY BY, WITH	I was *accompanied by* several advisors.
	The terms were *accompanied with* a plea for immediate peace.
ACQUITTED OF	He was *acquitted of* the crime.
ADAPTED TO, FROM	This machine can be *adapted to* farm work.
	The design was *adapted from* a previous invention.
ADMIT TO, OF	The clerk *admitted to* the error.
	The plan will *admit of* no alternative.
AGREE TO, WITH, IN	They *agreed to* the plan but *disagreed with* us.
	They *agreed* only *in* principle.

*The term *idiom* is also used to mean the characteristic expression or pattern of a dialect or language. In this sense of the word, we can speak of the *idiom* of speakers from South Boston, or we can compare English *idiom* with German or French.

ANGRY WITH, AT	She was *angry with* me and *angry at* the treatment she had received.
CAPABLE OF	This paint is *capable of* withstanding vigorous scrubbing.
CHARGE FOR, WITH	I expected to be *charged for* my purchase, but I didn't expect to be *charged with* stealing something.
COMPARE TO, WITH	He *compared* the roundness of the baseball *to* that of the earth.
	He *compared* the fuel economy of the Ford *with* that of the Plymouth.
CONCUR WITH, IN	We *concur with* you *in* your desire to use the revised edition.
CONFIDE IN, TO	My friend *confided in* me. She *confided to* me that she was interviewing for another job.
CONFORM TO, WITH	The specification *conformed to* (or *with*) the architect's original plans.
CONFORMITY WITH	You must act in *conformity with* our rules.
CONNECT BY, WITH	The rooms are *connected by* a corridor.
	That doctor is officially *connected with* this hospital.
CONTEND FOR, WITH	Because she needed to *contend for* her principles, she found herself *contending with* her parents.
DIFFER ABOUT, FROM, WITH	We *differ about* our tastes in clothes. My clothes *differ from* yours. We *differ with* one another.
DIFFERENT FROM*	Our grading system is *different from* yours.
ENTER INTO, ON, UPON	She *entered into* a new agreement and thereby *entered on* (or *upon*†) a new career.
FREE FROM, OF	The children were *freed from* the classroom and now are *free of* their teachers for the summer.
IDENTICAL WITH	Your reasons are *identical with* ours.
JOIN IN, WITH, TO	He *joined in* the fun *with* the others.
	He *joined* the wire cables *to* each other.
LIVE AT, IN, ON	The Wamplers *live at* 14 Neil Avenue *in* a Dutch colonial house. They *live on* Neil Avenue.
NECESSITY FOR, OF NEED FOR, OF	There was no *necessity (need) for* you to lose your temper. There was no *necessity (need) of* your losing your temper.
OBJECT TO	I *object to* the statement in the third paragraph.

38e

ex

*Different than is colloquially idiomatic when the object of the prepositional phrase is a clause:

FORMAL   This town looks *different from* what I had remembered.

COLLOQUIAL   This town looks *different than* I had remembered it.

†In many phrases, *on* and *upon* are interchangeable: *depend on* or *depend upon; enter on* or *enter upon.*

OBLIVIOUS OF	When he held her hand he was *oblivious of* the passing of time.
OVERCOME BY, WITH	I was *overcome by* the heat. I was *overcome with* grief.
PARALLEL BETWEEN, TO, WITH	There is often a *parallel between* fantasy and reality. This line is *parallel to* (or *with*) that one.
PREFERABLE TO	A leisurely walk is *preferable to* no exercise at all.
REASON WITH, ABOUT	Why not *reason with* them *about* the matter?
REWARD BY, WITH, FOR	They were *rewarded by* their employer *with* a raise *for* their work.
VARIANCE WITH	This conclusion is at *variance with* your facts.
VARY FROM, IN, WITH	The houses *vary from* one another *in* size. People's tastes *vary with* their personalities.
WAIT FOR, ON	They *waited for* someone to *wait on* them.
WORTHY OF	That candidate is *worthy of* our respect.

EXERCISE 38e

Provide the idiomatic prepositions needed in the following sentences.

1. The birdwatchers waited _____ hours and were rewarded _____ a glimpse of the rare woodpecker.
2. The sighting was important because this species of woodpecker was almost identical _____ a more common type.
3. The birdwatchers agreed _____ compare the foliage of the bird they had seen _____ that of the more common woodpecker.
4. Because the bird was so rare, there was the need _____ absolutely positive identification; otherwise, ornithologists would object _____ their findings.
5. When the birdwatchers presented their findings to their group, experts concurred _____ them _____ their findings.
6. Everyone in the birdwatching group joined _____ the congratulations for sighting the rare bird; the two lucky birdwatchers were so happy that they were oblivious _____ the time and stayed until midnight.
7. The next day the two birdwatchers headed back to the forest, accompanied _____ the president of their group.
8. To get there, they had to contend _____ a traffic jam on the freeway and were relieved to be free _____ the traffic when they finally reached the forest road.
9. When they got to the area where they had seen the rare woodpecker, the three birdwatchers were overcome _____ grief to discover that a bulldozer was leveling the trees in preparation for turning the area into a housing development.
10. The birdwatchers couldn't believe that anyone would be capable

38e

ex

_____ destroying the habitat of the rare woodpecker; therefore, they rushed off to the mayor's office to object _____ the destruction.

38f
Concrete and specific words contribute exactness to abstract and general language.

Abstract words name qualities, ideas, concepts: _honesty, virtue, poverty, education, wisdom, love, democracy._ **Concrete words** name things we can see, hear, feel, touch, smell. _Sweetness_ is abstract; _candy, honey, molasses,_ and _sugar_ are concrete. To describe people as _reckless_ is to describe them abstractly; to say _they ran two traffic lights in the center of town and drove eighty-five miles an hour in a restricted zone_ is to pin that recklessness down, to make it concrete.

General words refer to all members of a class or group. **Specific words** refer to the individual members of a class. _Vegetation_ is general; _grass, shrubs, trees, flowers,_ and _weeds_ are specific. _Animal_ is general; _lions, elephants, monkeys, zebras, cats, dogs, mice,_ and _rabbits_ are specific.

The classes abstract and concrete, and general and specific overlap with each other, and both are relative. The verb _communicate_ is both abstract and general. _Speak_ is concrete and specific relative to _communicate,_ but it is general compared to _gasp, murmur, rant, rave, shout,_ and _whisper. Music_ is concrete and specific relative to _sound_ but general compared to _classical music,_ which in turn is general compared to _Beethoven's Fifth Symphony. Dwelling_ is a general word; _apartment, cabin, barracks, house, hut, mansion, shack,_ and _tent_ are specific. But _dwelling_ is more specific than _building,_ which includes not only _dwelling_ but also _church, factory, garage, school,_ and _store._

All effective writing will use both abstract and concrete words, both general and specific. There are no substitutes for such abstractions as _fairness, friendship, love,_ and _loyalty._ But all abstractions need to be pinned down by details, examples, and illustrations. When not so pinned down, they remain vague and always potentially confusing. We can all quickly agree that taxes and justice should be _fair._ But until each of us has narrowed down by detail and example what he or she means by _fairness_ in these matters, we will not understand each other in any useful way.

Similarly, we cannot do without general terms. We would be hard-pressed to define _cat_ if we could not begin by putting cats in the general class _animal._ But as soon as we have done so, we must then name the specific characteristics and qualities that distinguish cats from, say, armadillos or raccoons. To say _Tom enjoys reading_ tells read-

38f

_ex_

ers very little until we know whether the reading consists of *Sports Illustrated, People,* and *Masters of the Universe* or of Dickens and Dostoyevsky.

Effective writing constantly weaves back and forth between abstract and concrete, between general and specific. It is the writer's use of the abstract and general that guides the reader, but it is the concrete and specific that allow the reader to see, feel, understand, and believe. *This lamp supplies insufficient light* informs us; *this fifteen-watt bulb gives no more light than a firefly in a jam jar* makes us understand what the writer means by *insufficient*.

Whenever you use abstract words, give them meaning with concrete details and examples. Whenever use general words, tie them down with specific ones. Try constantly to express yourself and your ideas in concrete terms; search for the most specific words you can find.

GENERAL The flowers were of different colors.

SPECIFIC The chrysanthemums were bronze, gold, and white.

GENERAL The cost of education has increased greatly.

SPECIFIC Tuition at many private universities has increased as much as 1,000 percent in the past three decades.

MORE SPECIFIC Tuition at Boston University was $300 in 1947; in 1982 it was $6,200.

SPECIFIC Mateo was a stocky man, with clear eyes and a deeply tanned face. His skill as a marksman was extraordinary, even in Corsica, where everyone is a good shot. He could kill a ram at one hundred and twenty paces, and his aim was as accurate at night as in the daytime.

MORE SPECIFIC Picture a small, sturdy man, with jet-black, curly hair, a Roman nose, thin lips, large piercing eyes, and a weather-beaten complexion. His skill as a marksman was extraordinary, even in this country, where everyone is a good shot. For instance, Mateo would never fire on a wild ram with small shot, but at a hundred and twenty paces he would bring it down with a bullet in its head or shoulder, just as he fancied. He used his rifle at night as easily as in the daytime, and I was given the following illustration of his skill, which may seem incredible, perhaps, to those who have never travelled in Corsica. He placed a lighted candle behind a piece of transparent paper as big as a plate, and aimed at it from eighty paces away. He extinguished the candle, and a moment later, in utter darkness, fired and pierced the paper three times out of four.

PROSPER MÉRIMÉE, *Mateo Falcone*

EXERCISE 38f

Revise the following paragraph, supporting the generalizations and abstractions with concrete and specific details so that the meaning of the paragraph is clearer and the language more exact. Before you begin to revise, list the abstract or general words you think need sharper focus.

> My sister is confused about where to go to college. She wants to major in science. She did well on the SAT, and she ranks high in her class. Lots of good schools have sent her information, but she doesn't know how to choose one. Because of our financial situation, my parents can't afford to help her very much. As a result, my sister has to find a way to pay for most of her education. Her counselor at school has suggested some ways she could do that. Eventually, I think my sister will decide on a school that's suitable for her, but until then, I guess she's going to be pretty anxious about the whole process.

38g

Apt figurative language can increase exactness.

Like concrete and specific words, figurative language can help readers understand your ideas. The basis of most figurative language lies in the comparison or association of two things essentially different but nonetheless alike in some underlying and surprising way. Inexperienced writers sometimes think figurative language is the monopoly of poets and novelists. In fact, it plays an important part in much prose and is one of the most effective ways of making meaning concrete. Notice how the following passage uses figurative language to illustrate a point about consumer spending:

38g

ex

> Any significant business recovery has to have the consumer's support, because the consumer sector accounts for two-thirds of GNP [Gross National Product]. So far there is no solid support—consumer spending is not advancing. And for good reason: Consumer incomes are growing slowly. . . . So consumers are not exactly dragging their feet. They are dancing as fast as can be expected.
>
> *Business Week*

The two most common figures of speech are simile and metaphor. **Similes** make direct and explicit comparisons, usually introduced by *like, as, as if,* or *as when,* as in *Jess is as changeable as the New England weather.* **Metaphors** imply comparisons, as in *Prisoned in her laboratory, she ignored the world.* The figure of speech used in *Business Week* above is a metaphor that compares consumers to dancers in step with the slow growth in personal income.

Both simile and metaphor require that the two things compared be from different classes so that their likeness, when pointed out, will be fresh and surprising. The consumer–dancer metaphor accomplishes this goal because we do not usually think of consumers as dancers stepping to the tune of the economy. The image adds liveliness to the economic discussion and helps personify the generalization *consumers*, increasing our understanding of the relationship between spending and income. If similes and metaphors are extended they must also be consistent.

> Up scrambles the car, on all its four legs, like a black beetle straddling past the schoolhouse and the store down below, up the bare rock and over the changeless boulders, with a surge and a sickening lurch to the skybrim, where stands the foolish church.
>
> D. H. LAWRENCE, Mornings in Mexico

> Writing a story or a novel is one way of discovering *sequence* in experience. . . . Connections slowly emerge. Like distant landmarks you are approaching, cause and effect begin to align themselves, draw closer together. Experiences too indefinite of outline in themselves to be recognized for themselves connect and are identified as a larger shape. And suddenly a light is thrown back, as when your train makes a curve, showing that there has been a mountain of meaning rising behind you on the way you've come, is rising there still, proven now through retrospect.
>
> EUDORA WELTY, One Writer's Beginnings

38g

ex

In the foregoing passage, Eudora Welty compares meaning to a mountain and writing to a journey—specifically, a train trip—a simile she uses frequently in *One Writer's Beginnings*. Extended throughout the book is the metaphor of memory, and life itself, as a journey: *"The memory is a living thing—it too is in transit."*

Apt figures of speech can do much to make writing concrete and vivid, and, by making one experience understandable in terms of another, they can often help clarify abstractions. But be careful when creating figures of speech; if they strain too hard, as in the first example below, they will miss their mark, falling flat or seeming too contrived. When two figures are *mixed* so that they create clashing images, as in the final three examples, readers will not only miss your point, they will find your writing ludicrous.

> Her smile was as warm as an electric blanket.
>
> Does your life have to be on the rocks before you will turn over a new leaf?
>
> She made her reputation as a big star early in her career, but she has been coasting on her laurels for the past ten years.

Grandmother's tiny fingers appeared to stitch the fabric with the speed of a pneumatic drill.

He held the false belief that in a capitalist democracy we can peer deep into the veil of the future and chain the ship of state to an exacting blueprint.

EXERCISE 38g(1)

Collect several examples of figurative language from newspapers and magazines. Look for some that are effective and some that are "mixed metaphors." Identify what is being compared, what image is being created. Then analyze why the effective ones work and why the ridiculous ones do not. You can begin by practicing on the following paragraph from the sports pages of a newspaper.

UCLA, given up for dead early in the season, and Illinois, which has rumbled to life after nearly two decades of forgettable football, collide Monday in the 70th Rose Bowl.

EXERCISE 38g(2)

Replace the mixed or incongruous figures of speech in the following sentences with more appropriate comparisons. Be prepared to explain why the original similes or metaphors are inappropriate.

1. After the scandal, the politician decided to dig in her heels and ride out the storm of criticism aimed at her.
2. I thought that skiing down the advanced slope would be a piece of cake, but halfway down I lost control and bit the dust in a huge drift of snow.
3. Learning that I'd have to move the five-hundred-pound refrigerator was the straw that broke the camel's back, so I called a professional moving company.
4. Just when we thought the game was going to be a runaway win, our opponents rolled out the big guns and knocked our socks off.
5. The failing student just could not seem to hammer home his point when he wrote an essay, so he threw in the towel and said he was finished with freshman English.
6. The new supervisor gained a foothold in the eyes of the workers when she stood up to the department manager.
7. I hit the ceiling when I fell down and broke my new watch.
8. Pointing out the importance of the safety rules they had learned, the SCUBA instructor warned the diving class that they'd have to toe the line when they took their first dive; otherwise, the instructor warned, somebody might crash in flames while underwater.
9. The receiver hit the nail on the head when he caught the fifty-yard bomb thrown by the rookie quarterback.
10. The witness felt like a tightrope walker as the prosecutor's questions entangled her in a web of deceit.

38g

ex

38h
Trite expressions obscure meaning.

A trite expression, sometimes called a **cliché,** or a **stereotyped** or **hackneyed phrase,** is an expression that has been worn out by constant use, as *burning the midnight oil, Father Time, raving beauties, man about town.* Many trite expressions are examples of figurative language that once was fresh but has lost its power because we have heard it too often. Several of the metaphors and similes in Exercise 38g(2) are trite expressions: *the straw that broke the camel's back* and *threw in the towel,* for example.

Words in themselves are never trite—they are only used tritely. We cannot avoid trite expressions entirely, for they sometimes describe a situation accurately, capturing a writer's or speaker's intended meaning precisely. But such expressions can also be the crutch of a lazy thinker who chooses the worn cliché rather than searching for the exact words that will best express an idea.

> But when inflation came down last year and the lingering recession and a strong dollar forced even the wealthiest business executives and foreign travelers to pinch pennies, the financial feasibility of scores of new hotel projects went down the tubes.
>
> *Business Week*

The writer of the above example has chosen expressions that accurately capture the meaning. But the *pinch pennies* metaphor and the slang phrase *down the tubes* have been so overworked that they cease to be effective. Together these expressions create a mixed image (pennies down the tubes) that is likely to strike many readers as funny—probably not the effect the writer intended.

What is your estimate of the person who wrote this?

> A college education develops a *well-rounded personality* and gives the student an appreciation for *the finer things of life.* When he or she finally graduates and leaves *the ivory tower* to *play in the game of life,* the student will also have the necessary *tools of the trade.*

This writer's language suggests that her thinking is not only trite but imprecise as well. The expressions *well-rounded personality* and *finer things of life,* for example, are so abstract and vague that readers will surely wonder just what, exactly, the writer means.

Effectively used, triteness can be consciously humorous. The string of trite expressions in the example below explodes into absurdity when the writer deliberately transposes the words in the two clichés in the last clause.

A pair of pigeons were cooing gently directly beneath my window; two squirrels plighted their troth in a branch overhead; at the corner a handsome member of New York's finest twirled his night stick and cast rougish glances at the saucy-eyed flower vendor. The scene could have been staged only by a Lubitsch; in fact Lubitsch himself was seated on a bench across the street, smoking a cucumber and looking as cool as a cigar.

S. J. PERELMAN, *Keep It Crisp*

Although trite expressions can be apt when they do capture meaning exactly, most of them, because they are so familiar, have lost their vigor and will lessen the effectiveness of what you have to say. Look instead for fresher, more original ways of expressing yourself, words that will enhance the meaning of your sentences rather than deaden it.

EXERCISE 38h

Identify all the clichés in the following passage. Then revise the passage, eliminating those expressions you think are too hackneyed to be effective and substituting fresher, more meaningful language.

Most students are ready to leave the college scene after four years of burning the midnight oil to make the grade. When they graduate at long last, many students want to enter the business world and get on the fast track. Many of these brand new graduates believe that the bottom line is making money. Therefore, they beat the bushes looking for the perfect job, a job where they can earn big bucks. Unfortunately, some of these people have to learn the hard way that reaching the top is tougher than they thought it would be. These new employees soon discover that the business world can be a real jungle: it's a dog-eat-dog situation in which each individual has to look out for number one. Climbing the ladder of success can be a risky business. For instance, one wrong move, and these up-and-coming employees may find themselves out on the street looking for another job. In the long run, it's probably a wise move for new graduates to plan their career moves carefully. With careful planning, a graduate doesn't have to learn the hard way that surviving in the business world isn't as easy as it looks.

39

dir

39

DIRECTNESS

The challenge to directness comes from two fronts—wordiness and vagueness. A wordy writer uses more words than are necessary to convey meaning; a vague writer fails to convey meaning sharply and clearly. Wordiness and vagueness are found together so often as to be nearly indistinguishable, as the following example shows:

WORDY AND VAGUE	He attacks the practice of making a profitable business out of college athletics from the standpoint that it has a detrimental and harmful influence on the college student and, to a certain degree and extent, on the colleges and universities themselves.
IMPROVED	He attacks commercialization of college athletics as harmful to the students and even to the universities themselves.

Sometimes wordiness is just awkwardness; the meaning is clear, but the expression is clumsy.

AWKWARD	The notion that present-day Quakers wear flat-brimmed dark hats or black bonnets and long dresses is a very common notion.
IMPROVED	Many people think that present-day Quakers wear flat-brimmed dark hats or black bonnets and long dresses.

Wordiness and vagueness obscure meaning. Your goal as a writer should be to say things as directly and economically as possible without sacrificing clarity and completeness. Readers are always grateful for writing that is concise, that makes every word count. The following sections discuss ways to spot and eliminate wordiness and vagueness in your writing.

39a

dir

39a
Wordy writing wastes readers' time and contributes nothing to meaning.

Constructions that contribute to wordiness often appear in clusters. Where you find one sort, you are likely to find another. Two that frequently appear as a pair are **nominals** and **weak verbs.** Other contributors to wordiness are roundabout constructions, unnecessary phrases and clauses, redundancy, and awkward repetition.

1. Nominals. Nominals are nouns created by adding suffixes to verbs: *establishment, completion, deliverance.* While there is certainly nothing wrong with these words, using unnecessary nominals in your writing tends to make it ponderous and slow-moving. The reason is that the verb, the word that conveys action in the sentence, has been transformed into a noun, an object. Learn to spot nominal suffixes such as *-ment, -tion, -ance* (also sometimes *-ity, -ize, -ness*) in your writing and to change unnecessary nominals back into verbs. Your sentences will be shorter and more vigorous.

WORDY NOMINALS	Strict *enforcement* of the speed limit by the police will cause a *reduction* in traffic fatalities.
REVISED	If the police strictly enforce the speed limit, traffic fatalities will be reduced.

2. Weak verbs. Vague, weak verbs such as *make, give,* and *take* often occur in combination with nominals as replacements for the stronger, more energetic verbs that have been changed into nouns. Another weak verb form, the passive-voice verb, also lengthens sentences and reduces vigor because it involves things being *done to* rather than things *doing.* Consequently, a sentence using a passive-voice verb requires a prepositional phrase to identify the agent, or *doer* of the action. Your writing will be less wordy if you choose specific, concrete, active-voice verbs.

WEAK VERB	At the next meeting, the city council *will take* the firefighters' request for a raise under consideration.
REVISED	At the next meeting, the city council will consider the firefighters' request for a raise.
PASSIVE VOICE	A decision *was reached* by the council members to amend the zoning laws.
REVISED	The council members reached a decision to amend the zoning laws.
	The council members decided to amend the zoning laws.

39a

dir

3. Roundabout constructions. Indirect and circuitous wording annoys readers and wastes their time because it detracts from quick, clear understanding of your meaning. As you revise your writing, you will often be able to strike out obviously unnecessary words or gain directness with slight changes. Words such as *angle, aspect, factor,* and *situation,* and phrases such as *in the case of, in the line of, in the field of* are almost never necessary and are common obstacles to directness.

WORDY	I am majoring in the field of biology.
REVISED	I am majoring in biology.
WORDY	Another aspect of the situation that needs to be examined is the matter of advertising.
REVISED	We should also examine advertising.

Expletives *(there is, there are, it is, it was)* frequently add unnecessary words and weaken the emphasis on a sentence's true subject. Your sentence may be more effective if you simply begin with the true subject. In other instances, a one-word modifier may convey meaning more economically.

WORDY	There were fourteen people in attendance at the meeting.
REVISED	Fourteen people attended the meeting.

WORDY	It is apparent that we can't agree.
REVISED	Apparently, we can't agree.

Weak and wordy constructions such as *because of the fact that, it was shown that,* and *with regard to* can often be reduced to a single word or eliminated.

WORDY	Due to the fact that the plane was late, I missed my connecting flight to San Antonio.
REVISED	Because the plane was late, I missed my connecting flight to San Antonio.

WORDY	With regard to the luggage, the airline will deliver it to our hotel this afternoon.
REVISED	The airline will deliver the luggage to our hotel this afternoon.

4. Unnecessary phrases and clauses. Wordiness often results from using a clause when a phrase will do, or a phrase when a single word will do. Needless constructions waste readers' time and lengthen sentences without adding meaning. Learn to spot such constructions, especially several piled together. Where appropriate, try reducing clauses to participial or appositive phrases or to single-word or compound modifiers. Try reducing phrases to single-word or compound modifiers, verbals (verb root plus *-ing*), or possessives with *-'s;* or leave them out if they don't contribute to meaning.

WORDY	This shirt, *which is made of wool,* has worn well for eight years.
REVISED	This *woolen* shirt has worn well for eight years. [The meaning of the wordy clause *which is made of wool* is conveyed as accurately, and more economically, by *woolen,* a single-word modifier.]

WORDY	The football captain, *who is an All-American player,* played his last game today.
REVISED	The football captain, *an All-American,* played his last game today. [The meaning of the clause modifying *captain* is more economically expressed as an appositive phrase.]

WORDY	The conclusions *that the committee of students* reached are summarized in the newspaper *of the college that was published today.*
REVISED	The conclusions *reached by the student committee* are sum-

marized in *today's college newspaper.* [One-word modifiers *(student, college)*, a possessive *(today's)*, and a participle *(reached)* have replaced wordy clauses and phrases.]

5. Redundancy. Expressions such as *I saw it with my own eyes* and *audible to our ears* are **redundant;** they say the same thing twice. Redundancies don't clarify or emphasize; they just sound stupid—especially ones with words that are already absolute and cannot logically be further qualified *(unique, perfect, dead,* for example). Typical examples include the following:

Redundant	*Direct*
advance forward	advance
continue on	continue
completely eliminate	eliminate
refer back	refer
repeat again	repeat
combine together	combine
circle around	circle
close proximity	close
few in number	few
cheaper in cost	cheaper, less costly
disappear from view	disappear
past history	history, the past
important essentials	essentials

Sometimes sentences become wordy through a writer's careless repetition of the same meaning in slightly different words.

39a

dir

WORDY	As a rule, I usually wake up early.
REVISED	I usually wake up early.
WORDY	In their opinion, they think they are right.
REVISED	They think they are right.
WORDY	After the close of the office at 5 P.M. this afternoon, Jones's farewell party will begin.
REVISED	After the office closes at 5 P.M., Jones's farewell party will begin.
WORDY	She is attractive in appearance, but she is a rather selfish person.
REVISED	She is attractive but rather selfish.

Similarly, some expressions are simply redundant or roundabout ways of saying things that could be stated in a single, precise word.

Wordy	*Direct*
call up on the telephone	telephone
this day and age	today
of an indefinite nature	indefinite

Wordy	Direct
at this point in time	now, today
by means of	by
destroy by fire	burn
at all times	always
in the near future	soon

6. Awkward repetition. Repetition of important words can be a useful way of gaining emphasis and coherence in your writing (see Section **42d**), but careless repetition is awkward and wordy.

AWKWARD   The investigation revealed that the *average teachers teaching* industrial arts in California have an *average* working and *teaching* experience of five years.

REVISED   The investigation revealed that industrial arts teachers in California have an average of five years' experience.

AWKWARD   Gas mileage of American cars is being *improved* constantly in order to *improve* efficiency.

REVISED   Gas mileage of American cars is being improved constantly to increase efficiency.

EXERCISE 39a(1)

Revise the following sentences to reduce wordiness.

39a

dir

1. Due to the fact that the writer was working on the autobiography of his life, he didn't have time to attend the conference.
2. A substitute speaker has been found by the members of the committee.
3. When I heard that I had won the contest, I screamed out loud.
4. My personal opinion was that the strengthening of the regulations had strengthened the department.
5. At this point in time, all the members of the committee have voted unanimously to accept the proposal about which we have been speaking.
6. The smaller car that my neighbor recently bought has saved her a lot of money lately.
7. The establishment of a branch campus in the nearby city is the future goal of the university.
8. The group which gathered to hear the speech was large in number.
9. The utilization of a more effective method of screening applicants will ensure that the best applicants are chosen for the job.
10. One of my goals in life is to get a better job by means of going to graduate school.

EXERCISE 39a(2)

Revise the following paragraph to eliminate wordiness and awkwardness.

It was one of the all-time worst experiences of my entire life. Due to the fact that this event occurred, I have vowed to myself never again to be involved in the delay associated with waiting for an airline flight which has been delayed or cancelled. In this particular instance, transportation from New York to San Francisco was my personal goal when I purchased my airline ticket for the flight. Little did I know then that I was purchasing a ticket that would also force me against my wishes to spend two nights waiting in an airline terminal in New York. First, my flight was initially delayed until a later time because of a snowstorm which had piled up ten inches of snow on the city. Because of the fact of my past experiences with delayed flights, I resigned myself to a delay, although I hoped that it would be of short duration. However, this particular delay turned out to be for a forty-eight-hour period as a result of my first and original flight being eventually cancelled after ten hours. I spent those hours situated on the floor of the terminal where I spent sleepless hours awake and staring at the clock as the minutes crept slowly by. At last my new flight was announced after I had waited forty-eight hours. When the agent at the ticket counter announced the new flight, I jumped quickly to my feet and ran hurriedly up the ramp to the plane, for I wanted to escape from the former scene of my misery as fast as I possibly could get away.

39b
Vague, pretentious, artificial diction obscures meaning.

Never be ashamed to express an idea in simple, direct language. Complicated, pretentious, artificial language is not a sign of superior intelligence or writing skill. If alternative forms of the same word exist, use the shorter. Choose *truth* and *virtue* over *truthfulness* and *virtuousness*. Choose *preventive* rather than *preventative*.

As many of the examples in Section 39a illustrated, wordy language is frequently also pretentious language; diction becomes more elaborate, showy, and self-conscious than the subject requires. Vague, abstract terms and euphemisms are other characteristics of pretentious language. Instead of *we decided against it,* someone writes *we have assumed a negative posture on the matter*—as if these words were better than simply saying no.

We all are familiar with this kind of diction—the pompous language of many government documents, military reports, scholarly articles, and business executives' defenses of a poor product or unprofitable year. Pretentious diction is all too frequently a means of disguising the truth rather than revealing it. Instead of admitting he wants to raise taxes, the President talks about "revenue enhancement." Rather than a press office, the Environmental Protection Agency has an "Office of Public Awareness." The military refers to a bombing raid as a "protective reaction strike," and the MX missile is named "the Peacekeeper." Instead of saying "You're fired," the boss explains that an employee is "the next candidate for staff reduction." Even when such language is meant to convey information honestly, we react negatively because we are used to associating it with bureaucratic smoke-screens. It's no wonder artificial diction of this type has come to be called *businessese, bureaucratese, gobbledygook,* and *bafflegab.* In his novel *1984,* George Orwell termed such doubletalk "Newspeak"—a language designed to supplant truth with vagueness.

Preferring simplicity does not mean you must make *all* writing simple. Naturally, highly complex or technical subjects call at times for complex and technical language—the jargon and style appropriate to the subject and audience (see Section **37c**)—as the following passage illustrates.

> One of the simplest ways of evolving a favorable environment concurrently with the development of the individual organism, is that the influence of each organism on the environment should be favorable to the *endurance* of other organisms of the same type. Further, if the organism also favors *development* of other organisms of the same type, you have then obtained a mechanism of evolution adapted to produce the observed state of large multitudes of analogous entities, with high powers of endurance. For the environment automatically develops with the species, and the species with the environment.
>
> A. N. WHITEHEAD, *Science and the Modern World* [his italics]

Within the context of its subject, purpose, and audience, this passage is neither vague, pretentious, nor artificial. It conveys its meaning directly. On the other hand, the following examples are wordy and vague.

39b

dir

ARTIFICIAL	Due to the fact that the outlet mechanism for the solid fuel appliance was obstructed by carbon, the edifice was consumed by fire.
DIRECT	Because the flue for the wood-burning stove was clogged with soot, the house burned down.
ARTIFICIAL	The athletic contest commenced at the stipulated time.
DIRECT	The game began on time.
ARTIFICIAL	It still looks favorable for beneficial crop moisture in central Indiana.
DIRECT	Chances for rain in central Indiana still look good. The soybeans could use a soaking.

Euphemisms, words or phrases substituted for those that are, for some reason, objectionable, have their place in effective writing. They express unpleasant things in less harsh, less direct ways: *perspire* for *sweat, elderly* for *old, intoxicated* for *drunk.* Most common euphemisms are associated with the basic facts of existence—birth, age, death, sex, body functions—and often seem necessary for politeness or tact. We may be more comfortable describing a good friend as one who is *stout* and *likes to drink* rather than as a *fat drunk*. In such contexts these terms are harmless.

But using euphemisms to distract readers needlessly from the realities of work, unemployment, poverty, or war is at best misleading and at worst dishonest and dangerous. Today we take for granted terms such as "sanitation engineer" (garbage collector), "funeral director" (undertaker), and "maintenance staff" (janitors). Such terms perhaps help protect the feelings of individuals and give them status; but the individuals themselves still have to pick up garbage, prepare bodies for burial, and sweep floors—in short, do work that is hard or unpleasant. And if the terms make us forget that reality, they are misleading. It is but a short step to language consciously intended to deceive. Such language gives us "peace-keeping force" (military troops), "strategic redeployment" (retreat), "visual surveillance" (spying), and "inoperative statements" (lies). Such phrases are downright dishonest, created for the sole purpose of distracting us from realities we need to know about. Slums and ghettos are no less slums and ghettos because a writer calls them the "inner city." And if you're fired, you're out of a job even if you've been "terminated" or "de-selected."

Keep your own writing honest and direct. Be alert to dishonesty and pretentiousness in the writing of others. Use emphemism if tact and genuine respect for the feelings of your audience warrant it, but resist temptations to slide into artificial diction that veils, rather than conveys, meaning.

39b

dir

EXERCISE 39b(1)
Supply more direct phrases for the following euphemisms.

1. preowned automobile
2. motion discomfort
3. resale shop
4. passed away
5. termination of employment
6. burial park
7. correctional facility
8. economically disadvantaged
9. hairpiece
10. men's room
11. substance abuse
12. inebriated

EXERCISE 39b(2)
Find several examples of "gobbledygook" or pretentious, artificial diction in newspapers and magazines. Translate these into direct, natural language.

EXERCISE 39b(3)
Revise the following passage, substituting more direct, natural language for the wordy, artificial diction and unnecessary euphemisms.

The city council determined that their priority for the next year should be to effect maximum utilization of available resources. As a result, the council decided to prioritize their taskings for the upcoming year. First they determined that the budget for the year precluded having to terminate any employees. Also, they reached a consensus action in which the expeditious use of tax money to erect a new waste disposal site was approved. Finally, they finalized plans for authorizing removal of inoperative vehicles from the streets by the city's law enforcement officers. At the conclusion of the meeting, the new council members commended themselves on the efficient enactment of the agenda for the evening.

40

SPELLING

Language existed first as speech, and the alphabet is basically a device to represent speech on paper. When letters of the alphabet have definite values and are used consistently, as in Polish or Spanish, the spelling of a word is an accurate index to its pronunciation, and vice versa. Not so with English. The alphabet does not represent English sounds consistently. The letter *a* may stand for the sound of the vowel in *may, can, care,* or *car; c* for the initial consonant of *carry* or *city; th* for the diphthong in *both* or in *bother.* Different combinations of letters are often sounded alike, as in *rec(ei)ve, l(ea)ve,* or *p(ee)ve.* In many words, moreover, some letters appear to perform no function at all, as in *i(s)land, de(b)t, of(t)en, recei(p)t.* Finally, the relationship between the spelling and the pronunciation of some words seems downright capricious, as in *through, enough, colonel, right.*

Much of the inconsistency of English spelling may be explained historically. English spelling has been a poor index to pronunciation ever since the Norman conquest, when French scribes gave written English a French spelling. Subsequent tampering with English spelling has made it even more complex. Early classical scholars with a flair for etymology added the unvoiced *b* to early English *det* and *dout* because they mistakenly traced these words directly from the Latin *debitum* and *dubitum* when actually both the English and the Latin had derived independently from a common Indo-European origin. Dutch printers working in England were responsible for changing English *gost* to *ghost.* More complications arose when the pronunciation of many words changed more rapidly than their spelling. The *gh* in *right* and *through,* and in similar words, was once pronounced much like the German *ch* in *nicht. Colonel* was once pronounced *col-o-nel.* The final *e* in words like *wife* and *time* was long ago dropped from actual speech, but it still remains as a proper spelling form.

The complex history of the English language may help to explain why our spelling is illogical, but it does not justify misspelling. Society tends to equate bad spelling with incompetent writing. In fact, only the misspellings tend to be noticed, not the quality of the writing, and correct spellings sometimes render faulty constructions invisible.

40a

Use preferred spellings.

Many words have a secondary spelling, generally British. Though the secondary spelling is not incorrect, you should use the spelling more widely accepted in our society, the American spelling. Here is a brief list of preferred and secondary spelling forms; consult a good dictionary for others.

*1. American **e***	*British **ae, oe***
anemia	anaemia
anesthetic	anaesthetic
encyclopedia	encyclopaedia
fetus	foetus
*2. American **im-, in-***	*British **em-, en-***
impanel	empanel
incase	encase
inquiry	enquiry
*3. American **-ize***	*British **-ise***
apologize	apologise
civilization	civilisation
*4. American **-or***	*British **-our***
armor	armour
clamor	clamour
color	colour
flavor	flavour
labor	labour
odor	odour
vigor	vigour
*5. American **-er***	*British **-re***
center	centre
fiber	fibre
somber	sombre
theater	theatre
*6. American **o***	*British **ou***
mold	mould
plow	plough
smolder	smoulder
*7. American **-ction***	*British **-xion***
connection	connexion
inflection	inflexion
*8. American **l***	*British **ll***
leveled	levelled
quarreled	quarrelled
traveled	travelled
*9. American **e** omitted*	*British **e***
acknowledgment	acknowledgement
judgment	judgement

40a

sp

40b
**Proofreading your manuscripts carefully helps
eliminate misspelling.**

In writing a first draft, you form words into sentences faster
than you can write them down. You concentrate not on the words you
are writing, but on the words to come. A few mistakes in spelling may
easily creep into a first draft. Always take five or ten minutes to proofread your final draft for spelling errors.

Lack of proofreading accounts for the fact that the words most
often misspelled are not, for example, *baccalaureate* and *connoisseur*,
but *too, its, lose, receive, accommodate,* and *occurred*. Most of us think
we can spell a familiar word. Either we never bother to check the
spelling in a dictionary, or we assume that a word pictured correctly
in our mind must automatically spell itself correctly on the paper in
front of us. This thinking accounts for such errors as omitting the
final *o* in *too*, confusing the possessive *its* with the contraction *it's*, and
spelling *loose* when *lose* is meant. You will never forget how to spell
receive, accommodate, occurred if you will devote just a few moments to
memorizing their correct spellings.

40c
Careful pronunciation aids correct spelling.

Many words are commonly misspelled because they are mispronounced. The following list of frequently mispronounced words
will help you overcome this source of spelling error.

accident*a*lly		note the *al*
accu*r*ate		note the *u*
bus*i*ness		note the *i*
can*d*idate		note the first *d*
envir*o*nment		note the *on*
Feb*r*uary		note the *r*
gover*n*ment		note the *n*
incident*a*lly		note the *al*
lib*r*ary		note the *r*
math*e*matics		note the *e*
prob*ab*ly		note the *ab*
quan*t*ity		note the first *t*
represen*ta*tive		note the *ta*
soph*o*more		note the second *o*
su*r*prise		note the first *r*
ath*l*etics	**NOT**	ath*e*letics
disas*t*rous	**NOT**	disast*er*ous
heigh*t*	**NOT**	height*h*
grie-vous	**NOT**	gre-*vi*-ous
ir-*rel*-e-*v*ant	**NOT**	ir-*rev*-e-*l*ant
mis-ch*ie*-vous	**NOT**	mis-che-*vi*-ous

However, pronunciation is not an infallible guide to correct spelling. Although, for example, the last syllables of *adviser, beggar,* and *doctor* are all pronounced as the same unstressed *ur,* they are spelled differently. Proceed cautiously when using pronunciation as a spelling aid, and check your dictionary whenever you doubt either your pronunciation or your spelling.

40d

Distinguish among the spellings of words that are similar in sound.

English abounds in **homonyms,** words whose sound is similar to that of other words but whose spelling is different: for example, *rain, rein, reign.* Some of the most troublesome homonyms are listed below.

all ready: everyone is ready
already: by this time

all together: as a group
altogether: entirely, completely

altar: a structure used in worship
alter: to change

ascent: climbing, a way sloping up
assent: agreement; to agree

breath: air taken into the lungs
breathe: to exhale and inhale

capital: chief; leading or governing city; wealth, resources
capitol: a building that houses the state or national lawmakers

cite: to use as an example, to quote
site: location

clothes: wearing apparel
cloths: two or more pieces of cloth

complement: that which completes; to supply a lack
compliment: praise, flattering remark; to praise

corps: a military group or unit
corpse: a dead body

council: an assembly of lawmakers
counsel: advice; one who advises; to give advice

dairy: a factory or farm engaged in milk production
diary: a daily record of experiences or observations

descent: a way sloping down
dissent: disagreement; to disagree

40d

sp

dining: eating
dinning: making a continuing noise

dying: ceasing to live
dyeing: process of coloring fabrics

foreword: a preface or introductory note
forward: at, near, or belonging to the front

forth: forward in place or space, onward in time
fourth: the ordinal equivalent of the number 4

loose: free from bonds
lose: to suffer a loss

personal: pertaining to a particular person; individual
personnel: body of persons employed in same work or service

principal: chief, most important; a school official; a capital sum (as
    distinguished from interest or profit)
principle: a belief, rule of conduct, or thought

respectfully: with respect
respectively: in order, in turn

stationery: writing paper
stationary: not moving

their: possessive form of *they*
they're: contraction of *they are*
there: adverb of place

whose: possessive form of *who*
who's: contraction of *who is*

your: possessive form of *you*
you're: contraction of *you are*

40e
Knowing spelling rules aids correct spelling.

1. Distinguish between *ie* and *ei*. Remember this jingle:

Write *i* before *e*
Except after *c*
Or when sounded like *a*
As in *eighty* and *sleigh.*

i before *e*	*ei* after *c*	*ei* when sounded like *a*
thief	receive	weigh
believe	deceive	freight
wield	ceiling	vein

EXCEPTIONS:

N*ei*ther sover*ei*gns nor financ*ie*rs forf*ei*t the h*ei*ght of th*ei*r surf*ei*t l*ei*sure to s*ei*ze the w*ei*rd counterf*ei*ts of f*ei*sty for*ei*gners.

CHRISTOPHER W. BLACKWELL

2. Drop the final e before a suffix beginning with a vowel but not before a suffix beginning with a consonant.

a. Suffix beginning with a vowel, final e dropped:

please + ure = *pleasure*
ride + ing   = *riding*
locate + ion = *location*
guide + ance = *guidance*

EXCEPTIONS:

In some words the final *e* is retained to prevent confusion with other words.

dyeing (to distinguish it from *dying*)

Final *e* is retained to keep *c* or *g* soft before *a* or *o*.

	notice + able	= *noticeable*
	change + able	= *changeable*
BUT	practice + able	= *practicable (c* has sound of *k)*

b. Suffix beginning with a consonant, final e retained:

sure + ly   = *surely*
arrange + ment = *arrangement*
like + ness   = *likeness*
entire + ly   = *entirely*
entire + ty   = *entirety*
hate + ful   = *hateful*

EXCEPTIONS:

Some words taking the suffix *-ful* or *-ly* drop final *e:*

awe + ful = *awful*
due + ly = *duly*
true + ly = *truly*

Some words taking the suffix *-ment* drop final *e:*

judge + ment   = *judgment*
acknowledge + ment = *acknowledgment*

40e

sp

The ordinal numbers of *five, nine,* and *twelve,* formed with *-th,* drop the final *e. Five* and *twelve* change *v* to *f.*

> fifth   ninth   twelfth

3. Final *y* is usually changed to *i* before a suffix, unless the suffix begins with *i.*

$$
\begin{array}{ll}
\text{defy} + \text{ance} & = \textit{defiance} \\
\text{forty} + \text{eth} & = \textit{fortieth} \\
\text{ninety} + \text{eth} & = \textit{ninetieth} \\
\text{rectify} + \text{er} & = \textit{rectifier} \\
\text{BUT} \quad \text{cry} + \text{ing} & = \textit{crying} \text{ (suffix begins with } i\text{)}
\end{array}
$$

4. A final single consonant is doubled before a suffix beginning with a vowel when (a) a single vowel precedes the consonant, and (b) the consonant ends an accented syllable or a one-syllable word. Unless both these conditions exist, the final consonant is not doubled.

stop + ing   = *stopping* (*o* is a single vowel before consonant *p* which ends word of one syllable.)

admit + ed   = *admitted* (*i* is single vowel before consonant *t* which ends an accented syllable.)

stoop + ing   = *stooping* (*p* ends a word of one syllable but is preceded by double vowel *oo*.)

benefit + ed = *benefited* (*t* is preceded by a single vowel *i* but does not end the accented syllable.)

40e

sp

EXERCISE 40e(1)

Spell each of the following words correctly and explain what spelling rule applies. Note any exceptions to the rules.

1. argue + ment	= ?		9. operate + ion	= ?
2. begin + er	= ?		10. perceive + able	= ?
3. cook + ing	= ?		11. pity + ed	= ?
4. dispense + able	= ?		12. prefer + ed	= ?
5. drive + ing	= ?		13. seventy + eth	= ?
6. lonely + ness	= ?		14. star + ing	= ?
7. negate + ion	= ?		15. true + ly	= ?
8. notice + able	= ?		16. urge + ing	= ?

---

5. Nouns ending in a sound that can be smoothly united with *-s* usually form their plurals by adding *-s*. Verbs ending in a sound that can be smoothly united with *-s* form their third person singular by adding *-s*.

Singular	Plural	Some Exceptions		Verbs	
picture	pictures	buffalo	buffaloes	blacken	blackens
radio	radios	tomato	tomatoes	criticize	criticizes
flower	flowers	zero	zeroes	radiate	radiates
chair	chairs				
ache	aches				
fan	fans				

6. **Nouns ending in a sound that cannot be smoothly united with -s form their plurals by adding es. Verbs ending in a sound that cannot be smoothly united with -s form their third person singular by adding -es.**

Singular	Plural	Verbs	
porch	porches	pass	passes
bush	bushes	tax	taxes

7. **Nouns ending in y preceded by a consonant form their plurals by changing y to i and adding -es. Verbs ending in y preceded by a consonant form their third person singular in the same way.**

Singular	Plural	Verbs	
nursery	nurseries	pity	pities
mercy	mercies	carry	carries
body	bodies	hurry	hurries
beauty	beauties	worry	worries

EXCEPTIONS:

The plural of proper nouns ending in *y* is formed by adding *-s* (*There are three Marys in my history class*).

8. **Nouns ending in y preceded by a, e, o, or u form their plurals by adding -s only. Verbs ending in y preceded by a, e, o, or u form their third person singular in the same way.**

Singular	Plural	Verbs	
day	days	buy	buys
key	keys	enjoy	enjoys
guy	guys		

9. **The spelling of plural nouns borrowed from French, Greek, and Latin frequently retains the plural of the original language.**

Singular	Plural
alumna (*feminine*)	alumnae
alumnus (*masculine*)	alumni
analysis	analyses
basis	bases

40e

sp

Singular	Plural
crisis	crises
criterion	criteria
datum	data
hypothesis	hypotheses
medium	media
phenomenon	phenomena

The tendency now, however, is to give many such words an anglicized plural. The result is that many words have two plural forms, one foreign, the other anglicized. Either is correct.

Singular	Plural (foreign)	Plural (anglicized)
appendix	appendices	appendixes
chateau	chateaux	chateaus
focus	foci	focuses
index	indices	indexes
memorandum	memoranda	memorandums
radius	radii	radiuses
stadium	stadia	stadiums

EXERCISE 40e(2)

Spell the plural of each of the following words correctly and explain what spelling rule applies. Note any exceptions to the rules.

1. alley	6. class	11. James	16. success
2. auto	7. crash	12. marble	17. synopsis
3. break	8. display	13. no	18. taco
4. bush	9. enemy	14. pose	19. time
5. buzz	10. hero	15. spy	20. wax

40f

sp

40f

Spell compound words according to current usage.

Compound words usually progress by stages from being written as two words, to being hyphenated, to being written as one word: for example, *door mat, door-mat, doormat*. Since these stages often overlap, the correct spelling of a compound word may vary. For the current spelling of a compound, take the advice of a good dictionary. (For the general use of the hyphen in compounds, see "Hyphen," Section **30**.)

THE
WHOLE
ESSAY

Almost all Americans can read and write. Thus we seem to be equal.
But very few Americans possess discipline in the habits of language
necessary for its advantageous use, and those few who do
effectively control the many who do not.

ROBERT PATTISON, *On Literacy: The Politics of the Word
from Homer to the Age of Rock*

41

THE WRITING PROCESS

The foregoing sections of this book have examined grammar, punctuation, word choice, and other sentence-level matters that concern the arrangement of language into patterns of meaning. These are important matters. Although writers are chiefly interested in focusing on deeper text levels—on their ideas—it is precisely through sentence-level surface features that readers gain access to writers' meaning. But now let us broaden our perspective to include matters concerning the writing of a whole document.

41a
What is meant by "the writing process"?

By studying what writers think about and do when they write, researchers have learned that writing involves a number of interrelated activities. These activities, or subprocesses, can be described as follows:

PLANNING

- generating ideas about the paper to be written. This activity is sometimes called "invention" or "the discovery process," because it helps readers find out what they know about a subject or need to learn about it before they write.

- creating goals for the paper and for the writing activity as a whole. Goals may be as global as "I want to convince my readers that geology is an exciting major" or as narrow as "I have too many topics in this paragraph; I need to focus it more." Ultimately, plans and goals should respond to the internal and external needs that prompted the writer in the first place.

- organizing and grouping concepts and ideas. This activity helps the writer explore topics being considered and think about possible ways to present them.

WRITING

- making the ideas visible and available to readers, whether on paper, computer screen, or through some other medium; using the brainstorming notes, outlines, or other results of planning activities to produce text.

- presenting the writer's meaning in a form that is accessible and meaningful to readers. This complex drafting activity involves everything from the physical act of shaping letters or making keystrokes to the mental processes of choosing words, forming sentences, arranging paragraphs, and structuring the organization of the document.

REVISING

- rereading the writing, either as it is being created or later, to test it against the writer's plans and goals.
- changing the writing, if the evaluation indicates that changes will help meet goals. Revision may involve changes in meaning (the addition or deletion of information), changes in surface features (such as spelling and punctuation), or both.

At times some of these activities seem to occur almost simultaneously. For example, a writer in the midst of drafting *(writing)* a sentence may *reread* two or three previous sentences to help recall how he intended to develop an idea *(planning)*. Or, while thinking about how best to conclude an essay *(planning)*, a writer may try out several possible final sentences *(writing)*, crossing out false starts *(evaluating)* until she is satisfied with the thought and its expression *(revising)*.

Not only are the activities of the writing process often embedded in one another, they are also **recursive.** That is, they occur over and over as writers work their way toward a finished product. Although a great deal of deliberate planning may be visible before a writer begins to draft, writers consciously and unconsciously check what they are creating against earlier goals, developing new plans and sometimes changing or modifying their goals as they write and revise. Although many writers like to put their work aside for a while before rereading it for revisions, nearly all writers make some revisions as they are drafting.

In other words, the process of writing is *not* a straight line from initial idea to completed form—first you plan, then you write, then you revise, then you're done. Instead, planning, writing, and revising can occur in any order, and again and again, as writers generate and test their words and ideas.

The following sections present a more detailed discussion of various activities in the writing process, along with techniques you can use in your own writing. We will also look at the activities of two writers: Brad Bolton, a student who needs to write a personal experience essay for his English composition class; and Tina Rodriguez, an office employee who needs to let her co-workers know about an upcoming staff meeting. Rough drafts and revisions of their work appear at the end of Section **41.** You should read Brad's and Tina's rough drafts before continuing with this section.

41a

plan

41b

Why do writers write?

Writers write from need—either their own need or the need of others, sometimes both. A personal diary, a memo to a co-worker, a newspaper article, a poem, an essay exam, a legal brief, a Broadway play, and a lab report all originate from someone's need for writing. Writing may be internally motivated, as is usually the case with diaries, or it may be externally motivated, as is the case with most college assignments.

Whether responding to a personal need or to the requirements of others, the writer becomes involved in a set of activities that eventually produces a **text**—the writing to be read. This set of activities or procedures comprises the writing process.

If writing occurs in response to someone's needs, it then makes sense to look at those needs when thinking about an effective written response. By answering a set of questions, we can identify and analyze the most important needs.

- Who will read this text: who is its **audience?**
- Should the writer's personality be evident in the text: what is the writer's appropriate **role** or **voice?**
- What should this text be about: what is its **subject?**
- What will this text be used for: what is its **purpose?**

These questions are interrelated, and so they can be addressed in any order. Start with the one you find easiest to answer, and go on from there. Also, keep in mind that you may want to reconsider your answers to the questions as your writing progresses. Writers often make discoveries that cause them to redefine their audience, role, subject, or purpose.

41b

plan

41c

Who is the audience?

Planning with your audience in mind can help increase the effectiveness of your writing. Try to picture your audience. What do you know about the reader, or readers? Are they familiar or unfamiliar to you? Are they familiar or unfamiliar with your subject? Ask yourself whether the best presentation for this specific audience is likely to be simple or complex, casual or formal, general or specialized. To communicate effectively, you will need to adjust your subject matter, your point of view, the kind of detail and explanation you use, even the words you choose to the audience you are writing for.

Remember, also, that just as you should consider the relationship between yourself—the writer—and your audience, as well as the relationship between yourself and your subject, so too the audience will have predispositions not only about the subject but also about you, the writer—whether you are personally known to them or not. All these factors have a role to play in the final outcome of your writing.

SPECIALIZED VERSUS GENERAL AUDIENCES

A **specialized reader** already knows a good deal about a subject. Attorneys who write articles for the *Harvard Law Review* do not have to define the legal terms they use: readers of the *Law Review,* other attorneys, already know them. Of course authors writing for *Car and Driver* magazine want to make their articles interesting, but they also know that people who purchase the magazine already have a high interest in automotive-related subjects.

Today, numerous publications exist for readers who have highly specialized interests: *Antique Monthly, Chemical and Engineering News, Idaho Farmer-Stockman, Model Railroader, Industrial Marketing, Yoga Journal, Big Bike Choppers, Skiing, Journal of Genetic Psychology.* Writers can take for granted the audience's interest in the subject matter as well as a certain level of knowledge about it. Such an audience can make sense of information, ideas, and specialized language, or jargon, that would be inappropriate for general readers.

What is true for these authors for specialized journals and magazines is true for you as well. The professor reading your political science paper, the friend reading your letter about a recent rock concert, the insurance agent reading your inquiry about a medical bill have expertise that makes them specialized readers in the subjects you are addressing to them.

A **general reader** may work in a highly specialized profession and have any number of particular interests, but when he or she turns to general-interest publications such as *Ebony, Newsweek, People, Psychology Today, Sports Illustrated,* or *The New Yorker,* the general reader expects to find articles that are written in standard, nontechnical language that can be easily understood, with definitions and explanations supplied for unfamiliar things. Writing aimed at a general readership assumes no special degree of knowledge about a subject or issue. These readers are like yourself; they wish to be informed without having to become experts in a subject to achieve a general understanding about it.

Brad Bolton, whose essay appears at the end of Section **41,** decided to write about his experiences as a student ambassador on a European summer exchange program. He found he needed to change his approach in several ways when he shifted from brainstorming in the form of a letter to the trip's teacher-leader to writing the essay for an audience of his college classmates. The teacher-leader, Judy, not only accompanied his student group but had been to Europe several times before that. She was familiar with the situation and, thus, was a

41c

plan

specialized audience. His classmates and English instructor, on the other hand, had not shared his experience. In fact, Brad could not assume that any of them had been abroad or had much knowledge about foreign travel. Because they comprised a more general audience, he had to adjust his essay accordingly, doing more describing and explaining.

When writing for either specialized or general readers, ask yourself questions such as

- What are the *common denominators*? What characteristics do I share with my readers: education, age, beliefs and attitudes, level of knowledge about and interest in the subject? Are there any other factors that have a bearing on my assumptions about the common ground shared with my readers?
- What are the crucial *differences* between me and my readers? What steps will I need to take to overcome or minimize the effects of these differences? Will I need to define terms, use analogies, include more explanation or background, provide more evidence and examples, use a special tone? Are my readers likely to be sympathetic, hostile, or indifferent? How will that affect what I write?

EXERCISE 41c

Write three short letters in which you discuss the need for an emergency loan. Write the first letter to a close friend or relative who may be able to help you. Write the second to a close friend or relative who you know cannot easily afford to lend you money. Write the third letter to the financial aid officer at your college or university. Share your letters with a classmate, explaining the approach you used for each and what considerations about the audience played a role in your approach.

41d

plan

41d

What is the writer's voice or role?

Depending upon the other factors that influence the final form of the document, the **voice** of the writer will be more evident or less evident. "Voice" refers to the way a writer "sounds" to a reader, the way we present ourselves to our audience, the authorial role we have chosen. In many types of writing—a scientific journal article on the moons of Saturn, for example, or a newspaper story about a train wreck—the writer is seemingly transparent, virtually absent except as a channel for information. The facts are at the forefront. In other types of writing, the author's presence can be detected more strongly. We feel that someone is "speaking" to us, even if not always using the "I" of the first-person pronoun.

How you choose to present yourself to your readers can have a definite impact on the way they perceive your message. In his essay,

Brad's voice is that of a peer to his classmates; in writing about his personal experiences, he uses standard though informal English, without a great deal of slang, because he wants to be understood clearly and also because an important person in the audience is his instructor, who may not be familiar with teenage slang. Read Brad's first draft now, if you have not already done so (pages 362–365).

Brad's early draft contained some clichés, which did not fit the role he had developed for himself in the paper—that of careful observer and presenter of fresh and lively detail. As he revised the draft, he realized that some of these phrases needed to be changed, not only because they were not effective description but also because they undercut his role as observant narrator.

While revising her memo, Tina also encountered a problem with voice. She realized that the tone she had originally taken was too stiff and formal for a memo addressed to her colleagues. Tina knew she wanted to encourage the staff members to think and act as a team, but the tone of her first version sounded as if she were giving orders to subordinates rather than offering her peers suggestions for a more productive meeting. In contrast to Brad's essay, where the use of first-person pronouns helps the readers feel they are seeing things through the writer's eyes, the frequent use of "I" in Tina's memo made her writing sound rather self-centered. Together, these factors led her to worry that her readers might think she was trying to seize control of the group and thus might resist following her suggestions. So she adopted a more casual, conversational voice in the final draft, using more plural pronouns. These changes helped her to position herself as a member of the team. Read Tina's first draft and final draft now, if you have not already done so (pages 360–361).

41e

plan

EXERCISE 41d

Practice using different authorial voices by writing two paragraphs as follows: (1) for a new scout manual, describe how to build and light a campfire; (2) for a friend, describe how you built a campfire but could not get it lit. (Use your imagination if you have never actually built a campfire.) To what extent would each paragraph make the reader aware of you the author, as distinct from you the participant? Why?

41e

What is the subject?

Sometimes your subject is predetermined by the needs of the writing situation, perhaps a class assignment or work assignment: *Write an essay on the causes of World War I. Prepare a sales forecast for the next quarter. Discuss the question of whether our club should choose the Children's Home or the Senior Citizen Center for this year's service project.* At other times you may have to develop the subject yourself: *Write a per-*

sonal experience essay. Write a term paper on the nineteenth-century American novel of your choice. Identify a business problem in the company you are studying and write a report about it.

In later discussions about planning, we will more thoroughly investigate the process of choosing a subject and generating ideas about it. For now, suffice it to say that the shape you give your subject depends to a great extent on its interaction with the other needs of the writing situation. For example, at the top of her planning sheet, Tina wrote *Subject: Agenda for Tuesday's Meeting.* Eventually, as she explored ideas for the memo, she realized that her goal was to encourage the staff to do some advance thinking in preparation for the meeting. Tina left the subject line on the memo more or less as she had initially drafted it, but the major topic she addressed in the text was the need for people to think about agenda issues before they came to the meeting.

Having a more open-ended task before him, Brad needed to provide some boundaries for his thinking about the personal experience essay. His planning began with the question "Which personal experience?" and progressed through a series of focusing activities. After rejecting several alternatives, he chose a recent and powerful experience, his summer trip to Europe as a student ambassador in a youth exchange program. The broad subject "my trip to Europe" demanded more space than the three or four pages the instructor had allotted for the assignment, so Brad knew he must narrow his focus. For further planning and initial drafting, he chose, then, the more limited subject "my most memorable experiences in Europe."

During their planning activities, both Tina and Brad discovered the necessary constraints of their writing tasks and adjusted the subjects accordingly. In Tina's case the task broadened from *deliver the agenda* to *encourage thinking about the agenda.* Brad narrowed his task from *tell about trip to Europe* to *tell about most memorable parts of trip.*

41f

plan

41f
What is the purpose?

Writers sometimes find themselves at cross-purposes with their subjects, audiences, and the needs of the writing task itself. You need to ask yourself just what your writing ought to accomplish. If the answer to the question is unclear, or if it disregards the needs of your audience and subject matter, you are likely to have trouble creating a satisfactory text.

For example, if a question on a history exam asks you to *defend* the Loyalists' actions during the American Revolution, then the purpose of your answer must be to *argue for* the validity of their viewpoint. If your answer only *explains* what the Loyalists did during the Revolution, you have misunderstood the purpose. You are likely to receive poor marks on the question because you only partially completed the required task, which was both to explain and to persuade.

As Tina worked on her memo, she had to clarify her purposes. She discovered that her initial purpose—inform staff of the meeting agenda—fell short of her actual purpose—persuade staff to think about agenda items before the meeting. Here Tina's writing benefited from the recursiveness of the writing process. She returned to planning activities before doing any further drafting. When she had discovered what she really wanted to accomplish, and thus what she wanted the memo to accomplish, she was able to write a memo better suited to her real goals.

One way to check your text for clarity of purpose is to compare what you have written to four categories of prose known as the *rhetorical modes*. Each of these categories—*narration, description, exposition,* and *argumentation*—fits a different rhetorical purpose.

1. Narration. The purpose of narration is to tell a story, to recount a sequence of events, to tell "what happened." The appeal of narration is universal: it is the first kind of discourse that children learn, in bedtime stories and in the tales relatives tell about their childhoods. We use narration constantly in our writing: on an insurance claim, to relate how an accident happened; on the job, to prepare a report about monthly sales calls: for an economics paper, to outline the sequence of events that led to the 1929 stock market crash.

Brad used narration in sections of his essay; it suited his purpose quite well—to tell what he did on his free day in London. For Tina, on the other hand, the narrative opening paragraph in the first draft of her memo was an important clue that she had misdefined her purpose. Rereading the draft, she wondered what her point was in narrating the sequence of events leading up to the staff meeting, information people already knew. That discovery led Tina to ask what her real purpose was and what her readers really needed to know. The final draft of the memo contains much less narrative, since its purpose is mainly persuasive.

41f

plan

2. Description. The purpose of description is to make readers see, feel, hear what the writer has seen, felt, or heard. Description often appears in combination with other modes and provides an important sense of immediacy—"you are there"—that readers need in order to fully grasp a writer's meaning. Brad's instructor commented on an early draft of his essay that he needed to "put flesh on the bones" of his experience. Referring to his passage about a famous British department store, she wrote, "We need to see concrete examples to understand why you were overwhelmed" (see p. 366). Without using the term, she was asking him to supply more description.

Description can be of two kinds: objective (or technical) and suggestive (or impressionistic). The first requires writers to reproduce, as a camera would, what they see. An appraiser for a mortgage company provides an objective description of a house:

> Lot size 120 feet wide by 150 feet deep. Exterior dimensions of house: 84 feet by 27 feet. Living area 1,620 square feet; 648 additional square feet in two-car garage. Seven rooms: three bedrooms, living room, dining room, kitchen, den; two baths. One brick fireplace. Central heat (gas); central air (electric). R-19 insulation rating. Three years old.

The appraisal contains no emotional reaction, no judgment of the house's appeal. The goal of the appraiser's objective description is to enable the mortgage company to set a fair loan value on the house.

The homeowner who wishes to sell the same house writes up a description that reads as follows:

> Practically new three-bedroom, two-bath, ranch-style brick home situated on a shade-tree-covered half-acre lot. Over 1,600 square feet of living area. Modern kitchen with built-in appliances. Walnut-panelled family room with brick fireplace and beamed ceiling. Formal living and dining rooms for gracious entertaining. Master bedroom suite with adjoining full bath. Oversized two-car garage. Large patio with gas grill. All of this is nestled beneath stately maples on beautiful, easily maintained grounds and is available with a mortgage at 10½% interest.

This description creates a much different impression from the appraiser's. The latter description may not be merely the product of the owner's desire to sell the house; it no doubt reflects an emotional attachment to the house.

41f

plan

3. Exposition. The purpose of exposition is to inform, to explain, to clarify—to make readers know or understand something about a subject. Exposition may sometimes appeal to emotions, as narration and description often do, but the primary purpose of exposition is to inform. Exposition is the principle mode used to write a manual for automobile owners, a recipe for Southern fried chicken, a physics textbook, a magazine article about the campaigns of presidential candidates.

Both Tina and Brad had expository purposes for sections of their text. Brad wanted to explain why certain experiences on his trip were especially memorable. Tina needed to inform her colleagues of what was planned for the Tuesday meeting.

4. Argumentation. The purpose of argumentation is to persuade the audience—to convince them of the rightness of a point of view and/or course of action. We encounter argumentation in debates and editorials. Most political speeches are a form of argumentation.

Argumentation often has an emotional component, as is the case in political speeches, for example. But truly persuasive arguments are based primarily on adequate evidence, sound logic, and a thorough understanding of opposing positions. (See Section **43** for a more developed discussion of persuasive writing.)

Tina wanted to persuade her readers to think about the agenda items. Consequently, her memo contains argumentative sections where she provides reasons for the action she is trying to convince her readers to take (see her final draft, paragraphs 2 and 3).

Knowing the characteristics and purposes of narration, description, exposition, and argumentation will help you recognize when and where they are appropriate in your writing. You will be better able to judge which mode is most effective for what you are trying to accomplish.

41g
Planning: techniques for generating and joining ideas

Planning occurs throughout the writing process, and especially at the outset when the initial goals are being set—when the audience, author's role, subject, and purpose are being identified, developed and shaped. The generative aspects of planning—the invention and exploration—are fundamental to retrieving from memory knowledge and information about a subject. Thus, many writers need a rather unstructured period during the planning activity, when ideas are allowed to flow freely. At other times, more systematic planning techniques can be used. The following discussion explains both unstructured and structured techniques that can be used in planning activities.

41g

plan

1. Free association. This technique uses no writing at all, but emphasizes simply letting the mind range freely over a subject to see what bubbles up from the memory. Free association can work well when you have a wide-open assignment. It also can be helpful if you are experiencing writer's block and need to stop trying to compose sentences. Instead of trying to impose structure on your ideas before they may be ready for order, just see what percolates from your thoughts.

2. Brainstorming and note jotting. This technique can be a good step to follow free association—when your mind is generating enough potentially useful ideas that you want to get some of them down on paper. Jotting does not involve a mental censor. Concentrate on your subject or some aspect of it. Then write down what comes from brainstorming, without censoring ideas as to their importance. You are trying to see what mental information is available, trying to encourage a focus without forcing it. Your jotting might take the form of a list, a series of random notes, some key words, or whatever will help you recall ideas later.

3. Free writing. Free writing, like free association, is meant to help you generate ideas by simply letting them flow without censorship or interruption. Do not worry about spelling, punctuation, grammar, or form. Just start writing, including everything that goes through your mind, to see what you may have to say.

Free writing can be helpful when you have a wide-open subject and also when you are searching for a subject. It can also help when you have too much information to deal with and cannot seem to get it under control. Rather than struggling, relax and free write about the subject for five or ten minutes. Useful groupings and relationships may emerge. If not, give yourself a break and return to brainstorming when you are refreshed.

Following is a portion of Brad's free writing, done on a computer with a word-processing program. He often used the computer when generating ideas, sometimes dimming the monitor's screen so he would not be tempted to censor or to correct what he was writing. In this case, Brad believed it might be easier to get the ideas flowing if he addressed his thoughts to someone, so his free writing took the form of a letter to the leader of his summer trip. You may find that this method of "talking" to someone, either in person, on screen, or on paper, helps you, too. Compare Brad's free writing with his essay drafts at the end of Section **41**. Note which ideas Brad used in each draft and how he developed those ideas.

Free writing

41g

plan

Dear Judy,

   We're supposed to write a personal experience essay for English class and I decided to write about last summer on the student ambassador trip. That sure was a lot of fun and I learned an awful lot about other people and countries. The trip was awesome—absolutely the most interesting thing that has happened in my life. Also learned a lot of things about myself. should I write about that? what I learned about people during our homestays or when we were traveling. Or should I stick to what I learned about myself? I suppose the two things are realy connected, maybe I can separate them—should they be separated? Anyway the parts of the trip that come to mind right now are shopping in London and . . . .

what else? . . . talking to french students on park bench in
Paris . . . . . Bavarian homestay cookout . . . . Austrian
homestay family . . . . the bike ride I took with Peter and
Patrick. Why these? anything in common??? What? What?? Judy,
you told us one of the most important things we would do as
student ambassadors would be talk to people. You were right.
What sticks in my mind the most is times where I <u>really</u>
communicated with people, never mind language barriers. Times
when I really exchanged viewpoints with people and learned
new things. Maybe I can write my essay around that idea.

4. Mind mapping. This technique is more structured than free writing but less structured than some other techniques (described below). Mind mapping emphasizes the free flow of ideas, but it also allows you to show relationships among ideas without forcing them into an organizational scheme. Start with the subject circled in the center of a page. Then, as you think of other ideas, add new circles radiating outward on the page. If ideas are related to one another, place them in overlapping circles, or connect the circles with lines. Your mind map can be as simple or as detailed as you choose. The mind map

Mind map

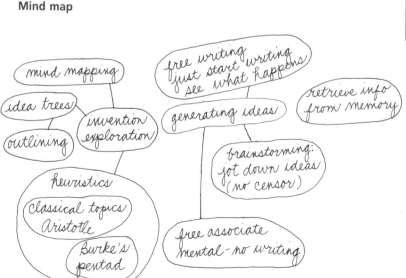

on page 337, used to plan this section of the *Prentice Hall Handbook,* shows how the technique is done.

Mind mapping is especially helpful if you want to collect ideas about aspects of a subject but find yourself stalled by the best order in which to present them. Seeing the ideas without a superimposed structure but in relationship to one another can help postpone the need to organize them until you have finished idea collection and are ready to think productively about organization.

5. Idea trees. This technique is a bit more structured than mind mapping; it represents ideas not only in relation to one another but also in hierarchical arrangements. Various such arrangements could be from greater to lesser, general to specific, main idea to supporting idea, and so forth, depending upon the subject and purpose of the tree. As the following example illustrates, idea trees can be useful for exploring the parts of a subject and also for organizing the presentation of ideas.

Idea tree

6. Outlining. Notes, lists, and idea trees are often types of **informal outlines.** Some writers use a **formal outline** as a blueprint for the paper they will write. An outline can be especially valuable when you must write against a deadline—an in-class essay or exam, for instance. It can keep you from discovering too late that you have confused issues, wandered from the main line of argument, left out important points, or maybe even failed to understand the question. Other writers use an outline as part of the revision process, preparing it after their paper has been written as a means of checking the structure and the development of ideas. Also, some assignments, such as research papers or long reports, require that a formal outline be submitted as part of the document.

The conventions of **formal outlining** are as follows:

a. Number and indent headings and subheadings consistently; do not use single headings or subheadings. Follow the rule "for every *I*, there must be a *II*; for every *A*, there must be a *B*." Any category of heading or subheading must have at least two parts. Here is a portion of Tina's working outline.

    I. Reasons for agenda
        A. Structure at meeting
            1. More efficient approach to business
                a. Most important topics first
                b. Least important topics if time
            2. Fewer irrelevant topics
        B. Preparation for meeting
   II. Agenda items for Tuesday

The following outline is **NOT** in correct form. It contains single subheadings, an indication of poor organization or incorrect partition. You cannot logically divide something into just one part. A single subheading should be incorporated into the heading of which it is logically a part, or it should be divided in two.

    I. Reasons for agenda
        A. Structure at meeting
   II. Agenda items for Tuesday
        A. Criteria for new staff jobs
        B. Growth areas
            1. data processing
                a. sales
        C. Proposal to Department Head

41g

plan

Also note that the incorrect outline contains same-level headings that do not represent the same classification principle. Items II. A. and B. are not of the same class; II. B. should be a subcategory of II. A. Items B. 1. and B. 1. a. are of the same class; they should have same-level headings. More logical divisions for the last part of the outline would be as follows:

   II. Agenda items for Tuesday
        A. Criteria for new staff jobs
            1. Anticipated growth areas
                 a. data processing
                 b. sales
            2. Currently overburdened area: accounting
        B. Proposal to Department Head

b. Follow either topic, sentence, or paragraph style throughout an outline, and use parallel grammatical structure. A *topic out-*

line uses a noun (or noun substitute) and its modifiers for each heading, as in the foregoing example. A *sentence outline* follows the same structure but uses a complete sentence for each heading. For an example of a sentence outline, see the sample research paper in Section **45j**. A *paragraph outline* gives a summary sentence for each paragraph of the paper and does not divide and subdivide headings into subordinate parts. Do not mix types in the same outline.

Remember also to make all parts within the same level or degree of the outline parallel in grammatical structure. Using consistent grammatical form emphasizes the logic of the outline as well as providing clarity and smoothness. Notice that in the last part of her revised outline, Tina wrote the modifier-noun phrase *Anticipated growth areas* and then the parallel modifier-noun phrase *Currently overburdened area*—not an unparallel construction such as *add to area currently overburdened.*

c. Avoid vague outline headings such as Introduction, Body, and Conclusion. These headings will not help you in planning, because they do not provide content clues. Also, if you are asked to submit an outline with your paper, such headings do not help your readers. Indicate in the outline what the introduction will include. If your paper is to have a formal conclusion, show in the outline what conclusion you will draw. Think of the outline as a table of contents for the reader, a preview of important information and its organization. Because it does provide such an overview, a formal outline often begins with a statement of the paper's thesis, as does the outline for the research paper in Section **45j**.

7. Heuristics. *Heuristics* refers to procedures for thinking systematically about a subject. Except for outlining, heuristics are the most structured planning techniques we will examine. Among the many heuristics available, two popular ones are Burke's pentad and Aristotle's topics.

a. Burke's pentad. This procedure involves exploring a subject as if it were a drama, using the five categories *act, scene, agent, agency,* and *purpose.* We can ask the following questions about a subject: "What happens to or with the subject *(act)?* When and where does the action take place *(scene)?* Who causes the action *(agent)?* How is the action carried out—who or what, by what means *(agency)?* Why does the action occur *(purpose)?* These "who, what, when, where, why, and how" questions can be helpful in discovering how much you know about a subject and whether there is anything you need to find out before you can start writing.

The pentad can also be quite helpful in checking what you are writing against the purpose you have identified. For example, if your purpose is to discuss the causes of teenage suicide but you find that most of your paper concentrates on the methods teenagers use to at-

41g

plan

tempt suicide, the pentad will show you that you have emphasized agency rather than purpose. You will need to adjust the focus of the paper, condensing the material on methods and developing material on reasons and motivations.

b. Aristotle's topics. The Greek philosopher Aristotle identi-fied four "common topics" to be used as keys for exploring the nature of a subject. These points of departure include (a) *definition:* what is it?; (b) *chronology:* what happened and in what order did things hap-pen?; (c) *comparison and contrast:* what are the similarities and the dif-ferences?; (d) *cause and effect:* what are the reasons and the results? The topics can provide helpful categories for organizing ideas as well as means for generating and exploring them. For example, if Brad Bolton had used Aristotle's topics as a heuristic for generating ideas about his essay assignment, he might have come up with something like the following.

DEFINITION:	What is my most memorable experience? What do I mean by memorable? What are the compo-nents required for a memorable experience?
CHRONOLOGY:	What happened that made my student-ambassa-dor experience memorable?
COMPARISON/CONTRAST:	How was my student-ambassador experience more memorable than other experiences? How was I different when I came back from the trip than before I left?
CAUSE/EFFECT:	Did some event(s) or person(s) on the trip cause me to change? What was responsible for making the trip so memorable? What have been the re-sults of this trip that made it more memorable than other trips?

41h

plan

EXERCISE 41g

1. Assume that you have been given an essay-writing assignment. The choice of subject is up to you. Applying the idea-generating tech-nique that you think will work best, come up with a subject and some ideas for a three-to-four page essay.
2. You have been assigned an essay on the subject of discrimination in America. Use another of the techniques described in Section 41g to generate ideas on this subject.

41h
Planning: subject boundaries and thesis statements

1. Setting the boundaries of your subject. Many of the idea-generating techniques previously discussed contain built-in methods for setting the boundaries of a general subject so that it fits the constraints of the writing task. An idea tree, for instance, is designed to move from general to particular aspects of a subject, from the whole to its parts, or from main idea to related supporting ideas. At some point in your planning activities you need to move from expanding the field of ideas to focusing on a few of them. You must choose those that look most promising for development and disregard the rest.

As we have noted, Brad engaged in setting boundaries and focusing his ideas when he decided which of his life's experiences he wanted to explore for his personal experience essay. He settled on his European trip and then had to do more focusing in order to select the few incidents that fit two important constraints. One of these constraints was external: the page limit set by the instructor. The other Brad eventually set himself: the controlling idea, or thesis, he was developing for his essay.

In planning an essay about his summer trip, Brad had to answer the question "*What* about the trip?" He had to refer to larger goals involved in the writing task. What, exactly, would be the purpose of the paper? Brad narrowed his purpose to explaining why the trip was his most memorable experience. He expressed this purpose as the controlling idea of his paper: *Probably the most memorable experience in my life is the trip I took to Europe* . . . [because it] *contributed to* [my] *general maturing.* . . ." Thus, Brad needed to select incidents that illustrated and supported the controlling idea.

His first draft shows that he initially chose four incidents for the essay—one each in London, France, Bavaria, and Austria. By the final draft, he had reduced the incidents to three. Brad omitted Bavaria not because it added too much length to the essay but because it did not add anything new to his illustration of the essay's controlling idea. This example shows how the focusing process is likely to be ongoing as you plan, write, and revise.

41h

plan

EXERCISE 41h(1)
For each general subject that follows, list three different, more focused subjects that could be derived from the general one. Then for each of those resulting subjects, list two even more limited subjects. Put your lists in the form of an idea tree. The general subjects are:

1. parents
2. music
3. jobs
4. equality
5. a subject of your choice

Following is an example of an idea tree using one general subject.

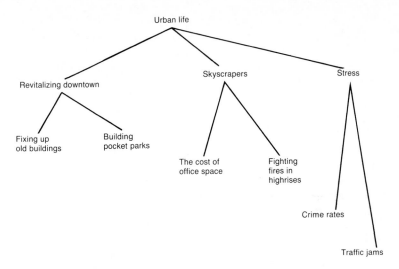

2. Expressing the controlling idea as a thesis statement.
Readers are notoriously impatient. They like to know what's going on. They appreciate being notified early in a paper about the subject and the direction you plan to go with it. In fact, it is to your advantage as a writer to indicate your goals and purposes early because sharing them not only makes your readers more attentive but also prepares them to understand the ideas you present.

A thesis statement is the most efficient means by which you can communicate your subject, goals, and purposes. It sets forth in a sentence or two the paper's controlling idea—its **thesis.** A thesis statement is *not* simply a statement of the paper's subject. "This paper is about the effects of industrialization on developing nations" is not a thesis statement. A thesis statement is an assertion; it answers the questions *What point does this paper make? What opinion does it offer? What stand does the writer take? What does the writer want us to focus on as we read this paper?* A carefully stated thesis introduces and summarizes the entire paper—puts into a nutshell the central idea, which the rest of the paper explores and develops.

Like any other statement, a thesis statement consists of a subject and a predicate. Your main topic is the subject. Writing a thesis statement is a matter of writing a predicate to go with that subject, a matter of stating the assertion you wish to make about the subject. Brad's thesis, expressed in two related sentences in his opening paragraph (see p. 362), asserts that his trip to Europe (subject) added to his maturity (predicate), and thus the trip (subject) is the most memorable experience of his life (predicate).

41h

plan

Not only does this thesis statement clearly present Brad's assertion about his subject, it also indicates his purpose (to explain why by telling the reader what happened), the main rhetorical modes he will use (exposition and narration), and the probable organization of the paper (cause and effect overall, chronology within sections).

A well-formed thesis statement helps you keep the paper unified, if you stick to the specific subject and direction it indicates. Because the thesis provides a basis for decisions about what to include and what to exclude, it also helps you organize your ideas. In addition, a well-formed thesis statement can give your paper an argumentative edge, a kind of dramatic interest. Even in a paper whose general purpose is to explain or describe, a thesis statement serves as the writer's commitment, a promise to the readers to make a clear point—in Brad's case, showing why this trip was memorable. The writer's task, then, is to support the thesis, to back it up with evidence, to explain what it means, to develop that explanation with details and examples, to convince readers that it is a valid assertion.

The most common problems that can weaken a thesis statement are lack of unity and lack of focus. A thesis should state a *single controlling idea*. The idea may be complex and have several parts, but it should be one idea nevertheless. A thesis statement should also be *focused;* that is, it should be restricted and specific enough for the reader to gain a clear idea of the subject and direction of your paper. The "original" sentences that follow have neither unity nor focus.

ORIGINAL		My difficulties in philosophy are unbelievable, but I'm doing OK in biology.
REVISION		Because I seem to be more comfortable with concrete things like frogs than with abstract ideas like existence, I am getting better grades in biology than in philosophy.
ORIGINAL		Kids face a lot of problems today and need help.
REVISION		Although being a teenager has never been easy, drug use, suicide, parental divorce, and unwanted pregnancy mean we need many more teenage counseling programs than are currently available.

41h

plan

The first sentence fails the test for unity because it contains two separate ideas with no indication of how—or if—they will be brought together. The paper that results from this thesis is likely to break into unconnected halves: one half devoted to biology, one half to philosophy. The second sentence remedies this problem by subordinating the ideas in a cause-and-effect relationship.

The first sentence also fails the test for focus because it uses vague generalities such as "are unbelievable" and "doing OK." Predicates that consist of *is* or *are* plus a vague modifying phrase or complement such as *good, interesting,* or *a serious problem* are usually too imprecise to be useful. Although general terms can be narrowed and defined elsewhere in a paper, readers appreciate a thesis assertion (such as that in the second, revised sentence) that supplies a specific subject and clear direction as quickly as possible.

Keep in mind that not every kind of writing needs an explicit thesis statement. Tina's memo, for instance, has a purpose statement that tells her readers why they have received the memo, but no actual thesis statement. The first sentence of the second paragraph, which expresses her goal of persuading her readers to prepare for the meeting, is the closest thing in the memo to a thesis sentence.

Some types of writing, such as business or technical reports, may have an overall purpose and clear goals that respond to needs known to writer and readers, but no single controlling idea that appears in a single statement. In fact, there may be different controlling ideas for different parts of a report. However, especially in essays that explain or argue a point, a clear thesis sentence is a great aid to the reader's understanding and recall.

Where you place a thesis sentence depends on your goals, your audience, the purpose of the essay, and how you intend to organize it. The most common position for the thesis statement in short expository and persuasive essays is in the opening paragraph. It may appear early in the opening paragraph, followed by sentences that further define or explain the assertion that the thesis makes. Or the thesis statement may be positioned at the end of the paragraph, following an introduction of the subject and some background information.

Although other locations for the thesis statement can work, remember that readers like a clear sense of what is going on. Be sure that your controlling idea is indeed controlling the paper, wherever the thesis is located. The principal argument for its early appearance in an essay is that readers will understand the relevance of your discussion better if you first tell them the main idea behind that discussion.

41h

plan

EXERCISE 41h(2)
Explain the flaws in the second "original" thesis sentence on page 344, and then explain how the revision corrects them. For practice in writing unified, focused thesis statements, revise the following thesis statements. If any of them are satisfactory as written, explain why.

1. People who drop out of school are stupid.
2. Farming isn't what it used to be, and a lot of farmers are going out of business.
3. Even though the conditions and weapons of warfare have changed greatly since World War I, the book *All Quiet on the Western Front* and the movie *Platoon* show that the lessons learned by soldiers during war have not changed.

4. Learning disabilities take many forms as well as many degrees of severity.
5. People's attitudes can often be seen in the way they treat others.

EXERCISE 41h(3)

Look for the thesis statement in (1) several editorials and letters to the editor in a local newspaper, (2) the "Essay" in *Time* magazine or an opinion article in another news magazine, (3) an informative article in a magazine for specialized readers. Choose one of them, write the thesis statement at the top of a page, and then make an outline of the editorial, letter, or article. How well does the author's thesis statement serve as the controlling idea?

EXERCISE 41h(4)

Using the subject you chose for an idea tree in Exercise 41h(1), write two unified, focused thesis statements for essays on that subject. These two statements should result in essays that go in different directions.

41i

Writing: getting organized

As you plan your essay, your ideas will begin to group together into an organizational scheme. After all, constructing a message for readers is not simply a matter of filling a sack with ideas. In fact, if you use Aristotle's topics, an idea tree, or an outline in your planning activities, you are organizing in a preliminary way. Most writers begin their first draft with a general notion of the order in which they want to present their points, an order that fits their purpose.

41i

write

Often, more detailed organizing occurs while writing and revising are underway. Tina, for example, made major changes in the organization of her memo after she had written the first draft. She changed the structure of her memo because she found the first version did not satisfy her plans as they had developed while she was writing. This "change of plans" happens to writers all the time: as we write, we discover things about our purposes and goals that we did not know when we began. This is normal. A preliminary organizing plan will help you when you start to write, but do not be afraid to change it if something else seems to work better.

The main thing to keep in mind as you write is that all the parts of your essay—every paragraph—should be related to the controlling idea that governs your paper. Each sentence should in some important way increase the reader's understanding of your main point. As you plan, write, and revise you will want to check your organization and development of ideas to be sure you have (1) eliminated things that are irrelevant to your focus and (2) made clear to your readers connections between ideas and paragraphs.

As you draft your paper, you may indeed find that you need to revise your thesis statement if your thoughts, and thus the structure of your essay, take a new turn. After all, the writing process is not only a recursive process, it is also a discovery process.

When they are trying to accomplish certain kinds of purposes, writers more or less naturally create certain organizational structures. Knowing the following common structures can help you shape your ideas to fit a particular purpose. Sample paragraphs of each type of organization appear in Section **42.**

1. Time. If you are writing narration—telling what happened—time order (also called chronological order) is a natural structure. When you write about an automobile accident or a historical event, you are likely to relate the events in the sequence in which they happened. Brad used chronological order for the sections of his essay dealing with events in London, Paris, and Austria. A chronology is also the appropriate structure for instructions: how to write a computer program, how to make a Caesar salad, how to use the library or overcome a fear of flying on airplanes.

2. Space. If you need to describe a scene or object, spatial order may be appropriate. You may focus the scene from where either you or the readers are located, and then move from left to right, top to bottom, front to back, inside to outside, or whatever spatial arrangement suits your purpose. Spatial order closely follows the order in which the eyes see or movie cameras move. One bit of information relates to the next in terms of position.

If you want to create an unusual descriptive effect, deliberately departing from normal spatial order might be your choice. Horror movies frequently violate the audience's spatial expectations to create a special atmosphere. The camera may first focus on glazed eyes, then on sprawled legs, then on a gaping mouth, and ultimately on a knife protruding from the chest to create the feelings of suspense, fear, and shock associated with a murder. You can use words in the same way.

41i

write

3. General to particular / particular to general. If you are explaining an idea or a concept, one of these structures can be useful. You might state the *general* idea first and then explain it by citing *particular* instances or examples of the generalization. The reverse is also possible: instances and examples first, summed up by a general statement. In his final draft, Brad used a particular-to-general organization when he first described his encounter with the French student and then concluded that the encounter was the reason he would never forget the evening in Paris (pp. 372-373).

These two organizational structures sometimes go by another name. Especially when applied to persuasive writing or logical analysis, the general-to-particular order may be called **deductive** organization, and the particular-to-general order may be referred to as **inductive** organization. When writers give reasons and explanations first and then present the central idea or conclusion to be drawn, they are using an inductive structure. If they present the conclusion/generalization/main idea first and then follow it with reasons and other explanatory detail, they are using deductive organization. Tina switched from an inductive structure to a deductive structure for the final draft of her memo because she decided that she needed a more direct approach for her readers and subject matter (pp. 360 and 361). Section **43** contains further discussion of deduction and induction.

4. Climax. If you are writing to persuade your readers, the order of climax can be very effective. Arranging evidence from least important to most important is a strategy used routinely in arguments and debates. When someone says "and last, but not least," you know he or she is about to deliver the crushing blow. Because climactic order, like a well-constructed play, achieves its big moment at the end, it also works well when you want to create suspense. Its drawback is that readers may get tired of waiting for you to come to the point.

5. Comparison and contrast. Writing that points out similarities compares; writing that notes differences contrasts. Frequently, but not always, comparison and contrast coexist in the same paper. Brad compared himself to the French student and noted a difference he found unusual: he doesn't care what language he speaks, but the French love to speak, and hear the sound of, their own language (p. 372).

Comparison and contrast are two of the most common structures for writing. This is not surprising when you remember that the principal way our minds process new information is to attach it to old information. We learn about the unknown by viewing it in terms of what we already know: how is it the same as (compared to) or different from (contrasted with) our previous experience? It makes sense, then, that writers naturally rely a good deal on comparison and contrast to communicate their ideas.

A special kind of comparison, called **analogy,** uses similarities between two things to imply other similarities or resemblances. To show how working for Company X is like belonging to a big family is to compare by analogy. For a more complete discussion of analogy, see Section **42.**

6. Analysis and classification. Analysis is the conscious process of trying to understand something by taking it apart, breaking it down into its smaller parts. Analysis is also sometimes called partition or division. For example, if you have decided on a career in nursing, at some point you will need to analyze the field—look at the kinds of nursing available—in order to decide which one—obstetric, pediatric, geriatric, surgical—you wish to practice. If you are trying to determine the cause of a business problem, you may want to analyze the business according to its components—manufacturing, distribution, marketing and sales, finance and accounting—to see where the problem lies. An important adjunct of analysis is classification; in fact, analysis makes classification possible. If you want to group items according to a common principle or characteristic, you classify them—put them into categories.

Suppose you were assigned an essay on the student body at your school. You would first analyze, then classify. In brainstorming about the subject, you would have to consider a variety of ways to distinguish one student from another. You could do so in terms of those who study diligently, those who study just enough to get by, and those who demonstrate no interest in their studies. When you assign several individuals to each of these categories, you are classifying according to study habits, a principle common to all students. Other classifications are possible: you might divide students according to their place of residence or their choice of career. Whatever classification you select for a paper depends on your purpose and derives from careful analysis.

Classification without analysis is called **stereotyping.** You stereotype if you classify a person or group without systematic and valid analysis. The outcome of stereotyping is often prejudice directed toward members of ethnic, political, sexual, racial, or religious groups. Before you put people or things into categories, be sure that you have fully and fairly examined the components that make up those people or things and have drawn valid conclusions about them.

7. Definition. If your purpose is to explain an abstract concept or something unfamiliar to your audience, you may find that definition is an appropriate organizational structure. If definition provides the overall structure for much or all of your paper, you will be writing an **extended definition.**

Definition is actually a form of comparison, beginning with the thing to be defined (the unfamiliar or unknown) and describing it in terms of things with which the reader is familiar. In addition, definition uses classification, first placing the thing to be defined within a broad category *(genus)* and then within narrower and narrower categories *(differentia)*. In the sentence definition *A crumpet is a light, soft bread similar to a muffin,* for example, *crumpet* (the unfamiliar) is compared to *bread* (the familiar) and further classified under the narrower categories *light* and *soft* to differentiate it from other types of bread. Section **43,** "Persuasive Writing," contains a full discussion of various types of definition.

8. Cause and effect. If your chemistry professor asks you to discuss the results of combining certain chemicals, you will develop your answer by the cause-and-effect method. If your English instructor asks you to write a paper on why you selected the college you attend, you will be expected to develop the paper using an effect-to-

41i

write

cause relationship. The decision is an effect, an already accomplished action; the reasons for your decision are the causes.

Cause-and-effect organization quite naturally falls into the pattern of (1) stating causes and describing or arguing what their consequences will be, or (2) identifying a problem or consequence and then explaining the causes. An organizational structure related to cause and effect is the *problem-solution pattern.* In analyzing the problem, you would first discuss causes and effects. Then you would probably switch to a thesis-support approach to present your solution and prove its validity.

9. Detail and example / thesis–support. If your purpose is to explain or persuade, it is very likely that a thesis supported by examples and details will provide the overarching structure for your paper. In fact, many of the papers you write in college can be effectively structured this way because many of your writing tasks will call for you to explain things to your readers or convince them of a point of view.

Even though you will frequently need to use cause-and-effect, comparison and contrast, definition, or one of the other types of organization discussed in this section, in many cases these structures will be subordinated to the larger goal of supporting your paper's thesis. They will often be a part of the larger web of details and examples you will need to get your point across clearly to your audience.

Because it is so basic to effective writing, detail and example/ thesis–support fits quite comfortably with other types of organization. A very common combination is detail and example with general-to-particular/particular-to-general order. Brad's paper illustrates another common combination: he used details and examples along with cause-and-effect to support his thesis that his trip to Europe was his most memorable experience because it helped him to gain maturity.

41j

write

EXERCISE 41i

Study the thesis statements you wrote for Exercise 41h(4). Which organizational structures seem appropriate for each statement. Why? Explain how the organization would support the thesis.

41j
Writing effective beginnings and endings

The beginning of a paper serves as a springboard into its subject and the assertion you are making about that subject. While there is no need to be "cute" in the introduction, it is important to think about the needs of your audience, purpose, and subject. The beginning should be strong enough to interest your audience in the subject and make them want to continue reading.

Journalists think in terms of writing a "hook" that will attract readers' attention and draw them into the story. Business people, on the other hand, write to get things done. For business readers, then, an effective beginning is one that clearly announces the subject and purpose of a document. Whereas an entertaining anecdote might be a good beginning for a magazine article, it probably would not be appropriate for the opening of a progress report from a manufacturing manager to corporate headquarters. The best advice is to consider the needs of your audience and purpose when evaluating the merits of a particular beginning or ending.

Important as a good beginning is, do not be overly concerned about it in your rough draft. If you think of a strong beginning, fine; but you may find that after drafting the paper your purpose is clearer and writing the opening is easier. Some people habitually compose the opening paragraph last, with good results. At least be prepared to perform major surgery on your opening. You may discover that the first few sentences you wrote in the rough draft were warm-ups and that a little revising will transform the third or fourth sentence into a good beginning.

EFFECTIVE BEGINNINGS

Following are some strategies for beginning papers effectively. They are almost certain to catch your reader's attention, so they well repay the time you spend to create them.

Consider beginning with a statement of fact, a startling statement, or an unusual detail.

41j

write

FACTUAL STATEMENT
Ninety-two percent of the students at State College live at home and commute.

STARTLING STATEMENT
There's a fine line between cheap and sleazy. I know. I recently drove right along it. Let me explain.

CARRIE DOLAN, " 'Little Lady' Suffers a Lapse of Luxury to Prove Boss Right"

UNUSUAL DETAIL
Grandmother Gardner didn't drink tea; she drank beer.

Consider beginning with a firm statement of opinion or a directly stated proposition.

OPINION
Stray dogs and cats are a nuisance, and they should be exterminated.

Television casts businessmen as villains. I have been writing about this for years and wondering what effect it had on viewers, particularly young ones. Recently, I explored the question . . . and confirmed my suspicion that youngsters do uncritically absorb business's overwhelmingly negative TV image.

BENJAMIN STEIN, "The Video Generation Gives
Business Low Ratings"

DIRECTLY STATED PROPOSITION — Because people who rarely talk together talk differently, differences in speech tell what group a man belongs to.

JAMES SLEDD, "Bi-Dialectalism: The Linguistics of
White Supremacy"

Consider beginning with a brief anecdote or incident that leads directly into your main topic.

BRIEF ANECDOTE — When Mark Twain left home at an early age, he had no great respect for his father's intelligence. When he returned a few years later, he was astonished at how much his father had learned in the meantime. I have been similarly astonished at how much both my father and mother have learned in the time I have been away from home.

Three-month-old Sameka Jackson is putting on a show for the child-development class. She demonstrates the standard reaction to bottle loss—a wail. Then, she shows how an infant tries to roll over. Sameka climaxes the exhibition by spitting up. Class discussion ensues.

JOHN HELYAR, "Will Mary Poppins Start Popping
Up All Over Chicago?"

41j
write

INEFFECTIVE BEGINNINGS

Avoid beginnings that are not self-explanatory. Don't make a reader refer to the title to find out the meaning of your paper's opening sentence. For example, a paper entitled "Nuclear Energy" that begins *Everyone is against it* opens vaguely and ineffectively, as does a paper giving instructions for building a model airplane that starts *The first thing to do is to lay all the parts on the table.*

Also avoid beginnings that start too far back. If you are writing a paper describing last Saturday's football game, get directly to the description; don't begin by explaining how you happened to go to the game. The writer of the following paragraphs should have begun with the second paragraph:

FATHER KNOWS BEST

You probably wonder from my title what I am going to write about. Well, it's a long story. It started back in 1970 when I was born. My mother announced to my father that I was a boy! "We're going to send him to State University!" my father exclaimed. So here I am at State, a member of the freshman class.

It was my father's idea from the first that I should come to State. He had been a student here in 1964 when he met my mother. . . .

If you want to complain about an assigned topic or apologize for what you have written, do so in a note attached to your paper. Never use your opening paragraph, or for that matter any part of your paper to do so.

> **COMPLAINT** Describing a building accurately is a very difficult task. Though it is a good assignment because it makes you look closely and observe details you would not otherwise notice, it takes considerable time and does not leave the student enough time to write the actual paper. I discovered this when I tried to observe and describe the university chapel.

> **APOLOGY** After trying unsuccessfully to write a paper describing my roommate, and then attempting to gather some new ideas on books I had read during the summer, I gave up and decided to write on my experience in reading *The Grapes of Wrath* by John Steinbeck. I hope this fits the assignment.

EFFECTIVE ENDINGS

With a strong opening, your paper gets off to a healthy start. A decisive conclusion lends it a finished, polished note. An effective ending echoes your introduction and brings your paper to a logical conclusion.

41j

write

Just as the nature of an introduction depends on the length and the complexity of the paper, so too does the conclusion. A paper of 500 words may require only a sentence or two, whereas a paper two or three times that length will probably need a paragraph to summarize its contents.

Consider concluding with a restatement of your thesis statement or with a quotation that illustrates your thesis.

> **THESIS RESTATED** Now that I have been here and have seen the school for myself, I am convinced that Father *does* know best. I have decided to enroll at State next term.

> **QUOTATION REFLECTING THESIS** I realize the image of chemistry is in such disrepair that it would take a major effort on all our parts to turn this around. . . . Most important, surely, is that we reach the general public and the politicians with the

message that chemistry is absolutely essential to our modern way of life. Let's revive the spirit once contained in the slogan, "Better things for better living through chemistry."

FRED BASOLO, "Let's Be Positive About Chemistry"

Consider summarizing the major ideas that you developed in your paper. A summary serves the double purpose of bringing your paper to a conclusion and of reminding your readers once more of the major points you discussed.

SUMMARY   As I have shown, all you need to build a model plane is a model to assemble, a little ingenuity, and a lot of patience. With these ingredients you can fill the friendly skies of your bedroom.

Consider a conclusion drawn from the facts you present. Especially if your purpose in a paper has been to argue a point of view, you need to write a conclusion that derives from the evidence or reasons you presented.

CONCLUSION
BASED ON
PRESENTED
FACTS

The fact that a state judge could seem almost casual about rape shows that beneath the new surface sensitivity, many of the cultural prejudices linger. "What we do in our society, whether it's in photography, films or language, is devalue sex," says Psychologist Groth, "and that gives the message that sex can become a weapon to degrade somebody." Such moral carelessness is what has made the U.S. violent in private, as well as in public.

MAUREEN DOWD, "Rape: The Sexual Weapon"

41j

write

Consider ending with a punch line. The punch-line ending usually contains an element of surprise or irony. It provides a twist, often somewhat humorous, that can be appealing, especially if it is consistent with the tone of the rest of your paper. The following ending effectively concludes an essay that argues that exercise can be a good remedy for writer's block.

PUNCH LINE   Give it a fair trial—three months, say, long enough for the novelty to wear off and for it to become a part of your routine. You may find, as I have, that exercise helps create a climate for the solution of writing problems. You may find only that it makes you feel better. On the other hand, it may be that all you get for your troubles is better health and longer life.

Listen, you can't win 'em all.

LAWRENCE BLOCK, "Fiction: Huffing and Puffing"

INEFFECTIVE ENDINGS

Don't end your paper by branching off into another aspect of the topic or by introducing new material. The ending of a paper should conclude what you have said. Readers are distracted and frustrated when you introduce at the paper's end a new, undeveloped idea. Don't conclude a description of how autumn appeals to you with a statement that says: "Even though autumn is a beautiful and exhilarating time of year, spring is still my favorite season." Such a sentence makes your reader wonder why you wrote about autumn in the first place.

And finally, never end your paper with an apology. Statements like the following harm a paper: "This is only my opinion, and I'm probably not really very well qualified to speak" or "I'm sorry this isn't a better paper, but I didn't have enough time." Such statements destroy the effect of whatever you have written. If you say that you have failed, your reader will probably agree with you.

EXERCISE 41j(1)

Look at articles in at least two different magazines (only one may be a news magazine). What sorts of beginnings and endings do you find? Do any of them fit the types discussed in Section 41j? Look at the beginning and ending of Brad's first draft (pp. 362 and 365). Do they fit any of the types discussed in Section 41j?

EXERCISE 41j(2)

Using one of the thesis statements you developed for Exercise 41h(4), write the rough draft of an essay. Try to notice the times when you stop drafting to do more planning or to reread and revise. In other words, try to become conscious of your own writing process—what you are doing when the writing goes well and what is happening when it does not.

41k

rev

41k

Revising: reviewing, evaluating, and rewriting

Throughout the writing process you will review what you have created, evaluate it to see if it fulfills the goals and purposes established during planning activities, and rewrite those portions that do not measure up. Changes that result from revision are of two fundamental, related types: surface changes and meaning changes. *Surface changes* are largely matters of correctness, convention, and style. Spelling, grammar, punctuation, sentence construction, word and sentence order, vocabulary choice are examples of surface changes. *Meaning changes* involve major additions of new content or deletions of existing content. Typical meaning changes include major changes in sentence and paragraph content, in the controlling idea and thesis statement, in organizational structure, in the authorial voice, in the purpose, or in the conception of the audience.

Sometimes revisions involving surface changes are referred to as *editing* and *proofreading*, while the term *revision* is reserved for activities involving meaning changes. However, sentence-level surface changes can certainly result in meaning changes. For example, the addition of a pair of commas that changes a restrictive modifier to a nonrestrictive one can substantially alter the meaning of a sentence and thus the whole gist of a paragraph. For this reason, revision here refers to any and all changes that result from reviewing and evaluating text—including proofreading for correctness and editing for word choice, sentence arrangement, paragraph construction, and so forth.

Although most people do some revising while they are drafting text, many writers like to make major revisions after they have finished all or a substantial part of their first draft. If the paper is long, they may revise after writing each section and then again when they have completed the entire paper. That way they can get a clearer sense of whether the text as a whole is measuring up to the goals they have set.

The key to revising is being able to see your paper critically. To *revise* means "to see again." Sometimes you may need at least a few hours, or even a few days, away from your writing to be able to revise it effectively. Being too closely involved with what you are writing can be a disadvantage to seeing it clearly and finding the weak spots. At other times, you may recognize the nagging sensation of "something wrong" while you are writing, and may find stopping right then and puzzling out the problem to be the most effective method. If you are afraid that stopping will cause you to lose an important train of thought, put a check mark or a brief note in the margin as a reminder for later revision, and go on with your writing.

Peer review can also be helpful in revising your paper. Ask another person to read your draft and point out errors and unclear, illogical, or poorly written spots. Having someone read your paper aloud to you, or reading it aloud yourself, can also reveal weaknesses you may have overlooked.

Many writers find it useful to separate reviewing for surface changes from reading for meaning changes. That way they don't fall victim to "memory overload," the problem of trying to pay attention to too many things at once.

At the end of this section appear the various drafts written by Brad Bolton and Tina Rodriguez. You will be able to see how they revised their texts between first and final drafts. In Brad's case, in addition to his own notes, you will also be able to see some of the comments his instructor wrote on his first draft.

Before reading their texts, review the following list of revision questions. Keeping these questions in mind will help you evaluate your own writing, as well as be a critical reader for Brad's and Tina's papers.

REVISION QUESTIONS

For meaning changes:

1. Do the choices of subject, purpose, and authorial voice or tone fit the needs of the audience and other constraints of the writing task? See Section **41c–f.**

2. Is the subject suitably focused? See Section **41h.**

3. Does the paper have a clearly stated or implied thesis? Do all the paragraphs support and develop the thesis—the controlling idea? In other words, does the paper show unity, clear and logical organization, and adequate development of ideas? Does it move in the direction you intend? See Sections **41h** and **41i.**

4. If you have used an outline (or other planning scheme), does the paper match that outline? If not, do your departures from it represent improvements? See Section **41g.**

5. Does each paragraph contain a specific topic sentence or indicate the topic clearly? See Section **42a.** Do all the sentences in each paragraph relate logically to the paragraph topic? See Sections **42b, 42c,** and **42g.**

6. Are all terms clearly defined and all assertions supported? See Section **43.**

7. Does the paper have an effective opening and a strong conclusion? See Section **41j.**

8. Finally, does the paper accomplish what you set out to do? Does it achieve its purpose and fulfill your goals? See Section **41f.**

41k

rev

For surface changes:

1. Is each sentence grammatically correct? Are there errors in pronoun or subject-verb agreement? See Sections **8** and **9.** In verb tense? See Section **5.**

2. Are the sentences complete? See Section **6a.** Are any sentences joined by a comma or by no punctuation at all? See Section **7.**

3. Are any sentences awkward or confusing because of dangling or misplaced modifiers? See Sections **11–14.** Are all the sentences logical and effective in their use of subordination, variety, parallelism, and emphasis? See Sections **31–34.**

4. Have you used correctly all commas, semicolons, periods, and other marks of punctuation? See Sections **19–24.**

5. Have you used correctly apostrophes, capitals, italics, abbreviations, and numbers? Are words hyphenated properly? See Sections

15–18 and **27–30.** If you used quoted material, did you quote and punctuate it correctly? See Sections **25–26.**

6.   Have you checked for misspelled words? See Section **40.** Use a dictionary to check any words you are not sure about. Are there any problems in usage—*lay* versus *lie,* for example? See Section **50.**

7.   Is the choice of words precise and appropriate for both your subject and your audience? See Sections **37–38.**

8.   Have you used words economically and effectively, avoiding wordiness and vagueness? See Section **39.**

EXERCISE 41k

Perform a final revision on the essay you drafted for Exercise 41j(2) or another document you have been writing recently. When you have finished, write a quick analysis of the types of changes you made during revision while you were drafting and the types of changes you made during the final revision. Did surface changes or meaning changes tend to occur more at one time than at the other? Were there more of either type than the other? How can this information help you improve your writing?

41l

A few words about word processing

Writing with a word processing program on a computer has become common on the job and at a number of colleges and universities. Both Tina and Brad, the writers featured in this section of the *Handbook,* used word processing to complete their writing tasks. If word processing is available to you, you should consider its advantages.

As shown previously in Section **41,** word processing can be useful for brainstorming. For some people, the computer screen stimulates creativity, giving them a sense of freedom to play with ideas— saving or deleting words as they choose. Being able to "see" their thinking on the screen in a form resembling print, undistracted by messy handwriting and crossed out sentences, is helpful to them. Some writers even see their computer screens as audiences, finding it easier to think about their readers' needs and expectations when they are using a computer.

Many writers also like the speed of word processing. They discover that, once they have mastered the keyboard, typing is much faster than writing with pen and paper and that they lose fewer ideas as a result. Furthermore, because the computer allows for the insertion of any number of lines between typed sections of text, it is possible to sketch in the bare bones of a paper—for example, an outline such as Tina prepared for her memo—and then draft paragraphs in between the headings without worrying about space constraints. You can hop easily around in the document at will, writing parts in any order that suits you.

Writers also like the ease with which the computer accommodates revisions. The ability to move words, sentences, even whole paragraphs and pages around with a few keystrokes enables writers to try out different arrangements of ideas, sentence structure, and word choice very quickly and easily—again without the clutter of messy hand-written cross-outs.

Ease of revision can be a drawback. Substituting revisions for previously written material deletes the old text. Thus, it is difficult to compare two versions without a printout of the previous draft; and dealing with a bunch of printouts can be both confusing and cumbersome. One way to remedy this problem is to type the revision just in front of the original material but not delete the original until you are satisfied that the revision is better. In other words, add as much new writing as you like, but think of it as an alternative. Only at the end, and perhaps after obtaining a printout and further considering the alternatives, delete all but the version you have decided to save as the final draft.

Probably the word processing characteristic writers cite most often is the way it facilitates creative revision: word processing positively encourages reviewing, evaluating, and rewriting. You can make changes in a draft without the visual mess and without the drudgery of recopying or retyping. But more and more writers are learning to rely on their computers for planning and invention as well. Most people who have learned to use the computer keyboard, even those who "hunt-and-peck" rather than touch-type, find that word processing frees them to concentrate on what they want to say and how they want to say it. As one writer said, "I feel free to create a text and move around inside it."

41l

Tina's memo: first draft with her notes for revisions

very busy people! Memo too unfocused — wastes time!!

To: Task force members
From: Tina Rodriguez
Date: March 14, 198–
Subject: Agenda for Tuesday's Meeting

redo first ¶ — condense background or omit

As you know, the company has been experiencing healthy growth over the past year. Orders have been increasing since October. In January, laid-off production employees were called back to work. Simultaneously, staff work has also increased. Earlier this month upper management decided to allocate new staff positions. Last week the vice president of human resources asked us to serve on a task force to investigate the staffing situation and recommend where new positions are critically needed. She says the budget allows for the creation of a total of six new jobs. I have been asked to set the agenda for our first meeting, which will be held on Tuesday at 9:30 a.m. in the third floor conference room.

too much background — readers know this stuff

memo starts too slowly — readers will quit before they get to the important info!

essential meeting info buried — move

awfully patronizing tone

I know some of you are probably not used to working from a set agenda. However, I feel that an agenda will provide structure for the meeting, promoting efficient handling of business. More important topics can be talked about first and less important matters can be ~~delt~~ dealt with if time permits. I also think that an agenda keeps people from spending time on ~~irelevant~~ irrelevant matters. An agenda distributed in advance also gives people the chance to think about topics beforehand and thus make better contributions to the meeting.

too many "I"'s — too much ego

Team = we

Here is the agenda I have set for Tuesday, along with time and decision goals:

sounds pretty dictatorial

move some of these reasons

* Develop criteria for creating new staff jobs
  Goal: Devise a formula for deciding how positions will be allocated
  Time: 30 minutes

this part OK

* Identify areas for new staff positions
  Goal: Choose areas that best fit criteria
  Time: 30 minutes

not enough time allotted here

* Select task force members to write report to vice ~~pres~~.
  Goal: Pick best author for each section
  Time: 15 minutes

president

* Other business: 15 minutes

I look forward to seeing each of you on Tuesday morning. If you have questions, please do not hesitate to ask.

stuffy business cliché — tired jargon

whole memo too long-winded — organization too round-about

Tina's memo: final draft after revision

```
     To:  Task force members
   From:  Tina Rodriguez
   Date:  March 14, 198–
Subject:  Agenda for March 18 meeting
```

The purpose of this memo is to let you know the agenda for our
first task force meeting, which is scheduled for next Tuesday at
9:30 a.m. in the third–floor conference room. The vice
president for human resources asked me to write up an agenda
based on the directions she gave us last week.

Since we will be trying to formulate some firm recommendations
about new staffing needs, this outline can help prepare us to
accomplish as much as possible on Tuesday morning. Below are
the major agenda items, along with time and decision goals:

```
    * Develop criteria for creating new staff jobs
        Goal:  Devise a formula for deciding how positions will
               be allocated
        Time:  30 minutes

    * Identify areas for new staff positions
        Goal:  Choose those areas that best fit criteria
        Time:  40 minutes

    * Select task force members to write report to vice
      president
        Goal:  Pick best author for each section of report
        Time:  10 minutes

    * Schedule date for next meeting. Other business.
        Goal:  Allow sufficient time for drafting report
        Time:  10 minutes
```

Having the agenda ahead of time should give everyone the chance
to think about issues beforehand. Also, a plan for the meeting
may help us handle business more efficiently and keep us from
going off on tangents.

Please call me at extension 523 if you have comments or
questions. See you all on Tuesday morning.

41

rev

WRITERS REVISING: THE WHOLE ESSAY

Read the following first draft of Brad Bolton's essay "My Most Memorable Experience." You don't need to revise his entire draft, but do mark the places where you think the essay needs improvement, as follows: (1) Make any surface changes you think are necessary; (2) Make notes about meaning changes you think would improve the essay. Then compare your revision suggestions with the changes Brad (blue ink) and his instructor (green ink) wrote on their copies of the draft. Finally, study the results of Brad's revision—the final draft, entitled "Truly a Learning Experience."

Brad's first draft

                  My Most Memorable Experience

Probably the most memorable experience in my life is the trip I took to Europe for six weeks. It is memorable for several reasons. They are: I explored new surroundings; I made lasting friends; and I experienced new cultures. All of this contributed to a general maturing that took place in me over the course of the six weeks that I spent in Europe. Here is how it happened.

London, England is the one city that I remember for the exploring that I did while there. In London on the last thursday of the trip I did some "real" exploring.

That morning at breakfast Judy, our teacher-leader, told us that we had the entire day free. We could do what ever we wanted. We were given our sack lunches and sent off. I, being an inexperienced shopper, don't like to shop for things that don't interest me. Consequently I went alone on this excursion. I planned to do some serious shopping, and I didn't want to waste time shopping for someone elses "important" items.

My first stop took me to that famed shopping

extravaganza, Harrods. Harrods is a stately, old
department store that just happens to serve the British
Royal family. I was overwhelmed at the selection and
quality of the merchandise that was on display there. I
can imagine what the employees thought of me as I gaped
at the fine merchandise on display. Such finery I had
never seen.

After purchasing two sweaters and thourghly
examining the first floor, I was hungry. I pulled out
my trusty map of London. Where to eat? Hmmn. . . ? Oh!
yes I've got a sack lunch. I almost forgot. I noticed
Hyde park was nearby, so I decided to walk there and
brown bag it in style.

As I look back, I realize that the day I spent in
London helped me to gain an independence that I had
never had before. I could actually take care of myself!
This, I feel, is an important step in my maturation
process.

As I look back, I can easily remember the night
Patti and I met a group of French students in Paris. We
were having a deep discussion on some important topic
when I noticed a group of students approach the area we
were sitting in the park. I became nervous. Since I
didn't speak French I had no way to communicate with
them. At first I thought that they were going to mugg
us. One of them asked me a question (in French of
course). I was astounded.

I replied, "I don't speak any French." This
seemed to puzzle them.

However, one replied, "Are you American?"

I almost freaked out! I couldn't believe that he

41

rev

spoke English. I replied, "You speak English! WOW!
How old are all of you? . . ."

From the conversation that ensued Patti and I
learned much about France and the French. We talked of
favorite rock groups, favorite languages, and common
pasttimes. During the whole conversation the one that
spoke English acted as a translator. Now as I look
back, I realize, I realize that this particular
experience helped to broaden my people-meeting skills.
This experience was fairly tipical. In almost every
city we were in we met and talked to total strangers.
These spontaneous talks I will never forget.

At our homestay in Bavaria (Germany), our hosts
threw a going away cookout part on the last night of our
stay. At the cookout we had steaks, baked potatoes,
bratwurst, pretzels, and of course beer. I think that
this particular experience is memorable because of the
good time that was had by all. We had a bon-fire,
around which we told tall tales and ghost stories until
the wee hours of the morning. Besides the tall tales, I
enjoyed talking with my hosts. The neatest thing was
their command of languages. The German youths could
speak at least two languages fluently, and they often
were knowledgable in a couple of other languages. I
remember we talked of politics, rock music, and common
interests. At the end I can remember many of my hosts
and travel companions crying because they all knew they
wuld mis their new friends and might never see them
again.

In Austria I spent an unforgettable week with the
Staudlbauer family. As I look back now I realize that

41

rev

the entire week I was learning about their culture. At
the time, however, I didn't think of the significance of
this particular homestay. One evening my homestay
mother cooked cooked a typical Austrian meal that
included Rindsbraten (pork roast), sauerkraut, knudel
(dumplings), and a salad. After dinner my homestay
father, Peter, and brother, Patrick, and I took a
liesurely bike ride on some of the nearby country roads.
While riding we spoke of politics, business, athletics,
farming, and life in general. The irony was that my
father said he didn't speak any English, but the entire
conversation was in English. I spoke very slowly and he
followed along the best he could, nodding where it was
appropriate. Occasionly he would say, "Ja." I think
that he knew more English than he led me to believe. As
time progressed I became very fond of Austrian customs
and my homestay family. On the last day of the homestay
I can remember seeing tears in Peter's eyes. I resolved
to someday go back and visit. As our bus left the small
town of 5,000 I can remember feeling a pang in my
throat. I, too, would miss the Staudlbauers.

   In summation I feel that the trip did several
things for me. It helped to broaden my views through
showing me different view points. It helped to increase
my independence through my exploration of the big cities
I visited. As I look back I realize that I am now more
mature. I'm not really sure if there was one incident
that has made me more mature, but instead I think it was
a more gradual process in which the entire trip played a
good part. All of this has made the trip a very
unforgetable part of my life.

41

rev

Brad's revision-in-progress (blue), with instructor's comments (green)

boring title!

My Most Memorable Experience *combine sentences*

When? Reader will want to ~~know~~
Probably, the most (memorable experience) in my life
is the trip I took to Europe for six weeks. (It is
22 B
memorable) for several reasons. They are: I explored new

surroundings; I made lasting friends; and I experienced

new cultures. All of this contributed to a general

maturing that took place in me over the course of the

six weeks that I spent in Europe. Here is how it

happened.

London, England is the one city that I remember
redundant
for the (exploring that I did while there.) In London on

the last Thursday of the trip (I did some (w)real(w) *25i*

exploring.)

no new ¶ (same topic)
That morning at breakfast Judy, our teacher-leader, *20 b*.

told us that we had the entire day free. We could do
whatever
~~what ever~~ we wanted. We were given our sack lunches and

sent off. ~~I, being an inexperienced shopper, don't like~~

~~to shop for things that don't interest me.~~ Consequently

Order of ideas:
I went alone on this excursion. I planned to do some *is this*

serious shopping, and I didn't want to waste time *chronology*

shopping for someone elses "important" items. *logical?*

was
My first stop ~~took me to~~ that famed shopping

extravaganza, Harrods. Harrods is a stately, old
tone: attempt at humor may seem like snobbery to some readers
department store that just happens to serve the British

Royal family. I was overwhelmed at the selection and

quality of the merchandise that was on display there. I

can imagine what the employees thought of me as I gaped

at the fine merchandise on display. Such finery I had
Put some flesh on these bones, Brad. We need to see
never seen. *Concrete examples to understand why you*
were overwhelmed.

41
rev

The Writing Process

After purchasing two sweaters and ~~thourghly~~ *thoroughly*
examining the first floor, I was hungry. I pulled out

my trusty map of London. Where to eat? Hmmn. . . ? Oh!
Effective use of present-tense "thoughts" to pull reader into the picture
yes! I've got a sack lunch. I almost forgot. I noticed

Hyde park was nearby, so I decided to walk there and

brown bag it in style. *What made it stylish? not clear*

Notice how often you repeat these phrases. (As I look back) (I realize) that the day I spent in
London helped me to gain an independence that I had *not enough previous evidence to support generalization*
never had before. I could actually take care of myself!

This, I feel, is an *wordy—why d remember London so well* important step in my maturation

process.

As I look back, I can easily remember the night
another student-ambassador
Patti and I met a group of French students in Paris. We
sitting on a park bench
were having a deep discussion ~~on some important topic~~
ing us
when I noticed a group of students approach ~~the area we~~
~~were sitting in the park.~~ I became nervous. Since I
20b
didn't speak French I had no way to communicate to them.
mug—why did you think
At first I thought that they were going to ~~mugg~~ us. One
so?
of them asked me a question (in French of course). I
Give reason
was astounded. *Why? Explain*

I replied, "I don't speak any French." This
seemed to puzzle them.

However, one replied, "Are you American?" *dialogue draws reader into scene. Good!*

I almost <u>freaked out</u>! I couldn't believe that he
spoke English. I replied, "You speak English! <u>WOW</u>!
voice: conflicting tones here—
How old are all of you? . . ." *slang jars with sophisticated vocabulary*
In
we discussed
~~From~~ the conversation that <u>ensued</u> ~~Patti and I~~
~~learned much about France and the French. We talked of~~
favorite rock groups, favorite languages, and common
sp (pasttimes). During the whole conversation the one that
spoke English acted as a translator. (Now as I look)

back, I realize ~~I realize~~ that this particular

not really the point

experience helped to broaden my people-meeting skills.

typical

This experience was fairly ~~tipical~~. In almost every

city we were in we met and talked to total strangers.

here's the point!

These spontaneous talks I will never forget.

audience—what's a homestay?

At our (homestay) in Bavaria (Germany), our hosts

30 b

threw a going away cookout part on the last night of our

stay. At the cookout we had steaks, baked potatoes,

bratwurst, pretzels, and of course beer. I think that

this particular experience is memorable because of the

yuck! horrible cliché—says nothing

good time that was had by all. We had a (bon-fire),

this & goes nowhere. French & Austrian examples make same point with better detail. Cut!

around which we told tall tales and ghost stories until

another cliché!

the wee hours of the morning. Besides the tall tales, I

37 b

enjoyed talking with my hosts. The neatest thing was

their command of languages. The German youths could

speak at least two languages fluently, and they often

were (knowledgable) in a couple of other languages. (I

(remember) we talked of politics, rock music, and common

interests. At the end (I can remember) many of my hosts

and travel companions crying because they all knew they

wuld mis their new friends and might never see them

again.

In Austria I spent an unforgettable week with the

Staudlbauer family. (As I look back now I realize) that

the entire week I was learning about their culture. At

the time, however, I didn't think of the significance of

Brad, this paragraph is mostly unfocused narrative

this particular homestay. One evening my homestay

mother cooked ~~cooked~~ a typical Austrian meal that

too many topics in ¶: controlling idea?

included Rindsbraten (pork roast), sauerkraut, knudel

(dumplings), and a salad. After dinner my homestay

father, Peter, and brother, Patrick, and I took a

~~*leisurely*~~ bike ride on some of the nearby country roads. *[leisurely]*

~~While riding~~ We spoke of politics, business, athletics, *[conversation,]*

farming, and life in general. ~~The irony was that~~ My *not father* *[ironically ironic]*

father said he didn't speak any English, but ∧the entire

conversation was in English. I spoke very slowly and he

followed along the best he could, nodding where it was *[audience: will readers know]* *[what's your point here?]*

appropriate. ~~Occasionly~~ *Occasionally* he would say, ("Ja.") I think *[what this word means?]*

that he knew more English than he led me to believe. As *[Ideas not related — need transition]*

time progressed I became very fond of Austrian customs

and my homestay family. On the last day of the homestay

(I can remember) seeing tears in Peter's eyes. I resolved

to someday go back and visit. As our bus left the small

town of 5,000 (I can remember) feeling a pang in my

throat. I, too, would miss the Staudlbauers. *[voice: very pompous language — not consistent with other vocabulary]*

In summation I feel that the trip ~~did several~~ *made me* *[.]*

~~things for me.~~ It helped to broaden my views through

showing me different view points. It helped to increase

my independence through my exploration of the big cities

I visited. (As I look back) (I realize) that I am now (more)

(mature.) I'm not really sure if there was one incident *[say something about friendships]*

that has made me more mature, but instead I think it was

a more gradual process in which the entire trip played a *[awful!]*

good part. All of this has made the trip a very

unforgetable part of my life. *[A weak ending, Brad. Also, check your final paragraph against your thesis paragraph. Consistent? Purpose fulfilled?]*

Brad's final draft

Truly a Learning Experience

Probably the most memorable experience in my life

is the six-week trip I took to Europe last summer as a

student ambassador in a youth exchange program. In

Europe I explored new surroundings, made lasting

friends, and experienced new cultures. All of this
contributed to a general maturing that took place in me
over the course of the six weeks. Here is a small
portion of how it happened.

London, England, is the one city that I remember
for the exploring that I did while there. In London on
the last Thursday of the trip, Judy, our teacher-leader,
told us at breakfast that we had the entire day free.
We could do whatever we wanted. We were given our sack
lunches and sent off. I planned to do some serious
shopping, and I didn't want to waste time shopping for
someone else's "important" items. Consequently, I
chose to go alone on my excursion.

My first stop was that famed shopping extravaganza,
Harrods. Harrods is a stately, old department store
that serves the British Royal family. I figured that if
it was good enough for Charles and Di, then it must be
good enough for me. I had been told what a fine store
Harrods was, but words just didn't do it justice.

Remembering Harrods now is like remembering
Christmas as a little boy. As I walked into this place,
a feeling of awe came over me. I simply stared in
wonder. But soon, like a boy at Christmas, I wanted to
examine the goodies. Browsing the first floor, I found
the men's section. In this area I saw the finest
clothing I had ever seen: pure cashmere sweaters in the
trendiest styles, velour robes that only wealthy
businessmen could afford to wear. Anything a man would
want, it was here.

I must have looked rather strange as I gaped at all
of the fine merchandise. I'm sure I looked much like

41

rev

the Russians shopping in New York at Bloomingdale's in the movie <u>Moscow on the Hudson.</u>

I had only covered one of Harrods six floors when my stomach reminded me that I was starved. Leaving the store in search of a place to eat, I pulled out my trusty map of London. Where to eat? Hmmn. . . ? Oh, yes! I've got a sack lunch. I almost forgot. I noticed that Hyde Park was nearby, so I decided to walk there and brown bag it in style on a park bench. Refueled, I then took the subway (the "tube," as Londoners call it) and rode to Oxford Circus, another of London's famous shopping districts.

I spent the afternoon in several department stores (none as impressive as Harrods), in a store that claimed to be the world's largest toy store, and in a store that advertised itself as London's largest record store—four floors of records and tapes! As I left the record store, I glanced at my watch and decided that I needed to find the hotel if I wanted to get fed that night. Heading toward the tube stop, I blended in with hundreds of other Londoners on their way home.

As I look back, I think that the day I spent shopping in London helped me to gain an independence that I had never before experienced. I discovered I could actually take care of myself in a totally unfamiliar foreign city. This is why London is still so memorable to me.

Sitting here at college, I recall a special evening in Paris. Patti, another student-ambassador, and I were seated on a park bench, enjoying a deep discussion. Everything was very peaceful in the park, a small one on

41

rev

a corner near our hotel. Suddenly there were intruders:
I noticed a group of students approaching us, about to
ruin the evening's peacefulness. I can remember a
feeling of nervousness came over me as the students sat
down next to us on one of the park's three benches. The
quiet, the deepening darkness, the approach of these
strangers . . . I had a weird feeling that we were about
to be mugged. I'm sure that I jumped three feet when
finally one of them spoke. I didn't know what he said,
because I don't speak any French.

"I don't speak French," I replied nervously and
slowly so that the strangers could understand me.

"You are Americans? No?"
I certainly hadn't expected any of them to address me in
English.

I responded, "You speak English?"

"Yes, I try," the student said.

In the following conversation we discussed the
differences between French and American school systems,
rock music, and favorite pastimes. Patti and I were
fascinated with the fact that the French student could
speak two languages. I asked many questions about his
mastery of English. Probably most fascinating—and
difficult to comprehend—was that all of these students
loved their native language. I really couldn't care
less which language I speak, while the French love to
hear the sound of their own language.

Looking back, I realize that during the entire
conversation I was learning about French culture. I
found the talking to the students very stimulating for
the simple fact that I was learning about their world.

41

rev

Furthermore, I enjoyed the spontaneity of the conversation. Meeting and talking with total strangers in the middle of a foreign city was a unique and exciting experience. For these reasons, I will never forget that evening in Paris.

In Austria, I spent a week living with the Staudlbauer family. Several of these "homestays" were part of our trip. Not until sometime later did I realize the significance of this particular homestay. One evening my homestay mother cooked a typical Austrian meal: Rindsbraten (pork roast), sauerkraut, knudel (dumplings), and a salad. After dinner my homestay father, Peter, and brother, Patrick, and I took a leisurely bicycle ride on some of the nearby country roads.

We spoke of politics, business, athletics, farming, and life in general. My father claimed that he didn't speak any English, but ironically the whole conversation was in English. As Patrick and I talked, I spoke slowly and Peter followed along as best he could, nodding where it was appropriate. Occasionally he would say "Ja" ("yes") in response or agreement. Although he may have felt he could not "speak" English, I believe he understood quite a bit. Any language barrier seemed much less important than his participation in the conversation. I really liked my homestay father for that.

When we said goodbye on the last day of the homestay, I saw tears in Peter's eyes. I, too, felt a pang in my throat as our bus left the small Austrian town of 5,000. I would miss the Staudlbauers, and I

41

rev

resolved to go back someday and visit. But next time I
intend to go back knowing how to speak German, so that I
can talk with Peter in his own language.

I feel that the trip has made me more mature. It
helped to broaden my views through exposing me to
different viewpoints. It helped to increase my
independence through my exploration of the big cities
that we visited. Most of all, the trip has taught me to
be open to new experiences and, especially, new people.
Again and again, strangers became friends—sometimes in
the course of several days, sometimes in the course of
an hour or two. Because of these things, last summer's
trip is an unforgettable part of my life.

42

EFFECTIVE PARAGRAPHS

What does the term "paragraph" really signify? If you say something like "a collection of sentences that should begin with an inden-
tion and that should explain a controlling idea," you would not be
wrong. That, in brief, is what paragraphing is all about. Because we
have spent a good deal of our lives reading paragraphs, we have expectations about what they should do—based on what we have seen
them do in the writing of others. Paragraphs package the writer's
meaning for the reader.

When you initially draft a paragraph, your major concern is
probably just getting your ideas down before you forget them. The
actual contents and shape of the paragraph are the result of your
planning decisions about your subject and purpose, attitude toward
the subject, the nature of the audience, the voice or role you have
assumed, and other goals that are part of the process of writing.

What, then, do readers expect the paragraph packages to provide? They expect things like *unity* that derives from a *controlling idea*
around which the paragraph is organized; *coherence* that links the
thoughts within the paragraph, as well as relating the paragraph to
those that precede and follow it; sufficient *development* to explain and
illustrate the controlling idea. You may ask, "Do readers really expect

these things? And how do I provide them if I'm busy fulfilling my plans and trying to get my ideas down?" The answer to the first question is yes: we know from research studies that unity, coherence, and development are important to readers' mental ability to perceive and understand meaning. The answer to the second question is you don't try to do everything at once: some effective paragraphing may come on the first try, but much of it will result from revision, looking at your rough draft paragraphs and reworking them.

Granted, these abstract terms—unity, coherence, and development—may not seem very meaningful to you, but you can recognize the problems that occur in paragraphs lacking any of these three elements.

PARAGRAPH LACKING UNITY

Club Tropic's beaches are beautiful, and the surrounding countryside is quite scenic. The quality of the food leaves a lot to be desired. Many vacationers enjoy the variety of outdoor activities and the instruction available in such sports as sailing and scuba diving. Unfortunately, security is poor; several vacationers' rooms have been broken into and their valuables stolen. Christmas in the Bahamas can make the thought of New Year's in Chicago bearable.

The paragraph lacking unity jumps from subject to subject with no clear sense of goal or purpose. What have scenery, food, sports, and security to do with each other? Until the author provides a controlling idea to unite the sentences and give them focus, we will never know.

Compare the following revision with the original version. Notice that the writer has supplied a controlling topic sentence at the beginning and eliminated those sentences that do not contribute to the paragraph's main idea. As a result, the paragraph's concluding sentence now makes sense.

42

¶

UNIFIED PARAGRAPH WITH TOPIC SENTENCE

For vacationers sick and tired of the frozen north, a week at Club Tropic can provide just the midwinter thaw they need. Club Tropic's beaches are beautiful, and the surrounding countryside is quite scenic. Many vacationers also enjoy the variety of outdoor activities and the instruction available in such sports as sailing and scuba diving. Christmas in the Bahamas can make the thought of New Year's in Chicago bearable.

The next example paragraph, showing lack of coherence, contains a topic sentence, and all the other sentences bear some relation to that controlling idea: vacationers' dissatisfaction. However, the individual sentences are not knit together in any meaningful way. Because ideas are not clearly connected, the paragraph doesn't "stick together."

PARAGRAPH LACKING COHERENCE

Club Tropic's isolation created dissatisfaction among some vacationers. The quality of the food was poor. People want a choice of entertainment in the evening. Most of us spent too much time together day after day. People expect to be able to go out for a meal if they feel like it.

Compare the following revision with the original. Notice how the writer has used transition words and a new organization, among other things, to establish logical relationships among ideas.

COHERENT PARAGRAPH

Club Tropic's isolation created dissatisfaction among some vacationers. Many people expect to be able to go out for a meal if they feel like it, but the club's location far from populated areas made that impossible. To make matters worse, the quality of the food was poor. The isolated location also forced people to spend all their time together—day after day. By evening nearly everyone was ready for a choice of food, entertainment, and company.

The following example paragraph, lacking development, leaves too many questions in the reader's mind.

PARAGRAPH LACKING DEVELOPMENT

A vacation at Club Tropic has its good points and bad points. The beaches are nice, but they may not be enough for some vacationers.

42

¶

Only one "good point" (nice beaches) is mentioned. Are there others? No example of a bad point is given, so how is the reader to judge whether nice beaches are enough to attract vacationers to Club Tropic? And what, exactly, does "enough" mean? If the reader is to understand the controlling idea, or even be interested in it, it must be explained and supported sufficiently. Compare the original with the following revision.

DEVELOPED PARAGRAPH

A midwinter vacation at Club Tropic has its good points and bad points. The beaches are clean and uncrowded. The surrounding countryside is lush and soothing to winter-weary eyes. Furthermore, being able to take sailing and scuba diving lessons, while friends back home shovel snow, makes the outdoor activities extra-enjoyable. On the other hand, several features of Club Tropic are substandard. The food is poor, and, because the club is isolated, eating elsewhere is impossible. Security could also be better, as thefts from several guests' rooms indicated. So, for some vacationers, nice scenery and fun activities may not be enough to offset the possibility of poor service and lax security.

By now you should have some idea of the differences between paragraphs with and without unity, coherence, and development. An important key, as always, is your reader. You may know perfectly well what you mean, what point you are trying to make in any given paragraph. You may be able to see it all in your mind's eye. But your readers cannot. They have not lived your life, do not necessarily share your perceptions, and should not be asked to "read between the lines."

When you ask your audience to infer or guess what you mean, to supply the connections between ideas, to think of examples that might support your generalizations or fill in the details that would put flesh on the bare bones of your statements, you are asking for trouble—for audience impatience and misunderstanding.

As in any piece of writing, your paragraphs should respond to the questions "What do I want to say?" "To whom do I want to say it?" "How do I want to say it?" These questions, as always, respond to the larger question "*Why* do I want to say it?" What is your goal, and have you constructed a paragraph that will accomplish that goal?

42a
Paragraph unity: using a controlling idea

A unified paragraph has a single clear focus, and all its sentences relate to that focus. As we noted in the Club Tropic example, any unrelated sentence seems to be off the subject and thus destroys the paragraph's unity. The focus for a paragraph is achieved by means of a **controlling idea** around which the paragraph is organized, just as the focus of a whole essay is achieved by means of a controlling idea. In an essay that idea appears in the thesis, either clearly implied or explicitly stated. Similarly, in a paragraph the controlling idea is clearly implied or, more commonly, explicitly stated in the **topic sentence.**

42a

¶ *un*

Like a thesis statement, a topic sentence presents the subject of the paragraph in the subject position of the sentence. The predicate contains the focus words, the assertion being made about the subject. Sometimes this main idea is expressed as a generalization, and the rest of the paragraph provides the supporting evidence, concrete examples, and explanatory detail. The first sample paragraph that follows in this section (p. 379) shows a topic-sentence generalization with supporting details.

The exact nature of a topic sentence will depend on the purpose of the paragraph. For example, some paragraphs are meant merely to deliver information without making a particularly forceful assertion about the information. A paragraph about parent-child bonding might have as its topic sentence *Touching is one of the main ways bonding occurs between a mother and her newborn* and then go on to describe other types of bonding behavior as well, without the reader's feeling the paragraph has become disunified. This topic sentence can be described as having rather loose control over its paragraph. Other topic sentences present stronger assertions, going beyond statements of fact to make arguable propositions. These types of topic sentences often exert strong control, defining more sharply what ideas are and are not relevant to the paragraph. The topic sentence *Some of the problems of psychologically disturbed children can be traced to a lack of bonding in infancy* allows for no digressions if the paragraph is to fulfill readers' expectations concerning unity. This paragraph will go about the business of showing a cause-and-effect relationship between parent-child bonding and psychological problems. Both types of topic sentences can be appropriate for their contexts; after all, paragraphs perform a variety of functions—from introducing a subject to providing transition between the events in a narrative to summarizing the points of an argument.

Research has shown that from the reader's standpoint the best place for a topic sentence is the beginning of a paragraph. Understanding will be quicker and more complete if the reader has a general idea of the subject and where the writer is headed with it. Topic sentences provide this information—which explains why your English teachers have often encouraged you to start your paragraphs with a topic sentence.

42a

¶ *un*

But we also know from observation that many excellent writers and many, many quite satisfactory paragraphs do not position the topic sentence first. The explanation is that what readers need is an initial sentence that orients them, provides an appropriate frame of reference for relating new information to what they already know (or have read), an opening sentence that readies readers to understand "what this is going to be about." This orienting sentence need not be the topic sentence.

The emphatic positions in paragraphs are the same as in sentences—first and last. As readers, we expect to find the key information first. If it's not delivered in the form of a topic sentence, then some other orienting words must be supplied. When they are not, we have to make inferences and build our own meanings—a time-consuming and risky business, since we are apt to create meanings quite different from the writer's intention.

The following paragraphs illustrate various placements for the topic sentence. When it is not positioned first in a paragraph, note how the writer initially orients the reader.

The topic sentence may be the first sentence of the paragraph. Such paragraphs state their central idea first and then add details supporting it. This kind of paragraph occurs in expository writing, but it also appears in persuasive and descriptive writing as well.

TOPIC SENTENCE FIRST

The ENCYCLOPAEDIA BRITANNICA, *although a valuable research tool, is difficult to read and hard to handle—hardly designed for the hasty researcher.* Each article is thorough and detailed, but the tiny print is extremely hard to read. To be assured of getting every fact and detail, the researcher needs a strong light and, unless his eyes are keen, a magnifying glass. To pick up a volume in the first place, one needs both hands. One doesn't balance a *Britannica* volume in one hand while scribbling furiously with the other. A table or desk to lay the volume open on is absolutely necessary. But even sitting comfortably at a desk with a *Britannica* presents problems. To avoid crushing or tearing the onion-thin pages requires slow, deliberate, careful moves. Haste or carelessness could easily result in obliterating the whole article one wishes to read. Given these disadvantages to using the *Encyclopaedia Britannica,* fly-by-night researchers should consider other general reference books.

Student paragraph

A paragraph's first sentence may combine a transition from the preceding paragraph with the topic statement of the new paragraph. In the following example, the references to Dawson's location and size allude to topics in the paragraph preceding the one reproduced here; the clause in italics states the topic of the example paragraph.

TRANSITIONAL INFORMATION AND TOPIC SENTENCE FIRST

Although it lay in the shadow of the Arctic Circle, more than four thousand miles from civilization, and although it was the only settlement of any size in a wilderness area that occupied hundreds of thousands of square miles, *Dawson was livelier, richer, and better equipped than many larger Canadian and American communities.* It had a telephone service, running water, steam heat, and electricity. It had dozens of hotels, many of them better appointed than those on the Pacific Coast. It had motion-picture theaters operating at a time when the projected motion picture was just three years old. It had restaurants where string orchestras played *Cavalleria Rusticana* for men in tailcoats who ate pâté de fois gras and drank vintage wines. It had fashions from Paris. It had dramatic societies, church choirs, glee clubs, and vaudeville companies. It had three hospitals, seventy physicians, and uncounted platoons of lawyers. Above all, it had people.

PIERRE BERTON, *The Klondike Fever*

42a

¶ *un*

The topic sentence may be the last sentence of the paragraph. Such paragraphs give details first and lead up to the main point in the final sentence.

TOPIC SENTENCE LAST

Beginning at breakfast with flying globs of oatmeal, spilled juice, and toast that always lands jelly-side down, a day with small children grows into a nightmare of frantic activity, punctuated with shrieks, cries, and hyena-style laughs. The very act of playing turns the house into a disaster area: blankets and sheets that are thrown over tables and chairs to form caves, miniature cars and trucks that race endlessly up and down hallways, and a cat that becomes a caged tiger, imprisoned under the laundry basket. After supper, with more spilled milk, uneaten vegetables, and tidbits fed to the cat under the table, it's finally time for bed. But before they fall blissfully asleep, the children still have time to knock over one more bedtime glass of water, jump on the beds until the springs threaten to break, and demand a last ride to the bathroom on mother's back. *Constant confusion is a way of life for parents of small children.*

Student paragraph

The topic sentence may appear first and last. In such paragraphs the last sentence repeats the idea of the first, frequently restating it with some amplification or a slightly different emphasis in the light of the intervening details or discussion.

TOPIC SENTENCES FIRST AND LAST

A metal garbage can lid has many uses. In the spring it can be used to catch rainwater in which a small boy can create a world of his own, a world of dead leaves and twigs inhabited by salamanders, small frogs, and worms. In the summer it can be turned on its top, the inside lined with aluminum foil, and used to hold charcoal for a barbecue. In the fall it can be used, with a similar lid, to frighten unsuspecting Halloween "trick-or-treaters." In the winter, if the handle is removed or flattened, the lid can be used by children to speed down snow-packed hills. *A garbage can lid covers garbage most of the time, but with a little imagination, one can uncover new uses for it.*

Student paragraph

42a

¶ *un*

Finally, the topic sentence may be—and often is—implied. Sometimes a writer may decide not to use an explicitly stated topic sentence. This is frequently the case in narrative and descriptive paragraphs, but it can also be appropriate in other types of writing. Your reader should be able to state the controlling idea if asked to do so. In the following paragraph by Joan Didion, for example, the controlling idea might be stated thus: "Though the sources of one's childhood imaginings are long lost, the record of those imaginings perhaps reveals lifelong habits of mind."

NO EXPLICIT TOPIC SENTENCE; IMPLIED CONTROLLING IDEA

My first notebook was a Big Five tablet, given to me by my mother with the sensible suggestion that I stop whining and learn to amuse myself by writing down my thoughts. She returned the tablet to me a few years ago; the first entry is an account of a woman who believed herself to be freezing to death in the Arctic night, only to find, when day broke, that she had stumbled onto the Sahara Desert, where she would die of the heat before lunch. I have no idea what turn of a five-year-old's mind could have prompted so insistently "ironic" and exotic a story, but it does reveal a certain predilection for the extreme which has dogged me into adult life; perhaps if I were analytically inclined I would find it a truer story than any I might have told about Donald Johnson's birthday party or the day my cousin Brenda put Kitty Litter in the aquarium.

JOAN DIDION, "On Keeping a Notebook"

EXERCISE 42a(1)

Following are two topic sentences, each accompanied by a set of statements. Some of the statements are relevant to the topic, some are not. Eliminate the irrelevant ones, and organize the rest into a paragraph.

1. The wreck on Route 64 at Mt. Nixon was caused entirely by careless and reckless driving by the driver of the Buick.

   When the wreck occurred the lights were green for the cars coming off the side road.

   A heavy truck loaded with hay was pulling out to cross the highway.

   The Buick came speeding down the main road, went through the stoplight, and crashed into the truck.

   You could hear the screeching of the tires and then the crashing and grinding of metal a quarter of a mile away.

   You could hear it in our house up the road.

   Both drivers dead, I will never forget that horrible accident.

2. We owe some of our notions of radar to scientific observation of bats.

   Most people hate bats.

   Bats are commonly considered unattractive, ugly creatures.

   They really look more like mice with wings than anything else.

   Scientists noticed that bats rarely collided with anything in their erratic flight.

   Keen eyesight could not be the reason for their flying the way they do, since bats are blind.

   It was found that bats keep sending out noises inaudible to people and that they hear the echoes of those noises.

   This principle whereby they fly safely was found to be similar to the main principle of radar.

42a

¶ *un*

EXERCISE 42a(2)

What is the topic sentence, expressed or implied, in each of the following paragraphs?

1. Restaurants have always treated children badly. When I was small my family used to travel a lot, and waitresses were forever calling me "Butch" and pinching my cheeks and making me wear paper bibs with slogans on them. Restaurants still treat children badly; the

difference is that restaurants have lately taken to treating us all as if we were children. We are obliged to order an Egg McMuffin when we want breakfast, a Fishamajig when we want a fish sandwich, a Fribble when we want a milkshake, a Whopper when we want a hamburger with all the fixings. Some of these names serve a certain purpose. By calling a milkshake a Fribble, for instance, the management need make no promise that it contains milk, or even that it was shaken.

ANDREW WARD, "Yumbo"

2.   Through photographs, each family constructs a portrait-chronicle of itself—a portable kit of images that bears witness to its connectedness. It hardly matters what activities are photographed so long as photographs get taken and are cherished. Photography becomes a rite of family life just when, in the industrializing countries of Europe and America, the very institution of the family starts undergoing radical surgery. As that claustrophobic unit, the nuclear family, was being carved out of a much larger family aggregate, photography came along to memorialize, to restate symbolically, the imperiled continuity and vanishing extendedness of family life. Those ghostly traces, photographs, supply the token presence of the dispersed relatives. A family's photograph album is generally about the extended family—and, often, is all that remains of it.

SUSAN SONTAG, "In Plato's Cave"

3.   Every writer has his own ways of getting started, from sharpening pencils, to reading the Bible, to pacing the floor. I often rinse out my mind by reading something, and I sometimes manage to put off getting down to the hard struggle for an unconscionable time. Mostly I am helped through the barrier by music. I play records while I am writing and especially at the start of each day one particular record that accompanies the poem or chapter I am working at. During these last weeks it has been a record by Albinoni for strings and organ. I do not always play that key record, but it is there to draw on—the key to a certain piece of work, the key to that mood. The romantic composers, much as I enjoy listening to them at other times, are no help. Bach, Mozart, Vivaldi—they are what I need— clarity and structure.

MAY SARTON, "The Art of Writing"

4.   An atmosphere that is a strange mixture of bleakness, tranquillity, and expectancy pervades the downstairs hall of the old gym early in the morning. As I walk from the chilly dawn outdoors into the basement of the old gym, I feel the dry heat on my face; although I assume that I am alone, I am surrounded by the impersonal noises of an antiquated steam-heating system. All the doors, which stand like sentries along the walls of the hallway, are locked, so that the deserted nature of that place and that hour are apparent; pipes hang from above, making the ceiling resemble the ugly, rarely viewed underside of a bizarre animal. I feel peaceful, however, in this lonely place, because of the silence. I know, moreover, that the

42a

¶ *un*

desertlike heat is a sign that preparation has been made for my arrival and a signal that the day of work is about to begin.

Student paragraph

5.   Fish *love* lures. They gather together in little lure-appreciation groups, called "schools," and howl with laughter when the lures go by. It's their major form of entertainment, and they don't want to lose it, so every now and then they draw lots and the loser has to bite the lure and get caught. This encourages the fishermen to continue.

DAVE BARRY, "How to Kill Fish"

42b

Paragraph coherence: organizing ideas

A coherent paragraph moves logically from thought to thought, knitting the thoughts together in an orderly way. The ideas should flow into one another so that their relation to the paragraph's main point is clear. Unfortunately, "flow" is difficult to define, although its absence is easy to detect.

You can apply several strategies to achieve coherence in your paragraphs as you write them or to check for it as you revise and edit them. One strategy is to use organizational structures both familiar to your reader and appropriate to the development of your paragraph's controlling idea. These structures are also used to organize whole essays (see Section **41**).

Organization can help readers understand your ideas because it provides a familiar shape, a built-in structural logic that can aid the reader. Organizational structure alone can't make a paragraph coherent; Sections **42c** and **42d** explain other types of structure necessary to coherent paragraphs.

42b

¶ *coh*

ORGANIZATIONAL OPTIONS

1. Time. Narrative paragraphs naturally arrange themselves in the order in which the events occur, as in this paragraph recounting the death of an eagle. Such ordering of events is *chronological.*

CHRONOLOGICAL ORDER

On her own, one of the female's bold hunting trips was to prove fatal. The male saw from high above that she was making an attack on a ground squirrel in a dry arroyo. Her path would take her over an embankment at low altitude. Hidden from her view were two hunters walking close to the bluff. The male tensed as he saw his mate approach the men. As her black form swept over the hunters, they whirled and raised their guns. The female saw, but too late. As she banked sharply, two shots sang out and one slug tore through her body, sending her crashing in a crumpled mass. Helpless and distraught, the male watched from above as the hunters stretched out the wings of his mate and examined their prize. With the fear of man reinforced in his mind, he turned away and mounted up to return to the safety of the back country.

KENT DURDEN, *Flight to Freedom*

Specific directions and explanations of processes also arrange themselves naturally in time order. The following directions for mixing powdered clay proceed step by step through the process.

CHRONOLOGICAL ORDER

Clay purchased in powder form is mixed with water to make it a plastic mass. To mix, fill a large dishpan or small tub about one-third full of water, sift clay over [the] water, one handful at a time, until [the] clay settles on top of the water to make a coating about 1 inch thick. Cover [the] pan with paper or cloth and let the unstirred mixture set overnight. On the following day mix and stir it thoroughly. If [the] mass is too thick to knead, add more water. If too thin, add dry clay. Clay is in a state to store when it is soft and pliable but does not stick to the hands. Since clay improves with aging in a damp condition, mix as far ahead of time of use as you can. Wrap [the] clay in damp cloth and store in a covered crock for at least one week before using.

HERBERT H. SANDERS, "How to Make Pottery and Ceramic Sculpture"

2. Space. Many descriptive paragraphs arrange themselves easily according to some spatial order, from east to west, from bottom to top, from near to far, from the center outward, and the like. In the following paragraph, the writer is describing the interior of her church's sanctuary. She carefully orders the details, always keeping the relative position of parts clear with such directional words and phrases as *over, above, on each side,* and with such descriptive verbs as *separated, line, hang, guard, flank,* and *arching.*

42b

¶ *coh*

SPATIAL ORDER

The sanctuary of the First Presbyterian Church is a study in nineteenth century architecture. *The sections* of contoured, crescent-shaped oak pews *separated by two main aisles line the wedge-shaped main floor. Over the main floor in the rear hangs a balcony* supported by two Greek columns whose decorative gilt tops complement similar ornamentation *at the front upper corners of the auditorium. Brass rails guard the balcony seats and separate* the raised *podium from the choir loft behind* it. *Above and on each side of the podium* are opera-box windows of beveled glass and brass. *Three stained-glass windows flank each side* of the sanctuary and, gleaming in the sunlight, depict such simple religious subjects as lilies, the cross, and Christ in his roles of Shepherd and

Comforter. The most distinctive feature, however, is the *huge fifteen-foot rotunda opening up the center* of the ceiling and arching its way to heaven.

Student paragraph

3. General to particular or particular to general. Many paragraphs begin with a topic sentence that makes a general statement, followed by sentences supporting the general statement with details, examples, and evidence. Other paragraphs reverse this order, presenting a series of details or reasons first and concluding with a general statement that summarizes.

In the following paragraph the author begins with a general statement—that teenage rejection-in-love is tormenting—and then she describes the specific behavior that constitutes the supporting particulars of the paragraph.

GENERAL-TO-PARTICULAR ORDER

Rejection-in-love is one of the most tormenting aspects of teenage life you will ever be forced to witness. Because it's like this: The first time a teenage boy ever gets serious about a girl, he realizes that she is a very highly evolved creature. That unlike his two best friends, Chuck and Ernie, she is actually able to carry on a conversation without bugging her eyes, belching, swearing, or kicking parking meters. So he tells this girl some *very important junk* about his innermost psyche, and if it works, great. If it doesn't—well, it doesn't become the end of the world; but the end of the world will certainly be visible from where he's sitting.

STEPHANIE BRUSH, "Understanding Teenage Boys"

42b

¶ *coh*

In the following paragraph, the author begins by asserting that disasters may not be as widespread as records indicate. To support this statement, she contrasts the range of events reported in the news with the relative normalcy of most people's typical day. She then states the "law" she has formulated on the basis of her perception of the true situation. The paragraph thus moves from general to particular back to general.

GENERAL-TO-PARTICULAR ORDER

Disaster is rarely as pervasive as it seems from recorded accounts. The fact of being on the record makes it appear continuous and ubiquitous whereas it is more likely to have been sporadic both in time and place. Besides, persistence of the normal is usually greater than the effect of disturbance, as we know from our own times. After absorbing the news of today, one expects to face a world consisting entirely of strikes, crimes, power failures, broken water mains, stalled trains, school shutdowns, muggers, drug addicts, neo-Nazis, and rapists. The fact is that one can come home in the evening—on a lucky day—without having encountered more than one or two of these phenomena. This has led me to formulate Tuchman's Law, as follows: "The fact of being reported multiplies the apparent extent of any deplorable development by five- to tenfold" (or any figure the reader would care to supply).

BARBARA TUCHMAN, *A Distant Mirror*

In contrast to the two preceding paragraphs, the following paragraph moves from particular to general. The writer, at the time the head of the Environmental Protection Agency, talks about people's particular frustrations with the agency first and then moves to the generalization that solutions to these frustrations do not depend on which political party is in power in Congress or the White House.

PARTICULAR-TO-GENERAL ORDER

When people get frustrated—understandably, to be sure—about why their dump isn't cleaned up or why there is still acid in the rain or asbestos in their schools, it is natural for them to look around for [somebody] to grab [by the lapels] and we are all they've got. I suppose this is bearable as long as we disabuse ourselves of the idea that these problems are susceptible to partisan interpretations. They are not. They are real, and in spite of what you may hear in the next five weeks [of the congressional election campaign], you can't vote them out of office.

WILLIAM RUCKELSHAUS, "Lapel Shaking"

4. Climax. Many paragraphs can be made coherent as well as more effective by arranging details or examples in order of increasing importance. The writer of the following paragraph arranged its examples—kinds of jobs—in order of climax. Drucker's evidence moves from those jobs in which skill at expressing oneself (the paragraph's subject) is least important to those in which it is most important.

42b

¶ coh

CLIMACTIC ORDER

If you work as a soda jerker you will, of course, not need much skill in expressing yourself to be effective. If you work on a machine, your ability to express yourself will be of little importance. But as soon as you move one step up from the bottom, your effectiveness depends on your ability to reach others through the spoken or the written word. And the further away your job is from manual work, the larger the organization of which you are an employee, the more important it will be that you know how to convey your thoughts in writing or speaking. In the very large business organization, whether it is the government, the large corporation, or the Army, this ability to express oneself is perhaps the most important of all the skills a man can possess.

PETER F. DRUCKER," How to Be an Employee"

5. Comparison and contrast. Some controlling ideas naturally suggest organization by comparison and contrast. Consider these topic sentences:

My brother is a natural student; I am a natural nonstudent.

Women have a long way to go before they have genuinely equal opportunity and recognition, but they have gone some of the distance since my mother finished high school.

Foreign wines may have virtues, but if we compare them carefully to their American counterparts, we'll choose the American.

Such sentences either directly assert or imply a contrast and almost require the writer to fill out the details of that contrast.

The paragraph that follows compares poetry and advertising, developing the assertion that they are alike in many ways by giving three examples of their similarity. The parallel constructions that mark the successive points of comparison and help give the paragraph coherence are in italics.

COMPARISON

Nevertheless, poetry and advertising have much in common. To begin with, *they both make extensive use* of rhyme and rhythm ("What's the word? Thunderbird!"). *They both use words chosen* for their affective and connotative values rather than for their denotative content ("Take a puff . . . it's springtime! Gray rocks and the fresh green leaves of springtime reflected in a mountain pool. . . . Where else can you find air so refreshing? And where can you find a smoke as refreshing as Salem's?"). William Empson, the English critic, said in his *Seven Types of Ambiguity* that *the best poems are ambiguous;* they are richest when they have two or three or more levels of meaning at once. *Advertising, too,* although on a much more primitive level, *deliberately exploits ambiguities* and plays on words: a vodka is advertised with the slogan "Leaves you breathless"; an automobile is described as "Hot, Handsome, a Honey to Handle."

S. I. HAYAKAWA, *Language in Thought and Action*

42b

¶ *coh*

In the preceding paragraph, the similarity between two things constitutes the central idea. But in many paragraphs, although the controlling idea does not state a comparison or contrast, it requires one. In the following paragraph, for example, the author contends that because beginning writers do not know how writing differs from speech, they proceed under false assumptions. Her assertion requires her to explain some of the contrasts between writing and speaking.

CONTRAST

Here the problem of unfamiliar forms merges with the second pedagogical problem—that *the beginning writer does not know how writers behave.* Unaware of the ways in which writing is different from speaking, he imposes the conditions of speech upon writing. As an extension of speech, writing does, of course, draw heavily upon a writer's competencies as a speaker—his grammatical intuitions, his vocabulary, his strategies for making and ordering statements, etc., but it also demands new competencies, namely the skills of the encoding process (handwriting, spelling, punctuation) and the skill of objectifying a statement, of looking at it, changing it by additions, subtractions, substitutions, or inversions, taking the time to get as close a fit as possible between what he means and what he says on paper. Writers who are not aware of this tend to think that the point in writing is to get everything right the first time and that the need to change things is a mark of the amateur. (Thus a student who saw a manuscript page of Richard Wright's *Native Son,* with all its original deletions and substitutions, concluded that Wright couldn't have been much of a writer if he made all those "mistakes.")

MINA SHAUGHNESSY, *Errors and Expectations*

In any comparison or contrast, it is important to arrange the points of similarity or difference clearly. The more extended the comparison, the more crucial clear ordering becomes. Note how careful the writer of the two following paragraphs is to keep the same order within the two paragraphs. In each, he speaks first of Roosevelt, then of Churchill; in each he moves back, at the end of the paragraph, to a telling final point of comparison. The careful ordering of the paragraphs helps keep them coherent.

COMPARISON AND CONTRAST

Roosevelt, as a public personality, was a spontaneous, optimistic, pleasure-loving ruler who dismayed his assistants by the gay and apparently heedless abandon with which he seemed to delight in pursuing two or more totally incompatible policies, and astonished them even more by the swiftness and ease with which he managed to throw off the cares of office during the darkest and most dangerous moments. *Churchill* too loves pleasure, and he lacks neither gaiety nor a capacity for exuberant self-expression, together with the habit of blithely cutting Gordian knots in a manner which often upsets his experts; but he is not a frivolous man. *His nature possesses a dimension of depth—and a corresponding sense of tragic possibilities, which Roosevelt's lighthearted genius instinctively passed by.*

Roosevelt played the game of politics with virtuosity, and both his successes and his failures were carried off in splendid style; his performance seemed to flow with effortless skill. *Churchill* is acquainted with darkness as well as light. Like all inhabitants and even transient visitors of inner worlds, he gives evidence of seasons of agonized brooding and slow recovery. *Roosevelt might have spoken of sweat and blood, but when Churchill offered his people tears, he spoke a word which might have been uttered by Lincoln or Mazzini or Cromwell but not Roosevelt, greathearted, generous, and perceptive as he was.*

ISAIAH BERLIN, "Mr. Churchill"

42b

¶ *coh*

A special kind of comparison is **analogy.** An analogy draws a parallel between two things that have some resemblance on the basis of which other resemblances are to be inferred; it compares the unfamiliar with the familiar or points up striking or unusual similarities between familiar things. When a comparison is drawn between a large city and an anthill or between a college and a factory or between the human nervous system and a telephone system, that is analogy. Although they may be quite inexact in many respects, parallels of this sort enable us to visualize ideas or relationships and therefore to understand them better, as the following analogy about a herd of African elephants illustrates.

ANALOGY

A herd of elephant, as seen from a plane, has a quality of an hallucination. The proportions are wrong—they are like those of a child's drawing of a field mouse in which the whole landscape, complete with barns and windmills, is dwarfed beneath the whiskers of the mighty rodent who looks both able and willing to devour everything, including the thumb-tack that holds the work against the schoolroom wall.

BERYL MARKHAM, *West with the Night*

In the paragraph that follows, the writer compares the student's job of managing time to that of the juggler's coordinating multiple tennis balls or Indian clubs.

ANALOGY

A college student trying to organize studies and activities is like a juggler trying to manage several tennis balls or Indian clubs at once. Each student takes several courses that have varying types and amounts of required work. He or she must learn to manage time so as to get all work for each course done on schedule. The task of the student in managing the work of four or five different courses alone is similar to that of the juggler coordinating four or five tennis balls at once. But in addition to four or five courses, the student must also fulfill responsibilities to perhaps two or three organizations and manage social activities with friends. If the student cannot learn to distribute time wisely among all these different demands, he or she may begin to feel like the juggler who has lost coordination; work and activities may begin to scatter in disarray, like the juggler's tennis balls which fall to the ground around him. In contrast, the student who learns to manage time effectively keeps studies and varied activities flowing smoothly, just as the juggler who successfully creates a smooth circle of six or eight flying tennis balls or Indian clubs.

Student paragraph

42b

¶ *coh*

6. **Analysis and classification.** Analysis takes things apart. Classification groups things together on the basis of their differences or similarities. You use them both every day. You break your days into morning, noon, and night; in the supermarket you look for pepper among the spices and hamburger in the meat department, because you know that's the way they're classified. Similarly in writing, in both individual paragraphs and entire essays, analysis and classification frequently can serve as guides to organization.

In the next example, the writer humorously analyzes the types of assignments that college students are asked to do during a semester. She classifies each assignment on the basis of the emotional effect it has on the student.

CLASSIFICATION

After the first semester at a university, a student may notice that homework assignments can be categorized according to the various emotional states they produce. For example, "The I'll-Do-It-Later-Tonight" assignment is a relatively easy assignment which takes no more than five or ten minutes and causes the student little inconvenience or worry. Related to this type is "The-I-Thought-I-Could-Do-It-Later-Tonight" assignment, which seems simple but is in reality much more than the student bargained for. This type often causes a sleepless night for the panicking student. "The-Impossible-Dream" assignment also causes the student a certain amount of panic. These assignments, also known as semester projects, are designed to take the majority of the semester to complete, and they seem to hang over the student's head like a dark cloud of doom. Much like this assignment, but perhaps even more traumatic, is "The-I'm-Going-To-Fail-This-Course" assignment. The purpose of this one is to rid the instructor of half the class. This assignment may be seriously pursued with genuine interest and yet remain incomprehensible. The student must face the fear of a low grade-point average if he or she encounters many assignments of this type. Of all the types of assignments, this is the most dreaded.

Student paragraph

42b

¶ *coh*

7. Definition. The logic of a paragraph sometimes requires that key objects or terms be defined. Definition is necessary to set the limits within which a topic or a term is used, especially in dealing with abstract matters. Full and exact paragraphs of definition are frequently important parts of papers, essays, and articles (see Sections **41i** and **43c**). Note that paragraphs of definition many times make use of details and examples, of comparison and contrast, and of restatement, in order to insure clarity.

The following definition first states the two basic elements of the fairy story—"a human hero and a happy ending." The author develops the paragraph by describing the kind of hero and the kind of story pattern that are the special marks of the fairy tale. Italics show the movement of the paragraph, a movement basically controlled by the progress of the hero from beginning to end of the tale.

DEFINITION

A *fairy story,* as distinct from a merry tale, or an animal story, *is a serious tale with a human hero and a happy ending. The progression of its hero is the reverse of the tragic hero's: at the beginning* he is either socially obscure or despised as being stupid or untalented, lacking in the heroic virtues, *but at the end,* he has surprised everyone by demonstrating his heroism and winning fame, riches, and love. *Though ultimately he succeeds, he does not do so without a struggle* in which his success is in doubt, for opposed to him are not only natural difficulties like glass mountains, or barriers of flame, but also hostile wicked powers, stepmothers, jealous brothers, and witches. *In many cases indeed, he would fail were he not* assisted by friendly powers who give him instructions or perform tasks for him which he cannot do himself; that is, in addition to his own powers, he needs luck, but this luck is not fortuitous but dependent upon his character and his actions. *The tale ends with the establishment of justice;* not only are the good rewarded but also the evil are punished.

      W. H. AUDEN, Introduction to *Tales of Grimm and Andersen*

In the two paragraphs that follow, John Holt defines intelligence. Holt relies upon contrast to develop his definition: intelligence is not, Holt tells us, what it is often said to be—an ability to score well or do well. Rather, it is a "way of behaving" in certain situations. We might call the development here a not-this-but-that development.

The three-sentence first paragraph sets the general contrast between the two definitions. The second moves initially to the more specific but quickly returns to the basic pattern. The italicized phrases will help you follow the controlling, not-this-but-that flow of the definition. The two paragraphs here could have been combined. By using two paragraphs, however, Holt is better able to draw attention to his description of how a person acts in a new situation—a description that is very important in clarifying his definition.

DEFINITION

42b

¶ *coh*

    When we talk about intelligence, we do not mean the ability to get a good score on a certain kind of test, or even the ability to do well in school; these are at best only indicators of something larger, deeper, and far more important. *By intelligence we mean* a style of life, a way of behaving in various situations, and particularly in new, strange, and perplexing situations. *The true test of intelligence is not how* much we know how to do, *but how* we behave when we don't know what to do.

    The intelligent person, young or old, meeting a new situation or problem, opens himself up to it; he tries to take in with mind and senses everything he can about it; he thinks about *it,* instead of about himself or what it might cause to happen to him; he grapples with it boldly, imaginatively, resourcefully, and if not confidently at least hopefully; if he fails to master it, he looks without shame or fear at his mistakes and learns what he can from them. *This is intelligence.* Clearly its roots lie in a certain feeling about life, and one's self with respect to life. *Just as clearly, unintelligence is not* what most psychologists seem to suppose, the same thing as intelligence only less of it. *It is an entirely different* style of behavior, arising out of an entirely different set of attitudes.

      JOHN HOLT, *How Children Fail*

8. Causes and effects. Some kinds of central ideas invite organization by an examination of causes or effects. Pollution and poverty exist. What causes them? What are their effects? What are the effects of television? Of the widespread use of computers? What are the causes behind the movements for equality of women, the popularity of football, the fluctuations in the unemployment rate?

In the paragraph that follows, the writer discusses the causes of a problem faced by his father, a high-school teacher, and other teachers. Note how many examples the writer gives of the causes of the effect, "shell shock" that teachers experience every day. The writer makes good use of parallel grammatical structure to reinforce the impact of the examples on the reader.

CAUSE AND EFFECT

My father is a public high-school teacher. He and the other teachers face a growing number of problems that seem to have no solutions. Having observed my father's behavior for several years, I have concluded that high-school teachers are suffering from a disorder formerly associated with war veterans—shell shock. Besides teaching five or six classes a day, teachers are also expected to sponsor clubs, coach athletic teams, raise money, head committees, chaperone dances, arrange parades, light bonfires, publish newspapers, and sell pictures. In my father's work, paperwork means more than just grading papers. It also means filling out a never-ending stream of forms that insure racial equality in the classroom, that provide free lunches to the needy, that reassure administrators that everything is in its place, and that even request more forms to be filled out. Discipline has also taken on a new meaning in public schools. Today, discipline means searching for drugs, putting out fires, disarming students, and breaking up gang fights. Faced with these daily problems and demands, it is no wonder that teachers like my father are becoming less like educators and more like soldiers suffering from combat fatigue.

Student paragraph

42b

¶ *coh*

EXERCISE 42b(1)

Assume you are writing an essay on the subject "so much to do, so little time." Write a paragraph with the topic sentence first. Then revise the paragraph, making the necessary changes so that the topic sentence comes last. Which organizational structure did your first paragraph follow? Which organizational structure resulted from placing the topic sentence last?

EXERCISE 42b(2)

You can see how the order of sentences in a paragraph contributes to its coherence if you examine a paragraph in which the original order has been changed. The following paragraphs were coherent as they were originally written, but the order of sentences has been changed. Rearrange each group of sentences to make a coherent paragraph.

1. (1) Landing a space capsule on Mars is technically complicated. (2) In 1971 one Soviet lander crashed and another stopped sending signals back after 20 seconds. (3) One of the Soviet 1974 attempts just flew past Mars. (4) Descending through Martian atmosphere is much trickier than landing on the airless moon. (5) The Soviets tried to land on Mars four times, twice in 1971 and twice in 1974. (6) Instruments on the second 1974 flight failed during descent, after transmitting usable signals for a few seconds.

2. (1) Language is full of symbols, but we also use signs or images that are not strictly descriptive. (2) Such things are not symbols. (3) We use spoken and written language to express the meaning we want to convey. (4) Although meaningless in themselves, signs have acquired a recognizable meaning through common usage or deliberate intention. (5) Some of these signs are mere abbreviations or strings of initials such as UN or UNESCO. (6) They are signs and do no more than denote the object to which they are attached. (7) Other signs are things such as familiar trademarks, badges, flags, and traffic lights.

3. (1) They fly in magnificent unison as they go further south to escape the cold. (2) The sight of the leaves covering the barren ground, additionally, indicates that cooler weather is approaching. (3) The fact that darkness arrives earlier in the evening makes one finally realize that the fall season has come. (4) There is nothing quite as visually exciting as noticing the signs which indicate fall is approaching. (5) Even during the day, the brisk wind compels a person to move at a quicker pace. (6) Obviously, the splendor of the fall season is unsurpassed. (7) Later in the afternoon, one notices that the birds, as well, are preparing for the onset of fall. (8) During the day one cannot help but notice the transformation of the leaves' colors from various shades of green to deep tones of red, gold, and brown.

42b

¶ *coh*

EXERCISE 42b(3)

Name appropriate organizational structures for paragraphs based on the following topic sentences. Explain your choices. Then write a coherent paragraph on one of the topics. Did that paragraph develop according to your original notion?

1. Shopping in a grocery store can be a study in personality types.
2. Attending a small college has disadvantages as well as advantages.
3. A distinction should be drawn between liberty and license.
4. Contemporary society places too much emphasis on test scores.
5. Finding a baby-sitter at the last minute on Friday night requires a considerable detective skill.
6. Students who cheat on exams, and the teachers who permit cheating, are the products of social conditioning.
7. To qualify as a "disaster area," a student's bedroom must have that lived-in look.
8. Slang is a puzzle to the uninitiated.
9. The best way to change a person's mind about a stereotype is to introduce him or her to someone who is an exception.
10. A poor diet can result in psychological as well as physical problems.

42c

Paragraph coherence: connecting ideas

In addition to the organizational "superstructures" that shape ideas into coherent paragraphs, hierarchical structures can be employed within paragraphs to achieve unity as well as flow. If the topic sentence or controlling idea appears at the top of the hierarchy (level 1) in the first sentence, then all the other sentences in the paragraph should relate to it as parallel or subordinate ideas. For example:

1. A good vacation means different things to different people.
   2. For some, the best vacation is the one that takes them away from home.
      3. They crave new sights, new sensations.
         4. A trip to the beach or the mountains refreshes the city dweller,
         4. while a trip to the city excites the country dweller.
   2. For others, a chance to stay at home is the best vacation.
      3. These folks want the ease and restfulness of familiar surroundings.
         4. They like lying around the house in old clothes.
         4. They enjoy puttering in the garden and talking to the neighbors.
      3. For them, the "new sight" or "new sensation" of not having to face the world or go to work in the morning is vacation enough.

You'll notice that the indentation technique used to examine the preceding paragraph (known as the Christensen method) looks very much like an outline. Like an outline, it reveals the relationships between main ideas and subordinate ideas. Thus, it reveals their interconnecting logic. The paragraph is well-knit, unified, and coherent, as can be seen from its structure of parallel and subordinate ideas. Each generality is supported by at least one level of specificity. You might want to check the relationships between elements in your own paragraphs by comparing sentence levels in this way.

42c

¶ *coh*

EXERCISE 42c(1)

Outline the following paragraphs using the Christensen indentation method illustrated in Section 42c. How do the levels of generality and specificity and the relationships between main ideas and subordinate ideas contribute to each paragraph's coherence? Do they help develop the paragraph's topic? Do you see any similarities in the structure of the two paragraphs that increase the coherence of the two taken together?

There was a time when the deathbed was a kind of proscenium, from which the personage could issue one last dramatic utterance, full of the compacted significance of his life. Last words were to sound as if all of the individual's earthly time had been sharpened to that point: he could now etch the grand summation. "More light!" the great Goethe of the Enlightenment is said to have cried as he expired. There is some opinion, however, that what he actually said was "Little wife, give me your little paw."

In any case, the genre of great last words died quite a few years ago. There are those who think the last genuinely memorable last words were spoken in 1900, when, according to one version, the dying Oscar Wilde said, "Either that wallpaper goes, or I do."

LANCE MORROW, "A Dying Art: The Classy Exit Line"

EXERCISE 42c(2)

Using the Christensen method, outline the paragraph you wrote for Exercise 42b(3). Revise the paragraph, incorporating changes the outline suggests for improving coherence.

42d

Paragraph coherence: connecting language

Besides positioning the ideas and sentences in a paragraph so that they relate logically to one another, you can use language cues that clarify relationships for readers. The most obvious ones are repeated key words and phrases, parallel grammatical structures, and transitional markers. Less obvious but equally helpful is using old information to introduce new information.

1. Repeated key words and phrases. Many well-constructed paragraphs rely on the repetition of key words and phrases, often with slight modification, to emphasize major ideas and carry the thought from sentence to sentence. Pronouns referring to clearly established antecedents in the previous sentence function in the same way. In the following paragraph the words and phrases that are repeated to provide clear links from sentence to sentence and produce a closely integrated whole are in italics.

42d

¶ *coh*

REPETITION OF KEY WORDS AND PHRASES

In discussing the pre-Civil War South, it *should be remembered* that the large plantation owners constituted only a small part of the *total Southern population.* By far the greater part of *that population* was made up of *small farmers,* and of course the slaves themselves. Some *small farmers* had acquired substantial acreage, owned three or four slaves, and were relatively prosperous. But most of the *small farmers* were terribly poor. They rented their land and worked it themselves, sometimes side by side with the slaves of the great *landowners.* In everything but *social position* they were worse off than the slaves. But it must *also be remembered* that they were as jealous of that superior *social position* as the wealthy *landowner* himself.

Student paragraph

2. Parallel grammatical structure. Using parallel grammatical structure in successive sentences is one of the most important ways of connecting them. Just as parallel grammatical form in coordinate parts of a single sentence emphasizes the coordinate relationship of the ideas, so parallel structure from sentence to sentence within a paragraph emphasizes the relationship of these sentences to the single idea of the paragraph. (See also Section **32.**)

PARALLEL GRAMMATICAL STRUCTURES

Life has often been described as a game, and if one is to play any game successfully, *he must know how to balance his skills* and blend them into the combination most effective for transferring potential into actual performance. *Regardless of how many times* a guard has held his man scoreless, *if he himself has not scored* for his team, his effort is incomplete. *Regardless of how many points* a forward or center averages per game, *if he has not guarded the lane* at every attempt of penetration by the opposition, he is inefficient. The most valuable player trophy is awarded to the player *who scores considerably, who grabs rebounds mechanically* off the backboard, and *who hustles relentlessly* from the initial center jump until the final buzzer sounds. A successful player at his life's game *must also balance his skills. If he always leads, people may tire* of following; *if he always follows, others may consider* him unworthy of a leadership position when he desires it. The secret, then, is to incorporate the two so that a mediocre character is transformed into an exceptional one.

Student paragraph

3. Transitional markers. A transitional marker is a word or a phrase placed at or near the beginning of a sentence to indicate its relation to the preceding sentence. The coordinating conjunctions *and, but, or, nor, so,* and *yet* are often used this way, particularly in informal writing, for they provide easy bridges from one sentence to another. But English provides a wide variety of transitional markers, as suggested in the lists below. Good modern writing uses the more formal markers sparingly. Be wary of cluttering your writing with unnecessary *however*'s, *moreover*'s, and *consequently*'s. But you should be equally careful to know them and to use them when they create clarity.

Here is a list of many of the common transitional words and phrases:

TO INDICATE ADDITION
again, also, and, and then, besides, equally important, finally, first, further, furthermore, in addition, last, likewise, moreover, next, second, third, too

TO INDICATE CAUSE AND EFFECT
accordingly, as a result, consequently, hence, in short, otherwise, then, therefore, thus, truly

TO INDICATE COMPARISON
in a like manner, likewise, similarly

TO INDICATE CONCESSION
after all, although this may be true, at the same time, even though,
I admit, naturally, of course

TO INDICATE CONTRAST
after all, although true, and yet, at the same time, but, for all that,
however, in contrast, in spite of, nevertheless, notwithstanding, on
the contrary, on the other hand, still, yet

TO INDICATE SPECIAL FEATURES OR EXAMPLES
for example, for instance, incidentally, indeed, in fact, in other
words, in particular, specifically, that is, to illustrate

TO INDICATE SUMMARY
in brief, in conclusion, in short, on the whole, to conclude, to summarize, to sum up

TO INDICATE TIME RELATIONSHIPS
after a short time, afterwards, as long as, as soon as, at last, at length,
at that time, at the same time, before, earlier, immediately, in the
meantime, lately, later, meanwhile, of late, presently, shortly, since,
soon, temporarily, thereafter, thereupon, until, when, while

Transitional words and phrases are italicized in the following:

TRANSITIONAL WORDS AND PHRASES
    As I have remarked, the pilots' association was now the compactest
monopoly in the world, perhaps, and seemed simply indestructible.
And yet the days of its glory were numbered. *First,* the new railroad
stretching up through Mississippi, Tennessee, and Kentucky, to
Northern railway-centers, began to divert the passenger travel from
the steamboats; *next* the war came and almost entirely annihilated
the steamboating industry during several years, leaving most of the
pilots idle and the cost of living advancing all the time; *then* the trea-
surer of the St. Louis association put his hand into the till and
walked off with every dollar of the ample fund; *and finally,* the railroads intruding everywhere, there was little for steamers to do,
when the war was over, but carry freights; *so straightway* some genius
from the Atlantic coast introduced the plan of towing a dozen
steamer cargoes down to New Orleans at the tail of a vulgar little
tugboat; and behold, in the twinkling of an eye, *as it were,* the association and the noble science of piloting were things of the dead and
pathetic past!

MARK TWAIN, Life on the Mississippi

42d

¶ *coh*

    4. Old information introducing new information. Like re-
peated key words or parallel grammatical structures, this technique

builds on readers' expectations by using repetition. People appreciate receiving new information by way of known information, so sentences that begin with the known (or previously mentioned) and then tie it to the unknown (newly mentioned) meet readers' expectations and replicate a familiar mental process. The following paragraph indicates this process with italic type for old information and boldface type for new information.

OLD INFORMATION INTRODUCING NEW INFORMATION

Basically a **word processor does** what a *typewriter does*, only better. The **main difference** between *them* is that on a *word processor* what you write is **stored as electronic or magnetic impulses,** instead of as *marks on paper*. *Word processors* can do this because **they're computers** that have been programmed to let you type in text, edit it, and have it printed out.

ARTHUR NAIMAN, *Introduction to WordStar*

Not every sentence above begins with old information. Because the writer's purpose is to define *word processor*, the paragraph begins with the term to be defined. But the unfamiliar is immediately explained by comparing it to the familiar (*a typewriter*), thus satisfying readers' expectations. Similarly, the second sentence starts with new information (*main difference*) but describes the difference (*electronic impulses*) in terms of the known and familiar (*marks on paper*).

Thinking carefully about readers' needs is important when you are building new information on top of old information. Readers can grow bored if known information is repeated needlessly. Use repetition and connections between the known and the unknown where readers need this type of assistance for understanding meaning, not where it merely slows down comprehension and makes them impatient.

42d

¶ *coh*

EXERCISE 42d

Make a coherent paragraph of the following statements. First, use the Christensen method (Section 42c) to help determine an appropriate order for the sentences. Then link them smoothly with connecting language to achieve coherence.

(1) This attitude shows a naive faith in the competency of secretaries. (2) Practicing engineers and scientists say they spend half their time writing letters and reports. (3) Many students foolishly object to taking courses in writing. (4) College students going into business think their secretaries will do their writing for them. (5) Students going into technical or scientific fields may think that writing is something they will seldom have to do. (6) Young business people seldom have private secretaries. (7) Their notion that only poets, novelists, and newspaper reporters have to know how to write is unrealistic. (8)

Other things being equal, people in any field who can express themselves effectively are sure to succeed more rapidly than those whose command of the language is poor.

42e

Paragraph development: filling in the gaps

Readers want details—they *need* details—to be able to understand your thinking. Consider, for example, the following paragraph from a letter written by an Alaskan to a friend in the Midwest whom he had not seen in several years.

> During the same summer you and Nancy were here, in August Faye and I were severely mauled by a grizzly bear on the Yukon River about 22 miles below Dawson. We spent three weeks in the Whitehorse hospital, and when we got home Faye was in and out of hospitals in Fairbanks and Anchorage all the rest of the winter and spring. It was kind of rough going there for awhile, but we're back in shape and back on the river again this winter.

You can imagine the reader's reaction. Bear! How big? Severely mauled! What do you mean by "severely"? Rough going! That must be the understatement of the year. Details, man, details! The paragraph is logically organized according to chronology, it is fairly unified and coherent, and it certainly has a controlling idea. But without adequate details, it obviously will not satisfy the reader.

The problem here is a misalignment of goals. The writer's goal was to reassure his friend that he and his wife are now all right by deemphasizing the mauling incident. Although this goal is also important to his friend, the friend's goal is to learn the details of the incident. The writer has focused on effects; the reader wants to know about causes.

42e

¶ *dev*

Not every paragraph is as dramatic as the preceding example, of course, or as frustrating in its lack of development. Still, all writers owe their audiences sufficient details, examples, evidence, and reasons to support the central idea adequately. A paragraph's controlling idea is usually a relatively general statement. To make readers understand what that general statement means and to keep them interested, you must explain and support it.

The following paragraph does not go far beyond its topic sentence:

> It is not always true that a good picture is worth a thousand words. Often writing is much clearer than a picture. It is sometimes difficult to figure out what a picture means, but a careful writer can almost always explain it.

The writer of this paragraph has given us no details that explain why it is not true that pictures are worth more than words, or any reasons for believing his topic sentence. The second sentence merely restates the topic sentence, and the final sentence does very little more.

Compare the following paragraph built on the same topic sentence.

It is not always true that a picture is worth a thousand words. Sometimes, in fact, pictures are pretty useless things. Far from being worth more than words, they can be downright frustrating. If you buy a new typewriter, would you rather have a glossy picture of it, or a 1,000-word booklet explaining how it works? If your carburetor is clogged, do you need a picture of the carburetor, or an explanation of how to unclog it? If you can't swim and you fall in the river and start gulping water, will you be better off to hold up a picture of yourself drowning, or start screaming "Help!"?

In contrast to the first writer, this writer has given us three concrete examples of how words may in fact be worth more than pictures. We may object that pictures of both the typewriter and the clogged carburetor would be helpful along with the words. But we understand what the writer means, and we've been kept interested.

EXERCISE 42e

Choose two of the following topic sentences and develop each into a meaningful paragraph by supporting it with details, examples, evidence, and reasons.

1. A first impression is not always a reliable basis for judgment.
2. The best surprise is no surprise.
3. Good news seldom makes the headlines.
4. Thank goodness the police are cracking down on drunk drivers.
5. A gifted child stands a good chance of receiving the wrong kind of education.
6. As the author Thomas Wolfe said, once you've left, "you can't go home again."
7. Keeping a detailed budget is more trouble than it's worth.
8. Fashions in clothes (books, slang, hairstyles, music, etc.) change from one year to the next.
9. People tend to fear the new or the unfamiliar.
10. No matter how old you are, you rarely *think* you're that old.

42f

¶ *dev*

42f

Paragraph development: deciding on length

A paragraph can *look* long enough and still not be adequately developed. Conversely, a paragraph can be too long, even though on a single topic, for a reader to digest easily. No magic number of sentences will predictably give you just the right paragraph length for every writing task.

Paragraph length is to some extent a function of readers' expectations. From experience, readers expect that paragraphs in novels or history books will be longer than paragraphs in newspaper articles or business letters. Readers' expectations also grow from their experience with content: a philosophical argument, for example, is likely to require longer paragraphs to accommodate extended explanations of complex ideas; an instruction manual, on the other hand, will use short paragraphs to mark off each step in a process.

Paragraph length is also a matter of visual appeal. The narrowness of a newspaper column makes lengthy paragraphs difficult to read. The undifferentiated letters and wide type blocks of a typescript need the white space of frequent paragraphing to provide a visual and a mental resting place for the reader. In the case of an instruction manual, the reader knows without actually comprehending the words but by simply observing the visual paragraph cues where the steps in the procedure are located. In short, effective paragraphing packages ideas into manageable chunks for readers so they can more easily absorb and understand information.

Although the frequency of paragraphing that readers expect in a given kind of writing is governed partially by custom, remember that where you mark a paragraph has a definite effect on meaning. Because readers expect the first sentence in a paragraph to be an orienting sentence, their specific interpretation of the paragraph will be shaped by that sentence, whatever it is. Thus you should not think of spacing to signal the start of a paragraph as an arbitrary act. Paragraphing defines a unit of coherent thought for your reader, and you'd best consider carefully how you want to control your reader's perception.

42f

¶ *dev*

A useful strategy is to think about paragraphs not only in terms of topics but also in terms of *aspects* of topics. If your development of a topic needs to be fairly lengthy to provide adequate support, divide it into manageable chunks—aspects or subtopics that will be easier for the reader to handle.

For example, Section **42e**'s grizzly bear paragraph would have been much more satisfying if divided in two: the first paragraph developing the details of the mauling, the second paragraph discussing the hospitalization and recuperation and ending with the reassurance that the couple was all right. Similarly, the paragraph developing the good points and bad points of the Club Tropic vacation (p. 376) might have been divided, with one paragraph devoted to good points and the other to bad points.

It is especially important to apply the techniques for achieving coherence when you divide a paragraph. The reader needs connecting language such as that described in Section **42d** to be able to see relationships between as well as within paragraphs.

Short, insufficiently developed paragraphs usually show a lack of attention to detail and an imperfect grasp of the full idea of the paragraph. When you want to revise short, choppy paragraphs, look for a controlling idea that might direct them. What is the overall point you want to make? Can several short paragraphs be combined and refocused under a single controlling idea? Or you might outline each paragraph by the Christensen indentation method (**42c**), looking for omissions in the paragraph's levels of supporting detail.

The following sample paragraphs are all insufficiently developed. The arguments are undirected, and the generalizations are inadequately supported by reasons, examples, and details. Simply stitching these fragments together would not produce a coherent, unified statement; instead, the entire statement would have to be thought through again and then rewritten.

> I am in favor of tightening the drunk driving laws in this state. Too many people are getting killed on the highway.
> For one thing, the legal drinking age is too low. For another, the legal blood alcohol limit is too high.
> The penalties are not stiff enough either. We ought to throw the book at people arrested for drunk driving.
> A light sentence or a suspended sentence doesn't save lives.

42f

¶ *dev*

EXERCISE 42f(1)

Revise the preceding sample paragraphs on drunk driving so that they are adequately developed, unified, and coherent and comprise a brief essay on the topic.

EXERCISE 42f(2)

Group the following sentences into two paragraphs. Provide transitional markers for the sentences, and, when possible, combine sentences.

> Martin Luther King was an ordained minister from Atlanta, Georgia. He gained prominence as a civil-rights leader during the 1950's and 1960's. In 1956 he led a boycott by Montgomery, Alabama, blacks against segregated city bus lines. After his success in Montgomery, he founded the Southern Christian Leadership Conference. This gave him a base to expand the civil-rights movement in the South and throughout the nation. In 1963 he organized a massive civil-rights march on Washington, D.C., which brought together more than 200,000 people. It was there that he delivered his famous "I Have a Dream" speech. In the years that followed, King broadened his political involvement. He continued to work for civil rights, but he also became an outspoken critic of the Vietnam war. His criticism of the war was based on his belief that the war was contributing to poverty in America. He argued that our valuable

national resources were being used to finance the war rather than to
fight poverty at home. In 1968 he planned another large-scale
march to Washington. It was to be called the Poor People's March.
He never fulfilled his wish though. In April of 1968 he went to
Memphis, Tennessee, to help settle a strike by sanitation workers.
While there he was assassinated.

EXERCISE 42f(3)

Read the following paragraphs and explain why you think the writer divided them into two instead of using one long paragraph. How have unity and coherence been maintained between the two paragraphs? State the controlling idea.

Many years ago a friend of mine took a room in an obscure hotel in the heart of the city. There was a blaze of street lights outside, and a few shadows. He had opened the window and retired, he told me, when something soft and heavy dropped on his feet as he lay stretched out in bed. Though he admittedly was startled, it occurred to him that the creature on his legs might be a friendly tomcat from the fire escape. He tried to estimate the weight of the crouched body from under his blankets and resisted the frightened impulse to spring up. He spoke soothingly into the dark, for he liked cats, and reached for a match at his bedside table.

The match flared, and in that moment a sewer rat as big as a house cat sat up on its haunches and glared into the match flame with pink demoniac eyes. That one match flare, so my friend told me afterward, seemed to last the lifetime of the human race. Then the match went out and he simultaneously hurtled from the bed. From his incoherent account of what happened afterward I suspect that both rat and man left by the window but fortunately, perhaps, not at the same instant. That sort of thing, you know, is like getting a personal message from the dark. You are apt to remember it a lifetime.

LOREN EISELEY, *The Night Country*

42g

¶ *con*

42g

Paragraph consistency

When you read effective writing, you may be struck by the fact that something more than mere adherence to an organizational principle seems to hold the sentences together. Such writing has an inner consistency that unites everything into an authoritative whole. In part, you are responding to the writer's care in situating both reader and writer, in indicating positions or roles for each. This positioning is largely a matter of point of view and tone.

1. Consistent point of view. Readers need to be on solid ground. Unnecessary shifts in person, tense, or number within a paragraph destroy the solid footing, leaving readers to wonder who is speaking and to whom (person), what the time sequence is (tense), and how many are being discussed (number). (See also Section **10.**)

UNNECESSARY SHIFT IN PERSON

A pleasant and quiet place to live is essential for a serious-minded college student. If possible, you should rent a room from a landlady with a reputation for keeping order and discipline among her renters. Moreover, a student ought to pick a roommate with a similar temperament. Then you can agree to and keep a schedule of study hours.

UNNECESSARY SHIFT IN TENSE

Every time I have seen one of Clint Eastwood's Dirty Harry movies, I suffered conflicting reactions. Harry Callahan, Dirty Harry, was a policeman who follows his own code of justice rather than the code of the law. Harry's justice amounts to vigilante action which he carried out by excessively violent means—usually with a handgun as big as a bazooka. These movies' brutal violence repulses me, but I could sympathize with Harry's feelings. Although reason tells us vigilante justice is wrong, especially in a law-enforcement officer, these films replaced audiences' reason with emotions that make such violence at least momentarily acceptable.

UNNECESSARY SHIFT IN NUMBER

Of great currency at the moment is the notion that education should prepare students for "life." A college graduate no longer goes out into the world as a cultivated individual. Instead students feel obliged to prepare themselves for places in the business world. Consequently, we are establishing courses on how to get and keep a mate, how to budget an income, and how to win friends and influence people—that is, how to sell yourself and your product. The study of things not obviously practical to a business person is coming to be looked upon as unnecessary.

42g

¶ *con*

Unnecessary shifts of this type disorient readers and make it impossible for them to trust the writer's control and understanding of the material.

2. Consistent tone. Tone is one of those matters that are clear enough until you try to define them. You know well enough what you mean when, if your neighbor has complained about your barking beagle, you remark that you don't mind his complaining but you don't like his tone. But when you try to describe exactly what it is you don't like, you find it extremely difficult. Tone is produced by an interplay of many elements in speech and writing. A writer's stance toward his or her subject and audience, the "voice" the writer uses, involve sentence structure, word choice, methods of organization and development, the kinds of examples, illustration, and details provided, and many other factors. Even punctuation or the use of sentence fragments can influence what the reader perceives the writer's tone to be.

The best way to increase your awareness of tone in writing is to study carefully a variety of effective paragraphs, asking yourself how you would describe their tone and then trying to determine how the writer has conveyed that tone. A writer's tone can be impersonal or personal, formal or informal, literal or ironic, sentimental or sarcastic, sincere or insincere, enthusiastic or indifferent, dogmatic or doubtful, hostile or friendly, condescending or respectful, modest or authoritative, serious or humorous. Obviously it can be a level in between any of these extreme pairs, or it can be a complex quality that can be adequately described only by a combination of several of these terms. By careful study of good writing, you can increase your awareness of the many factors that contribute to the control of tone.

An *appropriate tone* is one that reflects the writer's understanding of and respect for the needs and feelings of readers. It is not easy to state what will create such appropriateness in any particular paragraph or paper; but some things are generally to be avoided. Among them, these are the most important: talking down to your audience by repeating the obvious; talking over the heads of your audience, merely to impress them, by using words or allusions or examples they are unlikely to understand; being excessively dogmatic or sarcastic; being excessively or falsely enthusiastic.

This opening sentence of a student paper illustrates an extreme of inappropriate tone: *No one can tell me that people who vote for the characters on the Democratic ticket aren't putting their own selfish interests ahead of the true good of the country.* Whatever readers may think of this thesis, the writer's expression of it is offensive. The language is inappropriately hostile, the writer's attitude dogmatic. Readers have the immediate feeling that there is no point in reading further, since any sort of balanced or reasoned discussion suitable to the topic seems impossible.

Consistent tone requires maintaining a particular tone once you have set it. A jarring shift in tone may ruin the effect of a paragraph, even one that otherwise meets the tests of unity, coherence, and adequate development. The following paragraph from a student theme illustrates the point:

42g

¶ *con*

JARRING SHIFT IN TONE

Curiosity has developed ideas that have been vastly beneficial to humankind. We have seen humankind emerge from the age of great darkness into the age of great light. Today every hot-rod artist profits from the ideas of past inventors and every home has a kitchen full of push-button gadgets that it couldn't have without ideas. Above all, modern scientific theory leads us to a clearer and deeper comprehension of the universe. So we see curiosity is really a helpful tool.

The first two sentences and the next to last sentence of this paragraph set a serious, somewhat formal tone by such phrases as *vastly beneficial, we have seen humankind emerge*, the parallel phrases *age of great darkness* and *age of great light*, and *clearer and deeper comprehension of the universe*. But the language of both the third and last sentences, and the examples cited in the third sentence, depart completely from this tone of seriousness and formality. Having been prepared for comment about the great concepts of religion, politics, education, or science, readers are offered *hot-rod artists* and *push-button gadgets*. The effect is something like that of a cat meowing in a church service. When used deliberately, to achieve effects such as humor or irony, shifts of tone can be appropriate. However, the paragraph above shows uncontrolled writing rather than planned divergence from the tone initially established.

EXERCISE 42g(1)

The following paragraphs and paragraph parts are marred by inconsistent point of view (person, tense, number). Rewrite them to ensure consistency.

1.   Every time a nation is involved in a war it must face problems about its ex-soldiers after that war. The veteran is entitled to some special considerations from society, but how to treat them with complete fairness is a baffling problem. Livy reports that grants to the former soldier caused some troubles in the early history of Rome. There were many disagreements between them and the early Roman senators.

2.   Preparing a surface for new paint is as important a step in the whole process as the application of paint itself. First, be sure that the surface is quite clean. You should wash any grease or grime from the woodwork. The painter may use turpentine or a detergent for this. One must be careful to clean off whatever cleanser they have used. Then sand off any rough or chipped paint.

3.   One of the books I read in high school English was Dickens's *Tale of Two Cities*. In it the author tells of some of the horrors of the French Revolution. He spent several pages telling about how the French aristocrats suffered. The climax part of the book tells how a ne'er-do-well who failed in life sacrifices himself for another. He took his place in a prison and went stoically to the guillotine for him.

42g

¶ con

EXERCISE 42g(2)

Study the following paragraphs. Describe the tone of each and discuss the factors that contribute to it.

1.   For we're always out of luck here. That's just how it is—for instance in the winter. The sides of the buildings, the roofs, the limbs of the trees are gray. Streets, sidewalks, faces, feelings—they are gray. Speech is gray, and the grass where it shows. Every flank and front, each top is gray. Everything is gray: hair, eyes, window glass, the hawkers' bills and touters' posters, lips, teeth, poles and metal signs—they're gray, quite gray. Cars are gray. Boots, shoes, suits, hats, gloves are gray. Horses, sheep, and cows, cats killed in the road, squirrels in the same way, sparrows, doves, and pigeons, all

are gray, everything is gray, and everyone is out of luck who lives here.

WILLIAM H. GASS, "In the Heart of the Heart of the Country"

2.   Even though large tracts of Europe and many old and famous States have fallen or may fall into the grip of the Gestapo and all the odious apparatus of Nazi rule, we shall not flag or fail. We shall go on to the end. We shall fight in France, we shall fight in the seas and oceans, we shall fight with growing confidence and growing strength in the air; we shall defend our Island, whatever the cost may be. We shall fight on the beaches, we shall fight on the landing grounds, we shall fight in the field and in the streets, we shall fight in the hills; we shall never surrender; and even if, which I do not for a moment believe, this Island or a large part of it were subjugated and starving, then our Empire beyond the seas, armed and guarded by the British Fleet, would carry on the struggle, until, in God's good time, the New World, with all its power and might, steps forth to the rescue and liberation of the Old.

WINSTON CHURCHILL, *Speech at Dunkerque*

3.   My education and that of my Black associates were quite different from the education of our white schoolmates. In the classroom we all learned past participles, but in the streets and in our homes the Blacks learned to drop *s*'s from plurals and suffixes from past-tense verbs. We were alert to the gap separating the written word from the colloquial. We learned to slide out of one language and into another without being conscious of the effort. At school, in a given situation, we might respond with "That's not unusual." But in the street, meeting the same situation, we easily said, "It be's like that sometimes."

MAYA ANGELOU, *I Know Why the Caged Bird Sings*

42g

¶ *con*

4.   Boys evolve in a measurable, ordered, logical manner, up until the point where they suddenly *de*-evolve. And it all happens so awfully fast: Just yesterday, he was your dear little Mikey who used to love having *Bambi* read to him, and now he's on the phone to Grandma, using language that would embarrass the average lumberjack. One morning he was that moist little baby you used to feed Gerber's stewed apricots to, and the next morning he has a ring in his ear and a note from his homeroom teacher telling you he's been holding Competitive Belching Semi-Finals in social studies class again. And as a parent, you ask yourself, "Did I not raise this child to be a respectable member of Western Civilization, and is there really any hope at this point?"

STEPHANIE BRUSH, *"Understanding Teenage Boys"*

PARAGRAPHS FOR STUDY

There is no substitute for writing if you want to learn to do it well. However, reading is an integral part of this learning process. Research shows what many people have suspected for years: those who read widely, attentively, and often are usually better writers than those who do not. The reason is that frequent readers are more comfortable with language and familiar with a wider range of options and techniques for using language. Reading and analyzing what you read to understand how it is written can add to your own writing skills. Test your understanding of the principles of good paragraphs by studying the samples that follow. Analyze each to determine the controlling idea, the topic sentence if one is provided, the transitional markers and other means of achieving coherence, the organizational patterns, the level of development, and the tone. Identify what you believe to be the author's goal in each paragraph: what is it that he or she wants to accomplish?

Then **write a paragraph** explaining how one of the writers tries to accomplish his or her goal. Your paragraph should not be a summary of the paragraph's contents. It should be a discussion of the writing techniques the author has used and how successful these techniques are in accomplishing the goal.

42g

¶

1. Going to work for the Eclipse [computer] Group could be a rough way to start out in your profession. You set out for your first real [engineering] job with all the loneliness and fear that attend new beginnings, drive east from Purdue or Northwestern or Wisconsin, up from Missouri or west from MIT, and before you've learned to find your way to work without a road map, you're sitting in a tiny cubicle or, even worse, in an office like the one dubbed the Micropit, along with three other new recruits, your knees practically touching theirs; and though lacking all privacy and quiet, though it's a job you've never really done before, you are told that you have almost no time at all in which to master a virtual encyclopedia of technical detail and to start producing crucial pieces of a crucial machine. And you want to make a good impression. So you don't have any time to meet women, to help your wife buy furniture for your apartment, or to explore the unfamiliar countryside. You work. You're told, "Don't even mention the name Eagle outside the group." "Don't talk outside the group," you're told. You're working at a place that looks like something psychologists build for testing the fortitude of small animals, and your boss won't even say hello to you.

TRACY KIDDER, *The Soul of a New Machine*

2. The whole aim of good teaching is to turn the young learner, by nature a little copycat, into an independent, self-propelling creature, who cannot merely learn but study—that is, work as his own boss to the limit of his powers. This is to turn pupils into students, and it can be done on any rung of the ladder of learning. When I was a child, the multiplication table was taught from a printed sheet which had to be memorized one "square" at a time—the one's and the two's and so on up to nine. It never occurred to the teacher to show us how the answers could be arrived at also by addition, which we

already knew. No one said, "Look: if four times four is sixteen, you ought to be able to figure out, without aid from memory, what five times four is, because that amounts to four more one's added to the sixteen." This would at first have been puzzling, *more* complicated and difficult than memory work, but once explained and grasped, it would have been an instrument for learning and checking the whole business of multiplication. We could temporarily have dispensed with the teacher and cut loose from the printed table.

JACQUES BARZUN, *Teacher in America*

3.   The definition of equality varies from woman to woman. For some women, equality means being equal to men politically and socially. They feel that the traditional codes of chivalry are no longer applicable and resent men who open their doors, pull out their chairs, and help them with their coats. On the other hand, for some women, equality means that they should have the same opportunities and benefits as men yet also enjoy the tradition of chivalry. These women, although they may hold prestigious positions in government, education or medicine, don't resent a man who opens the door for them. Still for other women, equality is little more than a public interest story which has no effect upon their lives. They are secure in their lifestyles, whether domestic or not, and tend not to question the issue. Perhaps there is no one definition of equality for women but many, since each woman must decide how important equality is to her own self-esteem before she can determine what equality means.

Student paragraph

4.   For years, nuclear-power advocates have claimed that nuclear power is the most economical form of energy available; but in light of a few facts, one begins to doubt this claim. The cost of building the Sequoiah nuclear plant, for example, exceeded a billion dollars. For this astronomical amount of money, one can expect this reactor to be out of operation approximately thirty percent of the time. After thirty or forty years, it will become too "hot" to operate and will be shut down permanently. Even though the reactor will be shut down, it will still be highly radioactive and will have to be totally encased in concrete and lead—all at a cost of another few million dollars and guarded virtually forever. Nuclear power is neither cheap nor economical; it is both expensive and wasteful.

Student paragraph

42g

¶

5.   Often at my desk, now, I sit contemplating the fish. Nor does it have to be a fish. It could be the long-horned Alaskan bison on my wall. For the point is, you see, that the fish is extinct and gone, just as those great heavy-headed beasts are gone, just as our massive-faced and shambling forebears of the Ice [Age] have vanished. The chemicals still about me here took a shape that will never be seen again so long as grass grows or the sun shines. Just once out of all time there was a pattern that we call *Bison regius*, a fish called *Diplo-*

mystus humilis, and, at this present moment, a primate who knows, or thinks he knows, the entire score.

LOREN EISELEY, *The Night Country*

6.   The gym detonates, fifteen hundred throats in peril of rupture. The town's best game in years has ended in a tie, Hamilton equalling Hamilton. The crowd owes the night to Robbie Hodge, and no one begrudges him the credit. From the Garfield side comes "Hodge! Hodge! Hodge!" and the Taft side echoes. The sound builds until no words at all can be heard. It is almost like silence, the gym roaring for a performance that on Broadway gets a ten-minute curtain call and in Madrid two ears and a tail.

PETER DAVIS, *Hometown*

WRITERS REVISING: PARAGRAPHS

Michelle had drafted an essay on the Social Security system for her American government class. Typing with a word processing program on her computer, she could draft quickly and make corrections easily—with no evidence of the changes. The printout looked like a clean, finished essay. Appearances aside, Michelle knew that she had been pouring out her ideas without much attention to paragraphing. Below is a portion of her essay. Reparagraph it as you think necessary, looking for topic sentences, units of ideas, and transition markers. Then compare your version to Michelle's revision, which is also marked to show some alternative paragraphing possibilities. What differences in emphasis and meaning do the various paragraph changes make?

42

¶ *rev*

Draft

With only 116 million workers paying into the Social Security program and a whopping 36 million receiving benefits, it is overburdened. After fifty years of existence, the world's largest social program is on the verge of collapse. To understand the shortcomings of the Social Security system, we must be aware of the conditions under which and the intentions with which the system was created. In 1935 President Franklin Roosevelt signed the Social Security Act.

In those days 35 million workers supported the program with their payroll taxes, and only 106 thousand beneficiaries drew from the program. In addition, the average life span was shorter in 1935 than it is today. Because of the relatively small number of eligible retirees and the short life span, the average worker paid only a maximum of $30 per year, while beneficiaries received a maximum of $492 per year. Today, however, the maximum payroll tax is $2,792 annually, and only three workers support each beneficiary who receives up to $15,000 in benefits. To make things worse, the number of retirees is on the rise, and it will continue to rise as the baby boom generation ages. The bottom line is that the Social Security administration will operate at a deficit by the year 2020 despite corrective legislation passed by Congress in 1983 that was designed to make the program solvent for years to come.

Revision

42

¶ rev

With only 116 million workers paying into the Social Security program and a whopping 36 million receiving benefits, it is overburdened. After fifty years of existence the world's largest social program is on the verge of collapse.

To understand the shortcomings of the Social Security system, we must be aware of the conditions under which and the intentions with which the system was created. In 1935 President Franklin Roosevelt signed the Social Security Act. In those days 35 million workers supported the program with their payroll taxes, and only 106 thousand beneficiaries drew from the program. In addition, the average life span was shorter in 1935 than it is today. Because of the relatively

small number of eligible retirees and the short life span,
the average worker paid only a maximum of $30 <u>per year</u>.

Today, however, the maximum payroll tax is $2,792
annually, and only three workers support each beneficiary who
receives up to $15,000 in benefits. To make things worse, the
number of retirees is on the rise, and it will continue to
rise as the baby boom generation ages.

The bottom line is that the Social Security
administration will operate at a deficit by the year 2020
despite corrective legislation passed by Congress in 1983
that was designed to make the program solvent for years to
come.

43

PERSUASIVE WRITING

During your lifetime most of your writing will have a distinctly persuasive character. Your U.S. history exam may require that you write a short essay answering the question "What were the major causes of the Civil War?" Your English professor, explaining possible topics for a research paper, may say, "I don't want to read papers 'all about' a topic. I want you to digest your research and draw your own conclusions about the subject." Your company's regional manager may ask you for a proposal assessing several new sales strategies. The school board may decide to close your child's school, sending her to one in another neighborhood, and you and your neighbors may want to write a letter of protest.

All these writing tasks require more than assembling facts and information. They require analysis and logical evaluation so that the information builds a case that supports a stand on the issues. In short, few of us put words on paper, whether by desire or request, unless we have some point to make, some assertion to present (see Sections **41f**, **41h(2)**). Making an assertion places us in the realm of argument, because an assertion is a statement that can (or should) be supported with facts, with reasons—in other words, with evidence.

In each of the situations cited above, the audience evaluating the assertion and the supporting argument is clear: the professors, the regional manager, the school board. But even when you do not personally know your readers, making educated guesses about them and assessing their probable characteristics can be as important as thinking about the points you want to present.

In setting your goal for an argumentative paper, you should understand that three outcomes are possible. The first—most nearly ideal but also the most unlikely—is that you will change your reader's point of view from opposition to agreement with your own.

The second possibility is that you will be able to modify your reader's point of view, bringing it closer to your own. Although agreement may not be complete, you will have clarified and added to the reader's understanding, as well as having gained some acceptance and respect for your position on the issues. Modification is a reasonable goal, and of course you hope that the strength of your evidence will modify the reader's position substantially.

The final possibility is that you will not change your audience's mind at all. Even if your logic is faultless, readers can reject your argument for a variety of reasons that to you may seem thoroughly irrational.

Audience analysis, then, is extremely important to successful argumentation because anticipating audience reaction has a direct bearing on your goal. You will want to set your goal in accordance with the relative likelihood of the possible outcomes. Just presenting your own viewpoint is not enough. If you hope to have any effect on your readers, you need to consider their viewpoint as well.

Assessing the audience helps you decide on an effective approach. What is your readers' average age and level of education? What other factors such as sex, lifestyle, income, type of employment, political or geographic affiliation may make them more or less receptive to your point of view? Most important of all, is your audience likely to agree with you or disagree with you?

If your audience already agrees with you, your problem is clearly not to persuade them further. It is rather to get them to act. When Thoreau delivered his address "Civil Disobedience," he knew his audience was already opposed to slavery; his task was not to convince them of the evils of slavery but to inspire them to act on behalf of the antislavery cause. Thoreau's essay is full of emotionally charged language, passionate in its call for action.

How much emotion you can effectively communicate to readers will depend on the subject and the intensity of belief you and your readers share. A fist-shaking, tear-streaming appeal to vote down a proposed $2 increase in club dues is inappropriate. On the other hand, if you fail to express deep feelings when the occasion demands, your appeal will be equally ineffective. "Move us," the audience says to you. "Don't talk about a serious problem as if it were a minor inconvenience."

If readers are likely to disagree with you, you must take a dif-

43

log

ferent approach. No matter how strongly you believe that abortion is wrong or that welfare should be increased or that writing courses should not be required in college, there are nonetheless persuasive arguments for believing the opposite. You can assume that many of your readers will start out disagreeing with your point of view. If you want these readers to listen to your position, start out by recognizing theirs. If you begin by acknowledging their arguments, even admitting the strength of some of those arguments, you can then move on to suggest their weaknesses, and finally to set your own arguments against them (see Section **43f**).

If you go about the task of persuading with respect for readers' convictions, you will be much more likely to get them to listen. Your purpose is, after all, to persuade. If you say (or even suggest) that your readers are ignorant, stupid, or ridiculous to believe as they do, you will only antagonize them. You will never persuade them.

An effective argument is more, then, than an attempt to persuade readers that what you do or believe is right or just—or what others do or believe is wrong or unjust. At its most fundamental level, an effective argument is a statement of judgment or opinion that is supported with logical and persuasive evidence.

43a

Learning to recognize arguable assertions

The novelist Joseph Conrad wrote, "Every sort of shouting is a transitory thing, after which the grim silence of facts remains." A corollary to Conrad's statement is that some things are simply not debatable, in view of the evidence. It is important to recognize which assertions are arguable and which are not. Trying to argue an assertion that cannot be supported with valid reasons is pointless.

1. *A priori* is a term of logic meaning, roughly, "before examination." Assertions based on an *a priori* premise cannot be argued because such a premise can be neither proved nor disproved; people are simply convinced of its truth or untruth. *A priori* premises are beliefs so deeply held that they have the force of fact, although they cannot be supported by factual evidence.

Many deeply held and widely shared assumptions about human nature are *a priori* premises with cultural, racial, social, and moral or religious roots. If you argue from an *a priori* premise with someone who does not share that premise, you will find yourself arguing in circles or along parallel lines—but never toward resolution—because legitimate proof is not possible. For instance, when people passionately argue that one government or social system is better than another, they are often basing their position on different *a priori* premises. Or if one person believes, *a priori*, that human beings are basically good, altruistic, and trustworthy while the other person believes human nature is essentially wicked, selfish, and dishonest, then the two can never reach a conclusion about human nature. The premises are not provable, no matter how many examples each person cites.

A priori premises may change or be replaced over time, as attitudes toward gender roles in American society show. *A priori* assumptions underlying assertions about the "weaker sex," parenting, or inherently masculine and feminine characteristics are not nearly as widely shared today as they once were.

2. Subjective expressions of taste and nonrational reactions cannot be argued. The Latin *de gustibus non disputandum est*, "there is no disputing about tastes," is another way of saying subjective reactions do not lend themselves to reasoning. No matter how sound your logic that there is no lack of oxygen in an elevator stalled between floors, to a claustrophobic the sense of suffocation is real.

3. Matters of fact cannot be argued. If a fact is verifiable, there is no point in debating it. It can either be true (a *bona fide* fact) or false (not a fact), but in neither case is it a matter for argument because the record can be checked. The earth is round, or nearly so. This fact was verified by fifteenth-century explorers and more recently by means of space flights.

4. Statements involving unverifiable facts cannot be argued. While it is interesting to speculate about whether there is life after death, the answer is simply unknowable.

5. Statements based on insufficient facts cannot be argued conclusively. For instance, people enjoy arguing that life exists on other planets. Statistically, the odds favor extraterrestrial life forms. But we have no hard evidence at this point to prove the assertions. All we can say is perhaps; the jury is still out. Should information pointing one way or the other come to light, a conclusion may eventually be drawn. In the meantime, logical reasoning on the topic won't carry us very far.

43a

log

Keep in mind that facts are slippery and not necessarily static. What may be accepted as verifiably true this year may be proven false by next. Before sailors circled the globe, the populace accepted as fact that the world was flat. During the Middle Ages the plague that killed millions was attributed to God's wrath; people had no knowledge that fleas could transmit microorganisms from rats to humans and thus infect the population. What was once the "fact" of God's wrath is now regarded as a problem of hygiene. Correspondingly, what serves as fact today may be tomorrow's quaint, ignorant notion. Time and scientific inquiry have taught us that very little is immutably certain. The best we can do is draw conclusions from available data, deciding to formulate an argument when the supporting data warrant it.

EXERCISE 43a

Decide which of the following assertions are arguable and which are not. Be prepared to explain why each assertion does or does not lend itself to argument.

1. The film *E.T.: The Extraterrestrial* sold more theater tickets than any other movie in history.
2. Cotton handkerchiefs wrinkle more easily than polyester ones.
3. Whole wheat bread tastes better than white bread.
4. Suicide is a sin.
5. Small businesses employ more workers than all of the Fortune 500 companies combined.
6. One should always tell the truth.
7. "If man were intended to fly, he'd have wings."
8. The universe and everything in it was created in six days.
9. A good first-grade teacher is one who keeps the children quiet and in their seats.
10. People usually deserve what life dishes out to them.

43b

Learning the parts of an argument

An **assertion,** which states the stand or point of view on a topic (see Section **41h(2)**), is sometimes called a thesis, claim, or proposition. It must be supported by valid evidence if the reader is going to believe it.

Evidence is the part of an argument the reader is willing to accept as true without further proof. Most evidence can be categorized as either fact or opinion: that is, (1) a verifiable occurrence or experience or (2) a trusted judgment believed reliable because the source is knowledgeable, prestigious, and authoritative. We have already noted that facts can be slippery. In a later section **(43d)**, you will see that prestigious opinion also has its pitfalls if the source is not truly knowledgeable. Nevertheless, a plausible argument depends on evidence that is accurate, pertinent to the main assertion, and sufficient to support it.

Evidence often comprises a major portion of an argument, especially if the topic is controversial or complex. How much evidence is enough depends on the nature of your topic and the characteristics of your audience—on how likely the readers are to agree or disagree with your assertion.

You have probably experienced the frustration of reading on your English compositions the comments "not enough support" or "more examples needed." Bear in mind the benchmark of shared experience; that is, the more widely shared or commonly acknowledged an experience, the fewer examples you need to convince readers. The sun rises in the east. No one is going to argue with you. If in a paper on the value of home remedies, however, you offer as fact the statement that mustard-plasters are good for curing colds, you will have to cite a wide and representative sampling of incidents as well as testimony from respected medical authorities to convince your audience. Most readers would view your statement not as fact but as an assertion needing proof.

Evidence is only as good as its accuracy and your audience's willingness to accept it. Consequently, persuading the reader means looking at the evidence from the reader's point of view and then supplying statistics, illustrations, specific examples, personal experience, occurrences reported by authorities to validate the evidence in your reader's eyes.

Arguments also contain a third element, sometimes implied rather than stated, that shows the connection between the truth of the supporting evidence and the truth of the assertion. This third element is often called the **warrant.**

ASSERTION: We can expect college tuition to increase.

EVIDENCE: The cost of living keeps going up.

WARRANT: Since colleges are subject to the same economic pressures as everyone else, tuition increases will be necessary to meet rising costs.

Using an implied warrant, and a different order of presentation, the same argument might be written:

EVIDENCE: Because the cost of living keeps going up,

ASSERTION: we can expect college tuition to increase as well.

The words "because" and "as well" serve as the warrant, clearly implying the reason why or connection between the truth of the evidence and the truth of the assertion.

EXERCISE 43b

Find the assertion, evidence, and warrant in each of the following passages. If any of the parts is implied, point out the words that indicate the implied part or supply the missing words.

43b

log

1. I have a terrible sinus headache. Whenever the weather changes, I get one of these headaches, so we can expect rain before the day is over.
2. Most people are indifferent to local politics. Oh, they complain a lot about things, but only a minority of registered voters bothers to go to the polls when national candidates are not on the ballot.
3. And they lived happily ever after.
4. America's love affair with the big, flashy, luxury car is over. The energy crisis has seen to that.
5. If you don't behave yourself, Santa Claus won't bring you any presents.
6. The Surgeon General has determined that cigarette smoking is dangerous to your health.
7. National political conventions are merely ritualistic pageants. Their intended function, selecting the party's presidential candidate, has been taken over by the state primaries.
8. Some acreage in California's San Joaquin Valley is suffering from a

build-up of salt deposits, the result of irrigation without adequate drainage. Irrigation can bring life to crop lands, but it can also bring slow death.

9. No business can survive without some profit. Contrary to what some people believe, profits are not used primarily to line the pockets of company owners but to provide capital needed for investment in plant and equipment, the development of new products or services, the expansion of the work force—all important if a company is to survive in today's competitive marketplace.

10. It's no wonder that our state ranks among the highest in numbers of high school dropouts and among the lowest in SAT scores and numbers of students going on to college. We also rank among the lowest in teacher salaries and in state dollars allocated per student.

43c
Defining terms

Much senseless argument arises because people fail to agree on meanings. Readers have to understand your terms before they can follow your reasoning. The assertion *If the people of this country had believed the Vietnam war was right, we would have won it* is unsatisfactory on several counts, not the least of which is the slippery term *right*. The reader is bound to ask, "What do you mean by 'right'?"

The word *right* is an abstraction, and abstract terms are among the most difficult to define. However, the assertion itself could have provided some useful clues. Consider the statement *A good first-grade teacher is one who keeps the children quiet and in their seats*. This assertion defines *good* by using a concrete example: a teacher whose class is quiet and in place. Definitions, then, supply words or examples known and familiar to the reader, more easily understood than the term being defined, and show what items should be included or excluded from the category the term covers.

Definition by word substitution. Many terms can be satisfactorily defined by merely offering a synonym the reader is likely to know. This is particularly true for technical or other little-known terms. Often an **appositive**—another noun or a group of words used as a noun—placed immediately after the term will be useful for such a definition.

> cardiac arrest, stopping of the heart
> aerobic (oxygen-requiring) bacteria
> aquifer, a natural underground water reservoir
> layette, clothing or equipment for a newborn child

Formal definition. We learn about something new by discovering that it resembles things we already know and then by noting how it differs from them. Constructing a **formal definition**—sometimes called a *technical, Aristotelian, logical,* or *sentence definition*—requires exactly the same steps. First, we explain the class of things—the **ge-nus**—to which a term belongs, and then we determine how it differs from other things in that class—its **differentiation.** Formal definitions characteristically take the form *x is y;* that is why they are termed *sentence definitions.*

1.   The first step in formal definition is to put the term into the class of items to which it belongs. This process is called **classification.**

Term		Genus
A carpet	is	a floor covering.
A crumpet	is	a light, soft bread similar to a muffin.

In general the narrower the classification, the clearer the eventual definition.

NOT	A crumpet is a bread.
BUT	A crumpet is a light, soft bread similar to a muffin.
NOT	A rifle is a weapon.
BUT	A rifle is a firearm.

Indeed, a crumpet is classified as bread, but so is pumpernickel. Though *weapon* is a legitimate classification for *rifle,* the class includes more than is necessary (knives, spears, clubs, and so on).

2.   Distinguish the term from other members of its class. This process is called **differentiation.**

Term		Genus	Differentiation
A carpet	is	a floor covering	of woven or felted fabric usually tacked to a floor.
A crumpet	is	a light, soft bread similar to a muffin	baked on a griddle, often toasted and served with tea.

43c

log

Defining a term by genus and differentiation is analogous to the comparison and contrast methods of paragraph and essay development (see Sections **41i** and **42b**). The term is first classified according to similarity and then differentiated according to dissimilarity.

3.   Use parallel form in stating the term to be defined and its definition. Do not use the phrases *is when* or *is where* in definitions. (See also Section **14a.**)

NOT	A debate *is when* two people or sides argue a given proposition in a regulated discussion.
BUT	A debate is a regulated discussion of a given proposition between two matched sides.

4. Be sure the definition itself does not contain the name of the thing defined or any derivative of it. John Keats's line "Beauty is truth, truth beauty" is poetic, but not very helpful as a definition. Nothing is achieved when definitions are **circular,** when words are defined in terms of themselves.

> **NOT** A rifle is a firearm with *rifling* inside its barrel to impart rotary motion to its projectile.
>
> BUT A rifle is a firearm with spiral grooves inside its barrel to impart rotary motion to its projectile.
>
> **NOT** Traditionally, masculinity has been defined as the behavioral *characteristics of men.*
>
> BUT Traditionally, masculinity has been defined as the behavioral characteristics of courage, forcefulness, and strength.

5. Whenever possible, define a term in words that are familiar to the reader. It doesn't do much good to describe a truffle as "a fleshy, subterranean fungus, chiefly of the genus *Tuber,* often esteemed as food" if your reader won't know the meaning of *subterranean* or *fungus.* "An edible, lumpy plant that grows underground and is related to the mushroom" may be a much more understandable definition of *truffle,* depending on your audience.

Ordinarily, of course, you will define terms without being aware of giving them a genus and a differentiation. But it is always possible to check your definition against the criteria given above. Consider the following example from a student paper:

43c

log

> Finally, college is valuable to a person interested in success. By *success* I don't mean what is usually thought of when that word is used. I mean achieving one's goals. Everybody has goals to achieve, all of them very different. But whatever they are, college will give one the know-how and the contacts needed to achieve them successfully.

The specifications for definition help clarify why and how this unsatisfactory definition breaks down. If the statement that this paragraph makes about *success* is isolated, it comes out like this: *Success is the successful achievement of goals that know-how and contacts gained at college help one achieve.* First, this statement violates one of the principles of definition because it defines the word in terms of itself: *success is the successful achievement.* Next, the writer does not make clear what she means by *goals,* and the qualifying clause *that know-how and contacts gained at college help one achieve* does nothing to help us grasp her intended meaning because we do not know how she defines *know-how* and *contacts*. Hence, both aspects of good definition are violated: the terms are neither put into an understandable class nor really differentiated. What is said is that success means being successful, which is not a definition.

Extended definition. Many terms, particularly abstract words like *propaganda, democracy, happiness, religion, justice,* and *satisfaction,* require more than a formal definition if their meaning is to be clear. Extended definitions usually have a formal definition at their core but expand upon it using synonyms, examples, analogies, descriptions of operations and results, and various other explanations to show the reader more precisely what is meant. Extended definitions may be one paragraph long or longer; entire articles or even books can be structured as extended definitions.

The following paragraph illustrates a simple extended definition. Note that the first sentence in this definition gives a kind of dictionary definition of *induction*. *Induction* is put into a class of things— in this case *the art of reasoning*. It differs from other things in that class—in this case by being that kind of reasoning in which we first examine particulars and then draw a conclusion from them. This general definition is then developed in two parts: (1) by explaining the kind of scientific reasoning that is inductive, and (2) by explaining, through a series of specific examples, how our everyday reasoning is inductive.

EXTENDED DEFINITION

Induction is the kind of reasoning by which we examine a number of particulars or specific instances and on the basis of them arrive at a conclusion. The scientific method is inductive when the scientist observes a recurrent phenomenon and arrives at the conclusion or hypothesis that under certain conditions this phenomenon will always take place; if in the course of time further observation supports his hypothesis and if no exceptions are observed, his conclusion is generally accepted as truth and is sometimes called a law. In everyday living, too, we arrive at conclusions by induction. Every cat we encounter has claws; we conclude that all cats have claws. Every rose we smell is fragrant; we conclude that all roses are fragrant. An acquaintance has, on various occasions, paid back money he has borrowed; we conclude that he is frequently out of funds but that he pays his debts. Every Saturday morning for six weeks the newspaper boy is late in delivering the paper; we conclude that he sleeps on Saturday mornings and we no longer look for the paper before nine o'clock. In each case we have reasoned inductively from a number of instances; we have moved from an observation of some things to a generalization about all things in the same category.

NEWMAN AND GENEVIEVE BIRK, *Understanding and Using English*

43c

log

Extended definition can be used to clarify terms in an argument, but frequently it constitutes a whole argument—in and of itself—used not only to inform but also to persuade. In such a case the writer is trying to convince readers to share his or her beliefs in addition to clarifying a term. Thoreau wrote "Civil Disobedience" not only to explain the concept but also to justify it as a course of action. Alvin Toffler's book *Future Shock* provided our language with a new term, and the book is an extended definition of that term. But *Future Shock* does more than identify and describe a phenomenon: in Toffler's words the book's purpose is "to help us cope more effectively with both personal and social change. . . . Toward this end, it puts forward a broad new theory of adaptation." In short, *Future Shock* argues for a set of new attitudes and behavioral patterns.

EXERCISE 43c(1)

Examine the following definitions and be prepared to answer the following questions about each. Is the class (genus) to which the term belongs clearly named? Is the class narrow enough to be satisfactory? Does the definition clearly differentiate the term from other things in the class? Does the definition repeat the term it is defining? Is it stated in parallel form? If you think a definition is unsatisfactory, rewrite it.

1. A mail carrier's job is to transport the mail.
2. "Religion is the opiate of the masses."   KARL MARX
3. A thermometer measures temperature.
4. Gridlock is where traffic becomes so snarled that vehicles come to a standstill.
5. Grownups are big people with little senses of humor.
6. A coaster is a small piece of wood, plastic, or other material placed under a glass to keep watermarks from marring the tabletop.
7. Chaos is when everything gets out of control.
8. A touchdown pass is when the player throws the ball for a touchdown.
9. Skiing is strapping two boards to your feet, pushing yourself off the top of a mountain with two sticks, and praying you will live to see the bottom.
10. A computer manipulates pieces of electronic information. Each single piece of information, called a "bit," exists in electrical form as a high voltage or a low voltage.

43c

log

EXERCISE 43c(2)

Without using a dictionary, write formal definitions of two of the following terms. Then compare your definitions with those in the dictionary.

1. jump rope
2. knife
3. weather report
4. shoes
5. prayer

EXERCISE 43c(3)

Select one of the following terms and write a paragraph of extended definition. Use your first sentence to state a formal definition of the term and then clarify it in the rest of the paragraph.

1. diplomacy
2. suspense
3. competition
4. justice
5. pornography

43d

Planning an argument that is well supported, is logically sound, and does not resort to distortion

A convincing argument presents sufficient evidence to support its assertions and presents it in a manner that is logically error-free. Errors of logic in argument, called **fallacies,** weaken an argument, making it unreliable. Most fallacies fall into two categories: **fallacies of oversimplification** and **fallacies of distortion.** Common fallacies of oversimplification are **hasty generalizations, inadequate cause-and-effect relationships, false analogies,** and **either/or fallacies.**

1. Support and qualify all generalizations. A **generalization** asserts that what is true of several particulars (objects, experiences, people) of the same class (genus) is true of most or all particulars of that class. For example, *Drinking coffee in the evening always keeps me awake at night* is a generalization based on several particular experiences on separate evenings. Generalization is essential to thinking; without it, we could not evaluate experience—only accumulate isolated facts. Similarly, generalization is essential to argument, since evaluation is part of the argumentative process. In fact, generalizations often appear as topic sentences in paragraphs (see Section **42**).

43d

log

An argument's main assertion may be presented as a generalization: *Most people are indifferent to local politics.* Moreover, because arguments of any length or complexity are comprised of clusters or chains of smaller, related arguments whose proof supports the main assertion, the writer typically uses a number of generalizations in the course of convincing the reader. Thus, generalization is very important—but it has its dangers, as noted below.

Avoid hasty generalizations. Do not leap to conclusions on the basis of insufficient evidence. We all tend to generalize from a few striking examples, especially when they accord with what we want to believe. But unless examples are irrefutably typical, they can lead to fallacies, even absurd assertions.

PARTICULAR A	Mrs. Jones's son never gets home when his mother tells him to.
PARTICULAR B	Sally, the girl down the street, won't go to college though her father wants her to.
PARTICULAR C	My brother keeps telling his daughter not to go out with that boy, but she keeps right on doing it.
HASTY GENERALIZATION	Young people today don't obey their parents. [Does this generalization include Henry and John and Mike, who are always home on time? Or Katie, who is in college though she doesn't want to be? Or the brother's other daughter, who married the son of her father's best friend?]
PARTICULAR A	I know an Italian who is a bookie.
PARTICULAR B	The Italian who runs our neighborhood grocery once short-changed my neighbor.
PARTICULAR C	A man named Valenti was a gangster.
HASTY GENERALIZATION	Italians are crooks.

Hasty generalizations are dangerous because they make assertions about groups containing thousands of individuals on the basis of a small number of examples. And more often than not, the writer knows of examples that don't fit the generalizations but, giving in to the temptation to oversimplify, leaves them out.

To protect an argument's validity, as well as to be fair to your readers, never advance a generalization unless you can support it with sufficient evidence. Sometimes two or three examples may be enough, but sometimes you will need to analyze the evidence in detail. If you can think of exceptions to the generalization, you can be sure your readers will too; you should prepare a counterargument to handle them (see Section **43f**).

43d

log

Avoid broad generalizations. Be careful about using words such as *always, never, all, none, right, wrong* in generalizations. Broad generalizations, like hasty generalizations arise from inadequate evidence. Sweeping statements invite readers to start thinking of exceptions, to start picking apart your argument even before you've presented your evidence. Many an otherwise reasonable assertion has foundered for lack of *seldom* instead of *never, usually* instead of *always*.

OVERSTATED	Playing football always results in injury.
	Playing football results in injury.
QUALIFIED	Playing football sometimes results in injury.
	Playing football can result in injury.

Note that an overstated generalization need not specifically state that it applies to *all* people. By not making a qualification it clearly implies *all,* as in the second overstatement above. Similarly, words other than modifiers can act as qualifiers. For example, the verb *can* and *may* prevent overstatements, as in the second qualification above, where *can* implies possibility rather than certainty.

2. Don't assume that a cause-and-effect relationship exists between two facts simply because one follows the other in time. This inadequate assessment of cause and effect results in the fallacy of oversimplification known as **post hoc, ergo propter hoc** ("after this, therefore because of this").

> The Navy began allowing women to serve on its ships in the 1970's, and its preparedness has decreased steadily since then. [The newspaper columnist who made this statement ignored other important factors such as cuts in defense spending and a shortage of new vessels and equipment, all of which adversely affected the Navy's military strength.]

> I'm not surprised Bill had a heart attack. We warned him not to take that high pressure job at company *X*. [While a connection between stress and heart disease has been established, physicians point to diets high in cholesterol, lack of exercise, and smoking—long-term behavior that can contribute to heart attack. Bill's lifestyle more than likely made him a good candidate for a heart attack long before he changed jobs.]

3. Don't assume that because two circumstances or ideas are alike in some respects, they are alike in all respects. This fallacy, **false analogy**, shares some characteristics of broad generalizations. Because one or two points are analogous, it is very tempting to go overboard and claim two situations or concepts are wholly analogous. Political speeches are full of oversimplified, faulty analogies, as are moral diatribes.

43d

log

> I don't believe you can run a major U.S. company from abroad. George III tried to run the United States from Britain, and look what happened to him.
>
> SIR GORDON WHITE
>
> [About the only commonality between the eighteenth-century monarch facing the American Revolution and the head of a twentieth-century multinational corporation is the ocean between continents.]

> The United States is headed right down the road to oblivion, following in the footsteps of ancient Rome: too much luxury and leisure, too much sex and violence. The Roman orgy and bloody circus have their modern counterparts in American promiscuity and violent television programs. Like the Romans, we'll be conquered by stronger invaders one day. [This analogy fails to take into account

vast differences between ancient Rome and modern America—imperial dictatorship versus representative democracy, to mention just one.]

Analogy can be a useful persuasive tool, but keep in mind that while it can clarify, it can never prove a point. Analogy's value increases in direct proportion to the number of parallels you cite and decreases with every difference your reader thinks of.

4. Don't claim there are only two alternatives if, in fact, there are several. Either/or fallacies result if you oversimplify choices, proposing only two when several actually exist. Truth sometimes is an either/or sort of thing: either you passed the examination, or you failed it. But most things about which we argue are not as clearcut. Arguing as if only two possibilities exist when the facts justify a variety of possibilities is also known as the **all-or-nothing fallacy** or **false dilemma.** (These two fallacies are frequently distinguished from each other, but both involve ignoring alternatives.)

> Students come to college for one of two reasons: they come either to study or to party. Judging by Mack's attendance at campus mixers, I'd say he didn't come to study. [It's possible Mack studies very little, if at all. It's also possible he studies very efficiently and thus has free time to go to parties. Clearly, many combinations of studying and partying, to say nothing of the endless possibilities that include neither studying nor partying, are available to both the prudent and the not-so-prudent college student.]

> A woman can't have it both ways. She has to choose between career and family. [Statistics show that a significant proportion of married women and mothers in this country hold jobs. Somebody obviously has seen through the false dilemma to at least a third possibility.]

43d

log

5. Don't resort to distorted language or distorted logic. These tactics will weaken your argument. The surest way to damage your own position is to ignore counterarguments or, worse yet, divert attention from them by trying to appeal to your reader's prejudices and emotions. You may be successful in your diversion, but you will have avoided the real issues being discussed and failed the test of logical reasoning. In short, your argument will have been distorted and unfair.

One of the most common kinds of argumentative distortion is **slanted language,** words using **connotation** to appeal to emotion and prejudice (see Section **38**). Slanted language "twists out of shape," distorts meaning. For example, today words like *radical, permissive,* and *cover-up* produce negative responses from many people, while words like *freedom, responsibility,* and *efficiency* produce positive responses.

Consequently, the calculated—or careless—use of such words in argument tends to evoke emotional rather than reasoned reactions. If

Candidate Jones is described as standing for "free, responsible, and efficient government" while Candidate Smith is described as "a radical with a permissive philosophy," voters are likely to favor Jones over Smith without attempting to learn either candidate's actual position on inflation, government spending, unemployment, or anything else. It's not unusual to find diametrically opposed positions described by the same connotative language. "Fiscal responsibility" can mean a tax cut in one politician's campaign and a tax increase in another's.

Arguments can also be twisted and bent by **fallacies of distortion,** errors that misrepresent all or part of an argument's meaning. Among distortion techniques are **transfer, argument to the man, argument to the people, non sequitur, begging the question,** and **red herring.**

6. Don't associate an idea or term with a famous name in the hope of imbuing the former with characteristics of the latter. The erroneous technique of **transfer (argumentum ad verecundiam)** uses positive or negative association rather than reason as a basis for conclusion. When used negatively, transfer becomes a form of **name calling.** In either case, the hope is that characteristics will transfer, even when logically there is no connection—which explains the notable incongruity of professional football players' endorsements of pantyhose or popcorn poppers.

> We are the political party of Franklin D. Roosevelt and John Kennedy. Our campaign platform follows in that great democratic tradition.
>
> Schmaltz believes the federal government should decide the issue. He stands for big government, which is just another name for creeping socialism.
>
> If Miss America can get beautiful hair like this using X shampoo, you can too.

43d

log

Not to be confused with transfer, **argument from authority** is a legitimate form of persuasion. When you argue from authority, you cite the research and learned opinions of those considered to be experts on matters you are discussing. For example, if you are arguing for the value of a liberal arts education, you might cite the opinions of Father Theodore Hesburgh, the highly respected president of the University of Notre Dame for thirty-five years. Always remember, however, that argument from authority is persuasive only in so far as your audience acknowledges the authenticity and credibility of the authority you are citing.

7. Don't sidestep an argument by trying to discredit the person who proposed it. Argument to the man (argumentum ad hominem) ignores the point being argued and attacks a person's character instead. This distortion technique is similar to that of red herring [see Section **43d(11)**] because it substitutes a false issue for *bona fide* proof.

Furthermore, even though discredited for one thing, a person may be right about others.

> Why should you believe what Hartwell says about the needs of our schools? He is suspected of taking bribes. [Apart from the fact that Hartwell is only "suspected of taking bribes," what he has to say about school needs may be based upon extensive study and analysis.]

> Don't listen to Collins's arguments for abortion. She doesn't even like children. [That Collins doesn't like children says something about her. But her arguments for abortion may stem from deep conviction reached after long experience as a doctor.]

8. Don't sidestep an argument by appealing to the instincts and prejudices of the crowd. **Argument to the people (argumentum ad populum)** arouses emotions people have about institutions and ideas. When politicians evoke God, country, family, or motherhood, they are making such an appeal—as, for example, when candidates say they will protect the interests of the American family.

A slightly different fallacy that uses similar crowd appeal is the **bandwagon** approach. This fallacy says that what is right for the masses is right for the individual: one must go along with the crowd in belief or action. Obviously this is not true, as many incidents of mob rule have shown. Nevertheless, the bandwagon is a favorite ploy among advertisers (and children) who claim "everyone" is buying or doing something.

> Fifty million people can't be wrong! Drink Slurp-o!
> But Mom, all the kids are wearing shorts (or roller-skates or green wigs) to the prom!
> The responsible citizens of this state know that a vote for Jenkins is a vote for open and honest government.

9. Don't substitute inference for a logically sound conclusion. A **non sequitur** ("it does not follow") attempts a fallacious leap in logic, omitting proof.

> This is the best play I have seen this year, and it should win the Pulitzer prize. [Unless you have seen all the plays produced this year and are qualified to judge the qualities that make one a Pulitzer prize winner, it doesn't follow that the one you like best should win.]

> The problems we face today have been caused by the federal government. Elect Green to Congress. [Not only is the first assertion offered without evidence, but certainly we are given no proof that Green can solve the problems. Perhaps his strength lies in the fact that he has been in Omaha rather than Washington for the past four years.]

10. Don't assume the truth of something you are trying to prove. **Begging the question** is a fallacy that occurs when a premise requiring proof is put forward as true. A related fallacy is called **circular argument**.

> This insurance policy is a wise purchase. It covers all expenses related to cancer treatment. [While the policy may pay cancer-related expenses, the statement assumes the buyer will get cancer. If he or she does not, the policy will not have been a wise purchase.]

> His handwriting is hard to read because it is illegible. [This argument does not move from premise to conclusion but merely moves in a circle. *Illegible* means "difficult or impossible to read," so the author has said only that the handwriting is hard to read because it is hard to read.]

11. Don't introduce a false issue in the hope of leading your reader away from a real one. A most graphically termed fallacy, a **red herring** supplies a false scent in an argument, diverting the hounds from their quarry and leading them down an irrelevant trail. Usually the false issue elicits an emotional reaction, side-tracking the reader's attention from the real issue and the proof it needs.

> American cars really are superior to Japanese imports. After all, we should "buy American" and support our own economy rather than sending our dollars overseas. ["Buying American," a disguised appeal to patriotism, diverts attention from real issues such as mileage ratings, repair records, safety, and so on, exhibited generally by American cars as compared with Japanese cars.]

> I don't think Mary Ann should have been expelled from school for cheating on Professor Thompson's calculus test. Lots of people cheat on exams—they just don't get caught. Besides, everybody knows Thompson's tests are too hard anyway. [Neither the pervasiveness of academic cheating nor the difficulty of calculus tests is relevant to the issue. The author tries to justify Mary Ann's action with two red herrings—a bandwagon appeal and an attack on Thompson—both of which are beside the point.]

43d

log

EXERCISE 43d(1)

Explain what is wrong with the reasoning in the following statements, and try to identify the fallacies of oversimplification that occur.

1. Television is responsible for the violence in society today.
2. That girl my brother is seeing is a very bad influence on him; he met her at Christmas time and within a year he had dropped out of college.
3. Sex education gives kids too many ideas. There has been an increase in teenage pregnancies in our town every year since they started those sex education classes at the high school.
4. Your repeated failure to show up for work on time suggests either you don't like your job or you're lazy.
5. Welfare recipients are a lot like drones in a beehive. While the rest of us work to produce society's goods and services, they just consume and breed.

6. Any member of Congress who goes on a junket is just taking a vacation at the taxpayer's expense.
7. All this emphasis on "career training" has turned the university into an assembly line. Poke the students in at one end, keep piling on the required courses, and out they pop at the other end with a diploma but no individuality or ability to think creatively.
8. If you really loved me, you'd spend our anniversary here at home instead of going on that business trip.
9. World War I started during Wilson's term, World War II started during Roosevelt's term, and the Vietnam War escalated during Johnson's term; if we elect another Democratic president, he'll start another war.
10. Anyone who heads a large corporation got to the top by ruthless maneuvering and looking out for "number one."

EXERCISE 43d(2)

Explain the errors in reasoning in the following statements and try to identify the fallacies of distortion that occur.

1. My father raised his children with an iron hand, and we turned out all right. I intend to raise my son the same way. What was good enough for Dad is good enough for me.
2. Norma's house is always a mess. Anyone who's that disorganized at home couldn't possibly organize city government. I certainly wouldn't vote for her for mayor.
3. If you believe in the sanctity of the family, you'll agree that the books used in our schools should be chosen by us parents and not by the teachers. We are the ones who should decide what our children read.
4. He made very good grades in college so he's bound to do well in the business world.
5. The government must cut spending because economy in government is essential.
6. He knew how to run a lathe, but I didn't hire him because he spent a year in reform school and once a criminal, always a criminal.
7. How can you support the Equal Rights Amendment? Do you want women and men sharing the same restrooms?
8. In that TV commercial for Uppity Airlines, Herman Hero says their plane is the safest thing in the sky. He used to be an astronaut, so he must know what he's talking about.
9. Obviously a good golf game is the key to success in this company. Most of the rising young executives play golf, so I'd better practice my putting.
10. Senator Graft wouldn't have been charged with accepting bribes if there weren't some truth to it.

43d

log

43e

Brainstorming about your argument

In addition to the planning techniques described in Section **41**, you may want to try some of the following activities as you think about what to include in your argument.

1. **Pinpoint exactly what you want your reader to do after reading your argument.** Writing a sentence describing the actual results you would like to achieve helps you to clarify the purpose of your argument. It also helps you to begin thinking about your audience's needs and point of view.

2. **List the things that would motivate your audience toward the results you want.** Preparing such a list will help you think about approaches to take and reasons you will need to offer in your argument.

3. **Draw a flowchart of the things that need to happen in a reader's mind for him or her to accept your point of view.** In this way you can anticipate the audience's thought processes and, consequently, its objections to your viewpoint. This analysis will help you to prepare convincing counterarguments and especially to think about possible organizational structures. The points on the diagram can be turned into subheadings for an outline you can use when you draft the argument.

43f

Answering objections from the opposition

A successful argument takes into account counterarguments that the reader is likely to raise and tries to refute them fairly and reasonably. If counterpoints are indeed valid, the best strategy is to recognize their validity but provide sufficient evidence to substantiate the truth of your assertions overall. In fact, you may want to summarize the opposition's point of view before presenting your own. This strategy, named *Rogerian argument* after the psychologist Carl Rogers, involves describing the opposing position accurately and fairly. If you demonstrate that you understand and respect that point of view, your opponents are less likely to feel threatened or defensive and more likely to give your position a fair hearing.

43f

log

Another associated strategy is to find a common ground, a shared goal, one or more points on which you and your readers can agree. Establishing some common goals may help persuade your reader of the relevance of your overall point of view. For example, suppose your thesis is that science teachers should be paid higher salaries because they are in short supply and because better salaries will attract more scientists to teaching. While your readers may initially disagree with your assertion, if you can find common ground in the viewpoint that science education needs to be improved, you may be able to persuade your audience that higher salaries are the best means for accomplishing that goal.

EXERCISE 43f

Find a newspaper or magazine article, or better yet a person, expressing an opinion with which you disagree. Consider the opinion carefully and then restate it in your own words as accurately as you can. Ask another person to read your version and compare it to the original. Then write a counterargument that rebuts the original and supports your own point of view.

43g
Structuring your argument to fit your audience and goal

By definition, the rhetorical purpose of an argument is to persuade. Consequently, your broad goal is to change or modify your reader's point of view or move him or her to action. As we noted in Section **41** on the writing process, a number of organizational patterns lend themselves to persuasive purposes. The ones most commonly found in arguments are cause and effect, detail and example, particular to general, general to particular, and climax.

Order of climax, building from least important to most important, satisfies our natural preference for dramatic effect. In an argumentative paper you might state the opposition's viewpoint first and then provide counterarguments that first dispose of the weakest points and finally tackle the most important, difficult, or memorable issues.

Writers often structure arguments in either the particular-to-general or the general-to-particular order because these patterns parallel two fundamental logical processes: induction and deduction.

Inductive reasoning (as you learned from the example of extended definition in Section **43c**) proceeds from the particular to the general. *If* particular facts are shown to be true time after time or *if* a laboratory experiment yields the same result whenever it is run or *if* people in a wide and varied sampling respond the same way to a given question, *then* a general conclusion may be drawn. Repeated experimentation and testing led to the conclusion that the Sabin vaccine would prevent polio. Scientists use induction when they test and retest a hypothesis before stating it as a general truth. The scientific method proceeds by inductive reasoning.

Deductive reasoning proceeds from the general to the particular. From a general conclusion other facts are deduced. The validity of the deduction depends on the truth of the initial conclusion. Because you know that penicillin is an effective weapon against infection, seeking a doctor to administer it to you if you have an infection is valid deductive reasoning.

There is also an induction-deduction cycle of reasoning. Sound conclusions reached through induction may in turn serve as the basis for deduction. For example, over many years the National Safety Council has kept careful records of the occurrence and circumstances of highway accidents and has reached the valid conclusion that the proportion of accidents to cars on the road on holiday weekends is the same as the proportion on weekends that are not holidays. From this conclusion, arrived at inductively, you may deduce that you can travel as safely by car to a Memorial Day celebration as you can to church the Sunday before.

In this way, the arguments you construct may use both induction and deduction. Sometimes you reason from conclusions a reader accepts as true; sometimes you must prove the truth of the conclusions themselves. In either case, the assertions you make in the course of the argument should be adequately supported, and there should be no errors in the logic.

Remember that as with any writing task, your goal should help you shape your ideas into a successful argumentative paper. Accomplishing that goal may require a combination of organizational structures. To convince your readers of one point, you might need comparison and contrast. For another point, you might use time order, narrating a sequence of events that comprises a supporting example.

"Abolishing the Penny Makes Good Sense," the sample essay at the end of this section, follows an overall inductive pattern with details and examples to support its thesis. It uses analogy, contrast, and several other subordinate structures along the way, but on the whole the essay moves inductively through a series of illustrations supporting the author's contention that the penny is too expensive to be worth keeping around.

REVIEW EXERCISE A

Prepare a counterargument for at least one of the arguments stated below. Be sure your counterargument exposes any fallacious reasoning you find in the statements and does not itself contain fallacies. Also be sure to anticipate and defuse objections likely to be raised by the opposition.

43g

log

1. Although I help my nephew with his arithmetic assignments, he's still failing tests. He must not be paying attention, or else he's just stupid in math.
2. All these unnecessary environmental regulations are really not essential. Besides, the costs of pollution control are aggravating the national decline in productivity and the rise in inflation. The auto industry has suffered severe financial losses in recent years, and the energy crisis has made our country's deposits of high-sulfur coal crucial to our energy supply. What we need now is less environmental regulation, not more.
3. Since 1964 scores on Scholastic Aptitude Tests have been dropping. What's more, students graduating from high school today can neither read nor write nor do arithmetic at their grade level. Clearly, the minimum competency testing program used in Jacksonville, Florida, should be instituted nationwide. A student who can't pass these standardized tests shouldn't graduate.
4. My roommate will make a terrific veterinarian. She just loves animals. She's always bringing home stray dogs and cats. It really upsets her to see an animal suffer.
5. If a coat or suit becomes old, ragged, and out of style, we don't continue to wear it. We replace it with a new one. Similarly, employ-

ees who reach age 65 should be forced to retire to make way for younger people with energy and fresh ideas.

REVIEW EXERCISE B

The following problems are designed to direct your attention to some of the violations of logic that you encounter every day.

1. Analyze several automobile advertisements, several cosmetic or drug advertisements, and several cigarette advertisements in current magazines or on television on the basis of the following questions:
   a. What specific appeals are made? (For example, automobile advertising makes wide use of the bandwagon approach; cosmetic advertising often uses transfer methods.) How logical are these appeals?
   b. Are all terms clearly defined?
   c. What kinds of generalizations are used or assumed? Are these generalizations adequately supported?
   d. Is evidence honestly and fairly presented?
   e. Are cause-and-effect relationships clear and indisputable?
   f. Is slanted, loaded language used? What is the advertiser trying to achieve with the connotative language?

2. Read the following student editorial from a college newspaper and analyze its success as an argument by using the questions listed below.
   a. What is the author's apparent purpose? What action do you believe he wants readers to take?
   b. In your own words, what is the essay's assertion? Where is the assertion stated in the essay?
   c. What generalizations does the author make? Are they supported with adequate evidence?
   d. Does the author provide arguments that anticipate and diffuse counterarguments likely to be raised by the opposition?
   e. Do any parts of the argument rest on shaky assumptions or *a priori* premises?
   f. Is the author's reasoning sound? Does the argument contain fallacies? If so, what types?
   g. What is the author's tone? Does it change?
   h. Is any of the language unfairly slanted?
   i. Do you find the essay persuasive? Why or why not?

SELECTIVE DEMOCRACY

The President signed into law last week a bill banning radio and TV advertisements of any smokeless tobacco product. The law also called for one of the following three warnings to be placed on the packages of smokeless tobacco products: "This product may cause mouth cancer," "This product may cause gum disease and tooth loss," or "This product is not a safe alternative to cigarettes."

These warning labels, with the possible exception of the latter, are necessary and acceptable. Clear statements, such as those listed above, give people who are unqualified to assess the risks of tobacco themselves—in this case, anyone outside the medical field—information on the consequences of tobacco use.

However, taking from a company the opportunity to advertise its product is not only unfair; it is in direct contrast with the ideals and principles inherent in a democracy.

Once again, we see a company recognized as legally providing a product being refused the chance to use two of the most powerful media—television and radio. The Editorial Board's solution is, as it has been in similar matters in the past, quite simple: (1) make tobacco companies illegal and, on that basis, refuse to accept their advertising, or (2) recognize tobacco companies as legal and entitled to the rights other companies possess, and allow advertising for tobacco products on television and in other media.

In keeping with the second, and decidedly more democratic, approach, other businesses now prohibited from advertising on television and radio would be given the opportunity to use these and other media. Liquor and cigarettes would enjoy the same chance to reach the public as douches, Twinkies, and any other product.

It seems only fair.

REVIEW EXERCISE C

Read "Abolishing the Penny Makes Good Sense," the argumentative essay that follows. Use the questions listed in Review Exercise B2 to evaluate the essay. Which essay—"Selective Democracy" or "Abolishing the Penny"—is the more effective argument? Why?

ABOLISHING THE PENNY MAKES GOOD SENSE

An economist rarely has the opportunity to recommend a policy change that benefits 200 million people, imposes costs on virtually no one, and saves the government money to boot. But I have such a suggestion to offer the nation as a holiday gift: Let's abolish the penny.

Yes, the old copperhead has outlived its usefulness and is by now a public nuisance—something akin to the gnat. Pennies get in the way when we make change. They add unwanted weight to our pockets and purses. Few people nowadays even bend down to pick a penny off the sidewalk. Doesn't that prove that mining and minting copper into pennies is wasteful? Today, if it rained pennies from heaven, only a fool would turn his umbrella upside down: The money caught would be worth less than the ruined umbrella.

I have been antipenny for years, but final proof came about two years ago. I used to dump my pennies into a shoe box. Eventually, I accumulated several hundred. Dismayed by the ever-growing collection of useless copper, I offered the box to my son William, then 8, warning him that the bank would take the pennies only if he neatly wrapped them in rolls of 50. William, obviously a keen, intuitive economist, thought the matter over carefully for about two seconds before responding: "Thanks, Dad, but it's not worth it." If it's not worth the time of an 8-year-old to wrap pennies, why does the U.S. government keep producing the things?

43g

log

More than the time of 8-year-olds is involved. Think how often you have waited in line while customers ahead of you fumbled through their pockets or purses for a few—expletive deleted—pennies. A trivial problem. Yes, until you multiply your wasted seconds by the billions of cash transactions that take place in our economy each year. I estimate that all this penny-pinching wastes several hundred million hours annually. Valuating that at, say, $10 an hour adds up to several billion dollars per year. . . .

We also must consider the cost of minting and maintaining the penny supply. There are roughly 91 billion pennies circulating, and every year the U.S. Treasury produces 12 billion to 14 billion more, at a cost of about $90 million. Since this expenditure just produces a nuisance for society, it should be at the top of everyone's list of budget cuts.

There are no coherent objections to abolishing the penny. It has been claimed, apparently with a straight face, that eliminating pennies would be inflationary, because all those $39.99 prices would rise to $40. Apart from the fact that such increases would be penny-ante, the claim itself is ludicrous. A price such as $39.99 is designed to keep a four from appearing as the first digit—something the retailer deems psychologically important. In a penny-less society merchants probably would change the number to $39.95, not raise it to $40. Even if only one-fifth of all merchants reacted this way, abolishing the penny would be disinflationary.

Sales tax poses a problem. How would a penny-free economy cope with, for instance, a 7% sales tax on a $31 purchase, which comes to $2.17? The answer leads to the second part of my suggestion. Let all states and localities amend their sales taxes to round all tax bills to the next-highest nickel. In the example, the state would collect $2.20 instead of $2.17. The customer would lose 3¢ but—if my previous arguments are correct—would actually be better off without the pennies. What other tax leaves the taxpayer happier for having paid it?

Only tradition explains our stubborn attachment to the penny. But sometimes traditions get ridiculous. Surely the smallest currency unit a country uses should be related to its average income. Yet countries with lower standards of living than the U.S. have minimum currency units worth more than 1¢—while we have been minting the penny for two centuries. . . .

Sure, the penny has sentimental value. That motivates the last part of my suggestion. Rather than call in all the pennies and melt them, which would be too expensive and perhaps heartrending, the government should simply announce that it is demonetizing the penny . . . and let collectors take many of the pesky coppers out of circulation. After hobbyists and investors accumulated whatever stockpiles they desired, the rest could be redeemed by the government—wrapped neatly in rolls of 50, of course.

Let's get penny-wise and abolish the 1¢ piece. The idea is so logical, so obviously correct, that I am sure the new Congress will enact it during its first days in office.

ALAN S. BLINDER

43g

log

RESEARCH

Research is . . . the attempt to take external events and data and, by passing them through the sensibilities of the writer, to produce a text that reflects both the outer and the writer's inner worlds of meaning.

JAMES V. CATANO, "Navigating the Fluid Text"

Knowledge is of two kinds. We know a subject ourselves, or we know where we can find information upon it.

SAMUEL JOHNSON, Boswell's *Life of Johnson*

44

RESEARCH

Research is a basic human activity—as fundamental as a child's trial-and-error approach to learning about a hot stove, as sophisticated as a chemist's hypothesis-testing in the laboratory or an anthropologist's field study of tribal customs. Somewhere in between lies the research that students conduct while in college. Broadly, then, everyone engaged in the activity of acquiring knowledge, from the two-year-old to the nuclear physicist to the freshman writing a personal-experience narrative, is engaged in research.

Furthermore, research takes many forms. Observing people and events, performing laboratory experiments, tape-recording an interview, writing notes in the library, or comparing one's own experiences with those of someone else are all forms of research.

But research is not simply gathering data; it is selecting, organizing, analyzing, interpreting, and evaluating data so that valid statements can be made about some aspect of reality. To conduct research is to apply a systematic approach to obtaining information, drawing and testing conclusions, and sharing these conclusions with others. Research begins with what is known and moves into the unknown, with the aim of exploring some aspect of the world and making verifiable statements about it.

One end product of this process is the research paper. Whether the final form is an article in a scholarly journal or a magazine, a presentation at a business meeting, testimony before a congressional subcommittee, a patent application for a new drug, specifications for an improved automobile ignition system, or an essay for a college political science course, the results of the research process are often presented in writing at some stage so others can share and evaluate them.

This section and the next follow Jan Dunn, a student writer, as she collects material and writes a research paper for a course called "Social Change." The process Jan uses to plan her search strategy; gather her information; sort, evaluate, and organize it; and finally write the paper will show you an effective way to handle a research project.

44a

Planning a search strategy

The cornerstone of most research projects is a *preliminary* or *working bibliography*, a list of articles, books, and other sources you plan to consult in gathering your material. It is called a "working" bibliography because as your research progresses you will add to the initial list when you come across useful-looking references and you will delete items if you find information indicating that some sources may not be helpful.

Unfortunately, when faced with a research assignment, too many students begin by aimlessly thumbing the subject cards in the library's card catalog. They waste time and create frustration for themselves because they try to use the card catalog long before they are ready to benefit from the information it contains. With a good search strategy, you not only can save yourself time but can be reasonably certain you are developing an informed, balanced view of your topic.

Begin with knowledgeable people. Why reinvent the wheel? Before looking for books, talk to people. Once you have decided on the general subject area you want to explore, talk to professors, graduate students, or other researchers at your school who are likely to know something about your subject.

These people are often willing to help you learn about a subject and will probably be able to suggest relevant books and articles. They may even know of existing bibliographies you can use to begin your library search. Frequently such people can provide information about prevailing schools of thought on a subject and tell you about the most authoritative scholars and sources. In fact, your professors may be authoritative sources themselves. You may want to interview a professor, taking notes for later use in your research paper.

Because she was interested in computers, Jan Dunn decided she would like to write her research paper about the effects of computer technology on American society. Since her paper was for a class on social change, she thought she might explore the relationship between computer technology and social change, if any.

Jan began her search strategy by talking with her sociology professor. He helped her see that she would actually need to explore three topics: social change, the impact of technology in general, and the impact of computer technology in particular. Then she could formulate a thesis about their relationship.

44a

Tune your eyes and ears to your subject. Campus and community events can provide sources of information: special lectures, workshops, or programs that relate to your topic. Step up your reading of periodicals and newspapers. If your subject is a current one, you will probably discover useful articles in daily metropolitan newspapers or in weekly magazines such as *Time, Newsweek,* or *Business Week.*

Tell your friends and family about your topic. Jan's father gave her a tip about a relevant best-selling book, and he also remembered that *Time* magazine had devoted most of an issue to computers.

44b

Learning about your library's resources

Libraries have three principal kinds of holdings: a general collection of books; a collection of periodicals, bulletins, and pamphlets; and a collection of reference works.

General collection of books. The general collection includes most of the books in the library—all those that are available for general circulation. Some libraries have open shelves; that is, you can select books yourself. Other libraries keep the general collection in closed stacks; to obtain a book you submit a "call slip" bearing the call number, author, and title of the book. Then library personnel get the book for you. In either case, you first must obtain information from the card catalog (discussed later) so that your book can be located on the shelves.

Periodicals, bulletins, pamphlets. A **periodical** is a publication that appears at regular (periodic) intervals. Periodicals (also called *serials*) include popular magazines, specialized magazines, and professional or scholarly journals. General periodicals include both popular and specialized magazines such as *Time, Fortune, National Geographic, Road & Track,* and *Psychology Today.* Professional and scholarly journals include those such as *American Historical Review, PMLA, Journal of Organic Chemistry,* and *International Social Sciences Journal.* Both types of periodicals are good research sources, but remember that professional or scholarly journals will provide more detailed, learned investigations of subjects and are often considered primary sources. (Definitions of primary and secondary sources appear on page 455.)

Bulletins and **pamphlets** may or may not be periodicals, depending on whether they are issued as parts of a series or as separate, single publications. They are usually kept in the stacks with the main collection of books. Most libraries keep recent issues of magazines, journals, and newspapers in the open shelves of the reading room. Older issues are bound in volumes and shelved in the stacks. Back issues of major newspapers may be stored on microfiche or microfilm. Libraries usually do not allow periodicals to be checked out.

Periodicals are invaluable research aids because they contain the most recent material on a subject and reflect opinions current at the time of publication. Also, information is likely to appear in periodicals before it is published in books.

Reference materials. Your library's reference collection contains encyclopedias, dictionaries, indexes, directories, handbooks, atlases, and guides. These are usually located on open shelves in the main reading room, and they should not be removed from the reference area. Some of them, particularly indexes, may be stored on microfiche or in computerized data banks rather than in bound volumes.

You can use the subject, title, and author headings in reference works to find journal, magazine, and newspaper articles and to locate bibliographies. You can obtain statistics and biographical information in the reference collection or scan book reviews that will help you determine if a particular work is worth reading or not. You can also locate abstracts (summaries) of journal articles to help you decide whether you want to find and read a whole article.

44c

Using reference works to develop an overview of your subject

To benefit from sources that discuss your subject in detail, you first will need to gain a general view of it. Your library's reference collection—rather than the card catalog—is the best place to start. Reference works such as those listed on the following pages, and others that your reference librarian may suggest, can supply not only a subject overview but also numerous items for your working bibliography. As an illustration, Jan's search procedure in the reference collection of her college library is given below.

1. Checked encyclopedia for an overview of technology. Used one of the specialized ones, *International Encyclopedia of the Social Sciences,* which contained bibliography through the early 1960's.

2. Using subject headings in *Sociological Abstracts,* read its summaries of some journal articles on topic. Noticed several articles were published in one issue of periodical called *Daedalus.*

3. Looked up *Daedalus* in *Magazines for Libraries* to see what kind of reputation it has. Seems authoritative. Decided to locate this issue of journal. Also looked up *Technology Review* (mentioned in book recommended by Dad). *Magazines for Libraries* says it's published at MIT, is well written by leaders in field: "an important and authoritative quarterly." Planned to survey several issues.

4. Checked *Book Review Digest* to get opinions about *Appropriate Technology,* book recommended by sociology professor. Excerpts from review published in *Science* suggest its essays are written by knowledgeable people.

5. Noticed name "Harvey Brooks" in several bibliographies and references. Is one of the contributors to *Appropriate Technology.* Checked him in *Who's Who.* A professor at Harvard, he has impressive credentials.

6. Used *Essay and General Literature Index* to locate individual essays published in books.

7. Checked *Readers' Guide to Periodical Literature* to see which issue of *Time* magazine had article on computer as "man of year."

8. Got help from reference librarian, who showed me how to use Dow Jones News/Retrieval computerized database.

44c

Reference books can not only add to your working bibliography but help you decide whether sources are worth pursuing. Rather than reading randomly and perhaps missing important material, you can develop a planned approach for gathering the best available information.

Become familiar with the kinds of reference works available in your library and with the most important works of each kind. If you cannot find the book you want or if you do not know what sources will help you most, ask the reference librarian. Librarians are not simply custodians; they are teachers trained to show you effective ways of using the library as part of your search strategy.

The following is a representative list of reference books available in most libraries. Some reference books are revised periodicaly, appearing in new editions, or have supplements. You will usually want to look for the most recently published version.

GUIDES TO REFERENCE SOURCES

Brownstone, David, and Gorton Carruth. *Where to Find Business Information.* Directory to over 5,000 sources including data bases, information services, government publications, books, and periodicals.

Galin, Saul, and Peter Spielberg. *Reference Books: How to Select and Use Them.*

Gates, Jean Key. *Guide to the Use of Books and Libraries.*

Sheehy, Eugene P. *Guide to Reference Books.* Supplement.

Shove, Raymond H., et al. *The Use of Books and Libraries.*

Statistical Sources. A subject guide to locating statistics sources.

CATALOGS

Books in Print. Author and title indexes for *Publishers' Trade List Annual Subject Guide to Books in Print.*

Cumulative Book Index. Monthly listing of published books in English. Cumulated annually.

Monthly Catalog of U.S. Government Publications. 1895 to date.

National Union Catalog. Subject and author listings of Library of Congress holdings as well as titles from other libraries, motion pictures, recordings, and film strips.

Union List of Serials in Libraries of the United States and Canada. Lists of periodicals and newspapers. Supplemented monthly by *New Serial Titles.*

Vertical File Index. 1935—. Supplements to date. (Formerly called *Vertical File Service Catalog.* 1935–54.) Monthly, with annual cumulations. Subject and title index to selected pamphlet material.

GENERAL ENCYCLOPEDIAS

Chambers Encyclopedia. 15 vols.

Collier's Encyclopedia. 24 vols.

Encyclopedia Americana. 30 vols.

44c

Encyclopaedia Britannica. 30 vols.
Encyclopedia International. 20 vols.
New Columbia Encyclopedia. 1 vol.

DICTIONARIES, WORD BOOKS
Abbreviations Dictionary. International in scope.
Acronyms, Initialisms and Abbreviations.
American Heritage Dictionary. Good notes on usage.
Dictionary of American English on Historical Principles. 4 vols. 1938–44.
Dictionary of American Regional English.
Evans, Bergen, and Cornelia Evans. *A Dictionary of Contemporary American Usage.*
Fowler, Henry W. *Dictionary of Modern English Usage.* 2nd ed. Rev. by Sir Ernest Gowers.
Funk & Wagnalls New Standard Dictionary. Unabridged.
Oxford Dictionary of English Etymology.
Oxford English Dictionary. 13 vols. and supplement. 1888–1933. Also known as *New English Dictionary.* Unabridged.
Partridge, Eric. *A Dictionary of Slang and Unconventional English.*
Random House Dictionary of the English Language. Unabridged.
Roget's International Thesaurus. Several editions available.
Webster's Dictionary of Proper Names.
Webster's New Dictionary of Synonyms.
Webster's Third New International Dictionary. Unabridged.
Wentworth, Harold, and Stuart B. Flexner. *Dictionary of American Slang.*

YEARBOOKS
Americana Annual. 1924—.
Britannica Book of the Year. 1938—.
Congressional Record. 1873—. Issued daily while Congress is in session: revised and issued in bound form at end of the session.
Facts on File. A weekly digest of world events. 1940—.
Historical Statistics of the United States: Colonial Times to 1970. 2 vols. 1975. Supplement to *Statistical Abstract.* Both published by U.S. Bureau of the Census.
Negro Almanac. 1967—.
New International Year Book. 1907—.
Official Associated Press Almanac. 1969—. An almanac with longer articles, strong emphasis on statistical data and biographical information.
Statistical Abstract of the United States. 1878—.
United Nations Statistical Yearbook. 1945–1968. Monthly supplements.
World Almanac and Book of Facts. 1868—.

44c

ATLASES AND GAZETTEERS

Columbia-Lippincott Gazetteer of the World.

Commercial and Library Atlas of the World. Frequently revised.

Encyclopaedia Britannica World Atlas. Frequently revised.

National Geographic Atlas of the World.

New Cosmopolitan World Atlas. Issued annually.

The Times Atlas of the World.

Webster's New Geographical Dictionary.

GENERAL BIOGRAPHY

American Men and Women of Science.

Biographical Dictionaries Master Index. A guide to over 725,000 listings of biographies appearing in current dictionaries and collective biographical sources.

Biography Index. 1946—. Quarterly. Cumulated annually, with permanent volumes every three years.

Current Biography: Who's News and Why. 1940—. Published monthly with semiannual and annual cumulations.

Dictionary of American Biography. 17 vols., supplements.

International Who's Who. 1936—.

Webster's Biographical Dictionary.

Who's Who. (British) 1849—.

Who's Who in America. 1899—.

Who's Who of American Women. 1958—.

Who Was Who. 1897–1960.

Who Was Who in America. Historical Volume. 1607–1896.

BOOKS OF QUOTATIONS

Bartlett, John. *Familiar Quotations.*

Evans, Bergen. *Dictionary of Quotations.*

The Macmillan Book of Proverbs, Maxims, and Famous Phrases.

Oxford Dictionary of Quotations.

44c

MYTHOLOGY AND FOLKLORE

Brewer's Dictionary of Phrase and Fable.

Bullfinch, Thomas. *Bullfinch's Mythology.*

Funk & Wagnalls Standard Dictionary of Folklore, Mythology, and Legend. 2 vols.

Hammond, N. G., and H. H. Scullord. *The Oxford Classical Dictionary.*

Larousse World Mythology.

LITERATURE, DRAMA, FILM, AND TELEVISION

Aaronson, C. S., ed. *International Television Almanac.* 1956—.

Adelman, Irving, and R. Dworkin. *Modern Drama: A Checklist of Critical Literature on Twentieth Century Plays.*

Baugh, Albert C., ed. *A Literary History of England.*

Benét, William Rose. *The Reader's Encyclopedia.*

Bukalski, Peter J. *Film Research: A Critical Bibliography.*

Cassell's *Encyclopedia of World Literature.*

Cawkwell, Tim, and John Milton Smith, eds. *World Encyclopedia of the Film.*

Columbia Dictionary of Modern European Literature.

Contemporary Authors: A Bio-bibliographical Guide to Current Authors and Their Works. 1962—.

Dictionary of World Literary Terms.

Hart, J. D. *Oxford Companion to American Literature.*

Hartnoll, Phyllis. *The Oxford Companion to the Theatre.*

Harvey, Sir Paul, and J. E. Heseltine. *Oxford Companion to Classical Literature.*

————.*Oxford Companion to English Literature.*

Holman, C. Hugh. *A Handbook to Literature.*

International Encyclopedia of the Film.

Literary History of England. 4 vols.

Literary History of the United States. 2 vols.

MLA International Bibliography of Books and Articles on the Modern Languages and Literatures. Published annually since 1922.

New York Times Film Reviews, 1913–70.

Spiller, Robert E., et al., eds. *Literary History of the United States.*

Whitlow, Roger. *Black American Literature.*

Woodress, James, ed. *American Fiction 1900–1950: A Guide to Information Sources.*

HISTORY, POLITICAL SCIENCE

Cambridge Ancient History. 5 vols. Plates.

Cambridge Medieval History. 1967—.

Dictionary of American History. 8 vols.

Durant, Will, and Ariel Durant. *The Story of Civilization.* 11 vols.

Encyclopedia of American History.

Harvard Guide to American History. 2 vols.

Johnson, Thomas H. *Oxford Companion to American History.*

Langer, William L. *An Encyclopedia of World History.*

New Cambridge Modern History. 14 vols.

Political Handbook and Atlas of the World. Published annually.

Political Science: A Bibliographical Guide to the Literature.

Schlesinger, Arthur M., and D. R. Fox, eds. *A History of American Life.* 13 vols. 1927–48.

44c

THE ARTS

Apel, Willi. *Harvard Dictionary of Music.*

Bryan, Michael. *Bryan's Dictionary of Painters and Engravers.* 5 vols.

Canaday, John C. *The Lives of the Painters*. 4 vols.

Chujoy, Anatole, and P. W. Manchester. *The Dance Encyclopedia*.

Encyclopedia of Painting.

Encyclopedia of World Art. 15 vols.

Feather, Leonard. *Encyclopedia of Jazz*.

Fletcher, Sir Banister F. *A History of Architecture*.

Focal Encyclopedia of Photography. 2 vols.

Grove's Dictionary of Music and Musicians.

Myers, Bernard S. *McGraw-Hill Dictionary of Art*. 5 vols.

Osborne, Harold. *Oxford Companion to Art*. 1970.

Popular Music: An Annotated List of American Popular Songs. 6 vols.

Scholes, Percy A. *Oxford Companion to Music*.

Stambler, Eric. *Encyclopedia of Pop, Rock, and Soul*.

Thompson, Oscar, and N. Slonimsky. *International Cyclopedia of Music and Musicians*.

PHILOSOPHY, RELIGION

Adams, Charles, ed. *A Reader's Guide to the Great Religions*.

The Concise Encyclopedia of Western Philosophy and Philosophers.

Encyclopedia Judaica. 16 vols.

Encyclopedia of Philosophy. 4 vols.

Ferm, Vergilius. *Encyclopedia of Religion*.

Grant, Frederick C., and H. H. Rowley. *Dictionary of the Bible*.

New Catholic Encyclopedia. 17 vols.

New Schaff-Herzog Encyclopedia of Religious Knowledge. 12 vols. and index.

Universal Jewish Encyclopedia. 10 vols.

SCIENCE, TECHNOLOGY

Chamber's Technical Dictionary. Revised with supplement.

Dictionary of Physics.

Encyclopedia of Chemistry.

Encyclopedia of Physics.

Gray, Peter, ed. *The Encyclopedia of the Biological Sciences*.

Handbook of Chemistry and Physics. 1914—.

McGraw-Hill Encyclopedia of Science and Technology. 15 vols.

Universal Encyclopedia of Mathematics. 1964.

Van Nostrand's Scientific Encyclopedia.

SOCIAL SCIENCES, BUSINESS, AND ECONOMICS

Davis, John P., ed. *The American Negro Reference Book*.

Deidler, Lee J., and Douglas R. Carmichael. *Accountant's Handbook*.

A Dictionary of Psychology.

Encyclopedia of Educational Research.

44c

Encyclopedia of Human Behavior: Psychology, Psychiatry, and Mental Health.

Encyclopedia of Social Work. (Formerly *Social Work Yearbook,* 1929–1960.)

Good, Carter V. *Dictionary of Education.*

Greenwald, Douglas. *The McGraw-Hill Dictionary of Modern Economics.*

Heyel, Carl. *The Encyclopedia of Management.*

International Encyclopedia of the Social Sciences. 17 vols. Supplement.

Klein, Barry T., ed. *Reference Encyclopedia of the American Indians.*

Mitchell, Geoffrey D. *A Dictionary of Sociology.*

Munn, G. G. *Encyclopedia of Banking and Finance.*

Thomas Register of American Manufacturers. 1910—. Multivolume. Updated annually. Includes alphabetical listings of company profiles, also brand names and trademarks.

White, Carl M., et al. *Sources of Information on the Social Sciences.*

Using general and special periodical indexes. A library's catalog merely shows what periodicals are available. Periodical indexes, which are usually shelved in the reference section of the library, help you to locate the articles you need in those periodicals. Such indexes are usually classed as general or special indexes. **General indexes** list articles on many different kinds of subjects. **Special indexes** limit themselves to articles in specific areas. Representative lists of both kinds of indexes follow.

GENERAL INDEXES

Readers' Guide to Periodical Literature. 1900 to date. Published semimonthly; cumulated every three months and annually. The *Readers' Guide* gives entries under author, title, and subject for articles appearing in about 160 popular periodicals.

44c

This is the most widely known and used of the general indexes. Because many periodical indexes use systems very similar to that of the *Readers' Guide,* it is worth examining the sample entries below.

The headings for 1 through 5 are **subject entries;** 6 and 7 are **author entries.** Entry 8, a subject entry, indicates that an article indexed under the subject heading *Graffiti* was published in the June 1969 issue of *Science Digest,* volume 65, pages 31 through 33. Titled "Walls Remember," it was illustrated and unsigned. (All abbreviations and symbols used are explained in the first pages of any issue of the *Readers' Guide.*)

The second listing under entry 1 refers the user to a series of articles by D. Wolfle published in *Science* and titled "Are Grades Necessary?" The first article appeared in the issue of November 15, 1968 (volume 162, pages 745–746); the second and third appeared, respectively, in the issues for April 18 and June 6, 1969. Entry 2, under the subject heading *Graduate students,* indexes a review by D. Zinberg and P. Doty in the May 1969 issue of *Scientific American* of a book, *New Brahmins: Scientific Life in America,* by S. Klaw. The + that follows the page references is an indication that the review is continued on a page or pages past 140. Entries 3, 4, and 7 are cross-references to the places in the *Guide* at which the user can find the subject or author listed.

1 GRADING and marking (students)
Answer to Sally; multiple-choice tests. W. R. Link. Ed Digest 34:24–7 My '69
Are grades necessary? D. Wolfle; discussion. Science 162:745–6; 164:245, 1117–18 N 15 '68. Ap 18. Je 6 '69
ROTC: under fire but doing fine. il U S News 66:38 My 19 '69

2 GRADUATE students
New Brahmins: scientific life in America, by S. Klaw. Review
Sci Am 220:139–40+ My '69. D. Zinberg and P. Doty

3 GRADUATION. See Commencements

4 GRADUATION addresses. See Baccalaureate addresses

5 GRAEBNER, Clark
Profiles. J. McPhee. por New Yorker 45:45–8+ Je 7: 44–8+ Je 14 '69

6 GRAEF, Hilda
Why I remain a Catholic. Cath World 209:77–80 My '69

7 GRAF, Rudolf F. See Whalen, G. J. jt. auth.

8 GRAFFITI
Walls remember. il Sci Digest 65:31–3 Je '69

From *Readers' Guide to Periodical Literature,* July 1969, p. 73. Reproduced by permission of The H. W. Wilson Company.

Three other general indexes are valuable supplements to the *Readers' Guide:*

International Index. 1907–65. Became *Social Sciences and Humanities Index.* 1965–73. Divided into *Social Sciences Index.* 1974—, and *Humanities Index.* 1974—.

44c

Poole's Index to Periodical Literature, 1802–81. Supplements through January 1, 1907. This is a subject index to American and English periodicals.

Popular Periodicals Index. 1973—. An author and subject guide to popular articles appearing in about 25 periodicals not indexed by major indexing services.

SPECIAL INDEXES

These indexes list articles published in periodicals devoted to special concerns or fields.

The Bibliographic Index. 1938—. Indexes current bibliographies by subject; includes both bibliographies published *as* books and pamphlets and those that appear *in* books, periodical articles, and pamphlets.

Book Review Digest. 1905—. Monthly, cumulated annually. Lists books by author and quotes from several reviews for each. Covers 75 journals and newspapers.

Book Review Index. 1965—. Covers 230 journals and lists books that have one or more reviews.

Current Book Review Citations. 1976—. Indexes over 1,000 periodicals and includes fiction, nonfiction, and children's books.

Esssay and General Literature Index. 1934—. Indexes collections of essays, articles, and speeches.

New York Times Index. 1913—. Semimonthly, with annual cumulation. Since this index provides dates on which important events, speeches, and the like, occurred, it serves indirectly as an index to records of the same events in the other newspapers.

Ulrich's International Periodicals Directory. 2 vols. Lists 65,000 periodicals under the subjects they contain, with detailed cross-references and index, thus indicating what periodicals are in a particular field. Also indicates in what other guide or index each periodical is indexed, thus serving indirectly as a master index.

The titles of most of the following special indexes are self-explanatory.

Agricultural Index. 1916 to date. A subject index, appearing nine times a year and cumulated annually.

Applied Science and Technology Index. 1958 to date. (Formerly *Industrial Arts Index.*)

The Arts Index. 1929 to date. An author and subject index.

Articles on American Literature. 1900–1950. 1950–1967. 1968–1975.

Business Periodicals Index. 1958 to date. Monthly. (Formerly *Industrial Arts Index.*)

Dramatic Index. 1909–1949. Continued in *Bulletin of Bibliography,* 1950 to date. Annual index to drama and theater.

The Education Index. 1929 to date. An author and subject index.

Engineering Index. 1884 to date. An author and subject index.

General Science Index. 1978—. Supplements monthly except June and December.

Granger's Index to Poetry.

Index to Legal Periodicals. 1908 to date. A quarterly author and subject index.

Industrial Arts Index. 1913–1957. An author and subject index, monthly, with annual cumulations. (In 1958 this index was split into *Applied Science and Technology Index* and *Business Periodicals Index.*)

Monthly Catalog of United States Government Publications. 1905—.

Physical Education Index. 1978—. Covers not only physical education but sports in general. Published quarterly.

Play Index. 1978.

44c

Public Affairs Information Service Bulletin. 1915 to date. Weekly, with bi-monthly and annual cumulations. An index to materials on economics, politics, and sociology.

Quarterly Cumulative Index Medicus. 1927 to date. A continuation of the *Index Medicus,* 1899–1926. Indexes books as well as periodicals.

Short Story Index. 1953—. Supplements.

Song Index. 1926. Supplement.

United Nations Documents Index. 1950—.

PERIODICAL REVIEWS

Two reference books provide descriptions of periodicals found in most libraries. These books give publication information as well as types of subject matter, authors, and readers usually associated with a periodical. Such information can be helpful in evaluating a particular periodical's biases, authority, and credibility.

Farber, Evan I. *Classified List of Periodicals for the College Library.* 5th ed. 1972. Organizes scholarly and professional journals in the liberal arts and sciences by field. Does not cover technology or engineering.

Katz, Bill and Linda S. *Magazines for Libraries.* 4th ed. 1982. Describes most popular and many scholarly periodicals.

Using electronic databases. Accessing electronic databases of stored information is becoming increasingly widespread and thus increasingly important to library research. Many of these databases are available through information retrieval services to which libraries and individuals may subscribe; that is, the user pays a fee for "dialing up and logging on" to the service via computer, modem, and telephone. CompuServe, DIALOG Information Retrieval Service, Bibliographic Retrieval Service (BRS), and Dow Jones News/Retrieval are but a few of the many database vendors. Check with your librarian to see which ones may be available at your school. Through online computerized searches you can consult indexes, retrieve statistical information, examine law case records, check stock market prices, or look at research citations in education or a number of other fields. If your library has access to electronic databases, the library staff will show you how to use them.

44d

44d

Continuing your search at the card catalog

Once you have gained an overview of your subject, tentatively decided on a direction, and begun compiling a preliminary bibliography, you will be able to use the library's card catalog more effectively. This catalog lists alphabetically all the books and periodicals the library contains. Its cards tell you the call number you need to locate books on the shelves. Your library may list periodicals in a separate serials catalog, either on cards, microfiche, or computer printout. In fact, some libraries store their entire catalog listing on microform or in computer files.

Classification systems. The classification system on which a card catalog is based is a kind of map of library holdings. Library holdings are divided into categories with numbers or letters assigned to each. Consequently, if you know the numbers or letters for the general category you need, you occasionally might want to bypass the card catalog, go directly to the appropriate shelves, and browse through the books.

The chief purpose of a classification system is to permit easy retrieval of stored materials. To further that objective, every item in the library is given a call number. Be sure to copy the call number fully and exactly as it appears on the catalog card.

American libraries use either the Dewey decimal system or the Library of Congress system to classify books.

The Dewey system divides books into ten numbered classes:

000–099	General works	500–599	Pure science
100–199	Philosophy	600–699	Useful arts
200–299	Religion	700–799	Fine arts
300–399	Social sciences	800–899	Literature
400–499	Philology	900–999	History

Each of these divisions is further divided into ten parts, as:

800	General literature	850	Italian literature
810	American literature	860	Spanish literature
820	English literature	870	Latin literature
830	German literature	880	Greek literature
840	French literature	890	Other literatures

44d

Each of these divisions is further divided as:

821	English poetry	826	English letters
822	English drama	827	English satire
823	English fiction	828	English miscellany
824	English essays	829	Anglo-Saxon
825	English oratory		

Further subdivisions are indicated by decimals. *The Romantic Rebels,* a book about Keats, Byron, and Shelley, is numbered 821.09, indicating a subdivision of the 821 English poetry category.

The Library of Congress classification system, used by large libraries, divides books into lettered classes:

A	General works
B	Philosophy, Religion
C	History, Auxiliary sciences
D	Foreign history and topography
E–F	American history
G	Geography, Anthropology
H	Social sciences
J	Political science
K	Law
L	Education
M	Music
N	Fine arts
P	Language and literature
Q	Science
R	Medicine
S	Agriculture
T	Technology
U	Military science
V	Naval science
Z	Bibliography, Library science

Each of these sections is further divided by letters and numbers that show the specific call number of a book. *English Composition in Theory and Practice* by Henry Seidel Canby and others is classified in this system as PE 1408.E5. (In the Dewey decimal system this same volume is numbered 808 C214.)

If your library uses the Library of Congress classification system, you will find near the card catalog several volumes entitled *Library of Congress Subject Headings*. By looking up "key words" related to your topic in these volumes, you will learn which headings to check in the subject section of the catalog.

44d

If your library uses the Dewey decimal system, you will have to compare your list of key words directly with the catalog's subject cards to discover which ones are used as subject headings relevant to your topic. A reference book entitled *Sears List of Subject Headings* lists headings applicable to either the Dewey system or the Library of Congress system.

Besides **subject cards,** library catalogs also contain **author cards** and **title cards** (no title card is used when the title begins with words as common as "A History of . . ."). Following are author, title, and subject cards for a book Jan Dunn found by looking under the subject heading "Social History." Following the cards is an explanation of some of the information they contain.

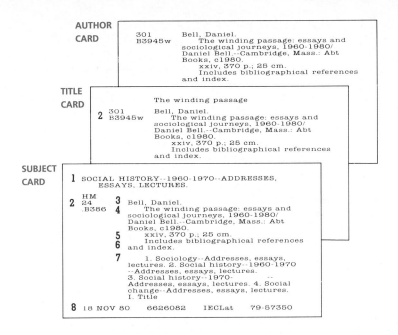

1. "SOCIAL HISTORY—1960–1970—ADDRESSES, ESSAYS, LECTURES" is a heading under which the card is filed in the subject section of the catalog.

HM
2. 24 gives the call number for the book in the Library of
.B386
Congress system.

301
B3945w gives the call number for this book in the Dewey decimal system. Except for the difference in the call number, catalog cards that use the Library of Congress system are identical with those in libraries using the Dewey system.

3. "Bell, Daniel" gives the name of the author (surname first). Some cards show the author's birth year after the name, followed by a dash if the author was living at the time the card was printed (e.g., "Wilson, John Harold, 1900—").

4. "The winding passage . . . 1980" gives the full title, the place of publication, the name of publisher, and the date of publication (copyright date). Note that library practice in capitalization differs from standard practice.

5. "xxiv, 370 p.; 25 cm." indicates that the book contains 24 introductory pages numbered in Roman numerals and 370 pages numbered in Arabic numerals. There are no portraits or illustrations in the book; if there were, they would be listed next as "ports." and "ils." The book is 25 centimeters high (an inch is 2.54 centimeters).

44d

6. Bell's book contains a bibliography and an index.

7. "1. Sociology . . . I. Title" are the **tracings** indicating that the book is listed in the catalog under four subject headings and one title heading. Subject headings are marked by Arabic numerals, and title headings are marked by Roman numerals.

8. "18 Nov 80 . . . 79–57350" contains library identification information such as the card's order number and the purchase date. The last few lines on some catalog cards also show the call numbers for both types of library classification systems and whether the book is held by the Library of Congress.

Two portions of a catalog card can be especially helpful in your search. The **contents note** (6) will tell you if the work contains a bibliography that you might use to find other related books or articles. The **tracings** (7) will show other catalog subject headings to check for additional books. For instance, under the heading "Social Change," Jan found several books that applied to technology's impact on society.

44e

Evaluating your selections

Once you have copied the author, title, and call number of the books and bound periodicals you've been adding to your preliminary bibliography, find them on the shelves if your library has open stacks. While you're at it, look at the books adjacent to the ones you've selected. Since books are classified by subject matter, you should expect to find other pertinent volumes nearby.

You'll save yourself some valuable time if you skim portions of the books you've chosen before you check them out of the library. Not every book that looked promising on a catalog card or in *Book Review Digest* will be worth carrying home. Jan decided some of her selections were of only limited value when she examined the following:

44e

1. **Table of contents.** It indicates which chapters might be useful.

2. **Preface.** It usually explains the book's purpose and the author's method. The preface may indicate that certain material has been omitted or included and why.

3. **Introduction.** It often gives a critical overview of the subject, establishing the focus and summarizing the approach taken.

4. **Glossary.** If included, it lists and defines terminology.

5. **Index.** It lists specific names, subjects, events, terms, and concepts covered in the book.

6. **Bibliography** and **footnotes** or **endnotes.** These may list additional important books and articles.

Students frequently carry home a mountain of books and begin reading from the top of the heap. No wonder research sometimes seems so laborious! Develop the habit of skimming your selections be-fore leaving the library. Five minutes spent glancing through its intro-duction, for instance, can tell you how pertinent a book will be to your research subject. Go back to the reference collection and see what *Book Review Digest* has to say about a book if you need to. Similarly, skim a few magazine and journal articles on your list. Rather than locating all of them in the stacks, check to see if any have been summarized in abstracts in the reference collection.

You'll want to narrow your sources to those that are most rele-vant and reliable. After all, your research paper will be judged on the merits of the evidence you present as well as on your use of that evi-dence.

44f
Distinguishing between primary and secondary sources

The difference between a primary and a secondary source is that the former is an original, first-hand report whereas the latter is second-hand information.

1. Primary sources include novels, short stories, poems, notes, letters, diaries, manuscripts, and other original documents; autobio-graphies; surveys, investigations, and interviews reported by the orig-inal recorder; original accounts of events by first recorders in news-papers and magazines.

2. Secondary sources include histories; biographies; encyclo-pedias and other reference works; essays, books, and articles that re-port or interpret the works of others.

When you use primary sources, you can evaluate the original information and draw your own conclusions, rather than depending on someone else's interpretation. Much of the time, however, you will probably have to rely on secondary sources. When you do, try to sep-arate fact from opinion and informed opinion from bias. Using sec-ondary sources written by well-respected authorities improves reliabil-ity, but keep in mind that even the most knowledgeable authorities often disagree. Comparing secondary sources with one another and with available primary sources often helps you to arrive at a balanced view of a subject.

44f

EXERCISE 44(1)

Draw a diagram of the reference room of your library, indicating on it the position of the following reference books and indexes.

1. *Encyclopaedia Britannica*
2. *Encyclopedia of Religion and Ethics*
3. *Jewish Encyclopedia*
4. *Dictionary of American History* (DAH)
5. *Dictionary of American Biography* (DAB)

6. *American Authors, 1600–1900*
7. *Who's Who*
8. *Facts on File*
9. *World Almanac*
10. *New English Dictionary* (NED), often referred to as *Oxford English Dictionary* (OED)
11. *General Card Catalog (if not in a separate room)*
12. *Readers' Guide to Periodical Literature*
13. *The New York Times Index*
14. *The Art Index*
15. *Business Periodicals Index*

EXERCISE 44(2)

Answer each of the following questions by consulting one of the standard reference guides listed in Exercise 44(1).

1. Where can you find information on the significance of the Menorah in Jewish history?
2. Among which tribe of American Indians is the highest development of shamanism found?
3. What did the word *gossip* mean in twelfth-century England?
4. Where can you find listed articles on French stained glass, printed in 1957 and 1958?
5. What was the first invention of Peter Cooper, American inventor, manufacturer, and philanthropist (d. 1883)?

EXERCISE 44(3)

To find a magazine article in *Readers' Guide* (or any periodical index), you must first know how to convert its information into conventional English. Demonstrate your familiarity with the *Readers' Guide* by examining the following excerpt and filling in the blanks.

44f

> **Job applications**
> *See also*
> Employment interviewing
> Courtesy and consideration: a plea to employers from a gypsy scholar. J. S. Goldberg. *Change* 15:8–10 Ja/F '83
> Does your résumé emphasize the right things? il *Glamour* 81:158 F '83
> Four personal ways to get a job. S. S. Fader. *Work Woman* 8:36+ Ja '83
> Résumés: how to write them. How to use them. M. Paul. il *Sr Sch* 115:19 F 4 '83
> Work resumes at 40 [women] C. Tuhy. il *Money* 12:81–2+ Ja '83

Articles on employment resumes are collected in the periodical index under the subject heading _____. These articles are arranged alphabetically by the _____ of the article. "Résumés: how to write them" is the title of an article written by _____. "il" means the article includes _____. "Sr Sch" is the _____ of the title of the periodical. The periodical's full title is spelled out in the _____ of the *Readers' Guide*. The article is in _____ 115, on _____ 19. "F   4   '83" stands for _____, the _____ the article was published.

EXERCISE 44(4)

Select a specific research subject of interest to you. Then use your library's resources to answer the following questions.

1. What are the titles of general or special encyclopedias (or handbooks or other general works such as textbooks) that have articles providing information on your subject?

2 If any of these articles contain relevant bibliographies, write down the full bibliographic information for a few of the most useful items.

3. What three subject headings found in the *Library of Congress Subject Headings* or *Sears List of Subject Headings* volumes are most closely related to your subject?

4. Examine the tracings on at least two relevant subject cards in the card catalog. Which tracings fit your subject best?

5. Names of people and organizations appear in the subject section of the card catalog. What names related to your subject are listed?

6. Using the subject headings in the catalog, look for the subject division "—Bibliography." If you find any book-length bibliographies, cite a few of those that look most useful.

7. Use the catalog subject headings and list two books that have bibliographies in them. Give the page numbers for the bibliography sections if they are listed on the catalog card.

8. In a book review index, locate reviews for one of the books relevant to your subject. Which book review index did you use? Where and when did the review originally appear?

9. List four periodical indexes (including one newspaper index and one collection of abstracts) showing useful articles on your subject. Write out the title, author (if any), and publication information for three articles. Using Katz's *Magazines for Libraries* and/or Farber's *Classified List of Periodicals for the College Library*, summarize their comments about the periodicals in which the articles are published.

10. Using the *Essay and General Literature Index*, give the following information pertaining to your research subject: (a) subject heading(s) used; (b) author of relevant essay; (c) title of that essay; (d) title of the book in which the essay appears; (e) call number of the book, if the library owns it.

45

45

THE RESEARCH PAPER

45a

Understanding the purposes of research papers

The aim of a research paper is not just to present information about a subject or to show that you can use the library and know correct documentation form. Although these skills are important, the purpose of a successful research paper should be to analyze and interpret information, to explore ideas and demonstrate their application.

Research projects usually start with a need for knowledge, or with an observation about what is known, and then systematically explore the subject with the aim of furthering the reader's understanding or breaking new ground. Consequently, research papers frequently test a theory, follow up on previous research, or explore a problem posed by other research or by events.

The opening section of a research paper typically introduces the broad subject and narrows it to the specific aspect the author intends to discuss. The opening often notes previous research, provides a context for the paper, or alerts the reader to points of view that will be explored later. The author's research method or approach may also be mentioned. And finally, the author indicates his or her point of view regarding the subject—the thesis or conclusions that the paper will demonstrate. Although these points may appear in a different order and with varying amounts of detail, they are usually all present in successful research papers.

45b

Determining your approach, directing your reading, focusing your subject

Knowing the general pattern and purposes of research papers will be helpful during your research process. Instead of taking notes with the nearly impossible aim of "learning everything," you can direct your reading. Once you have an overview of your subject, you may decide that you want to apply an accepted theory to a particular aspect of the subject. Or you may want to disagree with or modify someone else's conclusions, adding to and reinterpreting the evidence. Or perhaps your project requires careful observation, the recording of data, and then hypothesis formulation and testing. In any case, part of your research strategy should be deciding where you can make a contribution to the body of knowledge about your subject and then reading your sources with that goal in mind.

Jan Dunn, the student writer we met in Section 44 and whose research paper appears at the end of this section, thought very carefully about her audience. Naturally, since the paper was an assignment for a course, her primary reader was her sociology professor, who would expect her to approach her subject from a sound sociological perspective, as a serious researcher in the field.

In addition, because Jan was knowledgeable about computers (she had chosen computer science as her major), she wanted to address the doubts and fears of people unfamiliar with them. Although she believed some of these fears were irrational, she felt she previously had lacked the hard evidence to refute them. So Jan's secondary audience was people—some of them her classmates—who were suspicious of computer technology's effect on their lives. Since everyone in her class had to present a ten-minute oral report on his or her topic later in the term, she hoped her research would enable her to do a little educating when her turn came.

After she had read enough to know that opinions about technology's impact on society tended to be either very optimistic or very pessimistic, Jan began to think that neither point of view was satisfactory. Consequently, she directed her note-taking to those scholars who were less biased, who considered both sides. She was looking for a more balanced theory, and in fact she found several.

Jan also knew she couldn't discuss the whole subject of computer technology in a ten-page paper, so she began thinking about how to narrow the scope of her paper. As a result, she soon focused her research primarily on the technology most easily accessible to the greatest number of users—desk-top computers.

Having focused her subject, Jan was able to take notes more purposefully. She had a better idea of the types of background materials she needed to assemble, the range of views she wanted to present, and the kinds of information required to formulate her conclusions. She also felt confident that although she would probably assemble more evidence than she could include in her paper, nothing she read or took notes on now would be completely useless.

Now she was ready to sketch a rough outline to guide her note-taking, using the points that emerged from talking with her sociology professor and the insights gained from her preliminary reading:

I.   Points of view regarding technology/social change
    A.   Anti-technology
    B.   Pro-technology
    C.   Balanced view (decide on best one)
II.   Computer technology
    A.   Impact—pro
    B.   Impact—con
III.   Computer's acceptance (how widespread? facts!)
    A.   Evidence for and against acceptance
    B.   Application of social theory
IV.   Computer does/does not fit social needs

45c

This working outline differs from the final one Jan submitted with her research paper, of course. It would undergo several revisions as her research developed, but at this stage the outline served its purpose very well: to help Jan organize her thinking and plan her note-taking.

45c

Preparing exact bibliography cards for each source

You will need exact bibliography information for the "Works Cited" pages at the end of your research paper. Therefore, throughout your preliminary search carefully make an individual bibliography card for each article, book, or other source you think you might use. Follow this procedure consistently, even though it may seem tedious. Failing to get all the necessary bibliographic information when you are consulting a book, article, or reference source such as an index or the card catalog usually delays and inconveniences you later. At best, omitting a particularly useful piece of bibliographic information may make it necessary to look through several books, periodicals, or bibliographies to relocate exact information about a source.

The best method of keeping an accurate record is to write bibliography cards. The common card sizes are 3" × 5", 4" × 6", and 5" × 8". Researchers often use larger cards for note-taking and 3" × 5" cards for bibliographic entries.

Make out a separate card for each source. Although the exact information for various kinds of sources varies, all entries require three basic kinds of information: author, title, and publication information. The following bibliographic entries show the types of information and the form required for bibliographies using the conventions established by the Modern Language Association and described in the *MLA Handbook for Writers of Research Papers* (1984). It is the style guide for some eighty professional journals in the languages, humanities, and some social sciences. Other bibliographic and documentation forms are discussed on pages 482–486 (see also pages 518–522 for illustrations of MLA and APA styles in use).

Notice that different types of entries require different types of information. For example, if your source is a translation or an edited book, you will need the name of the translator or editor as well as that of the author. If your source is an article in a periodical, you will need to record the inclusive page numbers of the article. Writing the library call number on the bibliography card is also helpful for locating sources on the shelves later. You will also notice that the bibliography entries use shortened forms for publishers, such as Prentice for Prentice Hall or UP for University Press. They also use common abbreviations for months (Apr., Oct.) and for such things as "no date" (n.d.) and "translator" (trans.). A list of common scholarly abbreviations appears at the end of the bibliography samples on pages 468–469.

45c

FORM FOR BIBLIOGRAPHIC ENTRIES—"WORKS CITED"

Books

BOOK WITH ONE AUTHOR

Boorstin, Daniel J. <u>The Discoverers</u>. New York: Random, 1983.

The major parts of an entry—author, title, and publication information (place of publication, publisher, date of publication)—are each separated by a period, followed by two spaces. Give the author's name in its fullest or most usual form, last name first. Obtain the information for bibliographical entries from the title page of the work cited, not from library catalog cards, other bibliographies, or indexes. These other sources may omit capital letters or use different punctuation that is specific to the style conventions of those sources only. Instead, you must use the information as it is presented on the work itself. If the copyright date is not located on the title page, it usually appears on the copyright page—the back of the title page—with other publication information. In books published outside the United States, publication information may be located in the colophon (publisher's inscription) at the back of the book.

BOOK WITH TWO OR THREE AUTHORS

Bryan, Margaret B., and Boyd H. Davis. <u>Writing About</u>

    <u>Literature and Film</u>. New York: Harcourt, 1975.

Notice that in citations involving multiple authors only the first author's name is inverted. Other authors' names appear in normal order. If an entry requires more than one line of type, indent the second and any subsequent lines five spaces from the left margin.

BOOK WITH MORE THAN THREE AUTHORS

Brown, Herbert C., et al. <u>Organic Synthesis Via Boranes</u>. New

    York: Wiley, 1975.

Et al. is an abbreviation indicating that the work has more than three authors. Note that in the entry *et al.* should not be capitalized. If there are no more than three authors, list them as you would for a work with two authors.

BOOK IN EDITION OTHER THAN THE FIRST

Weidenaar, Dennis J., and Emanuel T. Weiler. <u>Economics: An</u>

    <u>Introduction to the World Around You</u>. 2nd ed. Reading:

    Addison, 1979.

When citing editions other than the first, it is correct to use *2nd, 4th, 17th,* etc. rather than *second, fourth, seventeenth,* and the like. *Edition* is abbreviated *ed.* If a work has a subtitle, as in the example above, be sure to use a colon between the main title and subtitle (even though some indexes and bibliographies may show the punctuation as a comma).

45c

BOOK IN A SERIES

Ryf, Robert S. <u>Henry Green</u>. Columbia Essays on Modern

    Writers 29. Ed. William York Tindall. New York:

    Columbia UP, 1967.

WORK IN TWO OR MORE VOLUMES

Morrison, S. E., and H. S. Commager. The Growth of the

    American Republic. 3rd ed. 2 vols. New York: Oxford UP,

    1942.

TRANSLATION

Eco, Umberto. The Name of the Rose. Trans. William Weaver.

    New York: Harcourt, 1983.

See also the entries and discussion under the heading "Book with Author and Editor."

REPUBLISHED BOOK (REPRINT)

Tuchman, Barbara W. A Distant Mirror: The Calamitous 14th

    Century. 1978. New York: Ballantine, 1979.

The publication date of the original hard cover printing is *1978. New York: Ballantine, 1979* is the publication information for the paperback reprint. Such information is important because although the reader needs to know exactly which edition was used in the research, it is also important to know when a work was initially published.

EDITED BOOK

Schorer, Mark, ed. Modern British Fiction. New York: Oxford

    UP, 1961.

BOOK WITH AUTHOR AND EDITOR

Melville, Herman. Billy Budd: Sailor. Eds. Harrison Hayford

      and Merton M. Sealts, Jr. Chicago: U of Chicago P, 1962.

Hayford, Harrison, and Merton M. Sealts, Jr., eds. Billy

      Budd: Sailor. By Herman Melville. U of Chicago P, 1962.

Compare the two entries for *Billy Budd*. The first one is appropriate for a paper about *Billy Budd* and/or Herman Melville. The second one is appropriate for a paper that discusses Hayford's and Sealt's work as editors. When an editor's name is the first (alphabetizing) information unit in an entry, *ed.* (editor) comes after the name and is not capitalized; otherwise, it precedes the name and is capitalized. (If there is more than one editor, make the abbreviation plural by adding an *s*.) The same distinctions apply to translations and *trans.* (translator) and other such works and contributors.

SELECTION IN ANTHOLOGY OR COLLECTION

Murray, Donald M. "Writing as Process: How Writing Finds Its

　　Own Meaning." <u>Eight Approaches to Teaching Composition</u>.

　　Ed. Timothy R. Donovan and Ben W. McClellend. Urbana:

　　NCTE, 1980.

The title of the selection appears first after the author's name and is enclosed in quotation marks. The title of the work in which the selection appears is listed next and is underlined or italicized. A period separates the two titles.

ANONYMOUS BOOK

<u>Norwegian Folk Tales</u>. Trans. Pat Shaw Iversen and Carl

　　Norman. Oslo: Dreyers Forlag, 1961.

Works without an author, editor, or other acknowledged "authorlike" person are alphabetized in "Works Cited" by the first important word in their title. They are not listed as *anonymous* or *anon.*

PAMPHLET

Latin, Giorgio Lilli. <u>Art in Italy</u>. Rome: Italian State

　　Tourist Dept., 1978.

UNPUBLISHED DISSERTATION

Stein, Robert A. "<u>Paradise Regained</u> in the Light of

　　Classical and Christian Traditions of Criticism and

　　Rhetoric." Diss. Brandeis U, 1968.

PUBLISHED CONFERENCE PROCEEDINGS

45c

<u>Quaker Education As Ministry</u>. Proc. of 4th Annual Conference.

　　Haverford: Friends Assn. for Higher Education, 1983.

Proc. is the abbreviation for *Proceedings.*

Articles in Reference Books

SIGNED ARTICLE

Goodwin, George C. "Mammals." <u>Collier's Encyclopedia</u>. 1976 ed.

UNSIGNED ARTICLE

"Universities." <u>Encyclopaedia Britannica: Macropaedia</u>. 1974 ed.

Familiar reference books, especially those that are reprinted frequently in new editions, are cited by edition-year only. When the abbreviation *ed.* appears with a year, it stands for *edition*, rather than *editor.* Full publication information is not necessary. However, less familiar reference works, or those that have been printed in only one edition, should be accompanied by full publication information, as in the entry that follows.

UNSIGNED ARTICLE IN FIRST EDITION

"28 July 1868 Reconstruction." The Almanac of American

History. Ed. Arthur M. Schlesinger, Jr. New York:

Putnam, 1983.

Periodicals

ARTICLE FROM JOURNAL WITH CONTINUOUS PAGINATION THROUGHOUT VOLUME

Palmer, Glenn E. "Computer Applications in the Freshman

Laboratory." Journal of Chemical Education

58 (1981): 995.

The title of the journal is followed by the volume number, the year of publication in parentheses, a colon, and the number of the page being cited. Some documentation styles may use *Vol.* for *volume* and roman instead of Arabic numerals. MLA style uses no abbreviation and Arabic numerals only. Notice that the colon is the only separating punctuation used after the journal title and that abbreviations such as *p.* or *pp. (page* or *pages)* are not used.

45c

ARTICLE FROM JOURNAL WITH EACH ISSUE PAGINATED INDEPENDENTLY

Mendelson, Michael. "Business Prose and the Nature of the

Plain Style." Journal of Business Communication 24.2

(1987): 3–11.

Because pagination begins over again with each issue of the journal rather than with each volume, it is necessary to give the issue number. Here the order is journal title, volume number, separating period, issue number, year of publication in parentheses, colon, and page numbers.

ARTICLE FROM WEEKLY OR BIWEEKLY PERIODICAL

Alexander, Charles P. "The Billion–Dollar Boys." Time 9

Jan. 1984: 46–48.

Notice that the date of the periodical's publication is inverted and presented in "military" or "continental" style as well as abbreviated: *9 Jan. 1984*. As in other periodical citations, the abbreviations *p.* or *pp.* are not used. Instead, the meaning of the numbers is indicated by their placement in the entry.

ARTICLE FROM MONTHLY OR BIMONTHLY PERIODICAL

Jordan, Robert Paul. "Ghosts on the Little Bighorn."

   National Geographic Dec. 1986: 787+.

The abbreviation + following the page number *787* indicates that the article continues, but not on consecutive pages.

ARTICLE FROM DAILY NEWSPAPER

Morris, Betsy. "Thwack! Smack! Sounds Thrill Makers of

   Hunt's Ketchup." Wall Street Journal 27 Apr. 1984,

   midwestern ed., sec. 1:1+.

This newspaper article carried a by-line, so the author's name is known. If the article were unsigned, it would be alphabetized in "Works Cited" by its title rather than by its author. For newspaper articles, give the date of publication, the edition if the paper is printed in more than one edition (either location or time of day, whichever is relevant), and the section number as well as the page number if the newspaper is divided into sections that are paginated separately. The citation given here refers to pages 1 and following of the midwestern edition of the *Wall Street Journal* for April 27, 1984.

SIGNED BOOK REVIEW

Morris, Jan. "Visions in the Wilderness." Rev. of Sands

   River, by Peter Matthiessen. Saturday Review Apr. 1981:

   68-69.

UNSIGNED ARTICLE OR REVIEW

"Form and Function in a Post and Beam House." Early American

   Life Oct. 1980: 41-43.

Government and Legal Documents

GOVERNMENT PUBLICATION

United States. Dept. of Health, Education, and Welfare.

   National Center for Educational Statistics. Digest of

   Educational Statistics. Washington: GPO, 1968.

45c

This entry shows an example of "corporate authorship." That is, an institution is considered the author, although clearly one or several people wrote the document. Corporate authorship is not uncommon for works from governmental and educational institutions, foundations, agencies, or business firms.

CONSTITUTION

```
U.S. Const. Art. 2, sec. 4.
```

COURT CASES

```
Bundy v. Jackson. 24 FEP Cases 1155 (1981).

Seto v. Muller. 395 F. Supp. 811 (D. Mass. 1975).
```

Methods for citing court cases and legal documents vary: the ones shown here are representative, however. The name of the case is given first, followed by identification numbers, references to courts and relevant jurisdictions (for example, "FEP Cases" means "Federal Employment Practices Cases"; "F. Supp." means "Federal Superior Court"), and the year in which the case was decided. The best guide for legal references is the most recent edition of *A Uniform System of Citation* (Cambridge: Harvard Law Rev. Assn.). It should be available in your college or university library.

Letters and Interviews

PUBLISHED LETTER

```
Mills, Ralph J. Jr., ed. Selected Letters of Theodore

     Roethke. Seattle: U of Washington P, 1968.
```

UNPUBLISHED LETTER

```
McCracken, Virginia. Letter to Colonel Thomas McCracken.

     1 July 1862.
```

INTERVIEWS

```
Silber, John R. Personal interview. 5 June 1979.

Kennedy, Senator Edward. Telephone interview. 3 May 1980.
```

Information Services, Computer Software

INFORMATION SERVICE

```
Beam, Paul. COMIT English Module. ERIC ED 167 189.
```

Material from information services is cited the same way as any other printed matter, with the addition of a reference to the source—

45c

in this case ERIC (Educational Resources Information Center). Be aware that information services, data banks, microform services, and other suppliers sometimes indicate how they should be cited in references. Follow their suggestions but adapt them to the particular documentation style you are using.

SOFTWARE

<u>SuperCalc</u>. Computer software. Sorcim, 1981. CP/M-based

microcomputer, disk.

For an entry documenting computer software, supply the following information: the author of the software (if known), the title of the program (treated like the title of any work and underlined or italicized), a descriptive label (Computer software), the name of the distributor, and the year of publication. Other information can be included at the end if it will be important to the reader. For example, this entry lists the type of computer on which the program can be used (CP/M-based) and its form (disk).

Films, Television, Radio, Recordings, Works of Art

FILM

<u>Children of a Lesser God</u>. Dir. Randa Haines. Paramount,

1986.

Films, television programs, movies, works of art, recordings, and the like are treated similarly to printed works except that the type of medium logically dictates the type of information to be included. The title of the work is always given. If the performer, composer, director, producer, or artist is of primary importance, then the name of that person will head the entry, appearing in the author position. If the work is more important than its creator or performer, then the title will occupy the lead position in the entry—as in the case of the audiotape *Footloose,* listed below. Provide whatever information the reader will need to identify or locate the work, such as dates of performances, broadcasts, or recordings; networks; recording companies; catalog numbers; etc. The following examples are representative.

45c

TELEVISION AND RADIO

<u>Casey Stengel</u>. Writ. Sidney and David Carroll. Perf. Charles

Durning. PBS, Boston. 6 May 1981.

Keillor, Garrison. "The News from Lake Wobegon." <u>A Prairie</u>

<u>Home Companion</u>. Minnesota Public Radio. WBAA, West

Lafayette, IN. 13 June 1987.

RECORD

Moussorgsky, Modeste. <u>Pictures at an Exhibition</u>. Leonard

Pennario, piano. Capitol, P–8323, n.d.

AUDIOTAPE; COMPACT DISC; VIDEOTAPE

<u>Footloose</u>. Audiotape. Perf. Kenny Loggins et al. Columbia,

JST 39242, 1984.

Beethoven, Ludwig van. <u>The Five Piano Concertos</u>. Perf.

Rudolf Serkin. Cond. Seiji Ozawa. Compact disc. Boston

Symphony Orchestra. Telarc, CD 80061–5, 1984.

Allen, Woody, dir. <u>Hannah and Her Sisters</u>. Videocassette.

HBO Video, 1985. 1 hr., 43 min.

WORK OF ART (PAINTING)

Picasso, Pablo. <u>A Woman in White</u>. The Metropolitan Museum of

Art, New York.

45d

Abbreviations

The following list contains many of the scholarly abbreviations you are likely to need in writing a bibliography or that you are likely to see while conducting research.

anon.	annonymous
art., arts.	article(s)
c., ca.	*circa* (about); used with approximate dates
cf.	*confer* (compare)
ch., chs., chap., chaps.	chapter(s)
col., cols.	column(s)
dir.	director, directed by
diss.	dissertation
ed., edn.	edition
ed., eds.	editor(s)
e.g.	*exempli gratia* (for example)
et al.	*et alii* (and others)
ERIC	Educational Resources Information Service
f., ff.	and the following page(s)
GPO	Government Printing Office
ibid.	*ibidem* (in the same place)
i.e.	*id est* (that is)
illus.	illustrator, illustrated by, illustration

introd.	introduction
l., ll.	line(s)
loc. cit.	*loca citato* (in the place cited)
ms, mss	manuscript(s)
n.b.	*nota bene* (take notice)
n.d.	no date (of publication) given
n.p.	no place (of publication) given
n. pag.	no pagination
no., nos.	number, numbers
NTIS	National Technical Information Service
numb.	numbered
op. cit.	*opere citato* (in the work cited)
p., pp.	page(s)
passim	throughout the work, here and there
perf.	performed by, performer
proc.	proceedings
prod.	produced by, producer
q.v.	*quod vide* (which see)
qtd.	quoted in
rev.	review, revised
rpt.	reprint, reprinted
sec.	section
sic	thus it is
trans., tr.	translator, translated
univ., U, UP	university, university press
v. (vs.)	versus (against)
vol., vols.	volume(s)

45e

Taking careful notes

Taking notes on cards is usually more efficient than writing them on full sheets of paper; cards are easier to carry and easier to rearrange when you are deciding on the organization for your paper. Limiting each note card to a single subject or even a single subtopic facilitates such rearrangements.

Use three types of notes: summary, paraphrase, and direct quotation. Some students write all their research notes as direct quotations from their sources. However, this method is tedious, time-consuming, and unnecessary. Furthermore, the act of transcribing prevents you from assimilating and evaluating the material as you read it. Take most of your notes in summary or paraphrase form, reserving direct quotations for material that is especially well stated or for points that might require the clout of a respected authority's exact words.

A **summary** is a brief note that captures information quickly without regard for style or careful expression. Your purpose is simply to record the facts or important points, to give a rough sketch of the material. (Be aware that summary notes differ in some important respects from the summary writing described in Section **46.**) Whenever

45e

you include a summary in your research paper, be sure to cite the source appropriately.

A **paraphrase** is a restatement of the source material in your own words, syntax, and style but preserving the tone of the original (humor, doubt, etc.) and of approximately the same length. A paraphrase uses the original author's idea and presents it in your own language. Since in paraphrasing you are borrowing someone's thoughts, you must document the source when you use the paraphrase in your paper.

A **direct quotation** records exactly the words of the original source (as well as the exact punctuation and even any spelling errors). Like summaries and paraphrases, direct quotations require citations in your paper crediting the source from which you copied them. Always put quotation marks around all the material you take word for word from any source. In general, use direct quotations only for particularly telling phrases or for information that must be rendered exactly as you found it.

Opposite are summary, paraphrase, and direct quotation notes Jan wrote as she read her resource material. Notice that each note indicates the source (complete bibliographic information is recorded on her bibliography cards) and shows the page numbers where the information appeared. She also has given each card a topic heading for easy sorting later.

Jan's notes reflect her evaluation of the material she read. The paraphrase card contains a comment in brackets where she noted the outdated viewpoint of the encyclopedia article. The direct quotation card contains two sets of ellipses. At these spots Jan decided not to copy original phrases that related detail unnecessary to the focus of her paper.

45f

45f

Writing the paper: do not plagiarize the work of others, either by accident or by design.

Plagiarism consists of passing off the ideas, opinions, conclusions, facts, words—in short, the intellectual work—of another as your own. Plagiarism is dishonest and carries penalties not only in academic environments but in all professions, as well as in copyright law.

The most obvious kind of plagiarism occurs when you appropriate whole paragraphs or longer passages from another writer for your own paper. Long word-for-word quotations are rarely appropriate to a paper, but if they ever are, you must indicate clearly that they *are* quotations and indicate their exact source. No less dishonest is the use of all or most of a single sentence or an apt figure of speech appropriated without acknowledgment from another source.

SUMMARY

Zorn, 17: C5 Humans' view of self

Compares artificial intelligence revolution (20th cent.) to Copernican revolution (1543):

Copernicus -- discovery that human beings not at center of solar system, let alone center of universe.

artificial intelligence -- humans not the only thing capable of logical "thinking."

PARAPHRASE

Merrill, 576 1968 attitude change: tech

He thinks it's strange that it has taken so long for a social science specialty to develop in the study of the social results of technology, especially since there has been a long-standing concern. The reason is that technology wasn't considered very interesting or very difficult to understand. [Obviously, that attitude has changed dramatically since the 1960s.]

DIRECT QUOTATION

Bell, 21 physical/intellectual tech.

"Physical technology -- the machine -- replaced human power at the manual level or raw muscle power ... or repetition of tasks; the new intellectual technology -- as embodied in a computer program ... substitutes algorithms for human judgments, where these can be formalized."

45f

    Suppose, for example, that you are working on a paper about families and have read a book by Jane Howard entitled *Families*. You have a note card on which you have written the partial sentence "Good families have a switchboard operator—someone who cannot help but keep track of what all the others are up to . . ." Your notes indicate that this is a quotation. But when you turn to writing your paper, this and other phrases from the same source seem so apt to your purposes in a slightly different context that you yield to temptation and write, as if in your own words, "All families need at least two things: someone around whom others cluster and someone who cannot help but keep track of what all the others are up to—a kind of switchboard operator." You have plagiarized just as badly as the writer who has appropriated a whole paragraph. The words are not yours, they are Jane Howard's, and honesty requires that you give her credit for them.

You are unlikely to copy directly from another writer without being consciously dishonest as you do so. But even though you acknowledge the source in a citation, you are also plagiarizing when you incorporate in your paper faultily paraphrased or summarized passages from another author in which you follow almost exactly the original's sentence patterns and phrasing. Paraphrasing and summarizing require that you fully digest an author's ideas and interpretations and restate them in your own words. It is not enough simply to modify the original author's sentences slightly, to change a word here and there. Consider the following original together with the sample paraphrases and summary:

ORIGINAL

The craft of hurricane forecasting advanced rapidly in the Sixties and early Seventies, thanks to fast computers and new atmospheric modeling techniques. Now there is a lull in the progress, strangely parallel to the lull in the storm cycle. The Center shoots for a 24-hour warning period, with 12 daylight hours for evacuation. At that remove, it can usually predict landfall within 100 miles either way. Longer lead times mean much larger landfall error and that is counterproductive. He who misses his predictions cries wolf.

WILLIAM H. MACLEISH, "Our Barrier Islands," *Smithsonian* Sept. 1980: 54.

45f

FAULTY PARAPHRASE

Hurricane forecasting made rapid progress in the sixties and seventies due to fast computers and new atmospheric techniques, but there is now a lull in the progress. The Warning Center tries for a 24-hour warning period, including 12 hours of daylight. That close to a storm, it can usually predict landfall within 100 miles either way. If lead times are longer, there will be a much larger error, which will be counterproductive (Macleish 54).

Even though the writer acknowledges the author (as indicated by the citation at the end of the paragraph), this is a clear example of plagiarism. The author has combined the first two sentences of the original and changed a few words here and there but in no way indicated that most of the paragraph's structure and phrasing is almost exactly that of the original.

IMPROVED PARAPHRASE

New techniques, together with computers, have significantly increased the accuracy of hurricane forecasting. Now it is possible to predict where a hurricane will hit land with an error of not more than 100 miles if a warning of 24 hours is allowed. If more than 24 hours is required, the error will be proportionately greater (Macleish 54).

This paraphrase successfully puts the information in the words of the researcher. Both the sentence structure and the phrasing are clearly the researcher's, not the original author's. But such a full paraphrase of a relatively simple passage is probably much more complete than someone researching hurricane warning problems and developments in a variety of sources would need. In many contexts, a simple, brief summary statement like the following might well be sufficient:

SUMMARY

With computers and new techniques, forecasters can now provide a 24-hour hurricane warning and predict within 100 miles either way where a storm will hit (Macleish 54).

EXERCISE 45e–f

For each of the following passages, write a summary note and a paraphrase note. If you think a passage contains subtopics that would best be handled as separate notes, prepare a summary and paraphrase for each subtopic. Be sure that you have avoided plagiarism: restate the original ideas in your own words. If you think that in a few spots there is no adequate substitute for the original language, put those words in quotation marks.

45f

1. "During the course of 'modernization,' values do change, but they do so slowly, and the core is resistant to assaults from reason or from new experience. Individuals prefer to live inconsistently, suffering from 'cognitive dissonance,' rather than to make conscious realignment of their value preferences."

   JOHN D. MONTGOMERY, "Beyond Appropriate Technology"

2. "There were several reasons for the royal progresses (court travels through the countryside) so important during the reign of Elizabeth I. These summer progresses were made for health reasons. After the court had stayed at one palace for a while, the place got dirty and smelly. The waste disposal system was very rudimentary, with wastes simply dumped into the castle moat. After a while the stench became unbearable, and the court had to leave so the place could be

cleaned. Also, after nine months of being in London and occupying herself with ruling the country, Elizabeth enjoyed going to the countryside where she could relax and engage in various activities such as hunting. Progresses were also made for economic reasons. The Queen's and her court's entertainment, lodging, food, and drink were paid for by the hosting town or hosting nobility. This took the strain off Elizabeth's pocketbook and placed the burden of cost, for a short time, elsewhere."

CHERYL THOMPSON, "The Elizabethan Royal Progress"

3. "In almost every college or university, the library is acknowledged by faculty, students, and administrators as the 'heart of the campus.' Yet on many college campuses the potential of the library goes unrealized. The library becomes an underutilized, expensive storehouse. Librarians are seen as, or what is worse, perform as keepers of the books, or, in the words of a Cambridge University faculty member, 'warehouse managers.' Consequently, library materials purchased to support the curriculum lie unused on the shelves. Students who frequent the library often use it as a study hall or as a convenient location for a social gathering. In addition when students have a course assignment or research paper that requires the use of library materials, they often perform poorly and spend more time than necessary. The reason for such poor performance is that most students do not have the necessary skills to effectively identify and use appropriate library materials."

CARLA J. STOFFLE, "The Library's Role
in Facilitating Quality Teaching"

45g
Learning when and how to use quotations

A research paper loaded with quotations or consisting of long quotations stitched loosely together with brief comments will almost always be an unsatisfactory paper. The point of research is to present in your own words the interpretations and judgments you have come to as a result of your investigation, making clear and accurate references to the sources you have consulted.

The almost irresistible temptation for inexperienced writers is to justify every major point they make in their research paper with a quotation from an authority. First, you are entitled to draw conclusions about your research subject; not everything you say requires backing up with a source. Second, make use of paraphrases and summaries instead of quotations in most cases where sources are cited. Frequently, the point can be made better in your own words, with proper citation, than in the words of the original.

Of course a research paper does lead to more direct quotation than you would ordinarily use in an essay presenting your own personal views. The nature of research requires that in establishing and supporting your points you work with evidence from a number of sources. A carefully researched paper on the changing roles of the family in the past four decades will obviously present more occasions for quotation from outside sources than a personal essay on your changing relationship with your own family.

Learning to use quotations wisely when you have good reason and learning how to fit them easily, naturally, and logically into your paper are signs of effective composition. Your *use* of a quotation, not the quotation itself, is part of your research contribution. When readers come upon a quotation, they should never feel that it has been "chopped" from the original source and "dropped" upon them suddenly. One of your tasks as a researcher and writer is to provide appropriate contexts for the quotations you are using. Consequently, it is often a good idea to mention the source or the importance of a quotation in the text of your paper. By providing an introductory phrase such as "according to a leading authority," or "a recent government study shows that . . . ," you not only supply a frame of reference for the quotation but you establish its authority and credibility in your reader's mind. Thus the quotation becomes an intrinsic part of the whole weave of your paper.

Many contexts can support the use of brief and—less frequently—long quotations. But the contexts in which they are most likely to be preferable to paraphrase or summary are those in which the original phrasing is striking, memorable, or lends concreteness or authenticity; the force of the statement is important and would be lost in paraphrase; the quotation is an example of what is being discussed; or, in writing about a writer or a literary work, the quotations exemplify the writer' style or typify a character, theme, or the like.

In her paper, Jan Dunn uses one quotation long enough to require setting off by indentation (see Section **25c**). She chose to quote Langdon Winner's paraphrase of W. W. Rostow's ideas, first, because she felt her paraphrase of Winner's paraphrase would be too many times removed from Rostow's original thoughts and, second, because the original language was itself specific and important enough to merit quoting. Her inclusion of this long quotation shows a situation in which its use is justified: when the ideas are most effectively conveyed in the words of the source.

45g

Jan provides a suitable introduction for the long quotation, making clear the purpose it serves and establishing the context in which it is to be understood (see page 501). She has also been selective, using ellipses to indicate omitted material extraneous to her purpose. Such omissions are permissible, even advisable, as long as they do not change the meaning of the original.

Like long quotations, short ones need to be fitted naturally into the flow of your paper. Short quotations should be worked smoothly into the syntax of your sentences; furthermore, they should be introduced in a way that establishes the connection between the source and the point you are making. Notice how the following examples by student writers achieve these goals with phrases such as *John Frederick Nims remarks, reports that, in Mary McCarthy's words, H. L. Mencken recorded . . . and observed that,* or *preaching that . . . those who tell us that.* (The numbers in parentheses are in-text page citations.)

> Not all Victorian women were the shy, timid, modest beings they are sometimes imagined to be. Elizabeth Barrett Browning once submitted a poem about women as sex objects which her editor rejected "for indecency." As John Frederick Nims remarks, "Who would have expected such a poem from a Victorian lady with three names?" (187).

> Any study of the music of Bela Bartok can well begin by taking note of the commanding presence of the man himself. Yehudi Menuhin, describing his first meeting with the composer, reports that he "felt at once that I was facing someone pared down to the essential core" (16).

> The book which is most informative about Mary McCarthy as a person is perhaps her *Memories of a Catholic Girlhood,* which reflects, in part, her early life with her great-aunt, who, in McCarthy's words, "had a gift for turning everything sour and ugly" (49).

> Distrust of and distaste for "new fangled inventions" is long. English writers of the nineteenth century denounced the arrival of the railroad in their beloved Lake country. Fifty years ago, H. L. Mencken recorded in characteristically pungent language his dislike for automobiles, phonographs, and movies, and observed that although he saw "potentialities" for the radio, he was convinced they would never be realized "so long as the air is laden and debauched by jazz, idiotic harangues by frauds who do not know what they are talking about, and the horrible garglings of ninth-rate singers" (272).

45g

> There is nothing like a time of inflation, declining productivity, burgeoning government expenditures, and increasing taxes to unleash a flood of conflicting economic theory. Our own period is fertile ground for such debate, and we find ourselves choosing sides between those who believe that only a return to the virtues of old-line capitalism can save us, preaching that we must untax the rich so they they may invest, since "the creation of wealth is the only salvation of the poor," (Abelson 21) and those who tell us that only a "fundamental restructuring of American society" (Fitzpatrick 383) will keep us from going down.

Whenever you make use of direct quotations in your writing, be sure to transcribe them accurately. Make it a rule to check and recheck each quotation, including its punctuation. Make sure that you understand the mechanical conventions of quoting material. Indicate omissions from a quotation by using ellipses (see Section **26c**), and make sure that what you retain is grammatically coherent. If you insert words of your own in the original, indicate your insertion by placing brackets around it (see Section **26a**). If the quotation contains a mistake or peculiarity of spelling or grammar, retain it in your quotation but indicate that it appears in the original by using *sic* ("thus it is") in brackets immediately following it (see Section **26b**).

EXERCISE 45g

Choose one of the passages from Exercise 45e-f and write a paragraph or two about the topic the passage discusses. Incorporate at least two direct quotations from the passage into your paragraph. Work them smoothly and naturally into your writing, avoiding "chop-and-drop" quotations. Be sure to use punctuation correctly, including any ellipses and brackets.

45h

Documenting your sources

One of the purposes of keeping accurate bibliography cards and careful notes that record your sources and distinguish carefully between direct quotation and summary or paraphrase is to provide you with the information you will need for documenting the source material you have used in your research paper. All the facts, ideas, interpretations, opinions, and conclusions of others that you incorporate in your own paper you must always acknowledge by documenting the sources—whether they be books, periodicals, interviews, speeches, or field studies.

Always acknowledge all direct quotations, charts, diagrams, tables, and the like, that you reproduce wholly or in part in your paper. Also, always acknowledge your paraphrases and summaries of the interpretations, opinions, and conclusions presented in your sources. Keep in mind that the interpretations and conclusions reached by researchers and scholars are in many ways more important contributions than the bald facts they may have gathered and are therefore even more deserving of acknowledgment.

You do not have to provide documentation for facts that are considered common knowledge. "Common knowledge" consists of standard historical and literary information available in many different reference books—the date of Lincoln's assassination, the dates of birth and death of John F. Kennedy, the fact that Charles Dickens created such characters as Uriah Heep and Mr. Micawber, or that Darwin's theory of evolution was the subject of great intellectual debate in the nineteenth century. Such information is considered common knowledge as far as documentation is concerned, even though it may be far from the tip of your tongue at the moment, even though you may, in fact, have learned it for the first time when you began your research.

In contrast, common sense will tell you that highly specialized facts—the cost of a six-room house in the 1830's, the number of Polaroid cameras sold between 1970 and 1980, the estimated population of Mongolia in 1950, the highest recorded tide in San Francisco Bay, or the number of earthquakes in Peru during the nineteenth century—are unlikey to be common knowledge.

In addition to information that is widely available and undisputed, facts agreed upon by nearly all authorities discussing a particular subject are considered common knowledge. As soon as you explore any subject to some depth, you will quickly come to see that certain material is taken as established fact while other material is disputed or has been established by some special investigation. A student writing on Wordsworth for the first time, for example, may not have known at the start that the *Preface to the Lyrical Ballads* was first published in 1800. But it will not take long to discover that everyone writing on the subject accepts this as an established fact. Such information will not need to be acknowledged. In contrast, the exact date of a particular poem may be a matter of dispute or may have been established by a scholar's diligent research. Information of this kind must be acknowledged.

45i
Using appropriate documentation form

Documentation is the means by which you acknowledge material you have borrowed from outside sources. As used in professional scholarship, documentation forms are complex and varied. Most forms have evolved from the demands of professional scholarship, itself a precise and exacting business. Furthermore, the preferred form for citations and bibliographic entries varies considerably among disciplines. Each of the natural sciences, the American Medical Association, the American Bar Association, such fields as linguistics, and many other groups and disciplines have their own preferred styles, each of which is described in the particular group's style manual. For any discipline in which you write, always check the professional publications and relevant style manuals to determine the appropriate documentation form. When you write for a specific course assignment, ask your instructor which documentation style he or she prefers.

In spite of their differences in detail, most disciplines use one of four basic systems: the name and page system, the name and year system, the number system, or the footnote system.

THE MLA NAME AND PAGE SYSTEM

The **name and page system** described by the Modern Language Association in its *MLA Handbook for Writers of Research Papers* (1984) uses **in-text citations** (rather than footnotes or endnotes) to acknowledge the words or ideas of outside sources where they are used in a paper. The only exceptions are content and bibliographical endnotes or footnotes. You will find examples of these exceptions on page 13 of Jan Dunn's research paper and definitions on the facing page.

All references cited in the text are listed alphabetically in a section at the end of the paper called *Works Cited*. As illustrated in Section **45c,** the "Works Cited" list functions as a bibliography, usually listing references by author's last name, if known, or by title if the author is not known. Sometimes a work will be listed by an editor's, translator's, or other person's name.

Using the MLA name-page documentation form, the work referred to in Jan Dunn's sentence "According to Naisbitt, the introduction of a new technology must be accompanied by a counterbalancing, human-centered response, or society will reject the technology (39)" is listed under *Naisbitt* in "Works Cited" as follows:

```
Naisbitt, John. Megatrends: Ten New Directions Transforming
     Our Lives. New York: Warner, 1982.
```

As the Naisbitt example shows, the name-page documentation system places relevant names (usually authors' names) and pages of the works being cited either directly in the text sentences or in parentheses in the text. What you cite in the text has a direct bearing on what you place in parentheses: that is, when information appears in a text sentence, it is not repeated in parentheses, as the following reference to Lundquist shows. Notice, in the parenthetical material referring to Klinkowitz, there is neither an abbreviation for "page" nor any punctuation between the author's name and the page number.

```
Kurt Vonnegut has been described as "a popular artifact which
may be the fairest example of American cultural change"
(Klinkowitz 16). According to critic James Lundquist, each of
Vonnegut's novels is a warning (15).
```

45i

Notice in the example above that the parenthetical reference is placed as close as possible to the documented material without disrupting the grammar or sense of the material. Usually this location is at the end of the sentence. Be sure to place the parenthetical information inside any concluding punctuation but outside any quotation marks, as shown above.

For the sake of readability, look for ways to integrate citations smoothly into your sentences. Your goal should be to keep parenthetical references concise. If you can do so in a convenient and readable fashion, integrate reference information into the text:

```
Hamlet's well-known "To be, or not to be" lines (56-89) in
```

> Act II, scene i are probably the most famous of Shakespeare's
>
> soliloquies and also probably one of the most misinterpreted.

rather than:

> The well-known "To be, or not to be" lines are probably the
>
> most famous of Shakespeare's soliloquies and also probably
>
> one of the most misinterpreted (<u>Hamlet</u>, II.i.56–89).

Besides at the end of a sentence, references may sometimes be placed conveniently at the ends of phrases or clauses, after statistics, and so forth. For example.

> Norton and Monroe's survey found that 57 percent of America's
>
> drivers do not use their seat-belts (73), but we suspect the
>
> percentage is much higher.

The name-page system enables readers to find a source in your bibliography and also the place in the source where the cited material appears. Giving the author's last name and the page number usually fulfills this purpose, but some cases require additional in-text information. For example:

TWO OR THREE AUTHORS; MORE THAN THREE AUTHORS

> The question then becomes whether "work produced by the
>
> institutional computer is looked upon as the work of the
>
> organization" (Pendergast, Slade, and Winkless 130); in
>
> contrast, the personal computer is identified with the
>
> individual (Elbring et al. 54).

WORK BY AN AUTHOR OF TWO OR MORE WORKS CITED; ANONYMOUS AUTHOR

> Vonnegut believes large families, whether biological or
>
> artificial, help sustain sanity (<u>Sunday</u> 66), and they nurture
>
> idealism. As the protagonist in <u>Jailbird</u> says, "I still
>
> believe that peace and plenty and happiness can be worked out
>
> some way. I am a fool" (57–58). This idealism endears
>
> Vonnegut to his readers ("Forty-Six" 79).

When a "Works Cited" section lists more than one work by the same author, in-text citations should contain the title (or a shortened version, such as *Sunday* for *Palm Sunday*) so readers will know which

45i

of the author's works you are referring to. For references to unsigned (anonymous) works, cite the title (or shortened form) and page number. The example above refers to an unsigned book review entitled "Forty-Six and Trusted."

LITERARY WORKS

```
P.D. James uses lines from a play by John Webster as clues in

her detective novel The Skull Beneath the Skin––for instance

in the note left at the murder scene (145; bk. 3, ch. 4):

"Other sins only speak; murder shrieks out" (Duchess of

Malfi, IV.ii.261).
```

Novels or plays that appear in several editions are best cited not only by page number (given first in the entry) but also by such information as chapter (ch.), part (pt.), or book (bk.) number, so that readers can follow your citations in editions other than the one you refer to. References to verse plays or poems customarily omit page numbers altogether, instead listing more helpful information such as division numbers (act, scene, canto, etc.) followed by line numbers. The arabic numerals in the citations of *Hamlet* and *The Duchess of Malfi* are line numbers.

MULTIVOLUME WORK; SEVERAL WORKS IN ONE CITATION

```
The last half–dozen years of Queen Elizabeth's reign began

with Shakespeare's Love Labours Lost and ended with her death

at age 70 (Harrison, vol. 2). As Harrison puts it, on March

24, 1603, the queen died "having reigned 44 years 5 months

and odd days" (2: 383). Historians regard her as a master of

statecraft (Johnson 2; Elton 46; Bindoff 377).
```

45i

When citing an entire volume as you would a general reference to an entire work, give the author and the volume number preceded by the abbreviation *vol.* When citing specific material in a multivolume work, give first the volume number and then the page number, but omit abbreviations, as in the second reference to Harrison, above. Here, 2 stands for Volume 2 and *383* is the page number. Note the use of a colon and a space to separate volume number from page number. When documenting several works in a single parenthetical reference, cite each as you normally would, separating the citations with semicolons. If multi-work references get too bulky, place them in a bibliographical endnote.

INDIRECT SOURCES

```
The failure of his play Guy Domville seems to have had

positive benefits for Henry James's later novels in that he

spoke of transferring to his fiction the lessons he had

learned from the theater, using those "scenic conditions

which are as near an approach to the dramatic as the novel

may permit itself" (qtd. in Edel 434; pt. 6, ch. 1).
```

It is always best to cite original sources in your work, but sometimes a secondary source may be all that is available. In that case, indicate the secondary nature of the source by using *qtd. in* (quoted in) followed by pertinent reference information. In the reference above, the source is indicated by author's name, page (434), and, since the book is divided formally into parts and chapters, by part and chapter numbers (pt. 6, ch. 1). Note that a semicolon and a space separate the main reference information (author and page) from the rest of the identifying information (part and chapter numbers).

You will find examples of these and other types of in-text citations in the sample research paper at the end of this section. Study them to familiarize yourself with the form and to see how information may be introduced smoothly into the text.

THE APA NAME AND YEAR SYSTEM

The **name and year system** is exemplified by the form described in the *Publication Manual of the American Psychological Association* (1983). So-called APA style is widely used in the social sciences. This system cites works in the text by the last name of the author and the year of publication. These citations of "name and year" permit readers to find full bibliographic information about the work in the reference list. If the author's name is mentioned in the text itself, only the year of publication is given in parentheses. If both author and year appear in the text, no parenthetical information is required:

```
Romonovic (1979) finds no correlation between the growth of

unemployment and urban unrest. However, in 1981 Kemper

reported conclusive evidence to the contrary. One study

(Bordman, 1983) points out that reliable statistics on the

subject are extremely scarce.
```

Page numbers are given for direct quotations and are inserted within the parentheses:

```
Selinki questions whether the research methods used to obtain
```

45i

```
the data "could ever have been considered valid" (1986, pp.
34–35).
```

When this system is used, all references are listed alphabetically by the author's last name at the end of the paper. If two or more studies by the same author are cited, they are listed in chronological sequence by year, the earliest first. If two or more studies by the same author with the same publication date are cited, they are arranged alphabetically and distinguished by lower-case letters after the year (Jones 1986a, Jones 1986b, and so on). The information given on each work in the listing is essentially the same as that required by the MLA form—author, title, and publication information—but entries differ in the order in which the information is arranged and in some mechanical details. Only the last name and initials of the author are given. Only the first word of the title is capitalized, if the work is a book.

```
Perkins, J. (Ed.). (1986). Neurotic characteristics as
     indicators of author success (2nd ed.). Englewood
     Cliffs, NJ: Prentice Hall.
Stretham, C.P. (1978). Achievement and longevity. New York:
     John Wiley.
```

If the work being listed is a periodical, only the first word of the article's title is capitalized. The article's title has no quotation marks around it, nor is it underlined. The title of the periodical in which the article appears is given in full upper and lower case letters and is underlined (for italics). The volume number is also underlined.

```
French, J. R. P., Ross, I. C., Kirby, S., Newlson, J. R., &
     Smyth, P. (1958). Employee participation in a program of
     industrial change. Personnel, 35, 16–29.
```

Notice that when referring to works with more than one author, all the authors' names are in inverted form and an ampersand (&) is used to indicate *and*. In the in-text citation, however, use the word *and* rather than an ampersand *(Bose and Page discovered that . . . .)* For works with two to five authors, in-text citations should give all the authors' names at the first reference; use the first author's name and *et al.* thereafter. For works with six or more authors, the first and all subsequent in-text references should list only the first author's name and *et al.*, with all names given in correct form in the reference list.

```
Wilson et al. (1987) believe that any planning system for the
semiconductor industry must be able to schedule for multiple
sites.
```

45i

```
Wilson, E. L., Sznaider, K. A., Jue, C., Russ, C., Rigodanzo,

    C. W., & Turner, L. T. (1987). A planning solution for

    the semiconductor industry. Hewlett-Packard Journal, 38,

    21-27.
```

A similar format is followed for magazine and newspaper articles. Use *p.* or *pp.* before page numbers in references to magazines and newspapers, but not in references to journals. If an article has no author, use a short title for the parenthetical citation, and in the references list alphabetize it by the first significant word in the title.

```
Gray, P. B. (1987, February 23). Taste buds atingle, recipe

    hounds keep stars under seige. The Wall Street Journal,

    pp. 1, 13.

Summer air fares gain altitude. (1987, June 22). Business

    Week, p. 54.
```

Pages 520–522 show part of Jan Dunn's research paper in APA style.

THE NUMBER SYSTEM

In the **number system** of documentation, used widely in the natural sciences and mathematics, if the author's name is mentioned in the text itself, the reference is indicated only by a number in parentheses. If the author's name is not mentioned, the reference given parenthetically in the text includes the author's last name followed by the appropriate number. References are numbered in this way sequentially throughout the text. In the list of references at the end of the paper, each item is given a corresponding number and listed in the *order of its occurrence in the text* (not in alphabetical order). In the text the reference will appear as follows:

```
Oliver (11) finds that only one type of halophyte, Salicornia

europa, or pickleweed, will germinate in water with a saline

content of 36 parts per thousand.
```

or:

```
Research indicates that only one type of halophyte,

Salicornia europa, or pickleweed, will germinate in water

with a saline content of 36 parts per thousand (Oliver 11).
```

The list of references would then show this entry:

```
11. Oliver, W. H. Salinity tolerance among halophytes. New

    York: Academic Press, 1978.
```

In a variant of the number system, used in the military and elsewhere, the reference list is made first. The entries are alphabetized and then numbered. A work is then cited in the text by the number already assigned to it in the reference list. Thus, for example, all references to Burton Ringwald's *Tennessee Battles,* entry 19 in the reference list, give only that number throughout the body of the paper.

THE FOOTNOTE (ENDNOTE) SYSTEM

The **footnote** (or **endnote**) **system** is a traditional documentation method used widely prior to 1984 in language and literature but now employed mainly in the disciplines of fine arts and humanities, such as religion and philosophy. This system documents in-text quotations, paraphrases, summaries, and the like, by means of a raised Arabic numeral immediately following the final word or punctuation mark of the citation. The consecutive numerals refer to corresponding documentation notes placed at the bottom of the page or gathered at the end of the paper.

Notes placed at the bottoms of pages are generally single-spaced, with double-spacing between them. When gathered as endnotes, they are double-spaced both within and between notes. The first line of each note is indented five spaces, the raised numeral appearing in the fifth space with no space between it and the first word of the note. Second and subsequent lines of a note are flush with the left margin.

As with other forms of documentation, the footnote system cites author, title, and publication information, including relevant page numbers. The major divisions of the note are separated by commas, and the entry is closed with a period. A sample of this documentation style follows:

According to A. G. Dickens, Puritanism "gave the cutting edge to the forces which shaped parliamentary, legal, and religious liberties" in America as well as in England.[1] Historian Elbert Russell points out that the relative tolerance of Oliver Cromwell's Puritan Commonwealth allowed dissenting religious sects to organize and spread their doctrines.[2] As a result, one sect—the Quakers—were to have a profound influence on the United States Constitution, particularly the First Amendment. Using William Penn's Great Laws for Pennsylvania as a model, "every one of the colonies enacted laws recognizing the right of conscience."[3] Later when the colonies had become states and were asked to ratify

45i

the new federal constitution, all refused until it was
amended to include a Bill of Rights for which Pennsylvania
and Maryland made the first proposals: "the rights of
conscience should be held inviolable."[4]

---

[1] A. G. Dickens, <u>Reformation and Society in Sixteenth-
Century Europe</u> (New York: Harcourt, 1966), p. 181.

[2] Elbert Russell, <u>The History of Quakerism</u> (Richmond, IN:
Friends United Press, 1979), p. 17.

[3] Harrop A. Freeman, "William Penn, Quakers, and Civil
Liberties," <u>Friends Journal</u>, 56 (October 15, 1982), p. 15.

[4] Ibid.

Footnotes 1 and 2 in the foregoing sample show the form for books.
Footnote 3 illustrates the form for a periodical. Footnote 4 illustrates
that references repeating an immediately preceding source may list
Ibid.—without a page number if the references are to the same page.
Subsequent references to a work already cited may be listed by author's last name and page number (for example: Dickens, p. 43.). If
more than one work by a single author appears in the notes, to avoid
confusion the author's last name, a shortened form of the title, and
page number are used in second and subsequent references (for example: Dickens, *Calvinism,* p. 75.). Depending on the discipline, papers using the footnote system may or may not have separate bibliographies.

Jan Dunn had a choice of several documentation styles for her
sociology paper. For example, she could have followed the style of the
Modern Language Association or that of the American Psychological
Association, both documentation forms being acceptable in the field.
Jan chose to use MLA conventions, illustrated in the following research paper. At the end of this section, the last few paragraphs of
her research paper are also reproduced in APA style, a form frequently used in the social sciences.

45j

45j

Sample research paper

Jan Dunn's research paper, presented in this section, is a successful student paper. For this assignment she had to choose a subject,
narrow its scope to a manageable focus, gather authoritative information from a number of sources, and then organize the information
clearly in a paper of approximately ten pages, excluding notes and
bibliography.

Jan's task as a researcher was not only to report information but also to evaluate it in a way that contributed to an understanding of the knowledge in the field. The assignment also required a thesis statement, a sentence outline, a bibliography in proper form, and appropriate documentation of evidence.

The commentary accompanying this paper explains Jan's writing process, as the preceding pages have outlined her research process. It details some of the writing and documentation problems she faced and solved.

45j

COMMENTARY

The format. The title of each part (outline, paper, endnotes, "Works Cited") is centered one inch below the top of the page. The text is double-spaced, with well-balanced left and right margins of about one inch. Small Roman numerals number the thesis and outline pages. Consecutive Arabic numerals number the pages of the paper itself, including the endnotes and bibliography.

The title page, thesis statement, and sentence outline. The first three sections give a quick summary of this research paper. The prefatory material falls into three divisions: (1) *the title*, which is a very general statement; (2) *the thesis statement*, which explains briefly what the paper attempts to do; and (3) *the outline*, which is a rather full statement.

45j

Technology with a Personal Touch:

Computers in American Society

by

Jan Dunn

Professor Alfred Hirsch

April 11, 198—

45j

Outline

<u>Thesis statement</u>: Among the reasons Americans have accepted computer technology is the fundamental one that it serves important social needs more than it interferes with them.

I. Despite the social costs of unemployment and impersonalization, the computer's impact is viewed as a positive form of technology by the social majority in America.

   A. The marketplace shows acceptance.

      1. Computers have become relatively affordable.

      2. Sales unit—and—dollar volume has soared.

   B. People foresee social and economic benefits.

      1. They expect computers to become commonplace in the home.

      2. They expect computers to increase productivity and raise the standard of living.

      3. They expect computers to improve the quality of education.

45j

II. Critics point to possible hazards associated with high technology as represented by computers.

   A. Loss of personal autonomy can result.

   B. A shift to high technology at the expense of traditional manufacturing can create widespread unemployment.

III. Attitudes toward the social impact of technology tend to fall into two camps.

   A. Technological determinism: technology drives social change.

Dunn ii

B. Cultural determinism: technology arises from human needs and, therefore, is a result rather than a cause of social change.

IV. Some scholars hold a more middle—of—the—road point of view.

A. Modern technology is both "culture—producing" and "culture—using."

B. Technology can satisfy traditional values, increasing satisfactory options for the majority of the members of society while sometimes limiting the available options for a minority.

V. The personal computer fits two fundamental aspects of the American character and is, therefore, perceived to be an "appropriate" form of technology.

A. Despite their differences, Americans believe themselves to be a unified nation with a collective character.

B. They also simultaneously glorify the independence and personal initiative characterized by the "pioneer spirit."

C. The computer supports both the need to belong to a group and the need to be autonomous.

1. Computer networks correspond to social networks.

2. The capability to log on and off at will, placing choice in the hands of the user, satisfies the personal need for power and control.

VI. Information workers rather than production workers largely comprise society today; thus the behavioral choices desired by this majority dictate the shape of our technology and our society——as can be seen in the computer's widespread acceptance.

45j

Paragraph 1. Jan introduces her broad subject, the social impact of computer technology, by reminding the reader of the computer's role in the routine activities of daily life. These familiar, everyday examples help prepare the reader for part of her argument: that computers have been accepted by the majority of Americans. Readers must agree with this point before Jan can go on to argue her thesis—*why* acceptance has occurred.

Paragraphs 2 and 3. In these paragraphs, Jan adheres to a general pattern followed for many research reports. She has introduced her broad subject, and now she mentions two predominant points of view concerning it—one pro, one con. In raising the main issues that she will explore in her paper—the costs and benefits of computer technology—she supplies the context for her investigation and indicates that she is joining an ongoing discussion important in the field. The issues raised briefly here will be explored in much greater detail as the paper develops.

1

Technology with a Personal Touch:

Computers in American Society

Evidence of computer technology in our daily lives is so
widespread that we scarcely notice it. Our monthly telephone
bills are computer-generated, as are the color graphics we watch
on television. The cars we drive are made from parts
manufactured by computer-controlled machines and engineered by
computer-aided design. We drink milk from cows whose feedings
have been computer-calculated, we buy milk from supermarkets
that use computerized inventory systems, and we read supermarket
ads in newspapers that are computer-typeset.

Undeniably, the computer allows things to be accomplished
faster, more reliably, and with less human effort. These are
some of the benefits. But there are also costs, social costs as
well as material and financial costs. The most obvious social
cost, the one that has attracted the greatest public notice, is
unemployment. Computers and computer-assisted equipment can be
used to replace people and the jobs they perform; computers can
do many tasks more cheaply and efficiently than human beings can.

A related social cost is the impersonalization or
dehumanization that computerization can bring to some aspects of
daily life. There's no doubt that an automatic teller machine
cannot compete with a friendly human when a person needs a smile
and a bit of cheerful small-talk as well as twenty dollars in
cash. A larger issue is the sense of loss of control people can
experience when large portions of their lives are in the
"hands" of machines. When confronted with technology that they
do not understand or trust, people tend to feel helpless,
victimized, and fearful.

45j

Paragraph 4. The fourth paragraph concludes the introduction and contains the thesis for which the rest of the paper provides support. Computer technology has been accepted because it supplies social benefits and serves social needs. Jan intends to show that the personal computer has helped facilitate this acceptance. With this introduction, Jan shows that she understands the nature of a research contribution and the pattern to be used in reporting it.

Paragraphs 5–7. At this point Jan turns to the specific evidence she has gathered during the course of her research. She uses statistics to show Americans' acceptance of the personal computer. Her rough draft actually contained fewer statistics. But she realized her evidence for the computer's popularity was thin—from a single source—so Jan returned to the library and located additional data to back up her point. She consulted business and industry sources, so that her information would be as authoritative as possible. Firmly establishing the computer's acceptance is necessary before she can explore the reasons for its positive reception. Notice that the Labe citation is to an unpaginated source, in this case from a computerized data retrieval service.

Time magazine provided several lively and effective phrases which Jan felt merited direct quotation: for example, the comparison between personal computers' popularity and Americans' love affair with the car and television.

45j

But Americans apparently have decided that the benefits outweigh the costs. Among the reasons they have accepted computer technology is the fundamental one that it serves important social needs more than it interferes with them. The personal computer, in particular, has been an effective means of shaping this acceptance.

Most people agree that the computer is having a dramatic social impact—so much so, in fact, that _Time_ magazine chose a computer rather than a human being as its 1982 "Man of the Year." _Time_'s publisher, John Meyers, believed that none of the human candidates had as much symbolic or historic importance as the computer (5).

Although computers have been around for over 30 years, they are now available to and owned by millions of users in relatively inexpensive desktop models for the office or home. Called personal computers, home computers, or microcomputers, they range in price from around $100 to $3,000 and up, depending on the power and sophistication of the system. Personal computer sales jumped by 115 percent worldwide in 1983 and grew a combined total of another 100 percent between 1984 and 1986, according to the high-tech research firm Dataquest. Dataquest projects annual sales of $49.5 billion and growth rates slightly over 9 percent for personal computers through 1991 (Schnurman B9). Although sales have leveled off from 1983 rates, industry specialists at the investment firm of Drexel Burnham Lambert, Inc. say the U.S. personal computer market will continue to grow, primarily in the business computer segment but with the home market "also showing signs of resurgent strength" throughout the decade (Labe n.p.). Comparing society's

45j

Paragraph 8. This paragraph provides transition to the next section of the paper. Jan uses terminology from the *Time* article (technological "upheaval" and "revolution") to lead into a discussion of the negative aspects of computer technology. She moves back and forth between pro and con points of view for the next several pages. Thus she is enlarging on the two camps of opinion she mentioned in the early paragraphs of the paper.

Paragraph 9. Jan neatly summarizes two lengthy works and several briefer citations in a couple of sentences. After reviewing a more extensive discussion of these sources in her rough draft, she decided she had belabored points not germane to her thesis. So she condensed the paragraphs into a summary and developed just one of those points—unemployment—in paragraph 10. Jan was still careful, however, to cite all her sources for the summary. Notice that the first reference cites an authority who is "qtd. in" (quoted in) an article written by someone else. "Qtd. in" makes clear that the information is secondhand reporting. The reference to Turkle cites those pages that most concisely summarize Turkle's overall thesis, a thesis explored throughout her book. For the reference to Zorn's article, as for the reference to Schnurman in paragraph 6, Jan observed MLA style but also followed the format recommendations that were listed in *NewsBank,* a microfilm information service. Sometimes microform, database, and information service sources will offer such guidelines for citing them in research papers.

acceptance of personal computers to "American love affairs with
the automobile and the television set," _Time_ says people are
receptive to and optimistic about the personal computer's impact
(Friedrich 14).

A poll conducted by Yankelovich, Skelly, and White showed
that 80 percent of the population believes home computers will
become as commonplace as televisions or dishwashers. About 67
percent thinks the "computer revolution" will raise production
and, hence, the nation's standard of living. Sixty-eight
percent believes computers will improve the quality of education
(Friedrich 14).

Time's writers chose to call the arrival of the personal
computer the end result of "a technological upheaval," "a
technological revolution" that is "now, quite literally,
hitting home" (Friedrich 14). For most people in American
society the words "upheaval" and "revolution" carry negative
connotations: we have been conditioned to see potential danger
in disorder and change. During the past several decades, we
have been particularly conditioned to see danger in many forms
of technology—sometimes with good reason. The Yankelovich poll
did, in fact, find that Americans were worried about
unemployment and dehumanization as negative consequences of
computerization.

Critics have frequently warned that the "computer age" may
bring massive unemployment as computerized robots take over
blue-collar manufacturing jobs. Others, including David
Burnham, author of _The Rise of the Computer State_, have
predicted a loss of personal autonomy as computerized data banks
track information about citizens and invade their privacy (qtd.

45j

Paragraphs 10-11. This discussion is derived from a personal interview and establishes a subtopic Jan returns to later in the paper. Not only does Professor Perrucci comment on the relationship between computers, high technology, and unemployment, but he talks about "smokestack" industries—a subject Jan will explore when she discusses social change. She originally placed the Perrucci interview closer to the end of the paper, but she eventually saw that is contributed effectively to the pro–con contrast between the general public attitude (paragraph 11) and that of the academic critics discussed in subsequent paragraphs. The questions raised in paragraph 11 provide an order of presentation for the viewpoints presented in paragraphs 12 through 17.

Notice in paragraph 10 that no in-text documentation appears with the Perrucci quotations. The reason is that the source is a personal interview that Jan conducted herself, not a written source. The Perrucci interview is, of course, listed with Jan's other sources in the "Works Cited."

45j

in Moskowitz 14). Some critics such as Sherry Turkle believe
that computers will lead to redefinitions of what makes people
human (12-25, 306-313). Others, including highly regarded
scientist Robert Jastrow, believe that as the machines gain
"intelligence" they will become the next step in evolution on
earth (Zorn C5).

Perhaps the most relevant personal threat to many Americans
is computer-related unemployment. During a recent interview,
sociology professor Robert Perrucci warned that the computer and
other technical marvels should not lull us into a "high-tech
ideology" presented as a cure-all for the nation's major
economic ills. "In a sense we are using this high-tech
ideology . . . to justify . . . getting out of the so-called
'smokestack industries,' " he says. Perrucci would be much more
sympathetic to those who are pushing high tech if they advocated
it as something that will enhance and contribute to America's
strength as a manufacturing society. He fears, however, that
high tech is being proposed as an alternative or a substitute,
abandoning millions of blue-collar workers. The linkage of home
computers to high-tech ideology is the aspect he finds most
troublesome: "It contributes to the kind of mentality or belief
that high tech in and of itself is the answer."

But the Yankelovich poll indicated that the majority of
Americans are less worried about the negative consequences of
the computer revolution than critics perhaps would like them to
be. Is this general acceptance the result of people's simply
giving in to technology determinism--a kind of join-or-get-
mowed-over-by-the-inevitable response? Or is it cultural
determinism, a widespread shift in values that has readied

45j

Paragraph 12. The twelfth paragraph begins Jan's development of the prevailing points of view respected scholars have toward technology. Notice that she uses correct form for the long quotation: indented ten spaces from the left, double-spaced, and without quotation marks. Only quotation marks that appear in the original are used in a displayed quotation.

Jan decided to omit the end of a sentence in the long quotation, so she correctly used four spaced periods—three ellipsis marks plus the concluding period—to indicate the omission.

Paragraph 13. The first part of this paragraph paraphrases Hannay and McGinn. Jan liked some of the original wording, particularly the phrase "survive, and . . . thrive," so she quoted that part exactly.

Her authoritative sources represent industry as well as academics. Because Jan is careful to let her reader know her sources' professional affiliations, the balance of points of view is evident. Citing sources by name and title not only establishes their credibility but also provides an introduction for her paraphrases and quotations.

45j

society to accept, in fact demand, this particular technology, even though it has objected to several other technologies (most notably nuclear energy and nuclear weapons)? Or has computer technology simply offered alternatives in keeping with existing traditional values and goals?

Speaking for the technological determinists, Langdon Winner, a professor of political science and technology studies at the Massachusetts Institute of Technology, notes that since the nineteenth century many people have come to believe technological change is "self-generating, self-determining, and in a true sense inevitable" (48). It is only a short jump to the conclusion that technological innovation drives social change. Winner writes:

> W. W. Rostow speaks of technological constraints that existed in "pre-Newtonian" times and asserts that when modern technology was lacking, social change was lacking as well. . . . But with the coming of Newtonian science and the industrial revolution, a pattern of linear growth was established that continues to the present day. In response to the developments in science and technics, the institutions of society and politics alter their structure in order to "absorb" the new technologies (47).

On the other hand, Bruce Hannay, a Bell Laboratories vice president, and Robert McGinn, a Stanford University professor of engineering, represent a more culturally deterministic point of view. They see technological developments as arising from basic human needs. They point out that humans have always needed protection from the environment and from other animals. Through

45j

Paragraph 14–15. Notice how smoothly the source materials have been blended in Jan's sentences. However, quotation marks, parenthetical page numbers, and references to author and source clearly signal readers that the material is borrowed. Jan uses paragraph 15 to evaluate Merrill's position relative to the two main schools of thought on technology and social change. She needs a bibliographical note, appearing at the end of the paper in the "Notes" section, to let her reader know where an overview of social change and extended definitions of cultural determinism and technological determinism can be found. A detailed discussion of these general theories would have been beyond the scope of her paper. Effective research writers learn that they must be discriminating about what to include in detail and what to mention only in passing, sometimes relegating large amounts of reading to just a reference.

Paragraphs 16–17. Here Jan introduces the point of view her research has suggested is the most relevant to her subject. Following a widely accepted research-report pattern, her paper surveys several theories before focusing on the one she intends to test against her topic. She quotes rather than paraphrases Ackerman, because she does not want to risk misrepresenting his viewpoint.

45j

technology, a human being attempts "to overcome his shortcomings and his vulnerability by extending his limited capacities. He thus enhances his power, which in turn often enables him to survive, and, on occasion, even to thrive" (35).

In the <u>International Encyclopedia of the Social Sciences</u>, Robert Merrill defines technologies as "the cultural traditions developed in human communities for dealing with the physical and biological environment" (577). He also explains that Western societies have institutionalized technological change. That is, they have developed social traditions for advancing or creating technology, "for producing new knowledge, processes, and products. Modern technologies are culture-producing as well as culture-using sociocultural systems . . ." (582).

In short, Merrill steers a path between the cultural determinists who view social change as shaped by cultural values, which in turn influence the choice and impact of technology, and the technological determinists who believe technological change drives social change.[1]

Social psychologist Werner Ackerman goes a step further. He suggests that an either/or view of the relationship between social change and technological innovation is simplistic. Neither technology as progress (i.e., "good") nor technology as alien and disruptive (i.e., "bad") produces useful ways of discussing social change. Rather than presenting a win-lose dilemma, his view suggests a sliding scale of behavioral choices (462).

Ackerman says that although options may be eliminated for some groups, technology provides new options for others--new "strategic possibilities" within their existing social

45j

Paragraph 18. In order to show why computers are achieving acceptance, Jan wanted to include a discussion of "appropriate technology," an alternative proposed by some technological determinists. At first she was tempted to give a lengthy analysis, including the movement's origins in the counterculture and ecology movements of the 1960's. After drafting several pages, she saw that she was wandering far from the main thrust of her research. In her final revision, Jan settled for a summary of the movement's objections to modern technology. She realized this was all she needed in order to position computer technology later.

Paragraph 19. Harvey Brooks provides a helpful bridge in Jan's discussion. Although she quotes only one of them, two long articles by Brooks were important to her research. The scholar offered one of the best-balanced views toward technology and society that she read. His suggestion about mixing technologies leads directly to an important conclusion Jan wanted to make about American culture.

45j

situation. Thus, new technology does not necessarily determine
new social behavior as much as it provides new opportunities for
people to fulfill their interests and demands: "It is quite
conceivable that the new behavioral alternatives are used in an
instrumental way to satisfy constant traditional values. . . .
The goals and values may have remained constant, but ways of
attaining them have been diversified" (462).

The most outspoken critics of modern technology disfavor
what they view as its tendency to subordinate humans to
machines. Proponents of "appropriate technology," these
critics object to technological interdependency, to increasingly
abstract and impersonal human relationships, to decisions made
by those who never see how the consequences affect other people,
to life affected by forces people cannot control, perceive, or
understand--all of which they claim result from technology's
social impact (De Forest 68). According to this point of view,
then, computer technology imposes another layer of bureaucracy,
another impersonal control system understood only by
specialists, that benefits a few at the expense of many. Anyone
who has ever experienced feelings of helplessness while trying
to get an incorrect charge removed from a computer-generated
bill can sympathize with this viewpoint.

Professor Harvey Brooks of Harvard University responds to
the technological determinists by pointing out that
"interdependence is a fact of modern life," which he sees
"little prospect of reversing . . . without great
impoverishment of life both in a material and in a spiritual
sense" (68). However, Brooks does think mixing different <u>kinds</u>
of interdependencies may substantially decrease people's <u>sense</u>

45j

Paragraphs 20–23. These paragraphs are among several in the paper containing no citations. Jan undoubtedly could have referred to source material to back up her point of view—a not-uncommon one. But, in fact, she had developed these ideas about the American character over a period of time from readings and discussions in high school and college classes as well as from her own general reading in magazines. Although not exactly the same kind of "common knowledge" as the date of Lincoln's assassination, the points about the pioneer spirit seemed to Jan to be widely accepted. So she provided the necessary circumstantial evidence but did not see a need to document it.

45j

of dependence on centralized, bureaucratic technological
systems. He cites the CB radio exisiting with the telephone as
an example of such a mixture (68). This technological
combination is a good illustration of two fundamental aspects of
the American character, aspects that have a direct bearing on
society's acceptance of computer technology.

Today we expect our technologies to give us rapid and
continent-spanning results the way our communications and
transportation systems do. A large part of our national
heritage is bound up in subduing and settling the wilderness,
conquering frontiers and linking them, making areas accessible
to people back in "civilization"--whether the frontiers be the
Mississippi, the Rockies, or the moon.

At the same time we have striven for national unity, our
national history has glorified the independent pioneer spirit.
The fact that America was discovered, mapped, and settled by
people on personal adventures makes our self-image as pioneers
unsurprising. The durability of this self-image can be traced
across American history from the pioneers rolling west in
covered wagons to the Pioneer spacecraft shooting beyond our
solar system.

Certain parts of the pioneer spirit, independence and
autonomy, are highly valued aspects of the American character.
Personal freedom of thought and action, whether actual or
imagined, lies at the very foundation of our system of
government and our expectations about human relations
at all levels of society.

America's technologically sophisticated, interlinked, and
efficient telephone systems do their part to sustain our

45j

Paragraph 24. Harvey Brooks supplied the telephone-CB radio comparison that Jan used as a springboard for her comments on the American character. In this paragraph she returns to the comparison to sum up her analysis and to lead into the final section of her paper— the personal computer's role in a culture characterized by simultaneous needs for togetherness and independence. The paragraph shows how a student can make a contribution to research. Jan read many sources; obviously she was not the first person to have thought about the topic. But thorough assimilation of her reading and thoughtful analysis enabled her to see connections between people's ideas. In paragraph 24 she draws together Brook's ideas and Naisbitt's high-tech–high-touch theory, connecting them with her own conclusion about how the personal computer fits into society.

Paragraphs 25–28. Networks are a key concept to Jan's thesis. At the end of paragraph 25 she uses a direct quotation to set up the relationship between interpersonal networks, computer networks, and technology appropriate to modern American society. Paragraphs 26–28 develop this relationship fully.

Ideally, she should have gone directly to Lipnack and Stamps, as the original source was footnoted in Naisbitt's book. However, *New Age* was not available in her library, so Jan had to settle for a second-hand report. She does indicate in the citation that the quotation is second-hand.

In paragraph 25 Jan refers again to Ackerman's theory regarding social values and change; paragraphs 27 and 28 are Jan's extension of the theory to personal computers and computer networks.

45j

national unity, our collective character, our interdependence.
The CB radio, on the other hand, recaptures some of the
trailblazer's independence, allowing asphalt cowboys and average
citizens alike limited but immediate and direct access to anyone
who is listening on their frequency. The telephone and the CB
may seem like mundane symbols, but they do show two important
and sometimes conflicting aspects of our value system.

In ways that correspond to Brooks's mixture of
technologies, personal computers fit in nicely with the social
needs and values of many Americans. The personal computer
enables people to be simultaneously interconnected and
independent—through a network they can enter and exit at will.
Because it is a type of technology that satisfies these two
important social needs, the personal computer has gained ready
acceptance in modern American society. The desktop computer has
what social forecaster John Naisbitt calls "high-tech/high-
touch."

According to Naisbitt, the introduction of a new technology
must be accompanied by a counterbalancing, human-centered
response, or society will reject the technology (39). He cites
interpersonal networks, such as those of the woman's movement of
the 1970s, as expressing the need for high touch in an American
society confronted with increasing amounts of technology. If we
apply Ackerman's criteria, we might say people have found
alternative ways to sustain and reinforce traditional values
associated with self-worth and self-importance. Writing in New
Age, Jessica Lipnack and Jeffrey Stamps draw an insightful
analogy: "Networks are appropriate sociology—the human
equivalent of appropriate technology" (qtd. in Naisbitt 193).

45j

Paragraphs 29–30. Jan worried that these paragraphs would seem rather unrelated to the focus of her paper. But she believed the shift from a manufacturing society to an "information society" was an important reason for the computer's acceptance. She particularly liked Daniel Bell's statement about the two types of technology characterizing the two halves of the twentieth century and paraphrased it in paragraph 30. Although she disliked relying so heavily on a single source, Naisbitt's discussion summarized most clearly and coherently ideas which had appeared piecemeal in a number of other sources.

Because Jan did not want to interrupt the flow of ideas with a definition of "content analysis" in paragraph 29, she used a content note. She felt her readers needed the definition to undertand how Naisbitt had reasearched his subject and arrived at his conclusions. Without such an explanation, she feared they would question the conclusions she drew from Naisbitt's evidence—especially since the last section of her paper relied heavily on this source. Content notes are appropriate in a situation such as this; however, never use them simply to cram in all the leftover bits of your research.

45j

But Naisbitt says networks have an even more fundamental
sociological function. He calls them the modern-day equivalent
of the ancient tribe, fulfilling the high-touch need for
belonging to a group while still focusing on the individual
(196-97). Networks locate people at "nodes," where many
threads of the communications web cross and from which
communication and action can be initiated.

In fact, the "tribe" can be global. An electronic
bulletin board user in a Montana town, for instance, can
communicate with another user in Ottawa, Canada. "It's a
community gathering place . . . like a bulletin board up in a
grocery store," explains a personal computer owner in Billings,
Montana, except that the "shoppers" may be from thousands of
miles away: "One of my friends is in Pennsylvania," reports the
Billings man, "and I've never even met the guy" ("Home
Computer Buffs" B3).

It's no wonder, then, that desktop computers have achieved
a high degree of acceptance. They offer access to a vast
information and communications network while allowing the people
at the nodes of this interconnected system (at their terminals
and minicomputers) a feeling of considerable autonomy at the
same time—in short, they confer a feeling of power and control.
It is necessary only to watch children playing with computers to
understand that this feeling of power is very real and very
satisfying.

Of the ten national trends revealed by Naisbitt's content
analysis[2] of America's newspapers and magazines, more than half
have a direct relationship to the increasingly widespread use of
computers in society. Like other observers, the social

45j

Paragraphs 31–32. Here Jan brings together the threads of her paper. Paragraph 31 drives home the connection between the information society and the operational role the computer fills in such a society. Further, it discusses how the personal computer has facilitated the acceptance of computer technology. In paragraph 32, Jan extrapolates from the personal computer in particular to computer technology in general with a restatement of the thesis, this time a more specific one than the general statement she used in the paper's opening paragraphs. She again identifies the pertinent social values (belonging and independence). She then reminds the reader that she has shown how the majority of Americans regard computers as beneficial (statistical and circumstantial evidence combined with Ackerman's theory). These factors explain the widespread public acceptance of computer technology.

45j

Dunn 11

forecaster sees a trend toward an economy based on the creation
and distribution of information rather than on industrial
manufacturing. Statistics show that information-related
occupations have increased from 17 percent in 1950 to 60 percent
today, whereas only about 13 percent of today's labor force is
involved in manufacturing; in fact, white-collar workers have
outnumbered blue-collar workers since 1956 (Naisbitt 12-14).

In other words, the shift from smokestack industries to
high-tech industries is over and done. Sociologist Daniel Bell
aptly states that whereas the machine was the symbol of the
first half of the twentieth century, "intellectual technology"
dominates the last half (21). We now have brain-intensive
industries, rather than capital- and labor-intensive industries,
employing more than half the work force in professional or
clerical jobs. For this majority, "the creation, processing,
and distribution of information is the job" (Naisbitt 15-16)
and frequently even the end product. Naturally, the behavioral
choices desired by this majority will dictate the shape of our
technology and our society.

In an information-dominated society, uncontrolled,
unmanaged, overwhelmingly proliferating information hinders
productivity rather than helping it. Computers help people
store, manage, select, and use the bulk of information upon
which their livelihoods depend. Personal computers, because
they are relatively small, "user-friendly," and right on top of
desks so that individuals can log on and off the communications
network at will, increase the user's sense of ownership and
control. They are indeed personal, in that they come to seem
like any other desktop tool--reference book, calculator,

45j

Jan's concluding paragraph is fairly short. She could have written "I have shown this, this, and this, which proves that," rehashing at some length material previously covered. Actually, the first few drafts of her ending were written that way. But believing that she had thoroughly developed the elements of her investigation and clearly expressed her conclusions throughout the paper, instead she ultimately chose to summarize her point of view in two strong final sentences. "If I have presented my research logically and effectively," she reasoned, "extra details will only weaken the impact of my ending paragraph."

telephone. And in fact these computers perform many of the same
functions—providing information, handling calculations, sending
and receiving messages—either by means of their own programs or
by means of their electronic links to the wider network. The
increasing number of people who have access to and the ability
to use personal computers enjoy a considerably expanded sphere
of knowledge, influence, and action.

    Thus computer technology satisfies some very basic and
sometimes conflicting American social values: the need to belong
and the simultaneous need to feel independent. As long as those
needs continue to be satisfied, and as long as the range of
behavioral choices continues to expand for the majority of the
population, computers will enjoy widespread public acceptance.

45j

Notes. Two types of notes may be used along with MLA-style in-text citations: bibliographical notes and content notes. Such notes are placed either at the end of the research paper (as endnotes) or at the bottoms of pages (as footnotes). Notes are indicated in the text by raised Arabic numerals.

Note 1 in Jan's paper is a **bibliographical note** referring the reader to a source not quoted but important as background reading. Because the whole book, rather than selections from it, was important to her research, Jan does not cite page numbers in the note. She does list the book in the "Works Cited." Bibliographical notes are also useful for documenting a number of sources that would make reading awkward if they were cited in the text.

Note 2 is a **content note.** Some editors and instructors discourage the use of such notes. They believe that if the information is important it should be included in the text; otherwise it should not appear at all. Others think a content note is permissible if the information is relevant but too digressive or complex to place in the text itself. Check with your instructor or refer to the style manual for the field before you use content notes. Certainly, avoid content notes that become essays lacking real relevance to the text.

Bibliography. The form presented on pages 518–519 follows MLA style and, therefore, is headed "Works Cited" rather than "Bibliography." Compare the entries listed in Jan's bibliography with those on pages 460–468 for a thorough explanation of MLA style as it pertains to various types of sources.

45j

Notes

[1] For an overview of schools of thought on social change, see Appelbaum.

[2] "Content analysis" is a long-term survey of a nation's newspapers and magazines to track topics and attitudes—which ones drop out of the news, which ones are added, and which ones remain current. This technique was used extensively during World War II and is still used widely by military intelligence and the CIA to gather information about foreign countries.

45j

Dunn 14

Works Cited

Ackerman, Werner. "Cultural Values and Social Choice of
      Technology." International Social Science Journal 33
      (1981): 447–465.

Appelbaum, Richard P. Theories of Social Change. Chicago:
      Markham, 1970.

Bell, Daniel. The Winding Passage: Essays and Sociological
      Journeys, 1960–1980. Cambridge: Abt, 1980.

Brooks, Harvey. "A Critique of the Concept of Appropriate
      Technology." Appropriate Technology and Social Values––A
      Critical Appraisal. Ed. Franklin A. Long and Alexander
      Oleson. Cambridge: Ballinger, 1980. 53–78.

De Forest, Paul H. "Technology Choice in the Context of Social
      Values––A Problem of Definition." Appropriate Technology
      and Social Values––A Critical Appraisal. Ed. Franklin A.
      Long and Alexander Oleson. Cambridge: Ballinger, 1980.
      11–25.

Friedrich, Otto. "The Computer Moves In." Time 3 Jan. 1983:
      14–24.

Hannay, N. Bruce, and Robert E. McGinn. "The Anatomy of Modern
      Technology: Prolegomenon to an Improved Public Policy for
      the Social Management of Technology." Daedalus 109 (1980):
      25–53.

"Home Computer Buffs Share Messages the Electronic Way."
      Billings (Montana) Gazette 18 Jan. 1986: B3.

Labe, P. "Personal Computer Industry." Drexel Burnham Lambert,
      Inc. 23 Apr. 1987: n.p. Dow Jones News/Retrieval Investext
      file 12, item 32.

45j

Dunn 15

Merrill, Robert S. "The Study of Technology." International
    Encyclopedia of the Social Sciences. 1968 ed.

Meyers, John A. "A Letter from the Publisher." Time 3 Jan.
    1983: 5.

Moskowitz, Daniel B. "Is Life with Computers So Insidious?"
    Rev. of The Rise of the Computer State, by David Burnham.
    Business Week 11 July 1983: 14.

Naisbitt, John. Megatrends: Ten New Directions Transforming Our
    Lives. New York: Warner, 1982.

Perrucci, Robert. Personal interview. 14 Feb. 1987.

Schnurman, Mitchell. "Computer Sales Growth." Dallas (Texas)
    Times Herald 6 Mar. 1987. NewsBank [microform],
    "Business," 1987, 26: B9–10, fiche.

Turkle, Sherry. The Second Self: Computers and the Human
    Spirit. 1984. New York: Touchstone/Simon, 1985.

Winner, Langdon. Autonomous Technology: Technics–Out–Of–Control
    as a Theme in Political Thought. Cambridge: MIT Press,
    1977.

Zorn, Eric. "What Do Computers Have in Mind for the Future?"
    Chicago Tribune 24 March 1982. NewsBank [microform],
    "Social Relations," 1982, 17:C4–6, fiche.

45j

45k

Sample excerpt in APA style showing name-date documentation system

Following is a repetition of paragraphs 30 and 31 of Jan's paper and her bibliography prepared according to the *Publication Manual of the American Psychological Association* (APA). Although these pages cannot show you all the documentation requirements of this style, you will be able to see the general name-date format and compare it to name-page MLA style.

In other words, the shift from smokestack industries to high-tech industries is over and done. Sociologist Daniel Bell (1980) aptly states that whereas the machine was the symbol of the first half of the twentieth century, "intellectual technology" dominates the last half. We now have brain-intensive industries, rather than capital- and labor-intensive industries, employing more than half the work force in professional or clerical jobs. For this majority, "the creation, processing, and distribution of information is the job" (Naisbitt, 1982, pp. 15–16) and frequently even the end product. Naturally, the behavioral choices desired by this majority will dictate the shape of our technology and our society.

In an information-dominated society, uncontrolled, unmanaged, overwhelmingly proliferating information hinders productivity rather than helping it. Computers help people store, manage, select, and use the bulk of information upon which their livelihoods depend. . .

References

Ackerman, W. (1981). Cultural values and social choice of
technology. International Social Science Journal, 33,
447–465.

Appelbaum, R. P. (1970). Theories of social change. Chicago:
Markham.

Bell, D. (1980). The winding passage: essays and sociological
journeys, 1960–1980. Cambridge, MA: Abt Books.

Brooks, H. (1980). A critique of the concept of appropriate
technology. In F. A. Long & A. Oleson (Eds.), Appropriate
technology and social values—a critical appraisal (pp.
53–78). Cambridge, MA: Ballinger.

De Forest, P. H. (1980). Technology choice in the context of
social values—a problem of definition. In F. A. Long & A.
Oleson (Eds.), Appropriate technology and social values—a
critical appraisal (pp. 11–25). Cambridge, MA: Ballinger.

Friedrich, O. (1983, January 3). The computer moves in. Time,
pp. 14–24.

Hannay, N. B., & McGinn, R. E. (1980, Winter). The anatomy of
modern technology: prolegomenon to an improved public
policy for the social management of technology. Daedalus,
109(1), 25–53.

Home computer buffs share messages the electronic way. (1986,
January 18). Billings (Montana) Gazette, p. B3.

Labe, P. (1987, April 23). Personal computer industry [on-line
database]. Drexel Burnham Lambert, Inc. (Producer). Dow
Jones News/Retrieval Investext (Distributor). (File 12;
Item 32).

45k

Technology

15

Merrill, R. S. (1968). The study of technology. In D. L. Sills

(Ed.), International encyclopedia of the social sciences:

Vol. 15 (pp. 576–589). New York: Macmillan.

Meyers, J. A. (1983, January 3). A letter from the publisher.

Time, p. 5.

Moskowitz, D. B. (1983, July 11). Is life with computers so

insidious? [Review of The rise of the computer state].

Business Week, p. 14.

Naisbitt, J. (1982). Megatrends: ten new directions

transforming our lives. New York: Warner Books.

Perrucci, R. (1987, February 14). Personal interview at Purdue

University.

Schnurman, M. (1987, March 6). Computer sales growth. Dallas

(Texas) Times Herald [Microform, NewsBank, 26: B9–10;

fiche].

Turkle, S. (1985). The second self: computers and the human

spirit. New York: Touchstone/Simon & Schuster. (Original

work published 1984).

Winner, L. (1977). Autonomous technology technics–out–of–

control as a theme in political thought. Cambridge, MA:

MIT Press.

Zorn, E. (1982, March 24). What do computers have in mind for

the future? Chicago Tribune [Microform, NewsBank, 17:C4–6,

fiche].

45k

SPECIAL
WRITING
APPLICATIONS

The only way some people know you is through your writing. It can be your most frequent point of contact, or your *only* one, with people important to your career. . . . To those men and women, *your writing is you*. It reveals how your mind works.

KENNETH ROMAN and JOEL RAPHAELSON, *Writing That Works*

46

SUMMARIES

The ability to summarize effectively—to strip a paragraph or a chapter down to its central meaning without distorting the author's original thought and approach—is extremely useful. On the job, you may be called upon to write a shorter version of a longer report or article. Or you may be asked to review a great deal of information and prepare a brief summary that highlights the main points. Writing summaries is also an excellent way to study. Having such summaries available is invaluable for later reference and review. And, of course, summary writing is an important tool for preparing a research paper. Section **45** explains the role summary notes play in library research.

Preparing summaries can also help you to read with greater accuracy as well as to write with greater conciseness and directness. You cannot summarize effectively if you have not read carefully, discriminating between principal and subordinate ideas. Such discrimination, in turn, will help you sharpen your own style and learn to revise the wordiness that creeps into writing.

Before you try to summarize a passage, read it carefully to discover the author's purpose and point of view. As you read, pick out the central ideas and notice how they are arranged. Be on the lookout for the author's own compact summaries, either at the beginning or end of a passage or at points of transition.

After studying the passage, you are ready to organize your summary, or **précis.** Ordinarily you will be able to reduce a paragraph—or sometimes a whole group of paragraphs—to a single sentence. Very complex paragraphs, however, may require more than one sentence.

Use a simple or complex sentence rather than a compound sentence to summarize a paragraph—unless the original paragraph itself is poorly organized. A compound sentence implies that there are two or more equally dominant ideas in the paragraph. If you find that you have written a compound summarizing sentence, recheck the paragraph to make sure you haven't missed some (perhaps implied) subordinating relationship. In determining the author's intent, be alert to such writing techniques as parallel clauses and phrases, which indicate ideas of equal weight, and transitional words and phrases, which show relationships among ideas.

Summarize ideas in the order in which they appear, but avoid following the wording too closely. If you try to preserve the flavor of the original too precisely, your summary will be too long. Do pick up the author's key terms and phrases, for they are useful in binding the précis together. Discard any figures of speech, digressions, or discussions that are not essential to the "trunk and main branches" of the paragraph. However, be sure that you have faithfully reflected the

46

author's point of view. Your task is to focus objectively on *someone else's* ideas, to produce an **informative abstract** of those ideas. (There may be times when you need to summarize someone else's ideas from your own viewpoint, including your evaluation of the ideas as a part of the summary. This is called a **critical abstract.** You should be sure you know which type of abstract is appropriate for the summary you are preparing.)

When you are through summarizing, you should have reduced the material to about one-third its original length. Study the following example:

> We very rarely consider, however, the process by which we gained our convictions. If we did so, we could hardly fail to see that there was usually little ground for our confidence in them. Here and there, in this department of knowledge or that, some one of us might make a fair claim to have taken some trouble to get correct ideas of, let us say, the situation in Russia, the sources of our food supply, the origin of the Constitution, the revision of the tariff, the policy of the Holy Roman Apostolic Church, modern business organization, trade unions, birth control, socialism, the League of Nations, the excess-profits tax, preparedness, advertising in its social bearings; but only a very exceptional person would be entitled to opinions on all of even these few matters. And yet most of us have opinions on all these, and on many other questions of equal importance, of which we may know even less. We feel compelled, as self-respecting persons, to take sides when they come up for discussion. We even surprise ourselves by our omniscience. Without taking thought we see in a flash that it is most righteous and expedient to discourage birth control by legislative enactment, or that one who decries intervention in Mexico is clearly wrong, or that big advertising is essential to big business and that big business is the pride of the land. As godlike beings why should we not rejoice in our omniscience?
>
> JAMES HARVEY ROBINSON, *The Mind in the Making*

This paragraph hinges on the sentence beginning *And yet most of us have opinions on all these.* . . . This sentence suggests the pattern that your summarizing sentence should take. The central idea of the paragraph is that we do not ordinarily take pains in forming our convictions on important matters, but we nevertheless express our opinions as a matter of right and even take delight in our apparent omniscience. The main clause of your summarizing sentence will express the second part of the central idea, retaining the author's ironic approach.

> We are godlike beings who delight in our ability to form and express convictions on birth control, on intervention in Mexico, or on the role of big business, without a moment's thought.

46

To preserve the author's qualification in the first part of the paragraph, however, you must precede the main clause with a subordinate clause.

> Although the few pains we take to understand such things as the situation in Russia, the sources of our food supply, the origin of the Constitution, the revision of the tariff, the policy of the Holy Roman Apostolic Church, modern business organization, trade unions, birth control, socialism, the League of Nations, the excess-profits tax, preparedness, and advertising in its social bearings give us little reason to have confidence in our opinions on these matters, we are godlike beings who delight in our ability to form and express convictions on birth control, on intervention in Mexico or on the role of big business, without a moment's thought.

But this "summary" is almost half as long as the original. To reduce it further, replace the specific examples with general terms.

> Although the few pains we take to understand such things as social, political, economic, religious, and medical issues give us little reason to have confidence in our convictions on these matters, we are godlike beings who delight in our ability to form and express such convictions without a moment's thought.

This summary, less than one-third the length of the original, would be acceptable for most purposes, but occasionally even a shorter summary is desirable.

> Although we have little reason to trust our convictions on the important issues of life, we delight in forming and expressing such opinions without a moment's thought.

> Clearly this last sentence does not express everything in Robinson's paragraph, but a summary is concerned only with the central thought; and the central thought is preserved in even the shortest statement above.

46

EXERCISE 46(1)

Write a two-sentence summary of the paragraph by Jacques Barzun on pp. 408–409.

EXERCISE 46(2)

Write a one-sentence summary of the same paragraph.

EXERCISE 46(3)

Try to write a one-sentence summary of the following paragraph. Does the effort tell you anything about the weakness of the paragraph itself?

Among the many interesting aspects of dietary training is the living together of the students. This allows each to get acquainted with people from all over the States and to exchange ideas and viewpoints from different sections of the country. By living in such a home, many girls grow into more mature individuals. It proves a good chance for girls who have always lived at home to become more independent. It also helps to establish feelings of self-sufficiency in those who have never before been on their own.

EXERCISE 46(4)

Select a magazine article totaling about three pages of text. Write a summary no longer than one-third the original. Exchange your summary with a classmate. Then, without reading his or her article, write a one-paragraph summary (four or five sentences) of your classmate's précis. Finally, compare the last two summaries with the two original summaries and with the articles, discussing how successful you each have been in distilling the main points. The comparison and discussion should help both of you sharpen your summary-writing skills.

47

ESSAY EXAMS

What you have learned from this handbook about effective writing applies to the special problem of writing essays for exams. You will be expected to write standard English, to organize material intelligently, and to provide evidence and detail to support generalizations. When you have several days to write a paper or a take-home exam, you spend a good part of the time on planning—thinking about the subject, gathering material, making notes, organizing your ideas, outlining. You also have time to revise your first draft, correcting errors and clarifying your meaning. However, you cannot expect to do all this in the limited time you have for an in-class exam. You are writing under pressure. Therefore, it saves time to go into essay exams knowing how to proceed.

47a

Preparing for exams

Most of your planning must be done before you go to the exam. How can you do that when you don't know what questions will be asked? You won't have free choice of subject; it will be chosen for you—or, at best, you will be allowed to choose from among two or three. You do know the *general subject* of the exam, however; it is the subject matter of the course or one part of the course. Your goal, then, is *to go to the exam having in mind a rough outline of the course segments and the contents of each.*

47

This process of outlining should begin with the first lecture or reading assignment and continue uninterrupted to the day of the exam. Take notes during lectures, underline key passages and make marginal notations in your textbooks, summarize your reading, look over your gathered material from time to time, evaluate it, and structure it. As you study, write a more formal outline based on an overview of the course material and any guidelines suggested by your instructor. Writing such an outline and studying it can help to fix the general subject in your mind.

Also think about your audience. What expectations will your instructor have concerning the subject matter and its treatment? What is the purpose of the exam? To answer these questions, think about the emphasis your instructor has placed on various topics during the term. As a general rule, the more time spent on a topic, the more important or complex the instructor judges it to be. Although you should review all relevant course material, you may be able to anticipate some exam questions if you think about topics and issues that have been stressed during the term. On the other hand, don't forget about readings that may have been assigned but not discussed. The exam may contain questions on this material, too. If you are not sure, by all means ask your instructor just how much material an exam will cover.

47b

Planning your answer

As soon as you see the specific questions in an exam, your subject is limited for you. Say, for example, your general subject was the history of Europe from 1815 to 1848—the segment of the course on which you are being examined. Now you are given fifty minutes to answer four questions, the first of which is *What were the four major political and social developments in Europe during the period of 1815–1848?* Or, your general subject was three stories by Nathaniel Hawthorne and two by Herman Melville—the stories you discussed in class. Now you are given fifty minutes to answer two questions, the first of which is this: *Hawthorne has been called a "moralist-psychologist." Define the term and evaluate Hawthorne's effectiveness as moralist-psychologist by making specific reference to two of his tales.*

Read the examination question carefully. Never start writing without thinking about what you are being asked to do. One of the most common errors students make during examinations is to read too hastily and consequently to misunderstand the question being asked. Underlining key words in the exam question can be helpful. For example, if the question says "compare and contrast," you are being asked to discuss both similarities *and* differences, not just one or the other. As you read an exam question, identify the task you are

47b

being asked to perform. Are you being asked to summarize or to analyze? Are you being asked to comment on a given statement, possibly to disagree with it, or to prove it by providing supporting evidence? Instructors think carefully about their exam questions; the wording will frequently provide you with a structure for your answer. The Hawthorne question, for instance, assigns two distinct tasks: defining and evaluating. If a student's response provides a thorough and well-supported evaluation but does not define "moralist-psychologist" adequately, his or her exam score will suffer despite the sound evaluation.

The European history question directs you to furnish information (what *are* the four major developments?). You have only about ten minutes to answer the question, so you will not be able to go into great detail. Don't try to fill up half a blue book with everything you know about the subject. In the second question, you are asked to define and evaluate; you must make a critical judgment on the basis of specific evidence in Hawthorne's stories. You have approximately twenty-five minutes to organize and write the essay. Make it a rule to take a minute or two to think about the question, and answering it will be easier.

Having done this, gather material and prepare a rough outline of the limited topic. Typical notes for the history question could include the following:

1815—Congress of Vienna

1848—Revolutions

Nationalism—C. of V. denied rights to Poles, Belgians, Greeks, etc.

Conservative-Liberal Conflict—Cons. anti-reform. Lib. underground

Industrial Expansion—Intro. of machines. Transportation—railroads, steam transport, etc.

Class conflict—Lower class vs. middle class

An answer to the question on Hawthorne could develop from the following notes:

How human beings behave (psych.) and how they ought/ought not to (moral)

"Ambitious Guest"—psychological study of human ambitions—moralistic application

"Wakefield"—integration of psych. and moral—people tied to systems

47b

After briefly studying such notes, you have only to number them in the order you wish to present them—and you have an outline.

As in all outlining and other such planning, you should not feel rigidly bound to the material and its structure. As you write, other ideas may come to you and a better structure may suggest itself. The student who answered the Hawthorne question, for example, decided to write on "Egotism" rather than "The Ambitious Guest." With time looking over your shoulder, though, you probably cannot afford to change your plans more than once.

47c

Writing a cover statement

On the basis of your notes you should now be able to begin your examination essay by writing a sentence or two that will serve as a thesis statement. The students who answered the above questions began as follows:

> Although there were no major conflicts among the European powers between the Congress of Vienna (1814–1815) and the Revolutions of 1848, important developments were taking place that would affect the future history of Europe. Four of these developments were the rise of nationalism, the conflict between the conservatives and the liberals, the conflict between the lower and middle classes, and the expansion of industry.

> Hawthorne is a moralist-psychologist who is concerned not only with *how* people behave but also with how they *ought* or *ought not* to behave. He is most successful when he integrates the two approaches, as in "Wakefield," and least successful when his moralizing gets away from him, as in "Egotism; or, The Bosom Serpent."

Often, of course, the pressure of the exam keeps you from composing such a thorough cover statement. If coming up with a good cover statement is delaying you, limit your opening to what is specifically required by the question (e.g., Define "moralist-psychologist"), then develop your ideas, and then conclude, after looking over what you have written, with the summary or evaluation (e.g., "Hawthorne, then, is most successful when. . . ."). In some examinations you will not be in a position to summarize or evaluate until you have addressed yourself to a number of particulars in the body of your answer.

Whether you begin your answer with a cover statement or not, resist the temptation, so powerful during the first few minutes of an exam, to start writing down everything you know. Don't begin to write until you have planned the direction you want your answer to take. And remember, your instructor is your audience: he or she knows the subject, so don't waste valuable time on writing background information or overexplaining facts.

47d

Writing your answer

Provide supporting evidence, reasoning, detail, or example. Nothing weakens a paper so much as vagueness, unsupported generalizations, and wordiness. Don't talk about "how beautiful Haw-thorne's images are and what a pleasure it was to read such great stories," etc., etc. If necessary, go back to your jotted notes to add supporting material. If you have written a cover statement, look at it again and then jot down some hard evidence in the space at the top of the page.

Say you have been asked to discuss the proper use of the I.Q. score by a teacher. Your notes read: *Intelligence—capacity for learning. Must interpret carefully. Also child's personality. Score not permanent. Measures verbal ability.* You have formulated this cover statement: *"Intelligence" is a vague term used to describe an individual's capacity for learning. The teacher must remember that I.Q. scores tell only part of the story and that they are subject to change.* Now you must provide the evidence. Think about specific I.Q. tests, specific studies that support your generalizations. Such notes as the following will help you develop your essay:

> 10% of children significant change after 6 to 8 years
> High motivation often more important than high I.Q.
> Stanford-Binet—aptitude rather than intelligence
> Verbal ability—children from non-English-speaking families—culturally divergent—low verbal score
> N.Y. study—remedial courses, etc.—40% improvement in scores

You now have some raw material to work with, material you can organize and clearly relate to your cover statement. Even if you do not fully succeed in integrating your data into a perfectly coherent and unified essay, you will have demonstrated that you read the material and have some understanding of it. Padding, wordiness, and irrelevancies prove only that you can fill up pages.

Must you never toss in a few interesting tidbits not specifically called for by the question? There is nothing wrong with beginning a discussion of the significance of the Jefferson-Adams correspondence with: "In their 'sunset' correspondence of more than 150 letters, Jefferson and Adams exchanged their ideas on world issues, religion, and the nature and future of American democratic society, almost until the day they both died—July 4, 1826." Although only the middle third of this sentence is a direct response to the question, the other information is both relevant and interesting. Such details cannot *substitute* for your answer, but they can enhance it, just as they would an out-of-class essay.

47e

47e

Taking a last look

Try to leave time at the end of the exam to read and revise what you've written. Check to see if you have left out words or phrases. See if you can add an additional bit of detail or evidence; you can make insertions in the margins. Correct misspellings and awkward sentences. See if your cover statement can be improved. You are not expected to write a perfectly polished essay in an exam, but make your essay as readable as you can in the time you have left.

EXERCISE 47

With a classmate, think of a question that might appear on an essay exam in one of your classes. Create the question as if you were the instructor preparing the test. Separately, outline an answer to the question, supplying the specific information, evaluation, organization, and presentation the question requires. Then compare your outlines and jointly determine where they can be improved with more facts, better analysis, clearer relationships between ideas, sharper focus on the tasks the question specifies.

48

BUSINESS CORRESPONDENCE

Academic and business writing require attention to the same elements of composition: purpose, audience, tone, style, grammar, mechanics, and organization. Because its fundamental goal is to help get things done, good business writing has efficiency as its hallmark. An efficient letter or memo makes its point quickly, often telling the reader what he or she most needs to know in the opening paragraph. Thus the reader learns the purpose of the correspondence without first having to wade through background information or detail. Besides being efficient, business correspondence should also be effective, the contents and tone persuasive. Readers appreciate correspondence that is straightforward but that also considers their needs and point of view. Tina Rodriguez's memos in Section **41** (pp. 360–361) show how one business writer revised her memo to make it more efficient in its delivery of information and more considerate of her readers' views and needs.

48a

48

Memos and letters

The most common types of business correspondence are the memorandum (memo) and the letter. The principal difference between the two is really only a matter of audience: a memo is *internal* correspondence written to your fellow employees, a letter is *external* correspondence written to someone outside your company or organization. A memo reflects this difference in its **routing information.** Instead of the return and inside addresses, salutation, complimentary close, and signature found on a letter, a memo provides this "sender-receiver" information in abbreviated form at the upper left of its first page.

```
TO:      Robin Kaufman, Sales Representative
FROM:    Jo Carter, District Manager  J.C.
DATE:    March 13, 198—
SUBJECT: April Sales Meeting Agenda

As we agreed on the phone yesterday,
the April sales meeting should be used to
develop new strategies for improving
the sales of our summer sportswear line.
Historically, the most unprofitable
territory has been New England, even though
```

Remember that most memos, other than personal notes, will frequently have more than one reader. Accurate and complete headings are important for routing, reference, and filing.

You may have noticed that Jo Carter's memo contains signed initials next to the name. Although initialing a memo is not mandatory, to do so indicates that the sender has reread and approved the memo after it was typed.

In most other respects, memos differ little from letters. Both are single-spaced with double-spacing between paragraphs and sections.

Visual cues are important in business correspondence. As the sample letters at the end of this section illustrate, paragraphs tend to be shorter than in an essay or research paper. Information may be presented in list form, and series may include bullets or dashes (see the Rodriguez memos, pp. 360–361, and sample letter 1) or numbers that would probably be omitted in an essay. One reason is that business correspondence often serves as a reference document. Consequently, the reader must be able to find items quickly. By dividing the discussion more frequently into subtopics and by providing more visual cues, the writer also aids the reader's understanding. In effect, these visual devices divide the document into manageable chunks of information that are easier for the reader's mind to process than are long, unbroken passages.

48b

48b
Parts of a business letter

The standard business letter has six parts: (1) the heading, which includes the return address and date; (2) the inside address; (3) the salutation; (4) the body; (5) the complimentary close; (6) the signature. Sample letter 1 illustrates a widely used format—**full block style**—with the six parts labeled.

Another common format is the **modified block style;** this style places the heading, date, complimentary close, and signature on the right side of the page (instead of flush left, as in the block style). The modified block format may use either indented or flush-left (not indented) paragraphs.

A more unusual business letter format is known as the **simplified format.** Simplified letters use full block style, with all parts flush at the left margin. The salutation and complimentary close are eliminated. A subject line appears where the salutation ordinarily would be placed. Like any block letter, this format is easy to type because no tab stops are needed. Furthermore, the subject is immediately clear, and the lack of salutation resolves problems when the name of the recipient is not known. The simplified format is useful for routine requests or when personalization is unimportant. Sample letter 2 shows the simplified format.

48c
Kinds of business letters

Letters of application. Though letters requesting information, registering complaints, and the like are probably those you will write most often, letters in which you apply for a job are almost certainly among the most important you will write. For application letters, keep the following advice in mind:

1.   Application letters are usually of two kinds: solicited applications and prospecting applications. You will write a **solicited application** letter when "applications are being solicited"; that is, when you know an opening exists because you have heard about the vacancy or seen it advertised. In addition to specifying the opening for which you are applying, mention the source of your information—newspaper advertisement, placement office posting, referral, or whatever. When you have no direct knowledge that an opening currently exists but you want to be considered if a job is available, your application letter is a **prospecting application** (see sample letter 1). In this case you identify the type of position you desire and briefly explain why you are interested in working for the company you are addressing.

2.   Describe those parts of your education or previous work experience that you believe prepare you for the job you want. If you are short on relevant paid work experience, it is certainly all right to discuss pertinent extracurricular activities or volunteer work that shows skills applicable to the job you are seeking. Be brief, direct, and factual, but at the same time present the information to your advantage; a job letter and accompanying resume should be persuasive documents as well as informative ones.

Don't just list your education and experience; *use* it to show the prospective employer how you are qualified to contribute to the company. Remember that the employer is the "buyer" and that you are "marketing" your credentials and skills. Although the tone of your letter should not be egotistical, neither should it be apologetic or pleading. There is no need to close with a line such as "I would be very grateful if you would be so gracious as to review my credentials. Thanking you in advance. . . ." Write a letter that is confident, courteous, and informative.

3. Offer to provide references. In some cases (part-time or summer jobs, for instance), you may want to list your references in the letter or on an accompanying sheet. However, if the purpose of your letter is to secure a job interview, standard practice is to offer to provide references upon request. If the interviewer decides you are a good job candidate, he or she will then request a list of your references. In any case, you should have contacted the people you intend to use as references and obtained their permission before you write an application letter. Remember that references must come from people who actually know your work first hand; a potential employer consulting one of your references will want to know specific things about your ability and your reliability. People for whom you have worked successfully and instructors with whom you have taken relevant courses are often among your best references.

4. An application letter is similar to a request letter: you are asking the reader to do something for you—consider you for a job interview. Consequently, you should use an action ending, as you would in a request letter. Since the next step in the employment process is usually an interview, you can end your letter by asking the reader to let you know when it would be convenient for you to come for an interview. A stronger, but permissible, ending is to say courteously that you will call to arrange an interview—as does the author of sample letter 1. Always tell the reader when, where, and how you can be reached if you are not available at your return address during the reader's business hours.

5. For many part-time or temporary jobs, it is sufficient to describe your qualifications in the body of your letter. For full-time positions it is wiser to present the information in clear, quickly readable form on a resume. This enables you to use your application letter to highlight particularly important information, to supply explanations, and to provide additional persuasive details, while conveniently presenting the necessary facts in the resume. Be sure to mention your resume in your letter. An accompanying resume follows sample letter 1.

48c

Request letters. Perhaps the most common kind of business letter is one asking someone to do something: give us information, send us something we have seen advertised, or correct a mistake. Such letters should be direct, businesslike, and courteous, even when you are registering a complaint.

Clarity is extremely important. The letter must directly state what you want the reader to do, and it must give the exact information the reader needs to meet your request. Notice that sample letter 2 concludes by telling the reader what results the writer expects. Conclusions of this type are called **action endings.**

Request letters can be grouped into two categories: (1) those with reader benefit—fulfilling the writer's request benefits the reader in some way; and (2) those without reader benefit—the reader has little or nothing to gain from fulfilling the request. Sample letter 2, although registering a complaint, falls into the reader-benefit category because the company clearly gains when its customers are satisfied and loses when they are unhappy.

What about requests without reader benefit? In such cases you are really relying on your reader's goodwill. Besides writing clearly, you should take up as little of the reader's time as possible, make your request reasonable, and—if you can—encourage the reader's goodwill, perhaps by paying an honest compliment. Requests for information can frequently be handled in this way.

Transmittal letters. If you are relaying information, answering a question, or sending some item such as a report or a piece of equipment, you may need to write a letter to transmit whatever you are sending. This type of letter has two main purposes: to say "here is the information (or item)" and to generate goodwill. Transmittal letters usually cite the reason for the transmittal, supply any necessary information about whatever is being transmitted, and include courteous remarks that will encourage the reader to view the writer and his or her firm in a positive light.

48d
Employment resumes

Following sample letter 1 is a resume showing a widely used, traditional format. This format works well when you want to emphasize your education and experience. Another format, which is effective if you want to emphasize capabilities, organizes information according to skills, placing education and a list of employers near the end of the resumé. This format may be advantageous for people whose work experience is varied or not continuous, or whose education or employment history is not obviously applicable to the job they are seeking.

Whatever format you use for your resume, list items in order of importance within each section. It is not necessary to list work experience, for instance, in chronological order. Organize the jobs from most important to least important in terms of their relevance to the position you want.

When writing your resume, remember that work experience applies not only to jobs for which you were paid but also to volunteer

48d

work, community service, leadership roles in campus organizations, and so forth. The only requirement is that the experience be relevant to the job for which you are applying. Similarly, you may want to list education that did not result in a degree. Consider for your resume and your job application letter evening classes, courses taken at a community center, art museum, or computer store—in short, any training that is relevant to your employment goal.

Use action verbs to describe your experience: *organized, developed, assisted, sold, built* instead of *duties included.* Talk about what you accomplished, goals you met or exceeded, skills you learned or demonstrated. Indicate any measurable results: *increased sales by $2,000, saved the sorority $700 on heating bills, increased the student newspaper's circulation by 20 percent.* Like your application letter, your resume should be persuasive.

Do not include information that is not pertinent to the job. For example, height and weight are not likely to be relevant. Laws forbidding job discrimination based on marital status, age, sex, race, or, religion have also changed the personal data appearing on resumes; employers cannot require this type of information from job applicants. For instance, if you are seeking a sales position that involves extended periods on the road or a job with a company that routinely transfers its employees, you might list willingness to travel or relocate under personal data; but you need not indicate whether you are male or female, single or married.

48d

SAMPLE LETTER 1: BLOCK STYLE

848 Plains Street
Fort Pierre, South Dakota 57067
April 4, 198– ── HEADING

Judith Stafford
Curator
W. H. Over Western Museum ── INSIDE ADDRESS
University of South Dakota
Vermillion, South Dakota 57069

Dear Ms. Stafford: ── SALUTATION

I believe I can offer practical ideas, backed by experience
in several museum settings, that will help the W. H. Over
Western Museum attract funding, increase community interest,
and improve quality——constant goals even in well-managed
facilities such as yours. I would like the opportunity to put
my ideas to work for your museum.

As the enclosed resume shows, my experience includes the
following museum operations:

   * collecting and cataloging specimens

   * researching and mounting exhibits

   * designing special children's programs

   * working with academics, students, funding agencies,
     the media, and the general public

   * writing successful grant proposals

One of the most rewarding aspects of this experience has been
seeing community participation broaden and financial
resources increase as a result of my efforts. I have a talent
for explaining things, as illustrated by the college teaching
award I received and the children's natural history program I
developed. This skill will be an asset for the educational
activities that are an important part of museum work.

My college and summer museum experiences have been a very
good introduction to my chosen career. I would like to talk
with you about employment possibilities at the W. H. Over
Western Museum and will call your office next week to see
about scheduling an interview. I look forward to meeting you.

BODY

Sincerely, ── COMPLIMENTARY CLOSE

John Lewkowski ── SIGNATURE

John Lewkowski ── TYPED SIGNATURE

48d

John Lewkowski
848 Plains Street
Fort Pierre, South Dakota 57067
605-555-9745

Employment Objective

A museum staff position leading eventually to a curatorship.

Education

B.A., Earlham College, Richmond, Indiana, 1988.
Major: history   Minor: biology   GPA: 3.85/4.00 = A

State University of New York, course in researching, cataloging, and mounting exhibits, summer 1986.

Experience

Museum volunteer, Joseph Moore Museum, Earlham College, 1986-88. Assisted director of small natural history museum. Developed traveling museum program for four local elementary schools. Identified and cataloged specimens, maintained exhibits.

Summer intern, Tippecanoe County Historical Museum, Lafayette, Indiana, 1987. Wrote grant proposal resulting in $10,000 award for archeological dig at 18th-century French and Indian trading settlement. Worked with state and federal agencies, university faculty, museum staff.

Laboratory assistant, Earlham College, spring term, 1988. Supervised freshman biology lab, prepared lab materials and specimens, answered students' questions, and graded lab reports. Was selected Outstanding Teaching Assistant in the Natural Sciences.

Honors and Activities

Earlham Alumni Scholarship, 1985-88
Outstanding Teaching Assistant, 1988
Earlham College tennis team, 1986-88

Personal Data

Speak and write French. Interests: travel and photography.

48

References Furnished Upon Request

SAMPLE LETTER 2: SIMPLIFIED STYLE

444 West Wilson Street
Madison, Wisconsin 53715
July 9, 198—

Cambridge Camera Exchange, Inc.
7th Avenue and 13th Street
New York, N.Y. 10011

INCOMPLETE SHIPMENT

The Minolta SRT 201 camera outfit I ordered from you on June
21 arrived today and appears to be in good working order.
However, your advertisement in <u>The New York Times</u> for Sunday,
June 16, listed six items as being supplied with this outfit,
including a film holder and a sun shade. Neither of these
items was included in the package I have just received, nor
do I find any notice that they will be sent at a later date.

I am sure that this omission is unintentional and that you
will correct it. Will you please let me know when I may
expect to receive the film holder and sun shade, as
advertised. If there is a dealer in the immediate area, I
would be happy to get them from him or her if you will
authorize me to do so at your expense.

Marilyn S. Conway

Marilyn S. Conway

48

GLOSSARIES

glos

What grammarians say should be has perhaps less influence on what shall be than even the more modest of them realize; usage evolves itself little disturbed by their likes and dislikes. And yet the temptation to show how better use might have been made of the material to hand is sometimes irresistible.

H. W. FOWLER, *Modern English Usage*

49

GLOSSARY OF GRAMMATICAL TERMS

This glossary provides brief definitions of the grammatical terms used in this text. Cross-references refer you to pertinent sections of the text. For further text references to terms defined, as well as for references to terms not included in the glossary, consult the index.

absolute phrase   Absolute constructions modify the sentence in which they stand. They differ from other modifying word groups in that (1) they lack any connective joining them to the rest of the sentence and (2) they do not modify any individual word or word group in the sentence. Compare *Seeing the bears, we stopped the car*, in which the participial phrase modifies *we*, with *The rain having stopped, we saw the bears*, in which the construction *the rain having stopped* is an absolute modifying the rest of the sentence. The basic pattern of the absolute phrase is a noun or pronoun and a participle. *(She having arrived*, we all went to the movies. We left about ten o'clock, *the movie being over.)* Such phrases are sometimes called **nominative absolutes,** since pronouns in them require the nominative case.

Absolute phrases may also be prepositional phrases *(In fact,* we had expected rain) or verbal phrases (It often rains in April, *to tell the truth. Generally speaking,* July is hot.)

For the punctuation of absolute phrases see **20e.**

abstract noun   See *noun.*

active voice   See *voice.*

adjectival   Any word or word group used to modify a noun. Some modern grammars limit the meaning of **adjective** strictly to words that can be compared by adding *-er* and *-est (new, newer, newest; high, higher, highest).* Such grammars apply the term **adjectival** to other words that ordinarily modify nouns, and to any other word or word group when it is used as an adjective. In such grammars the italicized words below may be called **adjectivals.**

LIMITING ADJECTIVES	*my* suit, *a* picture, *one* day
NOUNS MODIFYING NOUNS	*school* building, *home* plate, *government* policy
PHRASES MODIFYING NOUNS	man *of the hour*
CLAUSES MODIFYING NOUNS	girl *whom I know*

adjective   A word used to describe or limit the meaning of a noun or its equivalent. According to their position, adjectives may be (1) **attributive,** i.e., placed next to their nouns *(vivid* example; *a* boy, *strong* and *vigorous),* or (2) **predicative,** i.e., placed in the predicate after a linking verb (She was *vigorous*).

According to their meaning, adjectives may be (1) **descriptive,** naming some quality *(white* house, *small* child, *leaking* faucet); (2) **proper,** derived from proper nouns *(Roman* fountain, *French* custom); or (3) **limiting.**

Limiting adjectives may indicate possession *(my, his)*, may point out *(this, former)*, may number *(three, second)*, or may be articles *(a, the)*.
See **1b(1)** and Section **3**.

adjective clause   A subordinate, or dependent, clause used as an adjective.

> The man *who lives here* is a biologist. [The adjective clause modifies the noun *man*.]
>
> Dogs *that chase cars* seldom grow old. [The adjective clause modifies the noun *dogs*.]

See also **1d**.

adjective phrase   See *phrase*.

adverb   A word used to describe or limit the meaning of a verb, an adjective, another adverb, or a whole sentence.
According to function, adverbs may (1) modify single words (went *quickly, quite* shy, *nearly* all men); (2) modify whole sentences (*Maybe* he will go); (3) ask questions (*When* did he go? *Where* is the book?); or (4) connect clauses and modify their meaning (see *conjunctive adverb*).
According to meaning, adverbs may indicate (1) manner (*secretly* envious); (2) time (*never* healthy); (3) place (*outside* the house); or (4) degree (*quite* easily angered).
See **1b(1)** and Section **3**.

adverb clause   A subordinate, or dependent, clause used as an adverb.

> *When you leave,* please close the door. [The adverb clause, indicating time, modifies the verb *close*.]
>
> The sheep grazed *where the grass was greenest*. [The adverb clause, indicating place, modifies the verb *grazed*.]

Adverb clauses also indicate manner, purpose, cause, result, condition, concession, and comparison.
See **1d**.

adverb phrase   See *phrase*.

adverbial   A term used to describe any word or word group used as an adverb. Common adverbials are nouns in certain constructions (She went *home*), phrases (She went *in a great hurry*), or clauses (She went *when she wanted to go*). Compare *adjectival*.

adverbial conjunction   See *conjunctive adverb*.

adverbial objective   Sometimes applied to nouns used as adverbials. (They slept *mornings*. He ran a *mile*.)

agreement   A correspondence or matching in the form of one word and that of another. Verbs agree with their subjects in number and person (in *She runs,* both *she* and *runs* are singular and third person). Pronouns agree with their antecedents in person, number, and gender (in *He wanted his way, he* and *his* are both third person singular, and masculine). Demonstrative adjectives match the nouns they modify in number *(this kind, these kinds)*. See Section **8**.

49

glos

antecedent   A word or group of words to which a pronoun refers.

> She is a *woman who* seldom writes letters. [*Woman* is the antecedent of the pronoun *who.*]
>
> *Uncle Henry* came for a brief visit, but *he* stayed all winter. [*Uncle Henry* is the antecedent of the pronoun *he.*]

appositive   A word or phrase set beside a noun, a pronoun, or a group of words used as a noun, that identifies or explains it by renaming it.

John, my *brother*	Albany, that is, *New York's state capital*
his hobby, *playing handball*	modifiers, *words that describe or limit*

The appositives illustrated above are **nonrestrictive:** they explain the nouns they follow but are not necessary to identify them. When appositives restrict the meaning of the nouns they follow to a specific individual or object, they are **restrictive:** *my sister Sue* (that is *Sue*, not *Carol* or *Lisa*); *Huxley the novelist* (not *Huxley the scientist*). See **20c(2).**

article   The words *a, an,* and *the* are articles. *A* and *an* are **indefinite** articles; *the* is a **definite** article. Articles are traditionally classed as limiting adjectives, but since they always signal that a noun will follow, some modern grammars call them **determiners.**

auxiliary   A verb form used with a main verb to form a verb phrase. Auxiliaries are commonly divided into two groups. The first group is used to indicate tense and voice. This group includes *shall, will,* and the forms of *be, have,* and *do* (*shall* give, *will* give, *has* given, *had* given, *does* give, *is* giving, *was* given).

  The second group, called **modal auxiliaries,** includes *can, could, may, might, must, ought, should,* and *would.* These are used to indicate ability, obligation, permission, possibility, etc., and they do not take inflectional endings such as *-s, -ed,* and *-ing.* See Section **4.**

cardinal numbers   Numbers such as *one, three, twenty,* used in counting. Compare *ordinal numbers.*

case   The inflectional form of pronouns or the possessive form of nouns to indicate their function in a group of words. Pronouns have three cases: (1) **nominative or subjective** *(we, she, they),* used for the subject of a verb, or a subjective complement; (2) the **possessive,** used as an adjective *(their dog, anybody's guess);* and (3) the **objective** *(us, her, them),* used for objects of verbs, verbals, and prepositions. Possessive pronouns may also stand alone (The car is *his*). Nouns have only two cases: (1) a **common** case *(woman, leopard)* and (2) a **possessive** case *(woman's, leopard's).* See Section **2.**

clause   A group of words containing a subject and a predicate. Clauses are of two kinds: main, or independent; and subordinate, or dependent. **Main clauses** make independent assertions and can stand alone as sentences. **Subordinate clauses** depend on some other element within a sentence; they function as nouns, adjectives, or adverbs, and cannot stand alone.

MAIN	*The moon shone,* and *the dog barked.* [Two main clauses, either of which could be a sentence]
SUBORDINATE	*When the moon shone,* the dog barked. [Adverb clause]
	That he would survive is doubtful. [Noun clause]

See **1d.**

collective noun   A noun naming a collection or aggregate of individuals by a singular form *(assembly, army, jury)*. Collective nouns are followed by a singular verb when the group is thought of as a unit and a plural verb when the component individuals are being referred to (the majority *decides;* the majority *were* college graduates). See **8a(6)** and **8b.**

comma splice   A sentence error in which two independent clauses are joined only by a comma without a coordinating conjunction. See Section **7.**

common noun   See *noun.*

comparison   Change in the form of adjectives and adverbs to show degree. English has three degrees: (1) **positive,** the form listed in dictionaries *(loud, bad, slowly);* (2) **comparative** *(louder, worse, more slowly);* and (3) **superlative** *(loudest, worst, most slowly).* See **3e.**

complement   In its broadest sense, a term for any word, excluding modifiers, that completes the meaning of a verb (direct and indirect objects), a subject (subject complements), or an object (object complements).

VERB COMPLEMENTS	Give *me* the *money.* [*Money* and *me* are direct and indirect objects, respectively.]
SUBJECT COMPLEMENTS	Helen is a *singer.* She is *excellent.* [The noun *singer* and the adjective *excellent* refer to the subject.]
OBJECT COMPLEMENTS	We elected Jane *secretary.* That made Bill *angry.* [*Secretary* and *angry* refer to the direct objects *Jane* and *Bill.*]

complete predicate   See *predicate.*

complete subject   See *subject.*

complex sentence   See *sentence.*

compound   Made up of more than one word but used as a unit, as in compound noun *(redhead, football),* compound adjective *(downcast, matter-of-fact),* or compound subject (Both *patience* and *practice* are necessary).
See also *sentence.*

compound-complex   See *sentence.*

concrete noun   See *noun.*

conjugation   A list of inflected forms for a verb, displaying the forms for first, second, and third person singular and plural for each tense, voice, and mood. A synopsis of the third person singular *(he, she, it,* and singular nouns) forms for a regular and an irregular verb is shown on the following page.

49

glos

	SIMPLE FORM	PROGRESSIVE FORM
Active Voice		
PRESENT	*he/she* asks/drives	*he/she* is asking/driving
PAST	*he/she* asked/drove	*he/she* was asking/driving
FUTURE	*he/she* will ask/drive	*he/she* will be asking/driving
PRESENT PERFECT	*he/she* has asked/driven	*he/she* has been asking/driving
PAST PERFECT	*he/she* had asked/driven	*he/she* had been asking/driving
FUTURE PERFECT	*he/she* will have asked/driven	*he/she* will have been asking/driving
Passive Voice		
PRESENT	*he/she* is asked/driven	*he/she* is being asked/driven
PAST	*he/she* was asked/driven	*he/she* was being asked/driven
FUTURE	*he/she* will be asked/driven	*he/she* will be being asked/driven
PRESENT PERFECT	*he/she* has been asked/driven	*he/she* has been being asked/driven
PAST PERFECT	*he/she* had been asked/driven	*he/she* had been being asked/driven
FUTURE PERFECT	*he/she* will have been asked/driven	*he/she* will have been being asked/driven

Forms for first and second person singular and all plural forms may be described briefly as follows:

The present tense forms for other persons are *I/you/we/they* ask/drive.

The past and future tense forms for all persons are the same as those shown for the third person.

All perfect tense and passive voice forms that use *has* as an auxiliary in the third person use *have* in all other persons.

All perfect tense and passive voice forms that use *is/was* in the third person use *am/was* for the first person (*I*) and *were* in all other persons.

conjunction A part of speech used to join and relate words, phrases, and clauses. Conjunctions may be either coordinating or subordinating.

49

glos

Coordinating conjunctions connect words, phrases, and clauses of equal grammatical rank: *and, but, or, nor, for.*

Subordinating conjunctions join dependent clauses to main clauses: *after, although, as if, because, since, when.*

See **1b(2).**

conjunctive adverb   An adverb used to relate and connect main clauses in a sentence. Common conjunctive adverbs are *also, consequently, furthermore, hence, however, indeed, instead, likewise, moreover, nevertheless, otherwise, still, then, therefore, thus.* **Conjunctive adverbs,** unlike **coordinating** and **subordinating conjunctions,** are movable and can thus occupy different positions within the main clause in which they stand. See **21b.**

connective   A general term for any word or phrase that links words, phrases, clauses, or sentences. **Connectives** thus include conjunctions, prepositions, and conjunctive adverbs. See **1b(2).**

construction   A general term describing any related groups of words such as a phrase, a clause, or a sentence.

coordinate   Having equal rank, as two main clauses in a compound sentence. See Section **31a.**

coordinating conjunction   See *conjunction.*

correlatives   Coordinating conjunctions used in pairs to join sentence elements of equal rank. Common correlatives are *either . . . or; neither . . . nor; not only . . . but also; whether . . . or; both . . . and.* See **1b(2).**

dangling construction   A subordinate construction that cannot easily and unambiguously be linked to another word or group of words it modifies. See Section **12.**

declension   See *inflection* and *case.*

degree   See *comparison.*

demonstratives   *This, that, these,* and *those* are called **demonstratives** when used as pointing words. (*This* dinner is cold. *That* is the man.)

dependent clause   See *clause.*

derivational suffix   See *suffix.*

determiner   A word such as *a, an, the, his, our, your,* that indicates that one of the words following it is a noun.

direct address   A noun or pronoun used parenthetically to point out the person addressed, sometimes called **nominative of address** or **vocative.** (*George,* where are you going? I suppose, *gentlemen,* that you enjoyed the lecture.)

direct and indirect quotation   A direct quotation is an exact quotation of a speaker's or writer's words (sometimes called **direct discourse**). In **indirect discourse** the speaker's or writer's thought is summarized without direct quotation. See **25a.**

DIRECT	He said, "I must leave on the eight o'clock shuttle."
INDIRECT	He said that he had to leave on the eight o'clock shuttle.

49

glos

direct object See *object* and *complement.*

double negative The use of two negative words within the same construction. In certain forms, two negatives are used in the same statement in English to give a particular emphasis to a positive idea. (He was *not* entirely *un*prejudiced). In most instances, the double negative is nonstandard. (He *didn't* do *no* work. We *didn't* see *no*body.) See **37b.**

elliptical construction An omission of words necessary to the grammatical completeness of an expression but assumed in the context. The omitted words in elliptical expressions are understood *(He is older than I* [am]. *Our house is small, his* [house is] *large).*

expletive The word *it* or *there* used to introduce a sentence in which the subject follows the verb. See **1a, 33c,** and **39a(3).**

> *It* is doubtful that he will arrive today. [The clause *that he will arrive today* is the subject of the verb *is.*]
> *There* are two ways of solving the problem. [The noun *ways* is the subject of *are.*]

faulty predication A grammatical fault that results when a subject and its verb or a subject and its complement in a subject/linking verb/complement construction are mismatched in meaning. See Section **14.**

finite verb A verb form that makes an assertion about its subject. Verbals (infinitives, participles, gerunds) are not finite forms. All finite verbs can add *-s* in the third person singular of the present tense to show agreement with their subject. Nonfinite verb forms cannot make this inflectional change. See Section **4.**

function word A term used to describe the words, such as articles, auxiliaries, conjunctions, and prepositions, that are more important for their part in the structure of the sentence than for their meaning. They indicate the function of other words in a sentence and the grammatical relations between those words. Compare *lexical word.*

fused sentence (run-on) Two or more grammatically complete thoughts with no separating punctuation. See Section **7c.**

gender The classification of nouns and pronouns as masculine *(man, he),* feminine *(woman, she),* and neuter *(desk, it).* A few English nouns have special forms to indicate gender *(salesman, saleswoman; hero, heroine).*

genitive case The possessive case. See Section **2.**

gerund A verbal that ends in *-ing* and is used as a noun. Gerunds may take complements, objects, and modifiers. See **1b(3).**

idiom An expression established by usage and peculiar to a particular language. Many idioms have unusual grammatical construction and make little sense if taken literally. Examples of English idioms are *by and large, catch a cold, lay hold of, look up an old friend.* See **38e.**

imperative See *mood.*

indefinite pronoun A pronoun, such as *anybody, anyone, someone,* that does not refer to a specific person or thing.

49

glos

independent clause See *clause.*

independent element An expression that has no grammatical relation to other parts of the sentence. See *absolute.*

indicative See *mood.*

indirect object See *object.*

indirect quotation See *direct and indirect quotation.*

infinitive A verbal usually consisting of *to* followed by the present form of the verb. With a few verbs *to* may be omitted (heard her *tell;* made it *work*). Infinitives can serve as nouns (*To swim* is to relax), as adjectives (I have nothing *to say*), or as adverbs (We were ready *to begin*). See **1b(3).**

inflection Variation in the form of words to indicate case *(he, him),* gender *(he, she, it),* number *(mouse, mice),* tense *(walk, walked),* etc. **Declension** is the inflection of nouns and pronouns; **conjugation** is the inflection of verbs; and **comparison** is the inflection of adjectives and adverbs.

inflectional suffix See *suffix.*

intensifier A term applied to such modifiers as *much, so, too,* and *very,* which merely add emphasis to the words they modify. Words such as *actually, mighty, pretty,* and *really* often occur as vague intensifiers in colloquial English.

intensive pronoun Any compound personal pronoun ending with *-self* used for emphasis. (I did it *myself.* The dean *himself* wrote the letter.)

interjection A word or group of words that is grammatically independent and used to show mild, strong, or sudden emotion. (*Ych.* I hate caterpillars. *Say!* Let's go to a movie.)

intransitive verb See *verb.*

inversion A reversal of normal word order. (*Dejected, he left the witness stand. The verdict he clearly foresaw.*)

irregular verb A verb that forms its past tense and past participle by a change in an internal vowel, or by some other individualized change, as opposed to the usual addition of *-d* or *-ed* to the basic form of so-called **regular verbs,** as in *walk, walked, walked (begin, began, begun; do, did, done; fall, fell, fallen).* See Section **4.**

kernel sentence A term used in some contemporary grammars to describe one of a limited number of basic sentence patterns from which all grammatical structures can be derived. See **1a.**

lexical word Nouns, verbs, adjectives, and adverbs are sometimes termed lexical words, that is, words that carry most of the meaning in English, in contrast to *function words,* which indicate relationships among lexical words. Compare *function word.*

linking verb A verb that shows the relation between the subject of a sentence and a complement. (*He seems timid. The cake tastes sweet. She is my sister.*) The chief linking verbs are *be, become, appear, seem,* and the verbs pertaining to the senses (*look, smell, taste, sound, feel*). See Section **4.**

49

glos

main clause   See *clause.*

misplaced modifier   See *modifier.*

mixed construction   A grammatical fault that consists of joining as a sentence two or more parts that do not fit in grammar or meaning. See Section **14.**

modal auxiliary   See *auxiliary.*

modification   Describing or limiting the meaning of a word or group of words. Adjectives and adjective phrases or clauses modify nouns; adverbs and adverb phrases or clauses modify verbs, adjectives, or adverbs. See Section **3.**

modifier   A general term given to any word or word group that is used to limit, qualify, or otherwise describe the meaning of another word or word group. Adjectives, adverbs, prepositional and verbal phrases, and subordinate clauses are the usual modifiers in English. See Section **3** for adjectives and adverbs and Section **1** for various word groups as modifiers. For a discussion of misplaced modifiers, see Section **11.**

mood   The form of a verb used to show how the action is viewed by the speaker. English has three moods: (1) **indicative,** stating a fact or asking a question (The wheat *is* ripe. *Will* he *go?*); (2) **imperative,** expressing a command or a request (*Report* at once. Please *clear* your desk.); and (3) **subjunctive,** expressing doubt, wish, or condition contrary to fact (The grass looks as if it *were* dying. I wish he *were* more friendly.) See Section **5.**

nominal   A word or word group used as a noun. (The *blue* seems more suitable. *Eating that pie* will not be easy.) Compare *adjectival.* See Section **39a(1).**

nominative case   See *case.*

nonrestrictive modifier   A modifying phrase or clause that is not essential to pointing out or identifying the person or thing modified.

> Smith, *who was watching the road,* saw the accident.
>
> The lastest breakthrough, *reported last week,* has everyone talking.

> See Section **20c.**

noun   A word, like *man, horse, carrot, trip, theory,* or *capitalism,* that names a person, place, thing, quality, concept, or the like. Nouns usually form plurals by adding *-s,* and possessives by adding *'s,* and most frequently function as subjects and complements, although they also function in other ways. See **1a.**

Nouns are divided into various subclasses according to their meaning. The most common classes are the following:

Class	Meaning	Examples
common	general classes	*tiger, house, idea*
proper	specific names	*Chicago, Burma, Lee*
abstract	ideas, qualities	*liberty, love, emotion*
concrete	able to be sensed	*apple, noise, perfume*

49

glos

collective	groups	*herd, bunch, jury*
count	able to be counted	*chicken, slice, book*
mass	not ordinarily counted (not used with *a, an*)	*salt, gold, equality*

noun clause A subordinate clause used as a noun. *(What I saw* was humiliating. I shall accept *whatever he offers.)* See **1d.**

number The form of a noun, pronoun, verb, or demonstrative adjective to indicate one (singular) or more than one (plural).

object A general term for any word group or word that is affected by or receives action of a transitive verb or verbal, or of a preposition. A **direct object** receives the action of the verb. (I followed *him.* Keep *whatever you find.)* An **indirect object** indicates to or for whom or what something is done. (Give *me* the money.) The **object of a preposition** follows the preposition and is related to another part of the sentence by the preposition (We rode across the *beach).* See also *complement* and **1a** and **2c.**

object complement See *complement.*

objective case See *case.*

ordinal numbers Numbers such as *first, third, twentieth, sixty-fifth,* used to indicate order. Compare *cardinal numbers.*

parenthetical expression An inserted expression that interrupts the thought of a sentence. (His failure, *I suppose,* was his own fault. I shall arrive—*this will surprise you*—on Monday.)

participial phrase See *participle* and *phrase.*

participle A verbal used as an adjective. As an adjective, a participle can modify a noun or pronoun. The present participle ends in *-ing (running, seeing, trying).* The past participle ends in *-d, -ed, -t, -n, -en,* or changes the vowel *(walked, lost, seen, rung).* Though a participle cannot make an assertion, it is derived from a verb and can take an object and be modified by an adverb *(swimming the river, completely beaten).*

parts of speech The classes into which words may be divided on the basis of meaning, form, and function. The traditional parts of speech are: noun, pronoun, verb, adjective, adverb, preposition, conjunction, and interjection. See **1a** and **1b** and separate entries in this glossary.

passive voice See *voice.*

person The form of a pronoun and verb used to indicate the speaker (first person—*I am*); the person spoken to (second person—*you are*); or the person spoken about (third person—*she is*).

personal pronoun See *pronoun.*

phrase A group of related words lacking both subject and predicate and used as a single part of speech (see Section **1c**). Phrases may be classified as follows:

| PREPOSITIONAL | We walked *across the street.* |
| PARTICIPIAL | The man *entering the room* is my father. |

49

glos

GERUND	*Washing windows* is tiresome work.
INFINITIVE	*To see the sunset* was a pleasure.
VERB	She *has been educated* in Europe.

plain form   A term often used for the infinitive or dictionary form of a verb, as *run, stand, pounce.* See Section **4.**

positive, positive degree   See *comparison.*

possessive   See *case.*

predicate   The part of a sentence or clause that makes a statement about the subject. The *complete predicate* consists of the verb and its complements and modifiers. The *simple predicate* consists of only the verb and its auxiliaries. See **1a.**

predicate adjective   An adjective serving as a subject complement (We were *silent*). See *complement.*

predicate noun   A noun serving as a subject complement (He was a *hero*). See *complement.*

prefix   One or more syllables, such as *a-, mis-, sub-,* or *un-,* that can be added at the beginning of a word or root to change or modify its meaning: *a* + moral = amoral; *mis* + print = misprint; *sub* + standard = substandard; *un* + zipped = unzipped. See **36b.**

preposition   A word used to relate a noun or pronoun to some other word in the sentence. A preposition and its object form a **prepositional phrase.** (The sheep are *in* the meadow. He dodged *through* the traffic.) See **1c.**

prepositional phrase   See *phrase* and *preposition.*

principal clause   A main or independent clause. See *clause.*

principal parts   The three forms of a verb from which the various tenses are derived; the **present infinitive** *(join, go),* the **past tense** *(joined, went),* and the **past participle** *(joined, gone).* See Section **4.**

progressive   The form of the verb used to describe an action occurring, but not completed, at the time referred to (I *am studying.* I *was studying.*). See Section **4.**

pronoun   A word used in place of a noun. The noun for which a pronoun stands is called its **antecedent.** (See **1a** and **8b.**) Pronouns are classified as follows:

PERSONAL	*I, you, he, she, it,* etc.
RELATIVE	*who, which, that* I am the man *who* lives here. We saw a barn *that* was burning.
INTERROGATIVE	*who, which, what* *Who* are you? *Which* is your book?
DEMONSTRATIVE	*this, that, these, those*
INDEFINITE	*one, any, each, anyone, somebody, all,* etc.

49

glos

RECIPROCAL	*each other, one another*
INTENSIVE	*myself, yourself, himself,* etc.
	I *myself* was afraid. You *yourself* must decide.
REFLEXIVE	*myself, yourself, himself,* etc.
	I burned *myself.* You are deceiving *yourself.*

proper adjective   See *adjective.*

proper noun   See *noun.*

reciprocal pronoun   See *pronoun.*

regular verb   See *irregular verb.*

relative clause   A subordinate clause introduced by a relative pronoun. See *pronoun.*

relative pronoun   See *pronoun.*

restrictive modifier   A modifying phrase or clause that is essential to pointing out or identifying the person or thing modified. (People *who live in glass houses* shouldn't throw stones. The horse *that won the race* is a bay mare.) See **20c.**

run-on   See *fused sentence.*

sentence   A complete unit of thought containing a subject and a predicate. Sentences can be classified according to their form as **simple, compound, complex,** and **compound-complex.**

SIMPLE	They rested. [One main clause]
COMPOUND	They rested and we worked. [Two main clauses]
COMPLEX	They rested while we worked. [One main clause, one subordinate clause]
COMPOUND-COMPLEX	They rested while we worked, but we could not finish. [Two main clauses, one containing a subordinate clause]

sentence fragment   A group of words capitalized and punctuated as a sentence but not containing both a subject and a finite verb. See Section **6.**

subject   The person or thing about which the predicate of a sentence or clause makes an assertion or asks a question. The **simple subject** is the word or word group with which the verb of the sentence agrees. The **complete subject** is the simple subject together with all its modifiers. In *The donkey that Jones keeps in the back yard brays all the time,* donkey is the simple subject, and *the donkey that Jones keeps in the back yard* is the complete subject. See Section **1.**

subject complement   See *complement.*

subjective   See *case.*

subjunctive mood   See *mood.*

subordinate clause, subordination   See *clause.*

subordinator   See *conjunction.*

49

glos

substantive   A word or group of words used as a noun. Substantives include pronouns, infinitives, gerunds, and noun clauses.

substantive clause   A noun clause. See *clause.*

suffix   An ending that modifies the meaning of the word to which it is attached. Suffixes may be **inflectional,** such as the *-s* added to nouns to form plurals *(rug, rugs)* or the *-ed* added to verbs to indicate past tense *(call, called).* Or they may be called **derivational,** such as *-ful, -less,* or *-ize* *(hope, hopeful; home, homeless; union, unionize).* Derivational suffixes often, though not always, change the part of speech to which they are added. See *inflection* and **36b.**

superlative   See *comparison.*

syntax   The part of grammar that describes the structure and function of meaningful word groups such as phrases, clauses, and sentences, as opposed to **morphology,** the part of grammar that describes the formation, function, and classification of words.

transitive verb   See *verb.*

verb   A word, like *confide, raise, see,* which indicates action or asserts something. (See **1a.**) Verbs are inflected and combine with auxiliaries to form **verb phrases.** Verbs may be **transitive,** requiring an object (He *made* a report), or **intransitive,** not requiring an object (They *migrated*). Many can function both transitively and intransitively. (The wind *blew.* They *blew* the whistle.) **Linking verbs,** such as *be, become,* and *appear,* are followed by complements that refer to the subject. See Section **4.**

verb complement   See *complement.*

verb phrase   See *phrase.*

verbal   A word derived from a verb and able to take objects, complements, modifiers, and sometimes subjects but unable to stand as the main verb in a sentence. See *gerund, infinitive,* and *participle.* See also **1b(3)** and **1c.**

voice   The form of the verb that shows whether the subject acts **(active voice)** or is acted upon **(passive voice).** Only transitive verbs can show voice. A transitive verb followed by an object is **active** (They *bought* flowers). In the **passive** the direct object is made into the subject (The flowers *were bought*). See **1a,** and Section **5.**

word order   The order of words in a sentence or smaller word group. Word order is one of the principal grammatical devices in English.

50

GLOSSARY OF USAGE

Choosing the right word—or not choosing the wrong one—is one of the most difficult problems for writers. This glossary is intended to help you with some of the most commonly troublesome words and phrases. However, it is necessarily brief; you should keep a good college dictionary at hand and consult it both for words not listed here and for additional information about words that are listed.

For information about labels used in dictionaries, see Section **36.** The following two labels are used in this glossary:

COLLOQUIAL	Commonly used in speech but inappropriate in all but the most informal writing
NONSTANDARD	Generally agreed not to be standard English

In addition to specifically labeled words, some words and phrases are included here because, although widely used, they are wordy or redundant (e.g., *but that, inside of, in the case of*); vague and overused (e.g., *contact, really*); or objected to by many readers (e.g., *center around, hopefully* meaning *it is hoped, -wise* as a suffix). A few word pairs often confused (e.g., *imply, infer*) are included, but Section **38c** has a more extensive list of such pairs.

a, an *A* is used before words beginning with a consonant sound, even when the sound is spelled with a vowel *(a dog, a European, a unicorn, a habit). An* is used before words beginning with a vowel sound or a silent *h (an apple, an Indian, an hour, an uproar).*

accept, except To *accept* is to receive. To *except* is to exclude. As a preposition *except* means "with the exclusion of." *(He accepted the list from the chairman. The list excepted George from the slate of candidates. He asked why it included all except George.).*

actually Like *really*, frequently overworked as an intensifier.

adverse, averse These adjectives both mean "hostile" or "opposed." *Adverse*, however, means something is opposed to the subject; *averse* means the subject is opposed to something *(Cats are averse to adverse weather such as rain).*

advice, advise *Advice* is a noun; *advise* is a verb *(Don't ask for my advice unless you really want me to advise you).*

affect, effect As verbs, to *affect* is to influence, to *effect* is to bring about. *Effect* is more commonly used as a noun meaning "result." *(Recent tax reforms affect everyone. They are intended to effect a fairer distribution of taxes. The effects have yet to be felt.)*

agree to, agree with To *agree to* is to consent; to *agree with* means "to concur" *(I agree with Gail's opinion, and will therefore agree to the contract).*

ain't A contraction of *am not*, extended to *is not, are not, has not, have not.* Though often used in speech, it is strongly disapproved by the majority of speakers and writers.

a lot, alot The correct spelling is *a lot.*

all, all of Constructions with *all of* followed by a noun can frequently be made more concise by omitting the *of*; usually the *of* is retained before a pronoun or a proper noun; *all of Illinois*, but *all the money, all this confusion.*

50

glos

allude, refer   To *allude to* is to refer to indirectly; to *refer to* is to direct attention to *(When he spoke of family difficulties, we knew he was alluding to his wife's illness even though he did not refer directly to that).*

allusion, illusion   An *allusion* is an indirect reference; an *illusion* is a false impression *(He was making an allusion to magicians when he spoke of people who were adept at creating illusions).*

already, all ready   *Already* is an adverb meaning "previously" *(We had already left)* or "even now" *(We are already late).* In the phrase *all ready, all* modifies *ready;* the phrase means "completely prepared" *(We were all ready by eight o'clock).*

alright, all right   *All right* remains the only established spelling. *Alright* is labeled nonstandard in both the *New World* and *Random House* dictionaries, although *Webster's* lists it without a usage label.

also, likewise   Not acceptable substitutes for *and (We packed our clothes, our food, and* [not *also* or *likewise*] *our books).*

altogether, all together   *Altogether* means "wholly, completely"; *all together* means "in a group," "everyone assembled" *(She was altogether pleased with her new piano, which she played when we were all together for our reunion).*

alumnus, alumna   An *alumnus* (plural *alumni*) is a male graduate. An *alumna* (plural *alumnae*) is a female graduate. *Alumni* is now usually used for groups including both men and women.

among, between   *Among* implies more than two persons or things; *between* implies only two. To express a reciprocal relationship, or the relationship of one thing to several other things, however, *between* is commonly used for more than two *(She divided the toys among the three children. Jerry could choose between pie and cake for dessert. An agreement was reached between the four companies. The surveyors drove a stake at a point between three trees.).*

amount, number   *Amount* refers to quantity of mass; *number* refers to countable objects *(Large numbers of guests require a great amount of food).*

an   See *a, an.*

and etc.   *Etc.* (Latin *et cetera*) means "and so forth." The redundant *and etc.* means literally "and and so forth." See **16a(4).**

and/or   A legalism to which some readers object.

and which, and who   Use only when *which* or *who* is introducing a clause that coordinates with an earlier clause introduced by *which* or *who (John is a man who has opinions and who often expresses them).*

ante-, anti-   *Ante-* means "before," as in *antedate. Anti-* means "against," as in *anti-American.* The hyphen is used after *anti* before capital letters, and before *i,* as in *anti-intellectual.*

any more, anymore   Either spelling is correct. Meaning *now* or *nowadays,* the expression is used only in negative contexts *(He doesn't live here any more).* Used in affirmative contexts the expression is regional and should be avoided in writing *(What's the matter with you anymore?).*

anyone, everyone, someone   Not the same as *any one, every one, some one*. *Anyone* means "any person" *(He will talk to anyone who visits him)*. *Any one* means "any single person or thing" *(He will talk to any one of his neighbors at a time, but not more than one at a time)*.

anyplace   Colloquial for *any place.*

anyway, any way, anyways   *Anyway* means "nevertheless, no matter what else may be true" *(They're going to leave school anyway, no matter what we say).* Do not confuse it with *any way (I do not see any way to stop them). Anyways* is a colloquial form of *anyway.*

apt   See *liable.*

around   Colloquial as used in *stay around* meaning "stay nearby" and in *come around to see me.* As a synonym for the preposition *about, around* is informal and objected to by some in writing; write *about one hundred* rather than *around one hundred.*

as   In introducing adverbial clauses, *as* may mean either "when" or "because." Thus it is best avoided if there is any possibility of confusion. As a substitute for *that* or *whether (He didn't know as he could go)* or for *who (Those as want them can have them), as* is nonstandard. For confusion between *as* and *like,* see *like, as, as if.*

as . . . as, so . . . as   In negative comparisons, some authorities perfer *not so . . . as* to *not as . . . as,* but both are generally considered acceptable.

as, like   See *like, as.*

as to   A wordy substitute for *about (He questioned me about* [not *as to] my plans).* At the beginning of sentences, *as to* is standard for emphasizing *(As to writing, the more he worked, the less successful he was).*

at   Wordy in such constructions as *"Where are you eating at?"* and *"Where is he at now?"*

athletics   Plural in form, but often treated as singular in number. See **8a(10).**

awful, awfully   In formal English *awful* means "inspiring awe" or "causing fear." Colloquially it is used to mean "very bad" or "unpleasant" *(an awful joke, an awful examination). Awfully* is colloquial as an intensifier *(awfully hard, awfully pretty).*

awhile, a while   *Awhile* is an adverb and must modify a verb, an adjective, or another adverb. *A while* is an article with a noun. *(She said awhile ago that she would be gone for a while this afternoon).*

bad, badly   Often confused. *Bad* is an adjective and should be used only to modify nouns and as a predicate adjective after linking verbs *(She had a bad cold and felt bad* [not *badly]). Badly* is an adverb *(She hurt her leg badly* [not *bad]).*

basically   An overworked intensifier meaning "actually" or "really."

being that, being as (how)   Nonstandard substitutions for the appropriate subordinating conjunctions *as, because, since.*

50

glos

beside, besides   *Beside* is a preposition meaning "by the side of." *Besides* is an adverb or a preposition meaning "moreover" or "in addition to" *(He sat beside her. Besides, he had to wait for John.)*.

better   See *had better*.

between, among   See *among, between*.

bring, take   *Bring* should be used only for movement from a farther to a nearer location. *Take* is used for any other movement *(You may take my raincoat, but don't forget to bring it back with the other things you have borrowed)*.

bunch   Colloquial when used to mean a group of people or things *(a bunch of dishes, a bunch of money)*. Used in writing to refer only to things growing or fastened together *(a bunch of bananas, a bunch of celery)*.

bursted, bust, busted   The principal parts of the verb are *burst, burst, burst. Bursted* is an old form of the past and past participle, which is no longer considered good usage. *Bust* and *busted* are nonstandard.

but, hardly, scarcely   All are negative and should not be used with other negatives. *(He had only* [not *didn't have but*] *one hour. He had scarcely* [not *hadn't scarcely*] *finished. He could hardly* [not *couldn't hardly*] *see.)*

but however, but yet   Redundant. Use *but, however,* or *yet* but not two together *(I was ill, but* [not *but yet*] *I attended)*.

but that, but what   Wordy equivalents of *that* as a conjunction or relative pronoun *(I don't doubt that* [not *but that* or *but what*] *you are right)*.

can, may   Informally *can* is used to indicate both ability *(I can drive a car)* and permission *(Can I use the car?)*. In formal English, *may* is reserved by some for permission *(May I use the car?)*. *May* is also used to indicate possibility *(I can go to the movies, but I may not)*.

can't help but   This expression is redundant. Use either *I can't help (wondering if she saw us)* or the more formal expression *I cannot but help (wondering if she saw us)*.

case, in the case of   Wordy and usually unnecessary. See Section **39**.

censor, censure   To *censor* means "to examine in order to delete or suppress objectionable material." *Censure* means "to reprimand or condemn."

center around, center about   Common expressions, but objected to by many as illogical. Prefer *center on (The debate centered on* [not *centered around* or *centered about*] *the rights of students)*.

character   Wordy. *He had an illness of a serious character* means *He had a serious illness*.

cite, site   *Cite* is a verb meaning "to quote or mention"; *site* is a noun meaning "a particular place" *(I can cite the passage that refers the the site of the battle)*.

complected   A colloquial or dialect equivalent of *complexioned* as in *light-complected*. Prefer *light-* or *dark-complexioned* in writing.

complement, compliment   *Complement* comes from "complete" and means "to add to"; to *compliment* means "to flatter" *(Let me compliment you on that tie. It certainly complements your suit.)*.

complete   See *unique*.

conscious, conscience   *Conscious* is an adjective meaning "aware"; *conscience*, a noun, refers to one's sense of right and wrong. *(He was not conscious of his conscience)*.

consensus of opinion   Redundant; omit *of opinion*. *Consensus* means "a general harmony of opinion."

considerable   Standard as an adjective *(considerable success, a considerable crowd)*. Colloquial as a noun *(They lost considerable in the flood)*. Nonstandard as an adverb *(They were considerable hurt in the accident)*.

contact   Overused as a vague verb meaning "to meet, to talk with, to write," etc. Prefer a more specific word such as *interview, consult, write to, telephone*.

continual, continuous   *Continual* means "frequently repeated" *(He was distracted by continual telephone calls)*. *Continuous* means "without interruption" *(We heard the continuous sound of the waves)*.

continue on   Redundant; omit *on*.

convince, persuade   Widely used interchangeably, but many careful writers *convince* people that something is so, but *persuade* them to do something. The distinction seems worth preserving.

could of   Nonstandard for *could have*.

couple   Colloquial when used to mean "a few" or "several." When used before a plural noun, it is nonstandard unless followed by *of (We had a couple of* [not *couple*] *minutes)*.

credible, creditable, credulous   Sometimes confused. *Credible* means "believable" *(Their story seemed credible to the jury)*. *Creditable* means "praiseworthy" *(You gave a creditable violin recital)*. *Credulous* means "inclined to believe on slight evidence" *(The credulous child really believed the moon was made of cheese)*.

criteria   See *data*.

data, criteria, phenomena   Historically *data* is a plural form, but the singular *datum* is now rare. *Data* is often treated as singular, but careful writing still often treats it as plural *(These data* [not *this*] *are* [not *is*] *the most recent)*. *Criteria* and *phenomena* are plurals of the same kind for the singular forms *criterion* and *phenomenon*.

deal   Colloquial in the sense of *bargain* or *transaction (the best deal in town); of secret arrangement (I made a deal with the gangsters); and of treatment (I had a rough deal from the dean)*. Currently overworked as a slang term referring to any kind of arrangement or situation.

definite, definitely   Colloquial as vague intensifiers *(That suit is a definite bargain; it is definitely handsome)*. Prefer a more specific word.

50

glos

differ from, differ with   To *differ from* means "to be unlike." To *differ with* means "to disagree."

different from, different than   *From* is idiomatic when a preposition is required; *than* introduces a clause. See **38e.**

discreet, discrete   *Discreet* means "tactful" and comes from "discretion"; *discrete* means "seprate and distinct" *(Her criticism of their behavior was discreet, but she observed that the police report showed four discrete instances of public disturbance).*

disinterested, uninterested   Now frequently used interchangeably to mean "having no interest." The distinction between the two, however, is real and valuable. *Uninterested* means "without interest"; *disinterested* means "impartial" *(Good judges are disinterested but not uninterested).*

don't   A contraction for *do not,* but not for *does not (She doesn't* [not *don't*] *want a new dress).*

doubt but what   See *but that.*

due to   Some writers object to *due to* as a preposition meaning "because of" or "owing to" *(The fair was postponed because of* [or *owing to,* not *due to*] *rain).* Acceptable when used as an adjective *(My failure was due to laziness).*

due to the fact that   Wordy for *because.*

each and every   Unnecessarily wordy.

effect   see *affect, effect*

elicit, illicit   *Ellicit* is a verb meaning "to bring out or draw forth"; *illicit,* an adjective, means "illegal" *(The detective elicited a confession concerning an illicit drug sale).*

elude, allude   To *elude* means "to avoid or escape from"; to *allude* means "to refer to" *(I alluded to his elusive nature; he never seemed to be at home when we called).*

eminent, imminent   *Eminent* means "distinguished"; *imminent* means "impending or about to occur" *(The arrival of the eminent guest was imminent).*

equally as good   The *as* is unnecessary. *Equally good* is more precise.

etc.   See *and etc.* and **16a(4).**

everyone, every one   See *anyone.*

everywheres   Nonstandard for *everywhere.*

except   See *accept, except.*

expect   Colloquial when used to mean "suppose" or "believe" *(I suppose* [not *expect*] *I should do the dishes now).*

explicit, implicit   *Explicit* means "fully expressed"; *implicit* means "unexpressed," although capable of being understood. *(Although he never explicitly said no, his disapproval was implicit in his tone of voice).*

farther, further Some writers perfer to use *farther* to refer to distance and restrict *further* to mean "in addition" (*It was two miles farther to go the way you wished, but I wanted no further trouble*). Dictionaries recognize the forms as interchangeable.

fewer, less *Fewer* refers to numbers, *less* to amounts, degree, or value (*We sold fewer tickets than last year, but our expenses were less*).

field Wordy and overworked. Say, for example, *in atomic energy* not *in the field of atomic energy*. See Section **39.**

fine As an adjective to express approval (*a fine person*) *fine* is vague and overused. As an adverb meaning "well" (*works fine*) *fine* is colloquial.

flunk Colloquial; a conversational substitute for *fail*.

former, latter *Former* refers to the first-named of two; *latter* refers to the last-named of two. *First* and *last* are used to refer to one of a group of more than two.

function As a noun meaning "event" or "occasion," *function* is appropriate only when the event is formal (*a presidential function*). As a verb meaning "work," "operate," *function* is currently overused and jargonish (*I work* [not *function*] *best after I've had a cup of coffee*).

further See *farther, further*.

get A standard verb, but used colloquially in many idioms inappropriate in most writing. (*Get wise to yourself. That whistling gets me. You can't get away with it.*).

good and Colloquial as a synonym for *very* (*good and hot, good and angry*).

good, well *Good* is colloquial as an adverb (*The motor runs well* [not *good*]). *You look good* means "You look attractive, well dressed," or the like. *You look well* means "You look healthy."

graduate Either I *graduated from* college or I *was graduated from* college is acceptable, but I *graduated college* is nonstandard.

had better, had best Standard idioms for *ought* and *should*, which are more formal (*You had better* [or *had best*] *plan carefully.*) More formally: *You ought to* [or *should*] *plan carefully*). *Better* alone (*You better plan carefully*) is colloquial.

had ought, hadn't ought Nonstandard for *ought* and *ought not*.

hang, hung The principal parts of the verb are *hang, hung, hung*, but when referring to death by hanging, formal English uses *hang, hanged, hanged* (*We hung the pictures. The prisoners hanged themselves.*).

hardly See *but*.

have, of See *of, have*

he or she See **8b(1)** and **8c.**

himself See *myself*.

50

glos

hisself   Nonstandard for *himself.*

hopefully   *Hopefully* means "in a hopeful manner" *(They waited hopefully for money).* It is now widely used in the sense of "it is hoped" *(Hopefully, you can send me money).* Some readers object to this use.

hung   See *hang, hung.*

idea   Often used vaguely for *intention, plan, purpose,* and other more exact words. Prefer a more exact choice. *(My intention* [not *idea*] *is to become an engineer. The theme* [not *idea*] *of the movie is that justice is colorblind.).*

ignorant, stupid   The distinction is important. An *ignorant* child is one who has been taught very little; a *stupid* child is one who is unable to learn.

illusion   See *allusion, illusion.*

imply, infer   To *imply* means to suggest without stating; to *infer* means to draw a conclusion. Speakers *imply;* listeners *infer (They implied that I was ungrateful; I inferred that they didn't like me).*

in, into   *In* indicates "inside, enclosed, within." *Into* is more exact when the meaning is "toward, from the outside in," although *in* is common in both meanings. *(I left the book in the room and went back into the room to get it.)*

in back of, in behind, in between   Wordy for *back of, behind, between.*

incredible, incredulous   Something that is *incredible* is "unbelievable"; someone who is *incredulous* is "unbelieving" *(I was incredulous—surely I could not have won such an incredible amount of money).*

infer   See *imply, infer.*

ingenious, ingenuous   *Ingenious* means "clever"; *ingenuous* means "naive" *(Inventors are usually ingenious, but some are too ingenuous to know when they have been cheated).*

in regards to   Nonstandard for *as regards* or *in regard to.*

inside of, outside of   The *of* is unnecessary *(He stayed inside* [not *inside of*] *the house).*

in the case of, in the line of   See *case.*

irregardless   Nonstandard for *regardless.*

is when, is where, is because   Faulty predications in such sentences as: *A first down is when the football is advanced ten yards in four plays or fewer. A garage is where . . . . The reason is because . . . .* See **14a.**

its, it's   The possessive pronoun has no apostrophe. *It's* is a contraction of *it is.*

-ize   The suffix *-ize* is one of several used to form verbs from nouns and adjectives *(hospitalize, criticize, sterilize).* Writers in government, business, and other institutions have often used it excessively and unnecessarily in such coinages as *finalize, concretize, permanize.* Such coinages are widely objected to; it is best to limit your use of *-ize* words to those that are well established, and resist the temptation to coin new ones. See Section **39a(1).**

50

glos

judicial, judicious A *judicial* decision is one reached by the court or a judge, but a *judicious* decision is one showing sound judgment.

kind, sort These are frequently treated as plural in such constructions as *these kind of books* and *those sort of dogs*. Preferred usage in both speech and writing requires singular or plural throughout the construction, as in *this kind of book* or *these kinds of books*.

kind of, sort of Colloquial when used to mean *somewhat, rather (I was rather* [not *kind of*] *pleased*).

kind of a, sort of a Omit the *a*.

later, latter *Later* refers to time, but *latter* refers to the second of two *(Of the twins, Meg was born first. Peg, the latter, was born three minutes later.)*.

latter See *former, later*.

lay, lie To *lay* means "to place, put down" *(Lay the book on the table)*. To *lie* means "to recline" *(The dog lies on the floor)*. See **4c.**

learn, teach To *learn* means "to gain knowledge"; to *teach* means "to give knowledge" *(We learn from experience; experience teaches us much)*.

leave, let To *leave* is to depart; to *let* is to permit or allow *(I must leave now. Will you let me go?)*.

less See *fewer, less*.

let See *leave, let*.

liable, apt, likely Often used interchangeably. But careful writing reserves *liable* for "legally responsible," or "subject to," *likely* for "probably," and *apt* for "having an aptitude for" *(I am likely to drive carefully, for I am not an apt driver, and I know I am liable for any damages)*.

lie, lay See *lay, lie,* and see **4c.**

like, as, as if *Like* is a preposition; *as* and *as if* are conjunctions. Though *like* is often used as a conjunction in speech, writing preserves the distinction *(He looks as if* [not *like*] *he were tired)*. Note that *as if* is followed by the subjunctive *were*.

likely See *liable*.

loose, lose *Loose* means "to free." *Lose* means "to be deprived of." *(He will lose the dog if he looses him from his leash)*.

lots, lots of, a lot of Colloquial for *much, many,* or *a great deal (I had a great deal of* [not *lots of*] *money and bought many* [not *lots of* or *a lot of*] *cars)*. Note spelling: *alot* is incorrect.

mad Dictionaries recognize *mad* as a synonym for *angry,* or *very enthusiastic,* but some readers object to its use in these meanings.

manner Often unnecessary in phrases like *in a precise manner* where a single adverb *(precisely)* or a "with" phrase *(with precision)* would do.

may See *can, may*.

50

glos

may of Nonstandard for *may have.*

maybe, may be *Maybe* means "perhaps"; *may be* is a verb form. Be careful to distinguish between the two.

media A plural form (singular *medium*) requiring a plural verb *(The mass media are* [not *is*] *sometimes guilty of distorting the news).*

might of Nonstandard for *might have.*

most Colloquial as a substitute for *almost* or *nearly.*

must of Nonstandard for *must have.*

myself, yourself, himself *Myself* is often used in speech as a substitute for *I* or *me* but is not standard in writen English. Reserve *myself* for emphatic *(I myself will do the work)* or reflexive use *(I hurt myself).* The same applies to the forms *yourself, himself, herself,* etc.

nohow Nonstandard for *not at all, in no way.*

none The indefinite pronoun *none* may take either a singular or a plural verb, depending on its context *(None of the gold was stolen; None of the men were absent).* See **8a(2).**

nothing like, nowhere near Colloquial for *not nearly (I was not nearly* [not *nowhere near*] *as sick as you).*

nowheres Nonstandard for *nowhere.*

number See *amount, number.*

of, have In speech the auxiliary *have* in such combinations as *could have, might have,* etc., sounds very much like *of,* leading some people to write *could of, might of,* etc. All such combinations with *of* are nonstandard. In writing be careful to use *have.*

off of, off from Wordy and colloquial *(The paper slid off* [not *off of*] *the table).*

OK, O.K., okay All are standard forms, but formal writing prefers a more exact word.

on account of Wordy for *because of.* Regional for *because (She bought the car because* [not *on account of*] *she needed it).*

outside of Colloquial for *except (Nobody was there except* [not *outside of*] *Henry).* See also *inside of.*

over with Colloquial for *ended, finished, completed.*

per Appropriate in business and technical writing *(per diem, per capita, feet per second, pounds per square inch).* As *per your request* is inappropriate. In ordinary writing prefer *a* or *an (ninety cents a dozen, twice a day).*

percent, percentage Both mean "rate per hundred." *Percent* (sometimes written *per cent*) is used with numbers *(fifty percent, 23 percent). Percentage* is used without numbers *(a small percentage).* Avoid using either as a synonym for *part (A small part* [not *percentage*] *of the money was lost).*

perfect See *unique*.

persuade See *convince, persuade*.

phenomena See *data*.

plan on Colloquial in such phrases as *plan on going, plan on seeing,* for *plan to go, plan to see*.

plenty Colloquial as an adverb meaning "very, amply" (*I was very* [not *plenty*] *angry*). Note that as a noun meaning "enough, a large number," *plenty* must be followed by *of* (*I've had plenty of money*).

practical, practicable *Practical* means "useful, not theoretical." *Practicable* means "capable of being put into practice" (*Franklin was a practical statesman; his schemes were practicable*).

precede, proceed *Precede* is a verb and means "to come before." *Proceed* is also a verb but means "to move on, to advance" (*You must precede me in the line-up for graduation or the sergeant-at-arms will not let us proceed onto the stage*).

principal, principle As an adjective *principal* means "chief, main"; as a noun it means "leader, chief officer," or, in finance, "a capital sum, as distinguished from interest or profit." The noun *principle* means "fundamental truth" or "basic law or doctrine." (*What is my principal reason for being here? I am the principal of the local elementary school. That bank pays 5 percent interest on your principal. The textbook explained the underlying principle.*).

provided, providing Both are acceptable as subordinating conjunctions meaning "on the condition" (*I will move to Washington, providing* [or *provided*] *the salary is adequate*).

raise, rise *Raise, raised, raised* is a transitive verb (*They raised potatoes*). *Rise, rose, risen* is intransitive (*They rose at daybreak*).

real Colloquial for *really* or *very* (*real cloudy, real economical*).

reason is because See *is when* and **14a.**

reason why Usually redundant (*The reason* [not *reason why*] *we failed is clear*).

refer See *allude, refer*.

regarding, in regard to, with regard to Overused and wordy for *on, about,* or *concerning* (*We have not decided on* [not *with regard to*] *your admission*).

respectively, respectfully *Respectively* means "separately" or "individually"; *respectfully* means "full of respect" (*The participants in the debate were St. Lawrence High School and Delphi High School, respectively. The students respectfully stated their arguments.*).

right Colloquial or dialectal when used to mean "very" (*right fresh, right happy*). *Right along* and *right away* are colloquial for *continuously, immediately*.

rise, raise See *raise, rise*.

round See *unique*.

50

glos

said *Said* in such phrases as *the said paragraph, the said person* occurs frequently in legal writing. Avoid the use in ordinary writing.

scarcely See *but, hardly, scarcely.*

set, sit Often confused. See **4c.**

shall, will, should, would *Will* is now commonly used for all persons (*I, you, he, she, it*) except in the first person for questions (*Shall I go?*) and in formal contexts (*We shall consider each of your reasons*). *Should* is used for all persons when condition or obligation is being expressed (*If he should stay . . . . We should go*). *Would* is used for all persons to express a wish or customary action (*Would that I had listened! I would ride the same bus every day.*).

should See *shall.*

should of Nonstandard for *should have.*

since, because The subordinating conjunction *because* always indicates cause. *Since* may indicate either cause or time (*It has rained since yesterday. Since you need money, I'll lend you some*). Be careful to avoid using *since* in sentences where it could indicate either cause or time and thus be ambiguous. In *since we moved, we have been working longer hours,* it is unclear whether *because we moved* or *from the time we moved* is meant.

sit, set See *set, sit.*

so *So* is a loose and often imprecise conjunction. Avoid using it excessively to join independent clauses. For clauses of purpose, *so that* is preferable (*They left so that* [not *so*] *I could study*). *Because* is preferable when cause is clearly intended (*Because it began to rain, we left* [not *It began to rain, so we left*]).

some Colloquial and vague when used to mean "unusual, remarkable, exciting" (*That was some party. This is some car.*). In writing use a more specific word.

someone, some one See *anyone.*

sometime, some time Use one word in the sense of a time not specified; use two words in the sense of a period of time (*Sometime we shall spend some time together*).

somewheres Nonstandard for *somewhere.*

sort, sort of, sort of a See *kind, sort, kind of, sort of, kind of a.*

stationary, stationery *Stationary* means "not moving"; *stationery* is writing supplies.

straight See *unique.*

stupid See *ignorant, stupid.*

such Colloquial and overused as a vague intensifier (*It was a very* [not *such a*] *hot day*).

sure Colloquial for *surely, certainly* (*I was surely* [not *sure*] *sick*).

50

glos

sure and, try and   Colloquial for *sure to, try to.*

take and   Nonstandard in most uses *(Lou slammed* [not *took and slammed*] *the book down).*

teach, learn   See *learn, teach.*

than, then   Don't confuse these. *Than* is a conjunction *(younger than John). Then* is an adverb indicating time *(then, not now).*

that   Colloquial when used as an adverb *(She's that poor she can't buy food. I didn't like the book that much).*

that, which   *That* always introduces restrictive clauses; *which* may introduce either restrictive or nonrestrictive clauses. See **20c.** Some writers and editors prefer to limit *which* entirely to nonrestrictive clauses *(This is the car that I bought yesterday. This car, which I bought yesterday, is very economical.).*

theirselves   Nonstandard for *themselves.*

then, than   See *than, then.*

there, their, they're   Don't confuse these. *There* is an adverb or an expletive *(He walks there. There are six.). Their* is a pronoun *(their rooms). They're* is a contraction for *they are (They're too eager).*

these kind, these sort   See *kind, sort.*

this here, that there, these here, them there   Nonstandard for *this, that, these, those.*

thusly   Nonstandard for *thus.*

to, too   *To* is a preposition. *Too* is an adverb meaning *also (She laughed too)* or *more than enough (You worked too hard).* In the sense of *indeed* it is colloquial *(She did too laugh).*

toward, towards   Both are correct, though *toward* is more common in the United States, *towards* in Britain.

try and   See *sure and.*

type   Colloquial for *type of (This type of* [not *type*] *research is expensive).* Often used, but usually in hyphenated compounds *(colonial-type architecture, tile-type floors, scholarly-type text).* Omit *type* for such expressions wherever possible.

uninterested   See *disinterested, uninterested.*

unique   Several adjectives such as *unique, perfect, round, straight,* and *complete* name qualities that do not vary in degree. Logically, therefore, they cannot be compared. Formal use requires *more nearly round, more nearly perfect* and the like. The comparative and superlative forms, however, are widely used colloquially in such phrases as *the most unique house, most complete examination, most perfect day.* Their occurrence even in formal English is exemplified by the phrase *more perfect union* in the Constitution.

used to   In writing be careful to preserve the *d (We used to* [not *use to*] *get up at six every morning).*

50

glos

used to could   Nonstandard for *used to be able.*

wait on   Colloquial when used to mean "wait for"; *wait on* means "to serve, attend" *(We waited for* [not *waited on*] *the clerk to wait on us).*

you're, your   *You're* is a contraction for *you are. Your* is the second-person possessive pronoun. *(You're not going to eat your other doughnut, are you?)*

you was   Nonstandard for *you were.*

INDEX

Note: Numbers in **boldface** refer to section designations; other numbers refer to pages.
Thus, for example, the entry **40f:**324 refers to Section 40f on page 324.

ORGANIZATION CHART